CAPITALIST SOCIETY

Readings for a critical sociology

The Dorsey Series in Sociology

Editor   Robin M. Williams, Jr.   *Cornell University*

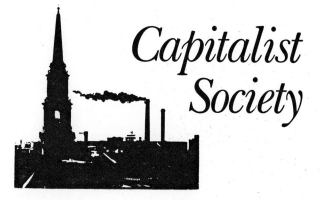

Capitalist Society

Readings for a critical sociology

Edited by

RICHARD QUINNEY
Brown University

1979

THE DORSEY PRESS Homewood, Illinois 60430
Irwin-Dorsey Limited Georgetown, Ontario L7G 4B3

Cover photo and cover design by Richard Quinney

ISBN 0-256-02233-X
Library of Congress Catalog Card No. 78–70955

Printed in the United States of America

1 2 3 4 5 6 7 8 9 0 K 6 5 4 3 2 1 0 9

PREFACE

The history of sociology is the development of generalizations about a particular type of society, one based on a capitalist mode of production with corresponding social relations. The contradiction within sociology is that—until very recent times—we have assumed these generalizations to be universal to all societies. In reality, however, our sociology is unique to Western, capitalist societies. A sociology quite different in substance and form is likely to emerge in the experience of developing socialist societies.

The objective of this book is to understand contemporary capitalist society in terms of its fundamental and distinguishing characteristics. Following the clear alternative to much of modern sociological theory—that of Marxist social theory— I have provided an intellectual framework that begins with the underlying capitalist mode of production and moves to the class structure of advanced capitalism, the capitalist state, culture and consciousness, social institutions, the problems and contradictions of capitalist society, and capitalist society in the world system. The substance of contemporary sociology is thereby covered, but the analysis is one that is critical.

In my own understanding of capitalist society and its transformation to a socialist society, I am attempting to integrate into a single paradigm an analysis of human history as being achieved through human action with symbols that allow us to unite our spiritual life and our material historical existence. The existential and essential task at hand is that of integrating our material subsistence with our spiritual life—for the purpose of both understanding our human history and acting in the fulfillment of our personal and collective being. We place ourselves within the prophetic tradition in which the human predicament is viewed according to the estrangement between existence and essence and the possibility of a unity with that which is vital to human and social life.

In the principle of socialism—with its prophetic voice—the fundamental questions of material existence and sacred essence are confronted. By combining a Marxist analysis and a theology of culture, we develop an understanding of the world and a way of transcending the contemporary historical condition. The ancient split between the sacred and the secular is overcome in the struggle for a new society. Regained is the dimension of depth in our encounter with reality.

February 1979   *Richard Quinney*

CONTENTS

CHAPTER 1

Introduction

We begin with the desire to understand the conditions of our contemporary historical existence. We recognize that we are at the same time products of our history and creators of it. People make their own history, Karl Marx noted, "but they do not make it just as they please; they do not make it under circumstances chosen by themselves, but under circumstances directly encountered, given and transmitted from the past."[1] The historical conditions of the time provide the setting for the possibilities of creation and development. While our daily struggle is one of transforming the existing order, of removing the conditions of oppression and making an authentic existence, the old social order will not perish until the productive forces and contradictions of that order have become obstacles to its further development. Thus history is made both subjectively and objectively, as the result of social and personal struggle *and* the transformation of the economic modes of production.

In the meantime, we must produce our means of subsistence. Production is the necessary requirement of existence and the primary process of social life. In the social production of our existence we enter into relations that are appropriate to the existing forces of production. It is this "economic" structure that provides the material foundation for our social and political institutions, for everyday life, and for social consciousness. Thus, all social life must be understood in terms of the objectives of production. In capitalist society—in a society based on a conflict between those who own and control the means of production and those who do not—the social and cultural life of any person or group of people is understood according to the relations produced by the capitalist system of production.

The growth of capitalism has meant the increasing division of society into social classes. Developing capitalist society is characterized by a growing struggle between the class that owns the means of production and the class that must sell its labor power. At the same time, the problems created by capitalist development must be dealt with in some way by capitalist society. For capitalism to continue—assuring further capital accumulation and legitimation of the capitalist system—the problems created by its own contradictions have to be regulated and controlled. A system that cannot generate a human existence, without altering beyond recognition its basic mode of production, responds by attempting to integrate the problems of its own creation into the overall system. Hence, the capitalist state has emerged to manage outside of the private sphere the problems of a developing capitalist economy.

The crisis of advanced capitalism is a crisis that is both material and spiritual. Materially, capitalism has reached a point at which it cannot advance economically or politically without altering the basic capitalist mode of production. The social problems created by the capitalist economic system can no longer be solved within the framework of capitalism. And the capitalist state, once a political means of dealing with the economic contradictions of capitalism, is nearing the end of its ability to accommodate the problems of developing capitalism; the capitalist state itself is increasingly subject to contradictions and crises.

Modern capitalism, rather than solving the structural contradictions, exacerbates the problems and creates new ones. The growing surplus population generated by the demands of advanced capitalism cannot be handled by the welfare state. What is being produced in capitalist society is an expanding reserve army of the unemployed and the unemployable. The capitalist state has neither the ability nor the financial resources to integrate the displaced and alienated population produced by the capitalist mode of production. More control and repression become necessary, and resistance to that control increases.[2] Capitalist society, on various levels, is in crisis; and it is a crisis that will continue to deepen until capitalist society is transformed into a socialist society.

Spiritually, as well as materially, capitalism is reaching the end of its era. In the realm of its own secular spirit, once characterized by an unquestioning enthusiasm for acquisitiveness and accumulation, the majority of the population finds little of the moral and personal support once provided by that spirit. The capitalist world is in disorder spiritually as it is materially. What is there to believe in when the material world no longer furnishes us with spiritual rewards and sustenance?

In the process of its material development, capitalism has all but destroyed the sacred spirit. Our advanced secular society leaves us without the religious symbolism and belief to be a real part of this world. Without apprehending the infinite and eternal questions beyond this world, we are neither of this world nor any other. We have lost our hold; our qualities have become those of the barren landscape that surrounds us. That we do cope in this world says something about the persistence of the human spirit. That we can rise above the material and secular realm of capitalism attests to the possibilities of divine providence in our own life and time.

The task of a critical sociology is to unmask the material and spiritual reality of our lives as experienced in the society in which we live, in a capitalist society. Our understanding of the social world is connected to our location in the class structure of advanced capitalism. Ideas—like people—are not detached from objective reality. They are dialectically related to social and economic foundations, having consequences that may be as contradictory as the locations from which they spring.[3] This makes our subjective world and our daily struggle even more important.

Our thought and our practice in sociology are related to the capitalist structures within which we operate and to the bourgeois roles we are assigned to perform. The normal knowledge we create and impart is supposed to fit into the conventional wisdom of a liberal education, providing the ideology for capitalist relations. The educational and agency structures within which we work have as their purpose the preservation of a capitalist society. Without dialectical thought, and without class consciousness and struggle, our efforts easily fulfill capitalist interests.

When we are not engaged in the socialist struggle, when we perform as petty-bourgeois intellectuals, our thoughts and actions are principally bourgeois. The condition is self-fulfilling: bourgeois intellectual life sets a priori limits to speculative-critical-dialectical thought, and without this kind of thought we tend not to become aware of other possibilities—of our true class interest in building a socialist society. Bourgeois thought is dependent on the inner logic of bourgeois (and petty-bourgeois) life.

Bourgeois thought and life are both tied to an Anglo-American empirical realism whose mission is essentially to serve as a check on social and class consciousness. Doubts about capitalism are kept from arising by concentrating on narrowly defined questions of law, freedom, and equality. Fredric Jameson observes in his book *Marxism and Form,*

> The method of such thinking, in its various forms and guises, consists in separating reality into airtight compartments, carefully distinguishing the political from the economic, the legal from the political, the sociological from the historical, so that the full implications of any given problem can never come into view; and in limiting all statements to the discrete and the immediately varifiable, in order to rule out any speculative and totalizing thought which might lead to a vision of social life as a whole.[4]

Dialectical thinking and living represent a threat to this form of class ideology.

Bourgeois ideology is a mystification of objective reality; it is not only a misrepresentation and distortion of the real world but a source of our continued alienation in the world. Bourgeois ideology is a corrupt form of consciousness that emerges from an identification with the capitalist class. It is a class consciousness, nevertheless, which has all the a priori limits conferred by identification with the bourgeoisie.[5] What is needed, instead, by all who engage in a critical sociology, is a class consciousness that is identified with the working class. For it is in a socialist society that the needs of all of us who labor can be satisfied. Through such consciousness we become the subjects (rather than the objects) in the transformation of human society.

Our engagement in sociology—in learning and in teaching—is a cultural production. The study of society is a product of human labor, and the same processes that produce other cultural productions also produce sociology. The productions of sociology are subject to the same forces that Marxist aesthetics has found to operate in the world of art and literature. How, then, are we to read and view the productions of sociology as a cultural form?

Like those who engage in other cultural productions, sociologists are engaged in a social practice. Our role is one of making something that has some cultural meaning in the existing society.[6] The commodities we produce, whether in the physical form of books or the transmission of ideas and consciousness in the classroom, are all shaped by the underlying capitalist mode of production. There is a connection (however dialectical) between the dominant mode of production and the content of our art—as well as its form.

A characteristic of all human beings, as Adolfo Sánchez Vázquez has noted, is "the creation or production of human objects through which essential human powers can be externalized."[7] The human need to produce originates in a need for material subsistence, but it is also in production that human creativity is necessarily exercised. Work is the basic human activity; it is an attempt to alter the subject-object relationship, to have control over our labors, to make us the movers of our history. It is at the same time the transcendence of our existence, to which we return with new light.

In capitalist society, however, there is an innate tendency to turn creative work (that is, art) into alien labor. Work no longer fulfills the human need for expression and communication; we no longer realize ourselves through creation. The alienation experienced in our work becomes the condition of the worker in all areas of life. Ownership and the control of life in general have been surrendered to alien hands.[8] Under capitalism the production of life itself is alienated. Our lives as well as our production of sociology tend to become subverted and alienated when they are lived in the context of capitalism. The creative essence of sociology is negatively affected when the student of social life is restrained by the inner need to produce.

The substance and form of all our productions, then, are expressions of the underlying structure of capitalism to the extent that production has become alienated under capitalism. Our productions in sociology are thus *mediated* by capitalism.[9] The final products of our labor (of our cultural work) are filtered through a multiplicity of mediations between the economic mode of production, the social structure, and the consciousness through which sociologists perceive reality. Through our productions we express the underlying structure of capitalism. Whether our expressions are critical and reflexive or merely reflections of capitalism is shaped by our ability to think dialectically and by our conscious involvement in the class struggle.

Cultural production differs from the positivistic-scientific mode of understanding in that it consciously seeks to transcend the objective, material world—in both theory and practice. Artistic culture as a way of seeing, feeling, and perceiving is prophetic in its forms and content. Not only does it penetrate beneath the surfaces of social reality to the underlying structures, but it aspires to go beyond that reality in actual life. Cultural production suggests how the world could be. It is a form of knowledge that has as its objective a transcendence of the everyday life of the existing order.

Reality thus may become transformed in the course of cultural production. Even momentarily, we are made to see the possibilities of another existence. The task of revolutionary theater according to Bertolt Brecht is not to reflect a fixed reality, but to demonstrate how character and action are historically produced, and so how they could have been different, and can still be transformed. "The play itself, therefore, becomes a model of that process of production; it is less a reflection *of,* than a reflection *on,* social reality."[10] The play is an experiment, testing its own presuppositions, just as it tests the reality within which it is produced. It becomes a public demonstration of its own form. It makes possible a transformation of reality as perceived and constructed by the audience in the course of the production. All art—I contend all critical sociology —aims to evoke. It aims to awaken in the observer, listener, or reader thoughts and emotions that lead to opposition and to action. Critical sociology when thus practiced is part of the class struggle, is part of socialist revolution.

Dialectical thought, as the basic thought form of critical sociology, is in its very structure self-conscious, and may be described as "the attempt to think about a given object on one level, and at the same time to observe our own thought processes as we do so: or to use a more scientific figure, to reckon the position of the observer into the experiment itself."[11] This is the Marxist dialectic, in which the thinker (the sociologist as theorist) is aware of his or her position in society and in history, and is conscious of the limits and possibilities of one's class position. Our thought, in the beginning, is situational, objectively determined. But with self-consciousness and class consciousness we transcend that restriction. "Thus our thought no longer takes official problems at face value, but walks behind the screen to assess the very origin of the subject-object relationship in the first place."[12] Dialectical thinking, thought about preexisting thought and its conditions, plays a necessary part in the process of transforming the dominant social and economic conditions of capitalist society.

In such a way we break the tie that has made the producer the product of the external world of capitalist production. Severing the bonds of the present, our thinking is now historical thinking; that is to say, thinking about the future. We see ourselves and our class (as well as our thought) as a part of the basic historical situation in which all of this takes place. We are now free with a relative degree of freedom to transcend existing conditions. We are in the class struggle for a new society. We are in a position—intellectually and socially—to think about and act upon the production of a socialist future.

A critical sociology is a form of *cultural politics.* We are creating (producing) a way of understanding and a way of living in the world. Our cultural production is specialized in speaking to other sociologists, but it is also popular as it becomes part of everyday consciousness and action. Although many of us will continue to work and study within that ideological apparatus known as the university, it is nevertheless one of the forums available to us for the dialectical expression of cultural production. Sociology as cultural politics has to be developed and practiced in this institution, as in other (and possibly alternative) institutions in capitalist society. The production of knowledge is a political act.

What we need to produce in the transition to socialism is a social theory that supports socialist development rather than capitalist development. This is a *socialist theory* that provides knowledge and politics for the working class, rather than knowledge for the survival of the capitalist class. In other words, the social theory appropriate to capitalism is quite different from the social theory needed for socialism. Moreover, as socialism develops, social theory will be modified from that necessary for the transition to socialism to that necessary for the further development of socialist society. For the moment, however, we need a social theory that allows us to move from late capitalism to the first stages of socialism.

As I have been arguing throughout, Marxist theory and practice provide the necessary basis for critical and socialist sociology. Increasingly social scientists are recognizing that Marxism is the one tradition that takes as its focus the conditions of capitalist society; it is the one form of analysis that is historically specific and locates the problems of our age in its material conditions. Thus the most dynamic and significant movement in the social sciences today is the development of a Marxist (or "neo-Marxist") social science. Marxism is the most suitable and all-embracing philosophy in which to produce our sociology. We will produce a sociology that takes us beyond capitalist ideology and practice to the everyday reality of the class struggle. As this takes place, we are creating the theory and practice for the transition to socialism.

The purpose of critical sociology in the transition to socialism is to subvert the capitalist hegemony that maintains its hold over the society. Critical sociology provides people with an understanding of their alienated and oppressed condition, and provides a means of expression that is the beginning of socialist revolution.[13] To engage in social theory under these conditions is to engage in educational, political, and cultural work. The production of socialist social theory assists in the development of class consciousness. "The intellectual," Theotonio Dos Santos observes, "considered not as an individual isolated in an ivory tower but as a militant intellectual of a class, is thus a key factor in working out and developing class consciousness."[14] A conscious culture of emancipation is being created.

Critical sociology, to conclude, is to serve in the struggle for a socialist society. As bourgeois sociology has served the captalist class under capitalism, a critical-Marxist sociology will assist in the transition to socialism and will serve the working class under socialism. In the struggle, sociological theory will be revised and practice will be altered to better achieve the goal of a socialist society. The only purpose in knowing the world is to change it. Our sociology does not stop with reflecting on the world, but rather is a part of the process through which the world is transformed.

In understanding social and moral life in capitalist society, we produce a theory and a practice that have as their objective changing the world. The importance of sociology is that it moves us dialectically to reject the capitalist order and to struggle for a socialist society. We are thus engaged in the working-class struggle—producing the conditions for our own development in history. The struggle is shared in common and goes to the core of our being. As the theologian and socialist Paul Tillich reminded us: "The most intimate motions within the depths of our souls are not completely our own. For they belong also to our friends, to mankind, to the universe, and to the Ground of all being, the aim of our life."[15] We are in the struggle together, always.

NOTES

1. Karl Marx, *The Eighteenth Brumaire of Louis Bonaparte* (New York: International Publishers, 1963), p. 15.

2. See Richard Quinney, *Class, State, and Crime:* *On the Theory and Practice of Criminal Justice* (New York: Longman, 1977), especially pp. 63–105.

3. These ideas are developed in my article "The

Production of a Marxist Criminology," *Contemporary Crises,* 2 (July 1978), pp. 277–292.

4. Fredric Jameson, *Marxism and Form: Twentieth-Century Dialectical Theories of Literature* (Princeton, N.J.: Princeton University Press, 1971), pp. 367–368.

5. See George Lukács, *History and Class Consciousness: Studies in Marxist Dialectics,* trans. Rodney Livingstone (Cambridge, Mass.: MIT Press, 1971). Also Richard Lichtman, "Marx's Theory of Ideology," *Socialist Revolution,* 5 (April 1975), pp. 45–76.

6. See Terry Eagleton, *Marxism and Literary Criticism* (Berkeley: University of California Press, 1976), pp. 60–76.

7. Adolfa Sánchez Vázquez, *Art and Society: Essays in Marxist Aesthetics,* trans. Maro Riofrancos (New York: Monthly Review Press, 1973), p. 61.

8. Karl Marx, *The Grundrisse,* ed. David McLellan (New York: Harper & Row, 1971), pp. 132–143.

9. See Stanley Aronowitz, "Culture and Politics," *Politics and Society,* 6 (no. 3, 1976), pp. 347–376.

10. Eagleton, *Marxism and Literary Criticism,* p. 65.

11. Jameson, *Marxism and Form,* p. 340.

12. Ibid., p. 341.

13. On the role of socialist knowledge in general, see André Gorz, *Socialism and Revolution* (New York: Doubleday, 1973), pp. 170–174.

14. Theotonio Dos Santos, "The Concept of Social Classes," *Science and Society,* 34 (Summer 1970), p. 186.

15. Quoted in Wilhelm and Mario Pauck, *Paul Tillich: His Life and Thought* (New York: Harper & Row, 1976), front matter.

CHAPTER 2

The capitalist
mode of production

Early capitalism was stimulated and given the necessary intellectual and spiritual support by the secular Enlightenment. Trade, commerce, and exploration among the European nations in the 16th and 17th centuries provided the material bases for procedures and forms that were unimaginable before that time, including commodity production and capital accumulation. The economic formation that we now know as the capitalist mode of production was made possible by the breakdown of feudal economic forms, the expansion of national empires, and the simultaneous growth of new ideas of a secular nature.

A series of transformations took place—in the transition from feudalism to capitalism—which resulted in a new social division of labor. Most important were the separation of the commercial (and eventually the industrial) from the agricultural, a distinction between manual and mental labor, and an opposition between the city and the country.[1] Mercantilism—by protecting enterprise within the nation—further enhanced the early development of capitalism. The colonies of the mercantile nations served as markets for exports and suppliers of raw materials to the mother countries. The extension of commerce into a world market system opened a new phase in the historical development of capitalism.

Capitalism as a system of production based on the exploitation of a working class by the capitalist class that owns and controls the means of production has gone through various stages of development in the subsequent history of capitalist societies. Capitalism has constantly transformed its own forces and relations of production; the whole of capitalist society is constantly being altered—within the basic framework of capitalist political economy. Thus, capitalism is always affecting the social existence of all who live under it.[2] This is the basic dynamic of capitalist development, an interdependence among production, the relations of production, and the social structure of institution and ideas.

An understanding of the social and moral life of capitalist society necessarily involves an investigation of the relationship between the development of capitalism and the social relations that correspond to this development. Moreover, as capitalism has developed, there has been an increasing discrepancy between the productive forces and the capitalist relations of production. Capitalist development, with economic expansion being fundamental to capitalism, exacerbates rather than mitigates the contradictions of capitalism. Workers are further exploited, the conditions of existence worsen, and the contradictions of capitalism increase. Capitalist development, in other words, and from another vantage point, creates the conditions for the transformation and abolition of capitalism, brought about in actuality by class struggle.

The United States has developed gradually as a capitalist society. The nascent capitalist economy of the colonial stage of American capitalism was, by and large, an economy of farming, shipping, and commerce. As manufacturing became increasingly important, the population grew rapidly and the urban centers grew in size and importance. Immigration continued to increase, to supply the needed labor for manufacturing in the growing factory system. From the time of the American Revolution to the Civil War, the United States was becoming a major industrial nation. The remainder of the 19th century was marked by unprecedented economic growth and expansion, making the United States the leading nation of industrial capitalism.[3]

Nevertheless, or as a consequence of the contradictions of capitalist development, the nation was beset with recurring economic depressions and recessions. More and more people were being adversely affected by developing capitalism. And by the turn of the century it was becoming clear that capitalism must be regulated and supported by the developing capitalist state. Advanced capitalism has now reached a point of increasing crisis—economic, political, social, and moral—brought about by the contradictions inherent in the capitalist mode of production.

NOTES

1. Eric J. Hobsbawm, "Introduction," in Karl Marx, *Pre-Capitalist Economic Formations*, ed. E. J. Hobsbawm (New York: International Publishers, 1965), pp. 9–65.

2. See Paul M. Sweezy, *The Theory of Capitalist Development* (New York: Monthly Review Press, 1968).

3. See the statistics and economic history presented in Jurgen Kuczynski, *A Short History of Labour Conditions under Industrial Capitalism in the United States of America, 1789–1946* (New York: Barnes & Noble, 1973); and Douglas C. North, *Growth and Welfare in the American Past: A New Economic History*, 2d ed. (Englewood Cliffs, N.J.: Prentice-Hall, 1966).

The critique of capitalism[*]

JOHN G. GURLEY

The economies of ancient Greece and Rome, and to a lesser extent Egypt, were built largely on slave labor. Roman society was succeeded in Europe by feudalism, a cellular rural society, the labor of which was performed by serfs and others tied to the land and dependent on their lords, and the production of which was mainly for personal use and local markets. During the 16th century, merchant capitalism began to make serious inroads on feudalism, which had already been under internal strain for at least two centuries. This impending replacement of one society by another was heralded by the growth of internal trade and the consequent rise of towns, the gradual breakdown of feudal obligations and the flight of serfs from the manor, and the overseas explorations to the East and to the New World. Trade, markets, money transactions, and towns all undermined the insular manorial system and the serfdom on which it was based. However, the rising class of commercial (and, later, industrial) capitalists required not only time but also revolutions to overturn the older order. While this sometimes bloody transformation was in process, the triumphal procession of the ascending bourgeoisie, with its trumpets blaring and cannons roaring, spread out from Western Europe to begin the transformation of virtually every corner of the world.

Paeans to capitalism

Karl Marx and his lifetime collaborator, Friedrich Engels, in their *Manifesto of the Communist Party* (1948), acclaimed the dynamism of this new society, which by their time was in full bloom, with such abandon as to baffle those later generations of readers who grew up imagining these authors to be bearded revolutionaries spewing forth nothing but vituperation. The bourgeoisie, Marx and Engels enthused, "during its rule of scarce one hundred years, has created more massive and more colossal productive forces than have all preceding generations together. . . . It has accomplished wonders far surpassing Egyptian pyramids, Roman aqueducts, and Gothic cathedrals; it has conducted expeditions that put in the shade all former Exoduses of nations and crusades." Marx and Engels were dazzled by the energy with which the bourgeoisie, over and over again, revolutionized production, applied science to industry, communications, and agriculture, built railroads, canals, electric telegraphs, and constructed machinery to produce even more machinery. The result was an enormous increase in all kinds of products, which required continually expanding markets to absorb them. This need, the *Manifesto* declared, "chases the bourgeoisie over the whole surface of the globe. It must nestle everywhere, settle everywhere, establish connections everywhere." It must batter down "all Chinese walls" and attempt to turn the entire world into its own image.

Marx and Engels could deliver these paeans because they viewed capitalism as the latest historical stage of social development, a stage that clearly surpassed earlier ones in its productive powers. However,

---

[*] From *Challengers to Capitalism: Marx, Lenin, and Mao*, by John G. Gurley (San Francisco Book Company, 1976), pp. 7–29.

they also believed that capitalism itself would be transcended by a still higher form of society—socialism—in which the workers would be the ruling class, the means of production would be collectively owned, and economic planning would guide production and distribution. Thus, they could be both admirers and critics of capitalism, commending the bourgeoisie for its conquest of the old aristocracy and the consequent release of new energy for economic activity, but at the same time recognizing exploitative, alienating, and oppressive features of the new society, all of which, they thought, would be overcome when the proletariat, the working class, successfully rose against the system. But, while Marx and Engels could praise and damn capitalism in the same breath, in truth they were predominantly critics, and very severe ones.

The materialist conception of history

Marx and Engels developed a theory about the movement of history that purports to explain why feudalism gave way to capitalism and why the latter will be succeeded by socialism. It is essential to understand this view of social development, which they called "the materialist conception of history," if one is to have any grasp of Marxism, for it lies at the heart of almost all Marxian reasoning today.

According to this theory, which is principally Marx's, people in a society, at any given time, have a certain level of productive ability. This depends on their own knowledge and skills, on the technology (machines, tools, draft animals, and so on) available to them, and on the bountifulness of the natural environment in which they live. These together are called "the material forces of production," or, in short, the productive forces. Marx alleged that the productive forces determine the way people make their living (for example, in

hunting and gathering, agriculture, or industry) and, at the same time, the way they relate to one another in producing and exchanging the means of life (for example, as lord and serf, master and slave, or capitalist and worker). These production and exchange relationships are what Marx called "the [social] relations of production." The productive forces plus the relations of production, which Marx referred to as "the economic structure of society," shape the "superstructure" of people's religious, political, and legal systems and their modes of thought and views of life. That is, people's material lives determine their ideas and their supporting institutions.

In a famous passage, which deserves careful attention, Marx summarized the theory that "became the guiding principle of my studies":

In the social production of their existence, men inevitably enter into definite relations, which are independent of their will, namely relations of production appropriate to a given stage in the development of their material forces of production. The totality of these relations of production constitutes the economic structure of society, the real foundation, on which arises a legal and political superstructure and to which correspond definite forms of social consciousness. The mode of production of material life conditions the general process of social, political and intellectual life. It is not the consciousness of men that determines their existence, but their social existence that determines their consciousness.

The key relationships are depicted below, with the main causal connections shown running upward but with downward reciprocal relations also present. These components are separated purely for expository purposes; in fact, each is by no means independent of the others.

That is essentially the materialist conception of history. Each of its major components will now be discussed more fully to give readers an opportunity to get their

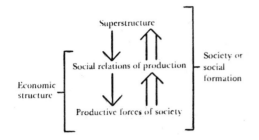

bearings. After that, the theory will be illustrated in several ways.

The productive forces.   The productive forces are the material means of production that people fashion and use to gain a livelihood from nature. Productive forces include machines, instruments and tools, raw materials, and natural resources; they also include human beings themselves—their knowledge, talents, aspirations, and needs. Productive forces develop through the labor and activity that people expend in extracting a living from their natural environment. Part of their development includes the growth of human abilities and needs. As people change their world, they develop their own capabilities as well as their desires to change the world still further. People thus make their living and themselves simultaneously. Human activity is, therefore, an integral part of the productive forces; an interpretation of the Marxian theory as being a form of "technological determinism" emasculates it by excising the human factor.

Human beings differ from animals in that they engage in purposeful productive activity—they *produce* their means of subsistence, consciously and not instinctively. At any one time, this purposive labor is performed with a certain technology, in a given environment, and within a particular class society—that is, it is performed within a certain mode of production. Human nature, according to Marx and Engels, is determined by the mode of production that people work in to maintain human life,

and since the mode of production changes, so does human nature.

Feudal man, for example, within his own mode of production, had different values, aspirations, abilities, and needs than has capitalist man within his higher mode of production. The change from the feudal to the capitalist mode of production, however, was made by human beings themselves, as they fashioned better tools, altered and controlled their environment, and, in this very process, changed themselves. Thus, capitalism could succeed feudalism not only because people designed superior technology, but also because, in the process of doing this, they changed their values and skills, their outlook on what is important, and so on.

This Marxian view of social development is important because it stresses that such development is not imposed on us from the "outside," nor do we simply adapt, in passive ways, to social changes. We, in fact, initiate those changes and, by so doing, make ourselves worthy of the new conditions. Thus, human nature, as seen by Marx and Engels, is essentially subject to change: man makes himself through productive activity.

The scheme below traces out these relationships which underlie the productive forces of the previous diagram.

The social relations of production.   According to Marx's formulation, the stage of development of society's material means of production—its productive forces—deter-

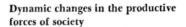

Dynamic changes in the productive forces of society

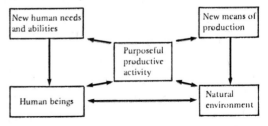

mines the social relations of production and exchange. The latter are the institutions and practices most closely associated with the way goods are produced, exchanged, and distributed. This includes property relations; the way labor is recruited, organized, and compensated; the markets or other means for exchanging the products of labor; and the methods used by the ruling classes to capture and dispose of the surplus product. The social relations of production are, in effect, the class structure of a society that is revealed in the work process. The mode of production of a society is seen principally through its class structure. A mode of production could be of the slave type, feudalist, capitalist, or anything else which describes the dominant manner in which people organize to make their living. Although societies may contain more than one mode of production, one mode is usually dominant.

As people change the world, they develop their own abilities and needs to change it further. Thus, productive forces grow over time. Sooner or later, the developing productive forces come into conflict with the prevailing class structure—the social relations of production. The newly developed ways that people extract a living from their natural environment become incompatible with the older ways they relate to one another in the work process. For instance, the rise of trade and commercial activity in the 16th century became incompatible with feudal relations in the countryside and with guilds in the towns.

This growing contradiction takes the form of a class struggle between the rising class associated with the new means of production and the old ruling class whose dominance was based on its control of the older, waning forces. This class struggle, under appropriate conditions, intensifies the contradiction between the means of production and the class structure until, as a result of revolution, new relations of production which are compatible with the superior productive forces are established. Thus, the bourgeoisie after 1500 gradually gained strength on the basis of new productive forces, such as sailing ships, improved weaponry, new energy sources, machinery, factory processes, accumulation of technical knowledge, and so on. These productive forces under their control enabled them to challenge successfully the older feudal ruling classes, whose privileged positions had depended on land rights and control of rural work processes as well as the judicial and military systems. The mode of production was changed, in a series of revolutions, sometimes spreading over a century or more, from feudalism to capitalism, from a class structure of lords and vassals, guildmasters and apprentices, to one of capitalists and wage-laborers. As Marx once put it, "The handmill gives you a society with the feudal lord; the steammill, society with the industrial capitalist." Even though coming from Marx, this is a grossly simplified aphorism that overemphasizes the technological to the neglect of the dialectical.

Marx has expressed these transformations in the following passage known by heart to many people around the world:

> At a certain stage of development, the material productive forces of society come into conflict with the existing relations of production or—this merely expresses the same thing in legal terms—with the property relations within the framework of which they have operated hitherto. From forms of development of the productive forces these relations turn into their fetters. Then begins an era of social revolution. The changes in the economic foundation lead sooner or later to the transformation of the whole immense superstructure.

The superstructure. Marx postulated that the economic structure of society molds its superstructure of social, political, and intellectual life, including sentiments, morality, illusions, modes of thought, principles, and views of life. The superstructure contains the ideas and systems of authority (political, legal, military, etc.) which support the class structure of that society—that is, the dominant position of the ruling class. In brief, how people make their living shapes their mental conceptions and supporting institutions. It follows that the transformation of the economic structure of society eventually causes the character of the superstructure to change—after ideological struggles, the overthrow of older systems of authority, and attrition have taken their toll. The defeat of the feudal ruling classes by the bourgeoisie, for example, not only opened the way for the further development of society's productive forces but in addition spelled the doom of feudal values, ideas, and institutions—all of which supported the feudal ruling classes but fettered the rising capitalists. The values associated with vows of homage and fealty, for instance, were vital to manorial life but simply got in the way of—and were incongruent with—commerce and market transactions.

Inasmuch as human beings change themselves by labor, it is clear that they alter, at the same time, at least some of their mental conceptions. They produce both material goods and their ideas. Thus, productive activity and the attending class struggles change not only the economic structure of society but the superstructure as well. Since this is so, interactions between the two are inevitable and are, in fact, both numerous and intricate. That is, the way people make a living determines their ideas, but these ideas in turn affect the way they make their living. However, modes of thought are shaped and limited, in the first place, by the mode of production. Accordingly, the ideas that become influential in a society cover only the narrow range reflecting the material activities and interests of the dominant class. Many ideas do not gain prestige because they conflict with real positions of class domination which themselves rest on a certain attained

level of the productive forces. For example, the current idea of "no growth" is incompatible with the fortunes of a capitalist class that are generated by industrial growth.

History is not the development of ideas, Marx and Engels tell us, but rather the development of productive forces, and the formation of ideas is explained by these underlying material changes. "Life is not determined by consciousness, but consciousness by life." Their theory of history "does not explain practice from the idea but explains the formation of ideas from material practice." This leads Marx and Engels to the conclusion that in every society the ideas of the ruling class are the ruling ideas. This does not mean that, at any given time, there is only a single set of ideas which serves the ruling class. The class structure of a society is often complex and the ideas of each class are likely to be expressed in complex ways in the superstructure. Therefore, revolutionary ideas may exist side by side with conventional ones because of the existence of a revolutionary class. (Marxism thus explains itself by the rise of an industrial proletariat in the first half of the 19th century.) But these revolutionary ideas can at best displace some other ideas; they cannot by themselves overthrow the prevailing class structure, which gave rise to the ruling ideas. So Marx and Engels write that "not criticism but revolution is the driving force of history." From the Marxist view this means, to use our previous example, that the idea of "no growth" can become dominant, not through criticism of the idea of "growth," but only by the revolutionary overthrow of the capitalist class.

The superstructure contains not only ideas but also institutions and activities that support the class structure of society—the state, legal institutions, family structures, art forms, and spiritual processes. The Marxian presupposition is that the superstructure of ideas and supporting institutions, although in some respects and to some degree capable of developing a life of its own, strongly reflects the economic structure of society. Thus, according to some Marxists, the prehistoric cave-wall paintings of animals in southern France and northern Spain reflected the magical need of hunters to depict their prey accurately and naturally. The later geometric pottery designs of settled agriculturalists, it is claimed, were reflections of the more abstract, mysterious forces that determined whether crops would prosper or die. This revolutionary change from hunting and gathering to settled agriculture, which occurred because of radically new productive forces (which in turn transformed the relations of production, also altered other elements of the superstructure, such as family structures, religions, rules and laws, governing bodies, the games played, and military organizations.

Marx regarded the religious world as "the reflex of the real world." Religion is a consolation for man's degraded condition; it is the imaginary realization of human perfection. It will finally vanish "when the practical relations of everyday life offer to man none but perfectly intelligible and reasonable relations with regard to his fellowmen and to Nature." For capitalism, Marx reasoned, "Christianity with its *cultus* of abstract man, more especially in its bourgeois developments, Protestantism, Deism, etc., is the most fitting form of religion." Engels carried the analysis further by linking some changes in religious views to changes in material life over a period of 2,000 years. But Engels was careful to note that once an ideology (such as a set of religious views) arises, it develops in part independently of the economic structure, subject to its own laws.

In Marxian thought, the state, a product of society at a certain stage of development, as a rule is the institution that protects the property and privileges of the ruling classes and preserves order among the oppressed and exploited classes. It is an instrument of class rule, the manifestation of the irreconcilability of class antagonisms. Nevertheless, Engels added: "By way of exception, however, periods occur in which the warring classes balance each other so nearly that the state power, as ostensible mediator, acquires, for the moment, a certain degree of independence of both." Marxists assert that over long periods the form of the state has changed—for example, from decentralized to centralized monarchies, to constitutional governments, bourgeois democracies, fascist dictatorships, and so on—in response to changes in economic structures. The state is the guarantor of a given set of property relations, and in capitalist society its highest function is the protection of private property. Marx believed that the bourgeois state would have to be smashed by the proletariat and a dictatorship of that class established in the new socialist society. As socialism gives way to communism, the state will wither away because, in a classless society, no organ of class rule is required. The state, however, as an administrator of things, such as a five-year plan, rather than an oppressor of subordinate classes, remains.

Dialectical materialism. Marx's view of social development has been called by others "dialectical materialism." The phrase refers to Marx's method of analyzing social change, a method that is strongly present in all of his major works. Marxian materialism reverses the idealist approach of viewing abstract ideas, concepts, and consciousness as divorced from real people and their activities. According to Marx, materialism begins with "real, active men, and on the basis of their real life-process demonstrates the development of the ideological reflexes and echoes of this life-process." The ideas in the human brain (morality, religion, and all the rest of ideology) do not live completely independent lives. A person, in trying to understand social history, should not start with these phantoms—with, say, the concept of "freedom"—for they are all sublimates of the real material life-process. For example, the 16th century is not explainable by "the idea of expansion," as though some people got this idea around 1500 and then proceeded to carry it out. Instead, the idea of expansion came from revolutionary changes in the economic structures of Western European societies, attended by transformations of the relations of production.

To understand the world, a person must begin with what is basic—with real human beings and their activities in the world. Marx and Engels felt that work was the most basic and most important of all human activities. Most of people's lives are spent working and much of the rest is spent in an environment which is shaped by the kind of productive technology available to them. For example, Indians lived in huts or tents near the rivers they fished, while early industrial workers lived in the company towns built around the factories. In both cases, the work process exerted an all-pervading influence on their lives, shaping the conditions of their existence and therefore of their thoughts. Marxian materialism maintains that ideas, philosophies, religions, and so forth all take form within the influence of real material conditions and are therefore determined by them.

Materialism is also at the base of the Marxian concept of social class, for classes are the result of people's lives being formed by the work process within a strict hierarchical work structure. Marx and Engels believed that two major classes, the bourgeoisie and the proletariat (along with several minor ones), emerged with capitalism. The bourgeoisie and the proletariat are distinct classes because the former owns and controls the physical means of production—raw materials, energy, and capital goods—while the latter owns only its labor-power and must sell it to the bourgeoisie to survive.

Although Marx believed, along with other materialists, that objects exist independently of human beings and their consciousness, still his materialism was quite different from that of the 18th century, as anticipated in the writings of John Locke. Bertrand Russell, in his *A History of Western Philosophy*, has best delineated this difference by pointing out that the older materialism regarded sensation of the subject as passive, with activity attributed to the object. Russell explains that in Marx's view, on the other hand, "all sensation or perception is an interaction between subject and object; the bare object, apart from the activity of the percipient, is a mere raw material, which is transformed in the process of becoming known." Consequently, knowledge is not passive contemplation, as Locke and others would have it. Rather, Russell continues, "both subject and object, both the knower and the thing known, are in a continual process of mutual adaptation." Russell then connects Marx's materialism to his economics:

> For Marx, matter, not spirit, is the driving force [of human history]. But it is matter in the peculiar sense that we have been considering, not the wholly dehumanized matter of the atomists. This means that, for Marx, the driving force is really man's relation to matter, of which the most important part is his mode of production. In this way Marx's materialism, in practice, becomes economics.

Marx stated that we can really know an object only by acting on it successfully. "And since we change the object when we act upon it," Russell appends, "truth ceases to be static, and becomes something which is continually changing and developing. That is why Marx calls his materialism 'dialectical.'" When a person gains knowledge through investigation of the material world he not only changes that world—and hence "the truth"—but changes himself at the same time, for in the process of knowing an object he acquires new information, abilities, and needs. This has been phrased very well by Ernst Fischer, the Austrian poet and critic, who wrote in *The Essential Marx:*

From the very start the species man has not appropriated the world passively but actively, through practice, labor, the setting of goals, the giving of form. As men *changed* the world they expanded and refined their ability to *know* it, and the growing capacity for cognition again enhanced their ability to change it.

What Fischer is describing is the dialectical relation between human beings and their natural environment, an important instance of the dialectical process that Marx and Engels believed pervaded human societies. In its broadest sweep, the dialectic method stresses the following elements:

1. All things are in constant change.
2. The ultimate source of the change is within the thing or process itself.
3. This source is the struggle of opposites, the contradiction, within each thing.
4. This struggle, at nodal points, brings about qualitative changes, or leaps, so that the thing is transformed into something else.
5. Practical-critical activity resolves the contradictions.

Formal logic, which has dominated Western thought for some 2,000 years, is based on the simplest and seemingly most commonsense axioms, such as A is equal to A and A is not equal to *non-A*. But by being based on axioms like these, which freeze reality into fixed categories, formal logic loses its ability to explain structural change. Thus, one difference between the bourgeois (traditional) and Marxian approach to economics is that the former postulates only *quantitative* change, with each element maintaining its basic identity as it grows or contracts, whereas Marxian change allows for *qualitative transformation,* with each thing capable of turning into something new by becoming a synthesis of itself and its opposite.

Marxian dialectics is the logic of constant change: A, which includes not only itself but its opposite, *non-A*, is in continuous evolution. The fundamental cause of change in all things lies in their internal contradictions, in the struggle of opposites, in their self-movement. Whatever *is* has emerged from something else. Capitalism has evolved out of feudalism; socialism will emerge out of the contradictions of capitalism, not because it is "a better idea." Within capitalism, wealth exists in unity with its opposite, poverty; the very same economic processes have created both wealth and poverty, and one cannot exist or even be defined independently of the other. Similarly, workers in capitalism can only be discussed in relation to their opposite, capitalists. The one is inconceivable without the other, and social change occurs as a result of the struggle between these opposites.

Dialectical thought, which Marx learned from the work of the German philosopher Hegel (1770–1831), has been called the power of negative thinking. This is because, according to the dialectical view, everything includes its opposite (its negative); a thesis has an antithesis. The struggle of these opposites leads to the transformation of the thesis into some other and higher form of being—a synthesis. The development of the thesis which results from the contradiction does not stop at the opposite of what it was, but rather moves to a synthesis of itself and its opposite. Thus, a thing or process is never simply this or that; it is always both. "The simple-minded use of the notion 'right or wrong,'" English philosopher Alfred Whitehead wrote, "is one of the chief obstacles to the progress of understanding." This is because right includes wrong and wrong contains right. Likewise, Engels wrote that one knows "that which is recognized now as true has also its latent false side which will later manifest itself, just as that which is now regarded as false has also its true side by virtue of which it could previously have been regarded as true. One knows that what is maintained to be necessary is composed of sheer accidents and that the so-called accidental is the form behind which necessity hides itself."

Marx can hardly be understood unless his dialectical approach is kept constantly in mind.

Applications of the Marxian theory. Engels emphasized that, in searching for explanations of historical change, one should not seek them "by deduction from fundamental principles" but instead should discover them "in the stubborn facts of the existing system of production." Further, the materialist conception of history can be successfully applied to a historical example, not by "mere empty talk," but only by "an abundance of critically examined historical material which has been completely mastered." One must also allow for many interactions among the elements of the historical episode being studied. For example, in some societies religion might inhibit the further development of the productive forces, while in other societies certain work institutions might play such a retarding role. If one does not make historical studies, Engels asserted, "the application of the theory to any period of history would be easier than the solution of a simple equation of the first degree."

Marx once complained, along the same lines, that a critic had tried to use his theory in a "super-historical" way:

He feels he absolutely must metamorphose my historical sketch of the genesis of capitalism in Western Europe into a historico-philosophic theory of the general path every people is fated to tread, whatever the historical circumstances in which it finds itself, in order that it may ultimately arrive at the form of economy which ensures, together with the greatest expansion of the productive powers of social labor, the most complete development of man. But I beg his pardon. (He is both honoring and shaming me too much.)

Marx then pointed out that, although ancient Roman society had seeds of capitalism within it, it nevertheless developed into slavery:

Thus events strikingly analogous but taking place in different historical surroundings led to totally different results. By studying each of these forms of evolution separately and then comparing them one can easily find the clue to this phenomenon, but one will never arrive there by using as one's master key a general historico-philosophical theory, the supreme virtue of which consists in being super-historical.

Marx and Engels, then, took pains to warn both friends and critics about the dangers of using the materialist conception of history in a mechanical and undialectical way, in which it is simply superimposed on any and all historical situations without regard to strong individual differences. The materialist conception of history provides a framework for analysis, a method, not ready-made answers.

The emergence of capitalism

Despite the fact that Marx's and Engel's analysis led to the conclusion that socialism would succeed capitalism, their sharpest focus was on capitalism itself, not on the future society. Marxism is concerned with the continuing evolution of the material and human world in all of its complexity, but most specifically it seeks to explain the dynamics of capitalism—the historical moment of its birth, its later development, and its future demise. Fundamental to that explanation, and the natural starting point, is an analysis of the forces that brought capitalism into being, a topic that will illustrate the use of the materialist conception of history and that will, at the same time, prepare us for an analysis of capitalism itself.

Capitalism has often been defined as either a commercial system (a money, exchange economy) or as a particular spirit of enterprise and profit rationality. These definitions, however, are historically imprecise, for both imply the existence of "capitalism" throughout most of history. Commercial and money systems reach back to antiquity, and the enterprising profit spirit of the Phoenician traders seems little different from that of the British East India Company or of our own exporters today. The first definition is vague; the second is idealist, in the sense that it assumes that elements of the superstructure lie at the heart of the system.

Marx defined capitalism by its mode of production. It is that mode of production in which the bourgeoisie, as owners of the means of production, directly opposes and exploits, in the production process, its antithesis, the proletariat, which owns only its labor-power and sells it as a commodity. The chief aim of the bourgeoisie is the production of surplus value (profits, rents, interest, executive salaries and bonuses). While capitalism produces its products as commodities, which are exchanged for money in a predominantly monetary economy, these exchanges are not the hallmark of the system. "The historical conditions of [capitalism's] existence are by no means given with the mere circulation of money and commodities," wrote Marx. "It can spring into life only when the owner of the means of production and subsistence meets in the market with the free laborer selling his labor-power." The heart of capitalism is not in the circulation but in the production sphere, where the laborer works under the control of the capitalist (to whom his labor belongs) and the product is the property of the capitalist. This definition clearly establishes capitalism as a special historical phenomenon, distinguishing it from its immediate feudal predecessor. In that earlier society, the bulk of the population, in possession of its own primitive tools, was tied to the land as serfs and vassals or united with its artisan capital in the guilds and in the homes. The definition also distinguishes capitalism from the classical periods of slavery, in which the slaves themselves were legally owned and exploited by others.

When capitalism is seen as a distinctive economic system, one must infer that there have been crucial points in economic development when qualitative changes occurred, when one system changed into another. Such abrupt changes are bound up with classes, the rise of the new class challenging and overcoming its predecessor, usually by force. When one ruling class replaces another, in response to the development of society's productive forces, that society undergoes a change in its mode of production, a qualitative transformation. Thus, development is not entirely gradual and quantitative but is at crucial times subject to "leaps," such as from feudalism to capitalism. The Marxian dialectical view, as we have already observed, is that the principal determinants of feudalism's decline lay within feudalism itself, within its own contradictions. This viewpoint does not rule out the impact of forces external to feudalism. As Mao Tse-tung has written about the dialectical approach: "It holds that external causes are the condition of change and internal causes are the basis of change, and that external causes become operative through internal causes. In a suitable temperature an egg changes into a chicken, but no temperature can change a stone into a chicken, because each has a different basis."

Maurice Dobb, a British Marxist economist who taught at Cambridge University for many decades, surmises that the growth of trade, starting around the 11th century, and the accompanying rise of towns were two forces external to feudalism that played their roles in weakening it. However, in his book *Studies in the Development of Capitalism,* he states that the main force was internal: "It was the inefficiency of feudalism as a system of production, coupled with the growing needs of the ruling class for revenue, that was primarily responsible for its decline." This led to overexploitation of the labor force, to the desertion *en masse* of serfs from their lords' manors, to the adoption by the feudal ruling class of expedients—commutation of labor services, leasing demesne lands to tenant farmers, etc.—and finally to the transformation of production relations in the countryside from feudal forms to commercial capitalist ones. Feudalism's internal contradictions destroyed that society, aided however by the external factors of the growth of trade and of market towns.

Feudalism had fairly well disintegrated by 1350–1400. However, the capitalist period did not begin until 1550–1600, 200 years later. Consequently, Dobb reasons, capitalism did not cause the decay of feudalism but itself developed from the crisis and decline of the old order. In the interval that elapsed between the beginning of feudalism's disintegration and the development of capitalism as a new mode of production, during the 1400s and 1500s, much wealth was accumulated by the rising bourgeoisie.

The merchant bourgeoisie gained its wealth through plunder abroad and through the acquisition of monopoly powers, allowing it to intervene profitably between producers and consumers. Dobb points out that this merchant bourgeoisie "compromised with feudal society once its privileges had been won," so that by the end of the 16th century it "had become a conservative rather than a revolutionary force."

The industrial bourgeoisie, on the heels of the merchants, concentrated capital in its hands through (1) speculative gains from land transactions, (2) usury, (3) profits from widening and freeing markets and from changing the mode of production to raise labor productivity, and (4) forceful acquisition of others' wealth. This rising industrial class came into conflict not only with the remnants of feudalism—urban localism and monopolies of the craft guilds—but also with "the restrictive monopolies in the sphere of trade in which

merchant capital" was entrenched. The political struggles of the 17th and 18th centuries reflected the complexities of these several antagonisms.

Thus, the whole period of capital accumulation by the bourgeoisie was an essential stage in the genesis of capitalism, a period that fell between the decay of feudalism and the real beginning of the bourgeois mode of production, a period Marx called "primitive [or original] accumulation." During this period there was both a transfer to and a concentration of wealth in bourgeois hands. This prior accumulation was necessary to enable the new bourgeoisie to break up or subordinate to capital the petty mode of production (independent small-scale agriculture and handicrafts) which was the legacy of feudal society.

However, according to Dobb, the formation of the bourgeoisie was not sufficient to usher in capitalism, because capitalism requires a laboring class dispossessed of its primitive means of production, with nothing left but its own labor-power—otherwise it would not be willing to work for others. Dobb explains: "The essence of this primary accumulation [consists in] the transfer of property from small owners to the ascendant bourgeoisie and the consequent pauperization of the former." That is to say, financial enrichment alone was not enough: it had to be enrichment of the few at the expense of the many. In short, the very same processes both enlarged and concentrated capital and simultaneously created "free" labor, free in the two senses that it could seek employment wherever it liked and that it had been freed of its possessions.

An embryonic English proletariat, for instance, was formed during the 1500s by the disbandment of feudal retainers, the eviction or release of peasants through land enclosures (for the raising of sheep) and changes in methods of tillage, the confiscation of lands of the Catholic Church (which tended to destroy feudal social relations and speed up enclosures), and by natural increases of the population. As a result, during this century a growing army of dispossessed people roamed the countryside as vagrants, whereupon, as Marx said, they were persecuted and harassed with "a bloody legislation against vagabondage." Later, in the 1600s and early 1700s—as land continued to be enclosed, as semi-feudal relations were redefined by landlords to the disadvantage of peasants, and as agricultural depression ruined many small landholders—some of the newly dispossessed sought work in rural domestic industry or as agricultural wage laborers and others drifted into towns and cities to seek employment in manufacturing workshops. By around 1750 the capitalist mode of production was fairly well implanted in agriculture, thus ensuring the existence of a relatively small group of large landowners (three-quarters of the land was owned by landlords) and a mass of dispossessed proletarian wage earners. Subsequently, the English proletariat was swelled by immigration of cheap labor from Ireland and Scotland, the enlistment of women and children into the ranks of wage labor, and rapid increases of population.

In *Capital*, Marx provided much detail on the early formation of the proletariat in England, which he called the classic case. "The expropriation of the agricultural producer, of the peasant, from the soil," Marx declared, "is the basis of the whole process." Marx stressed the role in this process of land enclosures, which took place from the late 1400s into the 19th century, and which replaced communal and semi-communal forms of landholding with private forms. Marx contended that enclosures were a crucial part of the transition from feudalism to capitalism and hence of the birth of the modern proletariat. The expropriation of peasants (accomplished not only by enclosures but in many other ways discussed by Marx) fash-ioned an "outlawed proletariat" that was then "whipped, branded, tortured by laws grotesquely terrible, into the discipline necessary for the wage system." This "free" labor was thus forced into wage relationships in agriculture, rural industry, and town enterprises.

Marx asserted that this process was repeated in European countries, though, he wrote, it "assumes different aspects, and runs through its various phases in different orders of succession, and at different periods." In Europe generally, the rising commercial capitalist classes acquired much wealth by spanning the globe in search of plunder and profit. In the meantime, European proletarian classes, dispossessed of means of production, were fashioned for the growing factories and manufacturing works. More and more, as time passed, concentrated capital met dispossessed labor on the labor markets.

In the New World, however, the early European capitalists did not find the process of developing profitable enterprises so simple. The seizure of North America with all of its natural resources and the "clearing" of the Indian population that accompanied British, French, and Spanish colonization prepared the way for the rise of American capitalism. Far from being based on the opening up of empty, virgin land, American capitalism was founded on the continual expropriation of a lightly populated but ecologically balanced land. Here the indigenous Indian population either died in great numbers from European diseases or fled into the continental interior. Capital found much potential natural wealth but little labor-power.

Historian Eric Williams, in his book *Capitalism and Slavery*, analyzes how this imbalance between the ready availability of capital in the form of land, raw materials, and liquid funds, on the one hand, and the lack of a sufficiently large labor force, on the other, led to slavery in the early period of capitalist development in the Caribbean. This imbalance, he explains, gave rise to a capitalist-generated slave mode of production and only later to capitalism itself. Throughout the Caribbean, as well as in North America, efforts were made to force Indians into service for production. The failure of these efforts led to heavy reliance, first, on white indentured servants (whose conditions of servitude approached slavery), convicts, and other temporarily unfree labor. But Indian slavery and white servitude were both inferior, from the capitalists' standpoint, to black African slaves, who proved to possess the cheapest and the best labor-power. When the slave trade and later slavery itself were abolished by the British, the sugar planters turned back to white labor and then to East Indians and to a lesser extent to Chinese coolies.

The reason for black slavery, Williams summarizes, "was economic, not racial; it had to do not with the color of the laborer, but the cheapness of the labor. . . . Slavery was not born of racism: rather, racism was the consequence of slavery. Unfree labor in the New World was brown, white, black, and yellow; Catholic, Protestant, and pagan." Capital sought labor-power wherever it could be found, enslaved it if it had to, bought it on markets if it could. Negro slavery, Williams adds, "was only a solution, in certain historical circumstances, of the Caribbean labor problem." When the sugar monopoly of the British West Indies impeded further economic progress by British industrial capitalists, they successfully attacked the slavery on which the monopoly rested. Economics, then, lay at the heart of both slavery and its abolition, though other factors clearly played important roles, especially in slavery's abolition.

Farther north, the American colonies during the 17th and 18th centuries were both pre-capitalist and capitalist in their modes of production. In the southern colonies, some strong elements of capitalism prevailed, for private capital sought profits through the production of commodities for a world market. But, just as in the Caribbean, capital encountered acute shortages of wage-labor that necessitated the employment of black slaves and white indentured servants in large numbers. This unfree labor was, in a sense, grafted onto the capitalist base. Marx wrote that the plantations represented the capitalist mode of production only in the formal sense, "since the slavery of Negroes precludes free wage-labor, which is the basis of capitalist production. But the business in which slaves are used is conducted by *capitalists*."

Such enslaved labor was used in the northern colonies, too, but there the mode of production began largely as pre-capitalist, in which many small freeholders (land owners) produced mostly for their own needs. However, the North very early witnessed the vigorous beginnings of commercial capitalism, too. But, for the most part, Marx wrote, the colonists in the North were not capitalists and did not carry on capitalist production.

In the first half of the 19th century, manufacturing and industry developed robustly in the northeastern states, and small-scale family farming burgeoned with the westward expansion. Indentured servitude vanished behind the opening of the western frontiers and in the face of heavy European immigration. Ultimately, northern capital and the farmers of the West came into armed conflict with the slavery mode of production in the South. Just as the English revolutions of the 17th century were, in large part, capitalist uprisings against absolutism and feudalism, and the French revolution of 1789 broke obstruction of feudal nobility and clergy to the further development of the French bourgeoisie, so the American Civil War served capital by expunging slavery as a mode of production that prevented the full continental development of the capitalist mode.

With regard to colonization generally, Marx observed that the capitalist mode of production was impossible so long as land was plentiful and cheaply available to labor, for this frustrated the formation of a working class that could be subjected to capitalist exploitation. A solution to the problem of the formation of a proletariat in such circumstances, as the problem appeared in Australia, was suggested by an English author, E. G. Wakefield. He proposed that the government should put a very high price on virgin land in order to compel the immigrants to labor long for wages before they earned enough money to buy land. Thus, the immigrants would have to be wage earners for an extended period before they could become independent peasants. Marx sarcastically commented that the money extorted from the worker by the sale of land at relatively prohibitive prices—violating, Marx noted, the sacred law of supply and demand—would be employed by the government to import more cheap labor from Europe into the colonies "and thus keep the wage-labor market full for the capitalists."

The danger of acute labor scarcity was also present in the United States at various times during the 18th and 19th centuries, largely because virgin land was so easily available to the working force (once the Indians were killed or driven off). The Homestead Act of 1862 exacerbated this tendency toward scarce labor by making land in the West available in lots of 160 acres to workers in the industrializing East, which threatened to raise industrial wages and lower profits. But this threat was mostly averted by the Immigration Act of 1864, which, as Charles and Mary Beard stated in *The Rise of American Civilization*, "gave federal authorization to the importation of working people under terms of contract analogous to the indentured servants of colonial times." By this and other means, the industrial capitalists managed to reproduce cheap labor despite the constant drains that occurred from the "reserve army."

The capitalist mode of production, these examples affirm, depends not only on the concentration of capital in the hands of a capitalist class, but also on the creation and continual reproduction of a working class that is dispossessed of or denied the means of production, and that has only its labor-power to sell. If individual members of this class "escape" to self-sufficiency through the slow accumulation of capital or by being the recipients of land grants, mechanisms are quickly brought into play to replenish the army of workers. This process has repeated itself, Marxists conclude, though with variation in detail, everywhere that capitalism has appeared or has been forced on a population.

Outside of Europe and America, the most notable growth of an indigenous capitalism has taken place in Japan. The rapid early growth of capitalism in the Meiji era (starting in 1968) was accompanied by pressure on the agricultural population similar to that which attended the emergence of capitalism in Europe. William Lockwood, of Princeton University, in his interesting work *The Economic Development of Japan*, has described this process vividly. He relates how masses of peasants were driven into tenantry and debt in the first 25 years of the Meiji period, and how an escape from this condition was made almost impossible by the high price of land, high rents, and usurious interest rates. "The mounting surplus of farm population had to find employment increasingly outside agriculture," he writes. "Those families which remained on the farm also sought supplementary income, either through part-time employment in local industries or through putting their reluctant daughters into the textile factories of the towns and cities." Japan, he says, thus repeated the earlier experience of many European countries, the pressures on the Japanese peasants being especially "reminiscent of those experienced by the English yeoman a century or more before."

Lockwood has also drawn a rough parallel between the ways some of the European and the Japanese proletariat were recruited. In Japan, low-wage female labor was recruited for the textile industries. "Wages were low, even by Japanese standards. . . . There were no factory laws. Any organization of workers to bargain collectively or strike was effectively forbidden under the Police Regulations of 1900." In general, Japanese industrialization along capitalist lines exhibited the same poverty, miserable working conditions, and lack of worker protection as appeared earlier in England.

Even today, in South Korea, Brazil, Iran, Indonesia, and wherever capitalist development is getting started, the same phenomena appear: a separation of the producers from their means of production, a concentration of ownership of the means of production in a capitalist class, and the formation of an urban proletariat, of cheap industrial labor, kept cheap mainly by oppressive means, whose surpluses are appropriated by capitalists, landowners, financiers, and bureaucrats. Lockwood seems a bit surprised that Japan experienced much the same development as Europe, a development that created both wealth and poverty, where the existence of the one depended on the existence of the other. Had he lived to see Japanese capitalism, Marx would not have been the least surprised. This has been the typical pattern of emerging capitalism everywhere.

READING 2-2 _____

Business as a system of power*

DOUGLAS F. DOWD

"The business of America," President Coolidge once remarked, "is business." More pointed, while also reflecting the subsequent progress of *big* business, was the famous statement 30 years later of Charles Wilson (of General Motors, and Secretary of Defense under Eisenhower); "What's good for General Motors is good for America." These pithy assertations, and others of the genre—"The public? The public be damned!"—have been much maligned by those with a loftier vision for America. But as matters now stand—that is, in the absence of fundamental institutional change —it is unquestionably true that when business is bad, Americans are badly off; when GM and the other giant corporations are in trouble, so is not only the entire economy, but the entire society.

In short, America is a business society, for better or for worse. It is, indeed, *the* business society, even in comparison with other capitalist societies. Unlike the others, we started that way; we have become even more so with the passage of time. If, in our own day, deep questioning of the performance of American society has become pervasive, is it not because business calculations rather than human needs and possibilities so much dominate the entirety of our lives—not only in industry, but in our foreign policies, our domestic politics,

* From *The Twisted Dream: Capitalist Development in the United States since 1776*, 2d ed. by Douglas F. Dowd, pp. 59–83, © 1977. Reprinted by permission of Winthrop Publishers, Inc., Cambridge, Massachusetts.

our schools, our health care systems, our environment, and even our culture?

That ours is so fully a business-like society and the most fully-developed of capitalist societies allows two major inferences about the historical development of the United States. First, *all* social activities—the production of all goods and all services from carrots to computers and from mechanics to ministers—have flourished or languished dependent upon the degree to which they have satisfied the finally financial criterion of *marketability.* Indeed, most Americans are unaware that other, essentially qualitative, criteria exist to be taken seriously. From the necessary evaluation of a business firm in terms of its income statement and balance sheet, American society has moved insensibly to evaluating virtually all activities in similarly quantitative and pecuniary terms: What does it cost? How much does he make? Will it sell? Is it profitable? So it is with our ways of speech, with paintings and movie stars, with professors and journalists, even with religious personages. The society has left or created no comfortable resting-place for means of evaluation, other than "the bottom line."

Second, if business criteria have made their way into all walks of life, the prime reason is that capitalist development has been so successful in its own terms in the United States. No other country has had so long and so impressive a history of expansion, production, and productivity, with over time our levels of per capita real incomes. Capitalism stresses material achievement as its promise. American capitalism has fulfilled that promise. If, in the process, large sections of the population have been shunted aside, exploited, and oppressed, left outside the charmed circle of material well-being drawn by the American Dream, then that is by no means unique to the United States where, in fact or in illusion, the majority has seen itself as

blessed to reside in the most blessed of all nations.

To say that American capitalist development has been successful for so long is to point to two other major aspects of our development: the persistent and remarkable profitability, and the easy and comprehensive access to power, prestige, and authority by American businessmen and those who live by their criteria. These two processes have sustained and reinforced each other, and they bear closer examination, which must continue to focus most heavily on the questions of *expansion* and *exploitation,* the alpha and omega of capitalist development.

Onward and upward with King Cotton

Expansion may be thought of as having two directions: upward, the growth of the economy in its productive capacity and its structure of production, and outward, the expansion of the land surface under the control or influence of the national economy.

The temporal and social advantages for capitalism in the United States were facilitated mostly by our *geographic* realities and possibilities. The meaning of the North American colonies to the British was slight by comparison with what could be made of the continent stretching westward from the lands the British had settled on the Eastern Seaboard. Given the limited maritime and military technology of the time, the new United States had virtually a free hand in moving into the wide open and very rich spaces to the west of the original 13 colonies, and much more was made of the original land space because of that expansion into the West.

Consider briefly what access to the West stimulated and allowed and, more subtly, what it required (most especially, canals and railroads). For the South, the western lands were both a life-saver and a boon—a life-saver because the South's techniques of cultivating tobacco and cotton had depleted the soils; a boon because the new and even richer lands fitted most profitably into rapidly expanding markets in the Old World (most importantly, cotton for England's burgeoning textile mills). The South's movement westward into Alabama, Mississippi, and Louisiana meant, of course, the wholesale destruction of Native Americans and of their remarkable and healthy societies, as well as a vast increase in the numbers of black slaves imported and bred for plantation cultivation.[1]

But the South's geographic and economic expansion was an essential part of the developing capitalist world-economy and, of course, profitable—to the plantation owners, to the merchants and shippers and financiers tied into plantation agriculture. Still more, the entire American economy depended very much upon the dynamism, the foreign exchange, and the internal trade generated by King Cotton in the first half of the 19th century. The importance of the South's economy in the United States was well-reflected in its power in the federal government. By any measure of population, land, or capital, the South's power was disproportionate, whether referring to the legislative, judicial, or executive branch of government. The South's power, not the moral issue of slavery, was the central issue leading to the Civil War; when the South lost, it was because the economic power of northern industry, agriculture, and finance had surpassed it. If we may judge the intentions of warriors by what they do after victory, the organization and functioning of the American federal government during and after the Civil War tells us that northern intentions were to adapt federal power to the needs of industrial, not planter, capitalism.

The North's economic strength rested on the commercial, industrial, and financial activities that had their small beginnings in colonial New England, New York, Pennsylvania, and New Jersey. The beginnings were small because of the less bountiful agricultural possibilities in the North as compared with the South. However, forced to diversify and to improvise, by the 1830s the small beginnings had become a torrent of economic life, with still greater dynamism lying squarely ahead.

Much of the North's early development had depended on the South, for the merchants of the North were heavily involved in the slave trade and in the associated rum and general mercantile trade in a series of "triangular" patterns linking North America with the Caribbean, Africa, and Europe. Veblen had a characteristically insightful and sardonic view of these northern activities:

The slave trade never was a "nice" occupation or an altogether unexceptionable investment— "balanced on the edge of the permissible." But even though it may have been distasteful to one and another of its New-England men of affairs, and though there always was a suspicion of moral obliquity attached to the slave-trade, yet it had the fortune to be drawn into the service of the greater good. In conjunction with its running-mate, the rum-trade, it laid the foundations of some very reputable fortunes at the focus of commercial enterprise that presently became the center of American culture, and so gave rise to some of the country's Best People. At least so they say.

Perhaps also it was, in some part, in this early pursuit of gain in this moral penumbra that American business enterprise learned how not to let its right hand know what its left hand is doing; and there is always something to be done that is best done with the left hand.[2]

The North's process of economic development soon became the most dynamic industrialization process in the world up to that time; it was weaning itself from its heavy southern diet even at that time it was gaining the most from it. Of the several factors that loom large in northern economic development, one whole complex related to westward expansion. It was as vital as it was timely.

The dream unfolds: Westward the course of empire

It is impossible to speculate beyond a certain point on what the United States would have been like had its geographic scope been confined to that of the original colonies. But we need not speculate. For the states north of the Mason-Dixon line, the trans-Appalachian West was not merely a beckoning frontier; it was a seemingly endless expanse of land teeming with excellent soils, waterways, minerals (including gold and silver), and forests. To exploit those lands, the United States had to import rising millions of people, dig canals and build the largest rail network in the world—30,000 miles by 1860, 53,000 by 1870, twice that by 1882, and over 210,000 miles by 1904—import capital, and develop a technology that could master the great spaces and complex needs of such a land. But these needs had another side to them: they offered boundless possibilities to a society dominated and led by people with their eyes on financial gain.

The millions of immigrants contributed not just labor power, but imagination and enterprise and energy. The transportation network required new private and public financial institutions, and it constituted an enormous demand for a whole range of products—most importantly, metals and machinery and coal, the heart of 19th-century industrial development. A new technology was required to dig canals, to tame the plains and the mountains with rails and powerful locomotives, and to exploit the surface and subsurface resources of America's varied lands. All this, taken together with a persisting labor shortage, meant that the United States became the first of all industrial nations to develop a comprehensive machine technology for all aspects of production—agricultural, mineral, manufacturing, and transportation.

The resulting high labor productivity, combined with the widespread ownership of land (relative to Europe) yielded a level and a distribution of income that provided the first *domestic* mass market for modern production. By the end of the 19th century, the structure of American production in both consumer and capital goods was broader and deeper than anywhere else in the world; and the process had just begun.

With unprecedented swiftness, the United States filled in its continental boundaries, and in doing so created an economy that dazzled the world. But the unprecedented swiftness was matched by unprecedented rapacity—a heedless exploitation of natural resources, and a pattern of human exploitation whose viciousness was obscured, on the one hand, by the widespread expectation that *everyone* would someday rise in the socioeconomic structure and, on the other, by the equally widespread indifference to the conditions of those (especially nonwhites) who in fact had no such prospects.

From all this, a process of economic expansion whose buoyancy and profitability, despite intermittent business panics and crises, transformed the northeastern quadrant of the United States into a businessman's Eldorado. Meanwhile, cities grew like mushrooms over the face of the nation —New York, Philadelphia, and Boston, of course; but also Chicago, Cleveland, Cincinnati, St. Louis, New Orleans, Omaha, and San Francisco. The growth of the cities, like the growth of the economy, was a response to business needs and possibilities; as for anything more complicated, that could wait—or be forgotten.

Survival and success in the expansionist process required passing the test of the market, the test of a fully commercialized society. Those who survived grew in strength, and they garnered the society's power, prestige, and authority. *Power* means the ability to decide, to influence, to control; *prestige,* both a source and a consequence of power, refers to the deference received by those who possess power in society; *authority* resides in those who have the weight of law, of custom, and of society's deepest values vested in them.

In the U.S., already by the close of the 19th century the strength of the business impulse had swept aside all noncommercial contenders for power, prestige, or authority—except those political figures who knew where the power lay. In practice, this meant a multitude of things; most especially it meant that what business needed, business got. When complications arose, it was almost always when one business group was in contention with another business group—small versus big business, farmers versus railroads, for instance. We now turn to the evolution of American business as "a system of power."[3]

Capitalism, American-style

Adam Smith's hopes for a benign capitalist order rested squarely on his prescription for a fully competitive economy. In such an economy, all firms would be small; that is, the percentage of a given industry's output produced by one firm (or by a few firms) would be insignificant as a percentage of the whole industry output. Without control over supply, each business would have to function in response to the free market; *with* control over supply, the powerful firm could control the market. Smith's policies were designed to eliminate the control provided by State-granted privileges and monopolies. He did not examine the future dynamics of the kind of private economy he sought. Marx and Veblen did.

The *general* development of capitalism was first analyzed and explained by Marx, who sought to understand "the economic laws of motion of capitalist society." Marx barely touched upon the American experi-

ence. His empirical focus was Great Britain in the mid-19th century. Britain was the leading industrial capitalist society of the time, and Marx was in Great Britain. As a contributing journalist to the *New York Tribune* in the 1850s and 1860s, Marx had occasion to observe and comment upon American developments; he never did more than that.

It was left to Veblen to initiate the first systematic critique of American capitalism. Born in the U.S. almost a half-century after Marx's birth, Veblen was well-situated to study the more advanced and specifically American experience.[4] Veblen did not have to imagine or speculate on the course of capitalist development in America since the time of Marx, let alone that of Smith. He lived and wrote when the full sweep of American business and industrial practices was in evidence. His starting-point was to distinguish between "business" and "industry":

The industrial arts are a matter of tangible performance directed to work that is designed to be of material use to man. . . . [The] arts of business are arts of bargaining, effrontery, salesmanship, make-believe, and are directed to the gain of the business man at the cost of the community, at large and in detail. Neither tangible performance nor the common good is a business proposition. Any material use which his traffic may serve is quite beside the business man's purpose, except indirectly, in so far as it may serve to influence his clientele to his advantage.[5]

In brief, business is a matter of making money; industry, of making goods.

Veblen was by no means unique in noting the aggressiveness and the "effrontery" of businessmen. But the way in which he combined this widespread view with a larger analysis doomed him to the role of a lonely and scorned prophet. In his *Theory of Business Enterprise* (1904) he foresaw the two leading developments of American capitalism as centering on the drive for monopoly and the steady build-up of the forces of economic depression; in

Absentee Ownership (1923) he was able to look around him and see his expectations confirmed. Another major probability as he saw it was an "increased unproductive consumption of goods," by which he meant the need to manipulate and persuade the population to buy unnecessary and trivial commodities, and the growth of arms production, accompanied by what he called "a strenuous national policy."

Precisely because the kind of competitive economy Smith desired would entail effective price competition, Veblen argued, businessmen would energetically move to eliminate the competitive structure that allowed and required it. Their view of price competition was effectively suggested when they described it as "cutthroat competition." Businesses, monopolistic or otherwise, continue to "compete." But the forms taken by modern business rivalry are not such as to reduce costs, prices, and profits to some optimal level, as predicated in the competitive model; quite the contrary. Price competition has been replaced by two major forms of business rivalry: (1) "nonprice competition," which takes the form of price-*increasing* advertising, packaging, and other forms of sales promotion; and (2) efforts to gain special privileges at all levels of government—to stabilize prices, to gain privileged contracts, to influence taxing and spending, labor and foreign policies, and the like. To recall an earlier observation, the *State* mercantilism that Smith fought against has been revived and joined by a *private* mercantilism. We can do no better than to refer to Veblen again:

This decay of the old-fashioned competitive system has consisted in a substitution of competitive selling in the place of that competitive production of goods that is always presumed to be the chief and most serviceable feature of the competitive system. That is to say, it has been a substitution of salesmanship in the place of workmanship; as would be due to happen so soon as business came to take precedence of

industry, salesmanship being a matter of business, not of industry; and business being a matter of salesmanship, not of workmanship. . . . Competition as it runs under the rule of this decayed competitive system is chiefly the competition between the business concerns that control production, on the one side, and the consuming public on the other side; the chief expedients in this business-like competition being salesmanship and sabotage. Salesmanship in this connection means little else than prevarication, and sabotage means a business-like curtailment of output.[6]

The hoped-for effects of a competitive economy need not depend upon the existence of textbook forms of "perfect" or "pure" competition. But they do depend upon the existence of pervasive and effective competition which, as data below will show, has little to do with the American reality. A competitive economy is one in which firms respond to the market, rather than setting the terms upon which the market responds to them. In such an economy there might be monopolies, but they would be under constant scrutiny and regulation, or they would be temporary. In the former case, which economists call "natural monopolies," the monopoly is justified by the technology of the industry; this is typical in utilities, where it is economically foolish to have duplicative large-scale water or gas-works, for example. The aim of the regulatory agency is to combine the advantages of large-scale production with the pricing results of a competitive industry where prices are set so as to attract the necessary amount of capital into the industry, but without the profits of monopoly. (In practice, those who sit on regulatory boards are predominantly from or in sympathy with those industries being "regulated.") Temporary monopolies, on the other hand, are presumed to disappear as soon as the new technology or unusual market circumstances giving rise to them are countered by long-run competitive forces.

What would *not* be, in an effectively competitive economy, is what exists in all the major capitalist countries today: patterns of concentrated power in all of modern industry and increasingly in trade, construction, finance, and in hitherto competitive sectors. To which must be added a State apparatus that, far from restraining private economic power, responds to it, represents it, and paves the way for it. Americans have become familiar with part of the pattern in recent years as they have become conscious of the so-called military-industrial complex. The relationships exemplified in that pattern are not new; they are merely the latest development in the always close ties between business and government in the United States.

Returning now to the question of business competition in the American economy, and assuming that the textbook model is neither necessary nor possible, did anything even approximating an effectively competitive economy ever exist in the United States? And if it did, how, why, and by what was it corrupted?

The invisible fist

Of the many points to be noted, perhaps the first is that the capitalist system posits the businessman as its dynamic center. He, the "entrepreneur," is expected to respond to stimuli and to overcome obstacles so as to produce what society needs and wants. But to do this, he must possess one form of power: ownership of productive assets. To the degree that he succeeds, he is likely to gain more economic power, and other forms of power as well.

In practice, the dice are loaded in favor of those who own and control society's productive assets; and they are a tiny percentage of the population. By design and by default, those who are *not* property owners are weak in influence and power. For the competitive system to work well

economically and socially in Adam Smith's terms, in short, those who are powerful must be *frustrated* in what they seek—that is, profits and power. The social rationale for a competitive capitalist economy is thus a curious one: market competition will prevent those who have power in the society from realizing their aims. In reality, competition is eliminated and the benign principles are abandoned, except for their half-lives in textbooks and rhetoric.

The point may be made in another way. Social and economic policies are decided upon and implemented by those with power. The laissez-faire society is one in which all sources of public policy-making over the economy are eliminated on principle. What is left is economic power alone, private economic power, and that resides solely in the hands of those who own and control the means of production. Not, certainly, in the hands of the propertyless wage-earner (who in Smith's time didn't even have the vote) ; not, of course, in the hands of Church or State, by design. So in a society devoid of social controls other than the market, the capitalist will do what he can to mitigate the one threat to his strength and profitability: he will seek to eliminate competition. There is nothing to stop him, and much—including the political power he picks up along the way— to help him. In 19th and 20th century America, the developing large-scale technology provided such assistance, for the small-scale structure implied by and required for a competitive economy is quite generally incompatible with modern technology, both on business and economic grounds. If a capitalist economy is made socially "safe" only by competition, what then remains of the social rationale for capitalism in the modern world?

Until the years just after the Civil War, the American economy may be said to have been effectively competitive. During that early period, businessmen's desires were no less profit-oriented than after the 1870s; what was different was technology and the extraordinary onrush of events associated with westward expansion. In the last quarter of the century, the westward movement began to stabilize while large-scale technology spread throughout the production process.

In the period before the Civil War (roughly speaking), there were, of course, large as well as small firms. The largest firms tended to be found in transportation, communications, finance, and trade; the occasional large *manufacturing* firm (in textile machinery, for example) had no substantial influence on the economy as a whole, which was changing its structure and growing so rapidly. Once more, however, the impact of the large-scale technology after the Civil War deserves emphasis.

The seller's impulse toward monopolization is a constant in history. (Thales, the ancient Greek philosopher, is known for his attempts to corner the market in olive oil.) That impulse becomes necessary and, when successful, much more profitable when it joins with the economics of modern—that is, large-scale—industry. The productive efficiency associated with modern industry is owed to the scale of production. This in turn entails not only widespread specialization in production, but also much in the way of expensive and long-lasting plant and equipment. The normal ups and downs of capitalist economic expansion and the intermittent glutting of markets combine with large-scale plants to yield destructive ("cutthroat") competition—price competition which entails selling below cost in bad times as a way to minimize losses. When that happens, or in order to prevent it from happening, the number of firms in a given industry shrinks, leaving the giants to endure and to prosper. For if eliminating competitors *diminishes* the prospects of price competition, it also *increases* the pos-

sibilities of enhancing profits in both bad and good times through controlling the market. ("Controlling the market" in this respect means controlling—that is, restricting—supply, something that cannot be accomplished in a competitive market.) Thus the key characteristic of modern business behavior becomes that of dominant firms restricting supply in order to dictate and sell at a desirable price, a process that distorts both the supply and demand sides of the market, and that gives the large firms access to broad power over society as well—in a society that systematically and in principle foregoes locating that power in *non*economic institutions.

From mergers to monopoly: The giants feed

Until about 1860, the corporate form of business was largely confined to transportation and finance. With few exceptions, the emergence of corporations in manufacturing awaited the new, large-scale technology that emerged and spread after the Civil War.

From 1873 until the mid-1890s the entire industrial capitalist world underwent what was then called "The Great Depression." Unlike the Great Depression of the 1930s, the most prominent feature of the earlier period was pressure on profits, rather than massive unemployment. That pressure was due to the steady and dramatic lowering of prices through the period, which was in turn the result of great increases in efficiency, combined with the inability to cut off domestic or foreign competition in the context of relatively free trade and relatively competitive market structures.

Consequently, that same period saw the first general attempts to control price competition through one form of business reorganization or another. "Gentlemen's agreements" not to cut prices, profit pools, and trusts (all of which maintained the separate identity of the member corporations) were all tried; but the form which won out was the merger. The process in which mergers occurred is called the *combination movement*. By the late 1890s, mergers or combinations (in which many firms were combined under one ownership and identity) became the rule; the years between 1897 and 1905 witnessed their first spectacular rush. During these years, over 5,300 industrial firms came under the control, finally, of 318 corporations, the most advanced and powerful firms in the economy.

The turn-of-the-century wave of mergers was seen as spectacular, until subsequent waves surpassed it. A higher peak was reached in the 1920s; then, after what has been called a "ripple" in the 1940s, the largest wave of all began, in the 1960s. Economists have speculated as to what conditions are associated with increasing or decreasing merger activity. The evidence of the past 70 years or so suggests that the only period in which the *rate* of merger activity declines is that of depression; the impulse toward bigness and power is otherwise persistent.

The first waves of mergers were an outcome of the combination of expanding technology and businesses' aims of avoiding competition and of making profits. Technology then led to centralization of production facilities in a given location (for example, steel in Pittsburgh). Since World War II, however, technological development has led to *de*centralization of productive facilities geographically; at the same time the *control* over those facilities has become ever more centralized, spreading not simply over one industry but many different industries. Let us examine the process more closely.

Initially, mergers took place in each industry as it began to employ modern, large-scale technology. Sometimes the process was more like warfare than business in the late 19th century. Mergers spread from transportation to manufacturing, to utilities and finance, to mining and construction and trade; by now mergers are the dynamic mode in all significant business, including entertainment, hotels and even agriculture, long considered the final preserve of effective competition.

The patterns of the merger movements are striking; most striking of all is the tidal wave that began during World War II and reached its historic peak in 1948–69. As *Fortune* points out, "from 1964 through 1966, there were 293 mergers in which the acquired companies had assets of more than $10 million; in the final three years of the decade there were 530. The average size of the transactions, $38 million in the first period, rose to $64 million during the second. In the peak year of 1968 the nation's top 200 industrial firms acquired a total of ninety-four large companies, with aggregate assets of more than $8 billion."[7]

Throughout all this merger activity there have been several subprocesses. At first, mergers were in one industry, where all the merging firms produced much the same product. These are called *horizontal* mergers, in which competitors in a given industry come under the ownership and control of one company (for example, one steel company buying out another). While those mergers continued, another form, vertical mergers, began to appear, especially in the 1920s, in which a company buys out its suppliers and/or its customers (for example, Ford gaining its own steel facilities; U.S. Steel buying out coal mines and a bridge-building company).

Horizontal mergers lead to concentration of power in a given industry, and to *oligopoly:* a few dominant sellers in an industry. Vertical mergers strengthen the hand of already large firms, while also creating higher barriers to entry by new firms. In the late 20s and early 30s another form of merger began to attract attention, as it does even more so today: the *conglomerate*, where the firms acquired by a corporation are *only* distantly related, if at all, to the industry of the acquiring firm. In the vast merger movement since 1950 all these forms —vertical, horizontal, and conglomerate— have been operating, with the conglomerate form taking the prizes for drama. The drama became especially vivid in the 1960s, with "the new conglomerates."

The expansion of the "new conglomerates" was dominated by eight companies: ITT, Gulf & Western, Ling-Temco-Vought, Tenneco, White Consolidated, Teledyne, Occidental Petroleum, and Litton Industries. "Each of these companies made acquisitions during the 1960s totaling more than a half-billion dollars; for six the asset value was over a billion dollars."[8] Of the various important aspects of this movement, one worth noting is that it has sped up the process of bringing traditionally "small business" industries—for instance, food processing, nonelectrical machinery, and textiles— under the control of giant corporations.

The early merger movements, whether horizontal or vertical in origin, led to the *concentration* of economic power within the affected industries. When we add the conglomerate mergers to the earlier movement we come to an additional characteristic: *centralization*. Furthermore, combined with the concentration and centralization of *private* economic power is the associated concentration and centralization of *public* power. The concentration and centralization of State power shows itself in the enormously enhanced powers of the federal government today as compared with, say, 1900; it is revealed even more pointedly in the extraordinary powers increasingly arrogated by the presidency—and, conversely, the declining powers of Congress and the separate states. The government at all levels represents the interests of many groups in American society, of course—doctors, organized labor, the aged, the poor— but it represents most and best the interests of the most powerful. The most powerful are unquestionably the most powerful business corporations. Let us examine some representative data suggesting their position in the American economy.

Facts are stubborn things

There is no mystery as to the size or the identity of America's giant corporations. *Fortune* annually publishes its "Fortune 500" and "Second 500," showing assets, sales, employees, income, and profits of the largest industrial corporations; their data in turn are derived from a multitude of governmental and private sources, all open to the public eye. Economists are fully aware of these data, but they have yet to alter conventional economic *theory* to fit the data—quite possibly because to do so in any systematic manner would require abandoning the entire structure of the theory. One respected conventional economist, understanding this, has said (in the convoluted language used by economists when they address each other) : "To argue that monopolistic deviations can be ignored because of their minor importance is to exhibit ideological bias. To argue that piecemeal antitrust leads to improvement is false. The only bias-free option is the option that leads to a centrally controlled economy. But how many believers in fact are prepared to accept this conclusion?"[9]

The information that follows concerns the concentration and centralization of control over productive assets, sales, profits, employment, and the like. The emphasis will first be on *industrial* (manufacturing and mining) *corporations,* of which there are about 215,000, and which do over 90 percent of all industrial business—the heartland of the economy. Unless otherwise specified, the data are for 1975:

1. The *sales* of the largest 500 industrials were $865 billion; their *profits* were $37.8 billion (after taxes) ; and they *employed* 14.4 million, amounting to about two-thirds of industrial sales, and about three-

quarters of total industrial profits and employment.

2. The *sales* of the second largest 500 industrials were $83 billion; their *profits* after taxes $3.3 billion; and their *employment* 1.9 million; each figure was 10 percent or less of the top 500's. The top and second 500 together left very little indeed for the remaining 99 percent of industrial business. The *sales* of the largest 1,000 industrial corporations totaled $948 billion; *gross national product* in 1975 (the total money value of all goods and services at their final stage) was less than twice that amount ($1,573 billion).

3. The top *ten* of the 500 (EXXON, GM, Texaco, Ford, Mobil Oil, Standard Oil of California, IBM, Gulf Oil, GE, and Chrysler) had *sales* of $214 billion in 1975, almost one-quarter of the sales of the top 500, more than two times the total sales of the second 500; the top 50 had over half the sales of the 500. Note that five of the top ten are oil companies, three are autos.

4. The *assets* of the top 500 industrials were $668 billion, of the second 500, $61 billion; the top ten had assets of $158 billion.

5. The industrial corporation with the greatest *assets* is EXXON: $33 *billion*. The company with the smallest assets of the top 500 in 1975 was Idle Wild Foods: $44 *million*—1/750th of EXXON's. EXXON's sales were $45 *billion;* Idle Wild Foods' $323 *million*—less than 1/100th of EXXON's, although both are in the top 500. EXXON's sales were almost half those of the second largest 500 combined.

6. The after-tax *profits* of the top ten industrials in 1975 were $9.2 billion, almost one-quarter of the profits of the first 1,000 industrials. EXXON alone had profits of $2.5 billion, more than one-quarter of the top ten's.

7. In short, the concentration of the economy is continued within the top 500 and top 1,000 corporations, where the bulk of industrial power is held by the very few.

8. What is true of industry is true in more and less degree of the rest of the economy. Thus, there were over 14,000 *commercial banks* in the U.S. in 1974, with assets of $927.5 billion. The assets of the 50 largest were $346 billion, and of the 10 largest $196 billion. That is, 50 banks had well over a third of the assets of all commercial banks. Ten banks had well over half of that, and three banks—Bank of America, Citibank, and Chase Manhattan —own half or more of the assets of the top ten banks. The same pattern is true of deposits; the top ten banks hold just over 35 percent of all commercial banks' deposits.

9. The *five* largest *insurance* companies (Prudential, Metropolitan, Equitable, New York, and Hancock, in that order), with assets of $232 billion in 1975, account for nearly half of the total life insurance in force.

10. In the utilities group, AT&T is of course the giant among giants: $80 billion in assets, accounting for one-third of the top 50 assets, revenues, net income, and stockholders' equity, and with 949,054 employees, more than any other company in any other business. In the world.

11. A final fact of a different sort: the top 500 do more and more business, but they do not necessarily hire more and more workers: they employed 14.6 million in 1970 and 14.4 million in 1975. In 1975, the top 500 laid off about 1 million employees, and four companies—GM, Ford, IT&T, and GE—accounted for one-fifth of that.[10]

These facts are striking in themselves. When they are seen as merely the latest stage of a continuing trend, they take on even more ominous overtones. In a similar examination of the top industrials, Ronald Müller points out that:

Between 1955 and 1970 the *Fortune* top 500 industrial corporations increased their share of total manufacturing and mining employment, profits, and assets from slightly more than 40 percent to over 70 percent. Whereas during the fifties the largest 200 were increasing their share of total industrial assets each year by an average of 1 percent, by the 1960's, this annual rate of increased concentration had doubled.

He goes on to add, regarding banking that:

From 1965 to 1970 the top fifty were increasing their share of total assets at more than double their expansion rate during the previous ten years. Federal Reserve Board studies show that almost all foreign deposits of U.S. banks are in the hands of the top twenty American global banks, with four holding 38 percent of these deposits, and twelve having 83 percent of all foreign banking assets. . . . Nine of the largest global banks account . . . for more than 26 percent of all total commercial and industrial lending by American banks . . . [and] these same nine hold 90 percent of the entire indebtedness in the U.S. petroleum and natural gas industry, 66 percent in machinery and metal products, and 75 percent in the chemical and rubber industries.[11]

Such are some of the facts of life of a concentrated economy. Economists seek to systematize these kinds of data with what are called concentration measures. Table 1 shows the percentages held by the largest four corporations in a given industry, using various measures.

Averitt's *Dual Economy* was used for

TABLE 1
Concentration in manufacturing industries

Percentage of sales, total assets, net capital assets, and profits after taxes accounted for by the four largest firms in each industry for 28 selected industry groups, fourth quarter, 1962

		Percent of total		
Industry	Sales	Total assets	Net capital assets	Profits
Motor vehicles	80.8	79.7	83.1	89.1
Aircraft	47.3	41.9	32.6	46.6
Other transportation equipment	30.3	44.2	59.9	51.6
Electrical machinery	34.4	35.6	41.5	44.4
Metalworking machinery	14.5	16.3	18.5	19.1
Other machinery	20.6	24.3	31.5	39.6
Primary iron and steel	40.2	48.0	48.8	44.3
Primary nonferrous metals	27.3	41.1	47.7	37.1
Other fabricated metal products	14.7	19.9	30.3	17.7
Stone, clay, and glass products	18.1	19.9	19.8	23.4
Furniture and fixtures	5.2	8.4	9.6	5.3
Lumber and wood products	21.2	31.0	41.5	48.6
Instruments	37.9	41.2	50.2	56.6
Miscellaneous manufacturing	16.3	33.1	34.3	25.2
Dairy products	42.9	48.8	47.4	73.9
Bakery products	33.6	39.6	38.2	52.8
Other food	12.5	13.2	14.9	20.1
Textile mill products	22.0	26.1	25.7	30.5
Apparel	4.9	7.7	11.4	7.4
Paper	20.7	23.2	22.3	35.0
Basic industrial chemicals	42.0	45.5	44.6	64.6
Drugs and medicines	31.0	29.2	33.3	32.6
Other chemicals	28.5	30.0	33.6	35.8
Petroleum refining	50.3	50.1	47.7	54.3
Rubber	48.1	55.0	56.4	51.6
Leather	26.7	32.1	35.4	28.8
Alcoholic beverages	41.4	47.2	30.8	58.3
Tobacco	70.9	72.7	68.8	72.5

Source: Bureau of Economics, Federal Trade Commission.

some of the foregoing data. In his conclusion, he calls for a new microeconomic theory to build around the concentrated "center" and the weak "periphery." Having provided us with the data and an analysis showing that these describe a permanent feature of the American "dual economy," Averitt comes forth with the surprising conclusion that "we can attain perpetual prosperity while retaining a high level of what the business community calls 'economic freedom.' "[12] His optimism depends upon his hopes for governmental "moral suasion," which he takes to be "more effective in highly concentrated industries dominated by center firms than elsewhere."[13] To have such hopes is to assume that private economic power is one thing and State power something else, something independent of private economic power.[14] In a capitalist society the shred of truth contained in those hopes is completely outweighed by the realities of power.

The data above have been concerned with the functioning of the domestic economy. The figures show that the corporations involved constitute the hard core of power in the United States. When we look at the latest development of business power —the *multinational* corporation—we see the emergence of a powerful tendency for the same pattern of concentration and centralization in the capitalist world economy. Multinational corporations' main features are an integral part of the functioning of the American overseas empire; here it is appropriate to examine only the general shape of the development.

What's good for America . . .

The multinational corporation, as its name suggests, has its origins and its headquarters in one nation, and it buys, invests, produces, and sells in many nations. As Stephen Hymer has pointed out,

The multinational corporation is in the first instance an American phenomenon. Its precursor is the U.S. *national corporation* created at the end of the 19th century when American capitalism developed a multi-city continent-wide marketing and manufacturing strategy. . . . Though many U.S. corporations began to move to foreign countries almost as soon as they completed their continent-wide integration, the term *multinational* came to prominence only after 1960. . . . National firms think in terms of the national market; multinational firms see the whole world as their oyster and plan manufacturing and marketing on a global scale. . . . The shift in business horizons is closely connected to the aeronautical and electronic revolutions which made global planning possible.[15]

In 1972, about $500 billion of the world's production was attributable to multinational corporations. Of that amount, about half was produced by American multinationals, about one-quarter by foreign-based companies which also operate in the United States (for example, Royal-Dutch Shell), and the rest by interproduction in other countries. The proportion of world production contributed by multinational corporations is now growing at the rate of about 10 percent per year. Were that rate to continue—and the turbulence and complexities of the world economy make it unlikely—the few hundred multinationals would generate about one-half of world production by the year 2000.

Naturally, almost all of the multinational corporations are among the very largest corporations in their own countries. Also, as might be expected, the emergence of this phenomenon for American corporations coincided with (was both cause and consequence of) our taking up primary status in the world economy from the 1920s on. Its most spectacular period of growth has been the past 25 years, the period in which the American economy has become internationalized, and the capitalist world-economy Americanized. The dynamic center of any future power struggle in the capitalist world-economy will surely find the multinationals taking leading roles.

The increasing proclivity of American corporations to locate their producing plants all over the world has vital consequences for the functioning of the American as well as other economies. Apart from what it means for the multinational corporations, it means a significant redistribution of productive jobs around the globe, and it affects resource flows, foreign policies, economic growth rates and patterns, and the international monetary system. Whatever surprises and shocks the future holds, some of them will be due to the growing importance of these giants, as much of what has happened in the recent past has been clothed with their purposes and their needs.

Necessarily, the emergence of the American multinational corporation, like the emergence of the national corporation, has been facilitated by the State, which is much accustomed to responding to business needs and possibilities first, and asking and being asked questions about what it means to society, later—often too late. The internationalization of the American economy and the Americanization of the capitalist world-economy could not be accomplished without great changes in our global military posture, by comparison with any earlier period. Thus, there is an additional matter to be stressed in viewing the evolution of American business as a system of power: its relationship with the State and within that the relationships between business and the military. Here only the bare outlines will be suggested.

Among the justifications for capitalism as a system was one that, running contrary to the facts, is still frequently put forward. It claims that a "free enterprise" system minimizes the role of the State, and that it encourages everybody to pursue their rational material interests. One by-product of such a system would be efficiency; another would be material well-being; still another

would be a government swayed by rational, meaning material, considerations.

But recently (that is, since about 1930), the United States has found itself confronted with developing needs and possibilities that cannot be resolved by a free market economy. There was the Great Depression of the 1930s, which only World War II resolved. There was the widespread unrest of that same period, taking the form of labor and socialist movements which, if they were closely threatening, seemed so to the business class. There was the growth of fearsome Communist nations, assumed to be expansive and threatening to American interests, or even to "freedom" in the entire world. There was an already voracious and growing need for industrial raw materials, for markets, and for investment outlets, as well as a need for strategic sites to protect our expanding economic and political interests. Closely related to these developments was the growth of corporations that became usefully, vitally, or fully dependent upon military contracts—contracts typically constructed on a cost-plus (that is, guaranteed profit) basis.

These developments, taken together with the long-standing cultivation of patriotic attitudes among Americans, combined to produce a military-industrial complex most profitable to a hundred or so very large and thousands of smaller business firms, and a working force that was in fact or in its job fears dependent upon war production. Almost all Americans saw these developments, combining economic, military, political, and ideological needs, possibilities, and appeals, neither as malign nor as unreal; they saw them as responsibilities thrust upon America's economic and moral strength—thrust upon them by hostile, crafty, enigmatic, and essentially peculiar foreigners. (Lyndon Baines Johnson once remarked, almost peevishly, "Those foreigners weren't reared like us.") Later, we shall have occasion to cast doubt on whether the United States was forced by foreigners and/or hostile events to take up the role of Number One in the world. Here we may say merely that the processes of the past decades had the at least temporary effect, salubrious from the viewpoint of American capitalism, of bringing the majority of the American people closer to traditional conceptions of American virtues, a consequence anticipated by Veblen in 1904:

The largest and most promising factor of cultural discipline—most promising as a corrective of iconoclastic vagaries—over which business principles rule is national politics. . . . Busi-

ness interests urge an aggressive national policy and business men direct it. Such a policy is warlike as well as patriotic. The direct cultural value of a warlike business policy is unequivocal. It makes for a conservative animus on the part of the populace . . . [and] directs the popular interest to other, nobler, institutionally less hazardous matters than the unequal distribution of wealth or of creature comforts. . . . There can, indeed, be no serious question but that a consistent return to the ancient virtues of allegiance, piety, servility, graded dignity, class prerogative, and prescriptive authority would greatly conduce to popular content and to the facile management of affairs. Such is the promise held out by a strenuous national policy.[16]

NOTES

1. See Paul Jacobs, Saul Landau, and Eve Pell, *To Serve the Devil* (New York: Vintage, 1971), in two volumes.

2. Thorstein Veblen, *Absentee Ownership and Business Enterprise* (New York: Huebsch, 1923; Viking, 1954), p. 171.

3. This perspective is put forth most explicitly by Robert A. Brady, *Business as a System of Power* (New York: Columbia University Press, 1943).

4. Lewis Corey, *The Decline of American Capitalism* (New York: Covici-Friede, 1934), is the first systematic Marxian attempt.

5. *Absentee Ownership*, p. 107.

6. Ibid., p. 78.

7. *Fortune*, April 1973. A useful and comprehensive analysis of mergers is Samuel Richardson Reid, *Mergers, Managers, and the Economy* (New York: McGraw-Hill, 1968).

8. John M. Blair, *Economic Concentration: Structure, Behavior, and Public Policy* (New York: Harcourt Brace Jovanovich, 1972), p. 285.

9. Andreas G. Papandreou, *Paternalistic Capitalism* (Minneapolis: University of Minnesota Press, 1972), p. 26.

10. The data presented are easily available. These are drawn primarily from Blair and Reid, both cited earlier, from Robert T. Averitt, *The Dual Economy* (New York: Norton, 1968), from various issues of *Fortune*, but especially those of May and June 1976, and from U.S. Bureau of the Census, *Statistical Abstract of the United States: 1975* (96th ed.), Washington, D.C., 1975.

11. Ronald Müller, "A Qualifying and Dissenting View of the Multinational Corporation," in George W. Ball, ed., *Global Companies: The Political Economy of World Business* (Englewood Cliffs, N.J.: Prentice-Hall, 1975), pp. 24–25.

12. Averitt, *Dual Economy*, p. 200.

13. Ibid.

14. Six case studies of how private and public power work together and separately to corrupt the presumed functions of both are collected in Robert L. Heilbroner et al., *In the Name of Profits* (New York: Warner Paperback, 1973). The studies are illustrative of a much larger whole.

15. Stephen Hymer, "The United States Multinational Corporations and Japanese Competition in the Pacific," an unpublished ms. which the late author kindly allowed me to use here. By the broadest definition, there are over 7,000 multinational companies in the world but fewer than 200 have about three-quarters of total assets, and comparable percentages of sales, income, employees, and so on. Since his tragic death, Hymer's doctoral dissertation has been published by the M.I.T. Press: *A Study of Direct Foreign Investments* (1976).

16. *Theory of Business Enterprise*, pp. 391–93. In today's world, where so much of this has already been accomplished, it may be necessary to point out that Veblen's intent is sardonic, and that all his writings were devoted to preventing such developments from occurring. David Halberstam's *Best and the Brightest* (New York: Random House, 1972) provides an extraordinarily detailed account of the personalities and policies of the 1960s, and abundant references back to the Truman and Eisen-

hower years. The treatment is journalistic rather than analytical, and the writing style is often indigestible, but those reading it will find that the Cold War in general and the Indochina War in particular were the outcome of some combination of private interest and capitalist ideology, rather than the interest of the American or any other nation's people, and that those making policy since (at least) 1945 did so in a continuous state of arrogance, ignorance, confusion, and systematic deception. Watergate's roots go deep.

READING 2–3

The scientific management of labor*

HARRY BRAVERMAN

The classical economists were the first to approach the problems of the organization of labor within capitalist relations of production from a theoretical point of view. They may thus be called the first management experts, and their work was continued in the latter part of the Industrial Revolution by such men as Andrew Ure and Charles Babbage. Between these men and the next step, the comprehensive formulation of management theory in the late 19th and early 20th centuries, there lies a gap of more than half a century during which there was an enormous growth in the size of enterprises, the beginnings of the monopolistic organization of industry, and the purposive and systematic application of science to production. The scientific management movement initiated by Frederick Winslow Taylor in the last decades of the 19th century was brought into being by these forces. Logically, Taylorism belongs to the chain of development of management methods and the organization of labor, and not to the development of technology, in which its role was minor.

Scientific management, so-called, is an attempt to apply the methods of science to the increasingly complex problems of the control of labor in rapidly growing capitalist enterprises. It lacks the characteristics of a true science because its assumptions reflect nothing more than the outlook of the capitalist with regard to the conditions of production. It starts, despite occasional protestations to the contrary, not from the human point of view but from the capitalist point of view, from the point of view of the management of a refractory work force in a setting of antagonistic social relations. It does not attempt to discover and confront the cause of this condition, but accepts it as an inexorable given, a "natural" condition. It investigates not labor in general, but the adaptation of labor to the needs of capital. It enters the workplace not as the representative of science, but as the representative of management masquerading in the trappings of science.

A comprehensive and detailed outline of the principles of Taylorism is essential to our narrative, not because of the things for which it is popularly known—stopwatch, speed-up, etc.—but because behind these commonplaces there lies a theory which is nothing less than the explicit verbalization of the capitalist mode of production. But before I begin this presentation, a number of introductory remarks are required to clarify the role of the Taylor school in the development of management theory.

It is impossible to overestimate the importance of the scientific management movement in the shaping of the modern corporation and indeed all institutions of capitalist society which carry on labor processes. The popular notion that Taylorism has been "superseded" by later schools of industrial psychology or "human relations," that it "failed"—because of Taylor's amateurish and naive views of human motivation or because it brought about a storm of labor opposition or because Taylor and various successors antagonized workers and sometimes management as well—or that it is "outmoded" because certain Taylorian specifics like functional foremanship or his incentive-pay schemes have been discarded for more sophisticated methods: all these represent a woeful misreading of the actual dynamics of the development of management.

Taylor dealt with the fundamentals of the organization of the labor process and of control over it. The later schools of Hugo Münsterberg, Elton Mayo, and others of this type dealt primarily with the adjustment of the worker to the ongoing production process as that process was designed by the industrial engineer. The successors to Taylor are to be found in engineering and work design, and in top management; the successors to Münsterberg and Mayo are to be found in personnel departments and schools of industrial psychology and sociology. Work itself is organized according to Taylorian principles, while personnel departments and academics have busied themselves with the selection, training, manipulation, pacification, and adjustment of "manpower" to suit the work processes so organized. Taylorism dominates the world of production; the practitioners of "human relations" and "industrial psychology" are the maintenance crew for the human machinery. If Taylorism does not exist as a separate school today, that is because, apart from the bad odor of the name, it is no longer the property of a faction, since its fundamental teachings have become the bedrock of all work design. Peter F. Drucker, who has the advantage of considerable direct experience as a management consultant, is emphatic on this score:

> Personnel Administration and Human Relations are the things talked about and written about whenever the management of worker and work is being discussed. They are the things the Personnel Department concerns itself with. But they are not the concepts that underlie the actual management of worker and work in American industry. This concept is Scientific Management. Scientific Management focuses on the work. Its core is the organized study of work, the analysis of work into its simplest elements and the systematic improvement of the worker's performance of each of these elements. Scientific Management has both basic concepts and easily applicable tools and techniques. And it has no difficulty proving the contribution it makes; its results in the form of higher output are visible and readily measurable.
>
> Indeed, Scientific Management is all but a systematic philosophy of worker and work. Altogether it may well be the most powerful as well as the most lasting contribution America has made to Western thought since the Federalist Papers.[1]

The use of experimental methods in the study of work did not begin with Taylor; in fact, the self-use of such methods by the craftsman is part of the very practice of a craft. But the study of work by or on behalf of those who manage it rather than those who perform it seems to have come to the fore only with the capitalist epoch; indeed, very little basis for it could have existed before. The earliest references to the study of work correspond to the beginnings of the capitalist era: such a reference, for example, is found in the *History of the Royal Society of London,* and dates from the middle of the 17th century. We have already mentioned the classical economists. Charles Babbage, who not only wrote penetrating discussions of the organization of the labor process in his day, but applied the same concept to the division of mental labor, and who devised an early calculating "engine," was probably the most direct forerunner of Taylor, who must have been familiar with Babbage's work even though he never referred to it. France had a long tradition of attempting the scientific study of work, starting with Louis XIV's minister Colbert; including military engineers like Vauban and Belidor and especially Coulomb, whose physiological studies of exertion in labor are famous, through Marey, who used smoked paper cylinders to make a graphic record of work phenomena; and culminating in Henri Fayol, a contemporary of Taylor, who in his *General and Industrial Management* attempted a set of principles aimed at securing total enterprise control by way of a systematic approach to administration.[2] The publication of management manuals, the discussions of the problems of management, and the increasingly sophisticated approach taken in practice in the second half of the 19th century lend support to the conclusion of the historians of the scientific management movement that Taylor was the culmination of a pre-existing trend: "What Taylor did was not to invent something quite new, but to synthesize and present as a reasonably coherent whole ideas which had been germinating and gathering force in Great Britain and the United States throughout the nineteenth century. He gave to a disconnected series of initiatives and experiments a philosophy and a title."[3]

Taylor has little in common with those physiologists or psychologists who have attempted, before or after him, to gather information about human capacities in a spirit of scientific interest. Such records and estimates as he did produce are crude in the extreme, and this has made it easy for such

critics as Georges Friedmann to poke holes in his various "experiments" (most of which were not intended as experiments at all, but as forcible and hyperbolic demonstrations). Friedmann treats Taylorism as though it were a "science of work," where in reality it is intended to be a *science of the management of others' work* under capitalist conditions.[4] It is not the "best way" to do work "in general" that Taylor was seeking, as Friedmann seems to assume, but an answer to the specific problem of how best to control alienated labor—that is to say, labor power that is bought and sold.

The second distinctive feature of Taylor's thought was his concept of control. Control has been the essential feature of management throughout its history, but with Taylor it assumed unprecedented dimensions. The stages of management control over labor before Taylor had included, progressively: the gathering together of the workers in a workshop and the dictation of the length of the working day; the supervision of workers to ensure diligent, intense, or uninterrupted application; the enforcement of rules against distractions (talking, smoking, leaving the workplace, etc.) that were thought to interfere with application; the setting of production minimums; etc. A worker is under management control when subjected to these rules, or to any of their extensions and variations. But Taylor raised the concept of control to an entirely new plane when he asserted as an *absolute necessity for adequate management the dictation to the worker of the precise manner in which work is to be performed.* That management had the right to "control" labor was generally assumed before Taylor, but in practice this right usually meant only the general setting of tasks, with little direct interference in the worker's mode of performing them. Taylor's contribution was to overturn this practice and replace it by its opposite. Management, he insisted, could be only a limited and frustrated undertaking so long as it left to the worker any decision about the work. His "system" was simply a means for management to achieve control of the actual mode of performance of every labor activity, from the simplest to the most complicated. To this end, he pioneered a far greater revolution in the division of labor than any that had gone before.

Taylor created a simple line of reasoning and advanced it with a logic and clarity, a naive openness, and an evangelical zeal which soon won him a strong following among capitalists and managers. His work began in the 1880s but it was not until the 1890s that he began to lecture, read papers, and publish results. His own engineering training was limited, but his grasp of shop practice was superior, since he had served a four-year combination apprenticeship in two trades, those of patternmaker and machinist. The spread of the Taylor approach was not limited to the United States and Britain; within a short time it became popular in all industrial countries. In France it was called, in the absence of a suitable word for management, "l'organisation scientifique du travail" (later changed, when the reaction against Taylorism set in, to "l'organisation rationelle du travail"). In Germany it was known simply as *rationalization;* the German corporations were probably ahead of everyone else in the practice of this technique, even before World War I.[5]

Taylor was the scion of a well-to-do Philadelphia family. After preparing for Harvard at Exeter he suddenly dropped out, apparently in rebellion against his father, who was directing Taylor toward his own profession, the law. He then took the step, extraordinary for anyone of his class, of starting a craft apprenticeship in a firm whose owners were social acquaintances of his parents. When he had completed his apprenticeship, he took a job at common labor in the Midvale Steel Works, also owned by friends of his family and technologically one of the most advanced companies in the steel industry. Within a few months he had passed through jobs as clerk and journeyman machinist, and was appointed gang boss in charge of the lathe department.

In his psychic makeup, Taylor was an exaggerated example of the obsessive-compulsive personality: from his youth he had counted his steps, measured the time for his various activities, and analyzed his motions in a search for "efficiency." Even when he had risen to importance and fame, he was still something of a figure of fun, and his appearance on the shop floor produced smiles. The picture of his personality that emerges from a study recently done by Sudhir Kakar justifies calling him, at the very least, a neurotic crank.[6] These traits fitted him perfectly for his role as the prophet of modern capitalist management, since that which is neurotic in the individual is, in capitalism, normal and socially desirable for the functioning of society.

Shortly after Taylor became gang boss, he entered upon a struggle with the machinists under him. Because this struggle was a classic instance of the manner in which the antagonistic relations of production express themselves in the workplace, not only in Taylor's time but before and after, and since Taylor drew from this experience the conclusions that were to shape his subsequent thinking, it is necessary to quote at length here from his description of the events. The following account, one of several he gave of the battle, is taken from his testimony, a quarter-century later, before a Special Committee of the U.S. House of Representatives:

Now, the machine shop of the Midvale Steel Works was a piecework shop. All the work practically was done on piecework, and it ran night and day—five nights in the week and six days. Two sets of men came on, one to run the machines at night and the other to run them in the daytime.

We who were the workmen of that shop had the quantity output carefully agreed upon for everything that was turned out in the shop.

We limited the output to about, I should think, one-third of what we could very well have done. We felt justified in doing this, owing to the piecework system—that is, owing to the necessity for soldiering under the piecework system—which I pointed out yesterday.

As soon as I became gang boss the men who were working under me and who, of course, knew that I was onto the whole game of soldiering or deliberately restricting output, came to me at once and said, "Now, Fred, you are not going to be a damn piecework hog, are you?"

I said, "If you fellows mean you are afraid I am going to try to get a larger output from these lathes," I said, "Yes; I do propose to get more work out." I said, "You must remember I have been square with you fellows up to now and worked with you. I have not broken a single rate. I have been on your side of the fence. But now I have accepted a job under the management of this company and I am on the other side of the fence, and I will tell you perfectly frankly that I am going to try to get a bigger output from those lathes." They answered, "Then, you are going to be a damned hog."

I said, "Well, if you fellows put it that way, all right." They said, "We warn you, Fred, if you try to bust any of these rates, we will have you over the fence in six weeks." I said, "That is all right; I will tell you fellows again frankly that I propose to try to get a bigger output off these machines."

Now, that was the beginning of a piecework fight that lasted for nearly three years, as I remember it—two or three years—in which I was doing everything in my power to increase the output of the shop, while the men were absolutely determined that the output should not be increased. Anyone who has been through such a fight knows and dreads the meanness of it and the bitterness of it. I believe that if I had been an older man—a man of more experience—I should have hardly gone into such a fight as this—deliberately attempting to force the men to do something they did not propose to do.

We fought on the management's side with all the usual methods and the workmen fought on their side with all their usual methods. I began by going to the management and telling them perfectly plainly, even before I accepted the gang boss-ship, what would happen. I said, "Now these men will show you, and show you conclusively, that, in the first place, I know nothing about my business; and that in the second place, I am a liar, and you are being fooled, and they will bring any amount of evidence to prove these facts beyond a shadow of a doubt." I said to the management, "The only thing I ask you, and I must have your firm promise, is that when I say a thing is so you will take my word against the word of any 20 men or any 50 men in the shop." I said, "If you won't do that, I won't lift my finger toward increasing the output of this shop." They agreed to it and stuck to it, although many times they were on the verge of believing I was both incompetent and untruthful.

Now, I think it perhaps desirable to show the way in which that fight was conducted.

I began, of course, by directing some one man to do more work than he had done before, and then I got on the lathe myself and showed him that it could be done. In spite of this, he went ahead and turned out exactly the same old output and refused to adopt better methods or to work quicker until finally I laid him off and got another man in his place. This new man—I could not blame him in the least under the circumstances—turned right around and joined the other fellows and refused to do any more work than the rest. After trying this policy for a while and failing to get any results I said distinctly to the fellows, "Now, I am a mechanic; I am a machinist. I do not want to take the next step, because it will be contrary to what you and I look upon as our interest as machinists, but I will take it if you fellows won't compromise with me and get more work off of these lathes, but I warn you if I have to take this step it will be a durned mean one." I took it.

I hunted up some especially intelligent laborers who were competent men, but who had not had the opportunity of learning a trade, and I deliberately taught these men how to run a lathe and how to work right and fast. Every one of these laborers promised me, "Now, if you will teach me the machinist's trade, when I learn to run a lathe I will do a fair day's work," and every solitary man, when I had taught them their trade, one after another turned right around and joined the rest of the fellows and refused to work one bit faster.

That looked as if I were up against a stone wall, and for a time I was up against a stone wall. I did not blame even these laborers in my heart, my sympathy was with them all of the time, but I am telling you the facts as they then existed in the machine shops of this country, and in truth, as they still exist.

When I had trained enough of these laborers so that they could run the lathes, I went to them and said, "Now, you men to whom I have taught a trade are in a totally different position from the machinists who were running these lathes before you came here. Every one of you agreed to do a certain thing for me if I taught you a trade, and now not one of you will keep his word. I did not break my word with you, but every one of you has broken his word with me. Now, I have not any mercy on you; I have not the slightest hesitation in treating you entirely differently from the machinists." I said, "I know that very heavy social pressure has been put upon you outside the works to keep you from carrying out your agreement with me, and it is very difficult for you to stand out against this pressure, but you ought not to have made your bargain with me if you did not intend to keep your end of it. Now, I am going to cut your rate in two tomorrow and you are going to work for half price from now on. But all you will have to do is to turn out a fair day's work and you can earn better wages than you have been earning."

These men, of course, went to the management, and protested that I was a tyrant, and a nigger driver, and for a long time they stood right by the rest of the men in the shop and refused to increase their output a particle. Finally, they all of a sudden gave right in and did a fair day's work.

I want to call your attention, gentlemen, to the bitterness that was stirred up in this fight before the men finally gave in, to the meanness of it, and the contemptible conditions that exist under the old piecework system, and to show you what it leads to. In this contest, after my first fighting blood which was stirred up through strenuous opposition had subsided, I did not have any bitterness against any particular man or men. My anger and hard feelings were stirred up against the system; not against the men.

Practically all of those men were my friends, and many of them are still my friends. As soon as I began to be successful in forcing the men to do a fair day's work, they played what is usually the winning card. I knew that it was coming. I had predicted to the owners of the company what would happen when we began to win, and had warned them that they must stand by me; so that I had the backing of the company in taking effective steps to checkmate the final move of the men. Every time I broke a rate or forced one of the new men whom I had trained to work at a reasonable and proper speed, some one of the machinists would deliberately break some part of his machine as an object lesson to demonstrate to the management that a fool foreman was driving the men to overload their machines until they broke. Almost every day ingenious accidents were planned, and these happened to machines in different parts of the shop, and were, of course, always laid to the fool foreman who was driving the men and the machines beyond their proper limit.

Fortunately, I had told the management in advance that this would happen, so they backed me up fully. When they began breaking their machines, I said to the men, "All right; from this time on, any accident that happens in this shop, every time you break any part of a machine you will have to pay part of the cost of repairing it or else quit. I don't care if the roof falls in and breaks your machine, you will pay all the same." Every time a man broke anything I fined him and then turned the money over to the mutual benefit association, so that in the end it came back to the men. But I fined them, right or wrong. They could always show every time an accident happened that it was not their fault and that it was an impossible thing for them not to break their machine under the circumstances. Finally, when they found that these tactics did not produce the desired effect on the management, they got sick and tired of being fined, their opposition broke down, and they promised to do a fair day's work.

After that we were good friends, but it took three years of hard fighting to bring this about.[7]

The issue here turned on the work content of a day's labor power, which Taylor defines in the phrase "a fair day's work."

To this term he gave a crude physiological interpretation: all the work a worker can do without injury to his health, at a pace that can be sustained throughout a working lifetime. (In practice, he tended to define this level of activity at an extreme limit, choosing a pace that only a few could maintain, and then only under strain.) Why a "fair day's work" should be defined as a physiological maximum is never made clear. In attempting to give concrete meaning to the abstraction "fairness," it would make just as much if not more sense to express a fair day's work as the amount of labor necessary to add to the product a value equal to the worker's pay; under such conditions, of course, profit would be impossible. The phrase "a fair day's work" must therefore be regarded as inherently meaningless, and filled with such content as the adversaries in the purchase-sale relationship try to give it.

Taylor set as his objective the maximum or "optimum" that can be obtained from a day's labor power. "On the part of the men," he said in his first book, "the greatest obstacle to the attainment of this standard is the slow pace which they adopt, or the loafing or 'soldiering,' marking time, as it is called." In each of his later expositions of his system, he begins with this same point, underscoring it heavily.[8] The causes of this soldiering he breaks into two parts: "This loafing or soldiering proceeds from two causes. First, from the natural instinct and tendency of men to take it easy, which may be called *natural soldiering*. Second, from more intricate second thought and reasoning caused by their relations with other men, which may be called *systematic soldiering*." The first of these he quickly puts aside, to concentrate on the second: "The natural laziness of men is serious, but by far the greatest evil from which both workmen and employers are suffering is the *systematic soldiering* which is almost universal under all the ordinary schemes of management and which results from a careful study on

the part of the workmen of what they think will promote their best interests."

The greater part of systematic soldiering . . . is done by the men with the deliberate object of keeping their employers ignorant of how fast work can be done.

So universal is soldiering for this purpose, that hardly a competent workman can be found in a large establishment, whether he works by the day or on piece work, contract work or under any of the ordinary systems of compensating labor, who does not devote a considerable part of his time to studying just how slowly he can work and still convince his employer that he is going at a good pace.

The causes for this are, briefly, that practically all employers determine upon a maximum sum which they feel it is right for each of their classes of employes to earn per day, whether their men work by the day or piece.[9]

That the pay of labor is a socially determined figure, relatively independent of productivity, among employers of similar types of labor power in any given period was thus known to Taylor. Workers who produce twice or three times as much as they did the day before do not thereby double or triple their pay, but may be given a small incremental advantage over their fellows, an advantage which disappears as their level of production becomes generalized. The contest over the size of the portion of the day's labor power to be embodied in each product is thus relatively independent of the level of pay, which responds chiefly to market, social, and historical factors. The worker learns this from repeated experiences, whether working under day or piece rates: "It is, however," says Taylor, "under piece work that the art of systematic soldiering is thoroughly developed. After a workman has had the price per piece of the work he is doing lowered two or three times as a result of his having worked harder and increased his output, he is likely to entirely lose sight of his employer's side of the case and to become imbued with a grim determination to have no more cuts if soldiering can prevent it."[10] To this it should be added that even where a piecework or "incentive" system allows the worker to increase his pay, the contest is not thereby ended but only exacerbated, because the output records now determine the setting and revision of pay rates.

Taylor always took the view that workers, by acting in this fashion, were behaving rationally and with an adequate view of their own best interests. He claimed, in another account of his Midvale battle, that he conceded as much even in the midst of the struggle:

His workman friends came to him [Taylor] continually and asked him, in a personal, friendly way, whether he would advise them, for their own best interest, to turn out more work. And, as a truthful man, he had to tell them that if he were in their place he would fight against turning out any more work, just as they were doing, because under the piecework system they would be allowed to earn no more wages than they had been earning, and yet they would be made to work harder.[11]

The conclusions which Taylor drew from the baptism by fire he received in the Midvale struggle may be summarized as follows: Workers who are controlled only by general orders and discipline are not adequately controlled, because they retain their grip on the actual processes of labor. So long as they control the labor process itself, they will thwart efforts to realize to the full the potential inherent in their labor power. To change this situation, control over the labor process must pass into the hands of management, not only in a formal sense but by the control and dictation of each step of the process, including its mode of performance. In pursuit of this end, no pains are too great, no efforts excessive, because the results will repay all efforts and expenses lavished on this demanding and costly endeavor.

The forms of management that existed prior to Taylorism, which Taylor called "ordinary management," he deemed alto-

gether inadequate to meet these demands. His descriptions of ordinary management bear the marks of the propagandist and proselytizer: exaggeration, simplification, and schematization. But his point is clear:

Now, in the best of the ordinary types of management, the managers recognize frankly that the . . . workmen, included in the twenty or thirty trades, who are under them, possess this mass of traditional knowledge, a large part of which is not in the possession of management. The management, of course, includes foremen and superintendents, who themselves have been first-class workers at their trades. And yet these foremen and superintendents know, better than any one else, that their own knowledge and personal skill falls far short of the combined knowledge and dexterity of all the workmen under them. The most experienced managers frankly place before their workmen the problem of doing the work in the best and most economical way. They recognize the task before them as that of inducing each workman to use his best endeavors, his hardest work, all his traditional knowledge, his skill, his ingenuity, and his good-will—in a word, his "initiative," so as to yield the largest possible return to his employer.[12]

As we have already seen from Taylor's belief in the universal prevalence and in fact inevitability of "soldiering," he did not recommend reliance upon the "initiative" of workers. Such a course, he felt, leads to the surrender of control: 'As was usual then, and in fact as is still usual in most of the shops in this country, the shop was really run by the workmen and not by the bosses. The workmen together had carefully planned just how fast each job should be done." In his Midvale battle, Taylor pointed out, he had located the source of the trouble in the "ignorance of the management as to what really constitutes a proper day's work for a workman." He had "fully realized that, although he was foreman of the shop, the combined knowledge and skill of the workmen who were under him was certainly ten times as great as his own."[13] This, then, was the source of the trouble and the starting point of scientific management.

We may illustrate the Taylorian solution to this dilemma in the same manner that Taylor often did: by using his story of his work for the Bethlehem Steel Company in supervising the moving of pig iron by hand. This story has the advantage of being the most detailed and circumstantial he set down, and also of dealing with a type of work so simple that anyone can visualize it without special technical preparation. We extract it here from Taylor's *The Principles of Scientific Management:*

One of the first pieces of work undertaken by us, when the writer started to introduce scientific management into the Bethlehem Steel Company, was to handle pig iron on task work. The opening of the Spanish War found some 80,000 tons of pig iron placed in small piles in an open field adjoining the works. Prices for pig iron had been so low that it could not be sold at a profit, and therefore had been stored. With the opening of the Spanish War the price of pig iron rose, and this large accumulation of iron was sold. This gave us a good opportunity to show the workmen, as well as the owners and managers of the works, on a fairly large scale the advantages of task work over the old-fashioned day work and piece work, in doing a very elementary class of work.

The Bethlehem Steel Company had five blast furnaces, the product of which had been handled by a pig-iron gang for many years. This gang, at this time, consisted of about 75 men. They were good, average pig-iron handlers, were under an excellent foreman who himself had been a pig-iron handler, and the work was done, on the whole, about as fast and as cheaply as it was anywhere else at that time.

A railroad switch was run out into the field, right along the edge of the piles of pig iron. An inclined plank was placed against the side of a car, and each man picked up from his pile a pig of iron weighing about 92 pounds, walked up the inclined plank and dropped it on the end of the car.

We found that this gang were loading on the average about 12½ long tons per man per day. We were surprised to find, after studying the

matter, that a first-class pig-iron handler ought to handle between 47 and 48 long tons per day, instead of 12½ tons. This task seemed to us so very large that we were obliged to go over our work several times before we were absolutely sure that we were right. Once we were sure, however, that 47 tons was a proper day's work for a first-class pig-iron handler, the task which faced us as managers under the modern scientific plan was clearly before us. It was our duty to see that the 80,000 tons of pig iron was loaded on to the cars at the rate of 47 tons per man per day, in place of 12½ tons, at which rate the work was then being done. And it was further our duty to see that this work was done without bringing on a strike among the men, without any quarrel with the men, and to see that the men were happier and better contented when loading at the new rate of 47 tons than they were when loading at the old rate of 12½ tons.

Our first step was the scientific selection of the workman. In dealing with workmen under this type of management, it is an inflexible rule to talk to and deal with only one man at a time, since each workman has his own special abilities and limitations, and since we are not dealing with men in masses, but are trying to develop each individual man to his highest state of efficiency and prosperity. Our first step was to find the proper workman to begin with. We therefore carefully watched and studied these 75 men for three or four days, at the end of which time we had picked out four men who appeared to be physically able to handle pig iron at the rate of 47 tons per day. A careful study was then made of each of these men. We looked up their history as far back as practicable and thorough inquiries were made as to the character, habits, and the ambition of each of them. Finally we selected one from among the four as the most likely man to start with. He was a little Pennsylvania Dutchman who had been observed to trot back home for a mile or so after his work in the evening, about as fresh as he was when he came trotting down to work in the morning. We found that upon wages of $1.15 a day he had succeeded in buying a small plot of ground, and that he was engaged in putting up the walls of a little house for himself in the morning before starting to work and at night after leaving. He also had the reputation of being exceedingly "close," that is, of placing a very high value on a dollar. As one man whom we talked to about him said, "A penny looks about the size of a cart-wheel to him." This man we will call Schmidt.

The task before us, then, narrowed itself down to getting Schmidt to handle 47 tons of pig iron per day and making him glad to do it. This was done as follows. Schmidt was called out from among the gang of pig-iron handlers and talked to somewhat in this way:

"Schmidt, are you a high-priced man?"

"Vell, I don't know vat you mean."

"Oh yes, you do. What I want to know is whether you are a high-priced man or not."

"Vell, I don't know vat you mean."

"Oh, come now, you answer my questions. What I want to find out is whether you are a high-priced man or one of these cheap fellows here. What I want to find out is whether you want to earn $1.85 a day or whether you are satisfied with $1.15, just the same as all those cheap fellows are getting."

"Did I vant $1.85 a day? Vas dot a high-priced man? Vell, yes, I vas a high-priced man."

"Oh, you're aggravating me. Of course you want $1.85 a day—every one wants it! You know perfectly well that that has very little to do with your being a high-priced man. For goodness' sake answer my questions, and don't waste any more of my time. Now come over here. You see that pile of pig iron?"

"Yes."

"You see that car?"

"Yes."

"Well, if you are a high-priced man, you will load that pig iron on that car to-morrow for $1.85. Now do wake up and answer my question. Tell me whether you are a high-priced man or not."

"Vell—did I got $1.85 for loading dot pig iron on dot car to-morrow?"

"Yes, of course you do, and you get $1.85 for loading a pile like that every day right through the year. That is what a high-priced man does, and you know it just as well as I do."

"Vell, dot's all right. I could load dot pig iron on the car to-morrow for $1.85, and I get it every day, don't I?"

"Certainly you do—certainly you do."

"Vell, den, I vas a high-priced man."

"Now, hold on, hold on. You know just as well as I do that a high-priced man has to do exactly as he's told from morning till night. You have seen this man here before, haven't you?"

"No, I never saw him."

"Well, if you are a high-priced man, you will do exactly as this man tells you to-morrow, from morning till night. When he tells you to pick up a pig and walk, you pick it up and you walk, and when he tells you to sit down and rest, you sit down. You do that right straight through the day. And what's more, no back talk. Now a high-priced man does just what he's told to do, and no back talk. Do you understand that? When this man tells you to walk, you walk; when he tells you to sit down, you sit down, and you don't talk back to him. Now you come on to work here to-morrow morning and I'll know before night whether you are really a high-priced man or not."

This seems to be rather rough talk. And indeed it would be if applied to an educated mechanic, or even an intelligent laborer. With a man of the mentally sluggish type of Schmidt it is appropriate and not unkind, since it is effective in fixing his attention on the high wages which he wants and away from what, if it were called to his attention, he probably would consider impossibly hard work. . . .

Schmidt started to work, and all day long, and at regular intervals, was told by the man who stood over him with a watch, "Now pick up a pig and walk. Now sit down and rest. Now walk—now rest," etc. He worked when he was told to work, and rested when he was told to rest, and at half-past five in the afternoon had his 47$\frac{1}{2}$ tons loaded on the car. And he practically never failed to work at this pace and do the task that was set him during the three years that the writer was at Bethlehem. And throughout this time he averaged a little more than $1.85 per day, whereas before he had never received over $1.15 per day, which was the ruling rate of wages at that time in Bethlehem. That is, he received 60 per cent higher wages than were paid to other men who were not working on task work. One man after another was picked out and trained to handle pig iron at the rate of 47$\frac{1}{2}$ tons per day until all of the pig iron was handled at this rate, and the men were receiving 60 per cent. more wages than other workmen around them.[14]

The merit of this tale is its clarity in illustrating the pivot upon which all modern management turns: the control over work through the control over the *decisions that are made in the course of work*. Since, in the case of pig-iron handling, the only decisions to be made were those having to do with a time sequence, Taylor simply dictated that timing and the results at the end of the day added up to his planned day-task. As to the use of money as motivation, while this element has a usefulness in the first stages of a new mode of work, employers do not, when they have once found a way to compel a more rapid pace of work, continue to pay a 60 percent differential for common labor, or for any other job. Taylor was to discover (and to complain) that management treated his "scientific incentives" like any other piece rate, cutting them mercilessly so long as the labor market permitted, so that workers pushed to the Taylorian intensity found themselves getting little, or nothing, more than the going rate for the area, while other employers—under pressure of this competitive threat—forced their own workers to the higher intensities of labor.

Taylor liked to pretend that his work standards were not beyond human capabilities exercised without undue strain, but as he himself made clear, this pretense could be maintained only on the understanding that unusual physical specimens were selected for each of his jobs:

As to the scientific selection of the men, it is a fact that in this gang of 75 pig-iron handlers only about one man in eight was physically capable of handling 47½ tons per day. With the very best of intentions, the other seven out of eight men were physically unable to work at this pace. Now the one man in eight who was able to do this work was in no sense superior to the other men who were working on the gang. He merely happened to be a man of the type of the ox—no rare specimen of humanity, difficult to find and therefore very highly prized. On the contrary, he was a man so stupid that he was unfitted to do most kinds of laboring work, even. The selection of the man, then, does not involve finding some extraordinary individual, but merely picking out from among very ordinary men the few who are especially suited to this type of work. Although in this particular gang only one man in eight was suited to doing the work, we had not the slightest difficulty in getting all the men who were needed—some of them from inside the works and others from the neighboring country—who were exactly suited to the job.[15]

Taylor spent his lifetime in expounding the principles of control enunciated here, and in applying them directly to many other tasks: shoveling loose materials, lumbering, inspecting ball bearings, etc., but particularly to the machinist's trade. He believed that the forms of control he advocated could be applied not only to simple labor, but to labor in its most complex forms, without exception, and in fact it was in machine shops, bricklaying, and other such sites for the practice of well-developed crafts that he and his immediate successors achieved their most striking results.

From earliest times to the Industrial Revolution the craft or skilled trade was the basic unit, the elementary cell of the labor process. In each craft, the worker was presumed to be the master of a body of traditional knowledge, and methods and procedures were left to his or her discretion. In each such worker reposed the accumulated knowledge of materials and processes by which production was accomplished in the craft. The potter, tanner, smith, weaver, carpenter, baker, miller, glassmaker, cobbler, etc., each representing a branch of the social division of labor, was a repository of human technique for the labor processes of that branch. The worker combined, in mind and body, the concepts and physical dexterities of the specialty: technique, understood in this way, is, as has often been observed, the predecessor and progenitor of science. The most important and widespread of all crafts was, and throughout the world remains to this day, that of farmer. The farming family combines its craft with the rude practice of a number of others, including those of the smith, mason, carpenter, butcher, miller, and baker, etc. The apprenticeships required in traditional crafts ranged from three to seven years, and for the farmer of course extends beyond this to include most of childhood, adolescence, and young adulthood. In view of the knowledge to be assimilated, the dexterities to be gained, and the fact that the craftsman, like the professional, was required to master a specialty and become the best judge of the manner of its application to specific production problems, the years of apprenticeship were generally needed and were employed in a learning process that extended well into the journeyman decades. Of these trades, that of the machinist was in Taylor's day among the most recent, and certainly the most important to modern industry.

As I have already pointed out, Taylor was not primarily concerned with the advance of technology (which, as we shall see, offers other means for direct control over the labor process). He did make significant contributions to the technical knowledge of machine-shop practice (high-speed tool steel, in particular), but these were chiefly by-products of his effort to study this practice with an eye to systematizing and classifying it. His concern was with the control of labor at any given level of technology, and he tackled his own trade with a boldness and energy which astonished his contemporaries and set the pattern for industrial engineers, work designers, and office managers from that day on. And in tackling machine-shop work, he had set himself a prodigious task.

The machinist of Taylor's day started with the shop drawing, and turned, milled, bored, drilled, planed, shaped, ground, filed, and otherwise machine- and hand-processed the proper stock to the desired shape as specified in the drawing. The range of decisions to be made in the course of the process is—unlike the case of a simple job, such as the handling of pig iron—by its very nature enormous. Even for the lathe alone, disregarding all collateral tasks such as the choice of stock, handling, centering and chucking the work, layout and measuring, order of cuts, and considering only the operation of turning itself, the range of possibilities is huge. Taylor himself worked with 12 variables, including the hardness of the metal, the material of the cutting tool, the thickness of the shaving, the shape of the cutting tool, the use of a coolant during cutting, the depth of the cut, the frequency of regrinding cutting tools as they became dulled, the lip and clearance angles of the tool, the smoothness of cutting or absence of chatter, the diameter of the stock being turned, the pressure of the chip or shaving on the cutting surface of the tool, and the speeds, feeds, and pulling power of the machine.[16] Each of these variables is subject to broad choice, ranging from a few possibilities in the selection and use of a coolant, to a very great number of effective choices in all matters having to do with thickness, shape, depth, duration, speed, etc. Twelve variables, each subject to a large number of choices, will yield in their possible combinations and permutations astronomical figures, as Taylor soon realized. But upon these decisions of the machinist depended not just the accuracy and finish of the product, but also the pace of production. Nothing daunted, Taylor set out to gather into management's hands all the basic information bearing on these processes. He began a series of experiments at the Midvale Steel Company, in the fall of 1880, which lasted 26 years, recording the results of between 30,000 and 50,000 tests, and cutting up more than 800,000 pounds of iron and steel on ten different machine tools reserved for his experimental use. His greatest difficulty, he reported, was not testing the many variations, but holding 11 variables constant while altering the conditions of the 12th. The data were systematized, correlated, and reduced to practical form in the shape of what he called a "slide rule" which would determine the optimum combination of choices for each step in the machining process.[17] His machinists thenceforth were required to work in accordance with instructions derived from these experimental data, rather than from their own knowledge, experience, or tradition. This was the Taylor approach in its first systematic application to a complex labor process. Since the principles upon which it is based are fundamental to all advanced work design or industrial engineering today, it is important to examine them in detail. And since Taylor has been virtually alone in giving clear expression to principles which are seldom now publicly acknowledged, it is best to examine them with the aid of Taylor's own forthright formulations.

First principle

"The managers assume . . . the burden of gathering together all of the traditional knowledge which in the past has been possessed by the workmen and then of classifying, tabulating, and reducing this knowledge to rules, laws, and formulae. . . ."[18] We have seen the illustrations of this in the cases of the lathe machinist and the pig-iron handler. The great disparity between these activities, and the different orders of knowledge that may be collected about them, illustrate that for Taylor—as for managers today—no task is either so simple or so complex that it may not be studied with the object of collecting in the hands of management at least as much information as is known by the worker who performs it regularly, and very likely more. This brings to an end the situation in which "employers derive their knowledge of how much of a given class of work can be done in a day from either their own experience, which has frequently grown hazy with age, from casual and unsystematic observation of their men, or at best from records which are kept, showing the quickest time in which each job has been done."[19] It enables management to discover and enforce those speedier methods and shortcuts which workers themselves, in the practice of their trades or tasks, learn or improvise, and use at their own discretion only. Such an experimental approach also brings into being new methods such as can be devised only through the means of systematic study.

This first principle we may call the *dissociation of the labor process from the skills of the workers.* The labor process is to be rendered independent of craft, tradition, and the workers' knowledge. Henceforth it is to depend not at all upon the abilities of workers, but entirely upon the practices of management.

Second principle

"All possible brain work should be removed from the shop and centered in the planning or laying-out department. . . ."[20] Since this is the key to scientific management, as Taylor well understood, he was especially emphatic on this point and it is important to examine the principle thoroughly.

In the human, as we have seen, the essential feature that makes for a labor capacity superior to that of the animal is the combination of execution with a conception of the thing to be done. But as human labor becomes a social rather than an individual phenomenon, it is possible—unlike in the instance of animals where the motive force, instinct, is inseparable from action—to divorce conception from execution. This dehumanization of the labor process, in which workers are reduced almost to the level of labor in its animal form, while purposeless and unthinkable in the case of the self-organized and self-motivated social labor of a community of producers, becomes crucial for the management of purchased labor. For if the workers' execution is guided by their own conception, it is not possible, as we have seen, to enforce upon them either the methodological efficiency or the working pace desired by capital. The capitalist therefore learns from the start to take advantage of this aspect of human labor power, and to break the unity of the labor process.

This should be called the principle of the *separation of conception from execution,* rather than by its more common name of the separation of mental and manual labor (even though it is similar to the latter, and in practice often identical). This is because mental labor, labor done primarily in the brain, is also subjected to the same principle of separation of conception from execution: mental labor is first separated from manual labor and, as we shall see, is then itself subdivided rigorously according to the same rule.

The first implication of this principle is that Taylor's "science of work" is never to be developed by the worker, always by management. This notion, apparently so "natural" and undebatable today, was in fact vigorously discussed in Taylor's day, a fact which shows how far we have traveled along the road of transforming all ideas about the labor process in less than a century, and how completely Taylor's hotly contested assumptions have entered into the conventional outlook within a short space of time. Taylor confronted this question—why must work be studied by the management and not by the worker himself; why not *scientific workmanship* rather than *scientific management?*—repeatedly, and employed all his ingenuity in devising answers to it, though not always with his customary frankness. In *The Principles of Scientific Management,* he pointed out that the "older system" of management

makes it necessary for each workman to bear almost the entire responsibility for the general plan as well as for each detail of his work, and in many cases for his implements as well. In addition to this he must do all of the actual physical labor. The development of a science, on the other hand, involves the establishment of many rules, laws, and formulae which replace the judgment of the individual workman and which can be effectively used only after having been systematically recorded, indexed, etc. The practical use of scientific data also calls for a room in which to keep the books, records, etc., and a desk for the planner to work at. Thus all of the planning which under the old system was done by the workman, as a result of his personal experience, must of necessity under the new system be done by the management in accordance with the laws of the science; because even if the workman was well suited to the development and use of scientific data, it would be physically impossible for him to work at his machine and at a desk at the same time. It is also clear that in most cases one type of man is needed to plan ahead and an entirely different type to execute the work.[21]

The objections having to do with physical arrangements in the workplace are clearly of little importance, and represent the deliberate exaggeration of obstacles which, while they may exist as inconveniences, are hardly insuperable. To refer to the "different type" of worker needed for each job is worse than disingenuous, since these "different types" hardly existed until the division of labor created them. As Taylor well understood, the possession of craft knowledge made the worker the best starting point for the development of the science of work; systematization often means, at least at the outset, the gathering of knowledge which *workers already possess.* But Taylor, secure in his obsession with the immense reasonableness of his proposed arrangement, did not stop at this point. In his testimony before the Special Committee of the House of Representatives, pressed and on the defensive, he brought forth still other arguments:

I want to make it clear, Mr. Chairman, that work of this kind undertaken by the management leads to the development of a science, while it is next to impossible for the workman to develop a science. There are many workmen who are intellectually just as capable of developing a science, who have plenty of brains, and are just as capable of developing a science as those on the managing side. But the science of doing work of any kind cannot be developed by the workman. Why? Because he has neither the time nor the money to do it. The development of the science of doing any kind of work always requires the work of two men, one man who actually does the work which is to be studied and another man who observes closely the first man while he works and studies the time problems and the motion problems connected with this work. No workman has either the time or the money to burn in making experiments of this sort. If he is working for himself no one will pay him while he studies the motions of some one else. The management must and ought to pay for all such work. So that for the workman, the development of a science becomes impossible, not because the workman is not intellectually capable of developing it, but he has neither the time nor the money to do it and he realizes that this is a question for the management to handle.[22]

Taylor here argues that the systematic study of work and the fruits of this study belong to management for the very same reason that machines, factory buildings, etc., belong to them; that is, because it costs labor time to conduct such a study, and only the possessors of capital can afford labor time. The possessors of labor time cannot themselves afford to do anything with it but sell it for their means of subsistence. It is true that this is the rule in capitalist relations of production, and Taylor's use of the argument in this case shows with great clarity where the sway of capital leads: Not only is capital the property of the capitalist, but *labor itself has become part of capital*. Not only do the workers lose control over their instruments of production, but they must now lose control over their own labor and the manner of its performance. This control now falls to those who can "afford" to study it in order to know it better than the workers themselves know their own life activity.

But Taylor has not yet completed his argument: "Furthermore," he told the Committee,

if any workman were to find a new and quicker way of doing work, or if he were to develop a new method, you can see at once it becomes to his interest to keep that development to himself, not to teach the other workmen the quicker method. It is to his interest to do what workmen have done in all times, to keep their trade secrets for themselves and their friends. That is the old idea of trade secrets. The workman kept his knowledge to himself instead of developing a science and teaching it to others and making it public property.[23]

Behind this hearkening back to old ideas of "guild secrets" is Taylor's persistent and fundamental notion that the improvement of work methods by workers brings few benefits to management. Elsewhere in his testimony, in discussing the work of his associate, Frank Gilbreth, who spent many years studying bricklaying methods, he candidly admits that not only *could* the "science of bricklaying" be developed by workers, but that it undoubtedly *had been:* "Now, I have not the slightest doubt that during the last 4,000 years all the methods that Mr. Gilbreth developed have many, many times suggested themselves to the minds of bricklayers." But because knowledge possessed by workers is not useful to capital, Talyor begins his list of the desiderata of scientific management: "First. The development—by the management, not the workmen—of the science of bricklaying."[24] Workers, he explains, are not going to put into execution any system or any method which harms them and their workmates: "Would they be likely," he says, referring to the pig-iron job, "to get rid of seven men out of eight from their own gang and retain only the eighth man? No!"[25]

Finally, Taylor understood the Babbage principle better than anyone of his time, and it was always uppermost in his calculations. The purpose of work study was never, in his mind, to enhance the ability of the worker, to concentrate in the worker a greater share of scientific knowledge, to ensure that as technique rose, the worker would rise with it. Rather, the purpose was to cheapen the worker by decreasing his training and enlarging his output. In his early book, *Shop Management*, he said frankly that the "full possibilities" of his system "will have been realized until almost all of the machines in the shop are run by men who are of smaller calibre and attainments, and who are therefore cheaper than those required under the old system."[26]

Therefore, both in order to ensure management control and to cheapen the worker, conception and execution must be rendered separate spheres of work, and for this purpose the study of work processes must be reserved to management and kept from the workers, to whom its results are communicated only in the form of simplified job tasks governed by simplified instructions which it is thenceforth their duty to follow unthinkingly and without comprehension of the underlying technical reasoning or data.

Third principle

The essential idea of "the ordinary types of management," Taylor said, "is that each workman has become more skilled in his own trade than it is possible for any one in the management to be, and that, therefore, the details of how the work shall best be done must be left to him." But by contrast:

Perhaps the most prominent single element in modern scientific management is the task idea. The work of every workman is fully planned out by the management at least one day in advance, and each man receives in most cases complete written instructions, describing in detail the task which he is to accomplish, as well as the means to be used in doing the work. . . . This task specifies not only what is to be done, but how it is to be done and the exact time allowed for doing it. . . . Scientific management consists very largely in preparing for and carrying out these tasks.[27]

In this principle it is not the written instruction card that is important. Taylor had no need for such a card with Schmidt, nor did he use one in many other instances. Rather, the essential element is the systematic pre-planning and pre-calculation of all elements of the labor process, which now no longer exists as a process in the imagination of the worker but only as a process in the imagination of a special management staff. Thus, if the first principle is the gathering and development of knowledge of labor processes, and the second is the concentration of this knowledge as the exclusive province of management—together with its essential converse, the absence of such knowledge among the workers—then the third is the *use of this monopoly over knowledge to control each step of the labor process and its mode of execution.*

As capitalist industrial, office, and market practices developed in accordance with this principle, it eventually became part of accepted routine and custom, all the more so as the increasingly scientific character of most processes, which grew in complexity while the worker was not allowed to partake of this growth, made it ever more difficult for the workers to understand the processes in which they functioned. But in the beginning, as Taylor well understood, an abrupt psychological wrench was required. We have seen in the simple Schmidt case the means employed, both in the selection of a single worker as a starting point and in the way in which he was reoriented to the new conditions of work. In the more complex conditions of the machine shop, Taylor gave this part of the responsibility to the foremen. It is essential, he said of the gang bosses, to "nerve and brace them up to the point of insisting that the workmen shall carry out the orders exactly as specified on the instruction cards. This is a difficult task at first, as the workmen have been accustomed for years to do the details of the work to suit themselves, and many of them are intimate friends of the bosses and believe they know quite as much about their business as the latter."[28]

Modern management came into being on the basis of these principles. It arose as theoretical construct and as systematic practice, moreover, in the very period during which the transformation of labor from processes based on skill to processes based

upon science was attaining its most rapid tempo. Its role was to render conscious and systematic, the formerly unconscious tendency of capitalist production. It was to ensure that as craft declined, the worker would sink to the level of general and undifferentiated labor power, adaptable to a large range of simple tasks, while as science grew, it would be concentrated in the hands of management.

NOTES

1. Peter F. Drucker, The Practice of Management (New York, 1954), p. 280.

2. See Sudhir Kakar, *Frederick Taylor: A Study in Personality and Innovation* (Cambridge, Mass., 1970), pp. 115–17; and Henri Fayol, *General and Industrial Management* (1916; trans., London, 1949).

3. Lyndall Urwick and E. F. L. Brech, *The Making of Scientific Management,* 3 vols. (London, 1945, 1946, 1948), vol. 1, p. 17.

4. See Georges Friedmann, *Industrial Society* (Glencoe, Ill., 1964), esp. pp. 51–65.

5. Lyndall Urwick, *The Meaning of Rationalisation* (London, 1929), pp. 13–16.

6. Kakar, *Frederick Taylor,* pp. 17–27, 52–54.

7. *Taylor's Testimony before the Special House Committee,* in Frederick W. Taylor, *Scientific Management* (New York and London, 1947), pp. 79–85; this is a single-volume edition of Taylor's three chief works, *Shop Management* (1903); *Principles of Scientific Management* (1911); and a public document, *Hearings before Special Committee of the House of Representatives to Investigate the Taylor and Other Systems of Shop Management* (1912), which is given the above title in this volume. Each of the three book-length documents in this volume is paged separately.

8. Frederick W. Taylor, *Shop Management,* in

Scientific Management, p. 30. See also Taylor's *The Principles of Scientific Management* (New York, 1967), pp. 13–14; and *Taylor's Testimony* in *Scientific Management,* p. 8.

9. *Shop Management,* pp. 32–33.

10. Ibid., pp. 34–35.

11. *The Principles of Scientific Management,* p. 52.

12. Ibid., p. 32.

13. Ibid., pp. 48–49, 53.

14. Ibid., pp. 41–47.

15. Ibid., pp. 61–62.

16. Ibid., pp. 107–109.

17. Ibid., p. 111.

18. Ibid., p. 36.

19. Ibid., p. 22.

20. *Shop Management,* pp. 98–99.

21. *The Principles of Scientific Management,* pp. 37–38.

22. *Taylor's Testimony before the Special House Committee,* pp. 235–36.

23. Loc. cit.

24. Ibid., pp. 75, 77.

25. *The Principles of Scientific Management,* p. 62.

26. *Shop Management,* p. 105.

27. *The Principles of Scientific Management,* pp. 63, 39.

28. *Shop Management,* p. 108.

CHAPTER 3

The class structure of advanced capitalism

Social and moral life in capitalist society—today as in the past—is affected not only by the economic conditions of production but also by the struggle between classes produced by these conditions. For the capitalist system to operate and survive, the capitalist class must exploit the labor (appropriate the labor power) of the working class. The capitalist class survives by appropriating this labor, and the working class exists as long as exploited labor is required in the productive process. Moreover, the amount of labor appropriated, the techniques of labor exploitation, the conditions of working-class life, and the level of working-class consciousness are an integral part of the historical development of capitalism. Class conflict thus permeates the whole of capitalist development: The history of the development of capitalism is the history of class struggle.

A class analysis begins with the recognition that, first, classes are an expression of the underlying forces of the capitalist mode of production and that, second, classes are not fixed entities but rather ongoing processes in the development of capitalism. On the abstract level, the class structure of developing capitalism is an expression of the antagonistic relation between two opposing classes, those who own and control the means of production and those who do not. One class, the capitalist class, exploits the labor power of the other class, the working class. The capitalist class survives by appropriating the surplus labor of the working class, and the working class, as the exploited class, exists as long as surplus labor is required in the productive process: each class depends on the other for its character and existence. In the concrete empirical analysis of specific capitalist societies at particular points in history, however, the class structure is seen to be much more complex.[1] The primary focus of such analysis, nevertheless, is on the nature of the class structure in relation to the present level of capitalist development.

Since capitalism is constantly transforming itself, it follows that class analysis must be attuned to the changes in class relations that occur in the development of capitalism. Although all stages of capitalist development involve a dialectic between ownership and nonownership, control and noncontrol, domination and resistance, the fundamental opposition between the capitalist class and the working class continues. Yet it is becoming apparent that a class analysis of advanced capitalism requires a more elaborate description of this relationship. The class structure of advanced capitalism is in transition; new forms are emerging within the dynamic of the capitalist mode of production.

Although the composition of classes changes under advanced capitalism, around new forms of economic activity and occupations, capitalist development does not give rise to major new classes within capitalism. Rather, it gives rise to what Marx described as *fractions* within classes.[2] The basic dialectic between the capitalist class and the working class still predominates, but added to this is a dialectic between fractions within these classes.

The expansion of capitalism, in fact, necessitates fractions within classes. These new fractions are of such importance that several class theorists have posited the formation of a new class of "petty bourgeoisie" (including civil servants, intellectuals, and professional workers).[3] However, although the subjective consciousness of the petty bourgeoisie may be different from that of the industrial working class, this does not mean that the fundamental objective antagonism within the capitalist mode of production has been altered in any important way. The class struggle between the working class and the capitalist class continues, and continues at an even faster and higher level under advanced capitalism.

The fractioning of the working class is taking place in response to the development of different sectors of the economy. This century has seen a tremendous shift in relative and absolute numbers from industrial labor to nonindustrial labor. The more capitalist industry has grown, the greater has been the demand for a mass of labor to provide the "unproductive" activities that are required for the diversion and distribution of capital goods. According to the classical Marxian labor theory of value, this *unproductive* labor is in contrast to *productive* labor.[4] That is, productive labor under capitalism consists of labor that produces commodity value for capital; money is exchanged for labor with the purpose of appropriating that value which it creates over and above what is paid (*surplus* value). Unproductive labor, on the other hand, is labor that is not exchanged for capital and that does not produce surplus value, hence, profit, for capitalists. Clerical, sales, and service workers (primarily employed by corporations and the state) make up the largest segment of the classical category of unproductive labor. Unproductive labor, that used by the capitalist for "unproductive" purposes, is increasing significantly under advanced capitalism.

The mass of workers now included in "unproductive" labor have been transformed into a modern commercial proletariat. This wage-working segment has become a major element in the capitalist mode of production.[5] In the process, these workers have lost many of the characteristics that formerly separated them from the traditional productive workers. Their growth in the labor force has brought them into the modern proletariat.

A large portion of these workers (including professional and technical workers, clerical and sales workers, and various other service workers) are employed by the *state*. In order to assure continuing accumulation under advanced capitalism, the capitalist state has expanded, employing new forms of labor to carry out the work of the state apparatus.[6] Workers are now involved in the functions of servicing (and controlling) the population and maintaining the legitimacy of the capitalist system. Work under late capitalism has become both productive and unproductive in the Marxist sense. That is, although profit still continues to be appropriated through the surplus value of labor, much labor is unproductive—or better, *indirectly productive*—in that the capitalist mode of production is being supported by other necessary forms of labor.

This has led some neo-Marxists to turn from a strictly labor theory of value, suggesting that in the present context such activities as science and technology are among the leading productive forces.[7] It is true that late capitalist development has transformed liberal capitalism into a system of welfare capitalism. The construction of a wide range of social policies is a vital characteristic of late capitalism. The social order is stabilized by the capitalist state, with its pervasive intervention into the economy and the population. Nevertheless, while legitimation and stabilization are secured by a large "unproductive" labor force, the appropriation of surplus value from the traditional productive labor force continues. The condition in late capitalism is that all labor is *production* in either the direct, surplus value sense or in the indirect, unproductive sense.[8] The present system needs both kinds of production in order to survive.

The dialectic of the class struggle assures a conflict within advancing capitalist society. The role that religion will play in this struggle, however, is yet to be realized. Because the development of capitalism has also meant the secularization of religion, even the relegation of the spiritual to a minor place in human social and moral life, we are left with few resources in our immediate past from which to draw. This makes the restoration of religious concern to the socialist movement even more acute—for socialism also (along with developing capitalism) has failed to attend to necessary religious needs. The socialist struggle requires a spiritual consciousness as much as a class consciousness. The transition to socialism is both political and religious. And ultimately the religious goal is one that transcends concrete political structures. The prophetic expectation speaks finally to that which is infinite and eternal.

NOTES

1. Theotonio Dos Santos, "The Concept of Social Classes," *Science and Society*, 34 (Summer 1970), pp. 166–193.

2. See Francesca Freedman, "The Internal Structure of the American Proletariat: A Marxist Analysis," *Socialist Revolution*, 5 (October–December 1975), pp. 41–83.

3. Nicos Poulantzas, *Classes in Contemporary Capitalism* (London: New Left Books, 1975); Anthony Giddens, *The Class Structure of the Advanced Societies* (New York: Harper & Row, 1975); and Barbara and John Ehrenreich, "The Professional-Managerial Class," *Radical America*, 11 (March–April 1977), pp. 7–31. See the class analysis in Erik Olin Wright, "Class Boundaries in Advanced Capitalist Societies," *New Left Review*, no. 98 (July–August 1976), pp. 3–41.

4. The Marxist formulation of productive and unproductive labor is discussed at length in Ian Gough, "Marx's Theory of Productive and Unproductive Labour," *New Left Review*, 76 (November–December 1972), pp. 47–72.

5. Harry Braverman, *Labor and Monopoly Capital: The Degradation of Work in the Twentieth Century* (New York: Monthly Review Press, 1974), pp. 293–423.

6. Gosta Esping-Andersen, Roger Friedland, and Erik Olin Wright, "Modes of Class Struggle and the Capitalist State," *Kapitalistate*, no. 4–5 (Summer 1976), pp. 186–220.

7. See James Farganis, "A Preface to Critical Theory," *Theory and Society*, 2 (Winter 1975), pp. 483–508; and Peter Laska, "A Note on Habermas and the Labor Theory of Value," *New German Critique*, 1 (Fall 1974), pp. 154–162.

8. See James O'Connor, "Productive and Unproductive Labor," *Politics and Society*, 5 (no. 3, 1975), pp. 297–336.

Who owns America?*

MAURICE ZEITLIN

Do you remember those full-page newspaper ads that showed a little old lady stroking *her* locomotive, supposedly owned by millions of ordinary Americans just like her? Or Standard Oil's gushing claim, "Yes, the people own the tools of production . . . . How odd to find that it is here, in the capitalism [Karl Marx] reviled, that the promise of the tool has been fulfilled." Well, it's happening again.

A current Texaco television commercial has Bob Hope asking us to "take a look at the owners of America's oil companies," and then leads us on a tour of a typical community made up of just plain folks like you and me. A recent book, received with much fanfare in the press, repeats the refrain. Its author, long-time management consultant and publicist Peter Drucker, tells us that an "unseen revolution" has wrought "a more radical shift in ownership than Soviet communism." Even more amazing, "the socialism of Marxist theory has been realized for the first time on American soil."

Not only are the means of production now in everyone's hands, but the U.S. Chamber of Commerce confides that the United States has become a "post-industrial society." College textbooks inform us that a "dramatic shift from blue collar to white collar, from brawn to brain [has] occurred," and the best-seller *Future Shock* rhapsodizes that "for the first time in human history," a society—*our* society—has "managed within a few short decades to throw off the yoke of manual labor." A book on "power in America" celebrates the passing of classes and suggests that we organize popular visits to "Newport, and bus tours through Grosse Pointe, for purely educational purposes—like seeing Carlsbad Caverns once." It is time, the author advises us, to shout, "The Working Class is dead. Long live the memory of the Working Class." And, summing it all up, a popular book on how to be a politician announces that "the economic class system is disappearing. . . . Redistribution of wealth and income . . . has ended economic inequality's political significance."

So, what has happened to classes? Who does own America, and how has it all been changing? Has the capitalist class really been "lopped off" at the top, as Harvard's Talcott Parsons once pithily put it? Has the ownership of American corporations become so dispersed that control has shifted to "professional managers" who are merely the "trustees" for all of us—"stockholders, employes, suppliers, consumers, and the public"—as Donald S. McNaughton, the chairman of Prudential Life, announced in a recent speech? Has the yoke of manual labor really been lifted? Is the working class now a mere memory? Or are the claims that prompt these questions really pseudofacts that are as plausible and persuasive as they are deceptive? The answer, I think, is clear: Economic inequality weighs as heavily and cuts as deeply as ever, and neither capitalists nor workers have vanished from American life.

Let's look first at who owns what. It's certainly hard enough to find out, even if,

---

* Reprinted by permission from *The Progressive*, 42 (June 1978) , pp. 14–21. Copyright © 1978, The Progressive, Inc., 408 West Gorham Street, Madison, Wisconsin 53703.

like Government economists, you have access to Internal Revenue Service (IRS) data. No law requires Americans to report their net worth, and besides, wealth is deliberately hidden, whether out of modesty or to avoid taxes. Still, an ingenious method of estimating wealth has been devised, to make the dead disclose what the living conceal. It is called the "estate multiplier technique," and it uses IRS data on estate tax returns. It treats those who die in any year as a "stratified sample" of the living on whose estates tax returns would have to be filed if they died during the year—that is, those with estates worth $60,000 or more. All told, only 4 percent of the adults in this country have estates as large as $60,000, counting *everything* they own, including cash in hand or under the mattress, and the mattress itself. But within that group, a minute number of Americans make up the real owners of America.

The Rose Bowl's 104,696 seats would still be half empty if only every adult American who owns $1 million or more in corporate stock came to cheer, and it would be even emptier if only those who have $100,000 in state and local bonds got a seat. If you counted all state, local, and Federal bonds (except U.S. Savings Bonds), and added Treasury bills, certificates, notes, and mortgages—and even foreign bonds—held by Americans in amounts of at least $200,000, you would still find well over a quarter of the Rose Bowl seats not taken. Only 55,400 adults have $1 million or more in corporate stock. A mere 40,000 have $100,000 or more in state and local bonds (all Federal tax exempt), and 73,500 adults have $200,000 or more if we count all bonds and debt-holdings.

This tiny owning class at the tip of the top, barely more than 1/20th of 1 percent of American adults, has a fifth of *all* the corporate stock, nearly two-thirds of the worth of *all* state and local bonds, and two-fifths of *all* bonds and notes. No wonder it

took five years of trying by an outstanding economist, James D. Smith, to get the IRS to allow him to study its information—and by then some of the data had been destroyed.

Contrast what this propertied class owns to what the rest of us have. Nine out of ten adults in the United States could sell everything they own, pay off their debts, and have no more than $30,000 left. Worse, more than half of all Americans would have a total "net worth" of no more than $3,000. The bottom half of all American families combined have only three cents of every dollar's worth of all the wealth in the country.

Back at the top, if we count up what the richest 1 percent of the population own, we find that they have a seventh of all the real estate in the country, more than half the corporate stock, and almost all the trust assets. They even had a seventh of all the *cash* in every checking and savings account and pocket and purse in America.

Summed up, that is a quarter of the net worth of the entire population held by the top 1 percent. If we take a slice as large as the richest 4 percent—everyone whose total net assets (i.e., subtracting debts) are worth at least $60,000—their combined wealth is more than a trillion dollars—enough to buy the entire national product of the United States and have plenty left over to pick up the combined output of a few small European countries, including Switzerland, Norway, Denmark, and Sweden.

So it's clear who owns America—but has this propertied class been slipping in its hold on the nation's wealth? Maybe, but if it slipped at all, it was not because of any egalitarian tendencies in American capitalism. It took the country's worst crash, the Great Depression, when many fortunes (and even a few of the fortune-holders) took the plunge from the pinnacle, to make a dent on what they own. Even the modest shrinkage that supposedly took place then is probably more apparent than real, because just before the crash there was a phenomenal rise in the price of stock, the biggest asset in the portfolios of the rich.

But since the end of World War II, there has been no change in their share of the nation's wealth; it has been constant in every year studied, at roughly five-year intervals, since 1945. The richest 1 percent own a quarter, and the top half of 1 percent a fifth, of the combined market worth of everything owned by every American. Remarkably, economic historians who have culled manuscript census reports on the past century report that on the eve of the Civil War the rich had the same cut of the total: The top 1 percent owned 24 percent in 1860 and 24.9 percent in 1969 (the latest year thoroughly studied). Through all the tumultuous changes since then—the Civil War and the emancipation of the slaves, the Populist and Progressive movements, the Great Depression, the New Deal, progressive taxation, the mass organization of industrial workers, and World Wars I and II—this class has held on to everything it had. They owned America then and they own it now.

Any notion that *income* has been redistributed, even though *property* is intact, is also illusory: The higher the income bracket, the higher the percentage in it that derives its income from the ownership of property. At the top, almost all income is in dividends, rents, royalties, and interest. Among all American families and unrelated individuals combined, not more than one in eight receives any stock dividends at all. Not one in a hundred receives even a dollar from any "trust or estate." But among those with incomes of $100,000 or more, 97 percent receive stock dividends and more than half receive inherited income directly from a trust or estate.

The 5 percent of Americans with the highest incomes take in almost half of all the income from property in the country. They receive 64 cents out of every dollar in dividends earned on publicly traded stock and 93 cents of the dividends on stock owned in "closely held corporations" (those having just a few owners). Furthermore, they take in 30 cents of every dollar earned in interest, 37 cents in rents and royalties, and 64 cents of every dollar in America coming from trusts and estates.

If we divide Americans into five brackets from low to high, and count all known income, the top fifth gets about 40 cents of every dollar of personal income. The bottom fifth gets just one nickel. That is a ratio of eight to one, and that ratio has remained almost exactly the same in every year since World War II ended. (Here, in the capitalism celebrated by the Advertising Council and Bob Hope, the gap between the top and bottom fifths is wider than in Britain, Holland, West Germany, or even Japan. Among industrial nations, only France has a wider gap.) And the *real income* gap between the top and bottom has been growing, though the ratio has stayed the same: The average real income difference between the top and bottom fifth, measured in constant 1969 dollars, rose from $11,000 to $19,000 in the 20 years between 1949 and 1969.

All those "redistributive efforts" and wars on poverty we have heard about have not made a dent in income distribution. The overall tax burden has probably become more *regressive* since World War II—taxes are taking an increasing bite of the incomes of people in the lower rather than in the higher brackets. One reason is that state and local taxes, which are typically more regressive than Federal taxes, have grown in comparison to Federal taxes—from 42 cents to every dollar of Federal taxes collected in 1950 to 51 cents in 1961 and 58 cents in 1970.

But even Federal taxes have become more regressive during the same years. Corporate taxes have gone down, from 27 cents of every Federal tax dollar received in 1950 to only 16 cents in 1970, and at the same time Social Security and payroll taxes have jumped from just 9 cents to 26 cents of each tax dollar pumped into Washington. So, when the impact of all taxes and all Government spending is taken into account —even though there has been a sizable increase in Government "benefits" to low-income Americans—the level of income inequality ("post-fiscal") has not changed since 1950.

The notion that classes are withering away in America rests not only on the mistaken assumption that the propertied have been lopped off at the top, but on the equally unfounded notion that the working class itself has been vanishing and the "white-collar" strata of the so-called middle class have been multiplying. So renowned a pundit as Harvard's John Kenneth Galbraith, among many others, believes the class struggle is a "dwindling phenomenon" because "the number of white-collar workers in the United States almost fifteen years ago overtook the number in the blue-collar working force and is, of course, now greater."

Of course? The sort of counting done here misses and distorts what has really happened; it confuses occupational composition with class lines. Since the 1900s, especially during World War II, and in quickening pace in recent years, women— and increasingly married women—have been moving into the labor force. About four out of ten people in the labor force are now women, and almost half of all women now have paying jobs or are looking for them. It is this influx of women into paying jobs that accounts for the growing number of "white-collar" jobs—mainly in "clerical or sales" work—in the past few decades. Of all working women, not even one in ten was a "clerical or sales" worker in 1900. By 1940, on the eve of World War II, the figure jumped to almost three

in ten, and it climbed until it reached more than four in ten in 1970.

At the same time, the proportion of women working in crafts or as operatives and laborers (except on the farm) dropped. It also dropped in so-called service occupations which, for women, are typically dirty and menial jobs as domestics or "food service" workers. Some "white-collar" jobs are now almost entirely filled by women—and ten occupations alone, among them waitress, typist, cashier, hairdresser and beautician, nurse and dietician, sales clerk, and teacher, account for more than two out of five employed women. Of all clerical and sales jobs, two out of three, and the same ratio in service jobs, are filled by women. In contrast, of all those working in crafts or as operatives and laborers (off the farm), only one in six is a woman.

Among men, meanwhile, the portion with clerical and sales jobs has not risen in three decades. Only 7 in a hundred men at work had clerical or sales jobs in 1900, and it rose to just 12 in a hundred by 1940. In the three decades since, the ratio has not grown at all: It is still about 12 in a hundred. In the same years, though, there has been a significant rise in the proportion of men classified as "professionals and technicians" by the U.S. Census—from 3, to 6, to 14 in a hundred. But many such "professionals" are vocational school products, and about four out of ten in the rapidly growing category of "technicians" are not college graduates. This, of course, is scarcely the image evoked by the terms *professional* or *technician*. Many are really highly skilled workers; advanced education or certification is not required to fill their jobs, nor does their work differ much in independence and control from the work done by those classified as "craftsmen."

The plain fact is that the category of "manual workers" has not shrunk at all in this century. Fewer than 40 in a hundred men worked in 1900 as a "craftsman, operative, or nonfarm laborer." In 1920, the figure rose to 45 in a hundred, and it has barely changed since: In 1970, 47 out of every hundred men in the labor force were classified as manual workers. But to this figure we must add many if not most of the men who are called "service workers"— U.S. Census category that hides a host of blue-collar jobs within its semantic recesses: janitors, porters, waiters, garage mechanics, dishwashers, and laundry workers. How many of the seven in a hundred men in such service jobs in 1970 should be identified as "real workers" is anybody's guess— and mine is that it is most. We must also add an uncounted number of jobs that strangely get catalogued in the Census as "white collar"—among them stock clerks, baggagemen, newspaper carriers ("sales"), and even mailmen. Their work is certainly —and often heavily—"manual labor."

A safe estimate, then, is that more than five of every ten men who work in this country are manual workers, maybe as many as six in ten—and this does not count the three out of a hundred who work as agricultural laborers. Perhaps the only real difference in the working class today compared to past decades is that many working men now count on their wives' (or daughters') earnings to make the family's ends meet.

In fact, their wives are typically manual workers themselves, for among employed women, the division is sharp between those whose husbands are workers and those who are married to "professionals" or "managers." Among the latter's working wives, only one in six is in manual (or service) jobs. But among the working wives of craftsmen, two in five have such jobs; among the working wives of operatives, almost one out of two; and among the wives of laborers, about two out of three. They certainly are not smuggling any middle-class values, loyalties, or way of life into the working class based on their own experience at work. For them, on the contrary, as for most men in America, the "yoke of manual labor" is yet to be lifted.

Besides, whatever the social images "manual labor" evokes or whatever pain it involves, in real class terms the distinction between it and "nonmanual" or "white-collar" employment is, at best, misleading. How does wearing a white collar lift you into another class? Perhaps there is more prestige attached, though even this is doubtful, particularly among workers themselves. For some "white-collar" workers there may be increased security, but how many cashiers, typists, or beauticians get "salaries" rather than hourly wages, or are less subject to layoffs than highly organized manual workers?

Since most "white-collar" employes are women, and don't wear collars, white or otherwise, anyway, the name itself surely fools us about what it represents. The vast majority of the clerical and sales workers of today are, in any event, not the respectable clerks of yesteryear. Their work is not only routinized and standardized, but they often work in offices that are larger than (and even as noisy as) small manufacturing shops—tending steno machines, typewriters, accounting machines, data processors, or keypunch equipment. They work in supermarkets and department stores with hundreds of others who punch in and punch out and wait to be relieved before they take a break. They are as bereft of control over their work and the products of their work as "manual" workers—in fact, they have *less* independence and control than such workers as crane operators and longshoremen. Beneath their nice clean collars (if they wear them at all), they are propertyless workers, entirely dependent for their livelihoods on the sale of their capacity to work. And this is the essence of working-class reality.

So, neither the working class nor the propertied class has yet departed our fair land. But do the propertied really make up a *capitalist* class? Haven't they, because ownership of the large corporations has become so dispersed, lost *control* of these decisive units of production in America? Of all the pseudofacts behind the notion that classes have withered away in America, none is as persistent as the doctrine of the "managerial revolution" of "unseen revolution" implied by these questions.

The claim is that there has been a "separation of ownership and control" in large corporations—that as the corporations have grown immense, as the original founders have died off or their fortunes supposedly dwindled, as their kids have taken to mere coupon-clipping and jet-setting, and as stock ownership has spread out widely, the capitalists have lost control of the means of production. The result, we are told, is that not capital but bureaucracy, not capitalists but "anonymous administrators," now control large corporations and hold decisive power in contemporary America. The "managers" have usurped their capitalist predecessors.

With the capitalists gone and the managers no longer their mere agents, the inherent conflict that used to exist between labor and capital also supposedly becomes a relic of the past. Instead, we now have not a system of class domination but an occupational order based on merit: "rewards" get distributed according to ability ("functional importance"). What's more, with capital dissolved and new managers motivated by other urges and the pride of professionalism in control, pumping out profit is no longer what drives the corporations in the new "post-capitalist society" we are alleged to be living in. Instead, they have become the "trustees," as Prudential's chairman said—and he was just paraphrasing Harvard economist Carl Kaysen's words of 20 years ago—for all of us in the "new industrial state."

The intent of such notions is clear: We are to believe that "labor" and "management" are just parts of the same team, doing different tasks. It is a theoretical shell game that hides the fact of class domination —of the ownership *and* control of the mines,

mills, and factories by a class whose lives are certainly made easier if we don't know they're there, right behind the "anonymous bureaucrats." It hides the simple but profound fact that they live on what the rest of us produce.

One reason that the illusion of managerialism persists is that it is incredibly difficult to figure out who does control a large corporation. And the illusion is nurtured, as the late Senator Lee Metcalf put it bluntly and accurately, by a "massive cover-up" of the principal owners. There are several closely related ways that capital really controls the corporations. First, the real owners do not actually have to *manage* the corporation, or hang around the executive suite with its top officers or directors, or even be formally represented on the board, in order to have their objectives realized—that is, to exert *control*. And how much stock it takes to control a corporation is neither fixed nor standard.

The few recent studies that claim to find "management control" in most large corporations simply assume that it always takes at least 10 percent of the stock in one pair of hands in order to assure control, but it does not work that way. If you own 10 percent of the stock in a corporation, you are supposed to report it to the Securities and Exchange Commission (SEC), but if the same percentage is split among several of your close associates, without any formal ties between you, or with a few of your relatives, you don't have to report it—and even if you *are* required to report, who is to know if you don't? When Senator Metcalf died, he had been trying for years to get at such information, but his staff so far has had to rely on its own investigations and volunteered data.

How much stock is needed to control a corporation depends on how big the other stockowners are—and who they are, and how they are connected—and how dispersed the rest of the stock is; it also depends on how deeply the firm is indebted to the same few large banks or other creditors. What sorts of ties the corporation has to others, and especially to big banks and other "financial institutions" allied with it, is also crucial. The ability to exert control grows with the number of other major firms in which any family, individual, or group of associates has an interest or actual control.

What a particular large holding of stock implies for any attempt at control depends to an unknown extent on who holds it. If it is held, say, by a leading capitalist family like the Mellons—who control at least four firms in the top 500 nonfinancials (Gulf, Alcoa, Koppers Co., Carborundum Co.) as well as the First Boston Corp., the General Reinsurance Corp., and Mellon National Bank and Trust (the 15th largest bank in the country, measured by deposits), and perhaps also, through the Mellon Bank's 7 percent shareholding, Jones and Laughlin Steel—the meaning is just not the same as if some otherwise unconnected shareowner held it.

Even in corporations that a family like Mellon does not control, the presence of its representative among the principal shareowners, or on the board, can be critical. So the late Richard King Mellon as one of the principal shareowners in General Motors carried a rather different clout in its corporate policy than, say, Billy Rose did in AT&T, though he was reputed to be one of its biggest shareowners. Precisely because the number of shareowners is so large and their holdings typically so minute compared to the few biggest shareowners in a large corporation, it may not take more than 1 or 2 percent of a company's stock to control it.

The critical holdings and connections that make control possible are invisible to the uninformed eye, and often even to the seasoned investigator. Senator Metcalf's staff found, for instance, that Laurance S. Rockefeller owns a controlling block of almost 5 percent of the voting stock in Eastern Airlines, though his name did not appear on the required listing of its 30 top stockholders for the Civil Aeronautics Board. Neither the SEC nor the CAB nor Eastern itself could find all the accounts in which his shares were held and aggregate them until they asked *him* to do it for them—in response to Metcalf's prodding.

This helps explain why even the "insiders" who work as financial analysts at *Fortune, Forbes,* or *Business Week,* with their immense research resources and excellent files, have to rely heavily on gossip to estimate the holdings of even the leading families in corporations they have long controlled. These holdings are hidden in a welter of accounts held by brokers, dealers, foundations, holding companies, other corporations, associates, intermediaries, and "street names" (as the fictitious firms that just hold stock for someone are called on Wall Street) or other "nominees."

The extent of a leading capitalist family's holdings is also concealed by a finely woven though tangled web of kinship relations. Apparently unrelated persons with entirely different surnames can be part of a single cohesive set of kindred united to control a corporation. In Dow Chemical Company, for instance, there are 78 dependents (plus spouses) of H. W. Dow who own a total of 12.6 percent of Dow's stock. So, without research aimed at penetrating the web of kinship, any effort to find out who really controls a large corporation is hobbled at the outset.

In an outstanding recent study, Philip Burch, Jr., mined the "inside information" presented over the years in the financial press and found that at least 60 percent of the 500 top industrial corporations are "probably" (236) or "possibly" (64) under the control of an identifiable family or group of associates. Even these estimates are probably short of the mark because, in Ralph Nader's words, "no one really knows who owns the giant corporations that dominate our economic life." My own guess is that behind the thick veil of nominees, there are real controlling owners in most if not all of the large corporations that now appear to be under so-called management control.

Even if some large corporations were not really controlled by *particular* owning interests, this would not mean power had passed to the "new princes" from the old economic royalists. The higher executives would still have only *relative* independence in their activities and would be bound by the *general* interests of capital. The heads of the large corporations are the main formal agents or functionaries of capital. Their personal careers, interests, and commitments are closely tied to the expansion of corporate capital. Some are among the principal shareholders of the companies they run, and most own stock that not only provides much of their income but ranks them among the population's largest stockowners—and puts them in the propertied few.

Typically, the managers also move in the same intimate circles as the very rich. You'll find them together at debutante balls, select clubs, summer resorts and winter retreats, and other assorted watering places; and their kids attend the same private schools and rush the same fraternities and sororities—and then marry each other. Scratch a top executive and the chances are he will prove to be related to a principal shareowner. Intimate social ties and entangling kinship relations, common interests, and overriding commitments unify the families of the heads of the largest corporations and their principal owners into the same cohesive, dominant class in America.

Finally, even if "management" alone had full control of the corporations, it would still have to try to pump the highest possible profits out of their workers and make the most of their investments. The conduct of management is shaped above all by the imperatives of capital accumulation—the competitive struggle among the giants (now global rather than national), the types of investments they make and markets they penetrate, and the relations they have with their workers. High managerial income and status depend, directly and indirectly, on high corporate profits. "Stock options" and bonuses and other forms of executive "compensation" aside from salaries are closely tied to corporate profit rates. Whatever their so-called professional motivations or power urges, their technocratic teamwork and bureaucratic mentality, managers' decisions on how to organize production and sales have to be measured against the bottom line: They dare not imperil corporate profitability.

The recent spate of articles in the financial press on "how to fire a top executive" —you have them "take early retirement"— and the new placement services now catering to them, are rather pointed indicators of what happens to supposed "management control" in times of receding profit margins. In 1974, a year of severe economic crisis around the world, about half of all the chief executives in the nation's top 500 firms were expected to be replaced—in what a weekly newsletter to corporate heads called "a wave of executive ousters" that would "cause the greatest disruption in the business community since the 1929 depression."

Any obvious lowering in profit rates is also reflected in a drop in the price of the corporation's stock; this squeezes its capital base and makes it an attractive—and vulnerable—target for takeover. And this, in turn, leads to executive ousters. In addition, with the marked centralization of huge shareholdings in the trust departments of a few of the biggest banks that administer the investment portfolios of the very rich—typically, they will not take a trust of under $200,000—the tremors would be deep and the impact rather painful for any managers who turned out a below-average rate of return. The banks must unflinchingly act as "trustees" only for the top investors and real owners who control the large corporations.

Any political strategy that ignores or distorts these realities or is blind to the deep class divisions in our country cannot meet the common needs of the majority of Americans. So long as the illusion persists that our economic life has been "democratized" or that a "silent revolution" has already interred capital, emancipated labor, and redistributed wealth and income, we can be sure that a real effort to achieve those aims will slated for yet another postponement.

READING 3–2

The internal structure of the American proletariat*

FRANCESCA FREEDMAN

Over the past few years, more and more people on the left have begun to grapple with the question of class analysis. The need for such theory has become greater as the movement has sought to expand beyond the closed circle of the universities and into the community and the workplace. Developing a class analysis that can give direction to the movement for revolutionary change is a difficult task, since the class structure originates and unfolds at the hidden level of the most essential economic relations of a given mode of production. These essential economic relations are the manner in which the economic surplus of a given mode of production is produced and appropriated. Under capitalism this takes the form of the appropriation of surplus value from the proletariat by the capitalist class for the purpose of further capital expansion.[1] Hence the development of two classes under capitalism—bourgeoisie and proletariat—that are mutually dependent and mutually antagonistic.

One obstacle to the development of an adequate Marxist class analysis is that Marx himself never treated class, per se, in depth. The last chapter in volume 3 of *Capital* is a fragment entitled "Classes"; after a page and a half the manuscript tantalizingly breaks off. Where *Capital* does deal with the class structure, it does so in abstraction, stripping the concept of class down to its bare essentials: the division of society into the prototype industrial proletariat, industrial capitalist, and landowner, with the first two clearly dominant in the analysis. Volume 3 of *Capital* does deal with the various fractions of the bourgeoisie, but there is no treatment of the fractions of the working class, nor the other less significant classes under capitalism—that is, an analysis of the *inner structure* of classes is by and large lacking.[2]

Marx wrote that the essential economic relations of society "take place behind the backs of the producers"; the class structure they create is hidden by the proliferation of social and ideological divisions that arise out of the productive and reproductive mechanisms of the system. These divisions are continually developing as the specific needs of the expansion of capital undergo transformations that are historically rooted in the stages of capitalist development. Thus, for example, we will see that the rise of monopoly capitalism enlarged those sectors dealing with the realization of surplus value (retail trade), the accounting of value (sales divisions of corporations), and the allocation of surplus value among the various fractions of the capitalist class

* From *Socialist Review*, 5 (October–December 1975), pp. 41–83.

(banks and other financial institutions). So also, the extension of the dominance of market relations into all aspects of daily life, traditionally the arena of the domicile and the family, created an extensive service sector. Similarly, the vast increase in the government sector was occasioned by the need to rationalize and smooth over the contradictions of the system sharpened by the rise of monopoly capitalism. In all these sectors, not only were existing occupations swollen by a great influx of labor, but also many new occupations appeared.

Hence, capitalism develops a multitude of functions that must be performed in order to reproduce itself—by service workers and office workers, as well as intellectuals, professionals, and government workers—jobs that clearly do not fall into the category of the industrial proletariat. This represents the conquest of the market in labor-power over almost all categories within society's division of labor as much as it represents the conquest of market relations in general over all areas of daily life. Nevertheless, the subjection of ever greater numbers of people to the wage-relation does not imply their subjection to the same conditions of work. On this concrete level of the proliferation of new categories of work, many factors— ideology, politics, consumption (income), race, and sex—*seem* to reorient the concept of class away from a definition purely linked to whether one sells one's labor-power in order to make a living or whether one expropriates surplus labor from others. The structural divisions that are hereby developed within a class (here, the working class) come under the category of class "fractions."

Class fractions and the use-value of labor-power

The category of fraction is linked to the *function,* or use-value, of labor. One of the central methodological contributions made by Marx to political economy was the separation of use-value from value (developed in chapter 1 of *Capital,* vol. 1). This becomes a guiding analytical tool for developing a theory of internal class structure. As we will see, the creation by capitalism of new functions and occupations—through the progressive development of the forces of production, as well as by the expansion of capital into new fields—does not mean a change in the basic economic relations between classes. Hence, it does not give rise to new classes within capitalism. Rather, it gives rise to new fractions within classes, grouped around different forms of economic activity or around the place occupied within these activities (since, for example, different types of work are pegged into different levels of the occupational hierarchy).

Capitalism structures the manner in which use-value considerations are developed; that is, it structures them around the process of capital accumulation, around the expansion of value. Marx writes:

With accumulation, and the development of the productiveness of labor that accompanies it, the power of the sudden expansion of capital grows also, because the technical conditions of the process of production themselves—machinery, means of transport, etc.—now admit of the rapidest transformation of masses of surplus product into additional means of production. The mass of social wealth, overflowing with the advance of accumulation, and transformable into additional capital, thrusts itself frantically into old branches of production, whose market suddenly expands, *or into newly formed branches.*"[3]

This process contains a dialectical interplay between the development of the forces of production—which brings into being new categories of wage-labor—and the social relations of production. Hence the manner in which these new categories of labor are organized and utilized is shaped by the capitalist framework. Monopoly capitalism transforms the structure of the wage-earning population. As Braverman notes, "It is thus clear that the investigation of the movements of *labor* . . . [is] but another form of the investigation of the movement of *value*."[4]

The fractioning process within the structure of the work force finds its reflection in the social and ideological structure of capitalist society. It both determines the manner in which the social and ideological structure operates and is determined by it. On the one hand, the expansion of capital necessitates divisions within the working population, corresponding to the creation of new use-value functions for labor. On the other hand, this labor is *unified* under the wage-relation. Based as it is on antagonistic relations between classes, capitalism develops an ideology that is authoritarian and hierarchical in nature. It responds to the *objective* unity of the working class by reproducing authoritarian and hierarchical relationships within that class, utilizing them to divide it on a social and *subjective* basis. Hence, the ideological structure of capitalism mediates consciousness and social rank; these then find their expression in objective phenomena, such as differing consumption patterns, levels of income, and degrees of autonomy—or the lack of it—on the job.

Nicos Poulantzas in his major work on classes[5] puts forth the concept of "global effects," in which class is defined by "its *place* in the ensemble of the division of labor which includes" economic, ideological, and political relations.[6] He says that while class is defined *principally* by its place in production, ideological or political considerations can play a determining role as well. By assigning a *determining* force to these ideological and political considerations, he draws no clear *qualitative* distinction between them and the relationship to the means of production in the determination of class status. Thus, to say that class is defined "principally" by its place in the

production sphere loses meaning in the absence of such a distinction. For example, he posits the formation of a "new" class of petite bourgeoisie—intellectuals, civil servants, and other "unproductive" workers. These are *wage-earners*, yet they have inherited the ideology of the old petite bourgeoisie (e.g., individualism, attraction to the status quo, aspirations to bourgeois status, etc.). It follows that ideological factors, according to Poulantzas, play a determining role in the creation of a "new" class.

Within this construct, Poulantzas maintains that classes become real only within the class *struggle;* that is, in the last analysis, it is only in self-conscious political action that a group can come to be defined as a class. This is, I think, an undialectical and even idealist[7] point of view. It is imperative, on the one hand, to separate the objective from the subjective for the purposes of analysis—to keep in mind Marx's famous distinction between a class *in* itself and a class *for* itself. Theotonio Dos Santos suggests that "the concept of class consciousness in Marxism does not correspond to the vulgar empirical idea of the consciousness that individuals have of their class status." To elaborate, he quotes Marx: "We cannot judge of such a period of transformation by its own consciousness; on the contrary, this consciousness must be explained from the contradictions of material life."[8]

Classes arise out of an objective material base; they form the human actors of the given relations of a certain mode of production. In this light, it is difficult for me to accept Poulantzas' creation of a new class, since the basic social relation of capitalism has not and cannot be changed—i.e., the relationship between the owners of capital and those who own nothing more than their own labor-power. Nevertheless, while I disagree with his use of the concept as a determinant of *class*, Poulantzas' "global effects" is useful for an analysis of class *fractions*. The economic relationship people have to the means of production determines ultimately the class to which they belong. However, their *place* in the system of production and reproduction, with its attendant relationship to ideology, politics, consumption, is one element determining membership in a class fraction.

At the same time, the subjective and objective must be united in a dialectical manner for a dynamic analysis of classes, since classes are in their essence the expression of the antagonistic contradictions upon which a mode of production is based. Thus, class struggle is the highest form in which these contradictions are expressed. Class struggle is a *derivation* of the material existence of classes, and it is the material contradictions giving rise to classes that create the potential for class struggle. However, the primary contradiction between classes (the contradiction over the expropriation and disposition of the surplus) also creates other, secondary contradictions that create divisions *within* classes and serve to obscure the essential relations *between* them. Such other contradictions are, for example, the contradiction between "mental" and "manual" labor—hence, contradictions between different levels of the occupational hierarchy; contradictions between male and female workers, who are often segregated into different job sectors, and similarly between blacks and whites who are often situated in different positions in the occupational hierarchy; even the contradiction between producers and consumers (for instance, imperialist wars create jobs for the working class, but also place material burdens on it in the form of taxes, sons and brothers lost, etc., and there are factories that provide employment while polluting working-class neighborhoods). These contradictions are determined by the primary class contradiction: for example, the growth of the sales sector under capitalism (advertising, sales divisions in corpora-

tions) was determined by capital's need to realize the surplus value created in the productive sector. Thus, the division between productive and unproductive workers (dealt with more fully below) does not entail the division of workers in these two sectors into different classes, but rather is based on the primary contradiction inherent in the creation of surplus value.

Methodology and the development of internal class structure

In order to develop a clear understanding of the factors that enter into an analysis of the structure of classes—the confusing array of primary contradiction and secondary contradictions—we must first arrive at a proper methodological approach. Marxist methodology enables one to root the investigation at the "pure" abstract level and then to *build from there* more concretely to an analysis that approximates reality more and more closely.

Marx developed the concept of the social totality, in which the underlying *real* movement of social forces was represented in a fetishized and distorted manner at the level of concrete everyday praxis. At this level, the *phenomenal* manifestation of social relationships appears to society *to be their real and only existence*, rather than being linked to the "essence" of the economic relation that underlies them. This "essence" is the abstract form in which the real *motive force* of a social relation lies. The phenomenon is the manifestation of the essence in social practice, yet it nevertheless appears to be independent of and contradictory to it. Hence, for example, the level of the *exchange* of commodities, the marketplace, is the phenomenal form in which production under capitalism is realized. It is the exchange of equivalents, which then appears as the real relation of capitalism. This masks the extraction of surplus value from the proletariat, which is predicated on the *unequal* distribution of the means of production between classes.[9] Viewing concrete phenomena isolated from their essence leads to "false consciousness." Nevertheless, the concrete *is* real—but must be understood in its abstract context if the richness of dialectical analysis is to be achieved.

Dos Santos develops this methodology as applied to class analysis. Investigation of class structure proceeds on the basis of different levels that are analyzed successively. The first level is that of the mode of production, where "social classes are the fundamental expression of the antagonistic relations" of the mode of production.[10] This level comprises an investigation of the *forces of production* (the level of technology and the organization of the labor-process), and the *relations of production* (the social relations that govern the production and reproduction of the system). With respect to classes, it is the latter—the social relations of production—that is crucial.

The driving force and raison d'être of capitalism is the production of surplus value. Surplus value is created because wages paid to workers are less than the value in goods or services produced by them; this residual is surplus value, which is then transformed into profit for the capitalists. The creation of surplus value demands a working class that owns no other means of production save its own labor-power. Hence the wage-relation, the instrument of the production of surplus value, becomes the worker's economic relation to society.

But the wage-relationship, while rooted in the production of surplus value, does not operate in this sphere exclusively. There are other wage-workers whose function is to facilitate, in a variety of ways, the extraction of surplus value, yet who produce no surplus value themselves. Thrust outside the arena of productive activity by the introduction of labor-saving techniques, masses of workers are chan-

neled into "entire industries and large sectors of existing industries whose only function is the struggle over the allocation of the social surplus among the various sectors of the capitalist class and its dependents."[11] These workers labor to reproduce capitalist society as a whole, while at the same time they neither own nor control the means of production. In fact, their economic relationship to society is the same as the workers' in the productive (surplus-value-producing) sphere—they are wage-laborers.

From its basis in wage-labor, the definition of the "social relations of production" widens to include other social relations that operate differently among various groups of workers: relations of supervision and subordination to authority, degree of autonomy on the job, relations between workers who plan the production process and those who execute it, etc. These all develop from the primary social relation of wage-labor, yet tend to create different kinds of consciousness among the different groups of wage-earners. In fact, as derivations, these social relations belong properly to the succeeding levels of analysis that Dos Santos puts forth.

The second level of methodology is that of social structure, within which Dos Santos includes two parts: (1) social developments that correspond to historically specific stages of capitalism—e.g., imperialism and monopoly capitalism; and (2) "new specific forms of relation among the components"; for example, the development of the sales and service sectors we have already mentioned. The third level is that of "social situation," and it is the most concrete level in this progression from the abstract to the concrete. Dos Santos writes:

We see . . . that as we differentiate the structure internally, we encounter a series of phenomena correlated with and dependent on the class structure. One of these phenomena is social stratification, which introduces a factor of hierarchization of the individuals of society, not only according to their class position, but also according to differences of income, profession, culture, politics, etc.[12]

The third and most concrete level is determined by the two preceding; on this basis a contradictory movement in capitalism comes into play.

With the generalization and development of capitalist production society is, as Marx predicted, more and more divided into two great classes, bourgeoisie and proletariat. Albert Szymanski, in his article "Trends in the American Working Class," estimated that "by 1969, 89.5 per cent of the labor force had become wage or salary earners, while only . . . 9.1 per cent were self-employed."[13] The other social classes under capitalism, the farmers and the petite bourgeoisie, have been more and more pressured out of existence by the power of capital. The movement of capital toward greater concentration and centralization leads to an intolerance of forms of commodity production that represent an earlier stage of capitalism. As these forms are absorbed, their agents must either seek to be included in the ranks of their annihilators or be forced into direct subjugation to them as wage-earners.

However, this progressive simplification of the underlying class structure of capitalism is accompanied by a simultaneous and contradictory movement toward complexity and differentiation within the ranks of the two major classes. Among the bourgeoisie, there occurs the differentiation into national and international sectors; small and large capital; financial, industrial, and commercial capital; and a parasitic, coupon-clipping bourgeoisie. Within the proletariat, the uniform subjection of ever-increasing numbers of the working population to the wage-relation is accompanied by two broad divisions. One is the *horizontal* differentiation into different economic sectors, corresponding to the second level of analysis developed by Dos Santos.

The second is *vertical* differentiation, treated below. On the one hand, there is a vertical differentiation between the various levels of the occupational hierarchy, often intersecting with racial and sexual divisions; it is this process that Dos Santos analyzes. On the other hand, capital's need to search for methods by which to cheapen the value of labor-power—to drive down wages—*tends* to diminish the privileges enjoyed by certain workers (in the form of job conditions, social status, and income), and thereby eliminate the distinctions between them and other workers. It is primarily through the degradation, or *de-skilling*, of the work process that this cheapening of labor-power is implemented. The process of de-skilling—accomplished first in the industrial sphere in the last decades of the previous century—is facilitated by the application of technology and the reorganization of work that wrests control and knowledge of the production process from the hands of the workers and places it in the hands of management.

The accumulation process that enables the introduction of capital and masses of labor (set free by mechanization) into the newly created sectors of the economy is not accompanied by a uniform upgrading of labor in the new occupations, but by its opposite. As Braverman points out, job structures become increasingly polarized between a narrowing minority at the top (who are still wage-workers and therefore still threatened potentially by capital's search to replace their functions by machines) and the greatly increasing majority at the bottom, in all industries, whose work loses its special quality to acquire more and more the character of "simple labor in the abstract."[14] Hence, there is a dialectical interplay between the tendency toward polarization and the tendency to reduce all labor to a common degradation.

As we have seen, this tendency toward what has been termed the "proletarianization" of many non-industrial (worker) job categories flows directly from the needs of capital in the accumulation process. As a *tendency* this process develops unevenly throughout the capitalist economy: first, in terms of the numbers of workers in the same job category subjected to it (many firms do not have the technical means at their disposal to make their work force more "efficient," in the sense of making it cheaper); second, the nature of the work performed may not be amenable to the de-skilling process. These are elements that counteract or retard the operation of this tendency. But more importantly, hierarchical social relations between different categories of workers remain in force, even while the tendency toward proletarianization erodes more and more their objective foundation. Some of this can be laid to the power of notions about the privileged "status" of certain jobs, despite the fact that they have become little more than pretensions.

At a more basic level, however, hierarchical distinctions are maintained because any more egalitarian form of the social organization of work would be counter to the social needs of capitalism, i.e., the need to reproduce the class system. In fact, as the objective conditions different groups of workers face become more alike, the need to divide them on an ideological basis becomes even more acute. As *objective* differences between workers decline, *subjective* divisions must be more frantically shored up by management, so that workers are kept from recognizing their essential unity as a class. I do not mean to imply the existence of a "conspiracy" on the part of capitalists to divide the working class structurally. The very anarchy of capitalist production inhibits the power of capitalists to act in a conscious, coordinated manner to impose artificial divisions on the working class. These divisions must *appear*—both to capitalists and to workers—to arise naturally out of the technical requirements

of production (regardless of the social formation to which they belong) or out of "human nature." Hence, divisions within the occupational hierarchy appear to arise out of the needs of "industrial society"; or, by extension, sexual divisions appear to arise out of the "natural," or "biological," relationship between men and women throughout eternity, and racial divisions are similarly given the appearance of biological and "cultural" determination.

Two forms of division into fractions

The working class is split into fractions according to the needs of capital; hence, different *forms* of fractioning develop in response to different needs. Thus, we see that the tremendous development of the social division of labor under capitalism brings about a differentiation of the labor force into different sectors of the economy. This is one way the fractioning of the working class takes place. In the 20th century, American capitalism has experienced a tremendous absolute and relative increase in the number of non-industrial workers. Jim Stodder, in his article "Old and New Working Class," points out that while the the most stable sector of the working class . . . in this century . . . this fairly stable plateau, having been reached by a steady climb throughout the capitalist era, appears to have rounded off around mid-century and is now gradually sloping down. . . . The three categories that can be subsumed under the general title of *service producers*—professional and technical, clerical and sales, and service workers . . . have all experienced a steady growth, which has accelerated in the last thirty years."[15]

The second major division of the working class results from the social necessity of capital to keep the working class split up along hierarchical lines, thereby enforcing class discipline. This creates an occupational hierarchy. Bourgeois social

74

FIGURE 1
Trends in the composition of the labor force

Percent of total labor force

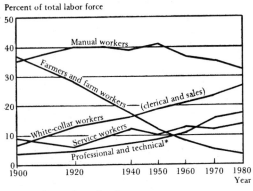

* Includes self-employed.

Source: *Historical Statistics of the United States, Statistical Abstract of the United States,* and *The U.S. Economy in 1980,* cited in Albert Szymanski, "Trends in the American Working Class," *Socialist Revolution,* No. 10 (1972), p. 100 and in Daniel Bell, "Labor in the Post-Industrial Society," *Dissent,* Winter 1972. Table reprinted from Jim Stodder, "Old and New Working Class," *Socialist Revolution,* 17 (September–October 1973).

science takes this occupational hierarchy for granted, without any analysis of the forces that created it—the existence of class struggle and the corresponding development by capital of methods to defuse that struggle. Bourgeois social science comes to define the occupational hierarchy as the class structure of society itself, proclaiming the existence of a "blue-collar class," a "white-collar class" (implicitly superior to the former), a "professional class," and a "managerial class." As is typical with bourgeois "science," the *appearance* of "class" differences is taken to be the reality. It is the task of Marxists to reveal the underlying class unity of the various levels of the occupational hierarchy, and then to put into this perspective the differences that separate these levels from one another.

These two major forms of fractioning relate to the two aspects of the reproduction of the class system under capitalism— the economic and social dimensions. The first form, the horizontal, is characterized by the production, allocation, and realization of surplus value. The second form,

the hierarchization of the job structure, is dominated by the need to enforce class discipline, both through the exercise of authoritarian relationships on the job and through the erection of social barriers between workers. Both these forms of fractioning are equally essential for the reproduction of the class system under capitalism.

The remainder of this article will examine these two forms of fractioning, as well as another division in the working class that has been discussed in Marxist literature: that between productive and unproductive workers. This is not meant to be an exhaustive investigation by any means. My purpose has been to lay out a method for analyzing the internal structure of the working class, rooted in the process of capitalist accumulation. I shall attempt to apply the analysis concretely in broad outlines only.

Occupational hierarchy

At the lowest level of the occupational hierarchy are those members of the industrial reserve army who constitute what Marx called the "floating segment." This segment is composed of workers who are continually repelled from and attracted to employment, depending on the demand for labor on the part of capital at any given time. Marx writes:

It is capitalistic accumulation itself that constantly produces, and produces in the direct ratio of its own energy and extent, a relatively redundant population of laborers, i.e., a population of greater extent than suffices for the average needs of the self-expansion of capital, and therefore a surplus-population. . . . But if a surplus laboring population is a necessary product of accumulation . . . on a capitalist basis, this surplus population becomes, conversely, the lever of capitalist accumulation, nay, a condition of existence of the capitalist mode of production. It forms a disposable industrial reserve army, that belongs to capital quite as absolutely as if the latter had bred it at its own cost. Independently of the limits of the actual increase of population, it creates, for the changing needs of the self-expansion of capital, a mass of human material always ready for exploitation.[16]

When employed, these workers are concentrated in unskilled, low-paying jobs that are subject to a high degree of job-tenure instability. In the United States, this segment is disproportionately made up of single non-white men, white or non-white women, and young, single males. In the consumption sphere it is this group that constitutes the "poor," along with the other segments of the reserve army of labor (with the exception of women married to employed males), and that depends heavily upon state welfare or unemployment benefits. Harry Braverman writes:

With the simplification of job operations and the spread of the number and variety of jobs for which the "qualifications" have been reduced to the minimums of simple labor, this stratum has grown to encompass large parts of the working population. An ordinary working life for many workers now consists of movement among a considerable number of jobs, so that such workers are in turn part of the employed and the reserve labor populations. This has been reflected in the system of unemployment insurance . . . ; it is in part a safeguard against the economic, social, and political effects of widespread and prolonged unemployment, and in part a recognition of the role workers play, now as part of the employed and now as part of the reserve armies of labor.[17]

This stratum of workers has existed since the establishment of industral capitalism in the United States. Although in the beginning years of industrialization there was a severe labor shortage, the importation of masses of immigrant workers helped to relieve this shortage and also supplied a surplus work force during recessions. In fact, the *over*-supply of workers afforded by immigration was crucial to the development of capitalism in the United States. It ex-

erted a downward pressure on wages and acted to enforce labor discipline. The fact that then, as now, a large part of this floating segment was composed of workers who were not white, not Northern European (except for the Irish), or not male, was crucial in creating antagonisms within the working class. The objective basis for such antagonisms resided in an industrial reserve army that constituted a threat against the job security of the employed. The subjective basis for antagonism was created by the racist and sexist ideology advanced by the bourgeoisie. This exacerbated intra-class divisions by reproducing the objective conditions that established it, given that more privileged workers would try to limit access to their own more stable areas of employment. Furthermore, when these workers joined the ranks of the employed, the secondary ideological effects of racism, sexism, and ethnism served to inhibit the development of class solidarity.

The second level of the occupational hierarchy is composed of unskilled workers in industrial, service, and office occupations. (It is important to mention here that a class fraction is not a simple unity. There are, for example, many unskilled workers who are very close to the fraction below them—often since they are the same people!) These workers are subject to poor wages and unstable employment. They generally lack union representation, which contributes to their poor working conditions. Other unskilled workers who hold jobs in highly unionized plants or industries (such as auto and steel) are closer to skilled workers with respect to income and job stability. Racial and sexual divisions are often correlated with job stability or income, with non-whites and women in a disadvantageous position.

There are real differences, even antagonisms, that develop between industrial and office workers. Office workers have rarely become involved in the struggles of industrial workers within or even outside their particular firms and industries—and vice versa. The industrial worker/office worker separation is linked to sexual divisions: that most office workers are female and most industrial workers are male (although in some industries, such as electronics and textiles, women dominate the industrial positions) has clearly exacerbated existing divisions.

Another crucial difference between office and industrial workers stems from how they relate to the means of production, as well as from the physical conditions of their work. While industrial workers are involved in the production of material goods and are aware that they are responsible, in some measure, for the daily reproduction of the life of the population, office workers are involved in the processing of paper, where the purpose of their work remains more or less hidden from them. And while industrial workers, by the very nature of their work, are concentrated in large numbers, only in the typing pools of large firms are office workers brought together in any significant numbers. Most office work goes on under very privatized conditions that reinforce an individualistic and passive relationship to the job. Even where office work takes on the quality of an assembly-line process, it is such in the organization of the work only, and not a physical assembly line. Hence office workers are still separated into different offices of the firm, with pneumatic tubes responsible for the flow of the materials they work with.

Service work is shaped by some of the conditions of both office and industrial work. On the one hand, a direct service is provided to the public which is quite palpable to the worker involved. On the other hand, except for telephone operators, the lack of "socialized" conditions of work is at least as pronounced for service as for office workers. In any event, service work does not begin to approach the degree of concentration typical of industrial work.

These differences are crucial, and suggest a separation of industrial, service, and office workers into distinct fractions. However, all three sectors exhibit common qualities, such as similar income levels and lack of control over the conditions of their work. The point to be made here is that these workers, seen as members of different fractions, are subject to different conditions because of their distinct locations in the economy, yet seen from the perspective of their membership within the occupational hierarchy, they experience many similar conditions. That is, they are unskilled (although "skill" is a mystifying concept under capitalism—most "semi-skilled" jobs take no more than a few weeks to learn) and therefore easily replaced by other workers. This helps to maintain their wages at a low level.

More and more office jobs are being reduced in skill and thus fit into this level in the job hierarchy—a process that involves the "proletarianization"† of office work already noted above. As Braverman writes:

The secretarial function is replaced by an integrated system which aims at centralized management, the breakdown of secretarial jobs into detail operations subdivided among production workers, and the reduction of the number of secretarial workers to one-half, one-quarter, or even smaller fractions of their former number. Among the subsidiary benefits management expects to derive from this arrangement is the reduction and thus cheapening of the skills of administrative employees.[18]

This process involves the endless repetition of small tasks, the mechanization of job functions, and the increasingly minute division of labor.[19] Along with these there is,

---

† By "proletarianization," I do not mean that the workers are just now becoming proletarians, since they have been that all along, but rather that the nature of the labor process in which they are engaged is coming more and more to approximate that of the industrial proletariat.

apart from the denigration of skilled work to unskilled and semi-skilled work that can be learned in a short period of time, the elaboration of fixed patterns of supervision and hierarchy. All this repeats the Taylorist "revolution" that so drastically changed the nature of the industrial workplace beginning with the turn of the century. Just as capitalism created a non-industrial work force, so do the social relationships of the industrial sphere extend to the arena of office work. For example, the subordination of the worker to the machine is becoming as ruthless for office workers as it has been for industrial workers, as any teletype operator can testify. One receptionist told Studs Terkel in an interview:

The machine dictates. This crummy little machine with buttons on it—you've got to be there to answer it. You can walk away from it and pretend you don't hear it, but it pulls you. You know you're not doing anything, not doing a hell of a lot for anyone. Your job doesn't mean anything. Because *you're* just a little machine. A monkey could do what I do. It's really unfair to ask someone to do that.[20]

In sum, industrial and non-industrial workers face increasingly similar job conditions. In response to this, stepped-up unionization drives among office and service workers are occurring.[21]

The third level in the occupational hierarchy is the category of skilled workers. These workers have by and large gained their skills in on-the-job training programs, or have taken short-term courses in schools that train them for one specific skill. Their job is to carry out the job tasks conceptualized by other workers. Some examples would be skilled industrial workers such as machinists, tool and die makers, lathe operators, etc., licensed practical nurses, and typist stenographers. Skilled industrial workers usually belong to strong unions; skilled workers in general have job stability and high wages in comparison with unskilled workers in the same industry, although the wages of skilled office workers,

such as secretaries, are often more on a par with those of many unskilled workers.[22]

The reverse side of the coin of the tremendous increase in unskilled jobs under capitalism is the progressive elimination of skilled jobs. On the one hand, mechanization and automation are causing the transfer of many job functions to unskilled and semi-skilled workers; on the other hand, control over the production process is increasingly transferred into the hands of management. This is an example of the polarization of job structures that Braverman describes. The category of skilled work in industry, for example, now encompasses the tending of machines more than the actual production of goods. The skilled jobs of lathe operator and tool and die maker are being taken over by computerized machines, and a work force drastically reduced in skill and numbers simply watches the machines and places the material to be processed on them.

The fourth level in the occupational hierarchy is composed of low- and middle-level technical workers such as technicians, grade and high school teachers, registered nurses—that is, workers who must have completed some form of higher education. The majority of these workers have acquired their job credentials from either two-year colleges or specific job-training programs in four-year schools. With the exception of the American Federation of Teachers, this sector has not been significantly unionized, although this situation has begun to change over the past few years. The American Federation of State, County, and Municipal Employees is one example of this recent increase in union activity. This change is an indication of the growing class consciousness of a group that is seeing its traditional privileges eroded by pressure from above and below (the polarization process we have discussed), and by the introduction of speed-up and the generally worsening conditions of work.

Workers in this level comprise the lowest rung of the so-called mental (or planning) stratum. Their position holds a certain amount of prestige and an often illusory promise of upward mobility. Under capitalism, the separation of mental and manual work accompanies the constant revolutionizing of the technical means of production and the division of labor. In industry, the alienation of direct producers from their product finds its reflection in the alienation of these same workers from any form of intermediate control during the production process. As machines become more and more complex, other workers must be trained to deal directly with them—maintaining or programming them but never actually producing anything themselves. The social relationship between technical workers and production workers is thereby eliminated, replaced by a fetishistic relationship to the machine, with one group of workers subjected to the machine and another dominating it. The separation of production workers from technicians is reflected in authority relations within the plant—as the latter are incorporated into the ranks of "management."

Technical workers in industry provide the best example of the division between their fraction and that directly below it, since it is in industry that the division between mental and manual labor is brought out most sharply. However, the fetishism of knowledge that distorts the unity between mental and manual workers as members of the same class operates in all occupational spheres. The reluctance of nurses, especially RNs, to become involved in hospital union organizing is an example of the perceived divergence of interests between these two types of workers. Yet regardless of whatever job satisfactions come from the skilled use of knowledge, technical workers hold no more control over the goods produced or the social organization of work than do the fractions below them.

The highest-ranking workers in the job hierarchy are middle-level management personnel, salaried professionals, university teachers and department heads, trade union bureaucrats (not including the highest level), and middle-level government bureaucrats. This fraction covers a continuum with respect to income, power, and prestige, in that workers in this fraction do not share equally in its privileges (for instance, associate professors are not equal to department heads of universities). I will analyze only the management group within this fraction, since it is representative to a significant degree of the other groups in the fraction and also possibly the most controversial segment.

Liberal sociologists of recent decades have pointed to the growth of managerial personnel as evidence of the emergence of a new "managerial" or "technocratic" class. But the growth of the managerial function within capitalism confirms nothing more nor less than the increased socialization of the means of production—that is, the concentration and centralization of capital. This process develops pari passu with the increasing social division of labor,[23] and hence creates a body of managers to coordinate the different operations of the firm. This constitutes no change in the property relations of capitalism, no creation of a new class. Rather, property relations become less personalized, more abstract, and achieve the *appearance* of independence from human relations.

This process has both a technical and a social aspect. The increasing complexity of capitalism encompasses the technical side: the departmentalization of the firm and the development of a corps of managers who are responsible for planning production, sales, advertising, accounting, etc. This is an aspect in the development of the *organization* of production. So, too, does it prefigure in certain respects the socialist form of organization through socialization of production and planning. However, the *social* manner in which this is accomplished (as well as the purpose to which it is put—

the expansion of capital) stamps it with an altogether different character than under socialism. The capitalist achieves an anonymity that serves to prevent the identification of exploitation with its human perpetrators. A group of managers is interjected between the capitalist class and the majority of the proletariat. These managers are the inheritors of the knowledge and control of the production process that have been wrested from the workers themselves, and they therefore represent the higher reaches of the polarization process that we have discussed. The purpose of management is control in the interests of capital—and this becomes the *use-value* of the labor-power of the salaried ranks of management. Managers become the *agents* of the control of social capital over social labor. Marx writes: "An industrial army of workmen under the command of a capitalist requires, like a real army, officers (managers) and sergeants (foremen, overseers) who, while work is being done, command the name of the capitalist."[24]

Marx clearly includes these "supervisory" workers in the ranks of wage labor, assigning them the position of skilled workers, whose wages, "like any other wage," find a definite market price:

The labor of supervision and management, arising as it does out of the supremacy of capital over labor . . . is directly and inseparably connected . . . under the capitalist system, with productive functions which all combined social labor assigns to individuals as their special tasks. . . . The capitalist mode of production has brought matters to a point where the work of supervision, *entirely divorced from the ownership of capital,* is always readily obtainable. It has, therefore, come to be useless for the capitalist to perform it himself.[25]

It must be re-emphasized here that *middle-level management* is part of the working class. Although these managers may be highly paid, their income is insufficient to allow them entry into the capitalist class— i.e., they cannot own significant amounts of corporate stock or other financial assets. Moreover, their income depends upon work, upon their receiving a salary. In contrast, the top ranks of management are drawn from the capitalist class itself; the fact that top-level managers receive a salary is not enough to put them into the ranks of the working class, since in this case the wage is merely a "judicial" relation.

At this level of the occupational hierarchy, ideological and political factors blur the distinction between middle-level management and those salaried personnel above it who have access to the ownership of capital. Ultimately, the distinction hinges on accessibility to capital and capital-earnings (to such a degree that they can form the bulk of income), where a quantitative increase in income must be associated with a qualitative change in class membership. This point is reached when the exchange-value of labor and occupational position allow for the purchase of stock or other forms of capital to a significant degree. People in this category are least likely to identify with the working class, and it is here that non-economic "global effects" operate to divide such workers from the fractions below them. The concrete conditions and the use-value of their work is such as to make identification with the capitalist class the very premise of their work; in the event of an anti-capitalist workers' movement there is little question that their political sympathies would lie with their employers.

Throughout this discussion of occupational hierarchy I have mentioned the correspondence between command over consumption and position within the hierarchy. While it is clear that income does not determine class fraction, but rather derives from it, the differing levels of command over consumption are an important secondary effect of class fractioning. Income bears on the mode of consumption (or "lifestyle"), the type of residential community, and the access to leisure options. All of these phenomena have clear ideological and political effects on subjective class identification. When goods are plentiful, for example, the kind of fetishized relationship to commodities that capitalism encourages tends to blunt the awareness of class conflict. However, the relative scarcity of goods, such as in a period of inflation and/or recession, can then bring a heightened sense of class conflict, since workers' expectations are so sharply violated.

Fractions in the production and reproduction spheres

We will not turn our attention to the second form of fractioning within the working class: that related to the sphere of the production and reproduction of the capitalist system. Apart from the obvious divisions that obtain between workers in the industrial, office, and service sectors, we will discuss two other types that relate to use-value functions—ideological workers and repressive workers. In addition, on the left there has been some recent discussion of unproductive workers. While this area is not specific to use-value functions, it does concern location in the (re) productive sphere, since it relates to place in the economic system and not to occupational stratification.

Unproductive workers. The question of how one integrates unproductive workers into a class analysis has plagued writings on the subject for some time. By "unproductive" workers I mean those who must sell their labor-power in order to live yet do not produce any surplus value, or, by extension, profit. Paul Baran gives another definition to the term *unproductive workers:* "Most generally [unproductive work] consists of all labor resulting in the output of goods and services the demand for which is attributable to the specific conditions and relationships of the capitalist system and which would be absent in a rationally ordered society."[26] The conclusion that often follows from this definition is that a social-

ist revolution would be counter to the objective interests of these workers and therefore they are not members of the working class. This is a *moral* definition, not a scientific one, and therefore at best only suitable for the purposes of polemics. Each mode of production creates a specific job structure tailored to its needs, and the fact that certain jobs can only be done under a specific mode of production and others are necessary to all says nothing about the differing *social relations* in each.[27] It is these social relations that are crucial to our discussion—and the general social relation of wage-labor to capital *unites* productive and unproductive workers under capitalism.

Poulantzas employs the correct definition of unproductive workers, but he seriously confuses their place in the class structure. First, he says that "the working class is not defined by *wages,* since wages are a juridical form in which the product is divided up according to the contract governing the buying and selling of labor-power." From this he concludes that wage-earning unproductive workers are not members of the working class but rather constitute a "new" petite bourgeoisie. Poulantzas does agree that class is determined by relationship to the means of production; what he fails to note here is that although wages are a juridical form, that form *expresses an economic relationship to the means of production*—the need to sell one's labor-power because one does not have ownership of the means of production. In my opinion, this is what is meant by "relationship to the means of production" rather than the specific value-creating nature of the production. To make the value-creating nature of the work a determinant of class would be mechanistic, ignoring the social and political effects of the wage-relationship.

It is thus clear that unproductive workers form part of the working class. The question is, do they form a separate fraction of that class, or are they simply part of other fractions (for instance, the various fractions of the occupational hierarchy) ? It is an important question, because since the tremendous rise in state activity under capitalism began (and government workers in advanced capitalist societies make up by far the greatest proportion of unproductive workers), this sector has been increasing greatly. I would argue that while unproductive workers do not directly produce surplus value, this is of minor importance, since they clearly are necessary for the functioning of the capitalist system and for the expanded reproduction of capital. The question arises: are the conditions of unproductive jobs different from those of similar levels in the surplus-value-producing sector? I believe not to any significant extent. Although there tends to be greater job security in government occupations, this has nothing to do with the non-surplus-value-creating nature of the work; other unproductive workers have no such job tenure conditions. Politically, it is more and more apparent—especially in the government sector—that unproductive workers have no unusual degree of class identification with their employers, since the growth of labor militancy in this sector has been phenomenal over the past few years. Finally, the unproductive nature of the work makes very little difference in the ability to exercise "critical force" against the capitalist system. Postal workers have already demonstrated their strength to do so, whereas many workers in the surplus-value-producing sectors would hardly be missed if they stopped work. For example, Broadway actors, who are productive workers, would be quite helpless to prevent the system from functioning if they went out on strike! The ability to apply "critical force" depends above all on the ability to mobilize *masses* of workers who are in sectors vital to the smooth operation of the production and reproduction of capital. Thus, if one is to give any meaning at all to the concept of fraction, in which ideological, political, and economic forces interact to differentiate one

fraction from another, one cannot make a separate fraction out of unproductive workers. In some capitalist countries, members of the government bureaucracy would constitute a separate fraction, owing to ideological and political factors, but even here their unproductive status is irrelevant to their inclusion in a separate fraction.

The office sector. The rise of office occupations is a result of the qualitative shift made by capitalism when it entered the monopoly stage. Monopoly capitalism represents the growth of social capital—the socialization of capital—where a numerically diminishing class must set into motion ever larger amounts of capital. Not only the scale of firms has increased, but also the functions for which they have taken responsibility. Vertical integration of industries, horizontal differentiation into different industrial sectors, and the increasing complexity of capitalist production have entailed a huge growth in the office operations of firms. Further, the growth of finance capital, which is a necessary component of the monopolization of capitalism as a whole, has meant an increase in the mass of office workers serving it.

Office labor within the firm is responsible for the *accounting* of value produced in the productive sphere (the industrial and private service sectors). It is therefore unproductive labor. The same holds for retail trade labor, which is responsible for the *realization* of value produced in the productive sphere. The left has tended to see the growth of labor in these unproductive sectors as significant of a basic change in capitalism: i.e., that the central problem of monopoly capitalism is the "absorption of surplus," the *sale* of values produced in the productive sphere. The corollary of this notion is that the composition of the work force is shifting decisively in favor of unproductive workers. I have seen no convincing evidence that such a basic shift is occurring. While it is true that office and retail trade labor have increased relatively to industrial and service labor, the latter two sectors, when taken together, are by far the largest category. Unproductive labor functions to facilitate the conversion of surplus value into fresh capital (excepting the government sector). But surplus value itself is created by productive labor alone. Because the wages of unproductive workers come out of the existing pool of surplus value, capitalism would simply be unable to support itself with a labor force composed predominantly of unproductive workers, since too much surplus value would be used up in wages and not enough would be available for its further self-expansion.

The service sector.

The growth of the service sector is part of a dual process: (1) The decline of labor in the goods-producing industries as technological change decreases the amount of labor required in the production process. This has led to the relative growth of the service sector vis-à-vis the goods-producing sphere, as well as to its absolute rise. The nature of service work is such that machinery can replace it only to a limited extent, since the consumption of a service is the consumption of the useful *labor* performed by the service worker.[28] (2) Capital's ceaseless search for new frontiers of economic activity. With the expansion of the service sector, the penetration of capital into domestic, community, and recreational activity raises the dependence of human beings on commodity relations to a higher level. Braverman writes:

The industrialization of food and other elementary home provisions is only the first step in a process which eventually leads to the dependence of all social life . . . upon the marketplace. The population of cities, more or less cut off from the natural environment by the division between town and country, becomes totally dependent upon social artifice for its every need. But social artifice has been destroyed in all but its marketable form.[29]

This process as it occurs under capitalism operates as a disciplining force on the working class, since the dependence on wages—which must cover ever more of the reproduction costs of the worker—becomes increasingly acute.

Labor that was previously involved in the non-commodity production of services (and therefore unproductive to capital) is wrenched out of that unproductive sphere and put to productive use in the expansion of capital. This process frees a great mass of female labor from its traditional role in the production of domestic use-values, making it available for exploitation on the labor market. Thus, consumption within the market sphere sets in motion a counter but inextricably linked reaction—the need to produce within the framework of capitalist commodity production. With the degradation of work skills and cheapening of labor-power the single-wage family can no longer provide for its needs. Thus women must enter the labor force, and, in a neat dovetailing process, they are channeled into those occupations that have been most closely connected to commodity relations: sales and service work, and the office work that goes with the circulation and production of commodities. In the case of service and retail sales work, these are precisely the areas that have made much of the traditional labor of women in the home obsolete.

The growing penetration of *large* capital into the service sector (and the progressive diminution of smaller, more "personalized" service businesses) has subjected this labor force to increasingly oppressive conditions of work. Service work was first proletarianized by its subjection to commodity production and the wage-relation; now, the "proletarianization" process expands to include the subjection to impersonal, "rationalized," proletarian conditions of work.

The supervisors of class peace.

Those who work in the sphere of the ideological

reproduction of capitalism present another division in the fractioning structure. These are workers in the schools and the media; their role is to transmit bourgeois ideology to the working class as a whole, and hence to ensure "harmonious" relations between the working class and the capitalist class (on the terms of the latter). The concrete use-value of their work is such as to encourage, even demand, identification with bourgeois ideology. The maintenance of an illusion of "objectivity" (so necessary to legitimize the function these workers play), and the latitude for criticism of certain aspects of capitalist society it permits, does not contradict in any way the basic identification with capitalism that the majority of these workers have. In order to function more rationally, capitalism needs its critics —so long as they do not overstep the bounds of criticism "from within" to question the very basis of the system. Of course for certain individuals within this fraction access to education has created an awareness of the contradictions of capitalist society. The role of ideological workers as legitimizers of the capitalist system hence contains two contradictory elements: criticism and apologetics. This, combined with their membership in a class whose interests contradict those of capital, makes it very difficult to project what political role will be played by these workers in the event of sharpened class struggle. Certainly, class struggle against capital will be carried on ideologically *within* this class fraction, between those members who defend the interests of the proletariat and those who defend the interests of the dominant class.

The category of *repressive* workers— police, foremen and supervisors, and soldiers—is perhaps the most controversial and difficult to analyze. This includes those workers whose labor has the use-value of ensuring the maintenance of the capitalist class structure. They are termed "repressive" workers since their role involves the open use of repressive mechanisms to en-

sure the "pax capitalista." In the case of policemen (and professional soldiers) the repressive mechanism is the actual or threatened use of physical force and legal punishment. For supervisors, the repressive mechanism is provided by the sanctions developed by the employer: firing, suspension, or docking pay.

The necessity for a police force within capitalism is quite obvious, since capitalism is a system of class conflict. The police must quell confrontations between workers and employers, or between oppressed groups and the state, which itself represents the interests of capital. (They must also exercise vigilance toward crimes committed by working-class people—caused by the poverty and social misery produced by capitalism). The requirements for foremen and supervisors arise out of the hierarchization of the job structure: this structure must have its specific social agents whose job is the supervision and maintenance of fractions within the working class.

These are the workers most often viewed by leftists as being either members of the "ruling class" or, at least, *not* members of the proletariat. This is a confusion of class *role* with class *membership*. The success of this role in reinforcing class discipline depends upon the subjective identification of these workers with the needs of the capitalist class. These workers are the least likely to act collectively according to their own class interest (although, in the case of the enlisted ranks of soldiers, their support or at least neutralization is possible and crucial for the success of a revolution). It is here that the link between a class "in itself" and a class "for itself" becomes the most problematic, since such workers will never make the transition from the former to the latter. Yet many of these workers, especially policemen, foremen, and military recruits, come from the most "traditional" working-class families, live in working-class neighborhoods, and have social relationships exclusively with workers from the "traditional" proletariat. At the same time, while in *value* terms (their status as wage-workers) they are members of the working class, in terms of the *use-value* of their labor they are clearly enemies of it.

Government workers. With the developing complexity of capitalist production there have emerged ever greater needs for its coordination. This coordination can be accomplished only to a limited extent within private production, since absence of planning is an inherent feature of capitalism. The contradictions of the system—the tendency toward explosive crises, unemployment, overproduction—become increasingly threatening to the basic survival of the system itself, since the greater complexity of the economy means that these contradictions can no longer be localized and isolated. The role of government in the economy therefore becomes crucial. It has a dual purpose: on the one hand, the proliferation of government activities becomes necessary to oversee the management of the capitalist system and to ensure the reproduction of class relations. As the inner contradictions of capitalism become more intense, government must step in to try to steer the anarchic forces at work onto a somewhat more stable course.[30] This occasions the great rise in the numbers of government workers.

On the other hand, government spending serves to reorganize what is produced and consumed, through military spending, social services, and the like. Government spending acts to intervene in the potentially explosive working out of the contradiction between growth in the production of physical goods under capitalism and the need to keep workers' wages down relative to capital. Marx termed this the primary contradiction of capitalism:

The *real barrier* of captialist production is *capital* itself. It is that capital and its self-expansion appear as the starting and the closing point, the motive and purpose of production.

. . . The limits within which the preservation and self-expansion of the value of capital resting on the expropriation and pauperization of the great mass of producers can alone move—these limits come continually into conflict with the methods of production employed by capital . . . which drive towards unlimited extension of production. . . . The means—unconditional development of the productive forces of society—comes continually into conflict with the limited purpose, the self-expansion of the existing capital.[31]

The job structure in the government sector has adopted that of the private sector as its model. The same patterns hold for both: job hierarchies, authoritarian work relationships, and similar wage-differentials. The only differences have been the relative security of government employment—which is presently being undercut—and the prohibition against strikes by public employees, which is being increasingly contested by government workers. As the "fiscal crisis of the state" becomes more acute we may expect that increased pressure on government workers will cause a corresponding rise in their organizing activities.

Conclusion: Political implications of the analysis of fractions

In this article we have analyzed the structure of fractions in the American working class. We have seen how as the class has grown to include the overwhelming majority of the United States' population it has also been split into many divisions which have emerged from the material needs of capitalism as it has developed historically. The development of these divisions within the working class is a concrete reality that poses some knotty questions for the left. The long-range question is how to overcome the fragmentation of the class and unite it politically around a program for socialist revolution. The objective unity of the class—that is, the unity of its wage-relation to capital—creates the potential for a broad-based mass socialist movement. A socialist revolution in the United States would not face the problem of a multiplicity of classes that characterized many third-world countries (e.g., China, with its lower, middle, and upper peasantry, craftsmen, merchants, national bourgeoisie, and comprador bourgeoisie).

At the same time, the political unification of the working class can only be accomplished under the leadership of the most genuinely revolutionary sectors of its population. Leadership of the class by sectors dominated by petit-bourgeois consciousness would probably lead a working-class movement toward social democracy, with its substitution of bourgeois forms of political struggle for mass initiative, of a loosely formed electoral party for a disciplined communist party (which, while participating in electoral contests, would go beyond them in its development of a revolutionary strategy). Hence, the short-range question facing the left is to identify which sectors of the working class are the most likely to lead a revolutionary movement to establish socialism. That is, which sectors are going to advance furthest in the anticapitalist struggle, and at the same time raise issues that can unite the class as a whole? Once these pivotal sectors are identified the left can focus its political activity on them, developing a base that can give weight and direction to the formation of a revolutionary party.

Socialists have traditionally seen the industrial working class as the sector that will provide this leading role. Recently certain groups on the left have questioned the assignment of the industrial proletariat to this role, pointing to the decreasing relative size of the industrial work force and the "proletarianization" of higher levels, such as professional and technical workers. Such "new working class" theorists have sought to focus their political activity at these higher levels. (Since many proponents of this theory are themselves members of this

"new working class," their political strategy involves remaining at their jobs and carrying on political work within that arena.)

In my opinion, however, the dichotomy "industrial working class vs. new working class" is misplaced. While professional and technical workers are certainly experiencing a degree of "proletarianization," to understand that sector as a political priority for the left seems to involve a fantastic leap. Not all workers are equally oppressed by capitalism, and this sector is qualitatively better off, in terms of income, job conditions, and occupational prestige, than the vast majority of other workers. Capitalism has "delivered the goods" to these workers to a significantly greater degree than it has to industrial and lower-level service, sales, and office workers. The "proletarianization" of these workers (job insecurity, speed-up, the threat of technological unemployment) is a relatively new phenomenon; hence they have only recently been faced with the necessity of defining their class position vis-à-vis the dominant class. Furthermore, the ideology of individualism, while certainly affecting all workers, is reinforced among these upper strata by professionalism, competition, and relatively higher income levels. Their willingness to participate in collective action with other sectors of their class, as well as their ability to take political struggle to its higher levels, is undermined by all the above factors. Finally, they constitute a distinct, although increasing, minority of the working class. This is not to say that no political work should be done among this sector—far from it. It *is* to say that the emphasis of the left should not be centered on it. While organizing among professional and technical workers may be a priority of *individuals* within the left, it should not be the priority of a socialist movement as a whole.

It seems more promising, therefore, to look at those non-industrial fractions of the working class that share the same general conditions as the industrial proletariat. The growth of the service, sales, and office sectors, with a concentration of low-paid workers subjected to poor, and worsening, job conditions, points to the greatest opportunities for the left outside of the industrial proletariat. The question now centers on three possibilities: (1) that the lower levels of service, office, and sales workers will supplant the industrial proletariat as the leading core of a revolutionary workers' movement; (2) that the differences between the two groups will be so lessened that together they can play the leading role; or (3) that the industrial proletariat will play the primary role. In the final analysis this question will only be resolved in practice, through the trial-and-error activities of the left and through future developments yet to come.

As we have seen, workers in the same fraction of the occupational hierarchy, while in different locations of the economy, experience many of the same working conditions, such as wage levels and degree of autonomy. Nevertheless, the separation of these workers into different spheres of economic activity cannot but have important effects on their consciousness. Marx pointed out that the very concentration of large numbers of workers under the same roof that occurs in industry was crucial in the development of class consciousness. Through this "socialization" of labor, workers develop the habits of cooperation and discipline that are not only important in the development of a working-class movement against capitalism but also in the preparation of the working class to manage socialist society after the defeat of capitalism. The fact that industrial workers are responsible for the physical reproduction of society, through the production of material goods, tends to develop an awareness on the part of these workers of their importance; they do not simply reproduce the goods of capitalism, but the necessities of life itself. Furthermore, with the production of material goods it is much easier to

quantify and tangibly identify the value produced. The worker produces something that is directly expropriated, and can see that it is sold for a much higher price than the wage received. Thus, the exploitation of the worker by the capitalist is more obvious than it is in non-industrial work.

This relationship is not so clear to non-industrial workers—productive and unproductive alike—nor are the material conditions for class unity so available. Office workers, for example, are not only separated from their co-workers in the workplace, occupying small, privatized offices (except for those in the typing pools of large firms), but the elaboration of a minutely divided hierarchy in the office is much more pronounced than in the industrial sphere. In the office, the receptionist, the clerk-typist, and the varying levels of secretaries who derive their status from their immediate superiors, are all divided from each other in an elaborate pecking order. Furthermore, the lack of mechanisms for job mobility within this structure intensifies these divisions. In the case of service workers, the pitting of the worker against the customer—for example, in hospitals and restaurants—militates against the development of an extensive class consciousness.

Industrial workers also have a much longer tradition of class struggle and representation by unions than the other groups of workers we have discussed. The unionization of workers is an indication of a certain level of class consciousness. Although a growing number of non-industrial workers are organizing into unions, they do not have the benefit of the lessons learned from years of struggle that industrial workers have. Yet unions have a dual nature under capitalism: on the one hand, they are the most basic defense organs of the working class, and, as such, they can become forums for militant class struggle. On the other hand, they are also institutions of discipline over the working class: in order to be able to "deliver the goods" to their membership unions must enter into a bargaining contract with the employer, thereby recognizing and legitimizing the existing class relations. Hence, they help to manage class struggle in ways that do not threaten the capitalist system. Their internal structure, the trade union bureaucracy, replicates bourgeois political structure; that is, they are democratic in form, and authoritarian in practice. This means that the rank-and-file, in order to advance the unions as organs of class defense, must struggle against the union bureaucracy as well as against the capitalist class. Rank-and-file struggle then becomes *political,* as well as economic. However, since unions are the most basic institution into which workers are organized *as a class,* the possibilities for this kind of struggle from below are much greater than in other social institutions with worker membership (for example, the existing political parties).

I have enumerated above some of the elements that operate to increase the class consciousness of industrial workers over that of other sectors of the class. However, there are other elements that could operate either to inhibit this development of industrial workers into the "leading core" of a revolutionary workers' movement or to raise non-industrial workers to at least the same position. These are: (1) the relative decrease of industrial workers as a percentage of the work force and the corresponding relative rise in the sales and service sectors; (2) the dead weight of bureaucracy in the old established industrial and craft unions which might operate as a brake on revolutionary activity by their members; (3) the feminist, third-world minority, and student struggles that may have an impact on the workplace, since many workers affected by these movements are in the non-industrial sphere (the majority of female workers are in service, retail, and clerical work).‡ This last point is crucial, since the struggles of women, minorities, and students have been primarily political in form, and through their critique of bourgeois ideology they have called into question some of the basic premises of the capitalist system. What this means in the long run is still unclear. However, in evaluating the trend toward political consciousness among these lower-level strata, their shared consumption level with industrial workers (they live in the same communities and even in the same households), and their increased tendency to share the same kinds of conditions on the job as factory labor, I am led to conclude that such sectors will, along with the industrial proletariat, form the pivotal elements of a revolutionary socialist movement. A strong base among these workers is therefore a necessary, although not sufficient, condition for an effective political organization of the left.

NOTES

1. Karl Marx, *Capital* (New York: International Publishers, 1967), vol. 3, p. 791.

2. Theotonio Dos Santos, "The Concept of Social Classes," *Science & Society,* vol. 34, no. 2 (Summer 1970), p. 172.

3. Marx, *Capital,* vol. 1, p. 632.

4. Harry Braverman, *Labor and Monopoly Capital* (New York: Monthly Review Press, 1974), p. 253.

5. Nicos Poulantzas, *Political Power and Social Classes* (London: Sheed & Ward, 1973).

6. Poulantzas, "On Social Classes," *New Left Review,* no. 78 (March–April 1973), p. 27.

7. Marx, *German Ideology* (New York: International Publishers, 1970), p. 14.

8. Dos Santos, pp. 177–78. The quote by Marx is from the preface to *A Contribution to the Critique of Political Economy.*

‡ For reasons of lack of space I have omitted the role of minorities and women in the capitalist economy, and therefore in the development of the working class. Many of the fractions we have dealt with here intersect with racial and sexual divisions, which operate to further *subjective* divisions within the class.

9. Marx, *Capital,* vol. 1, p. 76.

10. Dos Santos, p. 177.

11. Braverman, p. 255.

12. Dos Santos, p. 177.

13. Albert Szymanski, "Trends in the American Working Class," *Socialist Revolution,* no. 10 (1972), p. 103.

14. Marx, *Capital,* vol. 1, p. 73.

15. Jim Stodder, "Old and New Working Class," *Socialist Revolution,* 17 (September–October 1973), pp. 103–4.

16. Marx, *Capital,* vol. 1, pp. 630, 632.

17. Braverman, pp. 386–87.

18. Ibid., p. 346.

19. See Stanley Aronowitz, *False Promises* (New York: McGraw-Hill, 1974), chapter on "White Collar Proletarians," for a discussion of the nature of office work.

20. Studs Terkel, *Working* (New York: Pantheon, 1974), pp. 30–31.

21. A recent HEW report notes "a 46% increase in white-collar union membership between 1958 and 1968." U.S. Department of Health, Education, and Welfare, *Work in America* (Cambridge, Mass.: MIT Press, 1972).

22. Braverman, p. 355.

23. Ibid., p. 268.

24. Marx, Capital, vol. 1, p. 332.

25. Ibid., vol. 3, p. 386.

26. Paul Baran, *The Political Economy of Growth* (New York: Monthly Review Press, 1957), p. 32.

27. Marx, *Theories of Surplus Value* (Moscow: Progress Publishers, 1968), vol. 1, p. 157.

28. Marx, *Capital* (Moscow: Progress Publishers 1965), vol. 1, p. 187.

29. Braverman, p. 276.

30. See R. Boddy and J. Crotty, "Class Conflict, Keynesian Policies, and the Business Cycle," *Monthly Review,* October 1974.

31. Marx, *Capital* (New York ed.), vol. 3, p. 265.

READING 3–3

Intellectuals and the working class*

ERIK OLIN WRIGHT

Intellectuals have always had an ambiguous status both as actors in the history of Marxism and as categories within Marxist theory. On the one hand, the contribution of intellectuals to socialist movements is undeniable: as theorists, polemicists, revolutionary leaders. The most decisive advances in revolutionary theory have been made by men and women with considerable education, who spent a great deal of their time in intellectual activities. While it is unquestionably true that their ideas were nurtured through their contact with the masses, especially in the course of social struggles, nevertheless it is equally true that most important contributors to revolutionary theory were not themselves proletarians or peasants. They were intellectuals, and the systematic development of revolutionary theory is impossible to imagine without their contribution.

On the other hand, the very fact that most intellectuals are not unambiguously part of the working class has meant that they have always been viewed with some suspicion within revolutionary movements. Although as individuals intellectuals might be totally committed to a revolutionary project, as a social category intellectuals occupy privileged positions within bourgeois ideological relations and often privileged positions within bourgeois economic relations as well. The common designation by Marixsts of intellectuals as "petty bourgeois" reflects the reality of these privileges. The result is that while intellectuals as individuals have been essential for revolutionary movements, intellectuals as a social

* From *The Insurgent Sociologist,* vol. 8, no. 1 (Winter 1978), pp. 5–18.

category have often played a rather ambiguous role in working class socialist struggles.

This essay will attempt to explore the relationship of intellectuals to the working class and to class struggle. Two questions will guide the discussion: (1) *What is the location of intellectuals within the class structure of advanced capitalist societies?* (2) *What are the consequences of this class location for the role of intellectuals within socialist struggles?*

Part 1 will focus primarily on the first of these questions. After briefly surveying the major alternative ways in which Marxists have tried to understand the class location of intellectuals, I will advance the view that intellectuals must be understood as occupying a complex contradictory location within class relations. The premise of the discussion is that in order to analyze the roles of intellectuals in social struggles, it is first necessary to have a provisional grasp of their objective location within class relations. Part 2 of the essay will try to link the analysis of the class position of intellectuals to a discussion of their role in mediating the relationship between socialist theory and practice. Particular attention will be paid to the contradictory situation of Marxist intellectuals within bourgeois universities, although the analysis will be relevant to other categories of intellectuals as well.

PART 1: THE CLASS LOCATION OF INTELLECTUALS

Before proceeding it is necessary to define more precisely how I will use the expression "intellectual" throughout this discussion. The term *intellectual* has three interconnected meanings. First, "intellectual" designates a *general characteristic of all human activity,* namely that all activity involves in one way or another the use of the intellect, the mind. All activity, no matter how routinized, involves some mental

processes. Second, "intellectual" designates a *specific type of laboring activity;* laboring activity which is involved in one way or another with the elaboration and dissemination of ideas (rather than simply the use of ideas). Third, "intellectual" designates a *category of people:* people whose activity is primarily that of elaborating and disseminating ideas.[1]

One of the central characteristics of the division of labor in capitalist society is the tendency for intellectuals as a category of people to replace intellectuality as a type of laboring activity. This is usually expressed as the tendency for the progressive separation of mental and manual labor within capitalist society, that is, for a progressive separation of the activities of planning, designing, organizing, conceptualizing, from the activities of executing, producing, directly transforming nature. Instead of the elaboration and dissemination of ideas being part of everyone's laboring activity, such activity becomes tendentially restricted to specific categories of people: intellectuals.

The analysis in the following pages will concentrate on the third usage of the concept of intellectuals, intellectuals as a social category. The basic task, then, will be to sort out the class location of individuals whose central activity or function is the elaboration and dissemination of ideas.

Within Marxist theory there are at least five broad interpretations of the class position of intellectuals: (1) All intellectuals who are wage laborers are part of the working class. (2) Intellectuals can be divided into three categories: those who are tied to the working class, those who are tied to the bourgeoisie and those who are tied to pre-capitalist classes. (3) Intellectuals constitute one segment of the petty bourgeoisie, sometimes referred to as the "new" petty bourgeoisie. (4) Intellectuals largely fall into the "Professional and Managerial Class," which constitutes a distinct class, separate from both the working class and the petty bourgeoisie. (5) Intellectuals should generally be thought of as occupying contradictory locations within class relations at the economic and ideological levels. I will argue that each of these interpretations taps part of the reality of intellectuals in capitalist society, but that the fifth interpretation provides the most comprehensive basis for a rigorous understanding of intellectuals.

1. All intellectuals are workers. In this interpretation, the essential defining criterion for the working class is wage labor. Workers are defined as those people who do not own their own means of production, who are propertyless, and thus must seek employment from capital or the state in order to live. Regardless of what concrete activities they perform once they are employed, all people who have nothing to sell but their labor power are workers. In this perspective, while intellectuals may constitute a privileged stratum of the working class in terms of income, status, job security and other privileges, in terms of fundamental class relations they occupy the same position as industrial wage-laborers.[2]

There is a certain compelling quality to this simple polarization view of the class structure of capitalist societies and the treatment of intellectuals as workers. What it captures is the immanent tendency of capitalism towards polarization. The fundamental dynamics of the capitalist mode of production are embedded in the polarized relation of labor to capital, and at a high level of abstraction one can see all class positions in capitalist societies as being tendentially drawn into one polarized position or the other. But as an historical account of the actual class character of intellectual wage-labor, the view that intellectuals are firmly within the proletariat is inadequate for many reasons. Perhaps the most important issue in the present context is the assumption that the complex relationship between capital and labor can be captured by a single dimension, a single

criterion: selling and buying the commodity labor power. The relationship between capital and labor is fundamentally determined by what Marxists call the social relations of production, and the selling and buying of labor power constitutes only one aspect—albeit a very important aspect—of these relations. Two other dimensions of the social relations of production are especially important: the social relations of control over the labor of others within the labor process, and the social relations of control over one's own labor within the labor process. If the social relations of production represent a complex combination of several dimensions of social relations, then workers cannot be defined simply as wage laborers, but as wage laborers who also do not control the labor of others within production and do not control the use of their own labor within the labor process. In these terms, many intellectuals would be excluded from the working class, even though they do sell their labor power as a commodity.

2. Intellectuals belong to several different classes. This position is closely associated with the work of Antonio Gramsci.[3] Gramsci identifies three categories of intellectuals: those intellectuals who are organic intellectuals of the working class, "those who are organic intellectuals of the bourgeoisie and those whom he calls "traditional intellectuals," typically organic intellectuals of the feudal aristocracy. Rather than seeing the global category of "intellectuals" as having any genuine class unity either as part of the working class or of some other class, Gramsci identifies the class character of intellectuals with the specific function they play in the class struggle. Those intellectuals who contribute to the hegemony of bourgeois ideology comprise the intellectual stratum of the bourgeois class; those intellectuals who combat bourgeois ideology and contribute to the counter-hegemony of the proletariat are part of the working class; and those intellectuals who embody backward looking precapitalist culture reflecting the world view of the feudal aristocracy, constitute the traditional stratum of intellectuals. In the course of capitalist development, this latter category tends to be absorbed into the capitalist system as organic intellectuals of the bourgeoisie, and thus there is a general tendency for intellectuals to become polarized into two camps.

Gramsci's conception of intellectuals has the considerable merit of emphasizing the dynamic rather than static nature of class relations: class location must always be conceptualized in terms of class struggle, not simply in terms of a structure of positions. Nevertheless, it has a number of important limitations. In particular, by arguing that all intellectuals whose activity reproduces the hegemony of the bourgeoisie are part of the bourgeois class itself, Gramsci tends to minimize the objective antagonism between many of these intellectuals and the bourgeoisie. While it may be true, for example, that teachers contribute to the ideological hegemony of the bourgeoisie, it is also true that many categories of teachers are oppressed in various ways by the bourgeoisie. Some teachers, in fact, are even exploited by capital in tse technical sense of producing surplus value. Thus, while teachers may be *functionally* organic intellectuals of the bourgeoisie, *structurally* they are generally not members of the bourgeois class.

This conflation of functional and structural definitions of class location tends to obscure the contrete social relations within which intellectual labor is performed. It is one thing to argue, for example, that the director of a news network or a university is part of the bourgeois class, and another to argue that reporters and teachers are part of the bourgeoisie. It is of fundamental importance to distinguish between those intellectuals who control the apparatus of production of ideas (ideology), and those who merely work within those apparatuses.

Once this distinction is made, it becomes possible to talk about the proletarianization of intellectual labor—the progressive loss of any control over the immediate conditions of work by intellectual wage laborers. And this in turn makes it possible to talk about the increasing *structural* basis for class unity between certain categories of intellectuals and the working class, even though in functional terms they might remain "organic intellectuals of the bourgeoisie." This is not to deny the value of Gramsci's insights about the roles of intellectuals within the class struggle, and in particular his insistence on the importance of organic intellectuals of the working class for any revolutionary movement. The point is that such an analysis of functional relations to the class struggle is not a substitute for a critical decoding of the objective class character of given structural positions held by intellectuals.

3. Intellectuals are part of the petty bourgeoisie. The dissatisfaction with the simple polarization view of the class structure has led many Marxists to treat intellectuals as one segment of the petty bourgeoisie. In order to distinguish this segment from the traditional petty bourgeoisie of small shopkeepers and artisans, the intellectual–petty bourgeoisie has often been called part of the "new petty bourgeoisie." One of the most systematic advocates of this position at the present time is Nicos Poulantzas, especially in his recent book *Classes in Contemporary Capitalism* (London: NLB, 1975).

The view that intellectuals constitute a new petty bourgeoisie rests on two complementary claims: first, that intellectuals cannot be considered part of the working class, and second, that they share a fundamental similarity in class location with the traditional petty bourgeoisie.

A number of arguments are used to support the first claim: in addition to the rejection of wage labor as an adequate criterion for defining the proletariat, it has been argued by Poulantzas and others that intellectuals should be excluded from the working class because they are generally unproductive laborers[4] and because they do not engage in manual labor. While I agree with Poulantzas that intellectuals (or at least most intellectuals) are not an integral part of the working class, I disagree with the arguments he uses to defend this thesis.[5] Let us examine each of these arguments in turn.

In order to make the claim that unproductive labor as a whole is in a different class from productive labor, it is necessary to establish that this division corresponds to a division of *fundamental* class interests. The essential method for assessing such divisions of fundamental class interests is to decode rigorously the social relations of production and analyse the locations of specific categories of labor within those relations. Categories of labor which occupy similar positions within the social relations of production share, at the economic level, the same fundamental class interests. In these terms it is very difficult to maintain that unproductive labor occupies a distinctively different location within production relations from productive labor: like productive workers, many unproductive workers have absolutely no control over their labor process, are completely subordinated to capital, have no capacity to control the labor of others, and so on. Now, it may be true that most intellectuals do not fall into the working class on these dimensions of social relations (indeed, this is what I will argue in the discussion of contradictory locations), but it is because of their location on these dimensions and not because of their status as unproductive labor per se that they should be considered outside of the working class.

Poulantzas' argument for excluding intellectuals from the working class because they are mental laborers is more complex. For Poulantzas, the division between mental and manual labor constitutes the basic relationship of ideological domination/subordination in capitalist society (i.e., manual labor is subordinated to mental labor at the ideological level). Since classes must be defined at the ideological as well as economic levels, it follows, Poulantzas insists, that since mental labor dominates manual labor at the ideological level it cannot be part of the working class. Since intellectuals are one category of mental labor, it also follows that intellectuals are outside of the working class.

While Poulantzas may push this analysis too far—arguing that even secretaries and routinized salesworkers are mental laborers and thus dominate the working class ideologically—nevertheless, the central thrust of his argument seems to me substantially correct. I would only modify his position in one important respect: It is not enough simply to be mental labor to dominate the working class (even at the ideological level). It is also necessary to occupy a position of domination within ideological apparatuses. A mental laborer (such as a secretary) who lacks any control over the process of ideological production does not dominate the working class ideologically. In these terms, most intellectuals—people engaged in the elaboration and dissemination of ideas—would have some degree of control over the production of ideology, and thus would occupy a position of ideological domination with respect to the working class. This point will be developed at greater length in the discussion of contradictory locations within class relations below.

It is insufficient, of course, simply to establish that intellectuals are not part of the working class; it is equally important to understand what class they are part of. Two different sorts of arguments have been used to support the claim that intellectuals share a common class position with the petty bourgeoisie. First, as Judah Hill argued, certain categories of intellectuals—

especially professionals—can be viewed as "owning" their means of production even when they are employed by capital. That is, such intellectuals own their intangible intellectual skills (especially when such skills are certified in diplomas and licenses), and since these skills constitute the critical "means of production" of intellectuals, intellectuals should be seen as property-holders just like the traditional petty bourgeoisie.[6]

The central difficulty with this position is that it confuses an analysis of class defined in terms of market relations with class understood at the level of production relations. While it is certainly true, as Weber argued 60 years ago, that intellectuals possess certain special skills which give them certain advantages within the market, they do not necessarily have any real control *over the use* of those intellectual skills within production. Except in the case of self-employed professionals, most intellectuals give up considerable degrees of control over the use of their intellectual "means of production" when they accept employment by capital or the state. In order to maintain that certain categories of intellectual wage-laborers genuinely "own" their means of production, therefore, it is necessary to examine systematically the labor process within which they engage in intellectual labor and see the extent to which they actually retain self-direction of intellectual production. In general, intellectual wage-laborers would have much less control over their labor process than the traditional petty bourgeoisie.

The second argument supporting the claim that intellectuals are part of the petty bourgeoisie centers on an hypothesized unity of the ideologies of new and old petty bourgeoisie. This theme has been stressed by Poulantzas in his various works. Poulantzas argues that the very character of intellectual labor and the organizational structures within which it is performed in capitalist society guarantee that intellec-

tuals will be characterized by the essential elements of petty bourgeois ideology: individualism, veneration of the state, careerism, etc. In spite of the fact that intellectual wage-labor is involved in entirely different social relations of production from the petty bourgeoisie at the economic level—the petty bourgeoisie consists of independent producers within simple commodity relations of production while intellectuals are subordinated directly to capital within capitalist relations of production—nevertheless, Poulantzas argues, the congruence of their ideologies is so strong as to wield them into a single class.

Again, as in the simple polarization view of intellectuals, there is a compelling quality to this analysis. Certainly in terms of class consciousness, there are clear tendencies in many capitalist societies for intellectuals to have similar world views to the petty bourgeoisie, and at least in certain circumstances, to adopt similar political orientations. And yet, in the end, the view that intellectuals fall firmly into the petty bourgeoisie is as unsatisfactory as the view that they are part of the working class. To begin with, the claim that the ideologies of intellectual wage-laborers are essentially identical to the traditional petty bourgeoisie requires a very limited reading of ideology. For example, while both categories may hold highly individualistic ideologies, the individualism of the traditional petty bourgeoisie (be your own boss, rugged individualism) is entirely antithetical to the individualism of the employed intellectuals (organizational competitiveness, careerism). To equate the two is to obscure the fundamentally different social relations within which these individualistic ideologies operate.

Even more importantly, even if it were the case that the ideologies of intellectuals and the traditional petty bourgeoisie were identical, it would be unsatisfactory from a Marxist perspective to give such weight to consciousness and ideology that they can utterly obliterate the fundamental differences in economic relations which characterize most intellectuals and the traditional petty bourgeoisie. While wage labor may not be a sufficient criterion for defining class, it is certainly an important criterion, for it determines the basic contours of the relationship to capital. This difference in the relationship to capital means that there are basic—not just marginal—differences in the relationships of the petty bourgeoisie and intellectual wage-laborers to working class struggles and struggles for socialism. Specifically, because they are small property-owners, the petty bourgeoisie has a much more contradictory relationship to socialism than do intellectual wage-laborers. This is not to say that the class interests of intellectuals and workers are identical—indeed, if they were we would say that intellectual labor was part of the working class—but merely that those interests are generally less opposed to each other than are the interests of the working class to those of the traditional petty bourgeoisie.

4. Intellectuals are part of a Professional Managerial Class. If intellectuals should generally not be considered part of the working class, and if they are also not part of the petty bourgeoisie, then perhaps they should be considered part of a completely different class, a class which is distinct from the working class, the petty bourgeoisie and the bourgeoisie. This is essentially the claim of Barbara and John Ehrenreich in their analysis of the Professional-Managerial Class. They define the PMC as "consisting of those salaried mental workers who do not own the means of production and whose major function in the social division of labor may be described broadly as the reproduction of capitalist culture and capitalist class relations" (*"The Professional-Managerial Class," Radical America*, 11:2, 1977, p. 13). Most salaried intellectuals would certainly fall into the PMC by this definition. The question then becomes

whether the PMC can be really viewed as a "class" in the same sense that the bourgeoisie and the proletariat are classes, or whether what the Ehrenreichs are calling a class should be understood as some other kind of social reality. It is one thing to argue that the various categories grouped together under the label PMC have a certain internal unity, and another thing to identify the logic of that unity as a class unity.

The Ehrenreichs use two basic arguments to support the thesis that the PMC is in fact a class. First, they argue that the PMC is "characterized by a common relationship to the economic foundations of society—the means of production and the socially organized patterns of distribution and consumption" (p. 12). Second, they argue that the PMC is a class because it is "characterized by a coherent social and cultural existence," that is, that its members "share a common life style, educational background, kinship networks, consumption patterns, work habits, beliefs" (p. 12). This second argument is clearly dependent upon the first, for many other social categories which do not constitute classes are characterized by a coherent social and cultural existence (e.g., farmers, lumberjacks, sailors). It is only if it is established that the PMC in fact does occupy a common "relation to the economic foundations of society" that this second argument can be seen as reinforcing its existence as a class.

On what basis, then, do the Ehrenreichs argue that the PMC does constitute a distinctive location with respect to the means of production? Their essential argument is that the PMC is defined by a distinctive *function* in the social division of labor, namely the function of reproducing class relations. The concept of a common relation to the "economic foundations" of society is therefore identified with a common function in the division of labor, and positions which perform a common function are then viewed as constituting a class.[7]

As in Gramsci's analysis, the Ehrenreichs' discussion of functions is extremely important for any adequate understanding of intellectuals (or other members of the PMC), particularly in terms of their role in the class struggle. Nevertheless, such simple identification of the class location of intellectuals with their function in the social division of labor tends to collapse the structural and functional aspects of class into a single dimension, and this obscures rather than clarifies the essential class character of intellectual wage-labor. This is so for two basic reasons: (1) the problem of noncoincidence of structural positions with functions, and (2) the need to understand the social relations internal to the performance of functions. Let us look briefly at each of these issues.

Functions within a society, including the function of reproducing class relations, must be understood as *dimensions* of social relations, not *categories* of positions. While it is certainly true that some positions are more "specialized" than others in the function of reproduction, *every* position determined by capitalist relations of production to some extent or another contributes to the reproduction of those relations. Marx's analysis of commodity fetishism, for example, is in part an analysis of how the reproduction of capitalist relations of production is embedded in the very character of those relations rather than simply the responsibility of some specialized occupations. Manual workers on the production line, therefore, also perform the "function" of reproducing capitalist relations of production simply by participating in capitalist production.

In spite of this, it is true that some positions do become specialized in this function of reproduction. But it is equally true that even these specialized reproductive positions are generally not exclusively reproductive. Engineers, for example, do not merely function to reproduce capitalist class relations. They also design bridges and in other ways perform clearly productive

functions. Why should their class location be defined exclusively by their reproductive function? On what basis is it possible to establish which function is "more" important? And even if this can be determined, why should the dominant function necessarily have exclusive sway in determining class location? These questions illustrate some of the difficulties in making any simple identification of class and function.

The problem with a simple function = class conception becomes even clearer when we examine the social relations within which the specialized function of reproducing class relations takes place. If we examine some ideological apparatus—a school, a newspaper, a church—it is immediately clear that not all positions within that apparatus have the same structural relation to the functions of that apparatus. Some positions are involved in the control of the entire apparatus. Others involve control over specific activities within the apparatus, perhaps simply the activity of the position itself, but no control whatsoever over the apparatus as a whole. And finally, some positions are excluded entirely from any control over either the apparatus or specific activities within it. In terms of their relationship to the class structure as a whole, *all* positions within an ideological apparatus serve the "function" of reproducing capitalist class relations since the ideological apparatus itself serves this function. But clearly, different locations within the apparatus have entirely different structural relationships to this function than others.

The Ehrenreichs are quite aware of these gradations of positions within a single functional apparatus, and it leads them to argue that certain positions within the PMC are "closer" to the working class than others, while other positions are "closer" to the bourgeoisie. A registered nurse, for example, constitutes a position within the PMC close to the working class; an upper-middle manager in a corporation constitutes a position within the PMC closer to the bourgeoisie. The Ehrenreichs stress that the PMC is not a homogeneous class, but is characterized by an internal hierarchy of strata reflecting a range of structural locations within the common function of reproducing capitalist social relations.

Now, to say that both a registered nurse and an upper-middle manager are both members of the same class (albeit at different "ends" of the class) implies that they are "closer" to each other than they are to any other class. If this were not the case—if in fact registered nurses are "closer" to workers than to upper-middle managers—then it would make sense to see them as being within the same class. A registered nurse and an upper-middle manager might still have a certain commonality within class relations, but that commonality could not be understood as defining them within a single, coherent class. This is not a problem in the ambiguities at the "boundaries" of classes, but of the very logic of designating a set of positions within the social division of labor as a class.

The question of whether the PMC can be considered a class can thus be reposed as follows: Does it make sense to consider a set of positions that are in some sense situated "between" the working class and the bourgeoisie, in which some of these positions are closer to the working class and others closer to the bourgeoisie, a "class" in the same sense that the bourgeoisie and the proletariat are classes? There is a strong tradition within Marxism to assume that *every* position within the social division of labor *must* fall firmly into one class or another. If this assumption is accepted, then by default, all of the positions between the working class and the bourgeoisie must, of necessity, constitute a class.

But there is an alternative: instead of insisting that all positions within the social division of labor fall firmly into classes, some positions can be seen as *objectively torn between classes.* If classes are understood as social relations, not things, this implies that certain positions have a contradictory character within those social relations. On certain dimensions of class relations they share the characteristics of the bourgeoisie, on others they share the characteristics of the working class. If this stance is adopted, then it becomes very easy to talk about the sense in which some of these positions can be considered "closer" to the working class than others. They are closer precisely in the sense that their location within the social relations of production shares more characteristics with the working class than with the bourgeoisie. In this view, instead of seeing intellectuals as part of a distinctive class with its own coherence and unity, intellectuals would be understood as falling within a contradictory location within class relations.

5. Intellectuals occupy contradictory locations within class relations. Let me explain more rigorously exactly what I mean by the expression "contradictory locations within class relations." In a sense, of course, all class locations in capitalist society are "contradictory," since the very concept of class expresses fundamentally antagonistic relations. Some positions, however, are contradictory in a double sense: first, they reflect the basic antagonistic class relations of capitalist society, and second, they are objectively torn between the antagonistic classes of that society. Such positions do not have a class identity in their own right; their class character is determined strictly by their location between classes. It is because of this derivative nature of their class location that such positions are referred to as contradictory locations within class relations.

Since classes in capitalist society cannot be defined simply in terms of economic relations, neither can contradictory locations. It is essential to specify the contradictory character of certain positions at the level of political and ideological class relations as well as at the level of social relations of production. In the case of intellectuals, it will be especially important to examine their class location at the ideological level. In what follows, we will first examine contradictory class locations in terms of social relations of production, and then extend this discussion to class relations at the ideological level. The upshot, as we shall see, is that *intellectuals typically occupy a contradictory class location between the working class and the petty bourgeoisie at the economic level, but between the working class and the bourgeoisie at the ideological level.*

At the level of social relations of production, there are three basic contradictory locations within class relations in capitalist society:

1. *Managers* occupy a contradictory location between the working class and the bourgeoisie.
2. *Small employers* occupy a contradictory location between the bourgeoisie and the petty bourgeoisie.

3. *Semi-autonomous employees* occupy a contradictory location between the petty bourgeoisie and the working class.

These three class locations are schematically illustrated in Chart 1. The third category is especially important in the present context since much intellectual wage-labor falls into this location. Let us look at it a bit more closely.[8]

In order to understand the semi-autonomous employee category—the contradictory class location between the proletariat and the petty bourgeoisie—we need to look at the characteristic labor process of the petty bourgeoisie and the proletariat. The distinctive thing about the petty bourgeois labor process is that the petty bourgeois producer directly controls that labor process. In common parlance, the petty bourgeois is his or her own boss. The pace of work, the tools and procedures used, the scheduling of work, the product produced, etc. are all under the control of the direct producer. In capitalist production, on the other hand, the worker has at most marginal control over the immediate labor

CHART 1
**Contradictory locations within class relations
at the level of social relations of production**

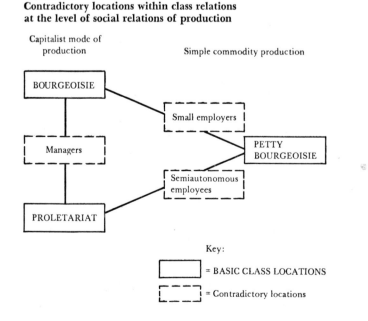

process. In the extreme case of the production line regulated by principles of scientific management, the worker becomes a human machine with no autonomy whatsoever. In these terms, semi-autonomous employees represent those wage laborers who, for a variety of reasons, maintain high levels of genuine control over their labor process. Like workers they are employed by capital (or the state), like workers they must sell their labor power in order to live, and like workers they do not control the apparatus of production as a whole. But unlike workers, and like the petty bourgeoisie, they do have real control over much of their labor process. This is often the situation of intellectual wage-labor. Perhaps the clearest example is an assistant professor, at least in an elite university. While assistant professors certainly do not have any control over the apparatus of education as a whole, they do have substantial degrees of control over what they teach, how they teach, what kind of research they do, how they spend their time, etc.

To describe a position as a contradictory location between the petty bourgeoisie and the working class means that such positions *simultaneously* share class interests with the working class and the petty bourgeoisie, but have interests identical to neither. They are objectively torn between the two classes. For such class positions, socialism simultaneously promises genuine liberation from the distortions and domination of capital and a reduction of the *individual* autonomy which they experience under capitalist conditions. That is, in a socialist society the labor process is controlled collectively by workers rather than either by capital or by individual laborers. This means that in many cases, especially for much intellectual labor, socialism implies a reduction in individual control over immediate laboring activity. It is in this sense that intellectual wage labor, to a greater or lesser extent, occupies a contradictory class location between the working class and the petty bourgeoisie.

Intellectual labor, however, cannot be analysed solely in terms of social relations of production. As the Ehrenreichs correctly emphasize, intellectuals play key roles in the reproduction of capitalist social relations and capitalist culture, and this means that it is essential to analyse their class location at the ideological level.

To do this we must first identify the basic class relations at the ideological level. Without going into a great deal of detail on this question, three basic class locations can be identified at the ideological level:

1. The *bourgeois class* location at the ideological level consists of those positions involving control over the process of ideological production as a whole, i.e., control over the bourgeois ideological *apparatuses*.

2. The *contradictory class* location at the ideological level consists of those positions which are involved in the elaboration and dissemination of bourgeois ideology, but not in the overall control of the apparatuses of bourgeois ideology.

3. The *working class* location at the ideological level consists of those positions which are excluded from either the control over the apparatuses as a whole or the elaboration and dissemination of ideology within those apparatuses.

In terms of the educational system, for example, the bourgeois position would be held by top education officials (boards of regents, chancellors, superintendents of schools); the contradictory location would be typically held by teachers; and the working class location would be held by secretaries, janitors, school cafeteria workers, etc.[9]

Let us now try to combine these two levels of analysis—contradictory locations at the level of production relations and at the level of ideological relations—in order to understand the class character of intellectual labor. So that this discussion will not be too abstract, I will focus specifically on the class location of teachers, although the analysis would apply to many other categories of intellectuals as well. By and large, teachers fall into the contradictory location between the petty bourgeoisie and the working class at the level of production relations. Historically, teachers have had fair amounts of control over their work process, but have generally had little to do with the control of the educational system as a whole. At the ideological level, on the other hand, teachers occupy a contradictory location between the bourgeoisie and the working class since teaching positions are one of the critical locations for the dissemination and elaboration of bourgeois ideology. Teachers are thus simultaneously located between the working class and the petty bourgeoisie and between the working class and the bourgeoisie.

This *disarticulation* between their class location at the economic and ideological levels has important consequences for the potential role of teachers (and other categories of intellectuals) in the class struggle. To the extent that teachers have a certain real level of autonomy at the level of social relations of (educational) production, they can potentially subvert bourgeois ideology at the level of ideological relations. There is thus a potential contradiction between the economic and ideological class location of educational workers, and this contradiction poses certain real threats to the bourgeoisie.

This potential contradiction is sharpest in institutions of higher education. In the United States at least, teachers in primary and secondary schools have much narrower autonomy in every respect than do teachers in higher education, and in particular they have less autonomy in terms of the ideological content of what they teach. In most places in the United States, if a primary school teacher were to attempt to seriously disseminate communist ideas in the classroom, she/he would almost certainly be out of a job. In colleges and universities the situation is more complex, and the autonomy of teachers is more of a reality. In spite of its ideological functions in supporting liberalism and creating the image of open and free discussion, "academic freedom" within the university does in fact create greater space for ideas which challenge bourgeois ideology. This is precisely why authoritarian regimes in capitalist societies are so insistent on imposing strict ideological controls within universities. If the relative autonomy of academics did not contradict their function at the ideological level, there would be no necessity for right-wing governments to purge so systematically the universities and schools. Conservatives may be somewhat paranoid in their estimation of the capacity of leftist academics to "poison" the minds of the young, but it is still true that the relative autonomy of teachers does create the possibility for real resistance to bourgeois ideology.

If this analysis is correct, it might well be asked: Why doesn't the capitalist class simply eliminate this "petty bourgeois" autonomy of university teachers and other categories of intellectual wage-labor? There have been times, of course, when precisely this happens. The extreme case is authoritarian bourgeois states in which the detailed content of educational activity is dictated from above, but less extreme forms (such as McCarthyism in the United States) occur within bourgeois democracies as well. Still, in most circumstances academics have had a certain measure of real autonomy in advanced capitalist societies, and this needs to be explained. Several factors seem especially important. First of all, while the relative autonomy of academics and other intellectuals within the social relations of production poses a potential threat to the bourgeoisie, this autonomy is also useful for the bourgeoisie. The strength of bourgeois ideology rests in part upon the claims of liberal freedoms, and these claims are embodied in the relative autonomy of intellectuals, including teachers. Furthermore, the bourgeois class needs intellectual production, it needs scientific research and imaginative reformulations of bourgeois ideology, and such intellectual production needs a certain level of autonomy to be effective. Finally, the bourgeoisie would potentially face considerable resistance from certain sections of intellectuals as well as the working class if the autonomy of intellectual labor were seriously attacked. The capitalist class might want to erode the autonomy of intellectuals, but in some circumstances the political and ideological costs might simply be too high.

As a result of these factors, the degree of autonomy of teachers within the social relations of production varies enormously across time and place. While teachers in general occupy a contradictory class location between the working class and the petty bourgeoisie at the economic level, certain teaching positions in certain times and places are much closer to the working class, other positions are much closer to the petty bourgeoisie. It is thus only a first step in the analysis to demonstrate that teachers occupy contradictory class locations. It is equally important to specify the variability within those relations and to examine the processes of change of the class location of given categories of teachers.

In the case of the United States, it appears that in the past decade and especially since the early 1970s, there has been a considerable proletarianization of many segments of teachers in higher education. Course loads have been increased, curriculums have been more administratively dictated, scheduling has been taken out of the hands of individual teachers, tenure-track positions have been replaced by short-term appointments with no job security, and so on. These transformations have produced a fairly deep bifurcation of the class situation of teachers in colleges and universities: in the elite institutions, proletarianization has occurred at a much slower pace,

or in some cases not at all; in junior colleges, community colleges and some undergraduate-oriented state universities, this erosion of the autonomy of teachers within the labor process has progressed very rapidly. Thus many teachers in such institutions have been drawn very close to the working class pole of the contradictory location between the working class and the petty bourgeoisie, while teachers at elite universities remain much closer to the petty bourgeois pole. As a result, one would expect very different patterns of class behavior on the part of academics in these two situations, in particular, very different possibilities for creating linkages between teachers and workers in various political and economic struggles. The much more successful unionization of university teachers in junior colleges and undergraduate-oriented state universities is one empirical indication of these trends.

At the ideological level, however, teachers remain in contradictory locations between the bourgeoisie and the proletariat in spite of the partial proletarianization of teachers at the economic level. While the autonomy within work may have decreased for many teachers, they still are actively engaged in the process of the elaboration and dissemination of bourgeois ideology. However, there are some developments within educational systems which indicate that teachers might be in a process of limited proletarianization at the ideological level as well as at the economic level. Perhaps the clearest example is the fairly extensive introduction of various forms of programmed learning through the use of computer technologies and other devices. Such machine-structured education undermines the role of teachers in the elaboration and dissemination of ideology. In the limiting situation, their responsibilities for actually disseminating ideology could be reduced to turning on machines rather than intervening as individuals within the process. Teachers would become machine-tenders rather than active participants in ideological production. In such a situation, the class location of teachers at the ideological level would move very close to that of workers (complete exclusion from the control over ideological production).

In more general terms, the variety of processes of routinization of the role of teaching in which the capacity of teachers to interject their own ideas into their teaching is reduced can be thought of as a process of ideological proletarianization within education. This does not mean that teachers simply dissolve into the working class at the ideological level, but it does mean that teaching positions play a less active role in the production of bourgeois ideology, and thus the situation of teachers at the ideological level would move closer to that of workers.

Such processes of ideological proletarianization of teachers should not be exaggerated. For the moment, most teachers still occupy a contradictory location within class relations at the ideological level. This generates a particularly complex set of pressures on teachers within the class struggle. On the one hand, although teachers occupy a contradictory class location between the petty bourgeoisie and the working class at the economic level, many teaching positions are unquestionably being proletarianized at the level of social relations of production. On the other hand, those same teaching positions still occupy contradictory locations between the bourgeoisie and the proletariat at the ideological level, and this location tends to tie them ideologically to the bourgeois class. The very ambivalent character of teachers unions and many teacher strikes reflects this disarticulation between the economic and ideological levels in the class location of teachers.

PART 2: INTELLECTUALS AND SOCIALIST STRUGGLES

So far in this essay we have focussed solely on the structural class location of in-

tellectuals, of people whose central activity is the elaboration and dissemination of ideas. I would now like to turn to the very problematic issue of the role of intellectuals in the struggle for socialism. In particular, I would like to examine the relationship between the objective class location of most intellectual labor (contradictory locations within class relations) and the contradictory character of their role within socialist movements. I will not discuss the problem of how intellectuals in general can be drawn into socialist movements, but rather will focus more narrowly on the question of their role within those struggles once they are involved.

In order to begin to explore this issue, we will first need to come to terms with the classic Marxist question of the relationship of theory to practice, if only in a provisional and schematic way. Once we have done this, we will examine how the contradictory character of the class location of intellectuals shapes their capacity to play a role in mediating the relationship between theory and practice.

Theory and practice

The problem of the relationship between theory and practice really involves three separate, but interrelated, dimensions: the relationship between theorists as producers of theory and practice; and the relationship between theorists and theory. The problem of the role of intellectuals in socialist struggles involves all three of these relationships. Let us examine each in turn.

1. Theory-practice dialectic. Most Marxist discussions of the general problem of the "unity of theory and practice" focus primarily on the relationship between theory as a conceptual apparatus and practice. This relationship can itself be dissected into two aspects. First, *the impact of theory on practice:* A central tenet of Marxism, especially since Lenin, has been that political practice—the activity of consciously transforming social relations and social structures—cannot be guided simply by the spontaneously-given ideological understandings of society, but must be guided by *scientific* revolutionary theory. As Lenin put it, without revolutionary theory there can be no revolutionary practice.

What precisely does this mean? It certainly does not imply that a scientific revolutionary theory provides a set of formulas for action or that such theory can provide complete predictions of the future upon which to base political strategies. Rather, the central rationale behind the claim that a scientific revolutionary theory should guide practice is that such theory provides us *with a systematic capacity to learn from our practice,* to learn from our mistakes and our successes. To "learn" implies that there are questions for which we do not already have the answers and that a method exists for genuinely answering those questions.[10] Historical materialism constitutes the scientific theory which enables us to produce new knowledge to be used in political practice.

The second aspect of the "unity of theory and practice" centers on the *impact of practice on theory:* Political practice provides the essential epistemological condition for the reconstruction of theory within Marxism. Historical materialism is a theory of the relationship between social structures and social practices, between structural constraints and the transformations of those constraints through struggle. It is the scientific theory of the contradictory determinants of social life. At any given time, as in any science, there are competing claims about those contradictory determinations within Marxism. While there may be a general consensus of sorts about many of the basic concepts of historical materialism, there is often intense dispute over specific propositions, particularly propositions dealing with the structural limits on class practices and the conditions for the transformation of those limits through class struggle.

How can such disputes within theory (and politics) be adjudicated? In part such disputes can be debated within theory itself—some propositions are more coherent than others; some involve purely ideological reasoning; etc. But ultimately, the most central debates within Marxism can only be advanced by studying the actual struggles attempting to transform social structures, either at the present or in the past. To state the issue in somewhat overly-positivistic terms, practice provides the "experimental conditions" for evaluating the adequacy of propositions within Marxist theory, and thus for reconstructing that theory in light of its inadequacies.[11]

2. *Theorist-practice dialectic.* Theory is produced by real human beings, embedded in real social relations within which they produce theory. Marxism, as a materialist theory of history, is also a materialist theory of Marxism, and this implies that the relationship of the theorist to practice itself constitutes one of the determinants of the development of Marxist theory.

While the relationship between theory and practice can be understood as providing the conditions for the generation of new *answers* within Marxist theory, the relationship of the theories to practice can be seen as providing the social conditions for the generation of new *questions.* The theory and research agendas of theorists do not come out of thin air. The problems with which they are preoccupied and which define the contours of the questions which they pose are critically shaped by the ways in which theorists are linked to political practice.

This is not a metaphysical claim, nor simply a psychological claim about the motivations and sincerity of the theorist. Rather it is a claim about the material relations necessary to sustain the asking of questions capable of advancing Marxist theory. Ultimately, this is a claim about the social relations which determine the *accountability* of theorists to given class and political constituencies.

Accountability implies that real mechanisms exist which shape the theorist's choice of questions and problems to be studied in ways which ensure their relevance to specific class interests. Theorists are accountable to the bourgeoisie to the extent that such mechanisms force them to define the relevance of their work by its contribution to bourgeois interests; they are accountable to the working class to the extent that they are linked to mechanisms which shape their work in terms of its relevance to that class's interests.[12]

There is a decisive asymmetry between the forms or mechanisms of accountability of theorists to the bourgeois class and to the working class in capitalist society. Accountability to the bourgeoisie is in many ways built into the very fabric of institutional relations of capitalist society. The pervasiveness of bourgeois ideology, the immediate reality of status systems and criteria for success, the competitive relations of intellectual production, and so on, all contribute to linking theorists to bourgeois interests. Furthermore, directly and indirectly these mechanisms are backed up by state power. In extreme situations this means that the repressive apparatus of the state can be brought to bear to impose class accountability (e.g., in the McCarthy period) ; in less extreme situations, it implies that the state uses its resources to underwrite the "selective mechanisms" which shape the activity of theorists (e.g., employment in state institutions, research grants, certification processes, etc.) . These diverse mechanisms, taken together, are in part what it means to say that the bourgeoisie is the "hegemonic class": bourgeois class practices have the capacity of substantially defining the range of relevant questions asked by theorists even when they are in-

capable of creating an ideological consensus of answers.

Accountability to the working class, on the other hand, has to be constantly produced through organized, collective resistance to capitalist domination. Accountability to the bourgeoisie is in many respects spontaneous within a capitalist society; *accountability to the working class can only be conscious accountability*. When speaking about the accountability of Marxist intellectuals to the working class within capitalist society, therefore, there is a sense in which such accountability is at least in part a *self-imposed accountability;* that is, it comes from the decision of theorists to participate in class practices in ways which produce this accountability.[13]

It is for this reason that such accountability is *always* problematic. The dominant institutions of capitalist society exert constant pressure on theorists, including Marxist theorists, to define their questions in terms of bourgeois practices. In the absence of a counter-accountability based on real links to working class practices, it is very difficult for a theorist to resist such pressures. This is not to argue that it is only through direct participation on the barricades that serious Marxist questions can be generated, but it does suggest that the greater the distance between the theorist and the real, practical struggles of the working class, the more difficult it will be for that theorist to be held accountable to the working class for the questions which are asked.

When the relationship of the theorist to practice is understood as a relationship of class accountability, it is clear that it must be viewed as a *variable* relationship, not an absolute one. Marxist theorists can be more or less accountable to the working class. Indeed, we can make an even stronger statement: under different historical conditions theorists may face different objective possibilities of accountability to the working class. Under conditions of a politically conscious, well-organized working class, with strong, mass-based revolutionary parties, a much higher level of accountability to the working class *as a class* is even possible than when the dominant forms of working class practice are reformist parties, trade unions, or other social movements. Participation in such movements may still provide real links to the working class, and they are still essential for countering the accountability to the dominant class. However, precisely because such movements tend of be organized around the immediate interests of the working class, they will provide a less effective mechanism of ensuring that theoretical work is directed towards the fundamental interests of that class. It is always important for Marxist theorists to be linked to the class practices of the working class in one way or another, but the available forms of such linkage and their effectiveness in influencing the theorist's work vary with historical conditions.

3. Theorist-theory dialectic. The production of theory is not simply a consequence of practical engagement with struggles to change the world; it is also a consequence of an engagement with theory itself. The subtitle to Marx's most important theoretical work, *Capital* is *A Critique of Political Economy*. Marx did not use as a subtitle, "a critique of bourgeois society," or "a critique of the capitalist mode of production"; he adopted the subtitle "a critique of *political economy.*" In doing so he emphasized that theory-construction is a process of transformation—the "critique" —of existing theory as well as a process of interpreting the world (in order to change it).

What specific role does the engagement with theory play in the production of Marxist theory? Schematically we can say that if the relationship between the theorist and practice provides the critical social basis for the questions asked, and the relation between theory and practice provides the historical conditions for the answers obtained, the relationship of theorist to theory provides the conditions for the production of the *concepts* (theoretical tools) necessary to generate those new answers from those questions. This is in part what Marx means by the process of "critique" itself: it is a process by which new concepts are produced through an assessment and criticism of the concepts of existing theory, in his case political economy.

If critique is the process by which new concepts are produced, then the elaboration and reconstruction of Marxist theory depends not simply on the social relations which provide the link of the theorist to political practice but also upon the social relations which provide the link between the theorist and theory. In terms of the theorist-theory dialectic, the development of Marxism as a scientific theory requires social relations which stimulate open and free debate over theoretical questions, which provide people with a sophisticated grasp of existing Marxist theory, allow for a strong ideological commitment to socialism along with an undogmatic commitment to Marxism, and so on. In the absence of social relations which produce these effects, theorists are unlikely to develop the conceptual tools necessary to grapple seriously with the questions posed through practice. History may produce the raw material for new answers, but without adequate concepts, the theorist may be unable to appropriate that history as new knowledge.

The class location of intellectuals and the relationship between theory and practice

The argument thus far can be summarized as follows: Because theory plays such an important role in shaping socialist political practice, it is important to understand the conditions necessary for the production and reconstruction of theory itself.

Three clusters of conditions have been elaborated: first, the relationship of the *theorist to political practice* shapes the *questions* which the theorist asks; second, the relationship of the *theorist to theory* shapes the elaboration of *concepts* needed to answer those questions; and third, the relationship between *theory and practice* determines the extent to which historical conditions allow for the discovery of new *answers.*

Let us now return to the problem of the class location of intellectuals. I will take as a particular case in point the problem of Marxist intellectuals located within bourgeois universities, although much of the analysis which follows would be relevant for other categories of Marxist intellectuals as well. I choose to focus on Marxist academics both because Marxists within universities have played a particularly important role in the development of Marxist theory in the United States and Western Europe over the past 50 years, and because it is the category of Marxist intellectuals about which I know the most. The issue, then, is this: In what ways does the complex class location of Marxist academics—contradictory locations between the petty bourgeoisie and the working class at the economic level and contradictory location between the bourgeoisie and the working class at the ideological level—shape their capacity to mediate the relationship between theory and practice? Or, to state the problem in the terms set out above, how does the contradictory character of their location within class relations affect the relationship of the theorist to practice and the theorist to theory?

First, let us look at the problem of the relationship of the theorist to practice. The central issue here, as stated earlier, is the problem of class accountability, particularly in terms of the questions asked by the theorist. Marxist theorists within bourgeois universities are under tremendous pressures to ask questions structured by

bourgeois problems, bourgeois ideological and political practices. Such pressures are often extremely direct, taking the form of tenure criteria, blacklisting, harassment, etc. But often the pressures are quite subtle, played out through the intellectual debates within professional conferences and journals. To publish in the proper journals one has to ask questions which those journals see as relevant, and such relevance is dictated not by the centrality of the questions to Marxism or to the revolutionary practice of the working class, but to the dilemmas and problems within bourgeois social science. Thus, the requirements of survival within the university necessarily push the theorist into a relationship of at least partial accountability to bourgeois class practices.

However, the theorist may simultaneously be accountable to the working class. Marxist theorists do not publish simply in bourgeois journals; they also publish in socialist and communist journals, newspapers, magazines. They do not simply attend professional conferences where debate is structured around the preoccupations of bourgeois ideological practice; they also attend political meetings and conferences where the issues are structured by quite different practices. They are not only tied to the bourgeoisie through their location within the university structure; they may be linked directly to the working class through their location within a party structure or their participation in various kinds of social movements. Through all of these processes, the questions asked by the theorist are held up to critical appraisal and accountability by social forces opposed to bourgeois domination.

Of these various modes of accountability to the working class, historically the most important has been membership in or class association with working class political parties, particularly various Communist Parties. Especially in certain Western European countries, such parties have provided the basic vehicle for sustaining a link between Marxist intellectuals and the working class. Such a link, however, was forged at a cost, for while they may have provided a basis for a certain level of class accountability, the internal structures of most Communist Parties have generally been unfavorable for a serious engagement of the theorist with theory. In particular, the existence of party lines on theoretical-scientific questions, on questions of the scientifically correct explanations of the world, has imposed real constraints on the practice of critique. It is one thing to insist on disciplined acceptance of strategic political choices made by a party (assuming that such choices are made through a process of genuine democratic political debate); it is quite another to insist on disciplined acceptance of "correct" scientific explanations of social life. While such party lines on matters of theory may be understandable given the severe conditions of ideological struggle waged against Communist Parties (and against the USSR), nevertheless, such discipline on theory systematically undermines the capacity of intellectuals within such party structures to produce and transform concepts.[14]

Marxist theorists have thus often been faced with a dilemma: the conditions which maximize their linkages to the working class have generally not been the conditions which maximize their capacity for critical theoretical work.[15] One of the responses to this dilemma has been the emergence of a tradition of Marxist theoretical practice within bourgeois universities, most notably in Western Europe, but more recently in the United States as well.

The possibility for the development of Marxism within bourgeois universities is a result of the contradictory character of the class location of the intellectuals. Whereas the contradictory class location of Marxist academics between the bourgeoisie and the working class at the ideological level generates contradictory pressures for accountability, the contradictory location of the academic theorist between the working class and the petty bourgeoisie creates the possibility for sustained critical theoretical activity. The semi-autonomous character of most intellectual production implies that theorists maintain some real control over the immediate conditions of theoretical production, and as long as such "petty bourgeois privileges" (control over the immediate conditions of production) are preserved, some space for the theorist/theory dialectic is created.

This argument has nothing to do with protecting the *income* privileges of professors. The critical issues are job security, control over one's work, work load, censorship, etc. Serious theoretical production cannot take place under conditions in which the theorist is fully proletarianized within the production relations of intellectual production. Defensive struggles against proletarianization within the university, therefore, are important for the very possibility of producing Marxist theory in the bourgeois university (i.e., of engaging in critical theoretical production). This does not imply, of course, that Marxist theory can *only* be produced within universities, but it does imply that if it is to be produced within the university at all, the contradictory class location of academics needs to be maintained.[16]

The preservation of the conditions of Marxist theoretical production within the university has, however, typically been obtained at a deep political cost: the relative isolation of Marxist theorists from the working class. Thus, although the contradictory location of academics makes possible the development of Marxism within the university, it simultaneously tends to displace the questions asked by Marxist academics from the central political problem of *making* a revolution.

To restate this dilemma in terms of our analysis of theory and practice: In the historical conditions of class struggle in Western Europe and the United States over the past half century, there has tended to be a contradiction between the conditions most favorable for the theorist-theory dialectic and those most favorable to the theorist-practice dialectic. This is a real contradiction, one that cannot be transcended by a simple "act of will" by individual Marxist theorists. The contradiction itself can only be transformed through collective political practices which transform the conditions within which Marxist intellectuals work and which make possible new forms of linkage between intellectuals and the working class.

NOTES

1. Gramsci distinguished between the first two of these concepts of intellectuals and the third by saying that "All men are intellectuals, one could therefore say; but not all men have in society the function of intellectuals" (*Selections from the Prison Notebooks,* ed. by Quintin Hoare and Geoffrey Nowell Smith, New York: International Publishers, 1971, p. 9).

2. A recent defense of this position can be found in an article by Francesca Friedman, "The Internal Structure of the American Working Class" in *Socialist Revolution,* no. 26 (1975).

3. See in particular Gramsci's important essay, "On Intellectuals" in *Selections from the Prison Notebooks,* op. cit.

4. Unproductive labor is being used here in the technical Marxist sense of labor which does not produce surplus value. This would include the labor of bank clerks, most salesworkers, government bureaucrats, etc. To say that labor is unproductive in this sense is not to say that it is unuseful, but merely to say that it does not produce new value (surplus value) for capital. For a more elaborate discussion of unproductive labor, see James O'Connor. "Productive and Unproductive Labor," *Politics and Society.*

5. For a much more detailed review and critique of Poulantzas' analysis of classes, see Erik Olin Wright, "Class Boundaries in Advanced Capitalist Societies," *New Left Review,* no. 96, 1976. This essay has been substantially revised and published as chapter 2 in Erik Olin Wright, *Class, Crisis, and the State* (London: New Left Books, 1978).

6. See Judah Hill, "Class Analysis: the United States in the 1970s, "Pamphlet, Class Analysis, P.O. Box 8494, Emeryville, California, 1975.

7. For an extended theoretical defense of such functional definitions of class relations, see G. Carchedi, *On the Economic Identification of Social Classes* (London: Routledge and Kegan Paul, 1977).

8. Because of space limitations, we will not systematically discuss managers and small employers in this essay. For a detailed discussion of these contradictory class locations at the level of production relations, see Erik Olin Wright, *Class, Crisis, and the State* (London: New Left Books, 1978), especially chapter 2, "The Class Structure of Advanced Capitalist Societies." The essential character of these locations can be very briefly summarized as follows: small employers are like capitalists in that they exploit labor power, but they are like the petty bourgeoisie in that they and members of their family directly engage in production themselves so that much of the surplus labor generated in production comes directly from their labor rather than simply from their workers. Managers are like capitalists in that they directly control the laboring activity of workers within production and may control the use of physical capital, and in some circumstances money capital, as well. They are like workers in that they are controlled by capitalists. They are excluded from control of the overall accumulation process and they sell their labor power as a commodity to capital.

9. It is important to remember throughout this discussion that we are talking about the class character of *positions,* not necessarily the class affiliation of the individuals within those positions. A teacher, for example, could be thoroughly engaged with working class struggles and even teach Marxist ideas in the classroom even though the teacher-position is a contradictory location at the level of ideology. Of course, in most circumstances there is a systematic relationship between the class affiliation of individuals and the class character of their positions—most teachers in fact teach bourgeois ideology. If it should happen that, as a result of class struggles, a large proportion of teachers within bourgeois educational apparatuses began to challenge bourgeois ideology, there would be a serious crisis of ideological hegemony. Under such circumstances one would expect extremely sharp struggles within the apparatus as attempts were made to reimpose bourgeois ideology on the teachers.

10. In contrast to such scientific theory, an "ideological" theory is one in which all questions are already answered by the theory (answers are "pre-given") and thus there exists no method for seriously answering new questions or generating new answers to old questions. In

these terms, Marxism functions both as an ideology and as a scientific theory: dogmatic Marxism (Marxism as an orthodox structure of immutable answers) functions as an ideology; scientific Marxism functions as a method for producing new knowledge about the world. The hallmark of Marxism functioning as an ideology is the use of quotes from Marx as a way of *validating an argument about the world* (as opposed to an argument about Marx). This is not to in any way deny the critical importance of studying Marx himself, but when Marx's words function as Authority, as a way of proving propositions about society, then Marx ceases to be a source of scientific method and instead becomes a source of ideological verification. This way of differentiating scientific theories from ideological theories is derived from the analysis by Louis Althusser in *Reading Capital* (London: New Left Review, 1970), although it departs from Althusser's discussion by seeing the possibility of Marxism itself functioning simultaneously as ideology and science.

11. Claus Offe develops this argument in an interesting way in his discussion of the problems of studying the state in his essay, "The Structural Problem of the Capitalist State" (reprinted in Von Beyme, ed., *German Political Studies, vol 1, 1975*, Beverly Hills: Sage, 1974). Offe argues that the critical dynamics of the capitalist state are those which exclude certain decisions or possibilities from the state altogether.

12. Accountability to the working class does not simply mean accountability to *workers*. Particularly in a society in which the struggles of the working class have been largely displaced from struggles over fundamental interests to struggles over immediate interests, accountability to workers as such cannot provide the material basis for ensuring that the questions asked by Marxist theorists serve the fundamental interests of the working class. Accountability, therefore, has to be the socialist political and ideological practice of the working class, not only to workers as such.

13. While it would be idealist to suppose that simply by an act of will a theorist can produce theory which serves the interests of the working class. It is not idealist to argue that theorists can choose to become embedded in a structure of social relations which can have the effect *on the theorist* of making the production of such theory possible. A theorist can choose to become linked to the working class in ways which establish the conditions for accountability, and thus which make possible sustained Marxist theorizing. It is in this sense that accountability is partially self-imposed: it requires an active choice by the theorist. The "default option," given that theoretical work is being done within a capitalist society, is accountability to the dominant class.

14. This argument does not imply that it is impossible to produce and transform theory within traditional Leninist parties, but merely that the process of theoretical innovation is impeded when a party imposes discipline on scientific questions. Such impediments obviously operate much more weakly on leadership cadre at the apex of the organizational structure, and this may be one of the reasons why theoretical innovation has tended to be the activity of top leadership more than middle-level and rank-and-file members.

15. Perry Anderson in *Considerations on Western Marxism* (London: NLB, 1975) discusses at great length this dilemma faced by Marxist intellectuals. Throughout most of the period since the 1920s, the only effective way for Marxist intellectuals to be systematically tied to the political practices of the working class was through the parties of the Third International, and yet membership in those Communist Parties acted as a serious constraint on their capacity to critically produce and transform theory. The rise of academic Marxism was one of the outcomes of this dilemma.

16. This argument about the conditions for the production of Marxist theory within bourgeois universities does not imply that in a revolutionary, socialist university, the production of theory will depend upon the preservation of petty bourgeois relations of production (semi-autonomous class locations) within intellectual production. While it is always risky to speculate on the nature of social relations in a socialist society. It would be expected that the relative *individual* autonomy of intellectual activity characteristic of the liberal bourgeois university would be replaced, or at least complemented, by new forms of *collective* autonomy, of collectively organized theoretical production.

The inner group of the American capitalist class*

MICHAEL USEEM

Like all social classes in the United States, the upper class contains distinct strata and fractions. However, relatively little has been known about the contours and implications of the internal differentiation of the upper class. Recent research suggests the presence of several divisions, and this paper evaluates the thesis that one of these divisions lies between an "inner group" and the remainder of the upper class.

Although upper, dominant, ruling, and capitalist class are frequently used interchangeably, our preferred label is capitalist since it connotes class standing primarily based on position in the private economy. Capitalist class can be defined as the set of people who own and/or manage business firms, or who have primary kinship ties to those holding such positions. This class is internally differentiated when subsets of class members hold distinct positions in the economy. At least limited differences in interests distinguish the positions, leading to different political outlooks, patterns of association, and forms of private and public influence.

Analysts have suggested that the capitalist class splits along three major axes. One divides those who own corporations from those who manage them. It is argued that owners are subject to the imperative of capital accumulation and maximization of profit while managers are subject to other imperatives, particularly corporate stability and growth (Berle and Means, 1932; Gordon, 1966). A second axis relates to divergent areas of economic activity.

Businessmen are divided into major interest groups, such as bankers and industrialists in one formulation (Fitch and Oppenheimer, 1970a, 1970b, 1970c), or managers of large, monopoly firms and executives of smaller competitive firms, in another model (Baran and Sweezy, 1966; O'Connor, 1973). A third axis differentiating the capitalist class relates to the integration of class interests. Most managers and owners, it is held, are primarily concerned with the interests of their own firm. In many instances, these interests clash with the overarching and long-term interests of American business. However, a small group of businessmen—the "inner group"—has acquired influence in diverse holdings. They are uniquely situated to help unite groups of firms and perhaps even to assist in integrating the interests of large numbers of corporations. Inner group members are likely to be particularly sensitive to the general needs of private enterprise that transcend individual corporate concerns (see Mills, 1956: 121–22; Domhoff, 1974; Zeitlin, 1974, 1976; Zeitlin, Ratcliff and Ewen, 1974; Soref, 1976).

The third inner group hypothesis contains important implications for how the capitalist class is organized to articulate and advance its collective interests. Unfortunately, this thesis has received the least analytic and empirical attention. Accordingly, this paper distinguishes key elements of the inner group hypothesis and considers new evidence bearing on its validity.

* From *Social Problems*, 25 (February 1978), pp. 225–240. © 1978 by The Society for the Study of Social Problems.

Inner group origins and functions

The inner group of the capitalist class can be defined as the set people who are in a position to exercise simultaneous influence over the activities of at least several major business firms. Circumstances permitting such influence would include ownership of a substantial fraction of several firms' stock, acting as a director of several corporations, controlling a resource that is critical to several firms, such as credit, and holding both a top executive position in one firm and at least one of the previously mentioned ties to another. Since the degree of control may range from influence over a few companies to a voice in the policies of many, the boundary between the inner group and the remainder of the capitalist class is diffuse rather than sharp. Those having the largest span of control are most central to the inner group.

Consider the positions of corporate director and top executive. If two or more of these positions are simultaneously occupied by the same individual, he or she will be in a situation to influence the policies of several firms. Such joint occupancy is expected for two reasons, both related to efforts at resource control. First, a firm is continuously faced with problems of controlling an uncertain and potentially unfavorable economic environment. One strategy for improving control is for the corporation formally to share top personnel with other firms whose policies are critical to the corporation's prosperity. This can be achieved by sharing a director or by having a top executive of one business sit on the board of the other company. Some such formal exchange between firms is, therefore, expected, particularly between financial and non-financial corporations. Credit is a crucial resource for most large industrial firms, and inclusion of a banking executive or director on their boards can help to ensure adequate financing. Moreover, the shared director or executive

is able to observe the institution in which an investment is made. Second, interlocking ties are likely to occur when wealthy individuals and extended families hold assets in several firms. One means for the wealthy to protect their investments is through actively overseeing and coordinating, as top executives and directors, the affairs of the several firms.

Studies confirm that both imperatives lead to inter-corporate sharing of directors and executives. Interdependent firms are disproportionately interlocked; financial institutions are heavily interlocked with non-financial institutions; wealthy individuals and families are well represented in top management and on the boards of firms in which their holdings are concentrated (Villarejo, 1962; Dooley, 1969; Burch, 1972; Allen, 1974; Sonquist and Koenig, 1975). As a result, a significant fraction of the capitalist class holds positions in two or more large corporations. In 1969, for instance, 8,632 individuals served as directors of the nation's largest 797 corporations, and nearly one-fifth (1,572) of the directors sat on at least two of the boards of these corporations (Mariolis, 1975: 433).

While these factors account for the existence of an inter-corporate network of executives and directors, the network itself may acquire an important new function, predictable by virtue of the special circumstances faced by those overseeing several firms. First, those with multiple positions are exposed to a broad range of business problems. Though still only a limited fraction of the entire range of corporate conditions, the diversity of experience is likely to foster a heightened awareness of the problems large companies have in common. Second, holding multiple positions tends to generate extensive bonds of acquaintance, cutting across industrial and regional lines, furthering the formation of a general class consciousness. Third, this group is also likely to have a strong voice in business circles because of its broad resource base. Since multiple position holders can mobilize several major firms on behalf of a policy, they are likely to be able to overrule narrowly oriented stands taken by other businessmen. Thus, those with multiple corporate positions are prone to exhibit greater class consciousness, social cohesion, and authority than those holding a single position. They should form, in short, an inner group with the capacity to specify and promote economic and political policies required for business activity in the United States, even when these positions clash with the immediate concerns of specific firms.

The presence of such a group would contradict an alternative "capitalist state" hypothesis on the organization of the capitalist class proposed by several analysts (Offe, 1973, 1974; Poulantzas, 1973: 123–141; O'Connor, 1973: 5–10). They contend that business firms are largely incapable, due to competition and isolation, of organizing and asserting their own general interests. Indeed, they argue that the inherent disorganization of the capitalist class requires the formation of a separate political authority to distill and protect capitalist interests. Thus, the state is necessary for "the liberation of the class interests" from the "fragmented, stubborn, and shortsighted empirical interests of single capital units" (Offe, 1973: 111).

In the inner group formulation, the capitalist class is seen as generating an instrument for the aggregation of its interests, with the inner group serving as a type of "vanguard" for the entire class. While the state also plays a role in promoting capital accumulation, many of its policies are fashioned by the inner group and merely implemented by the government. The role of the government in the capitalist state formulation is seen, by contrast, as more active. Lacking the capacity to organize itself, the capitalist class relies on the state to determine and implement the policies

required to sustain profitable business conditions. The contribution of the inner group is relatively minor. Thus, the validity of the inner group model has major implications for the organization of the capitalist class and its ability to promote its own general interests.

The inner group model

I will test the inner group model by examining whether inner group centrality is related to several predicted characteristics. Inner group centrality is assessed as follows. Though stock ownership, kinship, and other bonds are sources of multicorporate connections, the present study is limited to two inner group strands—top executive positions and directorships of major corporations. Serving as an executive or on a board of directors permits a person to help mobilize the firm's resources. Even greater control is possible if the person serves as both an executive and a director (the "inside director"). If two roles are held in different corporations (at least one as an "outsider director"), the individual is in a position to coordinate corporate policies. This brokerage role is even stronger if an executive position and several outside directorships are held. Thus, an appropriate though imprecise measure of centrality to the inner group can be based on (1) service as a corporate executive and (2) the number of outside directorships held with major corporations. The larger the number of outside directorships, the more central the individual; and, for a given number of directorships, holding an executive position further enhances centrality. The inner group model leads to the formulation of four research hypotheses on inner group centrality.

The wealth and financial executive hypothesis. The earlier discussion of the inner group suggests that those forming the core of the inner group are more likely to be wealthy and connected with financial institutions than are other big businessmen. Multiple corporate directorships will not necessarily be monopolized by financial executives and the wealthy, but both groups should be significantly over-represented.

The social cohesion hypothesis. Inner group members are likely to be more socially cohesive than are other members of the capitalist class. Bonds of acquaintance and friendship come from frequent interaction among inner group members attending board meetings and executive activities.

The political consciousness hypothesis. Since members of the inner group occupy similar institutional positions and, if the social cohesion hypothesis is correct, are in frequent contact, it is likely that the inner group will evolve a distinct political consciousness in two respects. First, interaction and shared roles generate similar outlooks, and the inner group should therefore have a more uniform perspective on political issues than other members of the capitalist class (Lazarsfeld and Merton, 1954). Second, the inner group should tend to have a high level of concern for the larger and long-range interests of corporations. The inner group is likely to hold an opinion differing from the remainder of the class on the appropriate role for government. Since welfare, labor, and other forms of government managed reforms can be costly to individual firms but valuable to all if the reforms maintain societal stability, inner group members are likely to be less opposed to state intervention in these realms than will be other capitalists (Weinstein, 1988; Kolko, 1963). The inner group is prone to embrace what Monsen and Cannon term a "managerial ideology" whose proponents are "convinced of the necessity of the expanded role of government to prevent deep depressions and possible radicalism" (1965: 47).

The influence hypothesis. The inner group will be over-represented on public and private decision-making bodies and will wield disproportionate influence within these councils. Inner group members' corporate connections should make them attractive members for community, business, government, and other advisory and policy-setting bodies. If the previous hypotheses are valid, the inner group's personal resources, social cohesion, and political consciousness should make them particularly effective participants in such organizations.

Research procedure

I will examine the inner group hypotheses with data from a survey of American college and university trustees. Though many trustees are not members of the capitalist class, the proportion of governing board members drawn from this class is large, and thus a sizable trustee survey will include a large number of businessmen. Under the auspices of the Educational Testing Service, Hartnett (1969) surveyed over 5,000 trustees in 1968, selecting the respondents through a disproportionate stratified cluster sample. Though university trustees are somewhat over-represented in the sample (compared to college trustees), the survey is a reasonable cross-section of the membership of college and university governing boards.[1]

The boundaries of the capitalist class cannot be defined precisely, but top executives and directors of major corporations should be included. The Hartnett survey asked whether the trustees were executives of a corporation whose shares are traded on a stock exchange and whether, during the past five years, they had been directors of a corporation whose shares were listed on a stock exchange. Since most large businesses have their stock on an exchange and most small businesses do not, these items separate those who oversee the nation's largest corporations from other trustees. Of the more than 5,000 respondents, 1,307 were executives and/or directors of large corporations (that is, a firm whose stock is traded on an exchange). This set of individuals is not, of course, a precisely representative sample of capitalist class members since all are college or university trustees, and most capitalists do not hold such positions. Though substantiating evidence is unavailable, it is likely that these trustees are more public-spirited and more often inner group members than other businessmen. This and other unknown biases are acceptable, since the present analysis relies on internal comparison of subgroups of the surveyed businessmen. A more serious problem is the small range of information acquired from respondents in a survey originally conducted for other purposes. Certain interesting dimensions were not measured and others were only marginally tapped. As a result, certain variables were unavailable or were indirectly indexed in the present study.

In the following discussion, I divide the businessmen into seven groups according to their executive and directorship positions. Two groups—executives (N = 265) and single-directors (294)—can be considered capitalists outside the inner group because they hold only one corporate position. A third group—single-director executives (200)—has a mixed membership which, unfortunately could not be separated. It includes executives serving on the board of their own corporation, who cannot be considered part of the inner group since their interests and influence are tied to a single corporation. But it also includes executives serving as an outside director for another corporation, who are at least marginal members of the inner group by virtue of their connections with two major firms. The four remaining groups are increasingly central members of the inner group: double-directors (145),

double-director executives (111), triple directors (sitting on three or more boards; 126), and triple-director executives (151). The range in inner group centrality can be illustrated by three members of the University of Pennsylvania governing board (1974–75):

Executive: Robert Galbraith Dunlop. Born in 1909 and graduating from the University of Pennsylvania in 1931, Dunlop joined the Sun Oil Company in 1933 and in 1974–75 was president and chairman of the board. He is a Presbyterian and is affiliated with the Republican Party.

Director Executive: Charles Brelsford McCoy. Also born in 1909, McCoy obtained degrees from the University of Virginia and M.I.T. and entered duPont de Nemours & Company in 1932. In 1974–75 he was president and board chairman of duPont, and he was serving as a director of First National City Bank of New York. He also sat on the board of two smaller firms (Diamond State Telephone Company and Wilmington Trust Company) and a local medical center, and he was a member of the Business Council.

Multiple-Director Executive: John Anton Mayer. Mayer was born in 1909 and obtained a bachelor's degree from the University of Pennsylvania. He was chief executive officer and chairman of the board of Mellon Bank N.A. and Mellon National Corporation in 1974–75, and he sat as a director of N. J. Heinz Co., Aluminum Company of America, PPG Industries, and General Motors. He was also on the governing board of Carnegie-Mellon University, Carnegie Institute, and Western Pennsylvania Hospital. He is an Episcopalian, and his exclusive social club affiliations include Duquesne (Pittsburgh) and Links (New York.) [2]

Wealthy individuals and financial executives in the inner group

One expects the wealthy to be overrepresented among the inner group. Though information is unavailable on the directors' and executives' personal assets, income data can be used to estimate their wealth. Of the general public aged 55 to 64 with incomes of more than $100,000 in 1962, 91 percent had personal assets valued at more than $500,000 (Projector and Weiss, 1966). Moreover, those with incomes in this range tended to derive the majority of it from corporate investments rather than salary. In 1966, for instance, 67 percent of the income of those earning over $100,000 came, on the average, from stock dividends and capital gains (Ackerman et al., 1972).

The respondents in the Hartnett study were asked to report their total annual family income from all sources before taxes. The percentage of the seven groups that received more than $100,000 is shown in Table 1. The fraction varied from 14 percent of the executives and 28 percent of the single directors to 57 percent of the triple-directors and 76 percent of the triple-director executives. Using the previous figures to estimate wealth from income, it can be inferred that approximately 12 percent of the executives and 25 percent of the single-directors held at least $500,000 in assets. By contrast, 52 and 60 percent of the central members of the inner group—triple-directors and triple-director executives—were likely to control personal assets in excess of half a million dollars.

The inferred relationship between wealth and inner group centrality is corroborated by observed patterns in the trustees' personal contributions to their college. They were asked to "indicate . . . the approximate amount of money [they] contributed to the college during the past five years," including corporate, foundation, and other money they directly controlled. A close association between inner group centrality and college contributions is apparent, as shown in Table 1. Among executives, 8 percent contributed over $30,000, and 31 percent of the single-director executives gave this amount. By contrast, 41 percent of the triple-directors and 58 percent of the triple-director executives were responsible for gifts exceeding $30,000. One in 3 of the triple-director executives personally contributed over $100,000, a level matched by only 1 in 50 of the executives.

It is possible that wealth is a consequence rather than a determinant of membership in the inner group. Executive stock options, bonuses, and high salaries facilitate the accumulation of personal wealth (Larner, 1970: 33–39; Fox, 1972). However, directorships provide little remuneration (Bacon, 1967: 28–79), and if wealth were largely a result of inner group membership, there should be little association between income and the number of directorships among the non-executives and executives taken separately. Yet it has been found that the fraction of non-executives with incomes in excess of $100,000 ranges from 28 percent of the single-directors to 57 percent of the triple-directors, and among the executives the

TABLE 1

Percentage of executives and directors with annual family incomes over $100,000 and college contributions over $30,000.

| Number of directorships | Incomes over $100,000 | | | | Contributions over $30,000 | | | |
| | Non-executive | | Executive | | Non-executive | | Executive | |
	Percent	(N) *	Percent	(N)	Percent	(N)	Percent	(N)
None	—	—	13.6	(263)	—	—	7.9	(253)
One	27.6	(291)	41.5	(199)	21.4	(285)	29.4	(196)
Two	37.2	(144)	61.3	(107)	20.1	(139)	35.2	(105)
Three+	57.1	(125)	76.2	(151)	40.8	(120)	57.6	(144)

* Number of cases on which percentage is based.

range is from 14 percent of those with no directorships to 76 percent of those with three or more directorships. A similar pattern is evident for the level of college contributions.

Another possibility is that the relation between wealth and inner group centrality is an artifact of a positive association between age and each of these factors. Top executive and multiple-directorship appointments tend to be acquired late in the business career; wealth is also accumulated over a lifetime. Age does show a substantial relationship with inner group centrality, with 25 percent of the executives but 55 percent of the triple-director executives in the survey reporting an age of 60 or over. However, income demonstrates only a modest relationship with age ($r = .106$). As a result, the multiple correlation of income with service as an executive and the number of directorships is only reduced by 3 percent when age is introduced as a control variable (in the form of a multiple-partial correlation coefficient).[3] Thus, it appears that high income and, by inference, wealth, is an important independent determinant of inner group membership. Whether membership is contingent on large individual holdings or on kinship ties with extended families that have large holdings remains to be established. It is likely that at least a fraction of the association is a matter of proper kinship rather than personal wealth alone.

Financiers should be over-represented among inner group members. The survey respondents were asked to classify their primary occupation in 1 of 30 categories, including manufacturing executive, merchandising executive, and an executive of a banking, investment, or insurance firm. While neither manufacturing nor merchandising employment showed a systematic relation with the number of corporate directorships held, employment in the financial sector did demonstrate such a pattern. Seventeen percent served as executives in the banking and insurance industries; for those holding no, one, two, and three or more corporate directorships, the percentages of financial executives are 9.8, 15.6, 18.3, and 25.2, respectively.

Inner group social cohesion

The inner group should exhibit greater social integration than the remainder of the capitalist class. Cohesion can be indirectly indexed by membership in exclusive social clubs in the nation's major cities. These clubs—familiar names include Links (New York), Pacific Union (San Francisco), and Somerset (Boston)—provide a convenient, relaxed, and private setting where businessmen establish and maintain informal acquaintance (Mills, 1956: 57–63; Baltzell, 1964: 362–374; Domhoff, 1974). Moreover, since affiliation with several clubs in different cities is common, members have an informal national network. Thus, club rosters disproportionately drawn from inner group ranks would indicate that a national social cohesion is more likely to be present within this group than among other class members.

The absence of club information or any data related to cohesion in the Hartnett survey required a special sample of college trustees. Of the 329 sampled trustees, approximately half (157) were either directors or executives of large corporations.[4] The small scale of the sample dictated combination of the single- and double-directors in the analysis. The relationship in this special sample between inner group centrality and membership in at least 1 of the nation's 40 major exclusive social clubs is shown in Table 2.[5] Affiliation with one or more of the clubs is held by 16 percent of the executives but by 50 percent of the triple-directors and 57 percent of the triple-directors executives. It is apparent that inner group members are heavily involved in the cohesion producing institution of the exclusive social club.[6]

TABLE 2
Percentage of executives and directors with
membership in an exclusive social club,
special trustee sample

Number of directorships	Non-executive		Executive	
	Percent	(N) *	Percent	(N)
None	—	—	16.0	(50)
One or two	26.5	(34)	25.0	(20)
Three or more ..	50.0	(26)	57.1	(28)

Analysis of variance†
Interact. F (1,153) = 1.05, n.s.
Director. F (2, 153) = 7.12, p < .001
Executive F (1,153) = 2.47, n.s.

* Number of cases on which the percentage is based.
† The analysis of variance criterion variable is the
number of exclusive social clubs.

Inner group political consciousness

The political consciousness of the inner
group is expected to be more uniform and
concerned with the long-range general interests of United States business. This difference should be especially apparent in
attitudes toward governmental social and
economic reforms. The increased regulation, taxes, and labor costs associated with
reform programs ensure the opposition of
business. However, reforms often yield
long-range benefits in the form of greater
economic and political stability, and the
inner group can be expected to place
greater emphasis on the latter than do
other businessmen. Opposition to government reform efforts is assessed here through
a combination of responses to several survey questions. One question asked the
businessman to classify his "political ideology or leaning" as "conservative, moderate, or liberal." Another question asked
of the "extent to which the political or
social views" of a set of prominent Americans, such as Richard Nixon, Nelson
Rockefeller, and William Fulbright, were
similar to those of the respondent. A
principal components factor analysis and
varimax rotation yielded a dominant first
factor related to general political persuasion. A low score on this factor meant the
businessmen identified his political ideology as conservative and found the views

of Barry Goldwater, Ronald Reagan, and
Richard Nixon as very similar to his own.
An unweighted sum of four major items
(political ideology, Goldwater, Reagan,
Nixon) is used to form a *political perspec-
tive* scale.[7]

Views of the administration of higher
education are also assessed. It is anticipated
that the inner group tends to stress the
college's autonomy more than do other
businessmen. Overt business interference
in the affairs of higher education can orient
the system to the immediate interests of
certain business firms, but it also threatens
to reduce the potential of higher education
for serving the general research and training needs of industry. Moreover, direct
corporate intervention, whatever the immediate gains, threatens higher education's
legitimacy, making it even more difficult
for the college system to meet the general
needs of advanced capitalism (see Poulantzas, 1969). The inner group, therefore,
is likely to oppose the imposition of repressive political policies and business
principles on higher education.

The respondents were asked their degree of agreement with 29 Likert-type statements on a range of educational policies.
A principal components factor analysis
and varimax rotation revealed a major
factor related to administrative treatment
of political and intellectual freedom and
dissidence on campus. A low score on the
factor implies the businessman felt the
administration should control the student
newspaper, screen campus speakers, expel
or suspend student protestors, discipline
students involved in off-campus civil disobedience, maintain a faculty loyalty oath,
and impose limits on the right of faculty
to express their opinions. An unweighted
sum of six items with the highest loadings
is used to form a *political tolerance* scale.[8]
The respondents' position on the use of
business principles in the administration
of a college is assessed through their level
of agreement with the assertion that "run-

ning a college is basically like running a business" and the importance they attach to "experience in high-level business management" in the selection of a new college president. The average response to these two items constitutes a scale labeled *business principles in education*.[9]

The three scales range in value from 1 to 5, with 1 representing the most conservative and 5 the most liberal political outlook. The means and standard deviations for the scales for each of the seven groups of businessmen are shown in Table 3. It is apparent that expectations of a more cohesive and more liberal consciousness within the inner group is generally disconfirmed by the evidence. The seven groups of businessmen exhibit nearly identical views on political issues in higher education. The group means demonstrate a range of only .23 in the case of political tolerance and .25 in the case of business principles in education (F-tests for equality of group means are all non-significant).

Similarly, the group dispersions are nearly identical (F-tests for homogeneity of group variances are non-significant).

Though the pattern is not entirely consistent, there is a moderate tendency for inner group centrality to be associated with a more conservative political ideology. The political perspective mean is 2.84 for single directors and 2.68 for executives, but it drops to 2.34 for triple-director executives. Much of this trend may be attributed to the fact that executives are substantially more conservative than non-executives (F-test significant at the .001 level). The smallest attitude dispersion is noted in the triple-director executive group, but there is little apparent relationship between group dispersion and inner group centrality (the test for variance equality is significant at the .04 level).

Contrary to the hypotheses on inner group consciousness, it is neither more uniform nor more liberal than that of other class members. Indeed, the core

TABLE 3
Means and standard deviations of executives and directors on three political ideology scales*

	Political perspective				Political tolerance				Business principles in education			
	Mean		Standard deviation		Mean		Standard deviation		Mean		Standard deviation	
Number of directorships	Non-executive	Executive	Non-executive	Executive	Non-executive	Executive	Non-executive	Executive	Non-executive	Executive	Non-executive	Executive
Three+ ..	2.79	2.34	1.00	.86	2.76	2.58	.72	.71	3.22	3.03	.87	.91
None	—	2.68	—	1.04	—	2.73	—	.71	—	2.97	—	.92
One	2.84	2.67	1.09	1.05	2.71	2.73	.79	.74	3.14	3.13	.96	.88
Two	2.68	2.63	1.13	1.05	2.64	2.81	.79	.82	3.12	3.16	.88	.92

Analysis of Variance

Homogeneity of variances, p = .04†
Interact. F (2,1271) = 2.67, n-s.
Director. F (3,1271) = 2.89, p = .03
Executive F (1,1271) = 11.06, p < .001

Homogeneity of variances, n.s.
Interact. F (2,1284) = 3.43, p = .03
Director. F (3,1284) = 0.52, n.s.
Executive F (1,1284) = 0.02, n.s.

Homogeneity of variances, n.s.
Interact. F (2,1281) = 1.24, n.s.
Director. F (3,1281) = 1.25, n.s.
Executive F (1,1281) = 0.62, n.s.

* The numer of cases are as follows: executives, 259–265; single-directors, 279–294; single-director executives, 194–200; double-directors, 139–145; double-director executives, 104–111; triple-directors, 119–126; triple-director executives, 145–150.
† Bartlett's test for homogeneity of variances.

members of the inner group—the triple-director executives—hold a more conservative general ideology than peripheral members.

Inner group influence

By virtue of their inter-organizational connections, inner group members are expected to exert greater influence on American society than are other class members. The disproportionate influence should be manifest in the group's more frequent membership on public and private decision-making bodies aside from their own corporations, its greater voice in the councils on which its members serve, and its greater capacity to mobilize resources for favored projects.

I assess the frequency of membership in public and private decision-making bodies in two ways. First, I judge participation rate by the businessmen's service on the governing bodies of organizations other than corporations and colleges, including such community organizations as a board of education, a church, or a service agency. Second, I measure frequency by the businessmen's participation in the affairs of nine major national business associations,

including the Business Council, the Committee for Economic Development, and the Council on Foreign Relations.[10] Data related to the first indicator are available in the Hartnett survey, but the absence of information related to the second index required reliance on the previously described special trustee sample.

The proportion of the corporate directors and executives serving on community organization governing boards and belonging to major national business associations is shown in Table 4. The fraction of trustees sitting on at least five community boards ranges from 32 percent of the executives and 47 percent of the single-directors to 58 percent of the triple-directors and 62 percent of the triple-director executives. Similarly, 12 percent of the executives but 29 percent of the triple-director executives are affiliated with one or more of the business associations. It is clear that the inner group is substantially over-represented on a variety of influential councils.

Not only should inner group members sit more often on decision-making bodies, but they also should play a more dominant role than other businessmen on such councils. Inner group members' disproportion-

---

TABLE 4
Percentage of executives and directors serving on community organization boards and belonging to major business associations

Number of directorships	Serving on five or more community organization boards*				Belonging to one or more business associations†			
	Non-executive		Executive		Non-executive		Executive	
	Percent	(N)‡	Percent	(N)	Percent	(N)	Percent	(N)
None	—	—	32.3	(263)	—	—	12.0	(50)
One	47.3	(292)	41.7	(199)	5.9	(34)	30.0	(20)
Two	53.1	(145)	47.8	(110)	5.9	(34)	30.0	(20)
Three+	58.4	(125)	61.6	(150)	15.4	(26)	28.6	(28)

Analysis of Variance §

Interact. F $(2,1273) = 2.19$, n.s. Interact. R $(1,153) = 0.00$, n.s.
Director. F $(3,1273) = 10.38$, p $< .001$ Director. F $(2,153) = 3.54$, p $= .03$
Executive F $(1,1273) = 1.33$, n.s. Executive F $(1,153) = 9.04$, p $= .003$

* Based on the Harnett trustee survey.
† Based on the special trustee sample.
‡ Number of cases on which the percentage is based.
§ The analysis of variance criterion variables are the number of community boards (five or more coded as five) and the number of business associations.

ate access to the potential support of several major corporations should give them high status; their voices should have a correspondingly greater weight in deliberations. This expectation can be examined in the case of decision-making in college governing boards. The respondents, all of whom are college trustees, reported their degree of involvement in 17 policy issues frequently brought before boards of trustees. These include faculty appointments, wage levels, investments, the campus budget and master plan, instructional methods, admissions policies, and student housing regulations. The businessmen indicated whether they decided, reviewed and advised, approved and confirmed, or were uninvolved in each area. An overall measure of *governing board influence* consists of the unweighted mean of an individual's influence on the 17 issues (the scale ranges from 1, high influence, to 4, low influence). The average influence of the seven groups is shown in Table 5. Though triple-director executives do report more influence than either single-directors or executives, the difference is very modest (and fails to reach the .05 level of statistical significance). Separate analysis of trustee influence on each of the 17 policy

areas reveals that sharpest differences appear in the area of financial matters, particularly investment decisions. Multiple-director executives exercise substantially more voice on investment of the institution's endowment than do other businessmen. (F-tests are significant at the .05 and .001 levels.)

The weakness of the relationship between inner group centrality and level of governing board influence might be related to differences in the time the trustees have available for board affairs. The degree of influence is likely to vary with the amount of time contributed to board activities, and it is possible that inner group members have competing commitments. This can be examined by introducing a measure of the time the businessmen spend each year on board-related activities.[11] As expected, governing board influence is related to the time measure ($r = .240$). However, time is not inversely related to inner group centrality, with inner group members reporting a slightly greater involvement than non-members.[12] It seems that inner group members are no less active and exercise only slightly more influence on governing board affairs than other businessmen. Inner group power appears to be a matter

TABLE 5

College governing board influence and fund raising success of executives and directors

Number of directorships	Mean influence on 17 college board decisions				Percentage raising $100,000+ for college during five years			
	Non-executive		Executive		Non-executive		Executive	
	Percent	(N) *	Percent	(N)	Percent	(N)	Percent	(N)
None	—	—	2.73	(265)	—	—	10.7	(224)
One	2.65	(294)	2.78	(200)	23.8	(231)	22.4	(161)
Two	2.69	(145)	2.64	(111)	35.1	(114)	45.5	(88)
Three+	2.62	(126)	2.56	(151)	51.0	(104)	55.1	(127)

Analysis of Variance†

Interact. F $(2,1285) = 2.31$, n.s.   Interact. F $(2,1041) = 0.49$, n.s.
Director. F $(3,1285) = 2.09$, n.s.   Director. F $(3,1041) = 38.87$, p < .001
Executive F $(1,1285) = 1.15$, n.s.   Executive F $(1,1041) = 0.08$, n.s.

* Number of cases on which the mean or percentage is based.
† The criterion variable in the fund raising analysis of variance is the dollar amount raised in seven steps (under $1,000; $1,000 to $9,999; $10,000 to $29,999; $30,000 to $99,999; $100,000 to $499,999; $500,000 to $999,999; $1,000,000 and over).

of over-representation on important decision-making bodies, rather than a decisive voice of its members within them.

It is also expected that inner group members have a greater capacity to mobilize resources for selected projects than do other businessmen. Obtaining financial support for their college can be seen as one such project, and the ability to generate backing is tapped through a question of the amount of money the trustee raised for his school during the preceding five years. The amount included "contributions generated by his efforts through direct solicitation or contacts," but it excluded funds personally contributed by the trustee. The percentage of the groups mobilizing over $100,000 for their college is shown in Table 5, and it is evident that inner group centrality is strongly related to resource mobilization. Eleven percent of the executives and 24 percent of the single-directors generated over $100,000, while this amount was raised by 51 percent of the triple-directors and 55 percent of the triple-director executives.

Discussion

It has been argued that strategies by the wealthy to control their business investments and by corporations to control their economic environments would both lead to interlocking ties among the large corporations. A substantial number of people do hold two or more of the top executive and directorship positions in large firms, and it was hypothesized that this inner group would be disproportionately drawn from the ranks of the wealthy and from among financial executives. Both patterns are observed.

I also reasoned that the inter-corporate foundation of the inner group could give it the role of informally but effectively identifying and promoting general business interests. Compared to the remainder of the capitalist class, the inner group was ex-

pected to have a high level of social cohesion, class consciousness, and influence on public and private affairs. Findings support the social cohesion hypothesis, with cohesion indexed by involvement in the acquaintanceship networks structured around exclusive social clubs. The influence hypothesis was also upheld. Inner group members were over-represented on the governing boards of community organizations and in the ranks of the major national business associations. They also demonstrated an exceptional capacity to mobilize financial resources, at least as measured by the private funds they generated for their college. However, within college boards and perhaps other governing bodies as well, individual inner group members do not appear to have a decisively greater impact than other businessmen.

The political consciousness hypothesis is disproven. The political ideology and views of college administration of the inner group were no more homogeneous than the attitudes of the remainder of the class. Nor were inner group perspectives more progressive and oriented toward general class interests than the perspectives of other businessmen. Several interpretations of these negative findings are possible.

First, it may be that inner group members do hold more class conscious and more homogeneous views on critical issues than do non-members, but the political measures available in this study were too unrefined to capture the differences. Second, inner group members may not have developed a commitment to general class interests. Third, there is the possibility that class consciousness is emergent in the inner group, but cleavages, such as those between industrial sectors, are more powerful determinants of business ideology at present and tend to undermine class consciousness (see, for instance, Christ, 1970; Seider, 1974; Russett and Hanson, 1975: 100–144).

The first possibility, emphasizing measurement shortcomings, is plausible and can be resolved only through further study. However, on the assumption that measurement error cannot fully explain the null results, the second or third interpretation may be correct, either implying that the inner group does not help integrate and express capitalist class interests. Without at least some commitment to generalized class interests, it is improbable that the inner group could promote policies to maximize long-range class concerns. This would leave the function of determining general business interests to an alternative mechanism or to the state. It is possible, of course, that the capitalist class is served well by neither its own institutions nor the government and is simply without effective leadership.

Though it appears unlikely that the inner group plays a forceful role in articulating general class interests, the likelihood is great that it assumes a more modest, integrating role in bridging a variety of splits in the business world. Interlocking directorships, for instance, break the nation's major corporations into a number of cliques, but at the same time the interlocking directors also link the cliques into a single national system (Schwartz et al., 1975; Sonquist and Koenig, 1975). Among the largest 1,131 corporations in 1962, for instance, 87 are directly or indirectly linked through the interlocking directorate (Schwartz et al., 1975: 53). Thus, the cohesion, influence, and extensiveness of the inner group enable it to help unit industrial and financial firms, monopoly and competitive corporations, old northeastern companies and new southwestern industries, and owner-controlled and manager-controlled firms. Although the inner group is apparently not the repository of capitalist class consciousness, it may help sustain what Giddens (1975: 111) calls "class awareness," a sense of common identity and community without explicit definition of class interests and opposing classes. Its role is perhaps that of an informal mechanism within the business community for resolving disputes, mobilizing resources for joint ventures, and disciplining corporate practices that pose a direct threat to other firms. It may also play an important role in representing immediate business concerns to other institutions, such as education, community organizations, and, of course, the government. It is likely that businessmen serving in high federal government posts are over-recruited from the inner group.[13]

Though the evidence is not definitive, it can be tentatively concluded that the capitalist class is differentiated along an axis of inner group centrality. Serving in several positions at the top of the major corporations, frequently holding large personal fortunes, and disproportionately employed in the financial sector, inner group members tend to form a relatively cohesive national network with considerable involvement in public and private affairs. The inner group, however, does not appear to have assumed a class organizing function. This problem remains to be solved by the state or some other institution.

NOTES

1. The nation's 2,231 higher education institutions in 1966–67 were divided into six levels, and a disproportionate sample was drawn from each: Ph.D. granting universities (100 percent sample), private non-doctorate universities (10 percent), public colleges (60 percent), private colleges (30 percent), public junior colleges (20 percent), and private junior colleges (20 percent). The 654 sampled institutions were asked to provide a roster of their governing board, and a list of 10,036 trustees was compiled from the 82 percent of the schools that cooperated. In 1968 a questionnaire was sent to all of these trustees, and a usable response rate of 52.5 percent was obtained (the rate ranged from 42 to 56 percent).

2. Biographical information is drawn from the 1974–75 edition of *Who's Who in America*.

3. Age is a five category variable (39 or under, 40 to 49, 50 to 59, 60 to 69, 70 and over). The college contribution multiple-partial correlation with age as the control variable is also approximately identical to the corresponding multiple correlation coefficient.

4. A stratified random sample of 39 private colleges and universities was drawn from the nation's 590 private non-sectarian schools in 1970, and information was sought on a random sample of ten trustees from each institution. Using seven standard biographical directories, adequate data were obtained on 84 percent (329) of the sampled trustees. Sampling details are reported in Useem, Hoops, and Moore, 1976.

5. The exclusive social clubs are the set developed by Domhoff (1970: 23–24).

6. Other studies have yielded similar results. In community studies, for instance, the local inner group is also a friendship group. Those holding top positions in several major organizations in the community exhibit greater social cohesion—as indexed by friendship—than do those who occupy only a single elite position (Perrucci and Pilisuk, 1970; Koch and Labovitz, 1976). Soref (1976) studied the directors of 30 large industrial firms and found that multiple directorships were disproportionately held by members of the "upper class," defined as individuals listed in the Social Register, graduates of exclusive preparatory schools, or members of 1 of the 40 exclusive social clubs. Similarly, comparing samples of single-directors of four or more large corporations, Koenig, Gogel, and Sonquist (1976) revealed a sharply contrasting club affiliation pattern—17 percent of the single-directors but 72 percent of the multiple directors belonged to an exclusive club.

7. The factor loadings for the political ideology, Goldwater, Reagan, and Nixon items are .574, .841, .793, and .670, respectively.

8. The six items and their factor loadings are as follows: "Faculty members should have the right to express their opinions about any issue they wish in various channels of college communication, including the classroom, student newspaper, etc., without fear of reprisal" (.463); "The administration should exercise control over the contents of the student newspaper" (.670); "All campus speakers should be subject to some official screening process" (.725); "Students who actively disrupt the functioning of a college by demonstrating, sitting-in, or otherwise refusing to obey the rules should be expelled or suspended" (.446); "Students involved in civil disobedience off the campus should be subject to discipline by the college as well as by the local authorities" (.498); "The requirement that a professor sign a loyalty oath is reasonable" (.492).

9. The inter-item correlation is .296.

10. The nine business associations are drawn from a roster developed by Domhoff (1975: 178). The list includes the organizations generally considered to be the primary national associations representing large business interests (Monsen and Cannon, 1965: 24–63; Domhoff, 1970: 111–250; Dye, 1976: 110–116). The nine organizations are the Advertising Council, Business Council, Committee for Economic Development, National Industrial Conference Board, Council on Foreign Relations, Foundation for American Agriculture, National Association of Manufacturers, National Chamber of Commerce, and the National Planning Association.

11. The respondents were asked to indicate the hours per year they spent on each of eight board-related activities (for example, attending board meetings, participating in committee work, soliciting contributions. A time measure consists of the average number of hours devoted to the eight areas.

12. The correlation of the time measure with service as an executive is .032 and with number of directorships is .071.

13. Studies of business recruitment to top government positions have not distinguished between the inner group and the remainder of the class but the studies do generally indicate that the businessmen are disproportionately drawn from the largest corporations and frequently are members of the exclusive social clubs, both suggesting some likelihood of inner group membership (Mills, 1956; Miliband, 1969; Kolko, 1969; Domhoff, 1970; Mintz, 1975; Freitag, 1975; Dye, 1976).

REFERENCES

Ackerman, Frank, Howard Birnbaum, James Wetzler, and Andrew Zimbalist
1972 "The extent of income inequality in the United States." pp. 207–18 in Richard C. Edwards, Michael Reich, and Thomas E. Weisskopf (eds.), The Capitalist System. Englewood Cliffs, N.J.: Prentice-Hall.

Allen, Michael P.
1974 "The structure of interorganizational elite cooptation: interlocking corporate directorates." American Sociological Review 39:393–406.

Bacon, Jeremy
1967 Corporation Directorship Practices. New York: National Industrial Conference Board.

Baltzell, E. Digby
1964 The Protestant Establishment: Aristocracy and Caste in America. New York: Random House.

Baran, Paul, and Paul Sweezy
1966 Monopoly Capital: An Essay on the American Economic and Social Order. New York: Monthly Review Press.

Berle, Adolph, Jr., and Gardiner C. Means
1932 The Modern Corporation and Private Property. New York: Harcourt, Brace & World (republished in 1967).

Burch, Philip H., Jr.
1972 The Managerial Revolution Reassessed. Lexington, Mass.: Heath.

Christ, Thomas
1970 "A thematic analysis of the American business creed." Social Forces 4:239–45.

Domhoff, G. William
1970 The Higher Circles: The Governing Class in America. New York: Random House.
1974 The Bohemian Grove and Other Retreats: A Study of Ruling-Class Cohesiveness. New York: Harper & Row.
1975 "Social clubs, policy-planning groups, and corporations: a network study of ruling-class cohesiveness." Insurgent Sociologist 5:173–84.

Dooley, Peter C.
1969 "The interlocking directorate." American Economic Review 59:314–23.

Dye, Thomas R.
1976 Who's Running America? Institutional Leadership in the United States. Englewood Cliffs, N.J.: Prentice-Hall.

Fitch, Robert, and Mary Oppenheimer
1970a "Who rules the corporations? Part 1." Socialist Revolution 1 (July–August): 73–107.
1970b "Who rules the corporations? Part 2." Socialist Revolution 1 (September–October):61–114.
1970c "Who rules the corporations? Part 3." Socialist Revolution 1 (November–December):33–94.

Fox, Harland
1972 Top Executive Compensation. New York: National Industrial Conference Board.

Freitag, Peter J.
1975 "The cabinet and big business: a study of interlocks." Social Problems 23:137–52.

Giddens, Anthony
1975 The Class Structure of the Advanced Societies. New York: Harper & Row.

Gordon, Robert A.
1966 Business Leadership in the Large Corporation. Berkeley: University of California Press (originally published in 1945).

Harnett, Rodney T
1969 College and University Trustees: Their Backgrounds, Roles, and Educational Attitudes. Princeton University Press.

Koch, A., and S. Labovitz
1976 "Interorganizational power in a Canadian community: a replication." Sociological Quarterly 17:3–15.

Koenig, Thomas, Robert Gogel, and John Sonquist
1976 "Corporate interlocking directorates as a social network." Unpublished.

Kolko, Gabriel
1963 The Triumph of Conservatism: A Reinterpretation of American History, 1900–1916. New York: Free Press.
1969 The Roots of American Foreign Policy. Boston: Beacon Press.

Larner, Robert J.
1970 Management Control and the Large Corporation. New York: Dunellen.

Lazarsfeld, Paul, and Robert K. Merton
1954 "Friendship as social process: a substantive and methodological analysis." Pp. 21–54 in Monroe Berger, Theodore Abel, and Charles H. Page (eds.), Freedom and Control in Modern Society. New York: Van Nostrand.

Mariolis, Peter
1975 "Interlocking directorates and control of corporations: the theory of bank control." Social Science Quarterly 56:425–39.

Miliband, Ralph
1969 The State in Capitalist Society. New York: Basic.

Mills, C. Wright
1956 The Power Elite. New York: Oxford.

Mintz, Beth
1975 "The President's Cabinet, 1897–1972: a contribution to the power structure debate." Insurgent Sociologist 5 (Spring): 131–48.

Monsen, R. Joseph, and Mark W. Cannon
1965 The Makers of Public Policy: American Power Group and Their Ideologies. New York: McGraw-Hill.

O'Connor, James
1973 The Fiscal Crisis of the State. New York: St. Martin's.

Offe, Claus
1973 "The abolition of market control and the problem of legitimacy (1)." Working Papers on the Kapitalistate 1:109–16.
1974 "Structural problems of the capitalist state: class rule and the selectiveness of political institutions." Pp. 31–57 in Klaus von Beyme (ed.), German Political Studies. London: Sage.

Perrucci, Robert, and Marc Pilisuk
1970 "Leaders and ruling elites: the interorganizational bases of community powers." American Sociological Review 35:1040–57.

124

Poulantzas, Nicos
 1969 "The problem of the capitalist state."
  New Left Review 58:67–78.
 1973 Political Power and Social Classes. Timothy O'Hagen, translator. London: New Left Books, and Sheed and Ward.

Projector, Dorothy S., and Gertrude S. Weiss
 1966 Survey of Financial Characteristics of Consumers. Washington, D.C.: Federal Reserve Board.

Russett, Bruce M., and Elizabeth C. Hanson
 1975 Interest and Ideology: The Foreign Policy Beliefs of American Businessmen. San Francisco: Freeman.

Schwartz, Michael, James Bearden, William Atwood, Peter Freitag, Carol Hendricks, and Beth Mintz.
 1975 "The nature and extent of bank centrality in corporate networks." Unpublished.

Seider, J. S.
 1974 "American big business ideology: a content analysis of executive speeches." American Sociological Review 39:802–15.

Sonquist, John, and Thomas Koenig
 1975 "Interlocking directorates in the top U.S. corporations: a graph theory approach." Insurgent Sociologist 5:196–229.

Soref, Michael
 1976 "Social class and a division of labor within the corporate elite: a note on class, interlocking, and executive committee membership of directors of U.S. industrial firms." Sociological Quarterly 17:360–68.

Useem, Michael, John S. Hoops, and Thomas S. Moore
 1976 "Class and corporate relations with the private college system." Insurgent Sociologist 6:27–35.

Villarejo, Don
 1962 "Stock ownership and the control of corporations: part 3." New University Thought (Winter) :47–62.

Weinstein, James
 1968 The Corporate Ideal in the Liberal State, 1900–1918. Boston: Beacon.

Zeitlin, Maurice
 1974 "Corporate ownership and control: the large corporation and the capitalist class." American Journal of Sociology 79:1073–1119.
 1976 "On class theory of the large corporation: response to Allen." American Journal of Sociology 81:894–903.

Zeitlin, Maurice, Richard Earl Ratcliff, and Lynda Ann Ewen
 1974 "The 'inner group': interlocking directorates and the internal differentiation of the capitalist class of Chile." Unpublished.

CHAPTER 4

The capitalist state

The capitalist state has emerged to manage politically the problems of a developing capitalist economy. Institutional forms within a growing state apparatus have been devised to meet the changing demands of capitalism. Between 1880 and 1920 new forms of state control were established in the United States for managing the problems brought about by the industrial stage of capitalism.[1] And since that time, as capitalism has moved to an advanced stage of development, the capitalist state has become even more important in regulating capitalist society and its problems. The economic and political structure of advanced capitalism is in the process of transformation, finally reaching the late stage of its development. Within the dialectics of this development is the emergence of social conditions—and a class consciousness—for the transformation to a socialist society.

A critical understanding of the state in capitalist society is very much in a process of formulation. Following the traditional Marxian interpretation, the state is intimately tied to civil society, especially to the class structure. The state appears to rest on the material, economic base of society: thus the Marxian characterization of the capitalist state as the managing committee of the capitalist ruling class. But the state is more than a mere instrument of the capitalist class; it is a social reality itself.[2]

The recent Marxian formulations of the state go beyond the instrumentalist notion that sees the state and its policies as direct outcomes of manipulations by the ruling class. Also expanded is the structuralist theory that describes the functions the state performs to reproduce capitalist society as a whole. In like manner, the Hegelian-Marxist perspective that emphasizes consciousness and ideology is being made more concrete, materialist, and historical.[3] The complex apparatus of the state in late capitalism is becoming evident.

The advancing capitalist state is losing much of its superstructural character. "The state is increasingly involved in accumulation, not just to protect the conditions of accumulation as earlier Marxist thinking emphasized, but to participate actively in the creation of those conditions."[4] Thus, the state itself is becoming a material force, a part of the substructure, at least a "middle structure." But more important, the state is seen dialectically as an apparatus that is developing in relation to the accumulation of capital under the late stages of advanced capitalism. The internal organization of the state is problematic, as it is being transformed in the course of the emerging contradictions of advanced capitalism. Class struggle itself, resulting from these contradictions, is transforming the state. The capitalist state is in transition.

The theoretical problem at this time is that of *linking* the class structure of advanced capitalism to the capitalist state. The starting point is the class character of the state. That is, how is the capitalist state really a *capitalist* state and not merely a state in capitalist society? Several "selective mechanisms" within the state apparatus either exclude anticapitalist interests from entering into state policy or assure the inclusion of capitalist interests in state policy. These structural features "put the State in a position to formulate and express class-interests more appropriately and circumspectly than can be done by representatives of the class—in the form of isolated units of capital."[5] The state thereby provides the necessary conditions for the continued accumulation of capital. Moreover, in periods of political crisis, as the selective mechanisms begin to break down, the state is forced to rely more and more on *repression* in order to maintain its class character. In acting negatively, the state attempts to exclude interests and forces that oppose or threaten the capitalist system. Class structure is thus translated into political power in the structure and operation of the capitalist state.

The state in advanced capitalism, therefore, is not simply an instrument for promoting the interests of a ruling class. Instead, the state secures the whole order of capitalism.

> The state does not patronize certain interests, and is not allied with certain classes. Rather, what the state protects and sanctions is a set of *rules* and *social relationships* which are presupposed by the class rule of the capitalist class. The state does not defend the interests of one class, but the common interests of all members of a *capitalist class society.*[6]

Thus, relating to the dynamics of class struggle is a new technocratic (and authoritarian) concept of politics, "a concept whose intention is no longer the seeing through of correct and just vital reforms, but the conservation of social relations which claim mere functionality as their justification."[7] There is the rise of a technocratic rationality in the late stage of capitalist development. It is embodied in the capitalist state and in its policies and practices of social control.

Class struggle, then, is being elevated and transposed into political struggle. The capitalist state increasingly relies on political repression in the class struggle. For the working class, class struggle becomes a political struggle. Marx argued that the conditions of developing capitalism would force the proletariat to move its struggle outside the factory and toward the state. Class struggle may continue to be the motive force of history, but that force is increasingly political and is more and more dominated by the dynamics of the capitalist state.

What is emerging is a new strategy of capitalist state policy. The control function of the state is being revised and expanded. Embodied in this development, however, is a dialectic between increased control and resistance to that control. This occurs particularly in the realm where control is most explicitly practiced, in the service organizations of advanced capitalism and in the management of the surplus population of the working class.[8] The expanded function of the state is a source of crisis in itself. The attempt by the state to control the problems generated by late capitalism is the basis of increased social conflict and political struggle.

The advanced stage of capitalist development signifies—at the same time—the end of a social and moral trend that has been accelerating since the beginning of capitalism: the trend toward religious skepticism and indifference. Advanced capitalist society has become the most secular society that the history of this world has known. Advanced capitalism is also advanced secularism. That developing capitalism and developing secularity have gone hand in hand is due to the internal demands of capitalism. An economy of exploitation requires an areligious ethic or spirit that legitimizes the further development of the economy as well as its present practices.

Nonetheless, the sacred religious spirit, however subterranean it may be, has continued in spite of the development of capitalism. And the rise of new theologies and religious movements attests to the persistence of the human need for the sacred. That the sacred must become a part of the world again is the message of a religious socialism. A socialism without the sacred would become a system as materialist and alienating as that of capitalism. What is emerging in the transition to socialism is a new religious concern, a concern which not only repudiates the essential secularity of capitalism but one that makes socialism whole by an integration of the sacred.

NOTES

1. Gabriel Kolko, *Main Currents in Modern American History* (New York: Harper & Row, 1976), pp. 1–33. On the nature of the state under advanced capitalism, see James O'Connor, *The Fiscal Crisis of the State* (New York: St. Martin's Press, 1973).

2. See Amy Beth Bridges, "Nicos Poulantzas and the Marxist Theory of the State," *Politics and Society*, 4 (Winter 1974), pp. 161–190.

3. On these traditions, see David A. Gold, Clarence Y. H. Lo, and Erik Olin Wright, "Recent Developments in Marxist Theories of the Capitalist State," *Monthly Review*, 27 (October 1975), pp. 29–43.

4. David A. Gold, Clarence Y. H. Lo, and Erik Olin Wright, "Recent Developments in Marxist Theories of the Capitalist State: Part 2," *Monthly Review*, 27 (November 1975), p. 42.

5. Claus Offe, "Class Rule and the Political System: On the Selectiveness of Political Institutions," mimeographed, 1973, p. 8. (A translation of chap. 3 of *Strukturprobleme des kapitalistischen Staates* [Frankfurt: Suhrkamp, 1972]).

6. Claus Offe and Volker Ronge, "Theses on the Theory of the State," *New German Critique*, no. 6 (Fall 1975), p. 139. Also Fred Block, "The Ruling Class Does Not Rule: Notes on the Marxist Theory of the State," *Socialist Revolution*, 7 (May–June 1977), pp. 6–28.

7. Claus Offe, "Advanced Capitalism and the Welfare State," *Politics and Society*, 2 (Summer 1972), pp. 479–488; and Larry Hirschhorn, "The Political Economy of Social Service Rationalization: A Development View," *Contemporary Crises*, 2 (January 1978), pp. 63–81.

8. Claus Offe and Volker Ronge, "Theses on the Theory of the State," pp. 145–147.

The ruling class does not rule[*]

FRED BLOCK

The Marxist theory of the state remains a muddle despite the recent revival of interest in the subject.[1] Substantial progress has been made in formulating a critique of orthodox Marxist formulations that reduce the state to a mere reflection of economic interests. However, the outlines of an adequate alternative Marxist theory are not yet clear. This is most dramatically indicated by the continued popularity in Marxist circles of explanations of state policies or of conflicts within the state that are remarkably similar to orthodox formulations in their tendency to see the state as a reflection of the interests of certain groups in the capitalist class. Many Marxists, for example, were drawn to interpretations of Watergate that saw it as a conflict between two different wings of the capitalist class.[2] This gap between theory and the explanation of actual historical events demonstrates that the critique of orthodox Marxist formulations has not been carried far enough. These earlier formulations—even when they have been carefully criticized and dismissed—sneak back into many current analyses because they remain embedded in the basic concepts of Marxist analysis.

This essay proposes two elements of an alternative Marxist theory of the state. The first element is a different way of conceptualizing the ruling class and its relationship to the state. This reconceptualization makes possible the second element—the elaboration of a structural framework which specifies the concrete mechanisms that make the state a capitalist state, whereas other structural theories have tended to analyze structures in an abstract and mystifying way.[3]

Although these two elements do not provide a complete Marxist theory of the state, they do provide a new way of thinking about the sources of rationality within capitalism. Contemporary Marxists have been forced to acknowledge that despite its fundamental irrationality, capitalism in the developed world has shown a remarkable capacity to rationalize itself in response to the twin dangers of economic crisis and radical working-class movements.[†] Since the present historical period again poses for the left the threat of successful capitalist rationalization, the understanding of the sources of capitalism's capacity for self-reform is of the utmost political importance. The traditional Marxist explanation of capitalist rationality is to root it in the consciousness of some sector of the ruling class. In this light, capitalist reform reflects the conscious will and understanding of some sector of the capitalist class that has grasped the magnitude of the problem and proposes a set of solutions. The alternative framework being proposed here suggests that the capacity of capitalism to rationalize itself is the outcome of a conflict among three sets of agents—the capitalist class, the

---

[*] From *Socialist Review*, 7 (May–June 1977), pp. 6–28.

[†] By "rationalization" and "capitalist reform," I am referring primarily to the use of the state in new ways to overcome economic contradictions and to facilitate the integration of the working class. Rationalization must be distinguished from strategies of forcing the working class to bear the costs of economic contradictions through dramatic reductions in living standards combined with severe political repression.

managers of the state apparatus, and the working class.‡ Rationalization occurs "behind the backs" of each set of actors so that rationality cannot be seen as a function of the consciousness of one particular group.

This argument and its implications will be traced out through a number of steps. First, I intend to show that critiques of orthodox Marxist theory of the state are flawed by their acceptance of the idea of a class-conscious ruling class. Second, I argue that there is a basis in Marx's writing for rejecting the idea of a class-conscious ruling class. Third, I develop a structural argument that shows that even in the absence of ruling-class consciousness, the state managers are strongly discouraged from pursuing anti-capitalist policies. Fourth, I return to the issue of capitalist rationality and describe how it grows out of the structured relationship among capitalists, workers, and state managers. Finally, I briefly analyze the implications of this argument for capitalism's current difficulties in the United States.

The critique of instrumentalism

The major development in the Marxist theory of the state in recent years has been the formulation of a critique of instrumentalism. A number of writers have characterized the orthodox Marxist view of the state as instrumentalism because it views the state as a simple tool or instrument of ruling-class purposes. First, it neglects the ideological role of the state. The state plays a critical role in maintaining the legitimacy of the social order, and this requires that the state appear to be neutral in the class struggle. In short, even if the state is an instrument of ruling-class purpose, the fact that it must appear otherwise indicates the need for a more complex framework for analyzing state policies. Second, instrumentalism fails to recognize that to act in the general interest of capital, the state must be able to take actions against the particular interests of capitalists. Price controls or restrictions on the export of capital, for example, might be in the general interest of capital in a particular period, even if they temporarily reduced the profits of most capitalists. To carry through such policies, the state must have more autonomy from direct capitalist control than the instrumentalist view would allow.

The critics of instrumentalism propose the idea of the relative autonomy of the state as an alternative framework. In order to serve the general interests of capital, the state must have some autonomy from direct ruling-class control. Since the concept of the absolute autonomy of the state would be un-Marxist and false, the autonomy is clearly relative. However, the difficulty is in specifying the nature, limits, and determinants of that relative autonomy. Some writers have attempted to argue that the degree of autonomy varies historically, and that "late capitalism" is characterized by the "autonomization of the state apparatus." But these arguments have an ad hoc quality, and they share an analytic problem derived from the phrase "relative autonomy from ruling-class control."

The basic problem in formulations of "relative autonomy" is the conceptualization of the ruling class. Relative autonomy theories assume that the ruling class will

‡ Each of these categories requires some definition "Capitalist class" or "ruling class" is used to refer to the individuals and families that own or control a certain quantity of capital. The cut-off point would vary by country or period, and it would necessarily be somewhat arbitrary, but the point is to distinguish between small businesses and large capitalist firms. The "managers of the state apparatus" include the leading figures of both the legislative and executive branches. This includes the highest-ranking civil servants, as well as appointed and elected politicians. "Working class" is being used in the broad sense. It includes most of those who sell their labor for wages, unwaged workers, and the unemployed.

respond effectively to the state's abuse of that autonomy. But for the ruling class to be capable of taking such corrective actions, it must have some degree of political cohesion, an understanding of its general interests, and a high degree of political sophistication. In sum, the theory requires that the ruling class, or a portion of it, be class-conscious, that is, aware of what is necessary to reproduce capitalist social relations in changing historical circumstances. Yet if the ruling class or a segment of it is class-conscious, then the degree of autonomy of the state is clearly quite limited. At this point the theory of relative autonomy collapses back into a slightly more sophisticated version of instrumentalism. State policies continue to be seen as the reflection of inputs by a class-conscious ruling class.

The way out of this theoretical bind, the way to formulate a critique of instrumentalism that does not collapse, is to reject the idea of a class-conscious ruling class. Instead of the relative autonomy framework the key idea becomes a division of labor between those who accumulate capital and those who manage the state apparatus. Those who accumulate capital are conscious of their interests as capitalists, but, in general, they are not conscious of what is necessary to reproduce the social order in changing circumstances. Those who manage the state apparatus, however, are forced to concern themselves to a greater degree with the reproduction of the social order because their continued power rests on the maintenance of political and economic order. In this framework, the central theoretical task is to explain how it is that despite this division of labor, the state tends to serve the interests of the capitalist class. It is to this task—the elaboration of a structural theory of the state—that I will turn after a brief discussion of the division of labor between capitalists and state managers.

A division of labor

The idea of a division of labor between non-class-conscious capitalists and those who manage the state apparatus can be found in Marx's writings.[4] Two factors, however, have obscured this aspect of Marx's thought. First, Marx did not spell out the nature of the structural framework in which that division of labor operated, although he hinted at the existence of such a framework. Second, Marx's discussion of these issues is clouded by his polemical intent to fix responsibility for all aspects of bourgeois society on the ruling class. Even when Marx recognizes that the ruling class lacks class consciousness, he still formulates his argument in such a way as to imply that the ruling class as a whole is in conscious control of the situation. Marx used the idea of a conscious, directive ruling class as a polemical shorthand for an elaboration of the structural mechanisms through which control over the means of production leads to control over the other aspects of society.

The tension in Marx's formulations is clearest in *The Eighteenth Brumaire* when he is explaining why the bourgeoisie supported Louis Napoleon's coup d'état against the bourgeoisie's own parliamentary representatives. He writes:

> The *extra-parliamentary* mass of the bourgeoisie, on the other hand, by its servility towards the President, by its vilification of parliament, by the brutal maltreatment of its own press, invited Bonaparte to suppress and annihilate its speaking and writing section, its politicians and its *literati*, its platform and its press, in order that it might then be able to pursue its private affairs with full confidence in the protection of a strong and unrestricted government. It declared unequivocally that it longed to get rid of its own political rule in order to get rid of the troubles and dangers of ruling.[5]

The passage suggests a division of labor and a division of interest between the extra-parliamentary mass of the bourgeoisie, primarily interested in accumulating profits, and the parliamentary and literary representatives of that class, whose central concerns are different. Marx uses the notion of representation as a substitute for specifying the structural relationship that holds together the division of labor.

In an earlier passage, in a discussion of the petit-bourgeoisie, he states what is involved in the idea of representation:

Just as little must one imagine that the democratic representatives are all shopkeepers or enthusiastic champions of shopkeepers. According to their education and their individual position they may be separated from them as widely as heaven from earth. What makes them representatives of the petty bourgeoisie is the fact that in their minds they do not go beyond the limits which the latter do not go beyond in life, that they are consequently driven theoretically to the same tasks and solutions to which material interest and socail position practically drive the latter. This is in general the relationship of the *political and literary representatives* of a class to the class that they represent.[6]

Marx here rejects the simple reductionism so common among his followers. For Marx, representation was an objective relationship—one did not need to be of a class, to be its representative. And, in fact, representatives and their classes did not always see eye to eye, since their different positions could lead to different perspectives. In sum, representatives are *not* typical members of their classes, and it is a mistake to attribute to the class as a whole, the consciousness that parliamentary or literary representatives display.

Marx's idea of representation suggests the general structural links between the capitalists and those who manage the state apparatus. Marx recognized that those in the state apparatus tended to have a broader view of society than the capitalists, although their view is still far short of a general understanding of what is necessary to reproduce the social order. After all, the state managers' preoccupation with the struggle for political power distorts their understanding. This is the source of the "parliamentary cretinism" that made Louis Napoleon a better defender of the bourgeoisie's interests than that class's own representatives. But if neither the ruling class nor its representatives know what is necessary to preserve and reproduce capitalist social relations, why then does the state tend to do just that? The answer is that such policies emerge out of the structural relationships among state managers, capitalists, and workers.

Subsidiary structural mechanisms

When Marxists put forward a radical critique of instrumentalist views of the state, they usually do so to justify reformist socialist politics. When one argues that the ruling class is diffused, lacks class consciousness and political sophistication, it seems to follow that if socialists could gain control of the levers of the existing state, they would be able to use the state to effect the transition to socialism. The logic is impeccable—if the state is not inherently a tool of the ruling class, then it can be turned into a tool of the working class. This reformist view shares with instrumentalism a personalistic reductionism—either the ruling class controls the state personally and directly or it does not control it at all, in which case the state can be used for other purposes. Neither view recognizes the structural mechanisms that make the state serve capitalist ends regardless of whether capitalists intervene directly and consciously. However, once these mechanisms are understood, it is possible to construct a critique of socialist reformism that is far more powerful than the critiques derived from the instrumentalist tradition.

Before considering the major structural mechanisms, it is necessary to consider a number of subsidiary mechanisms. The first of these includes all the techniques by which members of the ruling class are able to influence the state apparatus directly. Even though the members of the ruling class lack class consciousness, they are acutely aware of their immediate interests as capitalists and of the impact of the state on those interests. Capitalists, individually and in groups, apply pressure on the state for certain kinds of lucrative contracts, for state spending in certain areas, for legislative action in their favor, for tax relief, for more effective action to control the labor force, and so on. Needless to say, the pursuit of these various interests does not add up to policies in the general interest of capital. Even in the area of control of the labor force, where the common interest among capitalists is strongest, the policies that the capitalists demand might not even be in their own long-term best interest. Nevertheless, capitalists attempt to assure responsiveness by the state through various means, including campaign contributions, lobbying activities, and favors to politicians and civil servants. While these techniques are primarily used for increasing the state's receptivity to the special interests of particular capitalists or groups of capitalists, the overall effect of this proliferation of influence channels is to make those who run the state more likely to reject modes of thought and behavior that conflict with the logic of capitalism.

Included in the category of influence channels is the recruitment of ruling-class members into government service, and in recent years, into participation in various private policy-making groups that have a powerful impact on the formulation of government policies. Instrumentalists tend to see such individuals as typical members of their class, and their impact on the state is viewed as the heart of capitalist class rule. In the perspective being advanced here, this direct ruling-class participation in policy formation is viewed differently. For one thing, ruling-class members who devote substantial energy to policy forma-

tion become atypical of their class, since they are forced to look at the world from the perspective of state managers. They are quite likely to diverge ideologically from politically unengaged ruling-class opinion. More important, even if there were no politically engaged ruling-class members, there is still every reason to believe that the state and policy-making groups would advance policies that are in the interests of the ruling class. Marx's formulation cited earlier makes clear that one does not need to be of the ruling class to "represent" it politically; when there are no ruling-class individuals around, individuals from other social classes will eagerly fill the role of ruling-class "representatives."

All of the techniques of ruling-class influence, including direct participation, constitute a structural mechanism of subsidiary importance. The influence channels make it less likely that state managers will formulate policies that conflict directly with the interests of capitalists. But it is a subsidiary mechanism because, even in the absence of these influence channels, other structural mechanisms make it extremely difficult for the state managers to carry through anticapitalist policies. While instrumentalists argue that influence is the core of ruling-class control of the state, it is really more like the icing on the cake of class rule.

The same cannot be said of a second subsidiary mechanism—bourgeois cultural hegemony. The relevant aspect of cultural hegemony is the widespread acceptance of certain unwritten rules about what is and what is not legitimate state activity. While these rules change over time, a government that violates the unwritten rules of a particular period would stand to lose a good deal of its popular support. This acts as a powerful constraint in discouraging certain types of state action that might conflict with the interests of capital. However, simply invoking the existence of bourgeois cultural hegemony begs the problem of explaining how that hegemony is generated.

Here, too, there must be specific structural mechanisms that operate to make "the ruling ideas" consistent with class rule. However, the task of explaining these structural mechanisms is beyond the scope of this essay.

Major structural mechanisms

A viable structural theory of the state must do two separate things. It must elaborate the structural constraints that operate to reduce the likelihood that state managers will act against the general interests of capitalists. An understanding of these constraints is particularly important for analyzing the obstacles to reformist socialist strategies. But a structural theory must also explain the tendency of state managers to pursue policies that are in the general interests of capital. It is not sufficient to explain why the state avoids anti-capitalist policies; it is necessary to explain why the state has served to rationalize capitalism. Once one rejects the idea of ruling-class class consciousness, one needs to provide an alternative explanation of efforts at rationalization.

Both tendencies can be derived from the fact that those who manage the state apparatus—regardless of their own political ideology—are dependent on the maintenance of some reasonable level of economic activity. This is true for two reasons. First, the capacity of the state to finance itself through taxation or borrowing depends on the state of the economy. If economic activity is in decline, the state will have difficulty maintaining its revenues at an adequate level. Second, public support for a regime will decline sharply if the regime presides over a serious drop in the level of economic activity, with a parallel rise in unemployment and shortages of key goods. Such a drop in support increases the likelihood that the state managers will be removed from power one way or another. And even if the drop is not that dramatic,

it will increase the challenges to the regime and decrease the regime's political ability to take effective actions.

In a capitalist economy the level of economic activity is largely determined by the private investment decisions of capitalists. This means that capitalists, in their collective role as investors, have a veto over state policies in that their failure to invest at adequate levels can create major political problems for the state managers. This discourages state managers from taking actions that might seriously decrease the rate of investment. It also means that state managers have a direct interest in using their power to facilitate investment, since their own continued power rests on a healthy economy. There will be a tendency for state agencies to orient their various programs toward the goal of facilitating and encouraging private investment. In doing so, the state managers address the problem of investment from a broader perspective than that of the individual capitalist. This increases the likelihood that such policies will be in the general interest of capital.

Constraints on state policies

This is, of course, too simple. Both sides of the picture—constraints and rationalization—must be filled out in greater detail to make this approach convincing. One problem, in particular, stands out—if capitalists have a veto over state policies, isn't this simply another version of instrumentalism? The answer to this question lies in a more careful analysis of the determinants of investment decisions. The most useful concept is the idea of business confidence. Individual capitalists decide on their rate of investment in a particular country on the basis of a variety of specific variables such as the price of labor and the size of the market for a specific product. But there is also an intangible variable—the capitalist's evaluation of the general political/economic climate. Is the society stable; is the working class under control; are taxes likely to rise; do government agencies interfere with business freedom; will the economy grow? These kinds of considerations are critical to the investment decisions of each firm. The sum of all of these evaluations across a national economy can be termed the level of business confidence. As the level of business confidence declines, so will the rate of investment. Business confidence also has an international dimension when nations are integrated into a capitalist world economy. Multinational corporations, international bankers, and currency speculators also make judgments about a particular nation's political/economic climate which determine their willingness to invest in assets in that nation. This, in turn, will affect the internal level of business confidence and the rate of productive investment.

Business confidence is, however, very different from "ruling-class consciousness." Business confidence is based on an evaluation of the market that considers political events only as they might impinge on the market. This means that it is rooted in the narrow self-interest of the individual capitalist who is worried about profit. Business confidence, especially because of its critical international component, does not make subtle evaluations as to whether a regime is serving the long-term interests of capital. When there is political turmoil and popular mobilization, business confidence will fall, and it will rise when there is a restoration of order, no matter how brutal. It was business confidence that responded so favorably to Louis Napoleon's coup d'état, because he promised to restore the condition for business as usual, despite negative implications for the political rights of the bourgeoisie. The crudeness of business confidence makes capitalism peculiarly vulnerable to authoritarian regimes that are capable of acting against the general interests of capital.

The dynamic of business confidence as a constraint on the managers of the state apparatus can be grasped by tracing out a scenario of what happens when left-of-center governments come to power through parliamentary means and attempt to push through major reforms. The scenario distills a number of 20th-century experiences including that of Chile under Allende. From the moment that the left wins the election, business confidence declines. The most important manifestation of this decline is an increase in speculation against the nation's currency. Reformist governments are always under suspicion that they will pursue inflationary policies; a higher rate of inflation means that the international value of the nation's currency will fall. Speculators begin to discount the currency for the expected inflation as soon as possible.

This association between reformist governments and inflation is not arbitrary. Reformist policies—higher levels of employment, redistribution of income toward the poor, improved social services—directly or indirectly lead to a shift of income from profits toward the working class. Businesses attempt to resist such a shift by raising prices so that profit levels will not be reduced. In short, price inflation in this context is a market response to policies that tend to benefit the working class. The reformist government, faced with the initial speculative assault on its currency, has two choices. It can reassure the international and domestic business community, making clear its intention to pursue orthodox economic policies. Or, it can forge ahead with its reform program. If it pursues the latter course, an increased rate of inflation and an eventual international monetary crisis are likely.

The international crisis results from the combination of continued speculative pressure against the currency and several new factors. Domestic inflation is likely to affect the nation's balance of trade adversely, leading to a real deterioration in the nation's balance-of-payments account. It addition, inflation and loss of confidence in the currency lead to the flight of foreign and domestic capital and increased foreign reluctance to lend money to the afflicted nation. The initial speculative pressure against the currency could be tolerated; the eruption of an acute international monetary crisis requires some kind of dramatic response. The government may renounce its reformism or cede power to a more "responsible" administration.

But if the government is committed to defending its programs, it will have to act to insulate its economy from the pressures of the international market by imposing some combination of price controls, import controls, and exchange controls.

Escalation in the government's attempt to control the market sets off a new chain of events. These new controls involve threats to individual capitalists. Price controls mean that firms lose the ability to manipulate one of the major determinants of profit levels. Import controls mean that a firm may no longer be able to import goods critical to its business. Exchange controls mean that firms and individuals no longer are able to move their assets freely to secure international havens. The fact that assets are locked into a rapidly inflating currency poses the possibility that large fortunes will be lost.

These are the ingredients for a sharp decline in domestic business confidence. Why should business owners continue to invest if they must operate in an environment in which the government violates the fundamental rules of a market economy?

A sharp decline in business confidence leads to a parallel economic downturn. High rates of unemployment coexist with annoying shortages of critical commodities. The popularity of the regime falls precipitously. The only alternative to capitulation—eliminating controls and initial reforms—is sharp forward movement to socialize the economy. The government could put people back to work and relieve the shortages by taking over private firms. However, the political basis for this kind of action does not exist, even where the leaders of the government are rhetorically committed to the goal of socialism. Generally, the reformist government has not prepared its electoral supporters for extreme action; its entire program has been based on the promise of a gradual transition. Further, the government leaders themselves become immersed in the political culture of the state apparatus, militating against a sharp break with the status quo.

The outcome of this impasse is tragically familiar. The government either falls from power through standard parliamentary means—loss of an election, defection of some of its parliamentary support—or it is removed militarily. Military actions that violate constitutionality meet formidable obstacles in liberal capitalist nations, but when economic chaos severely diminishes the legitimacy of a regime, the chances of a military coup are enhanced. When the military intervenes, it does not do so as a tool of the ruling class. It acts according to its own ideas of the need to restore political order and in its own interests. Naturally, the removal of the reformist government leads to a rapid revival of business confidence simply because order has been restored. However, it should be stressed that this revival of business confidence might not be sustained, since there can be substantial conflicts between the interests of the military and the capitalists.

The key point in elaborating this scenario is that the chain of events can unfold without any members of the ruling class consciously deciding to act "politically" against the regime in power. Of course, such a scenario is usually filled out with a great deal of editorializing against the regime in the bourgeois press, much grumbling among the upper classes, and even some conspiratorial activity. But the point is that conspiracies to destabilize the regime are basically superfluous, since decisions made by individual capitalists according to their own narrow economic rationality are sufficient to paralyze the regime, creating a situation where the regime's fall is the only possibility.

Rationalization

The dynamic of business confidence helps explain why governments are constrained from pursuing anti-capitalist policies. It remains to be explained why governments tend to act in the general interests of capital. Part of the answer has already been suggested. Since state managers are so dependent upon the workings of the investment accumulation process, it is natural that they will use whatever resources are available to aid that process. In administering a welfare program, for example, they will organize it to aid the accumulation process, perhaps by ensuring certain industries a supply of cheap labor. Unlike the individual capitalist, the state managers do not have to operate on the basis of a narrow profit-maximizing rationality. They are capable of intervening in the economy on the basis of a more general rationality. In short, their structural position gives the state managers both the interest and the capacity to aid the investment accumulation process.

There is one major difficulty in this formulation—the problem of explaining the dynamic through which reforms that increase the rationality of capitalism come about. Almost all of these reforms involve an extension of the state's role in the economy and society, either in a regulatory capacity or in the provision of services. The difficulty is that business confidence has been depicted as so shortsighted that it is likely to decline in the face of most efforts to extend that state's role domestically, since such efforts threaten to restrict the freedom of individual capitalists

and/or increase the tax burden on capitalists. If the state is unwilling to risk a decline in business confidence, how is it then that the state's role has expanded inexorably throughout the 20th century?

Most theorists escape this problem by rejecting the idea that the capitalists are as short-sighted as the idea of business confidence suggests. Even if many members of the class share the retrograde notions implicit in the idea of business confidence, there is supposed to be a substantial segment of the class that is forward-looking and recognizes the value of extending the state's power. Theorists of corporate liberalism have attempted to trace many of the major extensions of state power in 20th-century America to the influence of such forward-looking members of the ruling class. However, the position of these theorists ultimately requires an attribution of a high level of consciousness and understanding to the ruling class or a segment of it, and assumes an instrumental view of the state where state policies can be reduced to the input of certain ruling-class factions.[7]

There is, however, an alternative line of argument, consistent with the view of the ruling class and the state that has been advanced in this paper. It depends on the existence of another structural mechanism —class struggle. Whatever the role of class struggle in advancing the development of revolutionary consciousness, class struggle between proletariat and ruling class in Marx's view has another important function. It pushes forward the development of capitalism—speeding the process by which capitalism advances the development of the productive forces. This is conservative in the short term, but progressive in the long term; it brings closer the time when capitalism will exhaust its capacity to develop the productive forces and will be ripe for overthrow. Class struggle produces this result most clearly in conflict over wages. When workers are able to win wage gains, they increase the pressure on the capitalists to find ways to substitute machines for people. As Marx described the cycle, wage gains are followed by an intense period of mechanization as employers attempt to increase the rate of exploitation; the consequence is an increase in the size of the industrial reserve army, as machines replace workers. This, in turn, diminishes the capacity of workers to win wage gains, until the economic boom again creates a labor shortage. While this description applies particularly to competitive capitalism, the point is that workers' struggles—in Marx's theory—play an important role in speeding the place of technological innovations. *Class struggle is responsible for much of the economic dynamism of capitalism.*

This pattern goes beyond the struggle over wages. From the beginning of capitalism, workers have struggled to improve their living conditions, which also means upgrading their potential as a labor force. For example, unbridled early capitalism, through child labor and horrendously long working days, threatened to destroy the capacity of the working class to reproduce itself—an outcome not in the long-term interests of capitalists. So working people's struggles against child labor, against incredibly low standards of public health and housing, and for the shorter day, made it possible for the class to reproduce itself, providing capitalism a new generation of laborers. In each historical period, the working class struggles to reproduce itself at a higher level of existence. Workers have played an important role, for example, in demanding increased public education. Public education, in turn, helped create the educated labor pool that developing capitalism required. Obviously, not every working-class demand contributes to the advance of capitalism, but it is foolish to ignore this dimension of class struggle.

In its struggles to protect itself from the ravages of a market economy, the working class has played a key role in the steady expansion of the state's role in capitalist societies. Pressures from the working class have contributed to the expansion of the state's role in the regulation of the economy and in the provision of services. The working class has not been the only force behind the expansion of the state's role in these areas. Examples can be cited of capitalists who have supported an expansion of the state's role into a certain area either because of narrow self-interest—access to government contracts, or because government regulation would hamper competitors—or because of some farsighted recognition of the need to co-opt the working class. However, the major impetus for the extension of the state's role has come from the working class and from the managers of the state apparatus, whose own powers expand with a growing state.

Once working-class pressures succeed in extending the state's role, another dynamic begins to work. Those who manage the state apparatus have an interest in using the state's resources to facilitate a smooth flow of investment. There will be a tendency to use the state's extended role for the same ends. The capacity of the state to impose greater rationality on capitalism is extended into new areas as a result of working-class pressures. Working-class pressures, for example, might lead to an expansion of educational resources available for the working class, but there is every likelihood that the content of the education will be geared to the needs of accumulation—the production of a docile work force at an appropriate level of skill. Or similarly, working-class pressures might force the government to intervene in the free market to produce higher levels of employment, but the government will use its expanded powers of intervention to aid the accumulation process more generally.

This pattern is not a smoothly working functional process, always producing the same result. First, working-class movements have often been aware of the danger of making demands that will ultimately strengthen a state they perceive as hostile. For precisely this reason, socialist movements have often demanded that expanded social services be placed under working-class control. However, working-class demands are rarely granted in their original form. Often, the more radical elements of the movement are repressed at the same time that concessions are made. Second, there can be a serious time lag between granting concessions to the working class and discovering ways that the extension of the state's power can be used to aid the accumulation process. There might, in fact, be continuing tensions in a government program between its integrative intent and its role in the accumulation process. Finally, some concessions to working-class pressure might have no potential benefits for accumulation and might simply place strains on the private economy. If these strains are immediate, one could expect serious efforts to revoke or neutralize the reforms. If the strains occur over the long term, then capitalism faces severe problems because it becomes increasingly difficult to roll back concessions that have stood for some time.

These points suggest that the tendency for class struggle to rationalize capitalism occurs with a great deal of friction and with the continuous possibility of other outcomes. Nevertheless, the tendency does exist because of the particular interests of the state managers. Where there is strong popular pressure for an expansion of social services or increased regulation of markets, the state managers must weigh three factors. First, they do not want to damage business confidence, which generally responds unfavorably to an expansion of the government's role in providing social services or in regulating the market. Second, they do not want class antagonisms to escalate to a level that would endanger their own rule. Third, they recognize that their

own power and resources will grow if the state's role is expanded. If the state managers decide to respond to pressure with concessions, they are likely to shape their concessions in a manner that will least offend business confidence and will most expand their own power. These two constraints increase the likelihood that the concessions will ultimately serve to rationalize capitalism.

Major reforms

This argument suggests that while some concessions will be made to the working class, the threat of a decline in business confidence will block major efforts to rationalize capitalism. Since business confidence is shortsighted, it will oppose even pro-capitalist reform programs if such programs promise a major increase in taxes or a major increase in the government's capacity to regulate markets. This leaves the problem of explaining the dramatic increases in the state's role that have occurred in all developed capitalist nations during the course of this century. The explanation is that there are certain periods—during wartime, major depressions, and periods of postwar reconstruction—in which the decline of business confidence as a veto on government policies doesn't work. These are the periods in which dramatic increases in the state's role have occurred.

In wars that require major mobilizations, business confidence loses its sting for several reasons. First, international business confidence becomes less important, since international capital flows tend to be placed under government control. Second, private investment becomes secondary to military production in maintaining high levels of economic activity. Third, in the general patriotic climate, it would be dangerous for the business community to disrupt the economy through negative actions. The result is that state managers have the opportunity to expand their own power with the unassailable justification that such actions are necessary for the war effort. Some of these wartime measures will be rolled back once peace returns, but some will become part of the landscape.

In serious depressions and postwar reconstruction periods, the dynamics are somewhat different. Low levels of economic activity mean that the threat of declining business confidence loses its power, at the same time that popular demands for economic revival are strong. In such periods, the state managers can pay less attention to business opinion and can concentrate on responding to the popular pressure, while acting to expand their own power. However, there are still constraints on the state managers. Their continued rule depends on their capacity to revive the economy. As government actions prove effective in reducing unemployment, redistributing income, or expanding output, the political balance shifts. Pressure from below is likely to diminish; business confidence re-emerges as a force once economic recovery begins. In short, successful reforms will tilt the balance of power back to a point where capitalists regain their veto over extensions of the state's role.

The increased capacity of state managers to intervene in the economy during these periods does not automatically rationalize capitalism. State managers can make all kinds of mistakes, including excessive concessions to the working class. State managers have no special knowledge of what is necessary to make capitalism more rational; they grope toward effective action as best they can within existing political constraints and with available economic theories. The point is simply that rationalization can emerge as a by-product of state managers' dual interest in expanding their own power and in assuring a reasonable level of economic activity. The more power the state possesses to intervene in the capitalist economy, the greater the likelihood that effective actions can be taken to facilitate investment.

Not every extension of state power will survive beyond those periods in which state managers have special opportunities to expand the state's role. After a war, depression, or period of reconstruction, the business community is likely to campaign for a restoration of the *status quo ante*. State managers in these new periods will be forced to make some concessions to the business community in order to avert a decline in business confidence. However, the state managers also want to avoid the elimination of certain reforms important for the stabilization of the economy and the integration of the working class. Self-interest also leads them to resist a complete elimination of the state's expanded powers. The consequence is a selection process by which state managers abandon certain reforms while retaining others. In this process, reforms that are most beneficial for capitalism will be retained, while those whose effects are more questionable will be eliminated. Again, the ultimate outcome is determined by intense political struggle.

Conclusion

The purpose of this essay has been to argue that a viable Marxist theory of the state depends on the rejection of the idea of a conscious, politically directive, ruling class. By returning to Marx's suggestions that the historical process unfolds "behind the backs" of the actors (including the ruling-class actors), it is possible to locate the structural mechanisms that shape the workings of the capitalist state. These mechanisms operate independently of any political consciousness on the part of the ruling class. Instead, capitalist rationality emerges out of the three-sided relationship among capitalists, workers, and state managers. The structural position of state managers forces them to achieve some consciousness of what is necessary to maintain the viability of the social order. It is this consciousness that explains both the reluctance of state managers to offend business confidence, and their capacity to rationalize a capitalist society. However, the fact of consciousness does not imply control over the historical process. State managers are able to act only in the terrain that is marked out by the intersection of two factors—the intensity of class struggle and the level of economic activity.

This framework has implications for a wide range of theoretical and political questions. One of the most critical of these concerns capitalism's capacity to overcome its current economic difficulties. Analysts on the left have predicted that the forward-looking segment of the American ruling class will favor a further extension of the state's role in regulating the economy as a means to solve the problems of stagflation.[8] This perspective exaggerates the capacity of capitalism to reform itself in "normal" periods, and is unable to account, for example, for the inability of British capitalism to rationalize itself during the long period of decline since the 1950s. The framework developed here predicts that while the working class and the state managers themselves might favor an expansion of state intervention, business confidence will effectively veto such changes. It is therefore quite possible that the American economy will continue in its present state of crisis for many years to come.

NOTES

1. For two surveys of recent Marxist work on the state—one polemical and the other dispassionate—see Alan Wolfe, "New Directions in the Marxist Theory of Politics," *Politics and Society*, vol. 4, no. 2 (1974); and David Gold, Clarence Y. H. Lo, and Erik Olin Wright, "Recent Developments in Marxist Theories of the Capitalist State," parts 1 and 2, *Monthly Review*, October and November 1975.

2. For critiques of such interpretations of Watergate, see Steve Weissman, "Cowboys and Crooks," in Steve Weissman, ed., *Big Brother and the Holding Company: The World behind Watergate* (Palo Alto, Calif.: Ramparts Press, 1974), pp. 297–310; and Stephen Johnson, "How the West Was Won: Last Shootout for the Yankee-Cowboy Theory," *Insurgent Sociologist*, Winter 1975, pp. 61–93.

3. My analysis has been influenced by the arguments of Nicos Poulantzas, particularly in his "Problems of the Capitalist State," *New Left Review* 58 (November–December 1969). However, my analysis differs from Poulantzas' in two important respects. He tends to attribute consciousness to particular fractions of the ruling class and he fails to explain adequately the mechanisms by which the state is structurally a capitalist state. In this regard, my position is closer to that of Claus Offe in a number of articles, including "Structural Problems of the Capitalist State," in Klaus von Beyme, ed., *German Political Studies* (Beverly Hills, Calif.: Sage Publications, 1976); and Claus Offe and Volker Ronge, "Theses on the Theory of the State," *New German Critique* 6 (Fall 1975).

4. In *The German Ideology*, Marx and Engels talk about a division of labor and of interests between capitalists and the producers of bourgeois ideology: ". . . so that inside this class one part appears as the thinkers of the class (its active, conceptive ideologists, who make the perfection of the illusion of the class about itself their chief source of livelihood), while the others' attitude to these ideas and illusions is more passive and receptive, because they are in reality the active members of this class and have less time to make up illusions and ideas about themselves." In Robert C. Tucker, ed., *The Marx-Engels Reader* (New York: Norton, 1971), pp. 136–37. This suggests an analogous division of labor between capitalists and state managers. In both cases, however, treating ideologists or state managers as part of the ruling class violates the idea that class is determined by one's relation to the means of production. In short, Marx and Engels in this passage are using the notion of the ruling class in a polemical sense.

5. *The Eighteenth Brumaire,* in ibid., p. 502.

6. Ibid., p. 502.

7. For a critique of corporate liberal theory, see Fred Block, "Beyond Corporate Liberalism," *Social Problems,* forthcoming.

8. See, for example, Stanley Aronowitz, "Modernizing Capitalism," *Social Policy*, May–June 1975; and James Crotty and Raford Boddy, "Who Will Plan the Planned Economy?" *The Progressive*, February 1975. Such analyses tend to assume that the contradictions of advanced capitalism can be solved or effectively eased through state action. The possibility exists that this is not the case. While it is virtually impossible to reach a conclusion on that issue, one can debate whether such expanded state intervention will even be attempted.

Class struggle and the capitalist state*

GOSTA ESPING-ANDERSEN, ROGER FRIEDLAND, and
ERIK OLIN WRIGHT

The relationship between class conflict and the structure of the state in capitalist society has been analyzed in a variety of ways. We shall review four perspectives: pluralist, instrumentalist, structuralist, and political class analysis.

Pluralist, instrumentalist, and structuralist perspectives

A liberal perspective, long dominant in American social science, views the state as a pluralist, aggregating mechanism in which agencies, programs, and legislation are substantive responses to the demands and interests of competing groups. The relationship between class structure and the state has generally been viewed in two ways, both perspectives viewing the state as a political market place. The first sees class and interest conflict mediated through party competition and generally assumes an automatic responsiveness of politically neutral state agencies (see for example Lipset, 1960; Lipset and Rokkan, 1967). The second pluralist approach sees state agencies as directly accessible to interest groups and classes for particularized, non-electoral control, and thus as bases of political power (e.g. McConnell, 1966). State bureaucracies become the battleground for specific interest groups, and competition between agencies for limited funding either reinforces or supplants party competition. The proliferation of programs and agencies on the one hand, and the differentiation of state levels on the other, is viewed as providing greater access for any interest to block gross injustice and at least secure a minimum foothold in the state (e.g. Rose, 1967, 1963).[1]

A second tradition sees the state as an "instrument" of the ruling class or dominant elite. This approach starts from a specific interpretation of Marx's superstructural view of the state:

The bourgeoisie has, at last, since the establishment of modern industry and the world market, conquered for itself, in the modern representative state, exclusive political sway. The executive of the modern state is but a committee for managing the common affairs of the whole bourgeoisie. (Marx, 1955)

A contemporary example of this view can be found in Sweezy's *The Theory of Capitalist Development*: ". . . state power must be monopolized by the class or classes which are the chief beneficiaries." Sweezy sees the state as, ". . . an instrument in the hands of the ruling classes for enforcing and guaranteeing the stability of the class structure itself" (Sweezy, 1942: 243). Frequently this view infers the power of capitalists from the class composition of the personnel who hold key administrative or legislative roles within the state. Miliband summarizes the conventional Marxist position:

. . . it has remained a basic fact of life in advanced capitalist countries that the vast majority of men and women in these countries has been governed, represented, administered, judged and commanded in war by people drawn from other, economically and socially superior and relatively distant classes. (1969: 67)

We shall refer to this approach as *instrumentalist*. The theory of "corporate lib-

* From *Kapitalistate*, 4–5 (1976), pp. 186–98.

eralism" is a sophisticated version of this approach (e.g. Hayes, 1964; Weinstein, 1968). This theory stresses the ability of progressive fractions of capital to preemptively determine the limits of reform through corporate financed, controlled, and staffed policy research and policy formation groups which originate model legislation and set the ideological boundaries within which partisan battles will be contained. The theory of corporate liberalism thus allows a political analysis of institutionalization and the cycles of capitalist participation.

A third general perspective on the state structure as determined by the systemic constraints and contradictions of capitalism. These constraints and contradictions need not affect state structure and function through overt political struggle and participation by individuals, interest groups, classes, or parties. Rather, to the extent that the survival of the system is dependent upon the containment and solution of recurrent crises, overt class participation may not be required at all. The emphasis of the *structuralist* Marxist approach is on the inherent dynamics and imperatives of the social formation in which the state is embedded. We will distinguish two structuralist Marxist approaches to the state, a political and an economic one.

The political variant of structuralism has been most fully developed by Poulantzas (1973, 1974, 1975) and Althusser (1971). As Poulantzas has written:

The relation between the bourgeois class and the state is an objective relation. This means that if the function of the state in a determinate social formation and the interests of the dominant class coincide, it is by reason of the system itself; the direct participation of members of the ruling class in the State apparatus is not the cause but the effect, and moreover a chance and contingent one, of this objective coincidence. (1972: 245)

Poulantzas argues that the state functions as the factor of cohesion in a social forma-

tion, that the bourgeoisie is incapable of achieving sufficient political unity as a class to attain hegemonic domination and therefore that state power must organize this class, and that state power only attains a unity to the extent that it corresponds to the bourgeoisie's interests.

In its more historical and dynamic forms, this structuralist approach attempts to locate destabilizing consequences of adaptation through changing state structure and function in accordance with the political economy as a whole. In its more mechanistic forms this approach is unable to locate specific actors and historically dynamic class conflict as a motor of structural change.

The economic structuralist approach to the state locates a series of functions that the state must perform to temporarily resolve economically determined contradictions. For example, Baran and Sweezy, in *Monopoly Capital*, attribute to the state the function of guaranteeing effective demand to avert realization crises to which monopoly capitalism is particularly prone. Altvater argues for the functional necessity of the state as an institution not internally constrained by the imperatives of surplus value production:

. . . the state can thus be conceived neither as a mere political instrument nor as an institution set up by capital, but rather as a special form of the accomplishment of the social existence of capital along with and besides competition, as an essential moment in the social reproduction process of capital. (1973: 99)

Thus the state is residually defined by the functions capital units cannot perform.

Both structuralist approaches to the state do not locate power in decision-making processes, elite preemption and cooptation, or the conversion of economic power into observable political power. Rather power is located in the ability of the state to reproduce class relations and class domination through structural relations that need not be immediately visible. Thus while the apparent determinants of state action may involve the political defeat of the bourgeoisie, the consequences of that state action reproduce and reinforce that class's domination. Poulantzas writes:

. . . a line of demarcation can always be drawn within which the guarantee given by the capitalist state to the dominated classes' economic interests not only fails to threaten the political relation of class domination, but even constitutes an element of this relation. (1973: 191)

A major analytic problem with the structuralist approach is its inability to explain *class action* that arises from class consciousness.[2] Class located individuals respond to the stimuli born out of the systemic logic, rather than act on the basis of self-conscious political practice.

On the other hand, the instrumentalist approach to the state tends to rely too heavily on observable class input into, and control of, policy formation. The instrumentalist perspective does not identify systemic constraints and imperatives that operate at all levels of society, including the state, which define and limit the range and form of possible class action. Thus, the instrumentalist perspective will tend to ignore the extent to which the demands and interests of the dominant class must take into account the limits of direct manipulation imposed by a historical social formation: internal state structure, state-economy relations, and economic structure.

The problem with both structuralist and instrumentalist approaches is, in fact, a much larger methodological one. To begin with, "systemic constraints" or "systemic imperatives" are not metaphysical abstractions. Rather, they are primarily products of historically specific struggles for class dominance. Present class action, class dominance, and class interests must be seen as present struggle arising out of and defined in terms of a structure which is historically determined.

Thus, an overemphasis on "structure" or "systemic logic" will tend to view class-originated inputs and demands as "passive" responses to stimuli born out of the structure. On the other hand, the class instrumentalist perspective will tend to be somewhat situational and voluntaristic since it does not relate present class action to the historically determined constraints of the system. The instrumentalist view of the state stresses the *political input* into the state and the importance of the unequal class distribution of power. The structuralist view of the state stresses the *political output* of state activity by which capitalist domination is reproduced and the cohesion of the social formation assured.

Neither approach contains a theory of the mechanisms that link political inputs and systemic constraints to the outputs of state activity. Neither approach can analytically distinguish the extent to which class action mediates between constraints and state structures, generates those constraints and structures, or at times is irrelevant to the relationship of economic constraints to the state.[3]

Political class struggle: An alternative view of the state

A fourth perspective is possible which focuses on state structure as an object of class struggle. The capitalist class attempts to create state structures which channel working class political activity in ways that do not threaten capitalist political dominance and objective interests. Working class challenge makes the success of such attempts problematic. A political class struggle perspective on the state tries to locate the state within the dialectical relationship between class dominance and systemic constraints.

There are two theoretical tasks to be accomplished in developing such a theory of the state. First, it is necessary to elaborate the nature of the internal structures of the state and their relationship to systemic contradictions. Second, it is necessary to understand the ways in which class struggle shapes, and is shaped by, those very structures.

An important approach is found in Claus Offe's work (1972, 1972, 1974). Offe attempts to analyze the extent to which the internal structures of the state permit it to pursue the interests of capital as a whole while simultaneously acting *with a degree* of "relative autonomy" from direct class domination, thereby assuring the legitimacy of its intervention. Offe distinguishes between the allocation and production functions of the state. Both functions support the process of private accumulation. The important difference lies in the way policies are made for the two functions. The allocation function refers to the ways that the public budget is allocated to regulate the capitalist market. Allocative policies are subject to direct political conflict, and therefore most clearly "instrumental" in character. Production policies, on the other hand, are more complex. These refer to state intervention to solve specific bottlenecks, externalities, or crises due to breakdowns in private capital investment upon which accumulation in the system as a whole is contingent. Production intervention involves some form of physical input into the production process. Due to lack of capitalist class cohesiveness, the state takes on responsibility for managing crises through production policy. With no direct class-originated policy guidelines, the state itself is forced to devise decision rules that reproduce private capital accumulation.

However, while Offe extensively discusses the internal structures of the state, he fails to relate them systematically to class struggle. This is apparent in his analysis of the welfare state (Offe, 1972). Offe tends to view the modern welfare state as a mechanism directed at "endemic systemic problems and unmet social needs" (1972:

42). The welfare state is not seen as the product of political and ideological class conflict; rather Offe points to its development in "relative independence from political controversy and ideological debate" (1972: 45). Welfare state structures exist independently of conscious political will and have thus some degree of autonomy to "compensate" for new problems which are byproducts of private capitalist growth. The state is seen as independent of direct class control, a technical apparatus for absorption of "newly created insecurities of political control which create immediate measures that avoid the socially destabilizing problem of the moment" (1972: 42).

Offe's conception of autonomy and his primary focus on the consequences of state intervention as a crisis-solver, lead him to ignore the extent to which classes are differentially able to shape the state machinery and voice specific demands for state action. In other words, the power and ability of the state to resolve recurrent crises do not seem to originate from people as much as from systemic "push-effects" (1972: 45).

Jim O'Connor's work on the fiscal crisis of the state is one of the few attempts to deal both with the relationship of internal structures of the state to contradictions in the accumulation process and with the relationship of class struggle to those state structures. O'Connor analyzes how crises of corporate profitability are transformed into crises of state bankruptcy given the constraints of a tax-dependent state. He also analyzes the ways in which class struggle limits the state's ability to rationalize capitalism and the ways in which state structures have been reorganized to make them more impermeable to working class challenge.

O'Connor suggests that the decline in Congressional power, long ago noted by Mills (1956), and the concentration of power in an increasingly depoliticized executive is required for state rationalization of capitalism. Various structural changes accomplish this centralization of state power: the use of revolving funds; refusal to prohibit transfers between appropriations; lump sum appropriations; the ability of the executive to mingle appropriations and bring forward unexpected balances of former appropriations; and the allocation, program planning, and policy controls increasingly vested in the Bureau of the Budget, Domestic Council, and the Office of the Management of the Budget. The consequence of this centralization of power within the national state structure has been to increasingly depoliticize, technicalize, if not make invisible, major decisions about the structure and level of taxation and expenditure.

We shall elaborate the theory of the state implicit in O'Connor's and Offe's work by arguing that the internal structure of the state is simultaneously a *product,* an *object,* and a *determinant* of class conflict. State structure is itself a source of power. The organization of political authority differentially affects the access, political consciousness, strategy and cohesion of various interests and classes. State structure is not neutral with respect to its effects on class conflict. The structure of the state intervenes between social needs and the way these needs are translated into political demands, between demands and state outputs, and between specific outputs and the ability to organize and raise new demands in the future.

Class struggle has repeatedly taken the form of political conflict over the structuring of state authority. As opposed to the "shell" requiring sudden and totalistic destruction posited by Lenin, Gorz (1964) has pointed to the critical role of structural change in the capitalist state as a starting point for the transformation of capitalist society. Gorz's strategic objective is *structural reform,* where the working class comes to control, if not constitute,

new centers of state power with authority to make decisions that respond to needs beyond the capabilities of capitalism—e.g., controls over profit levels, rates of investment, technological change, and social investments.[4] While it is very problematic whether or not the working class could actually control pieces of state power within the capitalist state, the critical point in the present discussion is that political challenge by the working class shapes the historical development of state structure. The actual structures of the state are thus not a simple reflection of capitalist interests, but a contradictory reflection of the class struggle between workers and capitalists.

The problem facing advanced capitalist social formations is *how can the capitalist state be structured so as to perform functions dictated by economic contradictions given the actual or potential existence of a politically organized working class?* As the state comes increasingly to be a necessary force in the development and regulation of the capitalist economy, as economic concentration and centralization render small disproportionalities and downturns increasingly dangerous and volatile, the political neutralization of an organized working class through structural change in the state has become more imperative for capitalist growth. Such structural change will always be contradictory, never completely successful. How successful such structural changes will be is contingent on the level of contradictions in the accumulation process and the organization and content of class struggle.

We shall review three historical examples of neutralization of politically organized and challenging segments of the working class through state structural change: the emergence of urban reform government; federal intergovernmental transfer programs for the central cities; and corporatist structures for national planning. In each case, structural change neutralized the political threat working class organization presented to capital accumulation.

Structural change: Urban reform government

City government has been restructured towards a reform government since the Progressive Era. This illustrates the ways in which state structural change allows the performance of functions critical to capitalist development despite the existence of a politically challenging working class. The movement for reform government was controlled by capitalist elites operating through the National Civic Federation and other corporatist policy organizations, who feared the rise of an urban, working-class-based Socialist Party movement (see Weinstein, 1968). Further, they were chary of the inefficiency and autonomy of political machines, the high cost of securing their own influence, and the potentially high ethnic working class influence over city expenditures and personnel. Given the need to radically expand city government functions at a time of rapid accumulation, industrialization, and urbanization, the reform governmental structure effected a political neutralization of city government unique in capitalist democracies, just when political challenge seemed most threatening (see Hays, 1969; Alford, 1973).

The reform movement developed a package of structural reforms which functioned to depoliticize city politics and insulate allocation and decision-making from class and ethnic political control: city manager form of executive, non-partisan and at-large elections, and small city councils. Through these various mechanisms reform government minimized the political organization, participation, and influence of working class and ethnic groups concentrated in the city, while at the same time increasing the influence of dominant interests over decision-making and allocation.

Non-partisan and at-large elections resulted in the elimination of party organization in general, and Socialist Party political organization in particular (Hamilton, 1972). At-large elections made it increasingly expensive for candidates to enter campaigns, thus favoring those with sufficient private resources to pay election expenses and those people most likely to be socially conspicuous in the community. Ward-based elections had increased the likelihood that local working class or ethnic leadership would be generated and decreased the electoral opportunities of middle or upper class candidates due to the restrictiveness of residential requirements based on relatively class homogeneous wards. At-large elections decreased the probability of electing working class party candidates because the percentage of the city as opposed to the ward determined election to the council, thus requiring a higher level of aggregate working class turnout in the city as a whole (see Williams and Adrian, 1969). Non-partisan elections made it difficult for any party organization to survive in local politics and, in contrast to most Western European countries, effectively dissociated city political conflict from national partisan politics. Working class candidates must rely on party organization for electoral financing, organization, visibility, and ideological identification through party label in order to get elected. Lacking a local, class-based party organization, manual workers have constituted a very small percentage of city council members in the U.S. in contrast to their percentage in the population.[5]

Under reform government, dominant business interests have more influence both at the city council level and through direct access to city agencies (see Miller, 1958a, 1958b; Morlock, 1973). Reform government functioned to increase the autonomy of city agencies from partisan electoral accountability. Agencies were thus more permeable to the most intensely interested, best organized and economically most powerful interests. Because agencies are more autonomous from partisan control, they are more vulnerable and must seek out interest groups upon which they can institutionalize relationships of political support.

The city machines supplanted by reform government had functioned to politically incorporate the mass migration of working class ethnics, many of whom brought with them socialist ideology and party identification. As Katznelson (1976) points out, the machines controlled both the political organization of social groups and the delivery of distributive outputs to those groups. While capitalist elites dominated the party machines, the high cost and uncertainty of that domination brought these structures into question. Hays (1969) has shown that it was the high cost of corruption for distributing favors for business that was one of the interests leading to capital support for reform. Scott (1969) argues that the machines required substantial financial support from capitalist elites in return for support of critical policy developments, while the machine controlled votes through delivery of patronage and distributive benefits to working class ethnic constituencies. The reformist restructuring of the city government is one illustration of how state structures have developed which effectively insulate areas of decision-making and allocation critical to capitalist interests from political accountability, thereby maximizing the translation of capitalist economic power into patterns of allocation and non-decisions favorable to those interests, while simultaneously minimizing the need for those capitalist interests to participate in manifestly political ways.

However, like all state structural change, the development of reform government has been internally contradictory. On the one hand, the departisanizing of city politics effectively destroyed the urban political party as an effective social control

mechanism without providing a satisfactory replacement. Thus, the new black urban proletariat which emerged during the post-WW II period was not initially politically absorbed, which was one of the important factors contributing to the violent and politically costly rebellions of the 1960s. On the other hand, reform government destroyed the politically powerful mayor as the centralizing role in the city political system. As a result, it is much more difficult in the reformed city to effectively rationalize and coordinate the fragmentary maze of highly autonomous city agencies (see Newton, 1973, 1974). The new forms of urban pork barrel politics have consequently pushed the city towards fiscal crisis without making the city a location for efficient production for capital as a whole.

Structural change: Intergovernmental grants to the cities

Presently, the central cities of the U.S. face a fiscal crisis which impinges upon city functions critical to capital and undermines the political domination of capitalist elites. As industry and upper income residents decentralize into a municipally fragmented metropolis, dissociating fiscal capacity from social needs, the central city fills up with an especially poor and often black segment of the working class. With their concomitant electoral power and potentially explosive demands for expenditures for adequate levels of basic social services, structural mechanisms (e.g. non-school special districts, regional authorities, inter-governmental project grants) have developed which insulate from popular control areas of policy-making and allocation upon which regional capital accumulation is dependent (see Feshbach and Shipnuck, 1973).

The structure of the federal intergovernmental transfer programs to the central cities was in the 1960s a particularly effective way by which state structures were politically insulated from challenging segments of the working class. Federal intergovernmental transfer programs and especially project grants located the origins of urban policy, and thus the limits of urban expenditure, outside the city. This favored those interests best able to organize on a national level—corporate policy groups, capitalist fractions like insurance companies, mortgage bankers, home building associations—and insulated policy formation from the poor and black who have been able to create electoral and nonelectoral challenges only on the local level. At the national level, black groups for example, have been loose ineffectual federations of local groups confined to legislative lobbying once the limits of substantive policy variations have already been defined (see Wolman and Thomas, 1970).

Further, the development of federal grants-in-aid has insulated urban agencies from political accountability. Federal programs have contributed to the proliferation of politically autonomous agencies with direct linkages to the federal bureaucracies and their administrative elites, making agencies more permeable to dominant capitalist interests which are best organized and have most at stake; and making any unitary, programmatic attack on urban problems impossible, thus contributing to the political fragmentation of lower class client groups. Without a unitary structure with the capacity to act, people who have most to gain from serious change have little incentive to politically participate (Newton, 1973).

Structures such as reform government and federal intergovernmental transfer programs depoliticize major segments of state power. Capitalist elites have been able to control the structure of city expenditures in ways that do not impinge upon the city functions critical to the continued profitability of the central city location, and which generate new fiscal resources without threatening the class-fragmented metropolis (Hill, 1974).

The proliferation of intergovernmental project grants for the cities has also been internally contradictory. For if such federal grants decreased the possibilities for political influence by the urban working class, they have also made rational policy formation by national and city executives even more difficult. At the national level the swelling national bureaucracies which resulted from the new federal urban programs were increasingly able to avoid Presidential control and become autonomous centers of policy formation. At the city level, both city managers and mayors were unable to control the federally funded city agencies because of these agencies' direct lines of communication to their federal sponsors. The erosion of urban executive power which resulted led finally to yet another structural change, revenue sharing, which promises new conflicts and contradictions.

Structural change: Corporatism

The emergence of corporatist structures to politically incorporate the organized working class, given the increasing role of state intervention in the economy, is a third example of structural change that attempts to insulate the political regulation of the economy from working class control.

A variety of analysts have linked the attempts at political incorporation of the organized working class into subordinate positions in corporatist structures to the increasing imperatives for state planning of capitalist development. Shonfield (1965) has argued that the emergence of the positive capitalist state which attempts to maintain full employment, regulate labor conflict, control inflation, and stabilize business cycles has been associated with the institutionalization of class conflict. Schmitter (1974) has analyzed the emergence of societal corporatism in advanced capitalist nations. Corporatism in general is characterized by:

. . . singular, non-competitive, hierarchically ordered, sectorally compartmentalized, interest associations exercising representational monopolies and accepting (de jure or de facto) governmentally imposed or negotiated limitations on the type of leaders they elect and on the scope and intensity of demands they routinely make upon the state. (1974: 99–100)

Schmitter argues that societal corporatism, a form of interest structuring not centrally imposed by an authoritarian state, emerges out of the decline of advanced pluralism. The institutionalization of class and interest conflict through societal corporatism assures state control and predictability of class conflict, the cooptation of working class elites in exchange for state guaranteed monopolization of working class access to state power. The process of corporatist development involves a variety of forms:

The modalities are varied and range from direct government subsidies for association, to official recognition of bonafide interlocuteurs, to devolved responsibilities for such public tasks as unemployment or accident insurance, to permanent membership in specialized advisory councils, to positions of control in joint public-private corporations, to informal, quasi-cabinet status, and finally to direct participation in authoritative economic and social councils. (Schmitter, 1974: 111)

Warren (1972) also has suggested the importance of politically incorporating the working class as a political requirement for capitalist planning given the need to assure wage control in the context of international trade competition. Political incorporation was critical if the politicization of profit levels and class shares of income was to be averted. The solution, according to Warren, was

The institutionalized integration of a bureaucratic trade union movement into the planning process, exchange for limited, but continuous economic and other gains for the working class —provided *all* independence of the movement is surrendered except over minor matters. (Warren, 1972: 8)

Warren suggests that the early adoption of wage policies in Norway, Sweden, and Holland was only possible because social democratic parties were in power and could induce trade union wage control. Warren points out that after the failure of deflationary measures in response to inflationary wage-price spirals, the United Kingdom, West Germany, Belgium, and Italy

. . . all ushered in planning plus wage policies under the aegis of newly formed social democratic governments or governments with social democratic participation; in all cases major sections of the ruling class specifically opted for social democratic participation in government; in all cases a certain political resurgence of the working class occurred at the same time as inflation was accelerating, and followed the exposure of the irrationalities of previous stop-go type policies, thus making the strategic problem of the integration of the working class into the new capitalism rather more urgent. (1972: 13)

Warren goes on to point out that with their incorporation into state planning, social democratic parties abandoned the socialist elements in their programs and stressed the efficiency with which the party could manage state planned, full-employment capitalism.

Corporatism is also an internally contradictory mode of incorporating the working class. The premise of a corporatist strategy is that the inclusion of selected leaders of working class organizations (especially unions, but also on occasion left parties) in formal state planning processes will reduce working class opposition to state policies without requiring massive concessions to popular demands. This outcome will occur only if two things happen: first, the incorporated leadership must be seen as legitimate by the working class, and second, the leadership must be sufficiently insulated from day-to-day mass pressures to accept the imperatives of planning in the interests of capital accumulation. And here lies the contradictory quality of corporatism: If the leadership of the incorporated working class organizations is sufficiently isolated from the working class so that state planning is insulated from popular pressures, then that leadership will tend to gradually lose legitimacy and thus cease to function as a means for integrating the working class. If, on the other hand, the leadership maintains close ties to the working class and remains a legitimate instrument of real working class organizations, then corporatist planning will be hampered by the constant pressures for accommodation with mass demands. The first of these possibilities undermines the cooptive function of corporatism and will tend to accelerate the disintegration of the incorporated organizations. This can already be seen in the case of social democratic parties in several European countries. The second of these possibilities undermines the planning function of corporatism and brings class struggle into the administrative heart of the state apparatus itself. In either case, corporatism, like other attempted structural solutions to political class struggle, remains an intensely contradictory strategy for the capitalist class.

In summary the three historical cases of reform government, federal intergovernmental urban transfer programs, and corporatist planning all suggest the importance of analyzing state structures as they mediate the relationship between classes (i.e. as a product and determinant of class conflict). Methodologically, this means that one cannot study a particular agency or legislative act in isolation from class struggle and the ways in which class struggle is internalized within the state. Consequently, in order to assess the contradictory ways by which state structure reproduces capitalist political domination it is necessary to analyze the location within state structures of the control of different policies and the location of political incorporation into the state of different class interests. Otherwise the state is likely to be seen as a neutral instrument or a functionalist thermostat for capital society.

The political struggles of the working class thus gain analytical importance absent from the "instrumental corporate liberal" and "structuralist" approaches. Political class struggle becomes the central determinant both of the restructuring of the state itself and of the contradictory consequences of that restructuring. To paraphrase Marx, capitalists may manipulate the state but they do not do so just as they please. The instrumental domination of the capitalist class is constrained by the structures of the state formed out of past class struggles, by the exigencies of current class struggles, and by the contradictory consequences of state activity for future class struggle.[6]

Summary

Our analysis can be summed up in several propositions:

1. State structures must be seen as the outcome of class struggle rather than as ahistorically given, perfect mechanisms for reproducing capitalist society and repressing the working class.

2. These structures mediate, in contradictory ways, the relationship between instrumental inputs into the state from the ruling class and functional outputs.

3. When successfully shaped by the capitalist class, these structures accomplish two critical tasks: (a) they limit state interventions within bounds compatible with the imperatives of capital accumulation; (b) they politically neutralize the working class in the sense of making its political demands congruent with the reproduction of capitalist social relations.

4. However—and this is very important —these structures are inevitably contradictory. They never provide a totally unproblematic solution to the challenge of political class struggle. The working class can

never be perfectly incorporated, totally neutralized. The political question for the working class is never whether or not contradictions exist within the state, but rather how intense those contradictions are and how they can be exploited by the working class.

Our discussion has largely focused on only one half of the dialectic between state structures and class struggle, namely the ways in which these structures are shaped by class struggle. It is equally important to see how the forms and directions of class struggle are shaped by the state. It is ultimately out of a dialectical theory of the relationship of class struggle to the state that a complete understanding of both will emerge.

NOTES

1. An excellent review and critique of the dominant American perspective can be found in James Sharpe, "American Democracy Reconsidered," *British Journal of Political Science,* 1973.
2. For Poulantzas, people are "agents" of the social structure (1973: 206), and not conscious, existentially generative actors. Poulantzas writes, ". . . political class struggle has nothing to do with a . . . process . . . 'acted' by . . . the class subject" (p. 77). Therefore it becomes impossible for this approach to specify the conditions under which the subjective interests of the capitalist class or members of it will coincide with the functions of the state.
3. For an extremely interesting critique of the instrumentalist perspective see Mollenkopf (1975). For a discussion of various strands of structuralist and instrumentalist theories of the state which parallels our analysis, see Gold, Lo, and Wright (1975).
4. In the U.S., black community movements have begun to realize the importance of structural change in the metropolis and city government as vital to their ability to politically organize for more generalized political power necessary to effect change. For example, May (1971) has described how a politically organized West Oakland community struggled not simply to assure community representation in programs affecting them, but to constitute a new center of power with *legitimate authority,* co-equal with the city council, to control all agencies relevant to their community. Not only the immediate political outcome but the capacity for future political organization, depends on the decision of whether to try to control existent state structures, or to restructure that apparatus.
5. In the four U.S. cities studied by Williams and Adrian, the median percentage of manual workers on the city council was 8 percent. Newton (1974) have pointed out that in Britain, where nationally integrated urban parties are organized around labor union support, manual workers and labor union leaders are much more likely to get elected to the council than in the U.S.
6. The general approach we have outlined allows us to understand how politics in advanced capitalist states has appeared pluralist despite the reality of capitalist domination of the state. Pluralism, as the phenomenal form of political conflict in capitalist societies, can be understood as one manifestation of the political neutralization of the working class. The empirical data of pluralist theory are thus saved, but raised to a higher analytic level.

REFERENCES

Alford, Robert, "The Limits of Urban Reform: Sociological Perspectives on the History of Urban Social Structure and Politics," paper delivered at the American Historical Association meetings, San Francisco, California, 1973.

Althusser, Louis, "Ideology and Ideological State Apparatuses," *Lenin and Philosophy* (New York: Monthly Review Press, 1971).

Altvater, Elmer, "Notes on Some Problems of State Interventionism," *Kapitalistate,* vol. 1, no. 1, 1973.

Baran, Paul and Paul Sweezy, *Monopoly Capital* (New York: Monthly Review Press, 1966).

Feshbach, Dan and Les Shipnuck, "Corporate Regionalism in the United States," *Kapitalistate,* vol. 1, no. 1, 1973, pp. 14–23.

Gold, David, Clarence Y. H. Lo, and Erik Olin Wright, "Recent Developments in Marxist Theories of the Capitalist State," *Monthly Review* 27 (November 1975).

Gortz, Andre, *Strategy for Labor* (Boston: Beacon Press, 1964).

Hamilton, Richard, *Class and Politics in the United States* (Wiley: New Press, 1972).

Hays, Samuel, "The Politics of Reform in Municipal Government in the Progressive Era," in

152

Callow, Alexander B., ed., *American Urban History* (Oxford: New York, 1969).

Hill, Richard Child, "Separate and Unequal: Governmental Inequality in the Metropolis," *American Political Science Review,* December 1974.

Katznelson, Ira, "The Crisis of the Capitalist City: Urban Politics and Social Control," in Hawley, Willia and Michael Lipsky, eds., *Theoretical Perspectives on Urban Politics* (Englewood Cliffs, N.J.: Prentice-Hall, 1976).

Lipset, Seymour Martin, *Political Man* (Garden City, N.Y.: Doubleday, 1960).

Lipset, S. M. and Rokkan, Stein, eds., *Party Systems and Voter Alignments* (New York: Free Press, 1967).

McConnel, Grant, *Private Power and American Democracy* (New York: Vintage, 1966).

Marx, Karl and Fredrick Engels, *Communist Manifesto,* S. Beer edition, 1955, pp. 11–12.

May, Judith, "Two Model Cities: Negotiations in Oakland," *Politics and Society,* Fall 1971, pp. 57–88.

Miliband, Ralph, *The State in Capitalist Society* (New York: Basic Books, 1969).

Miller, D. C., "Industry and Community Power Structure: A Comparative Study of an American and English City," *American Sociological Review,* vol. 23, 1956, pp. 9–15.

———, "Decision-Making Cliques in Community Power Structures: A Comparative Study of an American and English City," *American Journal of Sociology,* vol. 64, 1958, pp. 299–310.

Mills, C. Wright, *The Power Elite* (New York: Oxford University Press, 1956).

Mollenkopf, John, "Theories of the State and Power Structure Research," *Insurgent Sociologist,* vol. 3, 1975.

Morlock, Laura, "Business Interests, Countervailing Groups, and the Balance of Influence in 91 Cities," unpublished paper, 1973.

Morris, D. S. and Ken Newton, "The Occupational Composition of Party Groups on Birmingham Council: 1920–1960," Birmingham Faculty of Commerce and Social Science, discussion paper.

Newton, Kenneth, "Community Politics and Decision-Making: Some Lessons of the American Experience for British Research," unpublished paper, November 1973.

———, "Community Decision-Makers and Community Decision-Making in England and the United States," unpublished paper, 1974.

O'Connor, James, *The Fiscal Crisis of the State* (New York: St. Martin's Press, 1973).

Offe, Claus, "Advanced Capitalism and the Welfare State," *Politics and Society,* vol. 2, no. 4, 1972.

———, "Class Rule and the Political System: On the Selectiveness of Political Institutions," mimeographed, 1973b, translation of chap. 3 of *Strukturprobleme des kapitalistischen Staates* (Frankfurt am Main: Suhrkamp Verlag, 1972).

———, "The Theory of the Capitalist State and the Problem of Policy Formation," mimeographed, 1974.

Poulantzas, Nicos, "The Problem of the Capitalist State," in Blackburn, Robin, eds., *Ideology in Social Science* (London: Fontana, 1972).

———, *Political Power and Social Classes* (London, 1973).

———, "On Social Classes," *New Left Review,* March–April 1974, pp. 27–55.

———, *Fascism and Dictatorship* (London: New Left Books, 1974).

———, *Classes in Contemporary Capitalism* (London: New Left Books, 1975).

Rose, Arnold M., "Corruption, Machine Politics, and Political Change," *American Political Science Review,* vol. 63, December 1969.

Schmitter, Philippe C., "Still the Century of Corporatism?" *Review of Politics,* 1974, pp. 99–100 and 85–131.

Shonfield, Andrew, *Modern Capitalism* (New York: Oxford Press, 1965).

Sweezy, Paul, *The Theory of Capitalist Development* (New York: Monthly Review Press, 1942).

Warren, Bill, "Capitalist Planning and the State," *New Left Review,* vol. 72, 1972, pp. 3–29.

Weinstein, James, *The Corporate Ideal in the Liberal State* (Boston: Beacon Press, 1968).

Williams, Oliver and Charles Adrian, *Four Cities* (Philadelphia: University of Pennsylvania Press, 1969).

Wolman, Harold L. and Norman C. Thomas, "Black Interests, Black Groups, and Black Influences in the Federal Policy Process," *Journal of Politics,* vol. 32, November 1970, pp. 875–896.

The political economy of social service rationalization*

LARRY HIRSCHHORN

In the past several years, budget deficits at all levels of government, pressures from business groups concerned with the availability of capital, and tax resistance from over-burdened taxpayers have all led to significant reductions in social service spending. The food stamp program, education, public transit and hospital services have all been cut back to restore the fiscal balance of state, municipal and federal agencies. The immediate consequences are clear. The needy get less, employees are laid off, experimental programs are eliminated, and management techniques based on efficiency measures are introduced. The level of care falls.

These are the immediate consequences. But what are the long term consequences? Specifically, what impact does such a reduction and rationalization have, not only on clients, but on the political economy as a whole? We want to address this larger systemic question. We want to place social service rationalization in the broader framework of political economy.

To do this, we divide our paper into four sections. In section one we argue that the classical theory of the "welfare state" offers us one way of understanding the political economy of social service rationalization. This theory suggests that social service cutbacks in a depression or recession restore the basis for a renewed upswing in business. Rationalization is thus functional to capitalist development. In section two, however, we argue that welfare state theory presents an outmoded view of the relationship between social services and economic

development. It presumes that social services in particular and services in general play a subsidiary role in the development process, while industry and manufacturing labor are still the motors of productivity growth, market formation and social organization. In contrast, we argue that both state and private services have increasingly displaced industry as the organizing forces for development. Thus, in section three we argue that rationalization is no longer functional to capitalist development, it no longer restores the basis for a new cycle of accumulation. Instead, it further limits accumulation, stifles productivity growth, and restricts the development of new markets. Finally, in section four we show why state and corporate elites nevertheless persist in rationalization strategies. We argue that services growth and reorganization open up new areas of conflict that cannot be managed within the framework of traditional class politics. Rationalization thus sustains the old industrial system of social relations, but it consequently limits the development of what Marx called the productive forces. This argument points to a new "developmental" framework for examining social service growth and conflict. The political implications of this argument, however, take us beyond the familiar benchmarks of traditional class conflicts.

The welfare state and social service rationalization

The classical model. There is no fully developed theory of social services in most

* From *Contemporary Crises*, 2 (January 1978), pp. 63–81. © 1978 Elsevier Scientific Publishing Company, Amsterdam, The Netherlands.

theoretical views of the welfare state. But, if theoretical writings on both the welfare state and social services are examined, we think that the following synthetic framework emerges.[1]

In the welfare state, social service spending increases the real income of the working class. The working class can increase its standard of living by getting higher wages or more services (in kind or in cash). Thus, the division of national income between wages and profits (or consumption and investment) is the result of both the politics of wage setting and public spending and taxing.

Capitalists resist social service spending because it increases interest rates by shifting capital from the private to the public sector. As interest rates rise, investment falls, which leads in turn to a lower productivity growth in the economy as a whole. Thus, social service spending can become a "burden" on the private economy.

Workers and capitalists compete for resources both in the labor market (through the wage bargain) and in the public sector (through fiscal politics). Both too high a level of wages or social service spending can lead capitalists to reduce investment. The capitalists "go on strike" by withholding their money. Since total spending thus falls, employment also falls. In the ensuing recession or depression, capitalists will try to both lower wages and reduce social services.

We call this the "classical" conception. It has been amended in two ways. First, it is recognized that a certain minimal level of social services, particularly health and education, is required to maintain social cohesion and reproduce social structure. Workers must be able to read, while infectious diseases must be prevented. But the emphasis is on *minimums*. Just as too low a level of wages will diminish the worker's physical capacity, so will too low a level of social services undermine the rudiments of social life and social structure. However,

once minimal levels are reached, further expansion of service levels is unproductive.

Second, Keynesian economists have argued that social service spending (particularly cash subsidies such as unemployment insurance, food stamps, and housing allowances) need not always be a burden on the economy. In periods of unemployment, there are idle workers and machines. If the state increases social service spending, it can prevent large declines in consumer spending by protecting the basic living standards of the working class. If consumer spending is supported by public subsidies in this way, capitalists will be able to sell their product, inventories will not pile up in warehouses, and investment will not fall any further. Thus, social service spending can play an important "counter-cyclical" role in stabilizing the economy. It is not always a burden.

Yet, even with these amendments, the welfare state model of social services is unchanged in its basics. The immediate profit needs of capitalists still determine the optimal level of social service spending. The *size, scope,* and, with the Keynesian amendments, the *timing* of social service spending are all determined by the *existing* conditions of production.

The meaning of rationalization within this framework. In this framework the logic of rationalization is quite straightforward. Rationalization has three decisive impacts. First, as social spending and government borrowing fall, private capital is released from the public to the private sector. Corporations can then improve their liquidity positions (which are characteristically exposed at the beginning of a business downturn), pay off debts, write down bad investments, and thus establish a pool of capital for a new investment program.

Second, cutbacks in social services can increase the size of the available low-wage labor pool. High levels of social service spending allow people to stay off the labor market for relatively long periods of time as they look either for better jobs or choose non-work roles. Thus, for example, high welfare payments allow poor mothers to stay at home when their children are still infants, unemployment insurance allows workers to wait to be called back to their old jobs, while free or cheap education allows young people to choose the optimal time (from the point of view of their own plans) to look for their first full time job. Social service cutbacks generally eliminate or restrict the scope of these options. Instead, most people must choose any job they are offered.

Third, and finally, service cutbacks force service managers to streamline their programs so that only minimal standards of social and economic life are protected. Most often, this means that programs with short run payoffs to business are emphasized, while others, whose outcomes cannot be linked to immediate labor market conditions, are eliminated. In periods of service expansion, program content can be broadened to fulfill or give expression to a wide range of personal and social developmental needs—needs that cannot be justified by immediate profit considerations. Thus, for example, education programs for retired workers might be developed while health services for female-headed families might be expanded. In other words, in periods of service expansion social services can become the locus for the social development of the working class as a whole.

However, in periods of cutback, program content is usually narrowed. Vocationalism rules education, while curative medicine organized for the immediately productive part of the work force dominates health. This form of rationalization can thus maintain short run payoffs of social services to business. The profit rate is protected.

In all these cases the worker is demoralized. His or her capacity for resistance to "market dictates" is low. Under these conditions capitalists can force the reorganiza-

tion of economic structure, skills hierarchies and regional job deployment necessary for establishing the basis for a new cycle of accumulation. Indeed, this has been the basis for reorganizing the capitalist economy since the great enclosures of the late 18th and early 19th centuries.

Beyond the Welfare State: The new functions of services

Thus far, we have examined the theory of rationalization—as a process functional to capitalist development—within the analytic framework set by the concept of the welfare state. In other words, we have constructed a theory of rationalization based on a particular *paradigm* of the relationship between social services and economic development. We think, however, that this paradigm, the welfare state model of social services increasingly misleads us in our attempt to understand the reality of social services today. This implies in turn that our model of rationalization may also be incorrect. In contrast to the welfare state paradigm we propose instead that: (1) social services in particular and services in general increasingly play a leading or cutting edge role in economic development and, therefore, (2) social service rationalization is less and less functional to economic renewal and capitalist development. Let us examine each proposition in turn.

The new role for services. Recent neo-Marxist studies have pointed to the growing importance of the "reproductive" institutions of the political economy.[2] Whereas classical Marxist thinkers analyzed the labor process and market dynamics to the exclusion of family life, social services, state planning, research and development, communications and marketing dynamics, current writers emphasize that the *reproduction* of social structure, the *organization* of social life and the *circulation* of information and capital have become increasingly important to the process of capital accumulation. In turn, as they have become more important they have merged in function with the classically productive institutions of the factory, the office and the distribution system. Productivity, the rate of profit, the structure and size of markets—factors that were once determined in the market, on the factory floor and through the wage bargain—are now determined by a broader and more variegated set of institutions. Where Marx insisted that the reproduction of social organization, the circulation of capital and information, and the marketing of products determine only the *distribution* of surplus value, today's writers insist that these functions determine the levels and rates of surplus value. All this suggests that social services are not simply transfers of real income to the working class nor are marketing and communication services simply mechanisms for redistributing surplus value. Both create surplus value. The welfare state model of services, even with its amendments is incorrect.

Health and education. Health and education are no longer just transfers of real income (in the form of services) to the working classes. Recent studies on the sources of growth in advanced capitalism emphasize the importance of *human capital* in the form of both skill and adaptability as an increasingly important determinant of productivity and profits.[3] Education was, of course, always essential for socializing the working class to the rhythms and discipline of urban-factory life. (This was particularly important for the first generation of rural and/or foreign immigrants.) Punctuality and basic literacy had to be taught. But beyond this, little else was required. Indeed, the general tendency of capitalist development was to reduce the complexity of tasks once performed by artisans.

Today, however, capitalist profitability depends increasingly on an organized system of innovation. Writers often refer to the importance of innovation today without, however, making critical distinctions between the different systems of production management that have been developed in different and successive periods of capitalist development.[4] We can identify three critical systems: Taylorism, Operations Research and the system of Organized Creativity (Research and Development). As each system emerged a new stratum of educated workers was created. Moreover, as each system was developed the general stratum of educated worker became increasingly important for capitalist profitability. It is the last and most inclusive stratum, the stratum involved in the system of organized creativity, that highlights in clearest form the new and central role of health and education to profits and productivity. Let us briefly examine each of these systems in turn.

F. W. Taylor systemized the general method for increasing labor productivity *within an already established structure of machines and material inputs.*[5] When the capitalist decided on the product, the basic materials and the machine types, Taylor's system allowed him to engineer human motion so that profits could be maximized. Industrial engineers could eliminate all "wasteful" human motion by applying Taylor's *time and motion* techniques, while management could then apply Taylor's system of *rate setting* to minimize wage payments per unit of labor time. Capitalists could thus apply these two techniques to maximize profits within the confines of an already established technological process.

Operations research is qualitatively different from Taylorism because it shifts attention from the regulation of *labor* time to *time in general.* The operations researcher not only eliminates wasteful human movement but the wasteful or inefficient matching of inventory stockpiles, materials flow and market distribution per unit of time.

The operations researcher coordinates the different production steps *through* time so that there is a minimum of "down-time" of machines and warehousing of materials or products.

The operations researcher thus views the production process within a broader frame of reference than does the Taylor engineer. He cannot just maximize the productivity of particular production steps. Rather, the entire sequence of operations must be systematically and profitably integrated. Moreover, where the Taylor engineer could focus on factory operations alone, the operations researcher must examine the systematic interaction between factory and markets. If market sales fluctuate according to some pattern that can be discerned, then production must be meshed with that pattern if inventory costs are to be minimized. Thus, we can say that the shift from Taylorism to operations research represented a shift from *labor time* engineering to *systems* engineering.

Yet again, though the operations researcher assumes a broader scope and can therefore intervene at many more different points in the production process, he still must accept certain conditions, such as the relevant market, the basic materials and the broad characteristics of the machine technology, as given. His scope is broadened, but the key boundaries of action remain unchanged.

Finally, the last and present stage extends the organized system of intervention and planning beyond the confines of the systems engineer. Increasingly, capitalists try to organize the creative process itself by integrating scientists, engineers, market specialists and personnel managers in teams so that together they can design new products, new and appropriate materials, and new machine technologies in a coordinated and fully planned sequence of steps.

In this context, few parameters of production are taken as constant. Instead, the research team must determine which (monetizable) human needs are emerging, what products might best satisfy these needs, what materials would satisfy the performance criteria of the product, and finally what machinery would best process the materials. Profits are thus increased not by *economizing* labor time, nor by *optimizing* materials flow, but by *creating* and *servicing* a market. Taylorist engineers organized *labor* time, systems engineers organized total *production time*, whereas researchers and developers organize *social* time. In this sense we can say that the system for creating profits has moved from *human* engineering to *systems* engineering to *social* engineering.

This sequence is a "developmental" one in the sense that each new production system creates a new and broader system for making profits while at the same time making the older ones both more efficient and more "automatic" (from the point of view of the amount of management time required to operate the system). As a consequence the role of the educated worker has been affected in three interrelated ways. First, the educated worker must develop a progressively broader scope. Second, the worker must accept fewer and fewer conditions of production as given or fixed. Third, the worker must operate increasingly within teams. Together, these three dimensions suggest that profitability rests increasingly on an organized system of innovation in which a certain (but certainly growing) stratum of workers must operate increasingly in *open-ended* settings where goals, means and modes of coordination are *no longer specified.*[6] Instead, they must be created within and through the innovation process itself.

It is within this context that education becomes a productive force. When schools teach specific job skills we can say that the contents of education are derived from the specific conditions of production. But as the latter recede in significance as determinants of educated labor's work, the contents of education are no longer skills per se, but the learning process itself. Learning creativity, learning team work styles, learning to imagine become the leading edge determinants of education's new contents. As education turns in on itself, as it is derived less and less from specific conditions of production, it becomes in turn a productive force.

In sum, the educated worker, the technical, professional and managerial workers of today, must be trained to use not only a particular set of tools and concepts and manage a particular set of social relations, but in addition must also be trained to be adaptable, to learn new ways of organizing social, technical and conceptual systems. There is thus emerging an "innovation sector" of the economy located in research, human services, chemicals, planning, the design professions, marketing, communications, advanced machine tooling (computer controlled), in which profitability rests less on routinized work procedures and more on open-ended work protocols. As this sector develops, education becomes an increasingly important determinant of profit.

In this context, health services can also increase the "amount" of human capital, the adaptability and productivity of educated workers. It is now recognized that a person's health is clearly linked to his or her stress level.[7] The latter, however, is directly related to the amount and quality of change a person experiences. Thus, the more that profits are based on changing job and organizational protocols, the more does stress threaten the integrity and productivity of the work force. (Change, stress, and health are most often mediated through life-style changes, i.e. someone under stress begins to overeat, smoke, exercise less, sleep more poorly and neglect disease symptoms). Rapid innovation can thus undermine the work force that must in the end underpin the system of innovation itself. Thus health services, particularly life-style counseling therapy and health-education services, must be and in fact are being developed to socialize the experience and management of stress.

In sum, in a system of development based on innovation and qualitative change in the "input" of human effort (as against quantitative increases in the input of human labor time) health and education become productivity and profit increasing investments. They are not simply transfers of real income and services from the capitalist class to the working class.

Welfare. The recent expansion in welfare spending points to another new and increasingly central function of social services. In the past, social transfer policy was based on the presumption that most transfers would be employment related.[8] Thus, for example, social security payments to the aged were tied to past wage levels, while unemployment insurance was tied to the cycle of hiring and firing. Indeed, the architects of the first social security act argued that a federally directed and funded program for the aged, widowed and unemployed would eliminate all traditional "public welfare" spending funded by states and localities.

The facts of the post World War II welfare explosion proved them wrong. Welfare spending expanded in both good times and bad, and grew particularly fast in the upswing of the 60s. Many factors lay behind this growth, political militance being among the most important.[9] But studies revealed that the size of the *potentially eligible* pool of welfare recipients (as contrasted to the actual number of recipients) was determined in large part by deteriorating labor market conditions in many large cities.[10] Many young and minority people faced a life of structural unemployment or underemployment. They could not find work to maintain decent living standards (this was the root cause of family stress and break-up).

If we compare the growth of this "technologically superfluous" part of the labor force with the growth of the sector of highly educated workers, we confront what at first seems to be a paradox. How can the workforce be upgraded and displaced at the same time? Yet, a moment's reflection shows that these two developments are part of the same process of uneven and chronically unbalanced development. The Taylorist routinization of work in this modern period has increasingly displaced workers entirely from the labor force. (In the earlier period it destroyed craft labor and integrated the semi-skilled worker to the machine on a new basis.) However, where such rationalization is balanced by the growth of jobs rooted in innovation and human capital spending, private and public investment can be *on balance* employment increasing and skill upgrading. Thus, the growth of both a sector of highly skilled workers and a sector of displaced workers is a sign that the rate of expansion of the innovation sector is too low. The result is increasingly a tri-partite job structure, composed of workers in the innovation sector, displaced workers, and workers in old industrial jobs (steel, auto construction) who live on the knife-edge of skill upgrading or technological obsolescence.

Welfare spending plays a new role in this situation. It no longer provides stop-gap subsidies to those temporarily out of work. Rather, it must provide long term subsistence to individuals and families who can no longer play a productive role in the economy. Similarly, such structural employment weakens the ties of family and community that locate the individual in an ongoing social life. Welfare workers are thus pushed to reorder family and community relationships so that the process of social disintegration might be stopped (in this they often fail). Finally, if and when the state, as the result of political pressures from above or below, tries to upgrade the structurally displaced workers so that they might get jobs in the growth sector, the welfare system becomes the first point of attack. Job counseling, manpower training, the development of an upgrading system based on a combination of child care, job training and work experience programs all take place under the umbrella of the (public and non-profit private) welfare system.

In effect, the functions of the welfare system have changed. Welfare is no longer just a system of social control tied to immediate labor market conditions. Rather, the displacement and integration of people in the work system, a process once controlled by market forces, is increasingly controlled by the welfare system. Thus, in its tendencies, in its "laws of motion," welfare becomes a productive force as it translates productive potentials into actual job allocations. Thus, welfare services are not simply transfers of real income to the working class. Rather, they regulate the growth, structure and development of the "displaced population." In this way they play a decisive role in influencing patterns of accumulation and productivity development for the society as a whole.

Marketing. Not only social services but services in general have become central to the process of capital accumulation. The case of marketing is suggestive. In early stages of development consumption is low and much of the working class lives at near subsistence levels. But with rising productivity in the later stages, working class wages and consumption rise. Indeed, as Keynes emphasized, consumption must rise steadily if the rate of investment and thus the rate of full employment is to be sustained.

Yet, Keynesian theory focuses on economic aggregates. It ignores the social basis for mass consumption. When workers live at subsistence levels, consumption is organized by the simple biological needs for food, clothing and shelter. But mass consumption requires a social basis. It must be organized through a set of social institutions, roles and norms.

The suburban boom of the post World War II period is representative. Single family homes and consumer durables could be sold on a mass basis only when the prototypical nuclear-privatized family become the norm of working class life. Two factors made this possible. First, past political-economic and demographic trends had already weakened the older ethnic neighborhoods of large cities, e.g. street-car based suburbanization in the 1920s combined with the cut-off of immigration. Second, and more importantly, state policy and ideological management reinforced and channeled the resultant pattern of population dispersal and home life. Young people were offered historically low rates of downpayment and mortgage interest, women were pushed out of the jobs they had held during the war, and the mass magazines refurbished the cult of motherhood in modern dress.

The result was astonishing. The median age of marriage for men which declined at a rate of about 12 *days* per year from 1890 to 1940 fell 1.5 *years* from 1940 to 1950 or five times as fast. Similarly, from 1890 to 1940 there was almost no secular decline in the median age at first marriage for women (one-half year or 3.6 days a year). But from 1940 to 1950 the decline was 1.2 years or 1.4 months per year—about 12 times as fast as the previous trend. Young people were thus forming families earlier than ever before.[11] Consequently, the fertility rate *rose* for the first time since 1800.[12] Thus the post-war investment long cycle (which seems to have ended in 1965 when the rate of profit once again began to fall) depended ultimately on the *social organization* of consumption, based on the single family home, privatized durables consumption, the auto and a historically large family size. Without this consumption structure it is unlikely that investment and consumption would have risen to above depression or deep recession levels. Keynesian strategy notwithstanding, aggregate demand could not be simply maintained through quantitative strategies of taxing and spending but required in addition qualitative strategies for organizing consumption. The marketing of social images and the goods that complement them thus emerged as a key element in maintaining an acceptable rate of profit.

Today, of course, marketing has become supremely sophisticated. Marketing managers try to organize psychic structures as well as social behaviors. In particular, the emerging break-up of the stable nuclear family (as reflected in the growth of single parent homes, high divorce rates, serial marriages and a rising proportion of working and married mothers)[13] makes it harder to predict and control consumption patterns. Market strategists have thus sought to develop finer tools and concepts for analyzing and creating new consumption habits. (The concept of "life-style segmentation" has emerged as central.[14]) But as marketing extends its scope and impact, it faces new emerging counterpressures. As it more deeply penetrates the fields of value formation, life-styles and social relationships, it comes up against counter-images of social life forms from various sectors of the society. This is the broad basis for the recent growth in consumerism as the counterweight to marketing. The conflict that emerges as each develops in opposition to the other is one more sign of the increasing significance and centrality of marketing services to the accumulation process.

The limits of social service rationalization today

We have argued that services in general and social services in particular have become increasingly central to the process of economic development. Increasingly, they determine the rate of productivity growth and the rate of profit. In this sense we may say that services have become part of the "productive forces." Indeed, the growth and changing functions of services suggest that a new ensemble of productive forces is emerging. Increasingly, the organization of social life as represented by health, welfare and marketing, and the diffusion of information as represented by education, research and development and part of the communications industry, suggests that services have become the concrete or institutional embodiments of *information* and *organization* as productive forces. Similarly, aggregate labor time, that is the number of hours worked by the mass of semi-skilled laborers, has had a relatively smaller impact on profit than it had in earlier periods of capitalist development. This is the sense in which certain writers term the present period, the period of "disaccumulation," i.e. productive labor time is not expanded, or the beginnings of the post-industrial society.[15]

If we say that services are the institutional embodiments of new productive forces, then we can argue that social service rationalization *restricts the development* of these forces. Whereas, in the past, market dynamics limited the development of productive forces (in the form of unemployment, idle and machinery, cutbacks in investment), we would suggest that today the leading indicator of the balance between the retardation or expansion of productive forces is reflected in the dynamics of services development. Social service *rationalization*, that is, the restriction in the scope, level and dynamism of social services, is an indication that the productive forces themselves are being held back. Three examples are in order.

First, the cutback in welfare payments and food stamps lowers living standards and forces groups of people onto the low-wage market, e.g. young people, the "hidden minorities," women, etc. But today the high profitability sectors of production—steel, auto, paper, metal working—cannot profitably employ masses of unskilled and semi-skilled workers. As work is progressively rationalized, productivity is improved by displacing (or not hiring) workers. Nor will these workers be hired if, as Keynesians argue, aggregate demand is simply increased. If increases in sales lead to higher profit rates, the resulting higher rate of investment in more mechanized machinery will only displace more workers.

Thus, for example, the number of production workers in steel and auto fell throughout much of the post-war period. From 1953 to 1969 (two peak periods of employment) the number of production workers in primary metals production (steel, copper, etc.) fell by 85,000, and in auto by 31,000. In paper it fell by 173,000, while in other industries it rose by only a small amount over the period. Thus, while total employment rose 30 percent in that period, the total number of production workers in durable goods manufacturing rose only 6 percent.[16] Moreover, the number of non-production workers in durable goods manufacturing (a group composed of semi-skilled clerical labor and high skilled professional, technical and managerial labor) rose by 66 percent. In the long run, it seems that permanent job growth can take place only in the innovation sector where uncertain market, technical and organizational conditions make it unprofitable to routinize skills and protocols. In these settings routine spells obsolescence.

The data thus suggest that capitalist development is no longer based on the mass-employment of low-wage semi-skilled labor. Thus, if social service rationalization decreases living standards, many people will not be able to find work to maintain their incomes. Some, especially the young, will turn to crime. Other young people who remain in school will act out against teachers. Thus, the functions of welfare will simply be shifted onto the police and schools. Social costs will not fall.

Rationalizing education also has dysfunctional consequences. Matching skills to available jobs can increase the short run fit between work and school. Schooling will thus be profitable to business since the costs of training for necessary skills will be subsidized. But in the long run this form of vocational education will only limit the growth of profits. On the one hand, vocational skills in the stable high profit industrial sector become obsolete under the press of routinization. (This is happening rapidly to tool and die workers, perhaps the last remaining core of craft workers whose skills are still central to production.) On the other hand, productivity in the innovation sector depends less on fixed skills and more on learning capacity, flexibility, the ability to work in teams, and to work to irregular rhythms. A rationalized education system thus freezes workers into obsolescent molds of thought and skill.

Profitability is lowered in two ways. First, since Taylorism and operations research have been fully institutionalized, they can operate at a relatively low level of materials and time costs. They become less sensitive to overall fluctuations in business. But as education is cut back and vocationalized, the size and capacity of the innovation sector—the source of less obsolescence-prone jobs—is reduced. On balance, economic development becomes labor displacing and ultimately socially disorganizing. This tends to increase the *social* costs of production, via taxes and inflation, as the costs of social control (whether channeled through welfare, the police, schools, etc.) tend to increase. Second, since the size and capacity of the innovation sector is restricted, the rate of formation of new products and materials falls. But since new markets are the source of major new profit sources, restricting the innovation sector further depresses the profit rate.

Third, and finally, as rationalization disorganizes social life it *narrows* the range of possible consumption markets. In earlier periods of development the periodic destruction of working class life could estab-

lish a new and profitable basis for accumulation. Under these conditions lower wages allowed capitalists to increase the amount of machinery and equipment in place. Investment "fed on itself," as, for example, orders from railroad builders increased the demand for steel and increased steel production increased the demand for railroad cars (for the distribution of steel). Today, however, as Keynes emphasized, increased investment requires continuing increases in consumption.

Rationalization, however, can decrease consumption in two ways. First, it can reduce the scope of discretionary spending as increased service fees (for health and education) and decreased service levels (welfare, food and housing) reduce living standards. Second, continuous increases in consumption require periodic reorganizations of consumption patterns. For example, the rate of growth of auto sales slows down as the ratio of people to cars comes up against the limits imposed by transportation infrastructure, e.g. the miles of highways or the number of parking spaces. Similarly television sales slow down as televisions per family reach the limits imposed by family size and viewing habits. Most often the same commodity can penetrate new markets only if its cost and price fall so much that fundamentally marginal uses of the commodity become possible (this is what happened to radios with the development of transistor technology). In general, new consumption patterns require major reorganizations of social life forms, not just new gadgets. The present single family home-auto-nuclear-family complex imposes a definite consumption structure which can be shaped only within limits. Any new major consumer innovation, e.g. the computer in the home, requires a new pattern of social life.

But periods of austerity reduce the range of consumer experimentation. Under stress people look for moral support in old values and behaviors to shore up fragile family and community relations. (For example, the depression decade was culturally conservative.) They turn back to old patterns of social life which can support consumer markets of only below normal profitability (often the saturation of these very same markets led to the original business downturn). The disorganization of social life, once a strategy for increasing investment and profit, now only limits them.

In effect, rationalizing education and welfare and reducing living standards cannot increase the long term profitability of the economy. First, the reduction in living standards and the consequent spirit of austerity limit the rate of growth of new markets. Second, the growth of the innovation sector is restricted as the saturation of old markets provides corporations with little incentive to develop new products, materials and technical processes. Thus, the source of dynamic job growth is stifled. Third, the day by day routinization of older labor processes increases the social costs of production as the number of displaced, underemployed and part-time employed workers grows because the innovation sector grows so slowly. Rationalization progressively *disorganizes* economic and social life.

Summary. Let us summarize our argument thus far. First, we argued that services in general and social services in particular no longer play a secondary role in the accumulation process. Rather, increasingly they determine productivity growth and profit rates. In this sense, they constitute a new ensemble of productive forces. Second, we argued that social service rationalization, at one time functional to accumulation, now simply perpetuates low profit rates. This happened because social service cutbacks, the short run matching of social services and jobs, and the disorganization of social life imposed by austerity all limit the long term profit potential of the economy. Rationalization leads to stalemated developments.

The limits to social service expansion

If rationalization limits productivity why do elites in business and the state not develop a politics and policy of social service expansion? Here is where the key contradictions of late capitalist development emerge.

Marx argued that capitalism continually confronted and had to overcome the contradiction between the increasingly "socialized" productive forces and the privatized set of social relations, e.g. the property form. This proposition is abstract. It does not specify through what institutions and through which politics this contradiction emerges. We would suggest that in each historical period of capitalist development it takes on a different form.

In early periods of capitalist development, it was expressed as the tension between a system of production based on a "putting out" system in which property is family based and workers own their tools, and the larger more socialized factory system. Later, this same contradiction was expressed in the tension within the factory system and between capitalists who own the machinery and the mass of semi-skilled workers whose fundamentally *cooperative* work makes production possible.

We suggest that in the present period this tension is expressed over the expansion, contraction and development of services *because these services represent the new and most socialized forms of the productive forces.* In other words, because services represent the new productive forces the conflict over who will control their development emerges in the services sector. Consequently, while service rationalization limits the long term profit and productivity potential of the economy, it nevertheless allows elites in the corporations and the state to put a lid on this new locus of conflict. Three examples are in order.

First, we argued that health services become increasingly a productive force as preventive health emerges to counter the stressful impact on innovation and job change. Yet, even if preventive health seems necessary (from within the logic of social development) that does not mean it will emerge. On the contrary, since preventive health services must be based on the management of life-styles and ways of life, their extension raises conflict over the appropriate forms and modes of regulation of social life itself. In the last half-decade or so, for example, political health groups have appropriate their own health, to control emerged to argue that people must learn to appropriate their own health, to control their "own bodies," to root mental health counseling in community networks and, finally, to self-manage the forms and distribution of stress within communities. In other words, just as health emerged as a productive force the politics of appropriating health also emerged.

Second, we suggested that education becomes a productive force when flexibility and learning capacity become central to productivity and innovation. Yet again, even if this form of education seems necessary, that does not mean that it will emerge. As this form of education emerges (particularly at university levels) and specialized education declines in significance, people begin to demand the right to control the appropriation and utilization of their knowledge. When skills are narrow and knowledge specialized only managers and elites can integrate the broad range of skills and knowledge. People do not and generally cannot comprehend how this integration takes place. But as specialization breaks down, all people become increasingly involved and implicated in this process. They begin to demand the right to self-manage the development and utilization of knowledge. Thus, for example,

when universities and jobs expanded at a rapid rate in the 60s, students attacked disciplinary boundaries, they criticized research content, and they argued that university knowledge should be integrated with the general social life of the community. Again, as education emerged as a productive force the politics of appropriating education also emerged.

Third, and finally, insofar as welfare becomes a productive force, it subsidizes the social life of displaced communities and organizes the reintegration of people into the work system. When this happens, the welfare system becomes the locus for job development, for the integration of people and work. Welfare conflicts can become conflicts over who will control the translation of productive potentialities into actual work systems. Job development is politicized. For example, as welfare spending expanded in the 60s, welfare clients demanded the right to determine the amount and manner of welfare spending, the conditions and direction of manpower development, and the balance between work and family commitments. In effect, as the welfare system becomes a productive force, conflicts over job development, job allocation, and the integration of work and life began to emerge. Just as welfare began to structure the organization of social life within the nexus of work, so did conflicts over the pattern of this organization emerge.

New dimensions of conflict

We have seen that as services come to embody new productive forces, conflicts over who will control and appropriate these forces also emerge (that is why so many conflicts over social services in the 60s were phrased in social control terms). It is for this reason that elites favor a politics of social service rationalization. Yet, as they organize such a politics, they limit the further development of the productive forces, and the conflict between the socialized productive forces and the privatized social relations emerges in a new concrete form.

Indeed, something more is at stake. We would suggest that this conflict between forces and relations will be less manageable than ever before. The productive forces have never been more socialized than they are now. Health, education, our developing needs and our forms of social life reside within us, in our bodies, brains and social relations. How can they be fully appropriated and commodified for private profit based ends? In the past, the worker who sold his labor power could nevertheless retire to the private sphere of his family, his local neighborhood, his own beliefs and practices. But today the productive forces have become so socialized that corporate and state elites must invade the inner dimensions of our lives if they are to control them.

In this sense we think that today the capitalist pursuit of profits takes on an increasingly *totalitarian* form. Yet, as we saw in the 60s, this incipient totalitarianism can evoke at certain places and times an equally determined anti-totalitarian and democratic resistance. It is for this reason that elites must try to rationalize the services though in so doing they only perpetuate the state of stalemated development. Hence, capitalism enters a period of deep disaccumulation.

The final contradiction: The growth of unproductive services

Stalemated development and service rationalization become in the end self-fulfilling. Insofar as services are rationalized, production and marketing cannot be transformed. But in that degree that the latter are not transformed, disaccumulation takes place. Labor is displaced in industry and in services through the application of classical Taylorist techniques. Surplus labor

and hidden unemployment become endemic, the web of social life unravels, and services are pushed to cope with the contradictions of this decay. Schools become warehouses for misplaced and displaced youth, welfare bureaucracies become the loci for maintaining subsistence incomes, hospitals medicate men and women who face blocked careers and a decaying family life, and marketing channels the consequences of social decay along consumerist lines, e.g. the spread of alcoholism among youth and the dissemination of pornography. The final contradiction of service social development—of post-industrial development—becomes apparent. To the degree that services do not become developmental, to the degree that they do not transform production, marketing and job allocation, then to that degree do services become unproductive, wasteful and irrational. We face the "development of underdevelopment" at the center of late capitalist societies.

Today, social conflict can no longer be comprehended through the categories of factory, industrial worker, and rich versus poor. The stakes are higher than these terms allow. The socialization of the productive forces through services in this modern period of development forces all political actors to confront the new totalitarian project and the potential anti-totalitarian resistance. Services rationalization repress these conflicts by limiting the impact of the new productive forces. But in so doing, it further disorganizes social and economic life. Consequently, the totalitarian and anti-totalitarian forces must ultimately confront each other on an even more confused and disorganized plane of social life. It is this milieu, this strange combination of new productive forces, their stalemated development and the resulting disaccumulation that is establishing the present political context for resistance and action.

166

NOTES

1. For a critical review of the concept of the welfare state, see Titmuss, Richard (1968). "Welfare State and Welfare Society," in his *Commitment to Welfare*, New York: Pantheon.

2. See, for instance, O'Connor, James (1974). *The Fiscal Crisis of the State*, New York: St. Martin's Press.

3. I have discussed this literature at some length in my paper *Towards a Political Economy of the Service Society*, Working Paper no. 229, Institute for Urban and Regional Development, University of California, Berkeley, pp. 1–25.

4. The work of Kenneth Galbraith, e.g., *The New Industrial State*, is one example of a corpus of writing on innovation that does not make these distinctions.

5. Harry Braverman has discussed the history and logic of Taylorism at some length in his *Labor and Monopoly Capital*, New York: Monthly Review Press. 1975.

6. For a general theoretical view of open-ended work in innovation settings, see Schon, Donald A. (1973). *Beyond the Stable State*, New York: Norton.

7. See, for instance, the brilliant essay by Joseph Eyer, "Stress-related Mortality and Social Organization," unpublished, University of Pennsylvania, Department of Biology.

8. See Brown, J. Douglas (1972). *An American Philosophy of Social Security*, Princeton: Princeton University Press, pp. 56–59.

9. The significance of political militance is emphasized by Piven, Frances F. and Cloward, Richard P. (1971). *Regulating the Poor: The Functions of Public Welfare*, New York: Vintage, chap. 8.

10. The structure of these markets is discussed in Doeringer, Peter B. and Piore, Michael J. (1975). "Unemployment and the 'Dual Labor Market,'" *Public Interest*, Winter 1975.

11. For the relevant data, see Kreps, Juanita and Clark, Robert (1975). *Sex, Age, and Work: The Changing Composition of the Work Force*, Baltimore: Johns Hopkins University Press, p. 26.

12. Heer, David (1968). "Economic Development and the Fertility Transition," *Daedalus*, Spring, p. 452.

13. See, for instance, Glick, Paul C. (1975). "A Demographer Looks at American Families," *Journal of Marriage and the Family*, February. Also, Ross, Heather L. and Sawhill, Isabel V. (1975). *Time of Transition: The Growth of Families Headed by Women*, Washington, D.C.: Urban Institute.

14. See, for instance, Plummer, Joseph T. (1974). "The Concept and Application of Life-Style Segmentation," *Journal of Marketing*, January.

15. The concept of "disaccumulation" was first developed by Sklar, Martin (1969). "On the Proletarian Revolution and the End of Political-Economic Society," *Radical America*, May–June 1969.

16. *Manpower Report of the President: 1972*, U.S. Department of Labor, pp. 218, 215.

CHAPTER 5

Culture and consciousness in capitalist society

Under what conditions in the development of capitalism does social life become conscious political activity? When is social action of the working class consciously bound up in the larger class struggle, whereby an attempt is consciously made to change the condition of exploitation and to remove the domination of the capitalist class? This is not to imply that consciousness is simply determined by material conditions of class experiences. Rather, "class-consciousness is the way in which these experiences are handled in cultural terms: embodied in traditions, value-systems, ideas, and institutional forms. If the experience appears as determined, class-consciousness does not."[1] A political consciousness tends to develop under conditions of class oppression, but the specific form it takes and how it becomes manifested in either reactive or revolutionary activity vary in different times and places. During certain periods in specific places, especially in times of economic and institutional crisis under advanced capitalism, the oppressed realize their class affiliation, reject the capitalist's reified view of the world, and act to change their historical circumstances.[2] In a dialectical process, people change themselves, their consciousness, and their circumstances.

Our daily lives are lived in the tension and bond between the concrete historical situation and the unconditioned depth of our being. It is through the "here and now" of existence that we experience an awareness and realization of ultimate matters. The sacred and secular are thus joined: "History in all its spheres is the arena of salvation, the realm in which the demands of the unconditional are confronted. Salvation occurs in time and through community, in the overcoming of the demonic powers that pervert both personal and social life."[3] In life we come to know that which transcends life.

The sacred—the religious element of our being that is directed toward the unconditional—cannot be separated from the rest of culture. Following the theological tradition articulated by Paul Tillich, all sharp distinctions between the sacred and the secular are eliminated in a recognition of the common source of both religion and culture. "Religion," Tillich wrote, "is the substance of culture, culture is the expression of religion."[4] Implied here is a dialectical relationship between religion and culture: "Religion, in order to achieve realization, must assume form and become culture; in doing so it is religious in both substance and intention. But culture, even when it is not religious by intention, is religious in substance, for every cultural act contains an unconditional meaning, it depends upon the ground of meaning."[5] Yet when religion becomes cultural reality, it loses some of its depth and relatedness to the unconditional—becoming in various degrees "secularized." However, a new religious awareness may be rediscovered in the dialectic of cultural history. The history of a culture is in a broad sense the history of religion. The cultural history to which I am referring includes the mode of production and all material products, as well as the social institutions, patterns of thinking and acting, and all artistic creations—all aspects of human creation. Culture, in other words, is not merely the Marxian "superstructure," using a spatial metaphor, but is the totality of "base" and superstructure. Although religion is usually considered as being more directly an element of the superstructure, it is part of a dynamic that shapes the economic base of the culture.

A central proposition of the Marxist analysis of history is that there are deep contradictions and dynamic variations in the relationship between production and the superstructural elements. Moreover, when these forces are considered as the specific activities and relationships of real human beings, "they mean something very much more active, more complicated and more contradictory than the developed metaphorical notion of 'the base' could possibly allow us to realize."[6] When we talk about religion and its relation to culture, we are talking about an interconnected process and not a static condition.

Rooted deeply in the prophetic cultural tradition is the urge toward justice in human affairs. This urge becomes the divine will operating in history, providing the source of inspiration to all prophets and revolutionaries. In the cultural aesthetic of the prophetic we are made to see the possibilities of another existence. The aesthetic of all cultural production is a protest against existing arrangements and at the same time seeks to transcend them. Thereby, Herbert Marcuse observes, "art subverts the dominant consciousness, the ordinary experience."[7] The aesthetic of cultural creation allows us in form and substance to transcend the social determination of our work. The inner logic of the prophetic mode of cultural production is the creation of another sensibility which defies the dominant social institutions and modes of thought and belief. Prophetic criticism—in its aesthetic—reveals the essence of reality and suggests the potential of our essential nature. The critical function of a prophetic consciousness is its contribution to the historical struggle for human liberation.

The relation of culture and consciousness to the basic mode of production is especially important, in the sense of even shaping the substructure, when it is the *intention* of cultural creations to affect human life and influence historical development. And it is, indeed, the intention of religion (that is, life lived with the sense of ultimate concern) to be of consequence to the lives of people and institutions in this world as well as in any other.[8] Religion is a force that is constantly making and remaking culture. As with other human creations, it is from the beginning a practice. Religion is a practice that is continually shaping the conditions of the culture within which it is practiced.

Therefore we assume the relationship—dialectical and interdependent in both directions—between culture and religion. Religion is a vital and integral part of human history.

NOTES

1. E. P. Thompson, *The Making of the English Working Class* (New York: Random House, 1963), p. 10.

2. David Sallach, "Class consciousness and the Everyday World in the Work of Marx and Schutz," *The Insurgent Sociologist*, 3 (Summer 1973), pp. 27–37; and Bertell Ollman, "Toward Class Consciousness Next Time: Marx and the Working Class," *Politics and Society*, 3 (Fall 1972), pp. 1–24.

3. James Luther Adams, *On Being Human Religiously: Selected Essays in Religion and Society*, ed. and intro. Max L. Stackhouse (Boston: Beacon Press, 1976), p. 248.

4. Paul Tillich, *The Protestant Era* (Chicago: University of Chicago Press, 1948), p. xvii.

5. Adams, *On Being Human Religiously*, p. 245.

6. Raymond Williams, "Base and Superstructure in Marxist Cultural Theory," *New Left Review*, no. 82 (November–December 1973), p. 5.

7. Herbert Marcuse, *The Aesthetic Dimension: Toward a Critique of Marxist Aesthetics* (Boston: Beacon Press, 1978), p. ix.

8. José Míguez Bonino, "The Human and the System," *Theology Today*, 35 (April 1978), pp. 14–24.

READING 5-1 _____

Toward class consciousness in the working class[*]

BERTELL OLLMAN

I

Why haven't the workers in the advanced capitalist countries become class-conscious? Marx was wont to blame leadership, short memories, temporary bursts of prosperity, and, in the case of the English and German workers, national characteristics.[1] In the last 15 years of his life he often singled out the enmity between English and Irish workers as the chief hindrance to a revolutionary class consciousness developing in the country that was most ripe for it.[2] The success of this explanation can be judged from the fact that it was never given the same prominence by any of Marx's followers. Engels, too, remained unsatisfied. After Marx's death, he generally accounted for the disappointing performance of the work-

ing class, particularly in England, by claiming that they had been bought off with a share of their country's colonial spoils.[3] The same reasoning is found in Lenin's theory of imperialism, and in this form it still aids countless Marxists in understanding why the revolution Marx predicted never came to pass in the advanced capitalist countries.

Despite these varied explanations (or, perhaps, because of them), most socialists from Marx onward have approached each crisis in capitalism with the certainty that this time the proletariat will become class-conscious. A half-dozen major crises have come and gone, and the proletariat at least in the United States, England, and Germany are as far away from such a con-

* From *Politics and Society*, 3 (Fall 1972), pp. 1–24.

sciousness as ever. What has gone "wrong"? Until socialists begin to examine the failure of the proletariat to perform its historically appointed task in light of their own excessive optimism, there is little reason to believe that on this matter at least the future will cease to resemble the past. It is the purpose of this essay to effect such an examination.

II

"Men make their own history," Marx said, "but they do not make it just as they please; they do not make it under circumstances chosen by themselves, but under circumstances directly encountered, given and transmitted from the past."[4] In his writings, Marx was primarily concerned with the circumstances of social and economic life under capitalism, with how they developed and are developing. His followers have likewise stressed social and economic processes. As is apparent from the above quotation, however, the necessary conditions for a proletarian revolution were never mistaken for sufficient conditions: real, living human beings had to react to their oppressive circumstances in way that would bring needed change. The theoretical link in Marxism between determining conditions and determined response is the class consciousness of the actors.

The mediating role of consciousness is sometimes hidden behind such statements as: "The question is not what this or that proletarian, or even the whole of the proletariat at the moment considers its aim. The question is what the proletariat is, and what, consequent on that being, it will be compelled to do."[5] But compelled by what? Marx responds by "what the proletariat is." However, what the proletariat is is a class of people whose conditions of life, whose experiences at work and elsewhere, whose common struggles and discussions will sooner or later bring them to a consciousness of their state and of what must

be done to transform it.[6] Though industrial wage earners are in the forefront of Marx's mind when he speaks of proletariat, most of what he says holds for all wage earners, and he generally intends the designations "proletariat" and "working class" to apply to them as well.

Class consciousness is essentially the interests of a class becoming its recognized goals. These interests, for those who accept Marx's analysis, are objective; they accrue to a class because of its real situation and can be found there by all who seriously look. Rather than indicating simply what people want, "interest" refers to those generalized means which increase their ability to get what they want, and includes such things as money, power, ease, and structural reform or its absence. Whether they know it or not, the higher wages, improved working conditions, job security, inexpensive consumer goods, etc., that most workers say they want are only to be had through such mediation. Moreover, the reference is not only to the present, but to what people will come to want under other and better conditions. Hence, the aptness of C. Wright Mills' description of Marxian interests as "long run, general, and rational interests."[7] The most long-run, general, and rational interest of the working class lies in overturning the exploitative relations which keep them, individually and collectively, from getting what they want.

Becoming class-conscious in this sense is obviously based on the recognition of belonging to a group which has similar grievances and aspirations, and a correct appreciation of the group's relevant life conditions. For workers this involves divesting themselves of many current delusions—the list is as long as the program of the Democratic party—and acquiring a class analysis of capitalism akin to Marx's own. Such class consciousness also includes an *esprit de corps* that binds members of the class together in opposition to the common enemy.

As a social relation, class consciousness can also be seen to include the social and economic conditions in which recognition of class interests occurs (or can occur). Consequently, any large-scale exposition of this theory would have to involve an analysis of the major developments in capitalism —ranging from the factory floor to the world market—from Marx's time to our own. In providing the beginnings of such an analysis, Marxist writers have tended to underplay the psychological dimensions of the problem. Rather than denying their important contribution, my own focus on the individual worker is best seen as an attempt to redress the imbalance.

Finally, the step from being class-conscious to engaging in action aimed at attaining class interests is an automatic one; the latter is already contained in the former as its practical side. It makes no sense in Marx's schema to speak of a class-conscious proletariat which is not engaged in the activity of overturning capitalism. Workers bursting with revolt stage revolts, or at least prepare for them by participating in the work of a revolutionary party or movement. The revolution takes place when "enough" workers have become class-conscious, and, given the place and number of the proletariat in modern society, its success is assured. The essential step, therefore, is the first one. If class consciousness is to play the role Marx gave it of mediating between determining conditions and determined response it must be taken in a broad enough sense to include this action component.

Another approach to class consciousness is offered by Lukács who defines it as "the sense become conscious of the historical situation of the class."[8] By conceptualizing consciousness as a part of a class's objective conditions and interests, Lukács can treat theoretically what is only possible as if it were actual. However, if workers always possess class consciousness because they are members of a class to which such consciousness attaches, then we are not talking about real workers or, alternatively, "consciousness" applies to something other than that of which real workers are conscious. In any case, if all workers are class-conscious, in any sense of this term, we can no longer distinguish between those who are and those who are not, so that nothing concrete in the way of revolutionary activity follows from being class-conscious. Lukács only succeeds in avoiding our problem by begging the question.

A similar misconception, and one widespread in Marxist circles, has "class consciousness" referring to the workers' general resentment and feeling of being systematically cheated by the boss, where any aggressive action from complaining to industrial sabotage is viewed as evidence. Here, too, all workers are seen to be more or less class-conscious, and, as with Lukács, such consciousness leads nowhere in particular. Though obviously components of class consciousness, resenting the boss and the insight that he is taking unfair advantage are not by themselves sufficiently important to justify the use of this concept.

Nor is "class consciousness" a synonym for "trade union consciousness" as Lenin seems to suggest in *What Is to Be Done,* where he ties together the "awakening of class consciousness" and the "beginning of trade union struggle."[9] Despite this suggestion, an important distinction is made in this work between "trade union consciousness," or recognition of the need for unions and for struggle over union demands, and "socialist (or Social Democratic) consciousness," which is an awareness on the part of workers of the "irreconcilable antagonism of their interests to the whole of the modern political and social system."[10] Class consciousness, as I have explained it, has more in common with Lenin's notion of socialist consciousness, and Lenin, on one occasion, even speaks of "genuine class consciousness" with this advanced state of understanding in mind.[11]

III

For Marx, life itself is the hard school in which the workers learn to be class-conscious, and he clearly believes they possess the qualities requisite to learning this lesson.[12] Insofar as people share the same circumstances, work in identical factories, live in similar neighborhoods, etc., they are inclined to see things—the most important ones at least—in the same way. They cannot know more than what their life presents them with nor differently from what their life permits. However, the less obvious aspects of their situation, such as their own objective interests, often take some time before they are grasped. What insures eventual success is the ability Marx attributes to people to figure out, in the long run, what is good for them, given their particular circumstances. For Marx, no matter how dehumanizing his conditions, an individual is capable of seeing where his fundamental interests lie, of comprehending and agreeing to arguments which purport to defend these interests, and of coming to the conclusions dictated by them. It is such an ability that Thorstein Veblen labels the "calculus of advantage."[13]

Rather than the proletariat's conditions serving as a barrier to such rational thinking, Marx believes the reverse is the case. The very extremity of their situation, the very extent of their suffering and deprivation, makes the task of calculating advantages relatively an easy one. As part of this, the one-sided struggle of the working class—according to Engels, "the defeats even more than the victories"—further exposes the true nature of the system.[14] The reality to be understood stands out in harsh relief, rendering errors of judgment increasingly difficult to make.

The workers' much discussed alienation simply does not extend to their ability to calculate advantages, or, when it does—as in the matter of reification—it is regarded as a passing and essentially superficial phenomenon. Marx maintained that "the abstraction of all humanity, even the semblance of humanity" is *"practically* complete in the full blown proletariat."[15] A loophole is reserved for purposive activity, which is the individual's ability to grasp the nature of what he wants to transform and to direct his energies accordingly. Marx held that productive activity is always purposive, and that this is one of the main features which distinguishes human beings from animals.[16] Class consciousness is the result of such purposive activity with the self as object, of workers using their reasoning powers on themselves and their life conditions. It follows necessarily from what they are, both as calculating human beings and as workers caught up in an inhuman situation.

The workers are also prompted in their search for socialist meaning by their needs as individuals. For Marx, society produces people who have needs for whatever, broadly speaking, fulfills their powers in the state in which these latter have been fashioned by society. These needs are invariably felt as wants, and since that which fulfills an individual's powers includes by extension the conditions for such fulfillment, he soon comes to want the means of his own transformation; for capitalist conditions alone cannot secure for workers, even extremely alienated workers, what they want. Job security, social equality, and uninterrupted improvement in living conditions, for example, are simply impossibilities within the capitalist framework. Hence, even before they recognize their class interests, workers are driven by their needs in ways which serve to satisfy these interests. And, as planned action—based on a full appreciation of what these interests are—is the most effective means of proceeding, needs provide what is possibly the greatest boost to becoming class-conscious.

Though rooted in people's everyday lives, class consciousness is never taken wholly for granted. The main effort of socialists from Marx to our own time has been directed toward helping workers draw socialist lessons from their conditions. Marx's activity as both a scholar and a man of action had this objective. Viewed in this light, too, the debate initiated by Lenin regarding the character of a socialist party has not been over *what* to do, but rather over *how* to do it. Essential, here, is that among socialists the conviction has always existed that sooner or later, in one crisis or another (with the help of this form of organization or that), the proletariat would finally become class-conscious.

Both critics and defenders of Marx alike have sought to explain the failure of the working class to assume its historic role by tampering with his account of capitalist conditions. Thus, his critics assert that the lot of the workers has improved, that the middle class has not disappeared, etc., and, at the extreme, that these conditions were never really as bad as Marx claimed. His defenders have tried to show that it was relative pauperization he predicted, that big businesses are getting larger, etc., and, after Lenin, that imperialist expansion permitted capitalists to buy off their workers. Such rejoinders, however, whether in criticism or defense, miss the essential point that for the whole of Marx's lifetime the situation in the capitalist world was adequate, by his own standards, for the revolution he expected to take place.

Martin Nicholaus, in his widely read article, "The Unknown Marx," has argued that the mature Marx (Marx of the *Grundrisse*, 1858) put the socialist revolution far into the future, in effect after capitalism was thoroughly beset by problems of automation.[17] Though Marx does speak of such a possibility, this is not his first projection. Marx was dealing after all with trends in the capitalist economy, and particularly, though not exclusively, with their *probable*

outcome. On the basis of his research, he not only hoped for but expected revolutions on each downturn of the economic cycle. In 1858, the year of the *Grundrisse*, he wrote to Engels, "On the continent the revolution is imminent."[18] And 12 years later he declared: "The English have all the material requisites necessary for a social revolution. What they lack is the spirit of generalization and revolutionary ardor."[19] Does this sound like a man who thought capitalist conditions were not sufficiently ripe for the workers to make a revolution? Though it is true that Marx became progressively less optimistic (and always took account of other possibilities) he never really believed he was writing for a century other than his own.

If it was not conditions which failed Marx, it could only have been the workers. More precisely, the great majority of workers were not able to attain class consciousness in conditions that were more or less ideal for them to do so. Marx's error, an error which has had a far-ranging effect on the history of socialist thought and practice, is that he advances from the workers' conditions of life to class consciousness in a single bound; the various psychological mediations united in class consciousness are treated as one. The severity of these conditions, the pressures he saw coming from material needs, and his belief that workers never lose their ability to calculate advantages made the eventual result certain and a detailed analysis of the steps involved unnecessary.

IV

Class consciousness is a more complex phenomenon—and, hence, more fraught with possibilities for failure—than Marx and most other socialists have believed. With the extra hundred years of hindsight, one can see that what Marx treated as a relatively direct, if not easy, transition is neither. Progress from the workers' conditions to class consciousness involves not one but many steps, each of which constitutes a real problem of achievement for some section of the working class.

First, workers must recognize that they have interests. Second, they must be able to see their interests as individuals in their interests as members of a class. Third, they must be able to distinguish what Marx considers their main interests as workers from other less important economic interests. Fourth, they must believe that their class interests come prior to their interests as members of a particular nation, religion, race, etc. Fifth, they must truly hate their capitalist exploiters. Sixth, they must have an idea, however vague, that their situation could be qualitatively improved. Seventh, they must believe that they themselves, through some means or other, can help bring about this improvement. Eighth, they must believe that Marx's strategy, or that advocated by Marxist leaders, offers the best means for achieving their aims. And, ninth, having arrived at all the foregoing, they must not be afraid to act when the time comes.

These steps are not only conceptually distinct, but they constitute the real difficulties which have kept the mass of the proletariat in all capitalist countries and in all periods from becoming class-conscious. Though these difficulties can and do appear in other combinations, I believe the order in which they are given here corresponds to the inherent logic of the situation and correctly describes the trajectory most often followed. What we find then is that most workers have climbed a few of these steps (enough to complain), that some have scaled most of them (enough to vote for working-class candidates), but that relatively few have managed to ascend to the top.

To begin with, if we accept Marx's portrayal of the proletariat's dehumanization as more or less accurate, it is clear that there are workers who simply cannot recognize

that they have interests of any sort. They have been rendered into unthinking brutes ("idiocy" and "cretinism" are Marx's terms), whose attention does not extend beyond their immediate task.[20] Given the conditions which prevailed in Marx's time, many workers must have suffered from this extreme degradation. And, when treated like animals, they reacted like animals, tame ones. Marx, himself, offers evidence for such a conclusion in telling of occasions when the workers' already impossible lot worsened without raising any protest from them.

In 1862, during a depression in the English cotton trade, a factory inspector is quoted as saying, "The sufferings of the operatives since the date of my last report have greatly increased; but at no period in the history of manufacturers, have sufferings so sudden and so severe been borne with so much silent resignation and so much patient self-respect."[21] Even a member of Parliament from one of the worst affected areas cannot refrain from commenting, nor Marx from quoting, that in this crisis, "the laborers of Lancashire have behaved like the ancient philosophers (Stoics)." Marx adds, "Not like sheep?"[22]

What conclusion did Marx draw from these events, events which were by no means that unusual? None at all. Despite his angry retort, his purpose in relating this incident was to show the conditions in which the workers were forced to live and work, and not how uncomplainingly they had submitted to these conditions. So bludgeoned by life that they cannot conceive they have any interests, many workers are condemned to submit to their earthy travail with as much thought as an ox before the plow. Admittedly, this malaise was more prevalent when the working day averaged 14 hours than now when 8 hours is the rule, but I am not convinced that it has completely disappeared.

For workers who recognize that they are human beings with interests, the next step in becoming class-conscious is to see their interests as individuals in their interests as members of the working class. It is not immediately apparent that the best way to obtain a good job, more pay, better conditions, etc. is to promote the interests of one's class. On the contrary, the practical isolation that capitalism forces on all its inhabitants makes the very notion of shared interests difficult to conceive. It was Marx, himself, who noted that the individual in capitalist society is "withdrawn into himself, wholly preoccupied with his private interest and acting in accordance with his private caprice."[23] The character of the ensuing struggle is well brought out in Marx's definition of "competition," its all purpose label, as "avarice and war among the avaricious."[24] Throughout society, calculator meets calculator in the never ending battle of who can get the most out of whom. "Mutual exploitation" is the rule.[25]

With so much indifference and hostility ingrained in the way of life and outlook of everyone, it is not surprising that the competition between workers for a greater portion of the meager fare which goes to them as a class is no less intense. Marx is eminently aware that, "Competition makes individuals, not only the bourgeoisie, but still more the workers, mutually hostile, in spite of the fact that it brings them together."[26] This competition first rears its head at the factory gate where some are allowed in and others are not. Inside the factory, workers continue to compete with each other for such favors as their employer has it in him to bestow, especially for the easier and better paying jobs. After work, with too little money to spend, workers are again at each other's throats for the inadequate food, clothing, and shelter available to them.

The cooperation that characterizes industrial labor hardly offsets the atomizing affect of so much inner-class competition. The scales are even more unbalanced than this suggests, since the individual worker,

without a conception of his identity in the group, is incapable of appreciating the essential links between his own labor and that of his co-workers. Cooperation is something of which he is only dimly aware. So it is that both his social activity and product are viewed as alien powers. To be able to see one's interests as an individual in one's interests as a member of the working class under these conditions is no little achievement.

After workers realize they have interests, and class interests at that, it is essential next that they adopt Marx's view of what these latter are. I accept that there are objective interests which accrue to a class in virtue of its social-economic position, and, also, Marx's understanding of what these are for the workers, including their overriding interest in transforming the system. However, his belief that most workers will sooner or later come to agree with us has received little support from history. Without a doubt, this is the step at which the greater part of the proletariat has faltered.

When Samuel Gompers, the early leader of the AFL, was asked what the workers want, he answered, "More." And, as much as I would like to dispute it, this strikes me as an accurate description of how most workers have conceived their interests then and now. Most workers who have grasped that they have interests as workers have seen them in terms of getting a little more of what they already have, making their conditions a little better than what they are, working a little bit less than they do. As limited, cautious men, the workers have little, cautious designs. Their horizons have been clipped off at the roots. As with most of their other personal shortcomings, this is a result of the alienation Marx so eloquently describes. It is simply that their conditions have so limited their conceptions, that these conceptions offer them little opportunity to break out of their conditions.

While Marx was aware that most workers did not share his view of their interests, he refused to acknowledge the real gap which separates the two positions, or to devote serious study to its causes and likely consequences. Thus, when Jules Guesde came to London to seek Marx's advice about an election program, Marx could write, "With the exception of some trivialities which Guesde found necessary to throw to the French workers despite my protest, such as fixing the minimum wage by law and the like (I told him: 'If the French proletariat is still so childish to require such bait, it is not worthwhile drawing up any program whatever') . . . ."[27] But the proletariat, not only in France but throughout the capitalist world, were so "childish," and they remain so.

Marx's inability to grasp the staying power of the workers' trade union designs is due, in part, to his belief that the capitalists would not and could not accede to most of these demands; having got nowhere for so long, the workers would not fail to see that their real interests lay elsewhere. In part, he believed that whatever minor benefits they managed to force upon the capitalists could only be temporary, acquired in booms, in periods of rapidly expanding capital, and lost again in depressions. And, in part, he thought that whatever improvements withstood the test of time were so clearly insignificant that this fact would not be lost upon the workers themselves. These were the "crumbs" which, he said, do nothing to bridge the "social gulf" between the classes.[28] In capitalism, even when the workers get higher pay, this is "nothing but better payment for the slave"; it does not "conquer either for the worker or for work their human status and dignity."[29] The successes of the English Factory Acts in ridding capitalism of its worst abuses are treated in the same light.[30]

However, it is one thing for us to agree with Marx's characterization of such improvements as "crumbs" which do not win for the workers their "human status and dignity," and quite another to believe that most workers agree as well, or that they ever have, or that they ever will. On the contrary, the same conditions which so limit their horizons that a higher wage is considered the acme of their interests make it likely that a few dollars added to their pay packet will be regarded as a major success. In keeping with this Lilliputian perspective, rather than being disappointed with "crumbs," they will use their collective bargaining power to obtain more. Organized into unions, they have managed to retain many of the gains made in prosperous times through the reoccurring crises, and, with the steady growth of society's absolute product, they have succeeded in acquiring a higher standard of living than Marx thought possible. Given the time and the patience, even pyramids can be built of crumbs. But most workers have never wanted anything else, nor have they ever conceived of their interests in other terms.

Once workers accept that they have class interests and that Marx is right about what these are, the step they must take is to consider these interests more important than ties of nation, religion, race, etc. In the *Communist Manifesto* (1848) Marx declared that the proletariat had already lost both religious and nationalist attachments.[31] This is one conclusion he was later forced to qualify, at least as regards English and Irish workers. The hopes for a growing proletarian brotherhood received an almost fatal setback by the chauvinistic behavior of the European working class during World War I. With such divisions firmly entrenched in the psychology of most workers, an all too frequent reaction in time of economic hardship has been to seek for scapegoats among their class. It is against those who compete with them for scarce jobs, against fellow workers who can be easily distinguished because of their nationality, religion, or race that much of their pent up ire is directed.

One does not have to offer a theory of

where these prejudices come from and how they operate to hold that the weight Marx attached to them is seriously inadequate. Oddly enough, Marx provides the framework for such a theory in his account of alienation and the mystification which accompanies it, where we also learn that the tenacity of these prejudices is a function of the degree of distortion present. How could such deprived people be expected to operate with abilities they have lost? How could workers, who are manipulated more than any other group, overturn the results of this manipulation in their own personalities?

Besides causing conflicts among workers, the excessive attachment to nation, religion, and race is also responsible for a lot of inter-class cooperation, workers and capitalists of the same nation, etc., joining together to combat their alien counterparts.[32] In these circumstances, the hatred workers should feel for their exploiters, which is another requirement for class consciousness, is all but dissipated. The whole education, culture, and communication apparatus of bourgeois society, by clouding the workers' minds with noncontroversial orthodoxies, has succeeded admirably in establishing numerous links between the classes on trivial matters. Aren't we all fans of the Green Bay Packers?

The workers, with relatively few exceptions—depending on the country and the period—don't really and deeply hate capitalists, because they cannot distinguish them sharply enough from themselves, because they have never been able to set off a sufficiently unencumbered target to hate. Whatever class mobility exists—this is a more significant factor in America than elsewhere—merely serves to compound the problem. And if some workers are aided in making this distinction by having a capitalist with a long nose or different colored skin, they are more likely to become incensed against his religion or race than against his class.

One excruciating result of such bourgeois successes is that workers, including socialist workers, often admire capitalists more than they hate them. Workers who live vicariously through their employer are not limited to those with a stunted conception of their interests. And their envy is not of a man who has more, but who is in some sense better. Such an admission is already contained in the widespread drive for respectability and prestige, for "status." Actions acquire status according to a particular social code, which is set and promulgated in every society by the ruling social and economic class. To be interested in acquiring status is to submit to the social code that determines it. It is to accept the legitimacy of existing society, and to admit, however feebly, that one's interests as a citizen are somehow superior to one's interests as a worker.

Marx and Engels were often made aware of this failing, which affected many of their own stalwarts, particularly in England. If Tom Mann, one of the truly outstanding leaders of the English working class, was—as Engels relates—"fond of mentioning that he will be lunching with the Lord Mayor," what could one expect of the others?[33] Yet, Marx and Engels always treated this "bourgeois infection" (Marx's term) as something skin deep and of passing importance.[34] My own conclusion from such evidence, which has not diminished with the years, is that the vast majority of workers, including some devotees of Marxist parties, have never really and decisively rejected the society which has despoiled them, but have always been more concerned to be accepted by it than to change it.

The next step up the ladder to class consciousness is that workers must have an inkling, however vague, that their situation can be qualitatively improved. It does no good to know what they need and to have the proper likes and dislikes if they believe that nothing can be done about it. For, in this situation, lotteries and football pools remain the only escape from the lot that has befallen them. We have all heard such rejoinders as "The world will never change" and "Rich and poor will always be with us." What it is important to realize is that it is not only workers whose horizons stop at "more" who are afflicted with this pessimism, but also many who share Marx's conception of their interests. Clearly, the relevant question is how could people who are so battered by their reality believe otherwise? A vision requires hope, and hope requires a crack in the ceiling, such as few good landlords in any society permit.

Frederick Lessner, a working-class acquaintance of Marx, says of his introduction to Weitling's book, *Guarantees of Harmony and Freedom:* "I read it once, twice, three times. It was then it first occurred to me that the world could be different from what it was."[35] But how many workers would read this kind of book work even once? Yet, it was only through such sustained mental effort that a man who became a model for his class could obtain a major prerequisite for engaging in socialist activity, the idea that a more just society can be constructed. More recently, disappointment with the Soviet experiment has served as another kind of block to the workers' imagination.

Once workers who have accompanied us so far accept that change for the better is possible, the next hurdle is becoming convinced that they have something positive to contribute to this effort. A widespread phenomenon in our time, which we can only assume was also present in Marx's day, is the feeling of powerlessness, the self-reproach that there is nothing one can do which matters. Most people simply feel themselves too small and the establishment which requires overturning too large and imposing to see any link between individual action and social change.

Each person must make his own decision whether to join others for political action, and must justify to himself and, perhaps,

to his family the time and energy this new commitment will take. In this situation, even people with strong socialist views are prone to say, "One more, one less—it won't make any difference." Everything from going to vote to manning the barricades is affected by this doubt. Socialist views come coupled with the duty to act upon them only where the individual is convinced that somehow or other, sooner or later, his participation will count. In Marx's day, many of the most restless spirits among the European proletariat immigrated to the New World simply because they did not believe there was anything they personally could do to improve the old one.

Assuming we cross this hurdle, we are now confronted with workers who have grasped what Marx takes to be their interests, who possess the proper attitudes toward co-workers and capitalists, who believe it possible to create a better world, and who think that they can help effect this change—it is essential, next, that they consider the strategy advocated by Marx or their Marxist leaders to be the right one. Marx was thoroughly pragmatic when it came to the means for achieving social change, favoring the ballot where it could work and revolution where it could not.[36] Because national circumstances and traditions vary so greatly and because of the many peculiar "accidents" that cannot be systematized, Marx felt he was in no position to offer detailed advice; and, despite the reams written on Marx's theory of revolution, there is none. Most of his comments on this subject are very general, as when he says, the "social disintegration" will be "more brutal or more human, according to the degree of development of the working class itself."[37]

Nor did Marx ever speculate on what is the proper kind of political party or movement to make the revolution. The First International was a loose coagulation of working-class unions, educational associations, and parties whose first aim was to promote class consciousness. This, as we will recall, is also how Marx saw his task. When enough workers became class-conscious, they would know what to do and how to do it.

If Marx had no theory of revolution, he equally had no theory of democracy, and certainly felt no commitment to use "democratic" and "constitutional" methods. With his mixture of contempt and distrust for bourgeois democracy, his bias on the side of revolutions is a clear one. Once his followers were permitted to operate inside the constitution, however, many of them ceased thinking of their goals as outside it. For better or worse, they were determined to believe that it was possible to obtain what they wanted by obeying the rules (and even the customs) of the political game. What began as a tactical means became an end, displacing in the process their former end. Yesterday it was the Social Democrats and there are indications that the same metamorphosis is occurring in many Communist parties today.

Marx's correspondence is full of complaints against working-class leaders, many of them close students of Marxism, for their tactical bungling, usually for engaging in compromising actions with the bourgeoisie. He most often attributes their mistakes to personal faults, and, in this way, manages to exonerate their following. Ernest Jones, the Chartist leader, is described as the general of an army who "crosses over to the camp of the enemy on the eve of battle."[38] The army, apparently, was ready to fight. Again, my conclusion is more severe, for the evidence has been compounded many times over since Marx's day. The rules and practice of the capitalist political game, with its perpetual promise of the half-loaf, poisons the socialist rank and file as well as their leaders. For the workers to take up revolutionary tactics, it is essential that they be completely disillusioned with all reformist leaders and methods. But, in democracies, such leaders and methods are generally able

to secure a small part of what they promise. The result is that the workers are kept dangling, wed to solutions which cannot solve; yet, temptation, and with it hope, never ceases.

One final step remains. Once workers grasp what they need as workers, who their friends and enemies are, that a better world can be created, what must be done to create it, possess the confidence that they have something to contribute and that by avoiding the trap of reformism they can succeed, what is still required is that they have the ability when the time comes to act. An imprisoned class consciousness that cannot be translated into revolutionary action is no class consciousness at all. Waiting for the German proletariat to provide a revolutionary initiative which never came, Rosa Luxemburg—whose politics ran a close parallel to Marx's own—paid for the delay with her life. Yet, in the aftermath of World War I, Germany probably had more workers who had climbed all previous steps than any capitalist country either before or since. But when the opportune moment for action arrived, most of them held back. This does not excuse the betrayal of the German Social Democrats who argued against rebellion and helped put down the outbreaks that occurred; it only helps explain, at least in part, their unfortunate success. Luxemburg's fate may very well have been Marx's had he lived in a more troubled land at a more troubled time. Or, would he have read the handwriting which had been on the wall since 1848 or thereabouts and become—a "Leninist"?

Marx's mistake was to believe that understanding things correctly, in a way that calls for a particular action, necessarily leads to people taking this action. First of all, in the case before us, there is the very real fear of being hurt. Very few workers have the courage which comes with having nothing to lose, simply because they always have something to lose, their lives if nothing else. In recent years, of course, they have much more to lose, the growing number of objects which they have purchased. Because they have relatively few possessions, and ones they have worked very hard to obtain, the proletariat have become as petty as the petty bourgeoisie have always been about their goods. In this situation, the tendency is to look not at what one has to gain, but at what one has to lose in any radical change. This is the same affliction that the peasants have always suffered from.

But such last minute restraint can also be attributed to two related psychological mechanisms about which Marx knew very little. It has often been remarked how people in authority browbeat others to act against their recognized interests, how awe, respect, and habit combine to overturn the most rational conclusions. This falling into line under any circumstances is part of a syndrome which T. W. Adorno and others have popularized as the "authoritarian personality."[39] Rooted in the habit of taking orders, a habit which extends back to the earliest years of education and family training, it eventually succeeds in being felt as a duty. So great is the emotional compulsion to obey that the adult, who has been conditioned in this way, may actually feel physical pain when he disobeys.

How exactly this effect is created or the precise mechanism through which it operates cannot be gone into at this time. For my purposes, it is enough to state that it exists, and that the conditions in which most workers are raised—admittedly, more so in some cultures than in others—are only too well suited to producing authoritarian personalities. Thus in moments of crisis, many workers find themselves emotionally incapable of departing from long established patterns of subservience, no matter how much they rationally desire to do so.

The second psychological malfunction working to disrupt Marx's expectations is the security mindedness of the proletariat, what Erich Fromm has called their "fear of freedom."[40] People not only refuse emancipation because choosing against habitual patterns is painful, but because they irrationally fear what is to be chosen. What is new and unknown is more terrifying to many than the terror which is known. They think at least they have been able to live through the troubles they have had. How do they know they will be able to deal as well with the new troubles which await them?

People lack confidence in the future, essentially, because they lack confidence in themselves; but nothing in the lives of workers has enabled them to acquire such confidence. Again, those who are most in need of freedom are the very ones whose wretched, ego destroying existence has acted to make them afraid of freedom. In such straits, there will always be workers who desire to see the future conform to the past except at the limits of despair. This failing, admittedly, like the irrational need to obey, is more likely to afflict those who are not poised to act against the system. However, diseases—and what I have been describing are emotional diseases—generally have little respect for the political sophistication of their victims.

After removing workers for this, that, and the other shortcoming, and many for a combination of them (the actual combinations as I have indicated may vary), what is left? How many workers were class-conscious in Marx's time or are now? How many could have become class-conscious then or could become so now? How many workers who became class-conscious were able to remain so (for if character alters, it alters in both directions)?

V

From the foregoing account, it appears that consciousness is an extraordinary achievement of which very few workers at any time have shown themselves capable, and that there is little reason to believe this will change. Indeed, with greater inter-class mobility, increasing stratification within the working class, and the absolute (not relative) improvement in the workers' material conditions in our century, some of the factors which have helped bring about class consciousness where it did exist have lost much of their influence. The pessimistic import of such truths has led to the demise of more than one socialist and is at least partly responsible for the slight attention paid to problems of class consciousness by socialist writers.

Yet in trying to account for the past failures of the working class, my intention has not been to predict the future but to affect it. This is only possible, however, after frankly and fully admitting the real psychological as well as social barriers that exist to proletarian class consciousness. On the basis of the foregoing analysis, the problem with which socialists are confronted may be stated as follows: in order to have a revolution, there will not only have to be other severe crises in the capitalist system (these will occur), but a large segment of the working class will have to develop characteristics that will enable them to respond to one or another of these crises by becoming class-conscious.

This manner of posing the problem is not affected by differences of opinion regarding how quickly class consciousness can arise. The French events of May 1968 found workers climbing many of the steps to class consciousness in short order (just as the aftermath found many of them as quickly descending). Particularly impressive was the way workers initially rejected the gigantic wage increases won by their trade union leaders. Clearly, at this stage, a large number of workers wanted fundamental social change, though most were still uncertain as to what exactly that was or how to get it. The events of May were not only a result of preceding conditions and events, social, economic, and political, but as well of the ability of the most radical working class in any advanced capitalist country, with the possible exception of Italy, to respond as they did. And this response, when and to the limited degree that it occurred (whatever the guilt of the French Communist party), is evidence of the speed at which under certain pressures the barriers to class consciousness can be overcome. We have not been dealing, however, with how fast workers can become class-conscious, but with all such consciousness contains. While the complexity of this condition suggests slow or staggered development, it is clear that particular events can greatly speed the process.

It is time now to examine more closely the causes for Marx's own excessive optimism. Marx was forever expecting the proletariat to become class-conscious, essentially, because in his scheme for understanding man and society there is no niche put aside for their continued refusal to do so. We have already seen how the needs people have are conceptualized as one with the wants they feel for whatever it is that will satisfy these needs. Marx is aided (and, perhaps, even encouraged) in constructing this knot by the German language where *Bedingungen* means both "need" and "want." As a result, Marx is inclined to believe that people want or will soon come to want that for which they have needs, or, by extension, which serves as the means to acquire what they need. Yet, people may have needs for which they never consciously want relief, and others—as Freud has shown —of which they never become aware, and still others the means to the satisfaction of which they never directly want.

Marx's position that life-activity is purposive brings him to a similar conclusion whenever the self is treated as the object. But, again, the necessity Marx finds is one he himself introduces into his concepts. In fact, people may act without purpose, without consciously seeking any particular development or goals. It was such faulty conceptualization which led Marx to treat consciousness, despite qualifications to the contrary, as the mental reflection of surroundings and kept him from correctly estimating the real gap between objective and subjective interests.

In this manner, the link between conditions and character—for all the space it gets in Marx's writings—remains undeveloped. The problem of the receptivity of character to new influences, its malleability, particularly relative to age, is nowhere discussed. Marx is obviously correct in holding that the individual is to a remarkably high degree the product of his society, and that by changing his living conditions we change him, but there are at least two questions that still have to be answered: are the changes which occur in character always rational, i.e., in keeping with the new interests that are created? How long does it take for new conditions to produce new people?

Marx believed that the effect of conditions on character was rational and relatively quick acting. The evidence examined in this paper argues against such beliefs. Before attempting to modify Marx's conceptual framework, however, we must first realize that very little that passes for irrationality here is sheer madness. For the most part, it is a matter of too little attention paid to some factors and too much to others, or of the right amount of attention paid too late. Given where his calculations should take him and when, the individual's response to his environment is distorted; he has become fanatical in his devotion to some needs and a cold suitor to others.

One factor, in particular, which has received less than its due in Marx's writings is the sexual drive. Young people are more interested in sex, devote more time to thinking about and trying to satisfy this drive, and are immensely more effected by it (by not having sex even more than by having it) than most adults, even after Freud, would care to admit. If one doesn't eat, one starves to death. But what happens if one doesn't satisfy the sexual drive, or does so only rarely, hurriedly, and with a lot of guilt? One doesn't die, but how does such abstinence affect the personality? Which qualities does it reinforce and which does it weaken? There are no conclusive answers, but it is my impression that sexual repression among the workers, as among other classes, has contributed significantly to their irrationality.[41]

By the right amount of attention paid too late, I have in mind the time lag which exists between the appearance of new conditions and resulting changes in character. Though Marx accepted the necessity of some such lag, he did not make it long enough; nor did he properly estimate the potential for mischief which this delay carried with it. People acquire most of their personal and class characteristics in childhood. It is the conditions operating then, transmitted primarily by the family, which makes them what they are, at least as regards basic responses; and, in most cases, what they are will vary very little over their lives. Thus, even where the conditions people have been brought up in change by the time they reach maturity, their characters will reflect the situation which has passed on. If Marx had studied the family more closely, he surely would have noticed that as a factory for producing character it is invariably a generation or more behind the times, producing people today who, tomorrow, will be able to deal with yesterday's problems.

Even children, whose characters are more affected by existing conditions, don't become all these conditions call for, since the family, which is the chief mechanism through which society bears upon them, is staffed by adults whose outlook reflects the previous state of affairs. If, for adults, existing conditions come too late, for the young, who can do little about them in any case, they are reflected through a prism that both modifies and distorts the influence they would otherwise have. As a result, only in extreme cases do new conditions make people behave as they do (and these are generally young people); more often, old conditions determine their actions, and then, for the reasons given, this takes place in an irregular and distorted manner. In a society, such as capitalism, which is changing (albeit, in its superficial aspects) very rapidly, this means that the character of most people never catches up with their lives. They seem destined to be misfits, whose responses are forever out of date.

In order to allow for the irrationality which comes from this time lag, I would introduce into Marx's conceptual framework the idea of character structure, understood as the internalization of early behavior patterns, as organized habit. Such characterological hardening of the arteries derives whence character derives, but is a product apart, exercising a relatively independent influence on how one will respond to future events and conditions.

The idea of character structure does little violence to Marx's basic framework; the interactions he describes go on as before, except that something now mediates between conditions and response, between needs and wants, between objective and subjective interests, between activity and consciousness, something into and through which the one must be translated to become the other. As such, character structure is both a product of alienation and, with the real conditions of life, a contributing cause of alienated activity. With the introduction of this new factor we can better explain why workers so often find their inclinations in conflict with the demands of the current situation, why they consistently misunderstand and are incapable of responding to it in ways that would promote their interests. We can better explain, too, why people today are driven to act in ways that might have been rational a generation ago, in a war, a depression, or a boom which existed then but no longer does. The concept of character structure also helps account for the proletariat's "fear of freedom" and its

submissiveness before authority, which are, after all, simply attempts to repeat in the future what has been done in the past. Finally, character structure helps to explain the distorting sentiments of nation, race, and religion, as well as the worker's pessimism regarding a better form of society and his own role in helping to bring it about by treating them as expressions of early behavior patterns that, internalized within the individual, have acquired a dynamic and power of their own.

Thus, whenever the system has been in crisis, when it was in the workers' interests to construct new solutions, their character structure has disposed them to go on seeking old nostrums, where they can continue to act as they have been and know how to. To be sure, new social and economic conditions did develop with the growth of imperialism, workers' movements were often cursed with poor leadership at critical moments of their history, and capitalists have sought to exacerbate national and racial antagonisms—all this, as Marxists rightly maintain, has served to inhibit the development of proletarian class consciousness. What those who accept Marx's analysis have seldom admitted is that the character structure of most workers has also been at fault. With the introduction of this concept into Marx's framework, workers must be viewed not only as prisoners of their conditions, but of themselves, of their own character structures which are the product of previous conditions.[42]

VI

The introduction of the concept of character structure into Marx's scheme, substituting a sense of retarded rationality for the sense of irrationality toward which so much of this study seemed to point, has great significance for a socialist strategy. If, as part of their alienation, workers cannot react to their conditions, no matter how bad they get, in a rational manner, then all efforts to attain widespread class consciousness are doomed to failure. They are, that is, unless some manner can be found to affect their character structure during its formative years, to make sure that the behavior patterns internalized there never develop or, more to the point, never acquire the degree of durability they now have. Looked at in this way, the focal point of a socialist strategy must be those conditions which most affect the young. For it is possible to alter the character structure of workers by fighting against its construction, by counteracting the disorienting influence of family, school, and church, whatever in fact makes it difficult for the individual once he becomes an adult to make an objective assessment of his oppression and to act against it.

The concrete aims of radical activity, on the basis of this analysis, are to get teen-age and even younger members of the working class to question the existing order along with all its symbols and leaders, to loosen generalized habits of respect and obedience, to oppose whatever doesn't make sense in terms of their needs as individuals and as members of a group, to conceive of the enemy as the capitalist system and the small group of men who control it, to articulate their hopes for a better life, to participate in successful protest actions no matter how small the immediate objective, and to create a sense of community and brotherhood of all those in revolt. The purpose is to overturn (or, more accurately, to undermine) the specific barriers that have kept past generations of workers from becoming class-conscious. Full class consciousness can only occur later on the basis of adult experiences, particularly in the mode of production. Making allowances for exceptions on both ends of the scale, what can be achieved now is essentially a predisposition to respond to the conditions of life in a rational manner, what might be called a state of preconsciousness. Capitalism willing, and capitalism is periodically willing, revolutionary effects will follow.

To insist on the necessity of altering character structure is not to argue that only new men can create a new society, but to reaffirm that changes in both people and conditions are needed for a socialist revolution to occur. The opposition between idealism (where men are held responsible for transforming society) and vulgar materialism (where material conditions are) is, in any case, a false one. There is a constant, many-sided interaction going on, and the problem has always been how to capture (and conceptualize) the dynamics of this process so as to participate in it more effectively.

The conditions that now exist in the United States (more so than in other capitalist countries) are exceptionally well suited to the strategy I have been urging. In stressing the importance of social conditions in determining what people are and how they act, Marxists have not given sufficient attention to the fact that some conditions have a greater effect on what people are and others on how they act. This is chiefly because the people referred to in the two instances are not the same. Since we acquire the greater part of our character when young, it is conditions which most affect the young that most affect what people are (or what they are a generation later when the once young have become adults) ; whereas adults are the subject of conditions, generally more extreme, which are said to affect how people act.

Recent events have thrown up a number of important new conditions which exercise their predominant effect on what people are. Among these are the Vietnam War in which the young are expected to fight as well as to believe, a pause in the cold war and with it in anticommunist ideology, an increasingly evident racism that goes counter to taught ideals, the hunger and suffering seen daily on television, frequent disruption of community services and schools, growing unemployment among the newly trained and among incoming skilled workers of all sorts, the pill and drugs, and the new obscurantist puritanism that has arisen to combat both. In each case, a pattern of behavior in which the older generation grew up and which, through its transformation into character structure, contributed significantly to a passive acceptance of their lot is changing into behavior that in one or more respects opposes adolescents to the existing social and political system. It remains for socialists, especially young socialists, to make the most of these conditions, not to instigate a youth revolt (whatever that is) or to create an auxiliary of the working class, but to alter the character structure of the next generation of workers.

It is not possible for a paper that argues for a particular strategy to canvass all possible tactics that can be used to advance it. The choice of tactics requires detailed study of the time, place, and parties involved. Still, the strategy advocated here does suggest that the effort some radical groups are putting into high school "organizing" and publishing high school papers should be greatly expanded, especially in working-class districts, even at the expense of other activities in poor communities and among adult workers. Also, insofar as the aim is understood in the negative sense of breaking up existing behavior patterns, the hippies and Yippies—by holding up establishment ways and virtues to contempt and ridicule—may have as much to contribute as the more orthodox forms of protest. The means of keeping young people open to a rational calculus of advantages later in life may be quite different from those required to help them make the calculus itself. What exactly these means are needs further investigation, but for the moment I would not rule out any form of protest that increases or clarifies young people's discontent and their opposition to established authority.[43]

If the "revolution" is, as most socialists will admit, at a minimum decades away, then it is proper—given the conservative function of character structure and its greater malleability early in life—that we begin preparing for it among workers who will be around and relevant at the time. Samuel Gompers and his successors in the AFL–CIO sacrificed the revolutionary potential of the working class to the immediate needs of real workers; today, paradoxically, socialists with their limited means must pay less attention to real workers, certainly to workers over 30 (35?), so that they can help to develop a revolutionary working class.

NOTES

1. Instances of such explanations can be found in Karl Marx, *Letters to Dr. Kugelmann* (London, 1941), pp. 107, 135; Marx and Friedrich Engels, *Selected Correspondence*, ed. and trans. Dona Torr (London, 1941), pp. 249, 256–57, 350, 502; Marx and Engels, *Selected Writings*, vol. 1 (Moscow, 1951), p. 249; A. Lozovsky, *Marx and the Trade Unions* (New York, 1935), pp. 38, 58–59.

2. Marx, *On Colonialism* (Moscow, n.d.), p. 201. See, too, *Selected Correspondence*, pp. 280–81.

3. Engels, *Briefe an Bebel* (Berlin, 1958), pp. 82–83. See, too, Lozovsky, *Marx and the Trade Unions*, p. 61.

4. Marx, "Eighteenth of Brumaire," *Selected Writings*, vol. 1, p. 225.

5. Marx and Engels, *The Holy Family*, trans. R. Dixon (Moscow, 1956), p. 53.

6. Marx speaks of the proletariat on one occasion as "that misery conscious of its spiritual and physical misery, that dehumanization conscious of its dehumanization and therefore self-abolishing." Ibid., p. 52.

7. C. Wright Mills, *The Marxists* (New York, 1962), p. 115.

8. George Lukács, *History and Class Consciousness*, trans. Rodney Livingstone (Cambridge, Mass., 1971), p. 73.

9. V. I. Lenin, "What Is to Be Done?" *Selected Works*, 12 vols. (Moscow, n.d.), vol. 2, p. 77.

10. Ibid., p. 53.

11. Ibid., pp. 88–89. For a useful survey of other interpretations of class consciousness see H. Wolpe's "Some Problems concerning Revolutionary Consciousness," *The Socialist Register 1970*, ed. Ralph Miliband and John Saville (London, 1970), pp. 251–80.

12. According to Marx, "The contradiction between the individuality of each separate proletarian and labor, the conditions of life forced

upon him, become evident to him himself, for he is sacrificed from youth upwards and, within his own class, has no chance for arriving at the conditions which would place him in the other class." Marx and Engels, *The German Ideology*, trans. R. Pascal (London, 1942), p. 78.

13. Thorstein Veblen, "The Economics of Karl Marx: II," *The Place of Science in Modern Civilization and Other Essays* (New York, 1961), p. 441.

14. Engels, "Preface," Marx and Engels, *The Communist Manifesto*, trans. Samuel Moore (Chicago, 1945), p. 5.

15. *Holy Family*, p. 52 (my emphasis). For a discussion of the workers' alienation, see B. Ollman, *Alienation: Marx's Conception of Man in Capitalist Society* (Cambridge University Press, 1971).

16. Though encased in another set of concepts, this is one of the main conclusions to emerge from Marx's discussion and natural and species powers in the *Economic and Philosophic Manuscripts of 1844* (henceforth referred to as *1844 Manuscripts*), trans. Martin Milligan (Moscow, 1959), esp. pp. 74–76, 156–58.

17. Martin Nicholaus, "The Unknown Marx," *The New Left Reader*, ed. Carl Oglesby (New York, 1969), pp. 105–6.

18. *Letters to Dr. Kugelmann*, p. 107.

19. *Selected Correspondence*, p. 118.

20. *1844 Manuscripts*, p. 71.

21. Marx, *Capital*, vol. 3 (Moscow, 1959), p. 128.

22. Ibid., p. 135.

23. Marx, "Zur Judenfrage," Marx and Engels, *Werke*, vol. 1 (Berlin, 1959), p. 366.

24. *1844 Manuscripts*, p. 68.

25. Marx and Engels, *Deutsche Ideologie*, in *Werke*, vol. 3 (Berlin, 1960), p. 395.

26. *German Ideology*, p. 58.

27. Marx, *Letters to Americans*, trans. Leonard E. Mins (New York, 1953), p. 124.

28. Marx, "Wage Labor and Capital," *Selected Writings*, vol. 1, p. 91.

29. *1844 Manuscripts*, p. 81.

30. Marx, *Capital*, vol. 1, trans. Samuel Moore and Edward Aveling (Moscow, 1958), pp. 279 ff.

31. *Communist Manifesto*, p. 28.

32. *On Colonialism*, p. 301. In "Civil War in France" (1871), however, Marx still treats the German and French proletariat as if they were devoid of strong nationalist sentiment.

33. *Selected Correspondence*, p. 461.

34. Ibid., p. 147. In 1863, Marx wrote to Engels, "How soon the English workers will free themselves from their apparent bourgeois infection one must wait and see." Engels had just written him, "All the revolutionary energy has faded practically entirely away from the English proletariat and the English proletariat is declaring its complete agreement with the rule of the bourgeoisie." Ibid.

35. Frederick Lessner, "Before 1848 and After," *Reminiscences of Marx and Engels*, no editor (Moscow, n.d.), p. 150.

36. Engels tells us that Marx thought the transition to socialism in England, for example, might be peaceful and legal. Engels, "Preface to English Edition," *Capital*, vol. 1, p. 6.

37. Ibid., p. 9.

38. *Letters to Americans*, p. 61.

39. T. W. Adorno, *The Authoritarian Personality* (New York, 1950). Marx had some conception of this failing as it applied to German workers. Of them, he says, "Here where the workers are under the thumb of bureaucracy from childhood on and believe in authority, in the constituted authorities, it is a foremost task to teach them to walk by themselves." Lozovsky, *Marx and the Trade Unions*, p. 42.

40. Erich Fromm, *Fear of Freedom* (London, 1942), esp. pp. 1–19.

41. For an illuminating discussion of the role of sexual repression in helping to produce such irrationality, see Wilhelm Reich, *The Mass Psychology of Fascism*, trans. Theodor P. Wolfe (New York, 1946), esp. pp. 19–28, 122–43.

42. Useful discussion of the concept of character structure can be found in Reich's *Character Analysis*, trans. T. P. Wolfe (New York, 1961), esp. 22 ff; and in Hans Gerth and C. Wright Mills, *Character and Social Structure* (London, 1961), part 2. Another attempt to revise Marx's conceptual scheme is found in Marcuse's distinction (though barely suggested in Marx's writings) between "true" and "false" needs. *One-Dimensional Man* (Boston, 1964), p. 6.

43. For further discussion of some of the tactics advocated in this paper, see Reich's "What Is Class Consciousness?" trans. Anna Bostock, *Liberation*, vol. 16, no. 5 (October 1971), pp. 15–49. Though Reich devotes more attention to the problem of promoting class consciousness in adults than I feel is justified by his analysis of character structure, his stress on youth is unique in the serious literature on this subject. Reich's important contribution to Marxism in this area is summarized in B. Ollman, "The Marxism of Wilhelm Reich; or the Social Function of Sexual Repression," in *The Unknown Dimension: European Marxism since Lenin*, ed. Karl Klare and Dick Howard (Basic Books, 1972).

Ideology, the cultural apparatus, and the new consciousness industry*

ALVIN W. GOULDNER

There is a special connection, we have said, between the spread of modern ideologies with their historically special rationality, on the one side, and the unimodality and lineality of printed materials, on the other. Writing, and especially printed communication, then, is a basic grounding of "modern" ideologies, at least as we have come to know them. The future prospect of ideology will thus depend, in part, on the future of writing; on the production of writing and printed objects; on the consumption of writing and written objects; and, also, on the reproduction of audiences and markets for writings—"readers." Writers produce writings for readers. Hence anything that affects the production of writing, and the competition of printed objects for audiences, necessarily impinges on the role of ideology in the modern world. The position and structural character of ideologies are affected by changes in reading behavior, and by the changing interest in (or time available for) reading. We shall thus attempt to explore, with great tentativeness, some of the ways in which the recent, full-scale emergence of modern communication technologies and of the consciousness industry of which it is a part, may impinge on ideology and its prospect.

1

Hitherto, the fundamental symbolic means of ideology has been conceptual and linguistic. The relationship between ideology and society was mediated by the enormous development of printed matter. Ideology did not "reflect" society in a direct way but mediated the news and newspapers while, correspondingly, much of ideology's reciprocal impact on society was through its publication. Modern ideologies were made available, first, to readers, a relatively well-educated but small sector of the society—the "reading public" nucleated by a literate intelligentsia—and then through them to a larger public. Ideology was diffused via a relatively highly educated reading elite and spread to a larger public through written interpretations of "popularizations" of the ideology in newspapers, magazines, pamphlets, or leaflets, and through face-to-face oral communication in conversations, coffee shops, classrooms, lecture halls, or mass meetings.

In this "two step" model of communication, the dense information of complex ideologies is transmitted or "filtered down" to mass audiences by the media and, in particular, through a mediating intelligentsia. The mediating intelligentsia, then, serve partly as interpreters and partly as proprietors of those printed objects in which an ideology is defined as authoritatively exhibited. An intelligentsia may be said to have a proprietary relation to the printed object when (and to the extent that) they can certify readings of it as correct or incorrect, and certify others as possessing competent knowledge of it.

1.1

In contrast to the conventional printed objects central to ideologies, the modern communication media have greatly intensified the nonlinguistic and iconic component, and hence the *multi*modal character of public communication. The communication breakthrough in the 20th century begins with the spread of the radio and the cinema and is now coming to a culmination in the spread of television.[1] The worldwide diffusion of television marks the end of one and the beginning of a new stage in the communications revolution—the development of a computerized mass information system. We are presently at the early stages of a radically new communications era in which computerized information storage and retrieval systems will be integrated with "cable" television. The computer console will control the computer's information storage and order it to produce selective bits of information, making them directly available in offices and homes via television scanning through cable television, or through specially ordered print outs.

Television is not just an experience substitute *or* merely another experience; it is both, and hence is an historically new mass experience. Such ideologies as the television watchers accept must be successful in integrating and resonating the residual iconic imagery—"pictures-in-the-head"—generated by media-transmitted films as well as by their own "personal experience." In effect, this residual iconic imagery is a new, technologically implanted paleosymbolism; a type II paleosymbolism directly affecting, resonating, and reworking the type I paleosymbolism residual of early childhood experience. In brief, things people could not normally speak about are now being affected by other things they cannot speak about, in ways and with results they cannot speak about. To that extent, the *characterological grounding* of ideologies, normally changed only slowly and in the course of life experience, is being impinged upon and changed in new ways and, quite likely, at far more rapid rates. Television has instituted a new modality and tempo of experience.

If we can think of ideology and history as connected by the "black box" of personal experience, that black box has now been technologically amplified and we may therefore expect a decline in the *manifest* connection between ideologies and history, or people's social position in historical processes. In one way, this may be *experienced* as an "end of ideology," as the "irrelevance" of ideology, or as the "meaningless" or "absurdity" of life, of society, and culture. As the paleosymbolic materials of persons' character are now technologically touchable by six hours of television watching per day, which is to say, almost 40 percent of the person's waking day, the disjunction grows between the "personal" and the sociohistorical.

With such a technologically induced mass transformation of the paleosymbolic elements of character, changes will have to be made in the mass belief systems available, including the ideological. But it is not simply that different ideologies, ideologies having different public projects and appealing to different audiences, become necessary but, rather, that the entire lineal and activistic rationality of *any* kind of ideology—the very grammar of ideology—may be undermined. Television is a "you-are-there" participatory and consummatory activity. One is not commonly left with a sense that one needs to do something actively after a viewing. The viewing is an end in itself.

As a participatory experience, the viewers' sense of critical *distance,* one basis for the rationality premised by normal ideology, has been diminished. If there is residual tension after a viewing, it does not necessarily call for intellectual clarification of the kind provided for by ideology but for a "resolution" in the sense that a drama or piece of music may be "resolved." Ideology always implies a measure of rational social criticism, which is the specification of a social target and the readying of the self to change it. A *viewer's* participatory experience, when intellectualized at all, implies a *dramaturgical* criticism of an object to be consumed and experienced. Dramaturgical criticism does not prod a viewer to do something or change something, but simply to "appreciate" something in its givenness. The viewer presented with a negative dramaturgical criticism of something is not expected to produce a better showing, but to better "understand" it, to recommend others view or avoid viewing it, and to look forward to or avoid the next production by the same dramaturgist. Ideology implies rational criticism as preparation for action; dramaturgy implies the cultivation of the viewer's sensibility as the passive spectator of events as presented.

1.2

With the shift from a conceptual to an iconic symbolism, then, the very fundamentals shared by any ideology may be attenuated. The response prepared by the transition from a newspaper- to a television-centered system of communication may not take the form of ideological performances that vary around a common grammar of ideology, but of altogether differently structured symbol systems: of analogic rather than digital, of synthetic rather than analytic systems, of occult belief systems, new religious myths, the "discovery" of Oriental and other non-Western religions. In this, however, there is no "end" to ideology, for it continues among some groups, in some sites, and at some semiotic level, but it ceases to be as important a mode of consciousness of masses; remaining a dominant form of consciousness among *some* elites, ideology loses ground among the masses and lower strata. In consequence of television, it may be that the traditional undermining of "restricted" speech variants by the public school system is counter-balanced by tele-

vision's reinforcement of it, and that "elaborated" speech variants become increasingly limited to an elite.

The "end of ideology" thesis of the 1950s was rooted in a kind of optimism and in a tacit myth of progress. The idea was that ideology would be replaced by the victory of technological, scientific, and rational-pragmatic modes of consciousness; in short, by a "higher" mode of consciousness. The view suggested here is that the mode of consciousness likely to compete with ideology among the masses, at any rate, may not be more rationalism but less, not a higher rationalism but a lower. Ideology and the critics of ideology both remained rooted in the Enlightenment. The critics of ideology overlooked the fact that, when ideology faded, it need not be replaced by something more rational but by something that *they*—as Enlighteners—might regard as regressive and irrational. This is not to say that there were no limits to the Enlightenment's rationality that needed transcending, nor even that the Western drift to occultism and Oriental religions does not rest on certain irrationalities of present societies. It is, rather, to doubt that occultism and Oriental religions successfully surmount these irrationalities.

2

People who do not read can have only a kind of secondhand relationship to ideologies and ideological movements. If they are to be convinced, they must be convinced by other means or in some other way. Since there has been a profound change in the symbolic environment with the emergence of radio, cinema, and television, there must also be an important change in the role of ideology as a spur to, interpreter and director of, public projects. Correspondingly, certain places—such as schools and universities—or certain social strata—such as the relatively well-educated—remain structurally advantaged with respect to opportunities for ideological production and consumption.

With the growth of the system of mass education, the consciousness of the population of advanced industrialized countries becomes profoundly split: there is an intensification among some "elites" of the consumption and production of ideological objects; but at exactly the same time, there is also a growth of "masses." "Masses" are here defined as those to whom ideology is less central because their consciousness is now shaped more by radio, cinema, and television—being influenced more by the "consciousness industry" than by the ideological products of the "cultural apparatus."

2.1

In industrial countries there is considerable tension between the "cultural apparatus," largely influenced by the intelligentsia and academicians, and the "consciousness industry," largely run by technicians within the framework of profit-maximization and now increasingly integrated with political functionaries and the state apparatus. For that reason, such technicians may seek to avoid overt political acts, lest they offend potential markets as well as offend the political preferences of the industry's owners and managers, or political leaders and state functionaries. This is not at all to say, of course, that the content of the "entertainment" produced by the consciousness industry is apolitical. Far from it.

"The Cultural Apparatus" was a term that C. Wright Mills first used in a BBC broadcast in 1959 to refer to

all the organizations and *milieux* in which artistic, intellectual, and scientific work goes on, and to the means by which such work is made available to circles, publics, and masses. In the cultural apparatus art, science, and learning, entertainment, malarkey, and information are produced and distributed and consumed. It contains an elaborate set of institutions: of schools and theaters, newspapers and census bureaus, studios, laboratories, museums, little magazines, radio networks.

This formulation tends to conflate two different things whose separation repays analysis. One is the *sources,* the creative persons, circles, or milieux, in which or by whom critical reason is displayed and exercised, in which science and technologies are developed, and in which sensibility is symbolically evoked and explored. These *sources,* however, are quite distinct from the *media* through which they are conveyed to audiences and publics. If this distinction between sources and media is not made clearly, there is a tendency to blur the social marginality of the cultural apparatus, its ideological isolation and its political powerlessness. Correspondingly, to emphasize such a distinction is to indicate systematically that the producers of "culture" in modern society cannot communicate their work to mass audiences except by passing through a route controlled by media, and those who control the mass media, the consciousness industry.

This is not to say that the cultural apparatus is altogether devoid of its own media or has no control whatsoever over these. It does control certain magazines, theaters, and radio stations which are relatively small and, especially so, in the audience reached and in the influence exerted. The media directly under the influence of the cultural apparatus allows their members to communicate internally *with one another,* and thus to constitute themselves to some extent as a community; but they allow them little routine access to mass audiences. Often, they convey only elaborated codes.

Mills' discussion of the three stages through which, he held, modern culture was publicly supported essentially culminates in the consciousness industry. The first stage was the aristocratic patronage system, especially in Europe. The second was the bourgeois public for whom the cultural workman worked via the mediation of an anonymous market. The third was the one in which "Commercial agencies or political authorities support culture, but unlike older patrons, they do not form its sole public." It is in this last stage that (following Hans Enzensberger) what is called here the consciousness industry becomes the dominant force, as the medium of public communication.

Mills stresses that the earlier system in which cultural workers and buyers were integrated was unified only indirectly and as the unwitting product of the common taste of patrons or bourgeois publics. In contrast, however, in the third period now dominated by the consciousness industry, Mills notes that the definitions of reality, values, and taste once diffusely shaped by a cultural apparatus are now, however, "subject to official management and, if need be, backed up by coercion . . . the terms of debate, the terms in which the world may be seen, the standards and lack of standards by which men judge of their accomplishments, of themselves or of other men—these terms are officially or commercially determined, inculcated, enforced." Much the same point had been made (in 1954) by the dean of critical communications studies in the United States, Dallas W. Smythe, who remarked: ". . . as our culture has developed it has built into itself increasing concentrations of authority, and nowhere is this more evident than in our communications activities."[2]

Written at the end of the so-called silent decade of the 1950s, Mills' analysis minimized the conflict between the cultural apparatus and the consciousness industry. Mills then emphasized the subordination of American academicians and intellectuals to business values of usefulness and efficiency, and their gratitude for business philanthropy. "Joseph Schumpeter's notion that under capitalism intellectuals generally tend to erode its foundations," declared Mills, "does not generally hold true

of the United States." Mills was more nearly correct, if we take the focus of his remarks to be American intellectuals rather than Europeans. But, for the most part, however, we shall argue that it was Schumpeter who was correct.

There was a tendency on Mills' part to underestimate the alienation long felt by American cultural establishments from the society's dominant values. This alienation was fully visible at least as early as the American transcendentalists; it was an alienation that became more pronounced after World War I, as symbolized by Randolph Bourne's rejection of John Dewey's pragmatism; it was an alienation plainly visible during the Depression and the Marxism of the 1930s; and it was an alienation that would once again be evident only a few years after Mills' own talk on the cultural apparatus, a talk which, in itself, exhibited the very alienation whose absence it decried.

Speaking a decade after Mills, Herbert Gans remarked that "the most interesting phenomenon in America . . . is the political struggle between taste cultures over whose culture is to predominate in the major media, and over whose culture will provide society with its symbols, values and world view."[3] Gans also called attention to the continuing tensions "between the distributors and creators of culture,"[4] another expression of the conflict between the culture apparatus and the consciousness industry.

2.2

The tensions between the cultural apparatus and the consciousness industry are, in part, derived from the tensions that arise between any kinds of sellers and buyers. Here, however, there is the additional problem that those in the cultural apparatus are essentially small scale, handicraft workers who are ever in danger of domination by a narrowing circle of enormously powerful buyers. The buyers in the consciousness industry can establish prices and create political blacklists, exert continual economic and ideological pressure on the cultural workers, and violate the latter's sense of autonomy—of craftsmanship, of artistic or scientific integrity.

It is in part the very control exerted by the consciousness industry, on behalf of values opposed by cultural workers, that generates the latter's continuing critique of "mass culture." This bitterness is accentuated by the vulgarity of the standards that the consciousness industry is felt to impose. The relations between the two are also strained by the widespread feeling in the cultural apparatus that sheer contact with the consciousness industry is threatening to their deepest values. The consciousness industry is often viewed as a "dirty" business threatening the "purity" or authenticity of the cultural apparatus. Hans Enzensberger has noted sympathetically that, considering the nature of the consciousness industry, it is no wonder that "the temptation to withdraw is great." He adds, however, that "fear of handling this is a luxury a sewer-man cannot necessarily afford."[5]

2.3

An essential characteristic of the modern communication system is that it is a *mass media* system, which means that it can make an increasing number of low-cost messages available to an increasing proportion of the members of any society, and to an increasing number of societies throughout the world. This, in turn, has largely been a function of the technological innovation, the invention of printing, with which the communications revolution began. Enzensberger recently formulated a list of technological innovations in the last 20 years or so in communication: new satellites, color television, cable relay television, cassettes, videotape, video tape recorder, video

phones, stereophony, laser techniques, electrostatic reproduction processes, electronic high-speed printing, composing and learning machines, microfiches with electronic access, printing by radio, time-sharing computers, data banks. "All these new forms of media are constantly forming new connections both with each other and with older media like printing, radio, film, television, telephone, radar and so on. They are clearly coming together to form a universal system."[6] In the next 40 years, the symbolic environment and political systems of the world will, once again, be revolutionized by this newest communications revolution.

Both the cultural apparatus and consciousness industry parallel the schismatic character of the modern consciousness: its highly unstable mixture of cultural pessimism and technological optimism. The cultural apparatus is more likely to be the bearer of the "bad news" concerning—for example—ecological crisis, political corruption, class bias; while the consciousness industry becomes the purveyors of hope, the professional lookers-on-the-bright-side. The very political impotence and isolation of the cadres of the cultural apparatus ground their pessimism in their own everyday life, while the technicians of the consciousness industry are surrounded by and have use of the most powerful, advanced, and expensive communications hardware, which is the everyday grounding of their own technological optimism.

Cultural apparatus and consciousness industry thus each define the world quite differently and are, as a result, in a tense if somewhat one-sided relation with one another; one-sided in that the former worries more about the latter than the reverse. Clearly, the largest section of the populace in advanced industrial societies is now under the direct and immediate influence of the consciousness industry, while the cultural apparatus has little if any direct contact with this great public. In short, the cultural apparatus is largely without direct access to or influence on the rural peasantry or farmers, the poor, the blue-collar working classes, blacks, and women.

The differences between the cultural apparatus and the consciousness industry do not exactly parallel differences between the politically involved and the *apolitical*, or between the "left" and the "right" ideologies in politics. There are some tendencies in that direction, but they could be overstated. For example, there are some involved in the cultural apparatus whose fastidiousness makes politics boring or offensive to their sensibilities. Correspondingly, the consciousness industry, perhaps particularly in its pop-music sectors, often fosters a deviant subculture isolated from mainstream consciousness. As we suggested earlier, it sometimes generates a *counter-culture* that unwittingly undermines the very characterological and cultural requisites of the hegemonic class and the institutions that sustain it. It does so, of course, not because its personnel harbor a deliberate intent to sabotage, but from the most "respectable" of motives—to produce and sell whatever turns a profit—regardless of its consequences.

The cultural apparatus largely organizes itself in and around the modern university and its supporting facilities; it is therefore constantly threatened with isolation from the larger society and from any politically consequential following. In effect, the elites of the cultural apparatus surrender the mass of the populace to the consciousness industry, *so long as the elites continue to conceive of influencing others via ideology and ideological discourse.* For now, with the split between consciousness industry and cultural apparatus, ideology continues to ground an *elite* politics but loses effective influence over the masses.

Those who are ideologically mobilized and ready—the people of the cultural apparatus—are thus vulnerable to increasing political frustration, isolation, and impotence. The sense of self-identity and

achievement implicit in and reinforced by ideology is here threatened. Even the ideologically mobilized are now, under the conditions of this split, tempted toward the rejection of ideology itself. They, too are tempted toward a politics increasingly open to the irrational, in order somehow to make contact with the mass public from whom they have been cut off, and who do not respond to the conventional ideological appeals. Something of this was exhibited in what may be called the "Weatherman Syndrome," which is an impotence of the ideological that generates "days of rage," of violence and trashing, as a way of suppressing a sense of ineffectuality and of overcoming inclinations to passivity. In the Weatherman Syndrome—and in terrorism more generally—discourse ceases and ideology collapses into the propaganda of the deed. If the growth of the consciousness industry and its tensions with the cultural apparatus did not produce an "end to ideology" it certainly fostered a crisis for ideological discourse, making the limits on ideology's traditional modes of discourse all too evident.

2.4

There is now a growing mass of the populace in advanced industrial countries who are incapable of being reached by ideological appeals and who are insulated from ideological discourse of any political persuasion. It no longer seems merely mistaken, but is more nearly archaic, to think of the proletariat as an "historical agent" with true political initiatives in societal transformation. With the rise of the consciousness industry the inability of the proletariat to play such a role may now be beyond remedy. As E. P. Thompson has suggested: "So long as any ruling group . . . can reproduce itself or manufacture social consciousness there will be no inherent logic of process within the system which . . . will work powerfully to bring about its overthrow."[7] The conclusion is sound, however, only if we omit discussions of the contradictions of the consciousness industry itself.

Thus one may not conclude that the working class remains reliably controllable, even if it is continually vulnerable to the consciousness industry. Indeed, the proletariat in various countries, Italy, for example, may yet serve as the clean-up men of history, picking up power in the streets as their society's hegemonic class fumbles and collapses in the face of some abrupt crisis. But that is a far cry from being an historical agent with initiative and with a consciousness of its role.

The great and successful revolutions of the 20th century, in Russia and China, occurred in societies that were not only behind in general industrial development but, also, in the development of their communications technology. To this day, the Chinese Cultural Revolutions make important use of wall posters to mobilize their forces. Indeed, one might add that the Cultural Revolutions themselves seem to have been precipitated when Mao lost control over (and routine access to) Peking newspapers, which refused to print his criticisms of Peking's mayor.

3

In countries with an extensive development of the consciousness industry, talk of "revolutionary solutions" is primarily indicative of ideological rage at political impotence and of the fear of personal passivity. In other words, it is a symptom. At the same time, however, neither the continual readiness of the cultural apparatus for ideological arousal and mobilization, on the one side, nor the growth of deviant and countercultures among masses, on the other, can allow one to assume any persisting social stability and equilibrium. A potentially mobilizable mass coexists alongside of an easily arousable ideological elite.

Presently, the "stability" of modern society results in some large part from the mutual isolation of these sectors. Indeed, one should think of the present not as any sort of stable equilibrium but simply as a temporary "inertness." But whether that coexistence of mass and elite—an inert adjacency without much interaction and mutual influence—can long persist remains to be seen. Nevertheless, revolutionary solutions remain mythical so long as ideological elites and their cultural apparatus can reach masses only by going through the consciousness industry.

The paradoxical character of the present becomes even more visible if it is noticed that the *managers* of the consciousness industry, as of others, are also likely to be among the relatively well-educated, university-trained persons most extensively exposed to the cultural apparatus. Their ambiguous social role must yield an inevitable measure of ideological ambivalence. They cannot easily be dismissed by the cultural apparatus as philistine, illiberal, enemies of the mind. Indeed, the hegemonic elites have recently taken to accusing some in the consciousness industry of favoring the "left" and of being class traitors. This was, to some extent, the import of the Nixon-Agnew accusations against the press and of Daniel Patrick Moynihan's suggestion that university-trained journalists are one-sidedly critical of the *status quo*.

The tension between the consciousness industry and the cultural apparatus can become *a* center for a politics sensitive to the importance of the media and of the modern communications revolution. In one part, this will entail a struggle for public control and access to the burgeoning new communications technology. In another part, this politics will concern itself with the cultural apparatus's isolation from the mass media and the public they reach. The tension between the two exists in some measure because the consciousness industry has socially isolated the cultural apparatus and has successfully imposed an institutionalized form of tacit censorship on it. The political struggle between the two will, in part, concern itself with the maintenance or relaxation of this censorship.

But this is not a conflict in which the consciousness industry will be unambivalently opposed and solidary in its response to the cultural apparatus. The reliability and controllability of the technicians of the consciousness industry and even of some of its managers are, indeed, in question. For, as we have noted, they too have been exposed to the perspectives of the cultural apparatus and share its hostility to censor-

ship. Moreover to the extent that the cultural apparatus can produce products that capture and hold attention, and can be sold or used as a vehicle to sell other things, then the cultural apparatus *will* be given access to the media and publics controlled by the consciousness industry. A media-centered politics, then, will amplify the common values and hostility toward censorship shared by the consciousness industry and the cultural apparatus, building alliances around these. It will, at the same time, exploit the contradictions of the consciousness industry that dispose it to publicize any cultural outlook that helps maintain its own profitability.

NOTES

1. From 1946 to 1967, monochromatic sets in use in the United States increased from 8,000 to more than 81,000,000 while, in 1967 there were also some 12,700,000 color sets in the United States. This and other basic communication data are critically condensed in the solid volume by Melvin L. DeFleur, *Theories of Mass Communication*, McKay, New York, 1966.

2. Dallas W. Smythe, "Some Observations of Communications Theory," in *Sociology of Mass Communications*, Denis McQuail, ed., Penguin, London, 1972, p. 25.

3. Herbert J. Gans, "The Politics of Culture in America," in McQuail, ibid., p. 378.

4. Ibid., p. 380.

5. Hans Magnus Enzensberger, *The Consciousness Industry: On Literature, Politics, and the Media,* Seabury Press, 1974, p. 105. Enzensberger is one of the ornaments of the German intellectual life, whose independent neo-Marxism has a tough Voltairean glint.

6. Ibid., p. 99.

7. E. P. Thompson, "An Open Letter to Leszek Kolakowski," *Socialist Register,* Merlin Press, London, 1973, p. 75.

READING 5-3 _____

The aesthetic dimension*

HERBERT MARCUSE

In a situation where the miserable reality can be changed only through radical political praxis, the concern with aesthetics demands justification. It would be senseless to deny the element of despair inherent in this concern: the retreat into a world of fiction where existing conditions are changed and overcome only in the realm

* From *The Aesthetic Dimension: Toward a Critique of Marxist Aesthetics,* by Herbert Marcuse. Originally published in German, Copyright © 1977 by Herbert Marcuse. English version translated and revised by Herbert Marcuse and Erica Sherover, Copyright © 1978. Reprinted by permission of Beacon Press.

of the imagination. However, this purely ideological conception of art is being questioned with increasing intensity. It seems that art as art expresses a truth, an experience, a necessity which, although not in the domain of radical praxis, are nevertheless essential components of revolution. With this insight, the basic conception of Marxist asthetics, that is, its treatment of art as ideology, and the emphasis on the class character of art, become again the topic of critical reexamination.[1]

This discussion is directed to the following theses of Marxist aesthetics:

1. There is a definite connection between art and the material base, between art and the totality of the relations of production. With the change in production relations, art itself is transformed as part of the superstructure, although, like other ideologies, it can lag behind or anticipate social change.
2. There is a definite connection between art and social class. The only authentic, true, progressive art is the art of an ascending class. It expresses the consciousness of this class.
3. Consequently, the political and the aesthetic, the revolutionary content and the artistic quality tend to coincide.
4. The writer has an obligation to articulate and express the interests and needs of the ascending class. (In capitalism, this would be the proletariat.)
5. A declining class or its representatives are unable to produce anything but "decadent" art.
6. Realism (in various senses) is considered as the art form which corresponds most adequately to the social relationships, and thus is the "correct" art form.

Each of these theses implies that the social relations of production must be represented in the literary work—not imposed upon the work externally, but a part of its inner logic and the logic of the material.

This aesthetic imperative follows from the base-superstructure conception. In contrast to the rather dialectical formulations of Marx and Engels, the conception has been made into a rigid schema, a schematization that has had devastating consequences for aesthetics. The schema implies a normative notion of the material base as the true reality and a political devaluation of nonmaterial forces, particularly of the individual consciousness and subconscious and their political function. This function can be either regressive or emancipatory. In both cases, it can become a material force. If historical materialism does not account for this role of subjectivity, it takes on the coloring of vulgar materialism.

Ideology becomes mere ideology, in spite of Engel's emphatic qualifications, and a devaluation of the entire realm of subjectivity takes place, a devaluation not only of the subject as *ego cogito*, the rational subject, but also of inwardness, emotions, and imagination. The subjectivity of individuals, their own consciousness and unconscious, tends to be dissolved into class consciousness. Thereby, a major prerequisite of revolution is minimized, namely, the fact that the need for radical change must be rooted in the subjectivity of individuals themselves, in their intelligence and their passions, their drives and their goals. Marxist theory succumbed to that very reification which it had exposed and combated in society as a whole. Subjectivity became an atom of objectivity; even in its rebellious form it was surrendered to a collective consciousness. The deterministic component of Marxist theory does not lie in its concept of the relationship between social existence and consciousness, but in the reductionistic concept of consciousness which brackets the particular content of individual consciousness and, with it, the subjective potential for revolution.

This development was furthered by the interpretation of subjectivity as a "bourgeois" notion. Historically, this is questionable.[2] But even in bourgeois society, insistence on the truth and right of inwardness is not really a bourgeois value. With the affirmation of the inwardness of subjectivity, the individual steps out of the network of exchange relationships and exchange values, withdraws from the reality of bourgeois society, and enters another dimension of existence. Indeed, this escape from reality led to an experience which could (and did) become a powerful force in *invalidating* the actually prevailing bourgeois values, namely, by shifting the locus of the individual's realization from the domain of the performance principle and the profit motive to that of the inner resources of the human being: passion, imagination, conscience. Moreover, withdrawal and retreat were not the last position. Subjectivity strove to break out of its inwardness into the material and intellectual culture. And today, in the totalitarian period, it has become a political value as a counterforce against aggressive and exploitative socialization.

Liberating subjectivity constitutes itself in the inner history of the individuals—their own history, which is not identical with their social existence. It is the particular history of their encounters, their passions, joys, and sorrows—experiences which are not necessarily grounded in their class situation, and which are not even comprehensible from this perspective. To be sure, the actual manifestations of their history are determined by their class situation, but this situation is not the ground of their fate—of that which happens to them. Especially in its nonmaterial aspects it explodes the class framework. It is all too easy to relegate love and hate, joy and sorrow, hope and despair to the domain of psychology, thereby removing them from the concerns of radical praxis. Indeed, in terms of political economy they may not be "forces of production," but for every human being they are decisive, they constitute reality.

Even in its most distinguished representatives Marxist aesthetics has shared in the devaluation of subjectivity. Hence the preference for realism as the model of progressive art; the denigration of romanticism as simply reactionary; the denunciation of "decadent" art—in general, the embarrassment when confronted with the task of evaluating the aesthetic qualities of a work in terms other than class ideologies.

I shall submit the following thesis: the radical qualities of art, that is to say, its indictment of the established reality and its invocation of the beautiful image (*schöner Schein*) of liberation, are grounded precisely in the dimensions where art *transcends* its social determination and emancipates itself from the given universe of discourse and behavior while preserving its overwhelming presence. Thereby art creates the realm in which the subversion of experience proper to art becomes possible: the world formed by art is recognized as a reality. This experience culminates in extreme situations (of love and death, guilt and failure, but also joy, happiness, and fulfillment) which explode the given reality in the name of a truth normally denied or even unheard. The inner logic of the work of art terminates in the emergence of another reason, another sensibility, which defy the rationality and sensibility incorporated in the dominant social institutions.

Under the law of the aesthetic form, the given reality is necessarily *sublimated:* the immediate content is stylized, the "data" are reshaped and reordered in accordance with the demands of the art form, which requires that even the representation of death and destruction invoke the need for hope—a need rooted in the new consciousness embodied in the work of art.

Aesthetic sublimation makes for the affirmative, reconciling component of art, though it is at the same time a vehicle for the critical, negating function of art. The transcendence of immediate reality shatters the reified objectivity of established social relations and opens a new dimension of experience: rebirth of the rebellious subjectivity. Thus, on the basis of aesthetic sublimation, a *desublimation* takes place in the perception of individuals—in their feelings, judgments thoughts; an invalidation of dominant norms, needs, and values. With all its affirmative-ideological features, art remains a dissenting force.

We can tentatively define "aesthetic form" as the result of the transformation of a given content (actual or historical, personal or social fact) into a self-contained whole: a poem, play, novel, etc.[3] The work is thus "taken out" of the constant process of reality and assumes a significance and truth of its own. The aesthetic transformation is achieved through a reshaping of language, perception, and understanding so that they reveal the essence of reality in its appearance: the repressed potentialities of man and nature. The work of art thus re-presents reality while accusing it.[4]

The critical function of art, its contribution to the struggle for liberation, resides in the aesthetic form. A work of art is authentic or true not by virtue of its content (i.e., the "correct" representation of social conditions), nor by its "pure" form, but by the content having become form.

True, the aesthetic form removes art from the actuality of the class struggle—from actuality pure and simple. The aesthetic form constitutes the autonomy of art vis à vis "the given." However, this dissociation does not produce "false consciousness" or mere illusion but rather a counterconsciousness: negation of the realistic-conformist mind.

Aesthetic form, autonomy, and truth are interrelated. Each is a socio-historical phenomenon, and each *transcends* the socio-historical arena. While the latter limits the autonomy of art it does so without invalidating the *trans*historical truths expressed in the work. The truth of art lies in its power to break the monopoly of established reality (i.e., of those who established

it) to *define* what is *real*. In this rupture, which is the achievement of the aesthetic form, the fictitious world of art appears as true reality.

Art is committed to that perception of the world which alienates individuals from their functional existence and performance in society—it is committed to an emancipation of sensibility, imagination, and reason in all spheres of subjectivity and objectivity. The aesthetic transformation becomes a vehicle of recognition and indictment. But this achievement presupposes a degree of autonomy which withdraws art from the mystifying power of the given and frees it for the expression of its own truth. Inasmuch as man and nature are constituted by an unfree society, their repressed and distorted potentialities can be represented only in an *estranging* form. The world of art is that of another *Reality Principle,* of estrangement—and only as estrangement does art fulfill a *cognitive* function: it communicates truths not communicable in any other language; *it contradicts.*

However, the strong affirmative tendencies toward reconciliation with the established reality coexist with the rebellious ones. I shall try to show that they are not due to the specific class determination of art but rather to the redeeming character of the *catharsis.* The catharsis itself is grounded in the power of aesthetic form to call fate by its name, to demystify its force, to give the word to the victims—the power of recognition which gives the individual a modicum of freedom and fulfillment in the realm of unfreedom. The interplay between the affirmation and the indictment of that which is, between ideology and truth, pertains to the very structure of art.[5] But in the authentic works, the affirmation does not cancel the indictment: reconciliation and hope still preserve the memory of things past.

The affirmative character of art has yet another source: it is in the commitment of art to Eros, the deep affirmation of the Life

Instincts in their fight against instinctual and social oppression. The permanence of art, its historical immortality throughout the millennia of destruction, bears witness to this commitment.

Art stands under the law of the given, while transgressing this law. The concept of art as an essentially autonomous and negating productive force contradicts the notion which sees art as performing an essentially dependent, affirmative-ideological function, that is to say, glorifying and absolving the existing society.[6] Even the militant bourgeois literature of the 18th century remains ideological: the struggle of the ascending class with the nobility is primarily over issues of bourgeois morality. The lower classes play only a marginal role, if any. With a few notable exceptions, this literature is not one of class struggle. According to this point of view, the ideological character of art can be remedied today only by grounding art in revolutionary praxis and in the *Weltanschauung* of the proletariat.

It has often been pointed out that this interpretation of art does not do justice to the views of Marx and Engels.[7] To be sure, even this interpretation admits that art aims at representing the essence of a given reality and not merely its appearance. Reality is taken to be the totality of social relations and its essence is defined as the laws determining these relations in the "complex of social causality."[8] This view demands that the protagonists in a work of art represent individuals as "types" who in turn exemplify "objective tendencies of social development, indeed of humanity as a whole."[9]

Such formulations provoke the question whether literature is not hereby assigned a function which could only be fulfilled in the medium of theory. The representation of the social totality requires a conceptual analysis, which can hardly be transposed into the medium of sensibility. During the great debate on Marxist aesthetics in the early 30s, Lu Märten suggested that Marxist theory possesses a theoretical form of its own which militates against any attempt to give it an aesthetic form.[10]

But if the work of art cannot be comprehended in terms of social theory, neither can it be comprehended in terms of philosophy. In his discussion with Adorno, Lucien Goldmann rejects Adorno's claim that in order to understand a literary work "one has to transcend it towards philosophy, philosophical culture and critical knowledge." Against Adorno, Goldmann insists on the concreteness immanent in the work which makes it into an (aesthetic) totality in its own right: "The work of art is a universe of colors, sounds and words and concrete characters. There is no death, there is only Phaedra dying."[11]

The reification of Marxist aesthetics depreciates and distorts the truth expressed in this universe—it minimizes the cognitive function of art as ideology. For the radical potential of art lies precisely in its ideological character, in its transcendent relation to the "basis." Ideology is not always *mere* ideology, false consciousness. The consciousness and the representation of truths which appear as abstract in relation to the established process of production are also ideological functions. Art presents one of these truths. As ideology, it opposes the given society. The autonomy of art contains the categorical imperative: "things must change." If the liberation of human beings and nature is to be possible at all, then the social nexus of destruction and submission must be broken. This does not mean that the revolution becomes thematic; on the contrary, in the aesthetically most perfect works, it does not. It seems that in these works the necessity of revolution is presupposed, as the *a priori* of art. But the revolution is also as it were surpassed and questioned as to how far it responds to the anguish of the human being, as to how far it achieves a rupture with the past.

Compared with the often one-dimensional optimism of propaganda, art is permeated with pessimism, not seldom intertwined with comedy. Its "liberating laughter" recalls the danger and the evil that have passed—this time! But the pessimism of art is not counterrevolutionary. It serves to warn against the "happy consciousness" of radical praxis: as if all of that which art invokes and indicts could be settled through the class struggle. Such pessimism permeats even the literature in which the revolution itself is affirmed, and becomes thematic; Büchner's play *The Death of Danton* is a classic example.

Marxist aesthetics assumes that all art is *somehow* conditioned by the relations of production, class position, and so on. Its first task (but only its first) is the specific analysis of this "somehow," that is to say, of the limits and modes of this conditioning. The question as to whether there are qualities of art which transcend specific social conditions and how these qualities are related to the particular social conditions remains open. Marxist aesthetics has yet to ask: What are the qualities of art which transcend the specific social content and form and give art its universality? Marxist aesthetics must explain why Greek tragedy and the medieval epic, for example, can still be experienced today as "great," "authentic" literature, even though they pertain to ancient slave society and feudalism, respectively. Marx's remark at the end of *The Introduction to the Critique of Political Economy* is hardly persuasive; one simply cannot explain the attraction of Greek art for us today as our rejoicing in the unfolding of the social "childhood of humanity."

However correctly one has analyzed a poem, play, or novel in terms of its social content, the questions as to whether the particular work is good, beautiful, and true are still unanswered. But the answers to these questions cannot again be given in terms of the specific relations of production which constitute the historical context of the respective work. The circularity of this method is obvious. In addition it falls victim to an easy relativism which is contradicted clearly enough by the permanence of certain qualities of art through all changes of style and historical periods (transcendence, estrangement, aesthetic order, manifestations of the beautiful).

The fact that a work truly represents the interests or the outlook of the proletariat or of the bourgeoisie does not yet make it an authentic work of art. This "material" quality may facilitate its reception, may lend it greater concreteness, but it is in no way constitutive. The universality of art cannot be grounded in the world and world outlook of a particular class, for art envisions a concrete universal, humanity (*Menschlichkeit*), which no particular class can incorporate, not even the proletariat, Marx's "universal class." The inexorable entanglement of joy and sorrow, celebration and despair, Eros and Thanatos cannot be dissolved into problems of class struggle. History is also grounded in nature. And Marxist theory has the least justification to ignore the metabolism between the human being and nature, and to denounce the insistence on this natural soil of society as a regressive ideological conception.

The emergence of human beings as "species beings"—men and women capable of living in that community of freedom which is the potential of the species—this is the subjective basis of a classless society. Its realization presupposes a radical transformation of the drives and needs of the individuals: an organic development within the socio-historical. Solidarity would be on weak grounds were it not rooted in the instinctual structure of individuals. In this dimension, men and women are confronted with psycho-physical forces which they have to make their own without being able to overcome the naturalness of these forces. This is the domain of the primary drives:

of libidinal and destructive energy. Solidarity and community have their basis in the subordination of destructive and aggressive energy to the social emancipation of the life instincts.

Marxism has too long neglected the radical political potential of this dimension, though the revolutionizing of the instinctual structure is a prerequisite for a change in the system of needs, the mark of a socialist society as qualitative difference. Class society knows only the appearance, the image of the qualitative difference; this image, divorced from praxis, has been preserved in the realm of art. In the aesthetic form, the autonomy of art constitutes itself. It was forced upon art through the separation of mental and material labor, as a result of the prevailing relations of domination. Dissociation from the process of production became a refuge and a vantage point from which to denounce the reality established through domination.

Nevertheless society remains present in the autonomous realm of art in several ways: first of all as the "stuff" for the aesthetic representation which, past and present, is transformed in this representation. This is the historicity of the conceptual, linguistic, and imaginable material which the tradition transmits to the artists and with or against which they have to work; secondly, as the scope of the actually available possibilities of struggle and liberation; thirdly, as the specific position of art in the social division of labor, especially in the separation of intellectual and manual labor through which artistic activity, and to a great extent also its reception, become the privilege of an "elite" removed from the material process of production.

The class character of art consists only in these objective limitations of its autonomy. The fact that the artist belongs to a privileged group negates neither the truth nor the aesthetic quality of his work. What is true of "the classics of socialism" is true also of the great artists: they break through the class limitations of their family, background, environment. Marxist theory is not family research. The progressive character of art, its contribution to the struggle for liberation, cannot be measured by the artist's origins nor by the ideological horizon of their class. Neither can it be determined by the presence (or absence) of the oppressed class in their works. The criteria for the progressive character of art are given only in the work itself as a whole: in what it says and how it says it.

In this sense art is "art for art's sake" inasmuch as the aesthetic form reveals tabooed and repressed dimensions of reality: aspects of liberation. The poetry of Mallarmé is an extreme example; his poems conjure up modes of perception, imagination, gestures—a feast of sensuousness which shatters everyday experience and anticipates a different reality principle.

The degree to which the distance and estrangement from praxis constitute the emancipatory value of art becomes particularly clear in those works of literature which seem to close themselves rigidly against such praxis. Walter Benjamin has traced this in the works of Poe, Baudelaire, Proust, and Valéry. They express a "consciousness of crisis" (*Krisenbewusstsein*) : a pleasure in decay, in destruction, in the beauty of evil; a celebration of the asocial, of the anomic—the secret rebellion of the bourgeois against his own class. Benjamin writes about Baudelaire:

It seems of little value to give his work a position on the most advanced ramparts of the human struggle for liberation. From the beginning, it appears much more promising to follow him in his machinations where he is without doubt at home: in the enemy camp. These machinations are a blessing for the enemy only in the rarest cases. Baudelaire was a secret agent, an agent of the secret discontent of his class with its own rule. One who confronts Baudelaire with this class gets more out of him than one who rejects him as uninteresting from a proletarian standpoint.[12]

The "secret" protest of this esoteric literature lies in the ingression of the primary erotic-destructive forces which explode the normal universe of communication and behavior. They are asocial in their very nature, a subterranean rebellion against the social order. Inasmuch as this literature reveals the dominion of Eros and Thanatos beyond all social control, it invokes needs and gratifications which are essentially destructive. In terms of political praxis, this literature remains elitist and decadent. It does nothing in the struggle for liberation —except to open the tabooed zones of nature and society in which even death and the devil are enlisted as allies in the refusal to abide by the law and order of repression. This literature is one of the historical forms of critical aesthetic transcendence. Art cannot abolish the social division of labor which makes for its esoteric character, but neither can art "popularize" itself without weakening its emancipatory impact.

NOTES

1. Especially among the authors of the periodicals *Kursbuch* (Frankfurt: Suhrkamp, later Rotbuch Verlag), *Argument* (Berlin), *Literaturmagazin* (Reinbek: Rowohlt). In the center of this discussion is the idea of an autonomous art in confrontation with the capitalist art industry on the one hand, and the radical propaganda art on the other. See especially the excellent articles by Nicolas Born, H. C. Buch, Wolfgang Harich, Herman Peter Piwitt, and Michael Schneider in volumes 1 and 2 of the *Literaturmagazin*, the volume *Autonomie aer Kunst* (Frankfurt: Suhrkamp, 1972), and Peter Bürger, *Theorie der Avantgarde* (Frankfurt: Suhrkamp, 1974).

2. See Erich Köhler, *Ideal und Wirklichkeit in der Höfischen Epik* (Tübingen: Niemeyer, 1956; second edition, 1970), especially chapter 5, for a discussion of this in relation to the courtly epic.

3. See my *Counterrevolution and Revolt* (Boston: Beacon Press, 1972), p. 81.

4. Ernst Fischer in *Auf den Spuren der Wirklichkeit; sechs Essays* (Reinbek: Rowohlt, 1968) recognizes in the "will to form" (*Wille zur Gestalt*) the will to transcend the actual: negation of that which is, and presentiment (*Ahnung*) of a freer and purer existence. In this sense, art is the "irreconcilable, the resistance of the human being to its vanishing in the [established] order and systems" (p. 67).

5. "Two antagonistic attitudes toward the powers that be are prevalent in literature: *resistance* and *submission*. Literature is certainly not mere ideology and does not merely express a social consciousness that invokes the illusion of harmony, assuring the individuals that everything is as it ought to be, and that nobody has the right to expect fate to give him more than he receives. To be sure, literature has time and again justified established social relationships; nevertheless, it has always kept alive that human yearning which cannot find gratification in the existing society. Grief and sorrow are essential elements of bourgeois literature" (Leo Lowenthal, *Das Bild des Menschen in der Literatur* [Neuwied: Luchterhand, 1966], pp. 14 f.). (Published in English as *Literature and the Image of Man* [Boston: Beacon Press, 1957].)

6. See my essay "The Affirmative Character of Culture" in *Negations* (Boston: Beacon Press, 1968).

7. In his book *Marxistische Ideologie und allgemeine Kunsttheorie* (Tübingen: Mohr, 1970), Hans-Dietrich Sander presents a thorough analysis of Marx's and Engels' contribution to a theory of art. The provocative conclusion: most of Marxist aesthetics is not only a gross vulgarization—Marx's and Engels' views are also turned into their opposite! He writes: Marx and Engels saw "the essence of a work of art precisely not in its political or social relevance" (p. 174). They are closer to Kant, Fichte, and Schelling than to Hegel (p. 171). Sander's documentation for this thesis may well be too selective and minimize statements by Marx and Engels which contradict Sander's interpretation. However, his analysis does show clearly the difficulty of Marxist aesthetics in coming to grips with the problems of the theory of art.

8. Bertolt Brecht, "Volkstümlichkeit und Realismus," in *Gesammelte Werke* (Frankfurt: Suhrkamp, 1967), vol. 8, p. 323.

9. Georg Lukács, "Es geht um den Realismus," in *Marxismus und Literatur*, edited by Fritz J. Raddatz (Reinbek: Rowohlt, 1969), vol. 2, p. 77.

10. In *Die Linkskurve* vol. 3, no. 5 (Berlin: May 1931, reprinted 1970), p. 17.

11. *Colloque international sur la sociologie de la littératur* (Bruxelles: Institut de la Sociologie, 1974), p. 40.

12. Walter Benjamin, "Fragment über Methodenfrage einer Marxistischen Literatur-Analyse," in *Kursbuch* 20 (Frankfurt: Suhrkamp, 1970), p. 3.

The human and the system*

JOSÉ MÍGUEZ BONINO

It does not seem very difficult to show that there is a continuous and powerful biblical tradition of "denunciation" of and "resistance" to authoritarian governments, beginning with the early prophetic opposition to the establishment of absolute monarchy and the monarchic ideology in Israel and moving through apocalyptic anti-imperial theology to our Lord's clash with the Jewish religio-political establishment. Moreover the prophetic protest against authoritarianism seems to be directly related to the violation of the basic rights of certain individuals and groups. The episodes of Elijah and Ahab on Naboth's vineyard or Nathan's scathing condemnation of David come immediately to mind. The biblical protest against authoritarian governments often focuses on the betrayal of justice by those in power, as witnessed by practically all the "literary prophets" from Amos to Ezekiel. The biblical basis for the church's strong stand against authoritarianism thus seems well established.

Nevertheless, the interpretation of that tradition and, most of all, its rereading from within today's conditions and questions, are riddled with perplexing problems. On the whole, the church's interpretation of its "political duty" has not been based on the prophetic tradition but on a theology of order and the divine origin of political power, which is not absent from the Bible and which is usually anchored firmly in the traditional interpretation of Romans 13:1–5. Although there are notable exceptions, one can say that very early in the history of the Christian church the prophetic tradition was interpreted in a soteriological rather than in an ethical or ethico-political key.

This has been the dominant trend in large sectors of the Protestant tradition. The "privatization" of faith, the absolutization of the distinction between the secular (outward) and the religious (inner) realms, and the transcendent (otherworldly or eschatological) transposition of the prophetic vision, have combined to concentrate the church's relation to political authority into one single, formal duty: submission. It would be foolish to underestimate the powerful grip that this tradition still has on the mind and consciousness of Christians throughout the world.[1]

This interpretation has both been reinforced by, and in turn it has itself strengthened, a very basic theological conviction that political power is by its nature totally foreign and contradictory to the mission and method of Jesus, and consequently to Christian love as well. The former is in this view made synonymous with coercion and physical violence while the latter is seen as primarily operating subjectively and in face-to-face personal relations. This is the background against which Jesus' refusal of political power in the temptations, his rejection of a kingly messianic role, and even his cross are interpreted. Christians, insofar as they cannot avoid being caught in the "foreign" realm of political life—or even if they vocationally or by circumstances enter into it—cross over to an alien territory in which faith gives no direction except in terms of individual ethics. The cross is the negation of political power, and Christian love is the negation of political coercion. In pol-

---

* From *Theology Today,* 35 (April 1978), pp. 14–24.

itics, therefore, the Christians are seen to be practically on their own. Jesus Christ does not go with them into that area, or at least he does not have anything to say concerning the questions that arise there.

Certainly the concrete instances in which this general conception has crystallized are by no means homogeneous. Time, circumstances, social conditions, ideologies, and types of piety have shaped different responses. Some have affirmed the political realm as a legitimate field of Christian vocation, as part of God's creation. The content of that service, nevertheless, is determined by a different law—reason, natural law, or simple expediency. We have here some of the worst uses of the idea of "the two realms" (for which Lutherans usually take the blame but many other Christians faithfully practice). Others refuse to participate in political life, either by confining themselves to the "commerce" with the city that they cannot avoid (however much they may be participating unconsciously) and within what Max Weber called "the social strike" of the sects, or by attempting to build a "kingdom of Christ" where the law of love holds sway within the Christian community and wherein the Christian may exercise an earthly, yet not quite "public," Christian citizenship. Finally, the political realm interests the church insofar as the latter is also a part of the "human city" and suffers or profits from its conditions.

In this respect, the implicit or explicit theology in these relations has considered the political realm as totally extrinsic and basically irrelevant to salvation, but potentially beneficial or detrimental in an indirect way—by granting privileges to the church, by publicly supporting religion, or on the contrary by restricting religious freedom or restricting the "proper" task of the church. This ancillary function has so dominated the mind of the church that its support or resistance—even to the support of violent rebellion—to particular governments has hinged basically on the attitude of the state towards the church.[2]

This old and widespread theological and ecclesiastical tradition offers little help for today's questions, which do not emerge mainly at the level of official church-state relations or the *formal* problem of political participation, but center around the question of the Christian assessment of the *human content* of political systems and powers. On the specific question of the Christian mission *vis-à-vis* "authoritarian governments," we have to concede that basically the theological tradition is on the side of the latter. They know it and demand this support. When Christians begin to question the *content* of their politics and to relate their attitude to that content, authoritarian governments rightly claim that these Christians—whether individuals, groups, or ecclesiastical hierarchies—are departing from the tradition of the church and launching into an area in which they have no competence. It is in response to these circumstances that Christians have in the last few years begun to rediscover the political dimension of the prophetic message and to search in the history of the church for the sporadic surfacing of that prophetic stream. But we have to confess that we are just at the beginning of such a search and that we are far from having either adequately pondered or theologically articulated these insights.

Another source of problems involves the relation of individual freedom, distributive justice, and social order to different forms of government. This gives the impression of referring to entities or magnitudes which can be understood in themselves, as abstract notions to be discussed theoretically in relation to some theological "horizon of truth." As soon as we try to relate such notions to known and existent realities, we are bound to ask such questions as: "Whose freedom?" "Freedom for what?" "Freedom . . . within which social structure?" "What is to be 'justly distributed'?"

"How will it be produced?" "How is the production of what is to be distributed related to its distribution?" "The state" or "forms of government" do not stand by themselves in some sort of "ideological smorgasbord" from which we can pick according to our taste. The state stands in particular relation to a complex of economic, social, and cultural conditions. In order to give some relevance to our discussion, we are forced to engage in some social analysis of the specific social formations that serve as the context for reflection on the mission of the church.

What I would suggest, is a preliminary conversation about the social and theological frame of reference within which we want to tackle the consideration of the mission of the church in the political realm. For this discussion I am offering simply some notes under the rubrics of "analysis," "theological reflection," and "pastoral strategy." These notes will have some theoretical character, but I hope they may lead into a discussion that will clarify some of the concrete situations in which we are involved and which concern us very deeply.

Analysis of authoritarian governments

It would not be fruitful to start with an abstract notion such as that of "state" but with the concept of "social formation," an historically and geographically circumscribed society characterized by a more or less integrated and homogeneous economic system, political organization, and ideological perspective. Such social formations incorporate and are the result of the interaction of several dimensions or factors—economic, political, and cultural (among which I include here both culture in the classical sense, such as art, philosophy, etc., but also ideology and religion). We may leave aside the question as to whether any of these factors is finally determinant of the whole formation. But we can, I think,

grant at least that they condition each other and that in a given social formation one of these takes a dominant role (for example, religion in feudal society) .[3]

With this very simple perspective we may come back to our subject and focus on a rather broad social formation that we can characterize as "western capitalist society."[4] In relation to it I would suggest several brief theses for interpretation in order to locate more concretely the problem of "authoritarian governments," particularly as we face it in the countries of the so-called Third World.

1. *In a capitalist social formation the economic factor acquires a dominant role.* This seems clear from the history of the dominant western countries as well as from an analysis of the operation, expansion, conflicts, and stages of development of the western capitalist world.

2. *Freedom, justice, and order are indissolubly related to this society, both in their conception and in their operation to the economic instance.* This does not mean that they are solely economically determined or that they operate only at the economic level. But it does mean that we cannot understand them unless we relate them to the economic matrix in which they were—in their modern western form —conceived. The emergence of the political rights of the "citizen" is clearly related historically to the economic significance of the emerging bourgeoisie. The original relation of property to political rights is clear enough in this respect. The extension of "rights" to other sectors closely follows the weight that these sectors of society acquire in the productive process. The purely formal character of such rights for the "marginal"—those not integrated in the productive process—is another test of the same fact. A similar case can be made in relation to "justice" and "social order" within the western capitalist world.

3. *In the western capitalist society the political factor*—which has an integrative

function—*takes the form of the liberal democratic state, which both guarantees the preservation of the economic order and possesses a relative but real autonomy.* This point seems to me of great importance. In previous social orders—the feudal, for example—the identification of economic and political power is immediate, clearly visible, and ideologically justified. The modern democratic states serve the economic order in a more indirect way—by guaranteeing its unhindered development through non-intervention or by preserving (even through intervention in the economic realm) the social conditions indispensable for the functioning and expansion of the economic system. Thus, the liberal government may even defend the economically dominated classes against the dominant ones and set limits to the economic domination. This should not be interpreted as manifestation of a "classless" state, but as a service in which, through its relative autonomy, the liberal state may contradict the immediate interests of the dominant groups in terms of the long-range preservation of the system. "The New Deal," anti-trust laws, and the welfare state are good examples.

4. *The cultural factor—art, philosophy, religion, etc.—also receives in western capitalist society a significant autonomy, through which it best serves the economic instance by permeating the different floors of the social building with a cohesive outlook on reality which allows people to participate with good spiritual and religious conscience in the operation and expansion of the economic system.* The relation of the shaping of the basic traits of the human personality to the needs of the different stages of economic capitalist development and the role of religion in this development have been widely researched, and we need not take time with them now.

The problem of "authoritarian govern-ments," particularly as it appears in the Third World countries living within the capitalist system, has to be understood in relation to the crisis of the relation between the economic, political, and cultural instances as it was established in the classical form of capitalist western society. This relation is characterized by relative autonomy and indirect support. In the space provided by this relative autonomy, human rights and freedoms, including economic ones, found an ample space for development. But the limits of that space seem to have appeared particularly in the Third World countries. As the preservation of the bourgeois economic, political, and ideological "freedom" in the central countries of the system increasingly requires that some of the critical aspects of the economic development (inflation, unemployment, and exploitation of labor) be exported to the Third World, the conflicts between the periphery and the center of the system and within the peripheral societies escalate in such a way that they threaten the system itself. At this point, the political and cultural instances are recalled from their autonomy and required to serve the economic system *directly*. But some of these factors, such as art, literature, political parties, and the churches, have developed in their relative autonomy an ethos of their own which transcends the limits of the system, and they are not ready to surrender it. Thus, the western world is a house divided against itself, and confrontation and repression seem unavoidable.

Although we have talked here in schematic and somewhat abstract terms, we are referring to very concrete realities. Let us take for a moment the emergence of an authoritarian government of the military in Chile. I would here suggest three points of concentration for consideration:

1. The intervention takes place not in relation to the violations of the "letter

of the law"—that is, the basic democratic institutions—but, according to the military spokesmen, when "the spirit of the law"—the "essence of the nationality" or the Christian view of life or western civilization—is threatened. It becomes necessary, therefore, to do away with the political and cultural bourgeois order (the democratic state, cultural freedom) in order to safeguard that which is essential, namely western civilization. But what is left of western civilization once the liberal democratic state and the liberal culture have been amputated and even the religious institution, the church, is antagonized? However much one may declaim about one's devotion to that culture, only one thing is left: the economic system.

2. A new ideology, a new conception of the state, and a new definition of rights and freedom are then required. This, as we know, is "the doctrine of national security" which, as Comblin has so clearly shown, breaks with the whole western humanist tradition and becomes the support of the "new model of development" strictly along capitalist lines. In particular, the classical liberal definition of the "distinction of levels" between political life and religion has to be redefined, and the direct responsibility of religion, even its necessary symbiosis with the new ideology, has to be clearly defined. Military pronouncements are totally unambiguous at this point.

3. A clearer understanding of the absolutely necessary economic basis of the society is then required, which will make unmistakably clear that everything hinges on the defense of the capitalist economy. Therefore, it is not a matter of chance that the theory of Milton Friedman, the most explicit theorist of this order, is the basis for the new Chilean society. The relation of an authoritarian government, the corresponding ideology, the mission assigned to the church, and the economic system have been almost grotesquely asserted.

A theology of human survival

The thorough incompatibility of the Christian faith with the policies of the development of the western economic system is emerging in Latin America and in many other areas of the Third World not as a conscious or explicit challenge of the system. This takes place only among small groups of Christians. Rather, there is a growing cleavage between the humanistic themes developed by cultural, political, and religious thought during the last centuries and the inhuman and dehumanizing features displayed under the new authoritarian governments. As it has been tirelessly repeated, and as tirelessly ignored in western accounts of the conflict, the struggle did not originate at the theological level but out of everyday pastoral experience. It is there where hunger, exploitation, disease, and marginalization have shown their ugly faces. It is there where priests, ministers, petit bourgeois intellectuals, and students have begun to see the "western society" from its seamy side, from "the perspective of those who are below," and have felt the revulsive effect of this vision. This understanding and the commitments that were born from it in the 50s and 60s have met in the late 60s and 70s with the brutal reaction of the system in the establishment of "authoritarian governments," the use of torture and murder, and the numberless atrocities which are now well documented in so many places. This new situation seems to consolidate the conflict, into which bishops and church authorities, both in the Third World and in the western countries, are now drawn in defense of "human rights" and "minimal conditions for human survival." The body of evidence supplied by "episcopal letters" in Latin America alone during the last two years provides a moving evidence of this struggle.

It is only natural that Christians who find themselves in this struggle are compelled, for their own self-understanding as well as for the account and defense of their action, to reflect theologically on the basis and significance of an action, which is undertaken in many cases initially only as a "collateral service" but becomes more and more absorbing and exacting, to the point of death. The rediscovery of the prophets, of the dominical message of the Kingdom (Luke 4:18–19 or the *Magnificat*), of the very early manifestations of social protest in the New Testament and in the Fathers takes place as part of this effort. But this will not be enough to counteract the agelong interiorization of the previous tradition or the onslaughts of repression. It is necessary to uncover, behind and supporting all these prophetic witnesses, a unifying theological perspective, a fundamental focus, which is clearly and directly related to our faith in and commitment to the Tribune God whose will and purpose have been made known and effective in Jesus Christ. This is the theological task.

The so-called theology of liberation began to tackle that task at a particular point in the history of the conflict and in view of particular circumstances and needs of Christians participating in this struggle. This task has to be carried further in relation to the characteristics and problems that the new situation presents to us. What we confront is the unmasking of a system which is predicated on the annihilation of the human person as such, in the form of total subordination to humanity's economic function. For the capitalist order, as Friedman has so eloquently shown, human beings exist only as economic functions, producers or consumers, assets or liabilities, in the process of maximizing profit. Whatever threatens this function or does not fit into it has to be sacrificed—either metaphorically or literally. Over against this "theology of death," the Christian faith in the Creator, Reconciling, and Redeeming God has to proclaim and witness the gospel of life. In the simple words of Irenaeus,

"The glory of God is man alive." Over against a system and an ideology of death, Christian theology has to deepen and give content to the struggle for liberation in the exaltation and defense of human life as it was created by God, proleptically and vicariously lived by the *incarnate* Son, exalted at the right hand through the resurrection and ascension, and made available in history by the empowerment of the Spirit, until the final consummation in the Kingdom.

This may sound very simple—and even simplistic. But such a theological task is fraught with difficulties, because much of the Christian theology and symbolism has been a theology of death and human suppression and repression. What is required, therefore, is a rereading of fundamental aspects of Christian doctrine, not so much in order to change the content of doctrines but their function and perspectives from which they are developed. Have we, for instance, pondered the fact that the early church seems to have integrated the death of Jesus into its theological reflection as a saving event only in the light of the resurrection which was its earliest and fundamental confession? Why have we developed the doctrine of God's power on the model of autocratic authority and neglected early patristic insights into the Trinity as the power of love, moving in the "circulation" of the three persons and drawing into creative and transforming activity? Why have we neglected the eschatological reference of the sacraments, the seal of the new and authentic life, the covenant which is sealed by the shedding of blood but fulfilled in the banquet of the Kingdom? Why have we almost entirely substituted the model of arbitrary power and submission in humanity's relationship to God for the model of *covenant* which dominates the Old and New Testament? Why, finally, have we—particularly we Protestants—portrayed grace as a resignation of the human subject instead of the release and authorization of a new human "I," the new person in Christ, which has moved through death into life for a *bodily* and active human life which reaches towards the New Age?

If the proclamation of "God's glory as a living humanity" is the church's mission *vis-à-vis* "authoritarian governments" wed to an ideology of death, such proclamation cannot be done in the abstract. Three points seem to me of fundamental importance.

1. Such proclamation can occur only when the church lives for and with those on whom the system is daily inflicting its ministry of death: the poor, the marginalized, the persecuted.

2. Such proclamation cannot be abstracted from the specific conditions of the death that is rejected and the life that is exalted. It will have to be constantly nourished by the immediate reference to specific violations of human life and specific demands related to every aspect of life, and it will have to be informed and accompanied by a rigorous analysis of the dynamics of human life as it is lived within the conditions of a specific social formation.

3. Such proclamation must permeate every aspect of the church's life—its worship, fellowship, evangelism, organization. We cannot expect a theology of the resurrection to be truly significant when verbally proclaimed, or even socially declared in the framework of an alienating worship and in a castrating institution. Much more than prophetic declarations are necessary to make of the Christian churches a witness of God's blessing and defense of human life.

The shepherding of human life

These suggestions already touch on the question of "a pastoral strategy." Jaspers speaks of the "human vocation" as "the shepherding of being." For the disciples of the Incarnate Lord, in this time of death, it would be more fitting to define the mission of the church as "the shepherding of human life." This mission entails not some re-arrangement of the "quotas" of freedom, justice, and order within the existing system, but the struggle for a new social formation in which the relation between the economic, personal, and political life will be life-affirming, concerned with the freedom of human life and related to human concerns. This requires the emergence of a historical project which builds on objective conditions and which projects a different order.

Individual Christians and Christian groups will participate in different ways in this task. Their action is truly ecclesial action. But when we think of the mission of the churches as particular institutional entities, we are forced to recognize that their "shepherding of human life" cannot (even for sociological reasons) consist in the definition and advocacy of such a "historical project." The relation of mission to the necessary change is a more indirect one which can perhaps be subsumed under three areas:

1. The denunciation of "the system of death" in its specific violations of human life. Since a "Christian" legitimation is so important for the new authoritarian regimes with which we are dealing, this function of de-sacralizing the system of death is very important and significant. The violent reactions which its exercise evokes are a sign of its effectiveness.

2. The advocacy of basic human rights, of minimal space for human life even within the conditions of oppression. In other words, the churches can exercise the power and influence which they still possess for minimizing as much as possible the de-humanizing and destructive operation of the systems of repression. The defense of human rights means both the defense of "life" and the defense of "the access to the means of life."

3. The ministry to those who suffer, which is expressed in different forms of solidarity, in a pastoral service of encouragement and hope, in the provision within the churches of a "space of freedom" where the poor and marginals can assert their humanity.

These tasks are certainly modest. They will not change the system. But, if exercised in the perspective of a larger and more fundamental theological and social perspective, they may hasten the birth of a new day and help to shape the character of the new society.

NOTES

1. The idea of "submission" is the obverse side of a "political theology" which was present in different forms in the Near East, Greece, and Rome, and which understood the function of religion as the sacralization of power. The penetration of this political theology into the Christian church since the fourth century has been amply documented and debated.

2. We should not ignore the importance of the concept of "the Lordship of Christ" as political motivation, particularly in the Reformed tradition. But it seems to have expressed itself mainly in theocratic forms in which the state is given an ancillary position or as religious opposition to governments which were considered harmful to the church. Even the church struggle of the Confessing Church in Germany under Hitler does not quite escape this characterization! Aside perhaps from some experiments in Holland, which are not too encouraging in their outcome, it has not developed a positive content for political action. We notice the attempts by Visser 't Hooft (*The Lordship of Christ*), Karl Barth (*Bürgergemeinde und Christengemeinde*), and Roger Mehl (*Pour une Éthique Sociale Chrétienne*) to develop a political ethic on an "analogy" from Christology and ecclesiology.

3. Such a "dominant" role may not preclude that other factors—for example, the "economic" or the "political"—may be determinant in the last analysis. It would simply mean that "ultimate determination" operates in this particular case through another factor, i.e., the "religious." This is not an unimportant problem, but it need not concern us here.

4. I am by no means suggesting that the problem of a mission of the church in relation to authoritarian governments exists only in the western world. We are all well aware of its urgency and gravity in the socialist countries. I confine myself to the western world for three reasons. First, it is the area in which I live and with which I am more acquainted. Second, although formally there are striking resemblances in the characterizations and operation of "authoritarian regimes," we would need a totally different analysis even for the understanding of these similarities, for we would be dealing with historically and structurally related but different social formations. Third, it is in the west where the authoritarian governments make explicit religious claims and seek religious justifications.

CHAPTER 6

Social institutions in capitalist society

Although our location is in the material world, a comprehension of that world and our place in it requires an imagination that exceeds the details of finite daily existence. It is in both philosophy and religion, serving some of the same needs, that our imagination is enhanced. The myths and images of human nature and social life by which we live transcend our concrete historical situation.

The philosophy of Marxism, itself a universal form of thought without metaphysical premises, provides us with an analysis of human history as being achieved through human activity. The theology of Paul Tillich, which appeals to yet another human requirement and is also a critique of secular life, gives us symbols that help us to integrate our spiritual life with our historical existence. The task at hand is that of uniting these two universal forms of thought and belief into a framework for both understanding our human history and acting in the fulfillment of our personal and collective being.

Every social theory, and every theology, implies a conception of human nature. Added to this is an assessment of the ways in which and the extent to which this human nature is being realized in the contemporary historical context. Marxism begins with the vision of a "species-being," a basic (universal) human nature that is constantly being uncovered through historical action. As *human* beings, as species-beings, we are consciously creating our lives. As Karl Marx writes, "Conscious activity is the species character of human beings."[1] In productive life, especially in our work, life is creating life.

However, in the contemporary historical situation, under capitalism, our species-being (our basic human nature) is deprived. Under capitalism our work has become alienated; and "just as alienated labour transforms free and self-directed activity into a means, so it transforms the species-life of man into a means of physical existence."[2] Our otherwise productive activity is now directed against us; it has become independent of us and no longer belongs to us as producers. Work ceases to fulfill human needs, and the alienation experienced in labor becomes the condition in all areas of life.[3] Our lives and our institutions are subverted and alienating when lived and practiced in the historical context of capitalism.

From the analysis of alienation in contemporary society emerges the Marxian possibility of a revolution in conditions that will allow human beings to achieve the full potential of their self-creativity.[4] Since the conditions under which our self-creation takes place in present society are self-defeating, divorcing us from our essential function, transformation of the world becomes necessary. The Marxist critique of the secular political economy incorporates a call as well as a prescription for redemption.

The questionable character of human existence, as manifested in our time, is basic to Tillich's formulations. Involved in New Hegelian and Marxist intellectual circles between the two world wars, and politically active in the socialist movement, Tillich placed himself in a prophetic line that stems from Marx, and beyond Marx from the Old Testament prophets. In his own existentialism Tillich explored the "profound relationship" between the existence of the individual and the historical-political situation.[5] And the relationship is bound by the character of religion under capitalism, accounting ultimately for the meaninglessness and despair of our time.

Tillich thus accepted and utilized Marx's critique of bourgeois society, but went beyond its materialistic and antireligious basis. Tillich was drawn, in his own words, to the existential strain of Marx's thought: "to his struggle against the self-estrangement of man under capitalism, against any theory that merely interprets the world without changing it, against the assumption that knowledge is quite independent of the social situation in which it is sought."[6] For Tillich, as for Marx, economic materialism is a method of historical analysis and not a metaphysics. It does not imply that the "economic" is the sole principle for interpreting history.

> Economic materialism, however, does show the fundamental significance of economic structure and motives for the social and intellectual forms and changes in a historical period. It denies that there can be a history of thought and religion independent of economic factors, and thereby confirms the theological insight, neglected by idealism, that man lives on earth and not in heaven (or, in philosophical terms, that man lives within existence and not in the realm of essence)."[7]

Marxism is a necessary method of unmasking the hidden levels of secular reality. Its far-reaching religious and historical implications, however, are to be found in its prophetic elements. Socialism, Tillich observes, "acts in the direction of the messianic fulfillment; it is a messianic activity to which everybody is called."[8]

The problem in pursuing only the materialist method is that it denies the urgency of the very human nature that it seeks to unmask and recover. Such a materialist methodology for Tillich is a false and dogmatic conception of human nature and historical possibility. The urgency of immediate (material) needs actually is often transcended by other, less material needs. We must acknowledge that "even the most pressing needs are colored by their relationship to other needs, by the specific historical situation in which this constellation of factors has come to be."[9] A strictly materialist conception of human nature and historical conditions, in fact, is merely another manifestation of the corruptness of the capitalist order. A restricted materialist analysis is itself a part of the human predicament in contemporary culture. The spirit of the age not only affects our daily lives but our way of understanding our lives.

The methodology for understanding our world as well as our life within it suffers from the particular capitalist spirit that limits reality to the scientific and technical conquest of time and space. As Tillich describes the condition:

> Reality has lost its inner transcendence or, in another metaphor, its transparency for the eternal. The system of finite interrelations which we call the universal has become self-sufficient. It is calculable and manageable and can be improved from the point of view of man's needs and desires. Since the beginnings of the 18th century God has been removed from the power field of man's activities. He has been put alongside the world without permission to interfere with it because every interference would disturb man's technical and business calculations. The result is that God has become superfluous and the universe left to man as its master.[10]

Under capitalism our actual condition is mistakenly regarded as our essential condition. This condition is evident to varying degrees in the institutions of capitalist society, including work, family, education, health, and the environment we construct for ourselves. We continue to be the objects of our own history, left to drift without an ultimate end. This truly is the contemporary human predicament.

The need today is to go beyond the institutions of capitalism. Marxism provides the theoretical beginning for understanding life in capitalist society. At the same time, in spite of the materialist focus that it continues to receive from intellectuals, it embodies a consistency with Jewish and Christian theology. We have become, according to the prophetic Marx, estranged from our essential nature. True human nature, Tillich notes in his reading of Marx, is impossible under the conditions of capitalism; and true humanity can be achieved only in a protest against this estrangement.[11] Not only will human physical existence be revitalized but also psychic and social life.

A materialist perspective is solely this-world oriented: human beings are the measure of all things and have become their own gods—by assuming responsibility for the conditions of their own existence. Marx insisted that redemption is limited to the secular world. What the theology of Tillich offers, in the necessary task of restoring religious symbolism to revolutionary life, is the infinite quality of human life beyond the secular. The human situation, rather than being completely bound by time, is thereby "elevated into the eternal and the eternal becomes effective in the realm of time."[12] Reconciliation and redemption are realized through an apprehension of the transhistorical.

NOTES

1. Karl Marx, *Early Writings*, trans. and ed. T. B. Bottomore (New York: McGraw-Hill, 1964), p. 127.

2. Ibid., p. 128. On Marx's materialist conception of species-being, see James M. Glass, "Marx, Kafka, and Jung: The Appearance of Species-Being," *Politics and Society*, 2 (Winter 1972), pp. 255–71.

3. Karl Marx, *The Grundrisse*, ed. David McLellan (New York: Harper & Row, 1971), pp. 132–43.

4. See Stanley Aronowitz, "Culture and Politics," *Politics and Society*, 6 (no. 3, 1976), pp. 347–76.

5. See James L. Adams, "Introduction," to Paul Tillich, *Political Expectation* (New York: Harper & Row, 1971), pp. ix–x.

6. Paul Tillich, *Theology of Culture*, ed. Robert C. Kimball (New York: Oxford University Press, 1959), p. 109.

7. Paul Tillich, *On the Boundary: An Autobiographical Sketch* (New York: Scribner, 1966), pp. 87–88.

8. Tillich, *Theology of Culture*, p. 198.

9. Paul Tillich, *The Socialist Decision*, trans. Franklin Sherman (New York: Harper & Row, 1977), p. 114.

10. Tillich, *Theology of Culture*, pp. 43–44.

11. Tillich, *Political Expectation*, pp. 90–91.

12. Ibid., p. 91.

Women, labor, and family life*

JOAN B. LANDES

In its relatively short history, the movement of women's liberation has generated a number of political tendencies, ranging from liberal feminism to radical feminism, lesbian feminism, lesbian socialism, socialist feminism and Marxist feminism. Each group is linked in some fashion to a theoretical account of the grounds of women's oppression, the nature of family life and a strategy for women's liberation. Moreover, each theoretical account is characterized by a methodological orientation to the study of social reality.

In this article I will explore the methodological and theoretical implications of one such approach to women's liberation—Marxist feminism. My choice is not arbitrary. I hope to show that whereas Marxist feminism is one among many orientations, it alone provides the means by which the political perspectives of other approaches can be transcended. At the same time, it helps to resituate many of the most important insights of feminist groups. Before turning to Marxist feminism, it is necessary to examine the context out of which it emerged in the contemporary movement for women's liberation.

Feminist theorists seek to express a unity among women. Yet each attempt at a unified version of feminism seems to have divided rather than united the many feminisms within the movement. The movement's heterodoxy is reflected in the growing body of feminist works. Paradoxically, those writers who have sought to interpret the movement in its own terms, that is, without resorting to external evaluations, have invariably turned to such well-established social and philosophical approaches as functionalism, ego psychology, existentialism, Weberianism and structuralism. Each version of social science has offered a distinctive perspective on the questions raised by the movement. These differences cannot be resolved by verbal commitments to feminism. The fact is, feminism, set in the context of each of these approaches, not only looks but *is* very different. The explanations of oppression and the visions of liberation which ground the various theories of women's liberation reflect these differences.

The methodological strategies chosen by feminist theorists are extremely revealing of the political orientations of today's movement. For example, several writers who begin with an explicit commitment to socialist politics reintroduce liberal perspectives through the social science methods they employ. The best examples are two seminal works of the radical and socialist wings of the women's movement: *Woman's Estate* by Juliet Mitchell, and *The Dialectic of Sex* by Shulamith Firestone.

Mitchell argues for a Marxist approach to feminism.[1] Yet the method which she adopts diverges from a Marxist historical materialist approach to social reality. For example, the true subject of *Woman's Estate* is an abstraction called woman. This woman resists any historical or social definition. She is the same, or rather she is determined in the same way, inside different social classes. She performs the same "functions" within all societies. She is a product of an ideology generated through the socialization processes of the nuclear

* From *Science and Society*, 41 (Winter 1977–78), pp. 386–409.

family. The conceptual model for this family is borrowed from functionalist theory. Indeed Mitchell praises Talcott Parsons, especially for his analysis of socialization processes adding "no Marxist has provided a comparable analysis."[2]

The female subject of the overlapping structures which compose family life—reproduction, sexuality and socialization—is herself the product of an ideology which is considered eternal.[3] In other words, Mitchell suggests that the source of women's oppression is to be located first within a universal, atemporal ideology of womanhood which is translated into somewhat different practices in different societies. Both the ideology and the family practices possess an extremely durable character, so that woman, the subject of this ideology, possesses a disturbingly permanent social nature. As Mitchell states: "For though the family *has changed* since its first appearance, it *has also remained*—not just as an idealist concept but as a crucial ideological and economic unit with a certain rigidity and autonomy despite all its adaptations."[4] In this account, woman and the family are the embodiments of certain eternal ideas. The two are inextricably intertwined: "The Family 'makes' the Woman."[5] And one could add, woman is constituted over and over again. As in her second work, *Psychoanalysis and Feminism*, Mitchell is here concerned with the primary interrelationships, especially in the family, "between individual animals that make them human beings" and with the manner in which the little girl grows up in every culture to be *"like* her mother but the boy will grow up to be *another* father."[6] She emphasizes the overlapping nature of ideology, womanhood and family life. She also adopts a methodological orientation to her subject which is consistent with the thesis of eternality. By utilizing functionalist role theory, Mitchell de-emphasizes the historical character of social relations. Woman, the eternal subject of an eternal ideology, is an abstraction.

Mitchell subsumes classes within the category of group. This allows her the flexibility she needs to focus her analysis on sexual classes rather than economic classes. The title of her book expresses this emphasis: The two terms contain a reference to sex (i.e., woman) and a reference to social strata (i.e., estate—in its broadest sense). Class differences, according to Mitchell, split women off from one another, rather than sex divisions dividing workers. The liberation which Mitchell foresees is bound up with the process which functionalists label social change or modernization. Within a differentiated family of the future, Mitchell envisions the possibilities for a pluralistic situation in which no individual would be tied to a particular role or an ascribed status. No longer will biological motherhood necessarily be equated with social motherhood.

In short, Mitchell wishes to differentiate social roles in the one sphere which most functionalists have considered undifferentiable, i.e., the "natural." However, her argument amounts to a confirmation of what has already been, or is now being, affected by capitalism itself: the extension of market relationships to the sphere of personal life, which in the past provided an important, if insufficient and limited, support for individuals in an alienated social world. In broad terms, the earliest form of family life associated with capitalism was the productive unit whose working members included children, wife and employees or apprentices, all under the authority of the father-husband, *pater-familias.*[7] In the period of industrial capitalism this early productive household unit gave way among the bourgeois class to the characteristic privatized family, which functioned in part as a refuge from the alienated sphere of market and production relations. The family as refuge suggested an arena in which "relationships were not mediated through the market and the individual members were not competing with each other."[8] Within this new, non-productive family we find the fullest development of the role of non-working wife.[9] Only in the monopoly stage of industrial capitalism was this initially bourgeois family structure extended to some degree among the working classes. The bourgeois family was fully grounded in the economic relations of capitalist society. At the same time, the family possessed a limited amount of independence, which could function as the basis for protest against the most repelling aspects of modern industry. Likewise, the family upheld the importance of individual sexual love at a time when love was increasingly subordinated to property considerations. Thus, the family fostered an important element of anti-authoritarianism alongside the very real domination of wife by husband, and children by parents. However, within advanced capitalist society the private and autonomous family unit is undermined more and more by the tendency, arising out of the economy, to dissolve all independent cultural institutions.[10] In other words, the logic of capitalism is to abolish the distinctions within the capitalist totality and to turn against social formations which it initially fostered.[11]

To the extent that the classical bourgeois family was bound up with the oppression of women and children, it has been the object of attack by 19th and 20th century feminists. By limiting themselves to this one issue, however, contemporary feminists fall into the trap of endorsing the system responsible for the destruction of autonomous forms of social life which possess a real, if limited, moment of positive community. Full realization of such autonomy can occur only with the abolition of capitalism itself. Thus, Mitchell's shortcoming is further to affirm the social consequences of capitalist development through an uncritical reliance on sociological modernization theory. She seems to agree with many functionalists that human progress can be achieved only through greater specialization and differentiation of functional social relationships. She poses no alternative to formal equality and rationalization as a basis for a more liberated society. She never asks whether woman's present social existence might not encompass something more than a set of abstract functions. She appears to mistake the division of labor under capitalism for freedom. Finally, Mitchell fails to acknowledge the possibility that in creating a movement for the future which abolishes the alienated division of labor, men and women of the present might look backward as well as forward toward an ideal of community which survives in battered and incomplete form in today's family. Instead, Mitchell sees only one side of the family's multi-faceted character; in her view, it "embodies the most conservative concepts available; it rigidifies the past ideals and presents them as the present pleasures. By its very nature, it is there to prevent the future."[12]

Shulamith Firestone's vision of a contractual family resembles the image of differentiated family life just described. Firestone begins her works, *The Dialectic of Sex*,[13] by promising a dialectical and historical materialist approach grounded in sexual differences rather than class relationships. She claims that this change will allow not only for a comprehension of sexual oppression, but also for an orientation to class struggle. In fact, Firestone's classifications divide and separate, and only then relate to social factors. Relations, in her method, are always external because every factor is social and logically independent of every other factor. Firestone substitutes an exterior calculus to account for what she hopes will be the necessary relationships between working class revolution and feminist revolution. But what can be added can just as easily be subtracted. She offers no reason why sexual revolution cannot be achieved without class revolution. Sexual revolution seems to result from a series of technological changes—including, but not limited to, test tube babies—rather than a transformation of oppressive social relationships.

Firestone's vision of liberation is tied to a series of assumptions about individual freedom. Every person is free, on the basis of his or her individual rights and powers, to enter into contractual relations with every other person. These wholly instrumental relationships will be guided by quantitative considerations: the achievement of a specific objective for a limited amount of time. In other words, all human relationships in Firestone's world take the commodity form. All *things,* including one's person, are for sale. All arenas of life are now unequivocally characterized by capitalist social relations. The future family is so completely rationalized that even relations between parents and children are defined through contracts. Women's liberation is achieved on the terms of a privatistic, competitive and contractual world. Individuals are nothing more than monads who occupy fragmented spaces. "Liberation" here reverts to an early bourgeois conception of possessive individualism.[14]

Neither *Woman's Estate* nor *The Dialectic of Sex* offers feminists a way of transcending liberal political conceptions. These influential attempts to perfect Marxism by turning to one or another version of bourgeois social theory result in an ahistorical and abstract view of social reality. Lacking an historical awareness, Mitchell and Firestone reify basic elements of capitalism so that they reappear as transcendent aspects of all social life. Their attempts to articulate a universal theory of women's oppression reduce to biological arguments and abstract conceptions of women. By deploying functionalist and structuralist approaches, these writers reintroduce certain fundamental antinomies of bourgeois theory. In the end, the two most significant feminist attempts to go beyond classical Marxism regress behind it by accepting liberal perspectives.

These comments should not be taken to mean that feminism must be abandoned by Marxists as merely another version of bourgeois thought. In addition to the fact that there exists a long history of struggle on the part of working women around so-called women's issues, it is also true that within the socialist movement there have been many who have fought to incorporate the question of woman's emancipation within socialist practice.[15] Still, the record of Marxist attention to women's issues is uneven and there have been periods of what has been termed by one writer "proletarian anti-feminism" within the socialist movement.[16] Significantly, after a long lull of nearly 50 years there is now developing a body of literature extending the Marxist approach to the problems opened up by the contemporary movement for women's liberation. This literature also expands even further the questions traditionally explored by Marxists. As against earlier Marxist treatments of women's oppression which focused on female workers in industry, contemporary Marxist feminists are now concerned with the character of women's work within the family and its relationship to capitalist production.[17]

In contrast to liberal feminism, the Marxist approach to women's oppression is grounded in an understanding of women as social beings whose life activity, labor, takes an alienated form under capitalist social relations within the family or private sphere as well as in the sphere of commodity production. Those who focus on the social relations embodied in domestic labor within the working class family identify the peculiarly capitalist character of this work as well as the ties which bind the historical form of the oppression of women to the exploitative character of class relationships. The non–"gainfully employed" housewife and her work, housework, are revealed as products of the changes in the sexual division of labor and the structure of family life brought about by capitalist development. Therefore the negation of this specific form of domestic work does not signify the elimination of the family as such, but rather the supersession of a particular historical form of the family.

Before detailing some of the conclusions of the Marxist feminist debate over the character of domestic labor, it should be emphasized that these investigations proceed from an indispensable historical insight. As Lukács remarked, "Not until the rise of capitalism was a unified economic structure, and hence a—formally—unified structure of consciousness that embraced the whole society, brought into being."[18] The methodological analogue of this new reality is captured in the Marxist category of concrete totality. Persons, as well as things, are conceived in their dialectical and dynamic relationship to each other as well as to the whole, that is, in their integration in the totality. Reality is understood as a dynamic process undergoing historical transformation. The apparent facts on the surface of social life are seen as products of the reified appearance embedded in the capitalist totality itself.[19]

In this view, Marxist feminism rejects the commonplace assumption that what is empirically separate should be taken as such. As against the liberal feminist argument, these writers begin to explore the internal relationships which exist between community and workplace, private life and public existence, family and economy, reproduction and production. Whereas on the surface it may appear that the family is unrelated to economic life, the effort to elaborate a critical theory of society from a feminist perspective confirms that "what is immediate as sense perception is not concrete, but abstract . . . the alternative: the concrete is gained by mediation, by working through the immediate, not accepting it."[20] A critical dimension is attained by demonstrating how the so-called facts—i.e., what is affirmed as universal and unchangeable—are historically con-

crete and therefore subject to transformation. The apparently unchangeable nature of women's work in the home is shown to be an aspect of the capitalist totality.

Under capitalism, a worker's ability to labor is a commodity and is sold in the marketplace for wages. The precondition for this situation is an historical development by which the working class is stripped of any independent means of social production. As Marx stated:

> . . . the labourer instead of being in the position to sell commodities in which his labour is incorporated, must be obliged to offer for sale as a commodity that very labour-power, which exists only in his living self. . . . It [capital] can spring into life, only when the owner of the means of production and subsistence meets in the market with the free labourer selling his labour-power. And this one historical condition comprises a world's history. Capital, therefore, announces from its first appearance a new epoch in the process of social production.[21]

Marxist feminists point out that the separation of the working class from the means of production also entails the separation of the family unit from the sphere of production. However, the two spheres, while distinct, continue to be internally related. Both the family and the economy are the products of the same historical development. The production of labor power in its commodity form and the privatized consumption of manufactured articles as means of subsistence occur within the family unit associated with the rise of capitalism, which over time strips the family of any independent means of production. Therefore, the domestic labor process contributes to the historical production of the working class under capitalist relations of production.

Marxist feminists have asked whether the working class housewife falls under the category of productive labor which Marx reserved for that labor which exchanges with capital and increases capital by producing surplus value.[22] The arguments suggest that the housewife is not a productive laborer.[23] Wally Secombe concludes that the housewife is therefore an unproductive laborer, the category which Marx used to describe labor which exchanges with revenue resulting from profits, interest or rents. A more satisfying position on this definitional issue is advanced by Ira Gerstein and Lise Vogel, who argue that domestic labor is a distinctive form of social labor or productive activity which occurs within capitalism—that is, it is organized to some extent by capital itself, although it does not fall under the categories which Marx used to describe the sphere of commodity production proper. As Gerstein notes, "Labor power is the single and unique commodity in capitalist society which does not take place in a capitalist manner."[24] Or, as Secombe argues in his reply to his critics, whereas domestic labor does not fall directly under the law of value as does labor performed in the sphere of the production of surplus value, it, like all labor within capitalist society, is influenced by this law in decisive ways.[25] I take these arguments to mean that the housewife's labor is productive activity in the general sense of that term; it is a portion of the total or general social labor within society. Furthermore, although domestic labor does not produce surplus value, Secombe offers a compelling argument for the position that ". . . domestic labor creates value." He submits that the category of value is decisive in understanding any form of labor which occurs within a capitalist society since it expresses ". . . the relation of separated private labours to the total social labour in a society of generalized commodity production. Without this link the underlying connection between the domestic and industrial units cannot be adequately established; consequently, women's two labours are left to float analytically, to be related to one another only by way of the consciousness of women who move back and forth between them everyday."[26] In other words, it might be said that

a social formation exists which is marked by qualitative distinctions between different forms of social life. One such distinction appears in the separation between the domestic and industrial realms. But this appearance obscures the social relations which bind housework into the larger social division of labor; thus domestic labor is "equalized" with other labors in society through the continuous exchange of commodities, including labor power, within the marketplace.

This summary suggests that the debate over domestic labor has far-reaching implications for Marxist political practice. Many orthodox accounts of Marxism argue that the theory of alienation which grounds the concept of exploitation is situated by Marx in the social relationship between wage labor and capital at the point of production. Wage labor which is engaged by capital to produce surplus value is robbed of a portion of its total product which is appropriated by the capitalist. Consequently, the exploitative relations between wage labor and capital at the production site determine the form of the class struggle.

The definitional question—is or is not housework productive labor?—which preoccupies Marxist feminists when they investigate family life becomes another way of theoretically locating the point from which revolutionary change can proceed in capitalist society. These writers ask what relationship, if any, do housewives have to the class struggle. They ask whether the social conflicts which emerge around the sexual division of labor in the family and other specifically "women's issues" are an aspect of the movement to abolish capitalist social relations.

These are essential considerations for any feminist political strategy. Yet the literature in the housework debate either is unknown or is ignored by many feminists, even those in the socialist wing of the movement. It is important to note that the presentation of the character of women's work as either a definitional issue or a category dispute over whether or not housewives are exploited as workers, has been characterized by many as a sterile question. What is required is an extended discussion which can expand the insights already achieved in the housework debate by uncovering the material bases for such aspects of advanced capitalist social life as the commodity character of female sexuality, the unequal relation between men and women at work and at home and the property character of family life. These features of social existence are, of course, noted by many liberal and radical feminists. But they are treated in their works as either an attitudinal problem, a cultural artifact surviving from an earlier social structure or a universal feature of women's condition.[27] For Marxists the challenge is to reveal how such "facts" are themselves products of a given historical situation which can be altered.

Using an often-quoted passage from the *Economic and Philosophic Manuscripts* I will attempt to offer an approach to the alienated features of women's existence under capitalism which can resituate the insights of liberal and radical feminists and expand the discussion already begun within the Marxist feminist literature. In this work, Marx refers to the family as a product of the isolation, dehumanization, separation and distortion of social relationships which occurs under capitalism. He writes:

This *material,* immediately perceptible private property is the material perceptible expression of *estranged human* life. Its movement—production and consumption—is the *perceptible* revelation of the movement of all production until now, i.e., the realization of the reality of man. Religion, family, state, law, morality, science, art, etc., are only *particular* modes of production, and fall under its general law. The positive transcendence of *private property,* as the appropriation of *human* life, is therefore the positive transcendence of all estrangement—that is to say, the return of man from religion, family, state, etc., to his *human,* i.e., *social* exist-

ence. Religious estrangement, as such, occurs only in the realm of *consciousness,* of man's inner life, but economic estrangement is that of *real life;* its transcendence therefore embraces both aspects.[28]

This passage might be read to mean that all estrangement, including that which occurs within the family, will be abolished automatically upon the achievement of socialism. On such a reading, the so-called facts of continuing male privilege and female subordination in private and public life in contemporary socialist societies can be advanced as a way of disputing Marx's analysis. But to follow this line of argument requires a reintroduction of perspectives rooted in a naturalized conception of the sexual division of labor and of female biology so that women's inferiority is "proved" to be inevitable as long as women are women.

It would seem that Marx's own intention was to suggest the theoretical grounds for *political* action: the positive transcendence of an exploitative and oppressive social form. If feminists are to find the bases for a politics which can mediate between the present situation and a future society in which relations between the sexes are no longer oppressive in character, we must find an interpretation which does not force us to obliterate sexual distinction itself.

There is substantial evidence to suggest that when Marx wrote this passage he was concerned with family life in the bourgeois class. Indeed, just four years later, in *The Communist Manifesto,* Marx and Engels stated unequivocally:

On what foundation is the family, the bourgeois family, based? On capital, on private gain. In its completely developed form this family exists only among the bourgeoisie. But this state of things finds its complement in the practical absence of the family among the proletarians and in public prostitution.[29]

Eli Zaretsky and other writers have demonstrated that in the 20th century family life in the working class has assumed a new level of importance.[30] The shortening of the working day, the development of mass forms of consumption, the extension of mass culture, and the rise in the importance of subjectivity have together transformed working class family life. Such changes suggest that we must either abandon Marx's statement that the family is a particular mode of production which falls under the general law of private property or we must alter his emphasis. I propose that we do the latter and view the working class family as a specific mode of production—that is, "a definite form of activity . . . a definite form of expressing their life, a definite *mode* of life . . ."[31]—which is dominated by the alienated social processes of capitalist society as a whole.[32]

The formulation suggested here does not signify that the family merely copies the economic base or that alienation at work simply spills over into family existence. Rather, the reproduction of the working class within capitalism occurs not only at the office or plant, but in the family and other institutions of everyday life. In order to comprehend the reproduction of class relations from the vantage point of personal or family life, it is necessary to reject any theoretical orientation which takes as given the family's autonomy, independence or isolation from production "proper" and which therefore posits only external connections between production and the family's role as an agency of reproduction and socialization. The Marxist formulation emphasizes the existence of internal relations between family life and commodity production; the two spheres are qualitatively distinct but integrated aspects of one mode of production.[33] Exploitation of the working class in capitalism occurs not merely to the individual worker at his place of work, but also on a society-wide basis. Domestic labor reproduces the fundamental class relations of capitalist society not merely by the day, the week or the year,

but over a *lifetime*. The family viewed as a mode of production of capitalism has a class dimension. This is not merely because it is a "superstructural" reflection of the economic base, but rather because the reproduction of labor power occurs within the working class family.

Curiously, the sexual dimension of the reproduction of labor power appears to the family members as a "natural," even animal-like, aspect of human nature. Women, in particular, are linked to this realm of nature. Sexuality, in such a context, is repressed sexuality. The history of sexual relations and their social content harden into nature: sexuality becomes second nature. Accordingly, all attempts to present woman, sexuality and reproduction as products of a realm of nature reveal a ". . . history so long unliberated—history so long monotonously oppressive—that it congeals. . . . Second nature is not simply nature or history, but frozen history that surfaces as nature."[34]

The sexual division of labor within the working class family reflects a specialization of tasks that enables the worker's creative capacity to be transformed into a commodity to be bought and sold and thereby estranged from the worker. In order to repeat this process on a daily basis the housewife must purchase with the wage packet the means of subsistence for the entire family. As Marx demonstrated, the products produced by the worker stand opposed to the worker's entire family, who must now use their wages in order to live.

The capital given in exchange for labour-power is converted into necessaries, by the consumption of which the muscles, nerves, bones, and brains of existing labourers are reproduced, and new labourers are begotten. Within the limits of what is strictly necessary, the individual consumption of the working-class is, therefore, the reconversion of the means of subsistence given by capital in exchange for labour-power into fresh labour-power at the disposal of capital for exploitation. It is the production and reproduction of that means of production so indispensable to the capitalist: the labourer himself.[35]

Furthermore, the very kinds of products which are purchased and consumed by the working class family reflect the "imaginary appetites" or "false needs" which dominate capitalist production. Betty Friedan is right to suggest that there is a relationship between the general system of commodity production and the consumption of false needs by the American housewife.[36] She remains confused about this relationship because she cannot think of the family as anything but a bounded institution. In such a view, all economic and social influences are external to the organization of family life. What Friedan and other liberal feminists fail to see is that "the social does not 'influence' the private, it dwells within it."[37]

The working class family is pervaded through and through by commodity relationships. Enjoyment and leisure in the home occur through commodities. Yet people believe that the family is the only sphere left in which a person can be authentic; it is viewed as an arena of true subjectivity. Certainly useful labor goes into the production of the worker's labor power in the commodity form. In this process real human needs are satisfied through a form of social labor. At the same time, however, the subjective content of such relations with the family is constantly being undermined and cancelled by the universal tendency under capitalism for all social relations to assume the commodity form. Thus, husband and wife are deemed to "own" (have an investment in) one another and to "own" (have property in) their children. The life insurance policy purchased by the working man as a potential gift to wife and children becomes a testimony to the amount of sexual power he has to invest in their happiness.[38] Such is the power of money in capitalist society. As Marx recognized: "Money is the *pimp* between man's need and the object, between his life and his means of life. But *that which* mediates *my* life for me, also *mediates* the existence of other people *for me*. For me it is the other person."[39] Personal relations between man and wife within the private sphere of the family are mediated through money.

Today "liberated" marriage partners are counseled to draw up detailed contracts specifying their individual contributions to the marriage in order to facilitate a more efficient and equitable division of their mutual property should the marriage end in divorce. Indeed, the universal character of what appears as the particular sphere of personal life is best revealed in divorce, an increasingly common phenomenon. In divorce the very relations which were considered exempt from the alienated order of rights and property are directly subjected to that order as questions of property and monetary responsibility take precedence over all other matters.[40]

In *The Second Sex* Simone de Beauvoir pointed out that our sexual metaphors are metaphors of conquest. In fact, they are also metaphors of *ownership*. "To *take*" or "to *have*" one another is the language of a modern marriage ceremony. The language continues to express the core of marriage as recognized in the 18th century by Immanuel Kant. He wrote, "Sexual community is the reciprocal use made by one person of the sexual organs and faculties of another. . . . Marriage . . . is the union of two people of different sexes with a view to the mutual possession of each other's sexual attributes for the duration of their lives."[41] The most intimate relationship between persons are invaded by the language of things or commodity relations. Persons, in this view, are "owned" and "disposed" of like any other worldly object. Advertised schemes for contract marriage and computerized mating reveal even further that ". . . today even sex is assimilated into the relationship of exchange, into the rational 'give' and 'take.' "[42] Thus, sexual performance becomes a goal toward which man has to strive. And sexual conquests are *accumulated* and guarded against all potential competitors.[43] Women as well as men endeavor to accumulate lovers.

By focusing on the family sphere, Marxist feminism reveals the extent to which all human senses are reduced to the one sense of "having," to a one-sided gratification appropriate to the ownership of private property. Marxist feminism alters the conception of the autonomous family. It demonstrates that relations within the family are not "natural" relations. Indeed, it reveals that ". . . the family not only depends on the historically concrete social reality but it is socially mediated down to its innermost structure."[44] Both production and consumption within the family take an alienated form. The working class housewife, like the worker, is an alienated producer. The parallel between housework and labor performed within the modern office or plant, the extent to which both kinds of work are characterized by tedious, repetitive and fragmented tasks, is a manifestation of the internal relations which bind family to workplace under capitalism. The reproduction and care of children and aged family members are bound up with the production of the commodity labor power.

On the other hand, it is often argued that housework, unlike office or factory work, possesses aspects that are pre-capitalist—organic, non-rationalized.[45] Indeed, housework as a form of production does satisfy authentic needs. But the production which occurs in the working class family is not developed autonomously by the producers, for the family is itself a solidly capitalist relation. As such, it embodies a contradictory unit between production for use and production for exchange. As noted, production within the family is oriented toward exchange value obtained through the sale of labor power rather than around needs which can be satisfied in a more truly human form of production. Not surprisingly, the family expresses that which is

characteristic of all capitalist production: the triumph of exchange value over use value production. The tremendous development of the laborer as a productive force within capitalism is seen within the family as the one-sided, alienated, brutalized form of this development: even the worker's productivity exists only for capital.

The fetishization of female sexuality in commercial advertising is not the result of universal sex class privilege, as many feminists would have us believe. Rather, as Dalla Costa notes, under capitalism ". . . women are robbed of their sexual life which has been transformed into a function of reproducing labor power."[46] Men are also affected by a process of repression which amounts to the temporal as well as the spatial reduction of the libido. Capitalism's organization of the working day assigns sex to the hours during which much of the work which goes into the daily reproduction of labor power must be accomplished. The so-called free-space of leisure activity is also a sphere of domination. The repressive organization of sexuality amounts to its qualitative and quantitative restriction, so that genital sexuality comes to dominate all other forms of sexual gratification, becoming itself a means to a limited end—procreation.[47]

The naturalization of the family and woman in the ideologies of late capitalism —even within the feminist movement, as revealed in the works of Simone de Beauvoir and Shulamith Firestone—must be counterposed against the tendency toward commodity fetishism within capitalist society. Relations between persons take on the form of relations between things, they become reified; and relations between things take on the properties of human beings, they become personified. In Marx's words, commodity fetishism refers to "material relations between persons and social relations between things."[48] All ideologies which naturalize woman or the family thereby conceal the social relations between the housewife and her product, labor power. They treat the worker's labor as something which springs to life at the factory gates.

The view presented here reveals that the working class family is a mode of production and reproduction of the working class under capitalism, of the individual worker as a worker, and of the married woman as a housewife as well as a potential and frequently employed wage laborer. Indeed, women have always been employed as wage laborers under capitalism, from its origins down to the present.[49] The process of reproduction and production of the working class over generations involves the utilization of female labor as *both* wage labor and domestic labor.[50] There is a direct correspondence between the categories of jobs which women perform in the paid labor force and the kind of production which they perform in the home.[51] Like the male worker, the housewife experiences over the course of her own lifetime a split between her labor power and her personality, the result of the metamorphosis of her labor power into a thing or an object which she sells on the market.[52] And the necessity to transform her labor power into a commodity for sale is determined by the size of the wage packet offered to workers in various sectors of the economy, as well as the labor force requirements of capital at any point in time.[53]

The feminist literature is sensitive to the conservative content of the housewife's role within the family. This conservatism is directly related to the instruction which workers and future workers receive within the family. It is here that the family teaches workers to sell their labor power for the sake of consumption which they come to understand as leisure time. It teaches that leisure, not productive activity, gives meaning to life. Within the family, patterns of hierarchy (of men over women and of parents over children) serve to introduce workers to the hierarchical labor patterns

of the workplace. The ideology of the family helps to teach workers that these patterns are "natural" as well as legitimate. Also the family absorbs the shock of those who fail to achieve their "freedom" in the social division of labor.

The entire way in which workers live, as well as where they live, are aspects of capitalist alienation. There are no absolute divisions between family and factory in this respect. Housing developments are especially marked by the standardized character of the organization of physical space as well as the private lives of their residents. As Murray Bookchin notes, the featureless architecture of these buildings with their institutional corridors and office-like apartments suggests that ". . . the developments are bureaucratic institutions for *self-reproduction* and *self-maintenance,* just as the office skyscrapers are bureaucratic institutions for commerce and administration."[54] Women, in particular, are encouraged to regulate each family member's behavior not only inside the family but, more important, in such a way that the norms of correct behavior are projected outside the home. The good son or husband is a good worker as well.

Certainly, then, woman's role as producer of the commodity labor power possesses a conservative dimension insofar as her labor constitutes the production of the worker as a worker or the reproduction of the working class as a working class under capitalism. Hierarchy and repression are important features of this conservative content of the working class family and its female members. At the same time, the reproduction of the working class itself is founded upon the mediation of women's oppression within the class. The family also is a form of production within which social needs are met.

These considerations suggest the outlines of a full-scale investigation of capitalist society from the standpoint of the working class family. An examination of capitalist production as viewed from the vantage point of the family brings into prominence a series of contradictions. These contradictions are grouped around, or are aspects of, a central contradiction *in* capitalism and *for* it. To say that a contradiction exists in capitalism means that there is a contradiction between its content and its form; to say that a contradiction exists for it means that there is a contradiction between its mode of being and its essential transformation. To what central and secondary contradictions does the capitalist character of work point?

The central contradiction in capitalism posed by the nature of housework is that marked by the fundamental integration of housework into social labor (its *content*) and its privatized, isolated, "unproductive" (for capital, that is) *form*. Just as in the past, relations of exploitation in the factory have produced demands for unionization, higher wages, better working conditions, etc.—essentially for work reforms within the system—so now the social character of housework has led to well-intended but mistaken demands for wages for housewives. Those who have raised these demands have failed to grasp the character of this first contradiction. They have not understood that the awarding of a wage, if possible, would neither alter the relations of production nor the fact that the housewife already shares in the wage packet of the male wage earner. This is not to say that women should not struggle to force capital to bear an increasing share of the cost of the reproduction of labor power.

Housework's central contradiction for capitalism—which touches upon some broader aspects of alienation—is that between the way housework is now performed and a more truly human form of production not measured by labor time. The difficulties posed for post-capitalist societies by this contradiction are worthy of examination. A failure to understand it has clouded the vision of the socialist movement and has

contributed to the formulation of misconceived strategies which hope to liberate women "for production," ignoring how, as housewives, they already enter into it. As a form of alienated labor, housework cannot be transformed by "freeing" women to enter directly into the labor market. Nor can domestic work provide an alternative to capitalism if it serves to harken back to some earlier mode of production. Housework shows that whereas the subjugation of labor by means of the discipline of labor time may be the precondition for the emancipation of labor, it is not to be mistaken for emancipation itself. It is only in this *limited* sense that housework suggests, but cannot in itself offer, the vision of a form of production which is less, not more, alienated than the production of exchange value under capitalism.

These contradictions reveal a number of problems which also deserve serious examination. To begin with, the socialist call for "freeing" women for production has long since been heeded by capitalism itself. Since World War II married wmen have been entering the labor force in record numbers and, in contrast with the early part of this century, they now exceed the number of single working women. This development has sharpened and extended the antagonism between the property character of sexual relations under capitalism and the capitalist presupposition of a free laborer in a free market for labor. In other words, it has deepened women's consciousness of the contradiction between their status as proprietors of their personal capacities (mainly as sellers of labor power) and as objects of male sexual proprietorship. It is in this sense—and wholly within capitalism—that women's "liberation" from the home has fed potential political opposition to capitalist social arrangements.

Another aspect of this contradiction involves the antagonism between the ideology of femininity, which places women on a pedestal and encourages them to believe they can elevate their social status through marriage, and the exploitation of all working women on the labor market. For those women who seek security in their dependent but ostensibly respected positions as subordinate mates to their husbands, the real degradation experienced in the world of wage labor can produce knowledge of a conflict. It is here that the criticisms of the "feminine mystique" and the emphasis on transforming personal relations are useful for the theory and practice of the movement.

A major aspect of the contradiction between the form of women's work in the home and its social content is revealed by the housewife's integration into social labor and her isolation from the sphere of production of surplus value. Those who have advocated wages, not housework, have often noted the isolated housewife's attachment to conservative neighborhood institutions like churches, small businesses, schools, bingo nights, etc. For them, for the housewife to quit the home and join the union has been seen as a first step toward her liberation. Those who have advocated wages for housework, on the other hand, have also noted the potential for the community to become a locus of social struggle. While I have noted the limitations of the wages for housework demand,[55] the perception that housework is an aspect of the productive process challenges movements for social change more seriously to incorporate the insights of feminist theory in drawing up strategy. The investigation of domestic labor in the family thus has practical as well as theoretical implications. It is toward such considerations that further contributions to Marxist feminist theory should be directed.

NOTES

1. Juliet Mitchell, *Woman's Estate* (New York, 1971). Because of the emphasis in this article on the political and theoretical implications of Mitchell's version of socialist feminist theory, I have not attempted a critique of her second major work, *Psychoanalysis and Feminism* (New York, 1974), in which she argues for the relevance to feminists of Freud's discoveries.

2. Mitchell, *Woman's Estate*, p. 117.

3. For a similar conception of ideology from a theorist who has influenced Mitchell, see: Louis Althusser, "Ideology and Ideological State Apparatuses," in *Lenin and Philosophy and other Essays*, translated by Ben Brewster (New York, 1971).

4. Mitchell, *Woman's Estate*, p. 153 (her emphasis).

5. Ibid., p. 160.

6. Ibid., pp. 171, 170.

7. The following works should be consulted on this point: Margaret George, "From 'Goodwife' to 'Mistress': The Transformation of the Female in Bourgeois Culture," *Science & Society*, Summer 1973; K. V. Thomas, "Women and the Civil War Sects," *Past and Present*, no. 13 (April 1958); Sheila Rowbotham, *Hidden from History* (London, 1973).

8. Max Horkheimer, "Authority and the Family," in *Critical Theory*, translated by Matthew J. O'Connell et al. (New York, 1972), p. 114.

9. For an interesting account of women's resistance to this new role, as well as the mixed sentiments of men toward the idealized, nonproductive wife in turn-of-the-century United States, see: Ben Barker-Benfield, "The Spermatic Economy: A Nineteenth-Century View of Sexuality," in Michael Gordon, ed., *The American Family in Social-Historical Perspective* (New York, 1973).

10. On this point see: Horkheimer, "Authority and the Family."

11. Marx remarks in *Capital*, vol. I (New York, 1967), pp. 394–402, how with the development of machinery capital was led to exploit the labor of women and children, and in the process, to destroy the pre-existing family life among the working class. In the present period, the requirement of capital for cheaper labor entails a tendency to utilize women and to attack the role of housewife which was in an intervening period encouraged by these same economic forces.

12. Mitchell, *Women's Estate*, p. 156.

13. Shulamith Firestone, *The Dialectic of Sex: The Case for Feminist Revolution* (New York, 1970).

14. See: C. B. Macpherson, *The Political Theory of Possessive Individualism: Hobbes to Locke* (Oxford, 1962).

15. Among others, see: Clara Zetkin, "Lenin on

the Woman Question," in *The Emancipation of Women: From the Writings of V. I. Lenin* (New York, 1966); Frederick Engels, *The Origin of the Family, Private Property, and the State* (New York, 1972); August Bebel, *Women under Socialism* (New York, 1971); Alexandra Kollontai, *Communism and the Family* (London, 1971; Wilhelm Reich, *Sexpol: Essays 1929–1934*, ed. by Lee Baxandall (New York, 1972).

16. Werner Thonnessen, *The Emancipation of Women: The Rise and Decline of the Women's Movement in German Social Democracy, 1863–1933*, translated by Joris de Bres (London, 1969).

17. See: Mariarosa Dalla Costa and Selma James, *The Power of Women and the Subversion of the Community* (Montpelier, Bristol, England, 1972). Dalla Costa and James argue that the housewife is a productive laborer. For the alternative position that the housewife is an unproductive laborer, consider Wally Secombe, "The Housewife and Her Labour under Capitalism," *New Left Review*, no. 83, January–February 1973, 3–24. The position that the family constitutes a separate mode of production which does not fall under the laws of capitalist society has been argued in Margaret Benston, "The Political Economy of Women's Liberation," in Michele H. Garskof, ed., *Roles Women Play* (Belmont, California, 1971), pp. 194–205.

18. Georg Lukács, "Reification and the Consciousness of the Proletariat," in *History and Class Consciousness* (Cambridge, 1971), p. 100.

19. For a more developed treatment of this approach, see: Bertell Ollman, *Alienation: Marx's Conception of Man in Capitalist Society* (Cambridge, 1971), and "Marxism and Political Science: Prolegomenon to a Debate on Marx's Method," *Politics and Society*, vol. 3, no. 4, Summer 1973, 491–510; and Franz Jakubowski, *Ideology and Superstructure in Historical Materialism*, translated by Anne Booth (London, 1976).

20. Russell Jacoby, *Social Amnesia: A Critique of Conformist Psychology from Adler to Laing* (Boston, 1974), p. 59.

21. Marx, *Capital*, vol. I, pp. 168–170.

22. For a clarification of how Marx used the terms *productive* and *unproductive labor* in his own writings, see: Ian Gough, "Marx and Productive Labour," *New Left Review*, no. 76, November–December 1972, 47–72.

23. See note 17.

24. Ira Gerstein, "Domestic Work and Capitalism," *Radical America*, vol. 7, no. 5, October 1973, p. 114.

25. Wally Secombe, "Domestic Labour: Reply to Critics," *New Left Review*, no. 94, November–December 1975, p. 86.

26. Ibid.

27. See Firestone, *Dialectic of Sex*, and Simone de Beauvoir, *The Second Sex* (New York, 1952).

28. Karl Marx, *Economic and Philosophic Manuscripts of 1844*, ed., with an introduction by Dirk J. Struik (New York, 1964), p. 136.

29. Karl Marx and Frederick Engels, *Manifesto of the Communist Party* (Peking, 1972), p. 53.

30. Eli Zaretsky, "Capitalism, the Family, and Personal Life," *Socialist Revolution*, nos. 13–14 and 15, January–April 1973 and May–June 1973, 60–126, 19–70.

31. Karl Marx and Frederick Engels, *The German Ideology*, ed. by C. J. Arthur (New York, 1970), p. 42.

32. The theoretical formulation proposed in this article is on a high level of abstraction. Therefore, it is necessary to emphasize that variations exist among working class families due to the many regional, ethnic and racial divisions within the class. Moreover, the capitalist mode of production occurs within a variety of social formations. The reecnt study by John Berger and Jean Mohr, *A Seventh Man: A Book of Images and Words about the Experiences of Migrant Workers in Europe* (Baltimore, 1975), is a compelling description of the ways in which the traditional family relationships of male industrial migrant workers from southern Europe to the advanced industrial capitalist societies of northwestern Europe are transformed. The authors stress that a similar study should be done for migrant female laborers.

33. As argued in the text of this article, the integration of family and economy seems to intensify under advanced capitalism. In *Capital*, vol. I, Marx suggests that whereas capital requires that the working class reproduce itself as a class for production, it is not terribly interested in the form in which it maintains and reproduces itself. Also, he states that the worker performs necessary vital functions outside the process of production.

34. Jacoby, *Social Amnesia*, p. 31.

35. Marx, *Capital*, vol. I, p. 572.

36. Betty Friedan, *The Feminine Mystique* (New York, 1963), esp. pp. 206–232, chapter on "The Sexual Sell."

37. Jacoby, *Social Amnesia*, p. 104.

38. See Ernest Dichter, *The Strategy of Desire* (New York, 1960), p. 221, cited in Sheila Rowbotham, *Woman's Consciousness, Man's World* (Baltimore, 1973), p. 54.

39. Marx, *Economic and Philosophic Manuscripts*, pp. 165–166.

40. See Theodor Adorno, *Minima Moralia: Reflections from a Damaged Life*, translated by E. F. N. Jephcott (London, 1974), pp. 31–32.

41. Cited in Lukács, *History and Class Consciousness*, p. 100.

42. The Frankfurt Institute for Social Research, *Aspects of Sociology*, with a preface by Max Horkheimer and Theodor W. Adorno, translated by John Viertel (Boston, 1972), p. 131.

43. Rowbotham, *Woman's Consciousness, Man's World*, pp. 49–66.

44. *Aspects of Sociology*, p. 130.

45. See articles by Margaret Benston and Mariarosa Dalla Costa cited above, note 17.

46. Dalla Costa and James, *The Power of Woman and the Subversion of the Community*, p. 29.

47. For an excellent discussion of these points, see Herbert Marcuse, *Eros and Civilization: A Philosophical Inquiry into Freud* (Boston, 1966).

48. Marx, *Capital*, vol 1, p. 73. See also Richard Lichtman, "Marx's Theory of Ideology," *Socialist Revolution*, no. 23, April 1975, 45–76.

49. See Alice Clark, *Working Life of Women in the Seventeenth Century* (New York, 1968); Ivy Pinchbeck, *Women Workers and the Industrial Revolution, 1750–1850* (New York, 1961); Rowbotham, *Hidden from History;* Edith Abbott, *Women in Industry* (New York, 1910); Rosalyn Baxandall, Linda Gordon, and Susan Reverby, eds., *America's Working Women* (New York, 1976).

50 When the woman labors only at housework, her labor power is being expended although it is not being directly utilized by capital in the production of surplus value. So, whereas it is to the advantage of capital to maintain the working class family in its present form, there is a counter-tendency which suggests that capital might want to employ female labor power directly for commodity production. Over the course of capitalist development one can see both tendencies operating together as well as separately—that is, sequentially—depending upon the needs of capital at any given time.

51. See: Robert W. Smuts, *Woman and Work in America* (New York, 1971); Caroline Bird, *Born Female: The High Cost of Keeping Women Down* (New York, 1968).

52. See Lukács, *History and Class Consciousness*, p. 168.

53. We need to supplement our knowledge of dual labor markets by race and sex in order to account for the number of single, divorced or widowed women with children in the labor force who are among the most disadvantaged workers and for the disproportionate number of these women who are non-white. See: Valerie Kincade Oppenheimer, *The Female Labor Force in the United States* (Berkeley, 1970).

54. Murray Bookchin, *The Limits of the City* (New York, 1974), pp. 83–84 (my emphasis).

55. For a fuller argument on the inadequacy of the wages for housework demand, see my article, "Wages for Housework: Subsidizing Capitalism?" *Quest*, vol. 2, no. 2, Fall 1975, 17–30.

READING 6-2

Education and personal development*

SAMUEL BOWLES and HERBERT GINTIS

Every child born into the world should be looked upon by society as so much raw material to be manufactured. Its quality is to be tested. It is the business of society, as an intelligent economist, to make the best of it.

Lester Frank Ward
Education, c. 1872

It is not obvious why the U.S. educational system should be the way it is. Since the interpersonal relationships it fosters are so antithetical to the norms of freedom and equality prevalent in American society, the school system can hardly be viewed as a logical extension of our cultural heritage. If neither technological necessity nor the bungling mindlessness of educators explains the quality of the educational encounter, what does?

Reference to the educational system's

* From *Schooling in Capitalist America: Educational Reform and the Contradictions of Economic Life*, by Samuel Bowles and Herbert Gintis (Basic Books, 1976), pp. 125–148. © 1976 by Basic Books, Inc., Publishers, New York.

legitimation function does not take us far toward enlightenment. For the formal, objective, and cognitively oriented aspects of schooling capture only a fragment of the day-to-day social relationships of the educational encounter. To approach an answer, we must consider schools in the light of the social relationships of economic life. In this chapter, we suggest that major aspects of educational organization replicate the relationships of dominance and subordinacy in the economic sphere. The correspondence between the social relation of schooling and work accounts for the ability of the educational system to produce an amenable and fragmented labor force. The experience of schooling, and not merely the content of formal learning, is central to this process.

In our view, it is pointless to ask if the net effect of U.S. education is to promote equality or inequality, repression or liberation. These issues pale into insignificance before the major fact: The educational system is an integral element in the reproduction of the prevailing class structure of society. The educational system certainly has a life of its own, but the experience of work and the nature of the class structure are the bases upon which educational values are formed, social justice assessed, the realm of the possible delineated in people's consciousness, and the social relations of the educational encounter historically transformed.

In short, and to return to our persistent theme, the educational system's task of integrating young people into adult work roles constrains the types of personal development which it can foster in ways that are antithetical to the fulfillment of its personal developmental function.

Reproducing consciousness

. . . children guessed (but only a few
and down they forgot as up they grew
autumn winter spring summer) . . . .
e e cummings, 1940

Economic life exhibits a complex and relatively stable pattern of power and property relationships. The perpetuation of these social relationships, even over relatively short periods, is by no means automatic. As with a living organism, stability in the economic sphere is the result of explicit mechanisms constituted to maintain and extend the dominant patterns of power and privilege. We call the sum total of these mechanisms and their actions the reproduction process.

Amidst the sundry social relations experienced in daily life, a few stand out as central to our analysis of education. These are precisely the social relationships which are necessary to the security of capitalist profits and the stability of the capitalist division of labor. They include the patterns of dominance and subordinacy in the production process, the distribution of ownership of productive resources, and the degrees of social distance and solidarity among various fragments of the working population—men and women, blacks and whites, and white- and blue-collar workers, to mention some of the most salient.

What are the mechanisms of reproduction of these aspects of the social relations of production in the United States? To an extent, stability is embodied in law and backed by the coercive power of the state. Our jails are filled with individuals who have operated outside the framework of the private-ownership market system. The modern urban police force as well as the National Guard originated, in large part, in response to the fear of social upheaval evoked by militant labor action. Legal sanction, within the framework of the laws of private property, also channels the actions of groups (e.g., unions) into conformity with dominant power relationships. Similarly, force is used to stabilize the division of labor and its rewards within an enterprise: Dissenting workers are subject to dismissal and directors failing to conform to "capitalist rationality" will be replaced.

But to attribute reproduction to force alone borders on the absurd. Under normal conditions, the effectiveness of coercion depends at the very least on the inability or unwillingness of those subjected to it to join together in opposing it. Laws generally considered illegitimate tend to lose their coercive power, and undisguised force too frequently applied tends to be self-defeating. The consolidation and extension of capitalism have engendered struggles of furious intensity. Yet instances of force deployed against a united and active opposition are sporadic and have usually given way to détente in one form or another through a combination of compromise, structural change, and ideological accommodation. Thus it is clear that the consciousness of workers—beliefs, values, self-concepts, types of solidarity and fragmentation, as well as modes of personal behavior and development—is integral to the perpetuation, validation, and smooth operation of economic institutions. The reproduction of the social relations of production depends on the reproduction of consciousness.

Under what conditions will individuals accept the pattern of social relationships that frame their lives? Believing that the long-term development of the existing system holds the prospect of fulfilling their needs, individuals and groups might actively embrace these social relationships. Failing this, and lacking a vision of an alternative that might significantly improve their situation, they might fatalistically accept their condition. Even with such a vision they might passively submit to the framework of economic life and seek individual solutions to social problems if they believe that the possibilities for realizing change are remote. The issue of the reproduction of consciousness enters each of these assessments.

The economic system will be embraced when, first, the perceived needs of individuals are congruent with the types of satisfaction the economic system can objectively provide. While perceived needs may be, in part, biologically determined, for the most part needs arise through the aggregate experiences of individuals in the society. Thus the social relations of production are reproduced in part through a harmony between the needs which the social system generates and the means at its disposal for satisfying these needs.

Second, the view that fundamental social change is not feasible, unoperational, and utopian is normally supported by a complex web of ideological perspectives deeply embedded in the cultural and scientific life of the community and reflected in the consciousness of its members. But fostering the "consciousness of inevitability" is not the office of the cultural system alone. There must also exist mechanisms that systematically thwart the spontaneous development of social experiences that would contradict these beliefs.

Belief in the futility of organizing for fundamental social change is further facilitated by social distinctions which fragment the conditions of life for subordinate classes. The strategy of "divide and conquer" has enabled dominant classes to maintain their power since the dawn of civilization. Once again, the splintered consciousness of a subordinate class is not the product of cultural phenomena alone, but must be reproduced through the experiences of daily life.

Consciousness develops through the individual's direct perception of and participation in social life.[1] Indeed, everyday experience itself often acts as an inertial stabilizing force. For instance, when the working population is effectively stratified, individual needs and self-concepts develop in a correspondingly fragmented manner. Youth of different racial, sexual, ethnic, or economic characteristics directly perceive the economic positions and prerogatives of "their kind of people." By adjusting their aspiration accordingly, they not only reproduce stratification on the level of personal consciousness, but bring their needs into (at least partial) harmony with the fragmented conditions of economic life. Similarly, individuals tend to channel the development of their personal powers —cognitive, emotional, physical, aesthetic, and spiritual—in directions where they will have an opportunity to exercise them. Thus the alienated character of work, for example, leads people to guide their creative potentials to areas outside of economic activity: consumption, travel, sexuality, and family life. So needs and need-satisfaction again tend to fall into congruence and alienated labor is reproduced on the level of personal consciousness.[2]

But this congruence is continually disrupted. For the satisfaction of needs gives rise to new needs. These new needs derive from the logic of personal development as well as from the evolving structure of material life, and in turn undercut the reproduction of consciousness. For this reason the reproduction of consciousness cannot be the simple unintended by-product of social experience. Rather, social relationships must be consciously organized to facilitate the reproduction of consciousness.

Take, for instance, the organization of the capitalist enterprise. Power relations and hiring criteria within the enterprise are organized so as to reproduce the workers' self-concepts, the legitimacy of their assignments within the hierarchy, a sense of the technological inevitability of the hierarchical division of labor itself, and the social distance among groups of workers in the organization. Indeed, while token gestures toward workers' self-management may be a successful motivational gimmick, any delegation of real power to workers becomes a threat to profits because it tends to undermine patterns of consciousness compatible with capitalist control. By generating new needs and possibilities, by demonstrating the feasibility of a more thoroughgoing economic democracy, by increasing worker solidarity, an integrated and politically conscious program of worker involvement in decision-making may undermine the power structure of the enterprise. Management will accede to such changes only under extreme duress of worker rebellion and rapidly disintegrating morale, if at all.

But the reproduction of consciousness cannot be insured by these direct mechanisms alone. The initiation of youth into the economic system is further facilitated by a series of institutions, including the family and the educational system, that are more immediately related to the formation of personality and consciousness. Education works primarily through the institutional relations to which students are subjected. Thus schooling fosters and rewards the development of certain capacities and the expression of certain needs, while thwarting and penalizing others. Through these institutional relationships, the educational system tailors the self-concepts, aspirations, and social class identifications of individuals to the requirements of the social division of labor.

The extent to which the educational system actually accomplishes these objectives varies considerably from one period to the next. Recurrently through U.S. history these reproduction mechanisms have failed, sometimes quite spectacularly. In most periods—and the present is certainly no exception—efforts to use the schools to reproduce and extend capitalist production relations have been countered both by the internal dynamic of the educational system and by popular opposition.

We have identified the two main objectives of dominant classes in educational policy: the production of labor power and the reproduction of those institutions and social relationships which facilitate the translation of labor power into profits. We may now be considerably more concrete about the way that educational institutions are structured to meet these objectives. First, schooling produces many of the technical and cognitive skills required for adequate job performance. Second, the educational system helps legitimate economic inequality. The objective and meritocratic orientation of U.S. education reduces discontent over both the hierarchical division of labor and the process through which individuals attain position in it. Third, the school produces, rewards, and labels personal characteristics relevant to the staffing of positions in the hierarchy. Fourth, the educational system, through the pattern of status distinctions it fosters, reinforces the stratified consciousness on which the fragmentation of subordinate economic classes is based.

What aspects of the educational system allow it to serve these various functions? We shall suggest in the next section that the educational system's ability to reproduce the consciousness of workers lies in a straightforward correspondence principle: For the past century at least, schooling has contributed to the reproduction of the social relations of production largely through the correspondence between school and class structure.

Upon the slightest reflection, this assertion is hardly surprising. All major institutions in a "stable" social system will direct personal development in a direction compatible with its reproduction. Of course, this is not, in itself, a critique of capitalism or of U.S. education. In any conceivable society, individuals are forced to develop their capacities in one direction or another. The idea of a social system which merely allows people to develop freely according to their "inner natures" is quite unthinkable, since human nature only acquires a concrete form through the interaction of the physical world and preestablished social relationships.

Our critique of education and other aspects of human development in the United States fully recognizes the necessity of some form of socialization. The critical question is: What for? In the United States the human development experience is dominated by an undemocratic, irrational, and exploitative economic structure. Young people have no recourse from the requirements of the system but a life of poverty, dependence, and economic insecurity. Our critique, not surprisingly, centers on the structure of jobs. In the U.S. economy work has become a fact of life to which individuals must by and large submit and over which they have no control. Like the weather, work "happens" to people. A liberated, participatory, democratic, and creative alternative can hardly be imagined, much less experienced. Work under capitalism is an alienated activity.

To reproduce the social relations of production, the educational system must try to teach people to be properly subordinated and render them sufficiently fragmented in consciousness to preclude their getting together to shape their own material existence. The forms of consciousness and behavior fostered by the educational system must themselves be alienated, in the sense that they conform neither to the dictates of technology in the struggle with nature, nor to the inherent developmental capacities of individuals, but rather to the needs of the capitalist class. It is the prerogatives of capital and the imperatives of profit, not human capacities and technical realities, which render U.S. schooling what it is. This is our charge.

The correspondence principle

In the social production which men carry on they enter into definite relations which are indispensible and independent of their will. . . . The sum total of these relations of production constitutes . . . the real foundation on which rise legal and political superstructures, and to which correspond definite forms of social consciousness.

Karl Marx
*Contribution to a
Critique of Political Economy, 1857*

The educational system helps integrate youth into the economic system, we believe, through a structural correspondence between its social relations and those of production. The structure of social relations in education not only inures the student to the discipline of the workplace, but develops the types of personal demeanor, modes of self-presentation, self-image, and social class identifications which are the crucial ingredients of job adequacy. Specifically, the social relationships of education —the relationships between administrators and teachers, teachers and students, students and students, and students and their work—replicate the hierarchical division of labor. Hierarchical relations are reflected in the vertical authority lines from administrators to teachers to students. Alienated labor is reflected in the student's lack of control over his or her education, the alienation of the student from the curriculum content, and the motivation of school work through a system of grades and other external rewards rather than the student's integration with either the process (learning) or the outcome (knowledge) of the educational "production process." Fragmentation in work is reflected in the institutionalized and often destructive competition among students through continual and ostensibly meritocratic ranking and evaluation. By attuning young people to a set of social relationships similar to those of the workplace, schooling attempts to gear the development of personal needs to its requirements.

But the correspondence of schooling with the social relations of production goes beyond this aggregate level. Different levels of education feed workers into different levels within the occupational structure and, correspondingly, tend toward an internal organization comparable to levels in the hierarchical division of labor. The lowest levels in the hierarchy of the enterprise emphasize rule-following, middle levels, dependability, and the capacity to operate without direct and continuous supervision, while the higher levels stress the internalization of the norms of the enterprise. Similarly, in education, lower levels (junior and senior high school) tend to severely limit and channel the activities of students. Somewhat higher up the educational ladder, teacher and community colleges allow for more independent activity and less overall supervision. At the top, the elite four-year colleges emphasize social relationships conformable with the higher levels in the production hierarchy.[3] Thus schools continually maintain their hold on students. As they "master" one type of behavioral regulation, they are either allowed to progress to the next or are channeled into the corresponding level in the hierarchy of production. Even within a single school, the social relationships of different tracks tend to conform to different behavioral norms. Thus in high school, vocational and general tracks emphasize rule-following and close supervision, while the college track tends toward a more open atmosphere emphasizing the internalization of norms.

These differences in the social relationships among and within schools, in part, reflect both the social backgrounds of the student body and their likely future economic positions. Thus blacks and other minorities are concentrated in schools whose repressive, arbitrary, generally chaotic internal order, coercive authority structures, and minimal possibilities for advancement mirror the characteristics of inferior job situations. Similarly, predominantly working-class schools tend to emphasize behavioral control and rule-following, while schools in well-to-do suburbs employ relatively open systems that favor greater student participation, less direct supervision, more student electives, and, in general, a value system stressing internalized standards of control.

The differential socialization patterns of schools attended by students of different social classes do not arise by accident. Rather, they reflect the fact that the educational objectives and expectations of administrators, teachers, and parents (as well as the responsiveness of students to various patterns of teaching and control) differ for students of different social classes. At crucial turning points in the history of U.S. education, changes in the social relations of schooling have been dictated in the interests of a more harmonious reproduction of the class structure. But in the day-to-day operation of the schools, the consciousness of different occupational strata, derived from their cultural milieu and work experience, is crucial to the maintenance of the correspondences we have described. That working-class parents seem to favor stricter educational methods is a reflection of their own work experiences, which have demonstrated that submission to authority is an essential ingredient in one's ability to get and hold a steady, well-paying job. That professional and self-employed parents prefer a more open atmosphere and a greater emphasis on motivational control is similarly a reflection of their position in the social division of labor. When given the opportunity, higher-status parents are far more likely than their lower-status neighbors to choose "open classrooms" for their children.[4]

Differences in the social relationships of schooling are further reinforced by inequalities in financial resources. The paucity of financial support for the education of children from minority groups and low-income families leaves more resources to be devoted to the children of those with more commanding roles in the economy; it also forces upon the teachers and school administrators in the working-class schools a type of social relationship that fairly closely mirrors that of the factory. Financial considerations in poorly supported schools militate against small intimate classes, multiple elective courses, and specialized teachers (except for disciplinary personnel). They preclude the amounts of free time for teachers and free space required for a more open, flexible educational environment. The well-financed schools attended by the children of the rich can offer much greater opportunities for the development of the capacity for sustained independent work and all the other characteristics required for adequate job performance in the upper levels of the occupational hierarchy.

Much of this description will most likely be familiar to the reader and has been documented many times.[5] But only recently has there been an attempt at statistical verification. We will review a number of excellent studies, covering both higher and secondary education. Jeanne Binstock investigated the different patterns of social relations of higher education by analyzing the college handbooks covering rules, regulations, and norms of 52 public junior colleges, state universities, teacher-training colleges, and private, secular, denominational, and Catholic colleges. Binstock rated each school along a host of dimensions,[6] including the looseness or strictness of academic structure, the extent of regulations governing personal and social conduct, and the degree of control of the students over their cultural affairs and extracurricular activities. Her general conclusion is quite simple:

The major variations of college experiences are linked to basic psychological differences in work perception and aspiration among the major social class (occupational) groups who are its major consumers. Each social class is different in its beliefs as to which technical and interpersonal skills, character traits, and work values are most valuable for economic survival (stability) or to gain economic advantage (mobility). Each class (with subvariations based on religion and level of urban-ness) has its own economic consciousness, based on its own work experiences and its own ideas (correct or not) of the expectations appropriate to positions on the economic ladder above its own. . . . Colleges compete over the various social class markets by specializing their offerings. Each different type of undergraduate college survives by providing circumscribed sets of "soft" and "hard" skill training that generally corresponds both to the expectations of a particular social class group of customers and to specific needs for sets of "soft" and "hard" skills at particular layers of the industrial system.[7]

Binstock isolated several organizational traits consistently related to the various educational institutions she studied. First, she distinguished between behavioral control which involves rules over the student's behavior rather than intentions and stresses external compliance rather than internalized norms, and motivational control which emphasizes unspecified, variable, and highly flexible task-orientation, and seeks to promote value systems that stress ambiguity and innovation over certainty, tradition, and conformity. Second, Binstock isolated a leader-versus-follower orientation with some schools stressing the future subordinate positions of their charges and teaching docility, and others stressing the need to develop "leadership" self-concepts.

Binstock found that institutions that enroll working-class students and are geared to staff lower-level jobs in the production hierarchy emphasize followership and behavioral control, while the more elite schools that tend to staff the higher-level jobs emphasize leadership and motivational control. Her conclusion is:

Although constantly in the process of reformation, the college industry remains a ranked hierarchy of goals and practices, responding to social class pressures, with graded access to the technical equipment, organizational skills, emotional perspectives and class (work) values needed for each stratified level of the industrial system.[8]

The evidence for the correspondence between the social relations of production and education, however, goes well beyond this structural level and also sheds light on the commonality of motivational patterns fostered by these two spheres of social life. Juxtaposing the recent research of Gene Smith, Richard Edwards, Peter Meyer, and ourselves, the same types of behavior can be shown to be rewarded in both education

and work. In an attempt to quantify aspects of personality and motivation, Gene Smith has employed a relatively sensitive testing procedure, which he has shown in a series of well-executed studies[9] to be an excellent predictor of educational success (grade-point average). Noting that personality inventories traditionally suffer because of their abstraction from real-life environments and their use of a single evaluative instrument, Smith turned to student-peer ratings of 42 common personality traits, based on each student's observation of the actual classroom behavior of his or her classmates. A statistical technique called factor analysis then allowed for the identification of five general traits—agreeableness, extroversion, work orientation, emotionality, and helpfulness—that proved stable across different samples. Of these five traits, only the work-orientation factor, which Smith calls "strength of character"—including such traits as ". . . not a quitter, conscientious, responsible, insistently orderly, not prone to daydreaming, determined, persevering . . ."—was related to school success. Smith then proceeded to show that, in several samples, this work-orientation trait was three times more successful in predicting post-high-school academic performance than any combination of 13 cognitive variables, including SAT verbal, SAT mathematical, and high school class rank.

Our colleague Richard C. Edwards has further refined Smith's procedure. As part of his Ph.D. dissertation on the nature of the hierarchical division of labor, he prepared a set of 16 pairs of personality measures relevant to work performance.[10] Edwards argued that since supervisor ratings of employees are a basic determinant of hirings, firings, and promotions, they are the best measure of job adequacy and, indeed, are the implements of the organization's motivational system. Edwards, therefore, compared supervisor ratings of worker performance with the set of 16 personality measures as rated by the workers' peers. In a sample of several hundred Boston area workers, he found a cluster of three personality traits—summarized as rules orientation, dependability, and internalization of the norms of the firm—strongly predicting supervisor ratings of workers in the same work group. This result, moreover, holds up even when the correlation of these traits with such attributes as age, sex, social class background, education, and IQ is corrected for by linear regression analysis. Edwards found that rules orientation was relatively more important at the lowest levels of the hierarchy of production, internalization of norms was predominant at the highest level, while dependability was salient at intermediate levels.[11]

Edwards' success with this test in predicting supervisor ratings of workers convinced us that applying the same forms to high school students would provide a fairly direct link between personality development in school and the requirements of job performance.

This task we carried out with our colleague Peter Meyer.[12] He chose as his sample the 237 members of the senior class of a single New York State high school.[13] Following Edwards, he created 16 pairs of personality traits, and obtained individual grade-point averages, IQ scores, and college-entrance-examination SAT-verbal and SAT-mathematical scores from the official school records.[14]

As we expected, the cognitive scores provided the best single predictor of grade-point average—indeed, that grading is based significantly on cognitive performance is perhaps the most valid element in the "meritocratic ideology." But the 16 personality measures possessed nearly comparable predictive value, having a multiple correlation of 0.63 compared to 0.77 for the cognitive variables.[15] More important than the overall predictive value of the personality traits, however, was the pattern of their contribution to grades. To reveal this pattern, we first eliminated the effect of differ-

ences in cognitive performance in individual grades and then calculated the correlation between grades and the personality traits.[16] The results are presented in Figure 1.

The pattern of resulting associations clearly supports the correspondence principle and strongly replicates our initial empirical study of grading. The only significant penalized traits are precisely those which are incompatible with conformity to the hierarchical division of labor—creativity, independence, and aggressivity. On the other hand, all the personality traits which we would expect to be rewarded are, and significantly so. Finally, a glance at Figure 2 shows a truly remarkable correspondence between the personality traits re

FIGURE 1
Personality traits rewarded and penalized (in a New York high school)

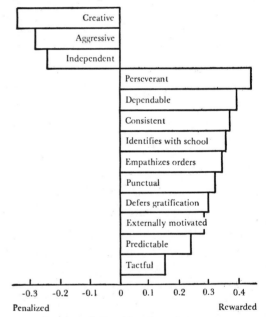

Partial correlation with grade – point average

Notes: Each bar shows the partial correlation between grade-point average and the indicated personality trait, controlling for IQ, SAT verbal, and SAT mathematical. The penalized traits (left) indicate creativity and autonomy, while the rewarded traits (right) indicate subordinacy and discipline. The data are from Samuel Bowles, Herbert Gintis, and Peter Meyer, "The Long Shadow of Work: Education, the Family, and the Reproduction of the Social Division of Labor." *Insurgent Sociologist,* Summer 1975.

FIGURE 2
Personality traits approved by supervisors

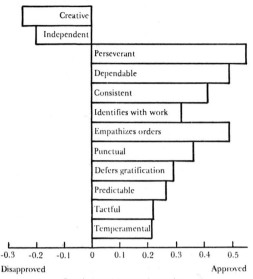

Correlation with supervisor rating

Notes: The pattern of personality traits indicative of supervisor approval correspond to those rewarded in high school. Each bar shows the correlation between supervisor rating and the indicated personality trait. The results are similar to Figure 1, except that aggressive is insignificant and temperamental significant in the sample of workers. The data are from Richard C. Edwards, "Personal Traits and 'Success' in Schooling and Work," *Educational and Psychological Measurement*, in press, 1976; "Individual Traits and Organizational Incentives: What Makes a 'Good Worker'?" *Journal of Human Resources*, Spring 1976, and are based on a sample of 240 workers in several government offices in the Boston area. All correlations are significant at the 1 percent level.

warded or penalized by grades in Meyer's study and the pattern of traits which Edwards found indicative of high or low supervisor ratings in industry.

As a second stage in our analysis of Meyer's data, we used factor analysis to consolidate the 16 personality measures into three "personality factors." Factor analysis allows us to group together those measured traits which are normally associated with one another among all individuals in the sample. The first factor, which we call "submission to authority," includes these traits: consistent, identifies with school, punctual, dependable, externally motivated, and persistent. In addition, it includes independent and creative weighted negatively. The

second, which we call temperament, includes: not aggressive, not temperamental, not frank, predictable, tactful, and not creative. The third we call internalized control, and it includes: empathizes orders and defers gratification.[17]

These three factors are not perfectly comparable to Edwards' three factors. Thus our submission to authority seems to combine Edwards' rules and dependability factors, while our internalized control is comparable to Edwards' internalization factor. In the case of the latter, both Edwards and Meyer's data depict an individual who sensitively interprets the desires of his or her superior and operates adequately without direct supervision over considerable periods of time.

Our theory would predict that at the high school level submission to authority would be the best predictor of grades among personality traits, while internalization would be less important. (The temperament factor is essentially irrelevant to our theory and might be expected to be unimportant.) This prediction was confirmed. Assessing the independent contributions of both cognitive measures and personality factors to the prediction of grades, we found that SAT math scores were the most important, followed by submission to authority and SAT verbal scores (each equally important). Internalized control proved to be significantly less important as a predictor. The temperament and IQ variables made no independent contribution.

Thus, at least for this sample, the personality traits rewarded in schools seem to be rather similar to those indicative of good job performance in the capitalist economy. Since moreover both Edwards and Meyer used essentially the same measures of personality traits, we can test this assertion in yet another way. We can take the three general traits extracted by Edwards in his study of workers—rules orientation, dependability, and internalization of norms—and find the relationship between those traits and

FIGURE 3
Predicting job performance and grades in school from the same personality traits

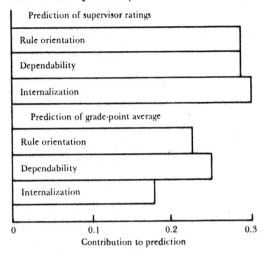

Prediction of supervisor ratings

Rule orientation

Dependability

Internalization

Prediction of grade-point average

Rule orientation

Dependability

Internalization

0   0.1   0.2   0.3

Contribution to prediction

Notes: The top three bars show the estimated normalized regression coefficients of the personality factors in an equation predicting supervisor ratings. The bottom three bars show the coefficients of the same three factors in an equation predicting high-school grade-point average. All factors are significant at the 1 percent level.

Sources: Bowles, Gintis, and Meyer (1975); Edwards (see full citations in Figures 1 and 2).

grades in Meyer's school study. The results, shown in Figure 3, exhibit a remarkable congruence.[18]

While the correspondence principle stands up well in the light of grading practices, we must stress that the empirical data on grading must not be regarded as fully revealing the inner workings of the educational system's reproduction of the social division of labor. In the first place, it is the overall structure of social relations of the educational encounter which reproduces consciousness, not just grading practices. Nor are personality traits the only relevant personal attributes captured in these data; others are modes of self-presentation, self-image, aspirations, and class identifications. The measuring of personality traits moreover is complex and difficult, and these studies probably capture only a small part of the relevant dimensions. Finally, both traits rewarded in schools and relevant to job performance differ by educational level,

class composition of schools, and the student's particular educational track. These subtleties are not reflected in these data.

For all these reasons, we would not expect student grades to be a good predictor of economic success. In addition, grades are clearly dominated by the cognitive performance of students, which we have seen is not highly relevant to economic success. Still, we might expect that in an adequately controlled study in which work performances of individuals on the same job and with comparable educational experience are compared, grades will be good predictors. We have managed to find only one study even approaching these requirements—a study which clearly supports our position, and is sufficiently interesting to present in some detail.[19] Marshall S. Brenner studied 100 employees who had joined the Lockheed-California Company after obtaining a high school diploma in the Los Angeles City school districts. From the employees' high school transcripts, he obtained their grade-point averages, school absence rates, a teachers' "work habits" evaluation, and a teachers' "cooperation" evaluation. In addition to this data, he gathered three evaluations of job performance by employees' supervisors: a supervisors' "ability rating," "conduct rating," and "productivity rating." Brenner found a significant correlation between grades and all measures of supervisor evaluation.

We have reanalyzed Brenner's data to uncover the source of this correlation. One possibility is that grades measure cognitive performance and cognitive performance determines job performance. However, when the high school teachers' work habits and cooperation evaluations as well as school absences were controlled for by linear regression, grades had no power to predict either worker conduct or worker productivity. Hence, we may draw two conclusions: First, grades predict job adequacy only through their noncognitive component; and second, teachers' evaluations of behavior in the classroom are strikingly similar to supervisors' ratings of behavior on the job. The cognitive component of grades predicts only the supervisors' ability rating—which is not surprising in view of the probability that both are related to employee IQ.

Why then the association between more schooling and higher incomes? We have indicated the importance of four sets of noncognitive worker traits—work-related personality characteristics, modes of self-presentation, racial, sexual, and ethnic characteristics, and credentials. We believe that all of these traits are involved in the association between educational level and economic success. We have already shown how personality traits conducive to performance at different hierarchical levels are fostered and rewarded by the school system. A similar, but simpler, argument can be made with respect to modes of self-presentation. Individuals who have attained a certain educational level tend to identify with one another socially and to differentiate themselves from their "inferiors." They tend to adjust their aspirations and self-concepts accordingly, while acquiring manners of speech and demeanor more or less socially acceptable and appropriate to their level.[20] As such, they are correspondingly valuable to employers interested in preserving and reproducing the status differences on which the legitimacy and stability of the hierarchical division of labor are based. Moreover, insofar as educational credentials are an independent determinant of hiring and promotion, they will directly account for a portion of this association.[21]

Finally, family background also accounts for a significant portion of the association between schooling and economic attainment. Indeed, for white males, about a third of the correlation between education and income is due to the common association of both variables with socioeconomic background, even holding constant childhood IQ.[22] That is, people whose parents have higher-status economic positions tend to achieve more income themselves independent of their education, but they also tend to get more education. Hence the observed association is reinforced.

Indeed, there is a strong independent association between family background and economic success, illustrated in Figure 4. For the large national sample represented there, children of the poorest tenth of families have roughly a third the likelihood of winding up well-off as the children of the most well-to-do tenth, even if they have the same educational attainments and childhood IQs. What is the origin of this effect? The inheritance of wealth, family connections, and other more or less direct advantages play an important role here. But there are more subtle if no less important

FIGURE 4
The effect of socioeconomic background on economic success is strong even for individuals with equal education and IQ

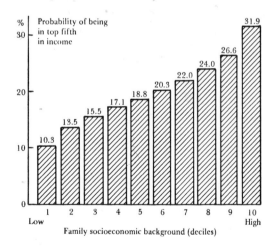

Notes: Each bar shows the estimated probability that a man is in the top fifth of the income distribution if he is from the given decile of socioeconomic background (as a weighted average of his father's education and occupational status and his parents' income), and if he has an average childhood IQ and average number of years of schooling. That is, it measures the effect of socioeconomic background on income, independent of any effects caused by education or IQ differences.

Sample: Non-Negro males from nonfarm backgrounds, aged 35–44.

Source: Samuel Bowles and Valerie Nelson, "The 'Inheritance of IQ' and the Intergenerational Reproduction of Economic Inequality," *Review of Economics and Statistics*, vol. 56, no. 1, February 1974.

influences at work here as well. We shall argue in the following section that the experiences of parents on the job tend to be reflected in the social relations of family life. Thus, through family socialization, children tend to acquire orientations toward work, aspirations, and self-concepts, preparing them for similar economic positions themselves.

Family structure and job structure

According to the materialist conception, the determining factor in history is, in the last resort, the production and reproduction of immediate life. But this itself is of a two-fold character. On the one hand, the production of the means of subsistence, of food, clothing, and shelter and the tools requisite therefore; on the other, the production of human beings themselves, the propagation of the species. The social institutions under which people of a particular historical epoch and a particular country live are conditioned by both kinds of production; by the stage of development of labor, on the one hand, and of the family on the other.

Friedrich Engels
*The Origin of the Family, Private Property,
and the State,* 1884

Family experience has a significant impact on the well-being, behavior, and personal consciousness of individuals, both during maturation and in their daily adult lives. The social relationships of family life —relationships between husband and wife as well as between parents and children and among children—have undergone important changes in the course of U.S. economic development. The prospect for future changes is of crucial importance in the process of social transformation.[23]

Rather than attempt a broad analysis of family life, we shall limit our discussion to a few issues directly linked to our central concern: the reproduction of the social relations of production. Like the educational system, the family plays a major role in preparing the young for economic and social

roles. Thus, the family's impact on the reproduction of the sexual division of labor, for example, is distinctly greater than that of the educational system.

This reproduction of consciousness is facilitated by a rough correspondence between the social relations of production and the social relations of family life, a correspondence that is greatly affected by the experiences of parents in the social division of labor. There is a tendency for families to reproduce in their offspring not only a consciousness tailored to the objective nature of the work world, but to prepare them for economic positions roughly comparable to their own. Although these tendencies can be countered by other social forces (schooling, media, shifts in aggregate occupational structure), they continue to account for a significant part of the observed intergenerational status-transmission processes.

This is particularly clear with respect to sexual division of labor. The social division of labor promotes the separation between wage and household labor, the latter being unpaid and performed almost exclusively by women. This separation is reflected within the family as a nearly complete division of labor between husband and wife. The occupational emphasis on full-time work, the dependence of promotion upon seniority, the career-oriented commitment of the worker, and the active discrimination against working women conspire to shackle the woman to the home while minimizing the likelihood of a joint sharing of domestic duties between husband and wife.

But how does the family help reproduce the sexual division of labor? First, wives and mothers themselves normally embrace their self-concepts as household workers. They then pass these onto their children through the differential sex role-typing of boys and girls within the family. Second, and perhaps more important, children tend to develop self-concepts based on the sexual divisions which they observe around them. Even families which attempt to treat boys and girls equally cannot avoid sex role-typing when the male parent is tangentially involved in household labor and child-rearing. In short, the family as a social as well as biological reproduction unit cannot but reflect its division of labor as a production unit. This sex typing, unless countered by other social forces, then facilitates the submission of the next generation of women to their inferior status in the wage-labor system and lends its alternative—child-rearing and domesticity—an aura of inevitability, if not desirability.

However, in essential respects, the family exhibits social patterns that are quite uncharacteristic of the social relations of production. The close personal and emotional relationships of family life are remote from the impersonal bureaucracy of the wage-labor system. Indeed, the family is often esteemed as a refuge from the alienation and psychic poverty of work life. Indeed, it is precisely because family structure and the capitalist relations of production differ in essential respects that our analysis sees schooling as performing such a necessary role in the integration of young people into the wage-labor system.

Despite the tremendous structural disparity between family and economy—one which is never really overcome in capitalist society—there is a significant correspondence between the authority relationships in capitalist production and family child-rearing. In part, this is true of family life common at all social levels. The male-dominated family, with its characteristically age-graded patterns of power and privilege, replicates many aspects of the hierarchy of production in the firm. Yet here we shall be more concerned with the difference among families whose income-earners hold distinct positions in this hierarchy.

As we have seen, successful job performance at low hierarchical levels requires the worker's orientation toward rule-following

and conformity to external authority, while successful performance at higher levels requires behavior according to internalized norms. It would be surprising, indeed, if these general orientations did not manifest themselves in parental priorities for the rearing of their children. Melvin Kohn's massive, ten-year study at the Natioanl Institute of Mental Health has documented important correspondences between authority in the social relationships of work and the social relationships of the family precisely of this type.

Kohn, in a series of papers and in his book, *Class and Conformity,* has advanced and tested the following hypothesis: Personality traits and values of individuals affect the economic positions they attain and, conversely, their job experiences strongly affect their personalities and values.[24] The most important values and behavior patterns in this interaction are those relating to self-direction and conformity,[25] with individuals of higher economic status more likely to value internal motivation and those of lower status more likely to value behavior that conforms with external authority. Thus, Kohn argues, individuals in higher-status jobs tend to value curiosity and self-reliance, to emphasize the intrinsic aspects of jobs such as freedom and choice, and to exhibit a high level of internalized motivation and a high degree of trust in interpersonal relationships. Conversely, people in lower-status jobs tend to value personal responsibility and the extrinsic aspects of jobs such as security, pay, and working conditions. Moreover, they exhibit more external motivations, a greater conformity to explicit social rules, and they are less trustful of others.[26]

Kohn goes on to inquire which aspects of jobs produce these results and concludes that the statistically relevant job characteristic is the degree of occupational self-direction, including freedom from close supervision, the degree of initiative and independent judgment allowed, and the complexity and variety of the job.[27] Thus, no matter what their economic status, whether white or blue collar, individuals with the same degree of occupational self-direction, tend to have similar values and traits. Self-direction versus close supervision and routinization on the job accounts for most of the status-related differences in personal preferences for self-direction, degree of internalized morality, trustfulness, self-confidence, self-esteem, and idea conformity.[28] He concludes:

In industrial society, where occupation is central to men's lives, occupational experiences that facilitate or deter the exercise of self-direction come to permeate men's views, not only of work and their role in work, but of the world and of self. The conditions of occupational life at higher social class levels facilitate interest in the intrinsic qualities of the job, foster a view of self and society that is conducive to believing in the possibilities of rational action toward purposive goals, and promote the valuation of self-direction. The conditions of occupational life at lower social class levels limit men's view of the job primarily to the extrinsic benefits it provides, foster a narrowly circumscribed conception of self and society, and promote the positive valuation of conformity to authority.[29]

There remains, however, an important discrepancy between our interpretation and Kohn's. What Kohn calls "self-direction" we feel is usually better expressed as "internalized norms." That is, the vast majority of workers in higher levels of the hierarchy of production are by no means autonomous, self-actualizing, and creatively self-directed. Rather, they are probably supersocialized so as to internalize authority and act without direct and continuous supervision to implement goals and objectives relatively alienated from their own personal needs. This distinction must be kept clearly in mind to avoid the error of attributing "superior" values and behavior traits to higher strata in the capitalist division of labor.

Kohn then went on to investigate the impact of work-related values on child-rearing. He began, in 1956, with a sample of 339 white mothers of children in the fifth grade, whose husbands held middle-class and working-class jobs.[30] He inquired into the values parents would most like to see in their children's behavior. He found that parents of lower-status children value obedience, neatness, and honesty in their children, while higher-status parents emphasize curiosity, self-control, consideration, and happiness. The fathers of these children who were interviewed showed a similar pattern of values. Kohn says:

Middle class parents are more likely to emphasize children's *self-direction,* and working class parents to emphasize their *conformity to external authority.* . . . The essential difference between the terms, as we use them, is that self-direction focuses on *internal* standards of direction for behavior; conformity focuses on *externally* imposed rules.[31]

Kohn further emphasized that these values translate directly into corresponding authority relationships between parents and children, with higher-status parents punishing breakdowns of internalized norms, and lower-status parents punishing transgressions of rules:

The principal difference between the classes is in the *specific conditions* under which parents —particularly mothers—punish children's misbehavior. Working class parents are more likely to punish or refrain from punishing on the basis of the direct and immediate consequences of children's actions, middle class parents on the basis of their interpretation of children's intent in acting as they do. . . . If self-direction is valued, transgressions must be judged in terms of the reasons why the children misbehave. If conformity is valued, transgressions must be judged in terms of whether or not the actions violate externally imposed proscriptions.[32]

In 1964, Kohn undertook to validate his findings with a national sample of 3,100 males, representative of the employed, male civilian labor force. His results clearly support his earlier interpretation: Higher-job-status fathers prefer consideration, curiosity, responsibility, and self-control in their children; low-status fathers prefer good manners, neatness, honesty, and obedience. Moreover, Kohn showed that about two-thirds of these social status–related differences are directly related to the extent of occupational self-direction. As a predictor of child-rearing values, the structure of work life clearly overshadows the other correlates of status such as occupational prestige or educational level.[33] He concludes:

Whether consciously or not parents tend to impart to their children lessons derived from the conditions of life of their own social class—and this helps to prepare their children for a similar class position. . . .

Class differences in parental values and child rearing practices influence the development of the capacities that children will someday need. . . . The family, then, functions as a mechanism for perpetuating inequality.[34]

Kohn's analysis provides a careful and compelling elucidation of one facet of what we consider to be a generalized social phenomenon: the reflection of economic life in all major spheres of social activity. The hierarchical division of labor, with the fragmentation of the work force which it engenders, is merely reflected in family life. The distinct quality of social relationships at different hierarchical levels in production are reflected in corresponding social relationships in the family. Families, in turn, reproduce the forms of consciousness required for the integration of a new generation into the economic system. Such differential patterns of child-rearing affect more than the worker's personality, as is exemplified in Kohn's study. They also pattern self-concepts, personal aspirations, styles of self-presentation, class loyalties, and modes of speech, dress, and interpersonal behavior. While such traits are by no means fixed into adulthood and must be reinforced at the workplace, their stability

over the life cycle appears sufficient to account for a major portion of the observed degree of intergenerational status transmission.

Conclusion

You will still be here tomorrow, but your dreams may not.

Cat Stevens

The economic system is stable only if the consciousness of the strata and classes which compose it remains compatible with the social relations which characterize it as a mode of production. The perpetuation of the class structure requires that the hierarchical division of labor be reproduced in the consciousness of its participants. The educational system is one of the several reproduction mechanisms through which dominant elites seek to achieve this objective. By providing skills, legitimating inequalities in economic positions, and facilitating certain types of social intercourse among individuals, U.S. education patterns personal development around the requirements of alienated work. The educational system reproduces the capitalist social division of labor, in part, through a correspondence between its own internal social relationships and those of the workplace.

The tendency of the social relationships of economic life to be replicated in the educational system and in family life lies at the heart of the failure of the liberal educational creed. This fact must form the basis of a viable program for social change. Patterns of inequality, repression, and forms of class domination cannot be restricted to a single sphere of life, but reappear in substantially altered, yet structurally comparable, form in all spheres. Power and privilege in economic life surface not only in the core social institutions which pattern the formation of consciousness (e.g., school and family), but even in face-to-face personal encounters, leisure activities, cultural life,

244

sexual relationships, and philosophies of the world. In particular, the liberal goal of employing the educational system as a corrective device for overcoming the "inadequacies" of the economic system is vain indeed. The transformation of the educational system and the pattern of class relationships, power, and privilege in the economic sphere must go hand in hand as part of an integrated program for action.

To speak of social change is to speak of making history. Thus we are motivated to look into the historical roots of the present educational system in order to better understand the framework within which social change takes place. Our major question will be: What were the historical forces giving rise to the present correspondence between education and economic life and how have these been affected by changes in the class structure and by concrete people's struggles? How may we shape these forces

so as to serve the goals of economic equality and liberated human development?

The historical development of the educational system reflects a counterpoint of reproduction and contradiction. As we have already seen, capitalist economic development leads to continual shifts in the social relationships of production and the attendant class structure. These social relationships have involved class conflicts which, throughout U.S. history, have periodically changed in both form and content. In important respects the educational system has served to defuse and attenuate these conflicts. Thus the changing character of social conflict, rooted in shifts in the class structure and in other relations of power and privilege, has resulted in periodic reorganizations of educational institutions. At the same time the educational system has evolved in ways which intensify and politicize the basic contradictions and conflicts of capitalist society.

NOTES

1. Herbert Gintis, "Welfare Criteria with Endogenous Preferences: The Economics of Education," *International Economic Review*, June 1974; Alfred Schutz and Thomas Luckmann, *The Structure of the Life-World* (Evanston, Ill.: Northwestern University Press, 1973); and Peter L. Berger and Thomas Luckmann, *The Social Construction of Reality: A Treatise in the Sociology of Knowledge* (Garden City, L.I., N.Y.: Doubleday and Co., 1966).

2. For an extended treatment of these issues, see Herbert Gintis, "Alienation and Power," in *Review of Radical Political Economics*, vol. 4, no. 5, Fall 1972.

3. Jeanne Binstock, "Survival in the American College Industry," unpublished Ph.D. dissertation, Brandeis University, 1970.

4. Burton Rosenthal, "Educational Investments in Human Capital: The Significance of Stratification in the Labor Market," unpublished honors thesis, Harvard University, 1972; and Edgar Z. Friedenberg, *Coming of Age in America* (New York: Random House, 1965).

5. Florence Howe and Paul Lauter, "The Schools Are Rigged for Failure," *New York Review of Books*, June 20, 1970; James Herndon, *The Way It Spozed to Be* (New York: Simon and Schuster, 1968); and Ray C. Rist, "Student

Social Class and Teacher Expectations: The Self-Fulfilling Prophecy in Ghetto Education," *Harvard Educational Review*, August 1970.

6. Binstock (1970), op. cit., pp. 103–106.

7. Ibid., pp. 3–4.

8. Ibid., p. 6.

9. Gene M. Smith, "Usefulness of Peer Ratings of Personality in Educational Research," *Educational and Psychological Measurement*, 1967; "Personality Correlates of Academic Performance in Three Dissimilar Populations," Proceedings of the 77th Annual Convention, American Psychological Association, 1967; and "Nonintelligence Correlates of Academic Performance," mimeographed, 1970.

10. Richard C. Edwards, "Alienation and Inequality: Capitalist Relations of Production in a Bureaucratic Enterprise," Ph.D. dissertation, Harvard University, July 1972.

11. Richard C. Edwards, "Personal Traits and 'Success' in Schooling and Work," *Educational and Psychological Measurement*, 1975; and "Individual Traits and Organizational Incentives: What Makes a 'Good' Worker?" *Journal of Human Resources*, 1976.

12. Peter J. Meyer, "Schooling and the Reproduction of the Social Division of Labor," unpub-

lished honors thesis, Harvard University, March 1972.

13. Personality data was collected for 97 percent of the sample. Grade-point average and test-scored data was available for 80 percent of the sample, and family background data was available for 67 percent. Inability to collect data was due usually to students' absences from school during test sessions.

14. The school chosen was of predominantly higher income, so that most students had taken college-entrance examinations.

15. The multiple correlation of IQ, SAT-verbal, and SAT-math with grade-point average (GPA) was r = 0.769, while their correlation with the personality variables was r = 0.25.

16. That is, we created partial correlation coefficients between GPA and each personality measure, controlling for IQ, SAT-V, and SAT-M.

17. We emphasize that these groupings are determined by a computer program on the basis of the observed pattern of association among the 16 variables. The fact that they are so clearly interpretable, rather than being hodgepodge, is a further indicator of the correctness of our analysis. We have not grouped the personality traits in terms of our preconceived theory, but observed rather how they are *naturally* grouped in our data.

18. This is taken from table 3 of Edwards (1975), op. cit.; and Samuel Bowles, Herbert Gintis, and Peter Meyer, "The Long Shadow of Work: Education, the Family, and the Reproduction of the Social Division of Labor," in *Insurgent Sociologist*, Summer 1975.

19. Marshall H. Brenner, "The Use of High School Data to Predict Work Performance," *Journal of Applied Psychology*, vol. 52, no. 1, January 1968. This study was suggested to us by Edwards, and is analyzed in Edwards (1972), op. cit.

20. See Claus Offe, *Leistungsprinzip und Industrielle Arbeit* (Frankfurt: Europäische Verlaganstalt, 1970).

21. See Ivar Berg, *Education and Jobs: The Great Training Robbery* (Boston: Beacon Press, 1971); and Paul Taubman and Terence Wales, *Higher Education and Earnings* (New York: McGraw-Hill, 1974).

22. Calculated from an estimated normalized regression coefficient of 0.23 on socioeconomic background in an equation using background, early childhood IQ, and years of schooling to predict income from 35–44-year-old males. This is reported in table 1 of Samuel Bowles and Valerie Nelson, "The 'Inheritance of IQ' and the Intergenerational Reproduction of Economic Inequality," *Review of Economics and Statistics*, vol. 56, no. 1, February 1974. The corresponding coefficients for other age groups are 0.17 for ages 25–34; 0.29 for ages 45–54; and 0.11 for ages 55–64 years.

23. Margaret Benston, "The Political Economy of Women's Liberation," *Monthly Review*, September 1969; Marilyn P. Goldberg, "The Economic Exploitation of Women," in David M. Gordon, ed., *Problems in Political Economy* (Lexington, Mass.: D. C. Heath and Co., 1971); L. Gordon, *Families* (Cambridge, Mass.: A Bread and Rose Publication, 1970); Zaretzky, "Capitalism and Personal Life," *Socialist Revolution*, January–April 1973; and Juliet Mitchell, *Woman's Estate* (New York: Vintage Books, 1973).

24. Melvin Kohn, *Class and Conformity: A Study in Values* (Homewood, Ill.: Dorsey Press, 1969).

25. Melvin Kohn and Carmi Schooler, "Occupational Experience and Psychological Functioning: An Assessment of Reciprocal Effects," *American Sociological Review*, February 1973.

26. Kohn (1969), op. cit.; chaps. 5 and 10.

27. Ibid., chap. 10.

28. Ibid., table 10–7.

29. Ibid., p. 192.

30. The occupational index used was that of Hollingshead, which correlates 0.90 with the Duncan index. Charles M. Bonjean, Richard J. Hill, and S. Dale McLemore, *Sociological Measurement: An Inventory of Scales and Indices* (San Francisco: Chandler, 1967).

31. Kohn (1969), op. cit., pp. 34–35.

32. Ibid., pp. 104–105.

33. Two problems with the Kohn study may be noted. First, we would like to have more direct evidence of the ways in which and to what extent child-raising *values* are manifested in child-raising *practices*. And second, we would like to know more about the impact of differences in child-rearing practice upon child development.

34. Kohn (1969), op. cit., p. 200.

Labor, capital, and class struggle around the built environment*

DAVID HARVEY

In this paper I will seek to establish a theoretical framework for understanding a facet of class struggle under advanced capitalism. The conflicts that will be scrutinized are those that relate to the production and use of the built environment, by which I mean the totality of physical structures—houses, roads, factories, offices, sewage systems, parks, cultural institutions, educational facilities, and so on. In general I shall argue that capitalist society must of necessity create a physical landscape—a mass of humanly constructed physical resources—in its own image, broadly appropriate to the purposes of production and reproduction. But I shall also argue that this process of creating space is full of contradictions and tensions and that the class relations in capitalist society inevitably spawn strong cross-currents of conflict.

I shall assume for purposes of analytic convenience that a clear distinction exists between (1) a faction of capital seeking the appropriation of rent either directly (as landlords, property companies, and the like) or indirectly (as financial intermediaries or others who invest in property simply for a rate of return), (2) a faction of capital seeking interest and profit by building new elements in the built environment (the construction interests), (3) capital "in general," which looks upon the built environment as an outlet for surplus capital and as a bundle of use values for enhancing the production and accumulation of capital, and (4) labor, which uses the built environment as a means of consumption and as a means for its own re-

production. I shall also assume that the built environment can be divided conceptually into *fixed capital* items to be used in production (factories, highways, railroads, and so on) and *consumption fund* items to be used in consumption (houses, roads, parks, sidewalks, and the like).[1] Some items, such as roads and sewer systems, can function both as fixed capital and as part of the consumption fund, depending on their use.

I will restrict attention in this paper to the structure of conflict as it arises in relation to labor's use of the consumption fund rather than its use of fixed capital in the immediate process of production. An analysis of this aspect of class struggle will do much to shed light, I believe, on the vexing questions that surround the relationship between community conflict and community organizing, on the one hand, and industrial conflict and work-based organizing on the other. In short, I hope to be able to shed some light on the position and experience of labor with respect to *living* as well as *working* in the historical development of those countries that are now generally considered to be in the advanced capitalist category. The examples will be taken from the United States and Great Britain. Some preparatory comments on the general theme to be pursued are in order.

The domination of capital over labor is basic to the capitalist mode of production—without it, after all, surplus value could not be extracted and accumulation would disappear. All kinds of consequences flow from this and the relation between labor

* From *Politics and Society*, 6 (no. 3, 1976), pp. 265–295.

and the built environment can be understood only in terms of it. Perhaps the single most important fact is that industrial capitalism, through the reorganization of the work process and the advent of the factory system, forced a separation between place of work and place of reproduction and consumption. The need to reproduce labor power is thus translated into a specific set of production and consumption activities within the household, a domestic economy that requires use values in the form of a built environment if it is to function effectively.

The needs of labor have changed historically and they will in part be met by work within the household and in part be procured through market exchanges of wages earned against commodities produced. The commodity requirements of labor depend upon the balance between domestic economy products and market purchases as well as upon the environmental, historical, and moral considerations that fix the standard of living of labor.[2] In the commodity realm, labor can, by organization and class struggle, alter the definition of needs to include "reasonable" standards of nutrition, health care, housing, education, recreation, entertainment, and so on. From the standpoint of capital, accumulation requires a constant expansion of the market for commodities, which means the creation of new social wants and needs and the organization of "rational consumption" on the part of labor. This last condition suggests theoretically what is historically observable—that the domestic economy must steadily give way before the expansion of capitalist commodity production. "Accumulation for accumulation's sake, production for production's sake," which jointly drive the capitalist system onwards, therefore entail an increasing integration of labor's consumption into the capitalist system of production and exchange of commodities.[3]

The split between the place of work and the place of residence means that the struggle of labor to control the social conditions of its own existence splits into two seemingly independent struggles. The first, located in the work place, is over the wage rate, which provides the purchasing power for consumption goods, and the conditions of work. The second, fought in the place of residence, is against secondary forms of exploitation and appropriation represented by merchant capital, landed property, and the like. This is a fight over the costs and conditions of existence in the living place. And it is this second kind of struggle that we focus on here, recognizing, of course, that the dichotomy between *living* and *working* is itself an artificial division that the capitalist system imposes.

Labor versus the appropriators of rent and the construction interest

Labor needs living space. Land is therefore a condition of living for labor in much the same way that it is a condition of production for capital. The system of private property that excludes labor from land as a condition of production also serves to exclude labor from the land as a condition of living. As Marx puts it, "the monstrous power wielded by landed property, when united hand in hand with industrial capital, enables it to be used against laborers engaged in their wage struggle as a means of practically expelling them from the earth as a dwelling place."[4] Apart from space as a basic condition of living we are concerned here with housing, transportation (to jobs and facilities), amenities, facilities, and a whole bundle of resources that contribute to the total living environment for labor. Some of these items can be privately appropriated (housing is the most important case) while others have to be used in common (sidewalks) and in some cases, such as the transportation system, even used jointly with capital.

The need for these items pits labor against landed property and the appropriation of rent as well as against the construction interest, which seeks to profit from the production of these commodities. The cost and quality of these items affect the standard of living of labor. Labor, in seeking to protect and enhance its standard of living, engages in a series of running battles in the living place over a variety of issues that relate to the creation, management, and use of the built environment. Examples are not hard to find—community conflict over excessive appropriation of rent by landlords, over speculation in the housing market, over the siting of "noxious" facilities, over inflation in housing construction costs, over inflation in the costs of servicing a deteriorating urban infrastructure, over congestion, over lack of accessibility to employment opportunities and services, over highway construction and urban renewal, over the "quality of life" and aesthetic issues—the list seems almost endless.

Conflicts that focus on the built environment exhibit certain peculiar characteristics because the monopoly power conferred by private property arrangements generates not only the power to appropriate rent but also yields to the owners command over a "natural monopoly" in space.[5] The fixed and immobile character of the built environment entails the production and use of commodities under conditions of spatial monopolistic competition with strong "neighborhood" or "externality" effects.[6] Many of the struggles that occur are over externality effects—the value of a particular house is in part determined by the condition of the houses surrounding it and each owner is therefore very interested in seeing to it that the neighborhood as a whole is well-maintained. In bourgeois theory, the appropriation of rent and the trading of titles to properties set price signals for new commodity production in such a way that a "rational" allocation

of land to uses can be arrived at through a market process. But because of the pervasive externality effects and the sequential character of both development and occupancy, the price signals suffer from all manner of serious distortions. There are, as a consequence, all kinds of opportunities for both appropriators and the construction faction, for developers, speculators, and even private individuals, to reap windfall profits and monopoly rents. Internecine conflicts within a class and faction are therefore just as common as conflict between classes and factions.

We are primarily concerned here, however, with the structure of the three-way struggle between labor, the appropriators of rent, and the construction faction. Consider, as an example, the direct struggle between laborers and landlords over the cost and quality of housing. Landlords typically use whatever power they have to appropriate as much as they can from the housing stock they own and they will adjust their strategy to the conditions in such a way that they maximize the rate of return on their capital. If this rate of return is very high, then new capital will likely flow into landlordism, and, if the rate of return is very low, then we will likely witness disinvestment and abandonment. Labor will seek by a variety of strategies—for example, moving to where housing is cheaper or establishing rent controls and housing codes—to limit appropriation and to ensure a reasonable quality of shelter. How such a struggle is resolved depends very much upon the relative economic and political power of the two groups, the circumstances of supply and demand that exist at a particular place and time, and upon the options that each group has available to it.[7]

The struggle becomes three dimensional when we consider that the ability of appropriators to gain monopoly rents on the old housing is in part limited by the capacity of the construction interest to enter the market and create new housing at a lower cost. The price of old housing is, after all, strongly affected by the costs of production of new housing. If labor can use its political power to gain state subsidies for construction, then this artificially stimulated new development will force the rate of appropriation on existing resources downwards. If, on the other hand, appropriators can check new development (by, for example, escalating land costs), or if, for some reason, new development is inhibited (planning permission procedures in Britain have typically functioned in this way), then the rate of appropriation can rise. On the other hand, when labor manages to check the rate of appropriation through direct rent controls, then the price of rented housing falls, new development is discouraged, and scarcity is produced. These are the kinds of conflicts and strategies of coalition that we have to expect in such situations.

But the structure of conflict is made more complex by the "natural monopoly" inherent in space. For example, the monopoly power of the landlord is in part modified by the ability of labor to escape entrapment in the immediate environs of the work place. Appropriation from housing is very sensitive to changes in transportation. The ability to undertake a longer journey to work is in part dependent upon the wage rate (which allows the worker to pay for travel), in part dependent upon the length of the working day (which gives the worker time to travel), and in part dependent upon the cost and availability of transportation. The boom in the construction of working-class suburbs in late 19th-century London, for example, can in large degree be explained by the advent of the railways and the provision of cheap "workman's special" fares and a shortening of the working day, which freed at least some of the working class from the need to live within walking distance of the work place.[8] The rate of rental appropriation on the housing close to the centers of employment had to fall as a consequence. The "streetcar" suburbs of American cities and the working-class suburbs of today (based on cheap energy and the automobile) are further examples of this phenomenon.[9] By pressing for new and cheap forms of transportation, labor can escape geographical entrapment and thereby reduce the capacity of landlords in advantageous locations to gain monopoly rents. The problems that attach to spatial entrapment are still with us, of course, in the contemporary ghettos of the poor, the aged, the oppressed minorities, and the like. Access is still, for these groups, a major issue.[10]

The struggle to fight off the immediate depredations of the landlord and the continuous battle to keep the cost of living down do much to explain the posture adopted by labor with respect to the distribution, quantities, and qualities of all elements in the built environment. Public facilities, recreational opportunities, amenities, transportation access, and so on, are all subjects of contention. But underlying these immediate concerns is a deeper struggle over the very meaning of the built environment as a set of use values for labor.

The producers of the built environment, both past and present, provide labor with a limited set of choices of living conditions. If labor has slender resources with which to exercise an effective demand, then it has to put up with whatever it can get—shoddily built, cramped, and poorly serviced tenement buildings, for example. With increasing effective demand, labor has the potential to choose over a wider range and, as a result, questions about the overall "quality of life" begin to arise. Capital in general, and that faction of it that produces the built environment, seek to define the quality of life for labor in terms of the commodities that they can profitably produce in certain locations. Labor, on the other hand, defines quality of life solely in use value terms and in the process may appeal to some underlying and very fundamental conception of what it is to be human. Production for profit and production for use are often inconsistent with each other. The survival of capitalism therefore requires that capital dominate labor, not simply in the work process, but with respect to the very definition of the quality of life in the consumption sphere. Production, Marx argued, not only produces consumption, it also produces the mode of consumption and that, of course, is what the consumption fund for labor is all about.[11] For this reason, capital in general cannot afford the outcome of struggles around the built environment to be determined simply by the relative powers of labor, the appropriators of rent, and the construction faction. It must, from time to time, throw its weight into the balance to effect outcomes that are favorable to the reproduction of the capitalist social order. It is to this aspect of matters that we must now turn.

The interventions of capital in struggles over the built environment

When capital intervenes in struggles over the built environment it usually does so through the agency of state power. A cursory examination of the history of the advanced capitalist countries shows that the capitalist class sometimes throws its weight on the side of labor and sometimes on the side of other factions. But history also suggests a certain pattern and underlying rationale for these interventions. We can get at the pattern by assembling the interventions together under four broad headings—private property and homeownership for the working class, the cost of living and the value of labor power, managed collective consumption of workers in the interest of sustained capital accumulation, and a very complex, but very important, topic concerning the relation to na-

ture, the imposition of work discipline, and the like. A discussion of the pattern will help us to identify the underlying rationale, and in this manner we can identify a much deeper meaning in the everyday struggles in which labor engages in the living place.

Private property and homeownership for labor. The struggle that labor wages in the living place against the appropriation of rent is a struggle against the monopoly power of private property. Labor's fight against the principle of private property cannot easily be confined to the housing arena, and "the vexed question of the relation between rent and wages . . . easily slides into that of capital and labor."[12] For this reason the capitalist class as a whole cannot afford to ignore it; they have an interest in keeping the principle of private property sacrosanct. A well-developed struggle between tenants and landlords—with the former calling for public ownership, municipalization, and the like —calls the whole principle into question. Extended individualized homeownership is therefore seen as advantageous to the capitalist class because it promotes the allegiance of at least a segment of the working class to the principle of private property, promotes an ethic of "possessive individualism," and brings about a fragmentation of the working class into "housing classes" of homeowners and tenants.[13] This gives the capitalist class a handy ideological lever to use against public ownership and nationalization demands because it is easy to make such proposals sound as if the intent is to take workers' privately owned houses away from them.

The majority of owner-occupants do not own their housing outright, however. They make interest payments on a mortgage. This puts finance capital in a hegemonic position with respect to the functioning of the housing market—a position that it is in no way loath to make use of.[14] The apparent entrance of workers into the petit form of property ownership in housing is, to a large degree, its exact opposite in reality—the entry of money capital into a controlling position within the consumption fund. Finance capital not only controls the disposition and rate of new investment in housing, but controls labor as well through chronic debt-encumbrance. A worker mortgaged up to the hilt is, for the most part, a pillar of social stability, and schemes to promote homeownership within the working class have long recognized this basic fact. And in return the worker may build up, very slowly, some equity in the property.

This last consideration has some important ramifications. Workers put their savings into the physical form of a property. Obviously, they will be concerned to preserve the value of those savings and if possible to enhance them. Ownership of housing can also lead to petty landlordism, which has been a traditional and very important means for individual workers to engage in the appropriation of values at the expense of other workers. But more importantly, every homeowner, whether he or she likes it or not, is caught in a struggle over the appropriation of values because of the shifting patterns of external costs and benefits within the built environment. A new road may destroy the value of some housing and enhance the value of other housing, and the same applies to all manner of new development, redevelopment, accelerated obsolescence, and so on.

The way in which labor relates to these externality effects is crucial if only because the housing market is in quantitative terms by far the most important market for any one particular element in the built environment. It would be very difficult to understand the political tension between suburbs and central cities in the United States without recognizing the fragmentation that occurs within the working class as one section of it moves into homeowner-

ship and becomes deeply concerned to preserve and if possible to enhance the value of its equity. The social tensions omnipresent within the "community structure" of American cities are similarly affected. Homeownership, in short, invites a faction of the working class to wage its inevitable fight over the appropriation of value in capitalist society in a very different way. It puts these workers on the side of the principle of private property and frequently leads them to appropriate values at the expense of other factions of the working class. With such a glorious tool to divide and rule at its disposal, it is hardly surprising that capital in general sides with labor in this regard against the landed interest. It is rather as if capital, having relied upon landed property to divorce labor from access to one of the basic conditions of production, preserves the principle of private propety intact in the face of the class struggle by permitting labor to return to the face of the earth as a partial owner of land and property as a condition of consumption.

The cost of living and the wage rate. Marx argued that the value of labor power was determined by the value of the commodities required to reproduce that labor power. This neat equivalence disappears in the pricing realm, but nevertheless there is a relation of some sort between wages and the cost of obtaining those commodities essential to the reproduction of the household.[15]

An excessive rate of appropriation of rent by landlords will increase the cost of living to labor and generate higher wage demands that, if won, may have the effect of lowering the rate of accumulation of capital. For this reason capital in general may side with labor in the struggle against excessive appropriation and attempt also to lower the costs of production of a basic commodity such as housing. Capitalists may themselves seek to provide cheap housing, as in the "model communities" typical of the early years of the industrial revolution, or they may even side with the demands of labor for cheap, subsidized housing under public ownership, provided that this permits the payment of lower wages. For the same reason the capitalist class may seek to promote, through the agency of the state, the industrialization of building production and the rationalization of production of the built environment through comprehensive land use planning policies, new town construction programs, and the like. Capitalists tend to become interested in such things, however, only when labor is in a position, through its organized collective power, to tie wages to the cost of living.

These considerations apply to all elements in the built environment (and to social services and social expenditures also) that are relevant to the reproduction of labor power. Those that are publicly provided (which means the bulk of them outside of housing and until recently transportation) can be monitored by a cost-conscious municipal government under the watchful eye of the local business community, and, perhaps, in an emergency situation such as that experienced in New York both in the 1930s and the 1970s, even under direct supervision by the institutions of finance capital. In the interests of keeping the costs of reproduction of labor power at a minimum, the capitalist class as a whole may seek collective means to intervene in the processes of investment and appropriation in the built environment. In much the same way that the proletariat frequently sided with the rising industrial bourgeoisie against the landed interest in the early years of capitalism, so we often find capital in general siding with labor in the advanced capitalist societies against excessive appropriation of rent and rising costs of new development. The coalition is not forged altruistically but arises organically out of the relation between the wage rate and the costs of reproduction of labor power.

"Rational," managed, and collective consumption. Workers mediate the circulation of commodities by using their wages to purchase means of consumption produced by capitalists. Any failure on the part of workers to use their purchasing power correctly and rationally from the standpoint of the capitalist production and realization system will disrupt the circulation of commodities. In the early years of capitalist development this problem was not so important because trade with noncapitalist societies could easily take up any slack in effective demand. But with the transition to advanced capitalism, the internal market provided by the wage-labor force becomes of greater and greater significance. Also, as standards of living rise, in the sense that workers have more and more commodities available to them, so the potential for a breakdown from "irrationalities" in consumption increases. The failure to exercise a proper effective demand can be a source of crisis. And it was, of course, Keynes's major contribution to demonstrate to the capitalist class that under certain conditions the way out of a crisis manifested as a falling profit rate was not to cut wages but to increase them and thereby to expand the market.

This presumes, however, that workers are willing to spend their wages "rationally." If we assume, with Adam Smith, that mankind has an infinite and insatiable appetite for "trinkets and baubles," then there is no problem, but Malthus voiced another worry when he observed that the history of human society "sufficiently demonstrates [that] an efficient taste for luxuries and conveniences, that is, such a taste as will properly stimulate industry, instead of being ready to appear the moment it is required, is a plant of slow growth."[16] Production may, as Marx averred, produce consumption and the mode of consumption, but it does not do so automatically, and the manner in which it does so is the locus of continuous struggle and conflict.[17]

Consider, first of all, the relationship between capitalist production and the household economy. In the United States in 1810, for example, "the best figures available to historians show that . . . about two thirds of the clothing worn . . . was the product of household manufacture," but by 1860 the advent of industrial capitalism in the form of the New England textile industry had changed all that—"household manufactures had been eclipsed by the development of industrial production and a market economy."[18] Step by step, activities traditionally associated with household work are brought within the capitalist market economy—baking, brewing, preserving, cooking, food preparation, washing, cleaning, and even child-rearing and child socialization. And with respect to the built environment, house-building and maintenance become integrated into the market economy. In the United States in the 19th century a substantial proportion of the population built their own homes with their own labor and local raw materials. Now almost all units are built through the market system.

The advent of the factory system was a double-edged sword with respect to the household economy. On the one hand it extracted the wage earner(s) from the home. In the early years of industrial capitalism it did so for 12 or 14 hours a day and, under particularly exploitative conditions, forced the whole household—women and children as well as men—into the wage-labor force (in this manner the wages of the *household* could remain stable in the face of a falling wage rate). Of these early years E. P. Thompson writes: "Each stage in industrial differentiation and specialization struck also at the family economy, disturbing customary relations between man and wife, parents and children, and differentiating more sharply be-

tween 'work' and 'life.' It was to be a full hundred years before this differentiation was to bring returns, in the form of labour-saving devices, back into the working woman's home."[19]

This "return" of commodities to the household is the other edge of the sword. The factory system produced use values for consumption more cheaply and with less effort than the household. The use values may be in the form of standardized products, but there should at least be more of them and therefore a material basis for a rising standard of living of labor. In the early years of industrial capitalism this did not in general happen. Laborers certainly worked longer hours and probably received less in the way of use values (although the evidence on this latter point is both patchy and controversial).[20] But the rising productivity of labor that occurs with accumulation, the consequent need to establish an internal market, and a century or more of class struggle have changed all of this. Consumer durables and consumption fund items (such as housing) have become very important growth sectors in the economy, and the political conditions and the material basis for a rising standard of living of labor have indeed been achieved.

The experience of labor in substituting work in the factory for work in the household has, therefore, both positive and negative aspects. But such substitutions are not easily achieved because they involve the nature and structure of the family, the role of women in society, culturally entrenched traditions, and the like. The substitutions are themselves a focus of struggle. The rational consumption of commodities in relation to the accumulation of capital implies a certain balance between market purchases and household work. The struggle to substitute the former for the latter is significant because its outcome defines the very meaning of use values and the standard of living for labor in its commodity aspects. The construction of the built environment has to be seen, therefore, in the context of a struggle over a whole way of living and being.

Techniques of persuasion are widely used in advanced capitalist societies to ensure rational consumption. Moral exhortation and philanthropic enterprise are often put to work "to raise the condition of the laborer by an improvement of his mental and moral powers and to make a rational consumer of him."[21] The church, the press, and the schools can be mobilized on behalf of rational consumption at the same time as they can be vehicles for genuinely autonomous working-class development. And then, of course, there are always the blandishments of the ad-men and the techniques of Madison Avenue.

It would be idle to pretend that "the standard of living of labor" has been unaffected by these techniques. But, again, we are dealing with a double-edged sword. They may in fact also exert what Marx called a "civilizing influence" on labor and be used by labor to raise itself to a new condition of material and mental well-being that, in turn, provides a new and more solid basis for class struggle.[22] Conversely, the drive by labor to improve its condition may be perverted by a variety of stratagems into a definition of use values advantageous to accumulation rather than reflective of the real human needs of labor. The human demand for shelter is turned, for example, into a process of accumulation through housing production.

Rational consumption can also be ensured by the collectivization of consumption, primarily, although not solely, through the agency of the state.[23] Working-class demands for health care, housing, education, and social services of all kinds are usually expressed through political channels, and government arbitrates these demands and seeks to reconcile them with the requirements of accumulation. Many of these demands are met by the collective provision of goods and services, which means that everyone consumes them whether he or she likes it or not. Capitalist systems have moved more and more towards the collectivization of consumption because of the need, clearly understood in Keynesian fiscal policies, to manage consumption in the interests of accumulation. By collectivization, consumer choice is translated from the uncontrolled anarchy of individual action to the seemingly more controllable field of state enterprise. This translation does not occur without a struggle over both the freedom of individual choice (which generates a strong antibureaucratic sentiment) and the definition of the use values involved (national defense versus subsidized housing for the poor, for example).

The built environment has a peculiar and important role in all of this. The bundle of resources that comprise it—streets and sidewalks, drains and sewer systems, parks and playgrounds—contains many elements that are collectively consumed. The public provision of such public goods is a "natural" form of collective consumption that capital can easily colonize through the agency of the state. Also, the sum of individual private decisions creates a public effect because of the pervasive externality effects that in themselves force certain forms of collective consumption through private action—if I fail to keep my yard neat then my neighbors cannot avoid seeing it. The built environment requires collective management and control, and it is therefore almost certain to be a primary field of struggle between capital and labor over what is good for accumulation and what is good for people.

The consumption fund has accounted for an increasing proportion of gross aggregate investment in the built environment since around 1890 in both Britain and the United States.[24] The housing sector in particular has become a major tool in macroeconomic policy for stabilizing economic growth, particularly in the United States where it has openly been used as a Keynesian regulator (not always, we should add, with success). And there are also strong multiplier effects to be taken into account. Housing construction, for example, requires complementary investments in other aspects of the built environment as well as in a wide range of consumer durables. The multipliers vary a great deal according to design and other considerations, but in all cases they are substantial.

These multipliers assume an added importance when we consider them in relation to the "coercive power" that the built environment can exercise over our daily lives. Its longevity and fixity in space, together with its method of financing and amortization, mean that once we have created it we must use it if the value that it represents is not to be lost. Under the social relations of capitalism, the built environment becomes an artifact of human labor that subsequently returns to dominate daily life. Capital seeks to mobilize it as a coercive force to help sustain accumulation. If our cities are built for driving, for example, then drive we must in order to live "normally" whether we like it or not. The highway lobby in the United States, the automobile, oil, and rubber industries and the construction interests, changed the face of America and used the coercive power of the built environment to ensure rational growth in the consumption of their products.[25] But labor is not oblivious to such pressures. The configurations of use values that capital urges upon labor may be resisted or transformed to suit labor's purposes and labor's needs—the automobile becomes, for example, a means of escape (we will consider from what very shortly).

Insofar as capitalism has survived, so we have to conclude that capital dominates labor not only in the place of work but in the living space by defining the standard of living of labor and the quality of life in part through the creation of built environ-

ments that conform to the requirements of accumulation and commodity production. To put it this strongly is not to say that labor cannot win on particular issues, nor does it imply that there is one and only one definition of use values for labor that fits the need for accumulation. There are innumerable possibilities, but the limits of tolerance of capital are nevertheless clearly defined. For labor to struggle within these limits is one thing; to seek to go beyond them is where the real struggle begins.

The socialization of labor and the relation to nature. Work and living cannot be entirely divorced from each other. What happens in the work place cannot be forgotten in the living place. Yet, we have a very poor understanding of the relation between the two.[26] The definition of "a use value for labor in the built environment" cannot, therefore, be independent of the work experience. We will consider two very basic aspects of this in what follows.

We tend to forget that the advent of the factory system required a quite extraordinary adaptation in social life. It transformed the rural peasant and the independent artisan into a mere cog in a system designed to produce surplus value. The laborer became a "thing"—a mere "factor of production" to be used in the production process as the capitalist desired. But the new economic order also required that "men who were non-accumulative, non-acquisitive, accustomed to work for subsistence, not for maximization of income, had to be made obedient to the cash stimulus and obedient in such a way as to react precisely to the stimuli provided." The habituation of the worker to the new mode of production, the inculcation of the work discipline and all that went with it, was and is still no easy matter. Consequently, "the modern industrial proletariat was introduced to its role not so much by attraction or monetary reward, but by compulsion, force, and fear. It was not allowed to grow as in a sunny garden; it was forged, over a fire, by the powerful blows of a hammer."[27] The consequences of this for the manner and forms of subsequent class struggle were legion. And, as Braverman points out, "the habituation of workers to the capitalist mode of production must be renewed with each generation."[28]

The inculcation of work discipline could in part be accomplished by training, threats, incentives, and cajolery in the work place. These were effective, but not in themselves sufficient. In the early years of industrial capitalism the problems were particularly severe because capitalism had not yet woven the "net of modern capitalist life that finally makes all other modes of living impossible."[29] And so originated the drive on the part of capital to inculcate the working class with the "work ethic" and "bourgeois values" of honesty, reliability, respect for authority, obedience to laws and rules, respect for property and contractual agreements, and the like. The assault on the values of the working class was in part conducted through religious, educational, and philanthropic channels, with the paternalism of the industrialist often thrown into the balance. But there is another component to this that is of particular interest to us here. The early industrialists in particular had to deal with workers both inside the factory and outside of it:

The efforts to reform the whole man were, therefore, particularly marked in factory towns and villages in which the total environment was under the control of a single employer. Here some of the main developments of the industrial revolution were epitomized: these settlements were founded by the industrialist, their whole raison d'être his quest for profit, their politics and laws in his pocket, the quality of their life under his whim, their ultimate aims in his image. . . . Great though the outward difference was between the flogging masters and the model community builders, "from the standpoint of control of labour both types of factory

management display a concern with the enforcement of discipline."[30]

This need to socialize labor to a work process through control in the living place is endemic to capitalism, but it is particularly noticeable when new kinds of work processes are introduced. Henry Ford's five-dollar, eight-hour day for assembly-line workers introduced in 1914 was accompanied with much puritanical rhetoric and a "philanthropic" control system that affected nearly every facet of the workers' lives:

A staff of over thirty investigators . . . visited workers' homes gathering information and giving advice on the intimate details of the family budget, diet, living arrangements, recreation, social outlook and morality. . . . The worker who refused to learn English, rejected the advice of the investigator, gambled, drank excessively, or was found guilty of "any malicious practice derogatory to good physical manhood or moral character" was disqualified from the five dollar wage. . . .[31]

Gramsci's comments on "Fordism" are perceptive.[32] There arose at that point in the history of capitalist accumulation a "need to elaborate a new type of man suited to the new type of work and productive process." This transformation, Gramsci argued, could only be accomplished by a skillful combination of force and persuasion—the latter including high wages, "various social benefits, extremely subtle ideological propaganda." Ford's puritanical and social control initiatives had the purpose of "preserving, outside of work, a certain psychophysical equilibrium which prevents the physiological collapse of the workers, exhausted by the new method of production." Workers had to spend their money "rationally, to maintain, renew and if possible to increase [their] muscular nervous efficiency." The fierce attack on alcohol and sexual activities was also a part of the comprehensive effort to inculcate "the habits and customs necessary for the new systems of living and working." The events that surrounded the introduction of Fordism are a classic example of the attempt by capital to shape the person in the living place to fit the requirements of the work place.

Our interest here is, of course, to understand the manner in which industrialists in general, and the community builders in particular, defined the quality of life for their workers and used the built environment as part of a general strategy for inculcating bourgeois values and a "responsible" industrial work discipline. We have already noted a modern version of this in the promotion of working-class home-ownership as a means to ensure respect for property rights and social stability—a connection that was recognized early in the 19th century in the United States.[33] But we are here concerned with the more direct forms of control of the living space. Bender suggests, for example, that the boarding-houses constructed to house the mill girls of Lowell in the 1820s "served as a functional equivalent of the rural family" and operated as "an effective adaptive mechanism" for the girls being drawn off the New England farms into the factories.[34] This same point was made most effectively in the design and functioning of those institutions concerned to deal with those who could not or would not adapt to the new style of life. As early as Elizabethan times, for example, madness and unemployment were regarded as the same thing, while the advent of industrial capitalism had the effect of defining physical sickness as inability to go to work. Both Pollard, in the British context, and Rothman, in the American, point out the connection between major social institutions—asylums, workhouses, penitentiaries, hospitals, and even schools—and the factory systems, which they closely resembled in layout and in internal disciplinary organization. The rehabilitation of the convict in Jacksonian America, for example, meant the socialization of the convict to something akin to an industrial work discipline.[35]

That there is a relationship of some sort between working and living, and that by manipulating the latter a leverage can be exerted on the former, has not escaped the notice of the capitalist class. A persistent theme in the history of the advanced capitalist countries has been to look for those improvements in the living place that will enhance the happiness, docility, and efficiency of labor. In the model communities, this kind of program is quite explicit. George Pullman, in his ill-fated experiment, built the town that bears his name in 1880 in order to

attract and retain a superior type of working-man, who would in turn be "elevated and refined" by the physical setting. This would mean contented employees and a consequent reduction in absenteeism, drinking and shirking on the job. Furthermore, such workers were expected to be less susceptible to the exhortation of "agitators" than the demoralized laborers of the city slums. His town would protect his company from labor unrest and strikes.[36]

And, we should add, the whole enterprise was supposed to make 6 percent on the capital invested. The Pullman strike of 1894 was a fitting epitaph to such a dream, demonstrating that direct unified control by the capitalists over the lives of labor in both the work place and the living place is an explosive issue.

The Pullman strike merely confirmed what had in any case been slowly dawning upon the capitalist producers throughout the 19th century. The direct confrontation between capital and labor in the living place exacerbates class tensions and conflict markedly because labor can easily identify the enemy—whether it be in company housing, the company store, company social services, or in the work place itself. It was no accident that some of the fiercest strikes and confrontations—such as Homestead in 1892 and Pullman in 1894—occurred in company towns. Under such conditions it is advantageous for the capitalist producers to seek out mediating influences that diffuse the target of labor's discontent. The privatization of housing provision, the creation of a separate housing landlord class, the creation of innumerable intermediaries in the retail and wholesale sector, and government provision of social services and public goods, all help to accomplish this. These measures also serve to socialize part of the costs of the reproduction of labor power and to facilitate the mobility of labor. For all of these reasons, the industrial capitalists seek to withdraw entirely from any direct involvement in the provision or management of the built environment.

The general proposition that Pullman had in mind, divorced from its paternalism and its tight, unified, and direct control aspects, is still important. The breakdown of the binding links of the old social order was clearly necessary if the new industrial work discipline was to be imposed upon the reluctant peasant or artisan. But this breakdown posed its own problems for social control and threatened the economic and social stability of the new order in a variety of ways. Bourgeois reformers sought to counter such threats and have long argued that proper housing, health care, education, and the like, are essential if workers are to become satisfied, virtuous, and solid citizens capable and willing to perform work tasks efficiently and thereby to do their bit to enhance the accumulation of capital.[37] Conversely, the typical industrial city, with its slums and overcrowding, its war of all against all, its signs of "moral degeneration" and vice, its dirt and grime and disease, was regarded as unconducive to the formation of a respectable working-class citizenry. Sometimes the reform strategy rests on a rather simple-minded environmental determinism—the idea that good housing creates good workers periodically appears on the stage of bourgeois reform thought, usually with not very effective consequences. But in its more sophisticated

form, bourgeois reform proved capable of tapping and organizing the relation between working and living in a manner that indeed did contribute to the reestablishment of social stability and to the creation of a relatively well-satisfied work force. And in the course of this effort, the reformers defined the meaning of a use value in the built environment for labor in a certain way. Capital seeks to intervene—this time indirectly through bourgeois reform and by means of ideological and political mechanisms—because to do so serves its own purposes and strengthens its hand in its historic struggle with labor. But as the Pullman strike epitomizes, labor is not always a willing and docile partner in such manipulations.

This brings us to the second aspect of the connection between working and living in capitalist society. Marx's materialist posture led him to regard the relationship to nature as perhaps the most fundamental relation ordering human affairs. This relationship is itself expressed primarily through the work process that transforms the raw materials of nature into use values. The mode of organizing this work process—the mode of production—is therefore the basis upon which Marx builds his investigations. To put it this way is not to engage in a simplistic economic determinism; it merely advances the thesis that the relation to nature is the most fundamental aspect of human affairs. Industrial capitalism, armed with the factory system, organized the work process in a manner that transformed the relation between the worker and nature into a travesty of even its former very limited self. Because the worker was reduced to a "thing," the worker became alienated from his or her product, from the manner of producing it, and, ultimately, from nature itself.[38]

That there was something degrading and "unnatural" about such a work process was apparent even to bourgeois consciousness. Indeed, the organization of the factory system appeared just as unnatural to the bourgeois as it felt to those who had to live out their daily lives under its regimen. This understanding, as Raymond Williams points out, was achieved by landed capital well before the industrial revolution:

The clearing of parks as "Arcadian" prospects depended on the completed system of exploitation of the agricultural and genuinely pastoral lands beyond the park boundaries. . . . [These] are related parts of the same process—superficially opposed in taste but only because in the one case the land is being organized for production, where tenants and labourers will work, while in the other case it is being organized for consumption. . . . Indeed it can be said of these eighteenth century arranged landscapes not only, as is just, that this was the high point of agrarian bourgeois art, but that they succeeded in creating in the land below their windows and terraces . . . a rural landscape . . . from which the facts of production had been banished.[39]

With the advent of industrial capitalism the penchant for actively countering in their own consumption sphere what they were organizing for others in the production sphere became even more emphatic for the bourgeois. The Romantic poets in Britain—led by Wordsworth and Coleridge —and writers like Emerson and Thoreau in the United States epitomized this reaction to the new industrial order. And the reaction did not remain confined to the realms of the ideologists. It was put into practice in the building of rural estates by the bourgeoisie, the establishment of the country mansion, the flight from the industrial city, and, ultimately, in the design of what Walker calls "the suburban solution."[40] The attempt to "bring nature back into the city" by writers and designers such as Olmsted and Ebenezer Howard in the 19th century, and Ian McHarg and Lewis Mumford in the 20th, attests to the continuity of this theme in bourgeois thought and practice.[41]

But if the bourgeoisie felt it, the artisan and displaced peasant experienced the alienation from nature very concretely, and they reacted no less vigorously whenever they could. William Blake, the spokesman for the artisan class, complained bitterly of those "dark satanic mills" and swore with his usual revolutionary fervor that we would "build Jerusalem in England's green and pleasant land." Faced with the brutalizing and degrading routine of the work process in the factory, the workers themselves sought ways to ameliorate it. In part they did so by resorting to the same mystifications as the bourgeoisie, and thus came to share a common romantic image of nature. When asked why the Lowell mill girls wrote so much about the beauties of nature, for example, the editor of their paper responded: "Why is it that the desert-traveller looks forward upon the burning, boundless waste, and sees pictured before his aching eyes, some verdant oasis?"[42] But merely to dream of some romantic idealized nature in the midst of the desert of the factory was scarcely enough, no matter how much it did to help the laborer through the long and tedious day. Consequently, as Bender reports: "Residents of Lowell made their periodic and appreciative contact with the natural landscape in a variety of ways. Besides using the cemetery and the public park, they sought nature through flights of fancy, through views from their windows, by walking out of the city (despite the non-trespassing signs . . .), and through summer visits to the country."[43]

The response rested on a mystification, of course, for it reduced "nature" to a leisure time concept, as something to be "consumed" in the course of restful recuperation from what was in fact a degrading relation to nature in the most fundamental of all human activities—work. But the mystification had bitten deep into the consciousness of all elements in society. To talk now of the relation to nature is to conjure up images of mountains and streams and seas and lakes and trees and green grass, far from the coal-face, the assembly line, and the factory, where the real transformation of nature is continuously being wrought.

But there is a sense in which this is a necessary and unavoidable mystification under capitalism. Without it, life would be scarcely bearable. And progressive elements within the bourgeoisie knew this to be as true for their workers as for themselves. Hardly surprisingly, therefore, the bourgeois reformers, often under the guise of moral universals and a romantic imagery, frequently sought to procure for their workers reasonable access to "nature." Olmsted, perhaps the most spectacular of these reformers in 19th-century America, saw that "the spontaneous interest of the worker was a more effective stimulus to work than any artificially imposed regimen," and it was a short step from this to proposing parks and sylvan suburbs as an antidote to the usual daily harassments of urban industrial life.[44] Turned into practice, in Olmsted's day primarily for the middle classes, but increasingly in modern times for the "respectable" working class, this solution to the problems of urban-industrial life has had a powerful effect upon the physical landscapes of our cities. The counterpoint between nature—represented by pastoral images of the country—and a work process represented by the urban and the industrial, is central to the history of the capitalist mode of production. And the counterpoint contains a tension between what Raymond Williams calls "a necessary materialism and a necessary humanity," adding:

Often we try to resolve it by dividing work and leisure, or society and the individual, or city and country, not only in our minds but in suburbs and garden cities, town houses and country cottages, the week and the weekend. But we then usually find that the . . . captains of the change, have arrived earlier and settled deeper; have made, in fact, a more successful self-division. The country house . . . was one of the first forms of this temporary resolution, and in the nineteenth century as many were built by the new lords of capitalist production as survived, improved, from the old lords. . . . It remains remarkable that so much of this settlement has been physically imitated, down to details of semidetached villas and styles of leisure and weekends. An immensely productive capitalism, in all its stages, has extended both the resources and the modes which, however unevenly, provide and contain forms of response to its effects.[45]

These "forms of response" serve to define in part the meaning of use values in the built environment for labor. The residents of the contemporary suburbs, whether workers or bourgeois, are no less anxious, for example, to banish "the facts of production" from their purview than were the 18th-century landlords because those facts are, for the most part, unbearable. And insofar as workers in conjunction with the capitalists have found ways to do just this, they have created an urban landscape and a way of life that are founded on what Williams calls "an effective and imposing mystification"—but a mystification that combines elements of necessity and cruel hoax. Hanging onto some sense of an unalienated relation to nature makes life bearable for the worker if only because it leads to a realistic appraisal of what has been lost and what potentially can be gained. But the romantic mystification of nature conceals rather than reveals the actual source of the sense of loss and alienation that pervades capitalist society. Bourgeois art, literature, urban design, and "designs for urban living" offer certain conditions in the living place as compensation for what can never truly be compensated for in the work place. Capital, in short, seeks to draw labor into a Faustian bargain: accept a packaged relation to nature in the living place as just and adequate compensation for an alienating and degrading relation to nature in the work place. And if labor refuses to be drawn in spite of all manner of seductions, blandishments, and a dominant ideology mobilized by the bourgeois, then capital must impose it because the landscape of capitalist society must in the final analysis respond to the accumulation needs of capital, rather than to the very real human requirements of labor.

The interventions of capital: A conclusion. Capital seeks to discipline labor as much in the home as in the factory because it is only in terms of an all-embracing domination of labor in every facet of its life that the "work ethic" and the "bourgeois values" necessarily demanded by the capitalist process can be created and secured. The promotion of homeownership for workers establishes the workers' allegiance to the principle of private property and therefore fits with this general stratagem. Sometimes conflicting with this drive we see that capital also needs to organize the consumption of the workers to ensure that it is cheap and rational from the standpoint of accumulation. The collectivization of consumption tends to take away the sense of individual responsibility and thereby undercuts the notion of bourgeois individualism if pushed too far. And running as a counterthread in all of this we see the need on the part of capital to promote in the work force a sense of satisfaction and contentment that will lead to spontaneous cooperation and efficiency in the work place. This condition cannot be cultivated without giving the worker at least the illusion of freedom of choice in the living place and of a healthy and satisfying relation to nature in the consumption sphere. Such illusions are pervasive but not always easy to sustain in the face of the realities enforced by the necessities of accumulation for accumulation's sake, production for production's sake. And the conditions in the work place can never be that easily concealed, no matter how mountainous the mystifications.

Nevertheless, the response of labor to its own condition is constantly subjected to the interventions and mediations of capital. As labor seeks to reorganize its mode of living to compensate for the degradations and disciplines of factory work, so capital seeks to colonize and pervert these efforts for its own purposes, sometimes to be turned cruelly against labor in the course of class struggle. Labor strives to raise its living standards by reducing the cost of living and increasing the use values it can command, but capital constantly seeks to subvert this drive, often through the agency of the state, into a reduction in the value of labor power and into "rational" modes of consumption understood from the standpoint of accumulation. As labor seeks relief from a degrading relation to nature in the work place, so capital seeks to parlay that into a mystified relation to nature in the consumption sphere. As labor seeks more control over the collective conditions of its existence, so capital seeks to establish collectivized forms of consumption and individual homeownership. The power of capital is omnipresent in the very definition of "a use value in the built environment for labor."

Conflicts in the living place are, we can conclude, mere reflections of the underlying tension between capital and labor. Appropriators and the construction faction mediate the forms of conflict—they stand between capital and labor and thereby shield the real source of tension from view. The surface appearance of conflicts around the built environment—the struggles against the landlord or against urban renewal—conceals a hidden essence that is nothing more than the struggle between capital and labor.

Capital may be omnipresent in such struggles, but it is neither omniscient nor omnipotent. The dynamics of accumulation require periodic rationalizations through crises that affect the working class in the form of bouts of widespread unemployment. At such moments the plans to coopt labor by the provision of "healthful and satisfying" living environments, by a contented relation to nature in the living place, go awry. In using the built environment as a coercive tool over consumption, capital ultimately coerces itself because it sets the conditions for the realization of values quite literally in a sea of concrete. And once committed, capital cannot go back. Pullman discovered this elemental fact in his ill-fated model town. When conditions of overaccumulation became apparent in the economy at large it became necessary to lay off workers, but Pullman could not do so because the profits to be had from the town were contingent upon full employment in the factory. The solution for the individual capitalist is to withdraw from the production of consumption fund items for the workers he or she employs. But the problem remains for the capitalist system as a whole. As problems of overaccumulation arise in capitalist societies—and arise they must—so the most well-laid plans of the capitalist fall by the wayside and the mechanisms for mystification, cooptation, disciplining labor, and inculcating the work ethic and bourgeois virtues, begin to crumble. And it is at just such times that labor recognizes that the bargain that it has struck with capital is no bargain at all but founded on an idealized mystification. The promises of capital are seen to be just that and incapable of fulfillment. And it also becomes evident that the needs of labor for use values in the built environment are incapable of being met by the captains of the system who promise so much but who can deliver so little.

Class consciousness, community consciousness, and competition

The phrase "the standard of living of labor" plainly cannot be understood outside of the context of actual class struggles fought over a long period in particular places around the organization of both work and living. This continuously shifting standard defines the needs of labor with respect to use values—consumption fund items—in the built environment. Individual workers have different needs, of course, according to their position in the labor force, their familial situation, and their individual requirements. At the same time, the processes of wage rate determination in the work place yield different quantities of exchange value to workers in different occupational categories. The social power that this money represents can be used to procure control over certain use values in the built environment. The way this money is used affects the appropriation of rent and the functioning of the price signals that induce the flow of capital into the production of new consumption fund items. We can envisage three general situations.

Consider, first, a situation in which each worker seeks independently to command for his or her own private use the best bundle of resources in the best location. We envisage a competitive war of all against all, a society in which the ethic of "possessive individualism" has taken root in the consciousness of workers in a very fundamental way. If the use values available in the built environment are limited, which is usually the case, then individuals make use of their market power and bid for scarce resources in the most advantageous locations. At its most elemental level this competition is for survival chances, for each worker knows that the ability to survive is dependent upon the ability to secure access to a particular bundle of resources in a reasonably healthy location. There is also competition to acquire "market capacity"—that bundle of attitudes, understandings, and skills that permits the worker to sell his or her labor power at a higher wage rate than the average.[46] Symbols of status, prestige, rank, and importance (even self-respect) may also be acquired by procuring command over particular resources in prestigious locations. These symbols may be useful in that they help a worker gain an easier entry into a particularly privileged stratum within the wage-labor force. And finally we can note that if the relation to nature in the work place is felt to be as degrading as it truly is, then there is a positive incentive to seek a location far enough away that the "facts of production" are in no way represented in the landscape. In other words, workers may compete to get as far as possible away from the work place (the automobile proves particularly useful for this purpose).

The competitive situation that we have here outlined is in most respects identical to that assumed in neoclassical models of land use determination in urban areas.[47] Individual households, such models assume, attempt to maximize their utility by competing with each other for particular bundles of goods in particular locations subject to a budget constraint. If it is assumed that the two most important "goods" being competed for are locations with lower aggregate transportation costs and housing space, then it can be shown with relative ease that individuals will distribute themselves in space according to (1) the distribution of employment opportunities, usually assumed to be collected together in one central location, and (2) the relative marginal propensities to consume transportation services and living space in the context of the overall budget constraint. Competitive bidding under these conditions will generate a differential rent surface that, in the case of a single employment center, declines with distance from the center at the same time as it distributes individuals by income in space. In this case the ability to appropriate differential rent is entirely created by competitive behavior within the working class. Also, if new development is typically distributed in response to the pricing signals set by such differential rents, then it is easy

to show that a spatial structure to the built environment will be created that reflects, to a large degree, social and wage stratifications within the labor force.

The second situation that we wish to consider is one in which collective action in space—community action—is important. The pervasive externality effects and the collective use of many items in the built environment mean that it is in the self-interest of individuals to pursue modest levels of collective action.[48] Workers who are homeowners know that the value of the savings tied up in the house depends on the actions of others. It is in their common interest to collectively curb "deviant" behaviors, bar "noxious" facilities, and ensure high standards of public service. This collectivization of action may go well beyond that required out of pure individual self-interest. A consciousness of place, "community consciousness," may emerge as a powerful force that spawns competition between communities for scarce public investment funds, and the like. Community competition becomes the order of the day.

This process relates to the appropriation of rent in an interesting way. Community control enables those in control to erect barriers to investment in the built environment. The barriers may be selective—the exclusion of low-income housing, for example—or more or less across the board, a ban on all forms of future growth. Actions of this sort have been common in suburban jurisdictions in the United States in recent years. The cartel powers of local government are in effect being mobilized to control investment through a variety of legal and planning devices. Homeowners may use these controls to maintain or enhance the value of their properties. Developers may seek to use such controls for rather different purposes. But "community consciousness" typically creates small legal "islands" within which monopoly rents are appropriatable, often by one faction of labor at the expense of another faction.

This latter situation gives rise to internecine conflicts within the working class along parochialist community-based lines. The spatial structure of the city is very different under these conditions compared to the product of individual competition.

The third kind of situation we can envisage is that of a fully class-conscious proletariat struggling against all forms of exploitation, whether they be in the work place or in the living place. Workers do not use their social power as individuals to seek individual solutions; they do not compete with each other for survival chances, for ability to acquire market capacity, for symbols of status and prestige. They fight collectively to improve the lot of all workers everywhere and eschew those parochialist forms of community action that typically lead one faction of labor to benefit at the expense of another (usually the poor and underprivileged).

Under such conditions the appropriation of rent cannot be attributed to the competitive behavior of individual workers or of whole communities. It has to be interpreted, rather, as something forced upon labor in the course of class struggle. A differential rent surface may arise in an urban area, but it does so not because labor automatically engages in competitive bidding, but because the class power of the appropriators is used to extract a rent to the maximum possible, given that resources are scarce and that they exist in a relative space. Because we witness a consequent social stratification (according to income) in space, and a development process that exacerbates this social ordering, we cannot infer that this is simply a reflection of individual workers expressing their "subjective utilities" through the market. Indeed, it may express the exact opposite—the power of the appropriators to force certain choices on workers no matter what the individual worker may think or believe. The power to appropriate rent is a class relation and we have to understand it that way if we are to understand how residential differentiation emerges within cities and the degree to which this phenomenon is the outcome of free or forced choices.[49]

The three situations we have examined —competitive individualism, community action, and class struggle—are points on a continuum of possibilities. We cannot automatically assume labor to be at any particular point on this continuum. This is something to be discovered by concrete investigations of particular situations. The United States, for example, appears to be more strongly dominated by competitive individualism and community consciousness compared to the more class-conscious working class in Europe. From the standpoint of capital, individual and community competition is advantageous because it then seems as if the appropriation of rent results from labor's own actions rather than from the actions of the appropriators themselves. The overt forms of conflict around the built environment depend, therefore, upon the outcome of a deeper and often hidden ideological struggle for the consciousness of those doing the struggling. This deeper struggle between individual, community, and class alignments and consciousness, provides the context in which daily struggles over everyday issues occur.

A conclusion

The capitalist mode of production forces a separation between working and living at the same time as it reintegrates them in complex ways. The superficial appearance of conflict in contemporary urban-industrial society suggests that there is indeed a dichotomy between struggles in the work place and in the living place and that each kind of struggle is fought according to different principles and rules. Struggles around the consumption fund for labor, which have been the focus of attention in this paper, seemingly arise out of the inevitable tensions between appropriators seeking rent, builders seeking profit, financiers seeking interest, and labor seeking to counter the secondary forms of exploitation that occur in the living place. All of this seems self-evident enough.

But the manner and form of such everyday overt conflicts are a reflection of a much deeper tension with less easily identifiable manifestations—a struggle over the definition and meaning of use values, of the standard of living of labor, of the quality of life, of consciousness, and even of human nature itself. From this standpoint, the overt struggles between landlord-appropriators, builders, and labor, which we began by examining, are to be seen as mediated manifestations of the deep underlying conflict between capital and labor. Capital seeks definitions, seeks to impose meanings, conducive to the productivity of labor and to the consumption of the commodities that capitalists can profitably produce. Like Dickens's *Dombey and Son*, capital deals "in hides but never in hearts." But labor seeks its own meanings, partly derived out of a rapidly fading memory of artisan and peasant life, but also out of the ineluctable imperative to learn what it is to be human. "Human nature" has, then, no universal meaning, but is being perpetually recast in the fires of restless struggle. And even though capital may dominate and impose upon us a predominantly *capitalist* sense of human

nature, the resistances are always there, and the internal tensions within the capitalist order—between private appropriation and socialized production, between individualism and social interdependency—are so dramatic that we, each of us, internalize a veritable maelstrom of hopes and fears into our present conduct. The human nature that results, with all of its complex ambiguities of desire, need, creativity, estrangement, selfishness, and sheer human concern, forms the very stuff out of which the overt struggles of daily life are woven. The manner in which these struggles are fought likewise depends upon a deeper determination of consciousness—individual, community, or class-based as the case may be—of those who do the struggling. From this standpoint it must surely be plain that the separation between working and living is at best a superficial estrangement, an apparent breaking asunder of what can never be kept apart. And it is at this deeper level, too, that we can more clearly see the underlying unity between work-based and "community"-based conflicts. They are not mere mirror images of each other, but distorted representations, mediated by many intervening forces and circumstances, which mystify and render opaque the fundamental underlying class antagonism upon which the capitalist mode of production is founded. And it is, of course, the task of science to render clear through analysis what is mystified and opaque in daily life.

NOTES

1. This distinction derives from Marx. See Karl Marx, *Capital* (New York: 1967), vol. 2, p. 210; and idem, *The Grundrisse* (Harmondsworth, Middlesex: 1973), pp. 681–87.

2. See Marx, *Capital*, vol. 1, p. 171.

3. This condition can be derived directly from Marxian theory by bringing together the analyses presented in Marx, *Capital*, vol. 1, pp. 591–640; vol. 2, pp. 515–16.

4. Marx, *Capital*, vol. 3, p. 773.

5. Ibid., chap. 37.

6. See David Harvey, *Social Justice and the City* (London and Baltimore: Edward Arnold, 1973), chaps. 2, 5.

7. For a more detailed argument see David Harvey, "Class-Monopoly Rent, Finance Capital, and the Urban Revolution," *Regional Studies* 8 (1974): 239–55.

8. John R. Kellet, *The Impact of Railways on Victorian Cities* (London: Routledge & K. Paul, 1969), chap. 11.

9. G. R. Taylor, "The Beginning of Mass Trans-

266

portation in Urban America," *Smithsonian Journal of History* 1, nos. 1–2; 35–50, 31–54; J. Tarr, "From City to Suburb: The 'Moral' Influence of Transportation Technology," in *American 'Urban History*, ed. Alexander B. Callow (New York: Oxford University Press, 1973); and David R. Ward, *Cities and Immigrants* (New York: Oxford University Press, 1971).

10. The McCone Commission Report on the Watts rebellion in Los Angeles in 1964 attributed much of the discontent to the sense of entrapment generated out of lack of access to transportation.

11. Marx, *Grundrisse*, Introduction.

12. Quoted in Counter Information Services, *The Recurrent Crisis of London* (CIS, 52 Shaftesbury Ave., London, W.1).

13. C. B. McPherson, *The Political Theory of Possessive Individualism* (Oxford: Clarendon Press, 1962); and J. Rex and T. Moore, *Race, Community, and Conflict* (London: Oxford University Press, 1975).

14. M. Stone, "Housing and Class Struggle," *Antipode*, vol. 7, no. 2 (1975); and David Harvey, "The Political Economy of Urbanization in Advanced Capitalist Societies: The Case of the United States," in *The Social Economy of Cities*, ed. G. Gappert and H. Rose (Beverly Hills, Calif.: Urban Affairs Annual, no. 9 [1975]).

15. The relation between values and prices in Marxian theory is highly problematic and involves us in the celebrated "transformation problem." To avoid making silly mistakes it is important to bear in mind that the value of labor power is not automatically represented by the wage rate.

16. T. R. Malthus, *Principles of Political Economy* (New York: Kelley, 1836), p. 321.

17. Marx, *Grundrisse*, Introduction.

18. Thomas Bender, *Toward an Urban Vision: Ideas and Institutions in Nineteenth Century America* (Lexington: University Press of Kentucky, 1975), pp. 28–29; and R. M. Tryon, *Household Manufactures in the United States, 1640–1860* (Chicago: University of Chicago Press, 1917).

19. E. P. Thompson, *The Making of the English Working Class* (Harmondsworth, Middlesex: 1968), p. 455.

20. Ibid., chap. 10; and E. J. Hobsbawm, *Labouring Men* (London: Weidenfeld and Nicholson, 1964), chap. 7.

21. Marx, *Capital*, vol. 2, p. 516; Dickens satirized the role of bourgeois philanthropy in relation to workers' consumption in *Hard Times*.

22. Marx, *Capital*, vol. 2, p. 408.

23. The theme of collective consumption has been examined in some detail by the French urbanists. See E. Preteceille, *Equipements, Collectifs, Structures Urbaines, et Consommation Sociale* (Paris: Centre de Sociologie Urbaine, 1975); and M. Castells, "Collective Consumption and Urban Contradictions in Advanced Capitalist Societies," in *Patterns of Advanced Societies*, ed. L. Lindberg (New York: 1975).

24. S. Kuznets, *Capital in the American Economy: Its Formation and Financing* (Princeton, N.J.: Princeton University Press, 1961).

25. See the accounts by J. Flink, *The Car Culture* (Cambridge, Mass.: M.I.T. Press, 1975); and H. Leavitt, *Superhighway—Super Hoax* (Garden City, N.J.: Doubleday, 1970).

26. An interesting attempt to look at this is J. E. Vance, "Housing the Worker: The Employment Linkage as a Force in Urban Structure," *Economic Geography* 42 (1966): 294–325.

27. S. Pollard, *The Genesis of Modern Management* (Cambridge: Harvard University Press, 1965), pp. 161, 207.

28. Harry Braverman, *Labor and Monopoly Capital* (New York: Monthly Review Press, 1974), p. 139.

29. Ibid., p. 151.

30. Pollard, *Modern Management*, p. 115.

31. Flink, *Car Culture*, p. 89.

32. All of the quotes that follow are to be found in Antonio Gramsci, *Selections from the Prison Notebooks* (New York: International Publishers, 1971), pp. 285–318.

33. Bender, *Urban Vision*, p. 197.

34. Ibid., p. 63.

35. See Michael Foucault, *Madness and Civilization* (New York: Pantheon Books, 1965); Pollard, *Modern Management*, p. 162; David Rothman, *The Discovery of the Asylum* (Boston: Little, Brown, 1971); and Samuel Bowles and Herbert Gintis, *Schooling in Capitalist America* (New York: Basic Books, 1976). The relation between school and factory is portrayed with extraordinary insight in Charles Dickens, *Hard Times*.

36. S. Buder, *Pullman* (New York: Oxford University Press, 1967), p. 44.

37. Much of this material as well as the argument is drawn from R. A. Walker, "The Suburban Solution" (Ph.D. dissertation, Department of Geography and Environmental Engineering, Johns Hopkins University, Baltimore, 1976).

38. Karl Marx, "The Economic and Philosophic Manuscripts of 1844," in *Karl Marx–Frederick Engels Collected Works*, vol. 3 (New York: 1975). See also A. Schmidt, *Marx's Concept of Nature* (London: 1971).

39. R. Williams, *The Country and the City* (London: Oxford University Press, 1973), p. 124.

40. Walker, "Suburban Solution."

41. Ebenezer Howard, *Garden Cities of Tomorrow* (London: 1955), wrote, for example, of "so

laying out a Garden City that, as it grows, the free gifts of Nature—fresh air, sunlight, breathing room and playing room—shall be retained in all needed abundance, and so employing the resources of modern science that Art may supplement Nature, and life may become an abiding joy and delight," p. 127.

42. Bender, *Urban Vision*, p. 90.

43. Ibid.

44. Bender discusses this aspect of Olmsted's thought in detail.

45. Williams, *Country and City*, p. 294.

46. See Anthony Giddens, *The Class Structure of the Advanced Societies* (London: Harper and Row, 1973), p. 103.

47. See, for example, W. Alonso, *Location and Land Use* (Cambridge: Harvard University Press, 1964); and E. S. Mills, *Studies in the Structure of the Urban Economy* (Baltimore: Johns Hopkins Press, 1972).

48. The theory of self-interested collective action is laid out in Mancur Olson, *The Logic of Collective Action* (Cambridge: Harvard University Press, 1965), but the theory of community is a mess that will require a good deal of sorting out.

49. I have attempted a preliminary analysis on this theme in David Harvey, "Class Structure in a Capitalist Society and the Theory of Residential Differentiation," in *Processes in Physical and Human Geography*, ed. M. Chisholm, P. Hagget, and R. F. Peel (London: Heinemann Educational, 1975).

CHAPTER 7

The contradictions and problems of capitalist society

Capitalist society is bound by its own contraditions. The advanced capitalist state cannot sustain private capitalist accumulation and, at the same time, legitimize the relations of advanced capitalism. On the economic level, the state cannot solve its own fiscal crisis that results from increasing state expenditures to assure private capital accumulation.[1] On the level of legitimation, the state cannot continue to maintain its credibility as it fails to solve the problems that it either creates or fosters in its promotion of the capitalist economy. Even its attempts at pacification through social services, on the one hand, and repression, on the other, are doomed to defeat both on the economic level and on the level of legitimation. Capitalist society is in a crisis that can be solved only in the transformation to a socialist society.

As the state expands as the primary instrument for advancing capitalism, it will necessarily have to develop stronger and more pervasive means of dominating the population. If the problems inherent to late capitalism cannot be solved by state intervention (by assisting capital accumulation and providing social services), the population will have to be more effectively controlled. Thus it is that the crisis of late capitalism signals the development of a new mode of human domination.[2] This is a domination that is in the first instance ideological, in restricting our conception of life chances and the problems of capitalism. Furthermore, it is a domination that is exercised in the physical control of our daily lives. The modern capitalist state is the agency of these forms of domination.

But, these facts notwithstanding, class struggle assures a conflict within capitalist society. The capitalist state, in not only failing to eliminate class struggle but in fact increasing it, contains the contradiction for its own ultimate demise. While expanding the function of the state means more state control, it also means that larger portions of the population become politicized. Especially for the "unproductive" segments of the population, the portion that does not reproduce itself through the productive labor market, there is increased involvement in the reproduction of the capitalist state—and the entire capitalist system. For state workers, students, the unemployed, welfare recipients, and housewives, a political consciousness develops around their condition, a consciousness that questions the legitimacy of the existing system.[3] The entire working class (productive and unproductive) is thus joined in a common political context.

A problem for the modern capitalist state is integrating the unproductive, nonsurplus-value portion of the population into the system of capitalist domination. Excluded from the traditional relations of capitalist domination—in the market economy—this new and increasing segment nevertheless must be controlled.[4] The problem cuts two ways: first, lack of integration generates its own sources of political rebellion, and second, integration actually politicizes this segment in the way that the working class in general is politicized. Either way, the emergence of a new and increasing fraction of the working class produces yet another crisis in the capitalist system. This is a crisis of legitimation that promotes a critical consciousness and further mobilizes the working class.[5] As the state attempts to promote and regulate capitalism further, it creates forms of work that cannot be successfully integrated into capitalist domination. The recourse for the state is domination through coercion, explicitly through crime control and criminal justice. For the worker, the capitalist system loses its legitimacy and political action becomes necessary.

The moral life of capitalist society is in crisis as well. The ultimate contradiction of capitalism is that it destroys the moral fabric of society. Contemporary capitalist society is caught in what Tillich calls a *sacred void*, the human predicament on both a spiritual and a sociopolitical level. Among the vacuous characteristics of present civilization are a mode of production that enslaves workers, an analytic rationalism that saps the vital forces of life and transforms everything (including human beings) into an object of calculation and control, the loss of feeling for the translucence of nature and the sense of history, the demotion of our world to a mere environment, a secularized humanism that cuts us off from our creative sources, the demonic quality of the political state, and the hopelessness of the future. We all experience the void:

> Little is left of our present civilization which does not indicate to a sensitive mind the presence of this vacuum, this lack of ultimacy and substantial power in language and education, in politics and philosophy, in the development of personalities, in the life of communities. Who of us has never been shocked by this void when he has used traditional or untraditional, secular or religious language to make himself understandable and has not succeeded and has made a vow of silence to himself, only to break it a few hours later? This is symbolic of our whole civilization.[6]

The void is historical, beginning, in the first part of the 19th century, with the emergence of capitalism and the breakdown of religious tradition under the impact of the Enlightenment and bourgeois liberalism. "First among the educated classes, then increasingly in the mass of industrial workers, religion lost its 'immediacy,' it ceased to offer an unquestioned sense of direction and relevance to human living."[7] Philosophies and popular movements have since attempted to restore or rediscover an ultimate meaning of life and a direction for living.

Recognizing the need for a new religious philosophy, and unable to accept the traditional and conventional political and religious views, Tillich sought a social and religious philosophy that would take seriously the social and economic situation of contemporary society. He found in socialism the best resources for dealing with the realities and for constructing a new social order. In making the "socialist decision," he urged others to enter into the socialist movement to pave the way for a future union of religion and socialist social order.

> We stand in a period of dissolution. A new age of unity is arising. Socialism will form its economic and social foundation. And Christianity stands before the task to convey to this development its moral and religious powers and thereby to initiate a great new synthesis of religion and social structure.[8]

Sensed here is the beginning of a new age in which the old order would give way to a socialist order combined with an awareness of the divine in human life.

NOTES

1. James O'Connor, *The Fiscal Crisis of the State* (New York: St. Martin's Press, 1973).

2. Trent Schroyer, *The Critique of Domination: The Origins and Development of Critical Theory* (New York: Braziller, 1973), pp. 238–47.

3. Jurgen Habermas, *Legitimation Crisis* (Boston: Beacon Press, 1975), pp. 66–70.

4. Claus Offe, "The Abolition of Market Control and the Problem of Legitimacy," *Kapitalistate*, no. 1 (1973), pp. 109–16.

5 Alan Wolfe, *The Limits of Legitimacy: Political Contradictions of Contemporary Capitalism* (New York: Free Press, 1977).

6. Paul Tillich, *The Protestant Era* (Chicago: University of Chicago Press, 1948), p. 60.

7. Paul Tillich, *Theology of Culture*, ed. Robert C. Kimball (New York: Oxford University Press, 1959), p. 106.

8. Quoted, from the German, in John R. Stumme, "Introduction," Paul Tillich, *The Socialist Decision*, trans. Franklin Sherman (New York: Harper & Row, 1977), p. xiii.

READING 7-1 ————————————————————————

The fiscal crisis of the state*

JAMES O'CONNOR

At present, the United States federal government employs about 2.5 million civilian workers in 80 departments and agencies and nearly 4 million members of the armed forces, and total state and local government, employment is roughly 8.5 million. In the federal government, employment is greatest in military and international relations agencies and the postal service, which employ 1 million and 600,000 workers, respectively. At the state and local level, employment is concentrated in the fields of education (4 million workers), health and hospitals (1 million), highways (550,000), and police protection (450,000).[1] In brief, a sizable part of the "new working class" employed in nondirectly productive, service, and similar occupations is employed by the state.

In addition to the 11 million workers employed directly by the state, there are countless wage and salary earners—perhaps as many as 25 to 30 million—who are employed by private capital dependent in

---

*From *The Corporations and the State: Essays in the Theory of Capitalism and Imperialism*, by James O'Connor (New York: Harper & Row, 1974), pp. 105–151. Copyright © 1974 by James O'Connor. Reprinted by permission of Harper & Row, Publishers, Inc.

whole or in part on state contracts and facilities. Workers in such industries as military and space, branches of capital goods, construction, transportation, and others, are *indirectly* employed by state capital. Further, tens of thousands of doctors, welfare workers, and other self-employed and privately employed professionals and technicians who use facilities provided by the state are also dependent in whole or in part on the state budget. Finally, tens of millions of men and women are dependent on the budget as clients and recipients of state services; these include nearly all students at all levels of education, welfare recipients, and users of public health, hospital, recreational, and other facilities.

There is no way to measure the total number of people who are related to each other through the state budget, and who are dependent on the budget for their material well-being; everyone is in part dependent on the state, and for millions of poor people, particularly minority people, this dependence runs very deep. Perhaps one-quarter to one-third of the labor force is wholly dependent on the state for basic necessities. And, historically, more and more people have looked to the state for that which they cannot provide themselves. Schools and colleges are bulging at the seams, the welfare roles expand, and state employment holds out the only hope of employment for millions of blacks, young people, retired workers, and women—between 1950 and 1966 the state sector accounted for 25 percent of the total growth of employment in the United States.

During recent years of high taxes and inflation, real wages and salaries of state workers have declined. Better known is the fact that federal, state, and local welfare, health, and education budgets are being frozen or cut across the entire country. And the growing poverty of the state spills over into the private sector, not only in the form of rising taxes that cut into real income, but also in rising prices for services. Because of the absence of new facilities constructed by the state, for example, hospital fees rose by 100 percent from 1957 to 1967, and are expected to rise more than 200 percent from 1968 to 1975.[2]

Progressively tighter budgets, constant or falling real wages and salaries of state employees, and declining welfare expenditures and social services in general have unleashed a torrent of criticism against the state by employees, dependents, and others. Public employee unions grow by leaps and bounds. The American Federation of State, County, and Municipal Employees grew from 150,000 members in 1950 to 400,000 today. Unions are calling more strikes, and strikes are fought for longer periods: in 1953 there were only 30 strikes against state and local governments; in 1966 and 1967, 152 and 181 strikes, respectively. In 1967–68 the American Federation of Teachers alone conducted 32 major walkouts and ministrikes that involved nearly 100,000 teachers.[3] In Massachusetts state employees have created an organization that cuts across occupational and agency lines, and that has mounted a demand for a 20 percent wage and salary increase. In New York 25 percent of the city's union membership are public employees. In the past few years, whole towns and cities have been brought to a standstill as a result of general strikes of municipal employees.

Practical criticism of the state has not been confined to local general strikes, still less to traditional labor union activity. State clients and dependents have been compelled to conduct their struggles around budgetary issues in highly unorthodox ways. Today there are few sectors of the state economy that remain unorganized. Welfare recipients have organized hundreds of welfare rights groups; student organizations have conducted militant struggles in small or large part over the control of the state budget for minority studies programs, student activities, and so on; blacks are struggling in countless ways to force the state to intervene on their behalf; public health workers, doctors, probation officers, prisoners, even patients in public mental hospitals have organized themselves, and seek better work facilities or better treatment and more finances and resources for themselves and the people whom they serve.

A serious revolt against high taxation is also developing. The forms of the present tax revolt are many and varied; the core cities are demanding that suburban commuters pay their "fair share" of city expenditures, and the suburbanites are resisting attempts to organize their communities into metropolitan governments; working-class residential districts organize tax referenda against downtown business interests; and property owners vote into office politicians who promise to reduce property tax burdens.

All of these activities—the demands mounted by state workers and dependents, on the one hand, and the tax revolt, on the other—both reflect and deepen the fiscal crisis of the state, or the gap between expenditures and taxation. Yet, by and large, these struggles have not been fought along class lines, and therefore do not necessarily pose a revolutionary challenge to the United States ruling class. In fact, the popular struggle for the control of state expenditures has been led by liberal forces, and, to a much lesser degree, by militant black and radical forces. And the tax revolt has been all but monopolized by the right wing.

Nevertheless, the state has been unable to develop traditional administrative solutions to these struggles, struggles in which the state itself is one of the contending parties. The state has not yet been able to encapsulate these struggles, nor has it been able to channel frustration, anger, and energy into activities which potentially do not threaten ruling class budgetary control. Whether or not the state can succeed in ameliorating these struggles, whether or not the state can prevent large numbers of people coming together in radical organiza-

tions around budgetary issues, and whether or not the contradiction between right-wing leadership of the tax revolt and liberal-left leadership of the fight for the control of expenditures can be resolved—these are some of the questions raised here.

A political framework for budgetary analysis

The developing economic struggles against the state are rooted in the structural contradictions of United States capitalism. Full comprehension and evaluation of these struggles requires a political framework for an analysis of the state budget. Budgetary theory is a branch of the theory of the state, and thus a brief sketch of the nature of state power is needed.

How do the main production relations in the United States express themselves politically? In the first place, the state is the economic instrument of the dominant stratum of the ruling class—the owners and controllers of the large corporations, who have organized themselves along both interest group and class lines.

Interest group organization, activity, and participation in the state have been studied by McConnell, Hamilton, Kolko, Engler, and others.[4] In Hamilton's words, "there are currently associations of manufacturers, of distributors, and of retailers; there are organizations which take all commerce as their province; and there are federations of local clubs of businessmen with tentacles which reach into the smaller urban centers and market towns. All such organizations are active instruments in the creation of attitudes, in the dissemination of sound opinion, and in the promotion of practices which may become widespread."[5]

In essence, these organizations are self-regulatory private associations which are ordinarily organized along industry rather than regional or other lines, owing to the national character of commodity markets. More often than not, these industry groups use the state to mediate between their members, as well as to provide needed credits, subsidies, technical aid, and general support. Some of the key industry and interest groups are the highway lobby (automobiles, oil, rubber, glass, branches of construction, and so on), the military lobby, oil, cotton textiles, railroads, airlines, radio and television, public utilities, banking, and brokerage. In agriculture, wheat, cotton, sugar, and other growers, together with cattlemen, are also organized into industry associations.

These and other interest groups have appropriated numerous small pieces of state power through a "multiplicity of intimate contacts with the government."[6] They dominate most of the so-called regulatory agencies at the federal, state, and local levels and many bureaus within the Departments of Agriculture and Interior, the Bureau of Highways, and a number of congressional committees. Their specific interests are reflected in the partial or full range of policies of hundreds of national and state government agencies, for example, the Interstate Commerce Commission and other regulatory bodies, Department of Defense, Corps of Engineers, United States Tariff Commission, and Federal Reserve Bank. "What emerges as the most important political reality," McConnell writes in a summary of the politics of interest groups,

is an array of relatively separated political systems, each with a number of elements. These typically include: (1) a federal administrative agency within the executive branch; (2) a heavily committed group of Congressmen and Senators, usually members of a particular committee or subcommittee; (3) a private (or quasi-private) association representing the agency clientele; (4) a quite homogeneous constituency usually composed of local elites. Where dramatic conflicts over policy have occurred, they have appeared as rivalries among the public administrative agencies, but the conflicts are more conspicuous and less important than the agreements among these systems. The most frequent solution to conflict is jurisdictional demarcation

and establishment of spheres of influence. Logrolling, rather than compromise, is the normal pattern of relationship.[7]

By itself, interest group politics is inconsistent with the survival and expansion of capitalism. For one thing, "the interests which keep [the interest groups] going," Hamilton writes, "are too disparate, and the least common denominator of action is too passive to bring into being a completely cohesive union."[8] For another, interest consciousness obviously leads to contradictory policies; enduring interest groups require a sense of "responsibility"—that is, class consciousness. For example, the attempt by regulatory agencies to maintain profitable conditions in a particular industry tends to freeze the pattern of resource allocation, establish monopoly conditions, and so on, which in turn retards capital accumulation and expansion in the economy as a whole. Foreign economic expansion thus becomes increasingly important, as a key mode of economic growth and as a way to transform interest group conflict into interest group harmony. And foreign expansion clearly requires a class-conscious political directorate.

The *class* organization of corporate capital—both its private activity and participation in the state—have been studied by Williams, Weinstein, Kolko, Domhoff, Eakins, and others.[9] These writers have shown that increasing instability and inefficiency attendant upon capitalist production increased investment risk and uncertainty, contributed to crises and depressions, and led to a deficiency of aggregate demand. By the turn of the century, and especially during the New Deal, it was apparent to the vanguard corporate leaders that some form of rationalization of the economy was necessary. And as the 20th century wore on, the owners of corporate capital generated the financial ability, learned the organizational skills, and developed the ideas necessary for their self-regulation as a class.

Thus, it was a class-conscious corporate directorate which controlled the War Industry Board during World War I, parts of the NRA and AAA, and the Office of War Mobilization, the last of the World War II planning agencies. Class-conscious corporate capital today profoundly influences or controls the Department of Defense, agencies within the Commerce and State departments, Treasury Department, Council of Economic Advisers, and Bureau of the Budget. Owing to the necessity of reconciling and compromising conflicts within the corporate ruling class and to the complex and wide-ranging nature of the interests of this class, policy is not dictated by a single directorate but rather by a multitude of private, quasi-public, and public agencies. Policy is formulated within the highly influential Business Advisory Council, in key ruling class universities and policy planning agencies such as the Foreign Policy Association and the Committee for Economic Development, and by the corporate-dominated political parties, and translated into law through legislation written and introduced by the federal executive. The president and his key aides thus have the supreme task of interpreting corporate ruling class interests, and translating these interests into action, not only in terms of immediate economic and political needs, but also in terms of the relations between corporate capital on the one side, and labor and small capital on the other.

This is the second way the production relations are expressed politically: the regulation of the social relations between classes in the interests of maintaining the social order as a whole. Around the turn of the century, labor, socialist, and populist forces posed a potentially serious threat to American capitalism. In a series of political moves designed to prevent popular movements from "removing the extremes of society"—capital and wage labor—the corporate leaders and the political directorate sought, in Marx's words, "to weaken their antagonisms and transform them into a harmonious whole." Lelio Basso writes that

"capitalism can function only thanks to the permanent intervention of the stage to organize the markets and ensure the process of accumulation."[10] The political meaning of this "permanent intervention" is that all elements of the population must be integrated into a coherent system, not rejected by it. Far and away the most important element is organized labor, which was taught a responsible attitude toward corporate capital and society as a whole. Specifically, this required regular cooperation between the leaders of organized labor, the corporations, and the state to head off mass social movements, transform collective bargaining into an instrument of corporate planning, guarantee a high level of employment and wages commensurate with productivity advances, and maintain labor's reproductive powers, with regard not only to the level of private consumption, but also to social insurance, health, education, and general welfare.

Class conflict thus tends to be bureaucratized, encapsulated, administered; qualitative demands originating on the shop floor are transformed by union leaders into quantitative demands that do not threaten "managerial prerogatives"; contradictions between labor and capital at the point of production are displaced or deflected into other spheres. Corporate capital's agencies for regulating the relations between organized labor and the unemployed and poor and itself are numerous—the National Labor Relations Board, National Mediation Board, Federal Mediation and Conciliation Service, Department of Labor, Social Security Administration, Department of Health, Education, and Welfare, congressional committees and subcommittees, and state employment agencies are some of the most important.

The state also regulates the relations between big capital and small capital, between capital based in different regions, and between capital in expanding sectors of the economy and capital in contracting sectors. Monopoly capital requires the political support of local and regional capital for its national and international programs, and thus cannot afford to antagonize the latter needlessly; subsidies must be granted to declining industries and to capital in underdeveloping regions. Deeply involved in managing relations within the ruling class as a whole, and permanently engaged in financing small capital support for monopoly capital, are, among other agencies, the Department of Agriculture, the Department of Commerce, many congressional committees, and federal grant-in-aid programs.

State capitalist budgetary principles and control

Many of these aspects of state power, which are not unique to monopoly capitalism, but which have taken special forms in the 20th century, are extremely expensive. Further, excepting interest group economic needs, to which the elected branch is highly responsive, the new functions of the state require a strong executive branch, supportive class-conscious elements in the Congress, and executive control of the state budget, because they require overall planning. The growth of, and centralization of power within, the executive branch, the multiplication of its functions, the decline of congressionally initiated legislation, the growth of bureaucratically managed governments at the state and local levels, the development of city manager governments, and the spread of the giant supramunicipal authorities—that is, the major trend of our times that signifies the removal of decision making from politics and the substitution of bureaucratic and administrative rule—constitute a familiar story.

Less familiar, but of equal importance, are the corresponding changes in budgetary control. Therefore a review of the changing state budgetary principles, in particular the

process through which the executive appropriated control of the budget, is required.

In the late 19th and the 20th centuries, technological innovations in production and the need to harmonize and stabilize production relations revolutionized the state finances and the budgetary principles on which they were based. The development of science and organized technology, the accumulation of large blocks of capital, and the concentration and integration of the work force needed to be regulated and controlled. As state capitalism and monopolistic industry developed, the budgetary principles of the liberal state were gradually discarded.

One change was the substitution of direct for indirect taxation; another was the surrender of the principle of balanced budgets; still another was the acceptance of an inconvertible paper monetary standard and a new role for loan finance. But most important, there was a steady expansion of state expenditures and an increase in the number and variety of state economic functions.

The evolution of the state budget as an increasing source of monopoly profits has gone hand in hand with the development of the state bureaucracy as the administrative arm of the giant corporations. This is particularly the case in the military, space, foreign loan, and research and development fields, where the lion's share of investment and production costs is borne by the general taxpayer while the profits accrue to the corporations. Further, there is the assumption of government rather than individual risk associated with the operation of the economy. The state underwrites business losses sustained during economic crises and arising from the anarchy of capitalist production. Direct lending, indirect lending via intermediaries, and loan insurance and guarantees socialize business risk and create huge government liabilities that can be guaranteed only by further private capital accumulation and growth—and hence more loans, subsidies, and guarantees. State capitalism is no temporary phenomenon that will be dismantled once capitalism finds its way back to "normalcy," but rather is the integrating principle of the modern economic era.

A brief review of the changing relationships between the representative and executive branches of the state is needed to fully comprehend the character and significance of the revolutionary change in the budget principles of monopoly capitalism. In Britain the budget was transformed into an instrument of the financial control of the crown by the rising middle classes during their struggle for political representation and, finally, political dominance. In the United States revolutionary warfare eliminated the crown, removing any analogous development. From the very beginning, a certain harmony between Congress and the executive existed because both represented more or less perfectly the interests of local and regional capital. The budget was from the start the expression of the material interests of the planter and merchant classes and, later, the farmers, and was always a source of private profit. By the late 19th century, the ascendancy of national capital and the giant regional interest groups began to drive a wedge between the representative and executive branches of the federal government. The latter became more and more responsive to national capital while the former still largely represents regional and local capital, as well as trade union and community interests.

Especially since the turn of the century, the control exercised by the representative body over-appropriations has become increasingly imperfect. The ways in which Congress has disabled itself include the establishment of revolving funds, the creation of government corporations, the refusal to prohibit transfers between appropriations, the authorization of the use of departmental receipts without limitation of amount, and the voting of lump-sum appropriations.[11] The attempt to reestablish control by way of large numbers of specific appropriations, "far from securing to Congress that completeness of financial control which is . . . its constitutional birthright, has served only to make the law less certain and to satisfy Congress with the name, rather than the substance of power."[12] Congressional control after funds have been appropriated has been equally imperfect. It is instructive to compare the situation in the United States with that in Britain, where parliamentary control after appropriations is relatively secure and the House of Commons is able to ensure that its policies are carried out "accurately, faithfully, and efficiently."[13]

Meanwhile class-conscious elements within the executive branch of the federal government have been eager to transform the budget into an instrument of national economic planning in accordance with the needs of national capital. With this aim in mind, the executive has hurried along the consolidation of its own financial powers by mingling appropriations, bringing forward the unexpended balance of former appropriations and backward the anticipated balance of future appropriations, and by incurring coercive deficiencies.[14]

Changes in the formal character of the state budget, however, have been the major steps toward executive financial control. At least three budgetary changes deserve mention. The first was the introduction of the "administrative budget," which coordinates expenditures proposed by the executive, and the creation of the Bureau of the Budget by the Budget and Accounting Act of 1920. The administrative budget is the basic instrument that coordinates the various activities of the congressional committees, which in turn are responsive to the specific industrial, regional, and other interests of private capital. It is the chief mode of "management and control by the Executive and Congress over activities financed with federal funds . . . which [once approved] becomes a tool of Executive control over the spending of the various departments, agencies, and government corporations."[15] In effect, the Act took the initiative away from Congress and gave it to the president. The class-conscious, corporate-dominated Institute for Government Research led the way. Many decades passed before Congress was willing to support the idea of coordinated executive expenditure proposals, and historically the individual executive departments had dealt directly with the specific congressional committees. Thus it was not until well into the 20th century (putting aside the post–Revolutionary War period) that the state was sufficiently independent of specific private interests to begin to impose its own discipline on the private economy.

The second change in the increasing executive domination of the budget is the gradual substitution of "line-time" budgets with "program" budgets. Line-time budgets are the net result of many specific competing forces, and classify expenditures in terms of the items to be purchased, while program budgets classify outlays on the basis of outputs and the resources necessary to yield certain outputs, and hence require some measure of resource costs—that is, some planning. The idea of program budgeting was first put forth in 1912 by the Taft Commission on Economy and Efficiency and the first applications were made by the Tennessee Valley Authority and the Navy Department. Beginning in 1961, program budgeting was introduced in the Department of Defense. For fiscal year 1968, 23 major departments and agencies were instructed to prepare program budgets, and many other departments were encouraged to do so.[16]

From an administrative point of view, program budgeting lays the basis for the application of marginal analysis and hence is attractive to many economists. Smithies,

for example, writes that "budgeting is essentially an economic problem in solving as it does the allocation of scarce resources among almost insatiable and competing demands."[17] In supporting program budgeting, this school of thought denies that budgetary issues are political issues and sees little or no difference between the allocation of resources by the household or business firm and the state. Critical analysis of the state and the state budget per se is replaced by an implicit acceptance of the given balance of private interests as reflected in the given composition of the budget. As one defender of program budgeting writes, "marginal analysis points to the need for continual reassessment of the pattern of expenditure *at the margin,* rather than being beguiled by arguments concerning the over-all 'necessity' of a particular program."[18] Other economists, however, clearly understand that the real significance of program budgeting is that it strengthens the executive office of the president in relation not only to the federal agencies but also to the Congress. The program budget, according to Burkhead, "becomes a technique, not for management at the operating level, but for the centralization of administrative authority."[19]

The third step toward executive control of the state finances was taken in 1963 when for the first time the budget contained an analysis of expenditures and receipts on a national income accounting basis. The national income budget is a more accurate measure of the impact of federal spending on general economic activity because it excludes purely financial credit transactions and it accounts for receipts and expenditures at the time of their economic impact rather than when cash receipts and payments are actually made. The national income budget represents an explicit recognition of the integral relation between the budget and the private economy and is a necessary precondition for overall fiscal planning.

In Congress there was for years no immediate sense of a loss of power. Congressional procedures for appropriating federal funds have remained unchanged for decades and the budget is still viewed by the representative branch as a set of individual and unrelated parts. It remains true that "taxes and expenditures are decided separately by the separate committees in each house, and although the bills on taxes and appropriations are passed by vote of the whole House and whole Senate, there is little evidence that the two groups of bills are related closely to each other when they are considered.[20] Similarly, the benefits and costs of the programs authorized in the specific appropriations bills are never analyzed or judged in relation to each other. Nor are the bills discussed or studied in detail by the full committees, and full House debate is rare. Each subcommittee of the House Appropriations Committee, for example, is still concerned with a different division of the government and "it is quite natural that a group of men familiar with a particular division of the executive branch will be inclined to take a parochial interest in its welfare."[21] In any event, only about 30 percent of federal expenditures is within congressional discretion to change from year to year. Finally, in recent years the military budget and weapons policies have been determined by the Department of Defense and the Armed Services committees without any real critical examination by the Congress.

In one sense, Congress still effectively "represents" the various parochial interests. But the executive increasingly interprets and coordinates these interests. This is an extremely subtle process and has few formal expressions, even though informal control is substantial. For one thing, any bill initiated by an individual congressman without "legislative clearance" from the Budget Bureau faces enormous obstacles. The Bureau has considerable control over the direction and timing of federal obligations incurred because it is the apportioning authority, hence augmenting its powers even more. During the Kennedy years, the Bureau, the Treasury, and the Council of Economic Advisors were organized into an informal group with the responsibility for overall fiscal planning, and began to exercise a powerful influence on the budget and general fiscal decisions. Thus, increasingly, budget policy is formulated by the executive without any attempt to revolutionize or "modernize" the appropriations process in the Congress itself. The effect of this shift in financial control to the executive has been succinctly described by Schlesinger:

The Congress, secure in its belief that the basic legislation has established policy, may view its annual consideration of the budget formulated by the experts simply from the standpoint of assuring the most economical attainment of legislative goals. Thus policy formulation, which is so intimately connected with the appropriations levels, may slip into organizational limbo and finally be unconsciously seized by the Bureau of the Budget—the one organization that, in theory, should be concerned with economy and efficiency, and should be divorced entirely from policy formulation.[22]

The general result is that budget issues cease to be political issues, and the budget becomes a more reliable planning instrument for the executive. In the past two decades, no major program introduced during previous administrations has been eliminated. The Republican administration in the 1950s even failed to reverse the upward trend of federal spending, including the expansion of outlays in the health, education, and welfare fields. In the contemporary period, only the executive can interpret the needs of private capital and private interests as a whole, and effectively act on these interpretations. So far as the operation of bourgeois democratic institutions is concerned, there is no need to add anything to the conclusion of one economist: "The relationship between the legislative and executive branches largely determines the success or failure of democratic government. Hence, the budget, because it is at the same time the most important instrument of legislative control and executive management, is at the very core of democratic government."[23]

Social capital expenditures

The budget reflects the particular and general economic needs of corporate capital, on the one hand, and the general political needs of the ruling class as a whole, on the other. Preliminary to an investigation of these needs, and their budgetary reflections, it should be stressed that there are no specific budgetary items that mirror *exclusively* any particular or general need. There are no hard-and-fast theoretical categories applicable to the analysis of the budget because there are no precise, real, historical budgetary categories. Individual expenditure items do not reflect with absolute precision any particular interest; quite the contrary, a particular item may express imperfectly a multitude of interests. To cite one outstanding example, state-financed railroad construction in the 19th century was determined by a combination of related economic and political factors.

Today there are few state expenditures that fail to serve a number of different, although related, ends. Johnson's War on Poverty aimed to simultaneously ensure social peace, upgrade labor skills, subsidize labor training for the corporations, and help finance local governments. Highway expenditures complement private investments in manufacturing and distribution facilities, encourage new private investments, link up the major metropolitan centers in accordance with the needs of the Department of Defense, facilitate the mobility of labor, and provide a kind of social consumption—or goods and services consumed in common. Outlays on other forms of transport, communications, water sup-

plies, utilities, and the like, also simultaneously provide inputs to private capital and services to the working class. Nevertheless, it is useful to categorize specific expenditures into four major groups, not for purposes of exposition, but rather because there is always a preponderant set of social forces determining the amount, type, and location of the particular facility.

The first major category of expenditures consists of facilities that are valuable to a specific industry, or group of related industries. These are projects that are useful to specific interests and whose financial needs are so large that they exceed the resources of the interests affected. They also consist of projects in which the financial outcome is subject to so much uncertainty that they exceed the risk-taking propensities of the interests involved. Finally, these are projects that realize external economies and large-scale production economies for the particular industries.

These projects fall into two subcategories: *complementary* investments and *discretionary* investments. Both types of investments, like private investments, increase the productive forces. But the first consists of facilities without which private projects would be unprofitable. Complementary investments are determined completely by the rhythm of private capital accumulation, or by the spheres that private capital has chosen to expand, and by the technical relations or coefficients between private investment and complementary activities. Complementary investments are thus a special form of private investment: their determination rests squarely on the determination of private commodity production and accumulation. And since private accumulation is increasingly social—since the economy is increasingly interdependent—there is no economic or technical limit on state expenditures for facilities which complement private facilities. The most dramatic examples of complementary investments are infrastructure projects in backward capitalist economies that specialize in the production of one or two primary commodities for export. The relationship between state and private capital is seen here in its pure form. Private investments in agriculture and mining completely determine the location, scale, function, and degree of flexibility of infrastructure projects. Railroads, ports, roads, and communication and power facilities are oriented to serve one or two industries making up the export sector.

The purpose of discretionary investments is to provide incentives for private accumulation. In practice, there is no hard line drawn between complementary and discretionary investments; highway extensions, for example, facilitate the movement of goods and also encourage new investments. While complementary investments are part of the normal rhythm of capital accumulation, discretionary investments are ordinarily made during times of crisis—when profitable opportunities for capital as a whole are lacking, or in the event that declining industries depress certain regions. Both kinds of investments are oriented by profit, although the latter may or may not raise the rate of profit.

In the context of the federal system and the fiscal crisis, which compels local governments to compete with one another for new tax-producing industrial and commercial properties by providing low-cost or free facilities to specific investors, and in the context of an industrial structure dependent on the state for contracts and subsidized to develop new technical "solutions" for "crime control," institutional administration, transportation systems, and so on, more and more discretionary investments are being financed by the state.

The most important state investments serving the interests of specific industries are highway expenditures. Domestic economic growth since World War II has been led by automobile production and suburban residential construction, which requires an enormous network of complementary highways, roads, and ancillary facilities. Rejecting public transportation, on the one hand, and toll highways, on the other, the state has "socialized intercity highway systems paid for by the taxpayer—not without great encouragement for the rubber, petroleum, and auto industries."[24] From 1944, when Congress passed the Federal Aid to Highways Act, to 1961, the federal government expended its entire transportation budget on roads and highways. Today approximately 20 percent of nonmilitary government spending at all levels is destined for highways; inland waterway and airport expenditures total less than $1 billion yearly; and railroads and local rapid transit receive little or nothing. And in area redevelopment schemes, highways receive the lion's share of the subsidies; more than 80 percent of the funds allocated by the federal government to Appalachia for economic development, for example, has been destined for road construction. The reason was that the federal planners needed the cooperation of the local governors, who together with electric power, steel, and other companies combined to block other "solutions."[25] The power of the "auto complex" has been documented many times; two more examples will suffice. In 1962 the combined forces of the truckers, port groups, and barge companies blocked legislation that sought to give the railroads more freedom to cut rates; in 1965 an attempt by Johnson to compel truckers to pay higher user charges failed completely.

Initiated and supported by the auto complex, sometimes along, and sometimes allied, with other industries, road transport nevertheless receives powerful support from the large part of private capital as a whole, as well as from the suburbs. From the standpoint of private capital the availability of truck transport is the key factor in location decisions. For the car-owning commuter, the transportation budget constitutes a giant subsidy, for two reasons. First, although the determinant of highway construction is found in the auto complex, highways have technical characteristics—mainly free access and unused capacity—that afford easy use by the car owner. Second, because "the auto owner enjoys a low marginal price per mile by auto once he commits himself to ownership" (because, in turn, he must meet fixed car payments), his use of public transportation is minimal.[26]

The social cost of auto transport is extraordinarily high, hence the enormous fiscal burden on the state. In the United States, about 20 percent of total product is spent on transportation (in the Soviet Union, roughly 7 percent), chiefly because of the high capital requirements of moving people from one destination to another, together with the existence of vast unused physical capacity—partial underutilization of highways during nonpeak hours and autos in transit, and full underutilization of autos during working hours.

Costs, and the fiscal burden, are also rising; it has become a standard complaint that the construction of freeways does not end, but rather intensifies congestion. The basic reason is that auto use is subsidized; hence expanding the freeway system leads to the expansion of the demand for its use. Furthermore, the state cannot free itself fiscally by constructing more freeways, because the freeway system has spawned more and more suburban developments—where road expenditures per capita are much greater than in the cities—at greater distances from the urban centers.

Further, road transport intensifies the fiscal crisis of the cities, owing to the removal of land from the tax rolls for freeways, access roads, and ancillary facilities. Simultaneously, the cities' commuting population places an extra burden on city expenditures in the form of traffic control, parking facilities, and the like.

For all of these reasons, not only does the social cost of transportation steadily rise,

but also transport costs borne by capital itself increase. Local capital and the state itself are responding to the monster created in Detroit, Akron, and other centers of the auto complex with programs for public transport, two of which have been implemented in San Francisco and Washington. But far from solving the transportation problem, these and other efforts are bound to add to the total irrationality of transportation patterns, and to the fiscal crisis. At present, there are more than 30 agencies at the federal level regulating or promoting particular modes of transport. Many of these agencies are in competition with one another, paralleling the competition for state funds among different branches of industry. To date, the federal government has been unable to rationalize and streamline transportation, because it has not been able to acquire sufficient independence from the conflicting and contradictory interests of particular industries to deprive the state agencies representing these specific interests of their independence.[27] Another reason to expect the transportation budget to rise in the future is that the development of rapid transport will push the suburbs out even further from the urban centers, and put even more distance between places of work, residence, and recreation. Far from contributing to an environment that will free suburbanites from congestion and pollution, rapid transport will simply displace the traffic jams to the present perimeters of the suburbs, thereby requiring still more freeway construction. The only general solution is planned urban development as a whole, and neither corporate capital nor local capital is willing or able to take this step.

Integrally related to transport outlays are urban renewal expenditures, which figure more and more in local, state, and federal budgets, and which are the main response to the decline in profits of downtown business interests. The decline in profitability in turn is attributable to the profoundly exploitative relationship that has developed between the suburb and the city.

It is in this context that urban renewal should be interpreted. The market still determines the contours of urban and regional development. More important, the supramunicipal authorities and quasi-public regional development agencies that control urban renewal *reinforce* the "decisions" of the market. The state budget has thus contributed to the dynamism of the downtown sections and the decay of the remainder of the city. Urban renewal expenditures are thus bound to expand in the future because they do not correct the irrationalities of capitalist development, but rather intensify them.

Specifically, spending on urban reconstruction takes the form of multiproject investments that harmonize the specific expenditure items in the interests of local capital as a whole. The main aspects of urban renewal include reconstruction of downtown areas in the interests of retailers suffering from sharp suburban competition; stadium and other recreational investments that seek to give restaurants, clubs, and so on, a new lease on life; multiplication of parking and other facilities for suburbanites working in downtown office buildings; deceleration of the deterioration of middle-class neighborhoods, and acceleration of the decline of working-class neighborhoods; in general, the re-creation and intensification of profitability conditions for builders, banks, utilities, retailers, brokers, and land speculators. To the degree that urban renewal reconstructs cities that complement suburban development, the development of the suburbs and the underdevelopment of the cities are intensified; to the degree that urban renewal reconstructs cities that compete with the suburbs, the underdevelopment of the cities is deaccelerated, at the expense of the duplication and multiplication of facilities of all kinds. In either case, urban renewal heaps new, expanding fiscal burdens on the state budget.

The second major determinant of state expenditures stems from the immediate economic interests of corporate capital as a whole. The budgetary expression of these interests takes many forms—economic infrastructure investments, expenditures on education, general business subsidies, credit guarantees and insurance, social consumption, and so on. In the United States, most of these forms appeared or developed fully only in the 20th century, although in Europe state capitalism emerged in an earlier period—in France, during the First Empire, generalized state promotion buoyed the private economy; in Germany, state economic policy received great impetus from political unification and war; in Italy, laissez faire principles did not prevent the state from actively financing and promoting accumulation in the major spheres of heavy industry; and everywhere liberal notions of small, balanced budgets and indirect taxation came face to face with the fiscal realities of wartime economies.

In the United States the budget remained small throughout the 19th century; transportation investments were chiefly private, and natural resource, conservation, public health, education, and related outlays were insignificant. The state served the economic needs of capital as a whole mainly in nonfiscal ways—land tenure, monetary, immigration, tariff, and patent policies all "represented and strengthened the particular legal framework within which private business was organized."[28] State subsidies to capital as a whole were confined to the state government and local levels and were largely the product of mercantile, rather than industrial capital, impulses.[29]

In the 20th century, however, corporate capital has combined with state capital to create a new organic whole. Corporate capital is not subordinated to state capital, or vice versa, but rather they are synthesized into a qualitatively new phenomenon, rooted in the development of the productive forces and the concentration and centralization of capital. More specifically, the rapid advance of technology has increased the pace of general economic change, the risk of capital investments, and the amount of uncontrollable overhead costs. Further, capital equipment is subject to more rapid obsolescence, and there exists a longer lead time before the typical investment is in full operation and thus is able to pay for itself.[30] The development of the production relations has also compelled corporate capital to employ state power in its economic interests as a whole, and socialize production costs. The struggles of the labor movement have reinforced the general tendency for the rate of profit to decline, and have thus compelled corporate capital to use the state to mobilize capital funds from the liquid savings of the general population. And, finally, the onset of general realization crises has forced large-scale business to use the budget to subsidize the demand for commodities.

The most expensive economic needs of corporate capital as a whole are the costs of research, development of new products, new production processes, and so on, and, above all, the costs of training and retraining the labor force, in particular technical, administrative, and nonmanual workers. Preliminary to an investigation of the process of the *socialization* of these costs, a brief review of the relationships between technology and production is required.

The forces of production include available land, constant capital, labor skills, methods of work organization, and, last but not least, technology, which is a part of, but not totally identified with, the social productive forces. The advance of technology, the uses of technology, and its distribution between the various branches of the economy are all determined in the last analysis by the relations of production. The transformation from a labor-using to a labor-saving technology in mid-19th-century Europe was caused not only by competition but also by the disappearance of opportu-

nities for industrial capitalists to recruit labor "extensively" from the artisan and peasant classes at the given wage rate. During the last half of the 19th century, the established industrial proletariat faced less competition, their organizations were strengthened, and they were better able to win wage advances. Thus, it was partly the class struggle that compelled capital to introduce labor-saving innovations.

Despite the rapid advance of technology during the first half of the 20th century, until World War II the industrial corporations trained the largest part of their labor force, excluding basic skills such as literacy. In the context of the further technological possibilities latent in the scientific discoveries of the 19th and 20th centuries, this was a profoundly irrational mode of social organization.

The reason is that knowledge, unlike other forms of capital, cannot be monopolized by one or a few industrial-finance interests. Capital-as-knowledge resides in the skills and abilities of the working class itself. In a free labor market—that is, in the absence of a feudallike industrial state that prohibits labor mobility, a flat impossibility in the capitalist mode of production—no one industrial-finance interest can afford to train its own labor force or channel profits into the requisite amount of research and development. The reason is that (excepting the patent system) there is absolutely no guarantee that their "investments" will not seek employment in other corporations or industries. The cost of losing trained manpower is especially high in those corporations that employ technical workers with skills that are specific to a particular industrial process.

World War II provided the opportunity to rationalize the entire organization of technology in the United States. As Dobb writes, "a modern war is of such a kind as to require all-out mobilization of economic resources, rapidly executed decisions about transfer of labor and productive equipment, and the growth of war industry, which ordinary market-mechanisms would be powerless to achieve. Consequently, it occasions a considerable growth of state capitalism. . . ."[31] The intervention of the state through government grants to finance research programs, develop new technical processes, and construct new facilities, and the forced mobilization of resources, converted production to a more social process. The division of labor and specialization of work functions intensified, industrial plants were diversified, the technical requirements of employment became more complex, and, in some cases, more advanced. The end result was a startling acceleration of technology.

At the end of the war, corporate capital was once again faced with the necessity of financing its own research and training its own technical work force. The continued rationalization of the work process required new forms of social integration in order to enable social production to advance still further. The first step was the introduction of the GI Bill, which socialized the costs of training (including the living expenses of labor trainees) and eventually helped to create a labor force that could exploit the stockpile of technology created during the war. The second step was the creation of a vast system of lower and higher technical education at the local and state level, the transformation of private universities into federal universities through research grants, and the creation of a system exploiting technology in a systematic, organized way that included not only the education system, but also the foundations, private research organizations, the Pentagon, and countless other federal government agencies. This system required enormous capital outlays, a large expansion of teaching and administrative personnel, an upgrading of teachers at all levels, together with programs of specialized teaching training, scholarships, libraries; in short, vast new burdens on the state budgets. In turn, this

reorganization of the labor process, and, in particular, the free availability of masses of technical-scientific workers, made possible the rapid acceleration of technology. With the new, rationalized social organization of technology and the labor process completed, technical knowledge became a main form of labor power and capital.

The continued substitution of "mind" work for manual work is bound to place a growing burden on state budgets at local, state, and federal levels. Equally important, the increased demand for higher education will add to the fiscal crisis. Education remains "private property" in the sense that the material benefits from training accrue not to society at large but to the technical worker himself.

Another rising expense facing corporate capital as a whole consists of investments in economic infrastructure—plant and equipment for education and research; water, power, and similar projects; and harbor, air, and other transportation facilities. Specific industries or groups of related industries normally do not provide the political impetus for these expenditures; rather regional or corporate capital as a whole does. These kinds of economic infrastructure ordinarily serve a wide variety of industries, either precede or coincide with private capital accumulation, and generate many-sided, long-term economic effects. They are also capital-intensive projects that are characterized by large "indivisibilities"; they require large original capital outlays and normally are constructed in large, discrete units. To cite one example, the Boeing 747 jetliner makes many existing air terminal facilities obsolete, and will require the construction of entirely new airports, rather than a gradual modernization of existing facilities.

These projects place a growing burden on the state budget for three reasons: first, their absolute size is increasingly large, owing to their capital-intensive and "indivisible" character; second, monopoly capital needs more economic infrastructure, because of the increased complexity and interdependence of production; and, third, state and local governments seeking to attract branch plants of large corporations by subsidizing infrastructure projects tend to produce an oversupply of projects. For all these reasons, federal outlays and grants-in-aid and state and local bond issues for "capital improvements" will continue to expand.

The social expenses of production

Still another fiscal burden heaped on the state by corporate capital is the *expenses of selling*. From a theoretical standpoint, the need for state spending destined to underwrite private commodity demand is limitless. Capital "accumulates or dies" and in the absence of regular increases in private commodity demand, which in the current era require fresh state subsidies, accumulation comes to a halt. Moreover, a few particular commodities receive the greatest share of state subsidies. Highways and education receive the most direct subsidies and private suburban housing and development receive the greatest indirect subsidies. Politically, it is difficult for the state to shift resources from highway construction to other modes of transportation, from suburban residential development to urban housing, and from social consumption in the suburbs to social consumption in the cities. This introduces an element of *inflexibility* in the budget, and tends to intensify the overall fiscal crisis.

The uncontrolled expansion of production by corporate capital as a whole creates still another fiscal burden on the state in the form of outlays required to meet the *social costs of private production* (as contrasted with the socialization of private costs of production, which we have discussed above). Motor transportation is an important source of social costs in the consumption of oxygen, the production of crop- and

animal-destroying smog, the pollution of rivers and oceans by lead additives to gasoline, the construction of freeways that foul the land, and the generation of urban sprawl. These costs do not enter into the accounts of the automobile industry, which is compelled to minimize its own costs and maximize production and sales. Corporate capital is largely unwilling to treat toxic chemical waste or to develop substitute sources of energy for fossil fuels that pollute the air. And corporate farming—the production of agricultural commodities for exchange alone—generates still more social costs by minimizing crop losses (and thus costs) through the unlimited use of DDT and other chemicals that are harmful to crops, animals, water purity, and human life itself.

By and large, private capital refuses to bear the costs of reducing or eliminating air and water pollution, lowering highway and air accidents, easing traffic jams, preserving forests, wilderness areas, and wildlife sanctuaries, and conserving the soils. In the past these costs were largely ignored. Today, owing to the increasingly social character of production, these costs are damaging not only the ecological structure, but also profitable accumulation itself, particularly in real estate, recreation, agriculture, and other branches of the economy in which land, water, and air are valuable resources to capital. The portion of the state budget devoted to reducing social costs has therefore begun to mount.

Another major category of state expenditures consists of the expenses of stabilizing the world capitalist social order: the costs of creating a safe political environment for profitable investment and trade. These expenditures include the costs of politically containing the proletariat at home and abroad, the costs of keeping small-scale, local, and regional capital at home, safely within the ruling corporate liberal consensus, and the costs of maintaining the comprador ruling classes abroad.

These political expenses partly take the form of income transfers and direct or indirect subsidies, and are attributable fundamentally to the unplanned and anarchic character of capitalist development. Unrestrained capital accumulation and technological change create three broad, related economic and social imbalances. First, capitalist development forces great stresses and strains on local and regional economies; second, capitalist growth generates imbalances between various industries and sectors of the economy; third, accumulation and technical change reproduce inequalities in the distribution of wealth and income and generate poverty. These imbalances not only are integral to capitalist development, but also are considered by the ruling class to be a sign of "healthy growth and change." What is more, the forces of the marketplace, far from ameliorating the imbalances, in fact magnify them by the multiplier effects of changes in demand on production. The decline of coal mining in Appalachia, for example, compelled other businesses and able-bodied workers to abandon the region, reinforcing tendencies toward economic stagnation and social impoverishment.

The political containment of the proletariat requires the expense of maintaining corporate liberal ideological hegemony, and, where that fails, the cost of physically repressing populations in revolt. In the first category are the expenses of medicare, unemployment, old-age, and other social insurance, a portion of education expenditures, the welfare budget, the antipoverty programs, nonmilitary "foreign aid," and the administrative costs of maintaining corporate liberalism at home and the imperialist system abroad—the expenses incurred by the National Labor Relations Board, Office of Economic Opportunity, Agency for International Development, and similar organizations.

The second major cost of politically containing the proletariat at home and abroad (not to speak of the socialist world) consists of police and military expenditures required to suppress populations in revolt. These expenditures place the single greatest drain on the state budget. A full analysis of these expenditures would require detailed development of the theory of imperialism, which cannot be undertaken here. However, we can identify those factors in the arms race, the structure of the "military-industrial space complex," the wars against national liberation struggles abroad, and the physical suppression of revolutionary movements at home that are likely to force the ruling class to expand the military budget in the foreseeable future.

First, the continuous expansion of social production, the extension of capitalism into the Third World, and the proletarianization of the world population enlarge the arena both for capital accumulation and for class conflict. The increasing instability of the world capitalist social order, the transformation of nationalist movements led by compromise-minded national bourgeoisies into national liberation struggles led by revolutionary armies, and the birth of new socialist societies have all required greater levels of military expenditure in the "mother country."

Second, a large and growing military establishment is needed to initiate technological advance in *civilian* production.

Third, not only is the economy as a whole more dependent on rising military expenditures, but also the major "private" military contractors have established permanent beachheads in the state budget, and thus have a permanent stake in the arms race itself. The largest 50 defense contractors received 58 percent of all military orders during World War II, 56 percent during the Korean War, and 66 percent in 1963–64.[32] In military production, "the initiative, risk-bearing and similar manifestations of enterprise appear to have become characteristics of the buyer rather than the seller,"[33] and thus the big military contractors cooperate readily with government defense programs independent of the rationality of these programs for overall ruling class interests.

The final expense of stabilizing the world capitalist social order consists of the funds needed to keep local and regional capital securely within the corporate liberal political consensus at home and the costs of maintaining the comprador ruling classes abroad. The latter take the form of foreign aid: in particular, balance-of-payments assistance through the International Monetary Fund; infrastructure loans by the World Bank and AID that economically strengthen export industries in the Third World and politically harden the rule of local bourgeoisies whose economic interests are based on export production, processing, and trade; and outright military and nonmilitary grants-in-aid.

At home corporate capital must make alliances with traditional agricultural interests (especially those of the Southern oligarchy) and small-scale capital. In the Congress, the votes of Southern and Midwestern farm legislators and other representatives bound to local and regional economic interests—for example, shipping, soft coal mining, and the fishing industry—are indispensable for the legislative victories of corporate liberal policies. Support for federal programs in the areas of urban renewal, education, health, housing, and transportation by state legislators, municipal governments, and local newspapers, TV stations, and other "opinion makers" is equally important.

The political support of small businessmen, farmers, and other local and regional interests is extremely costly. Billions of dollars of direct and indirect subsidies are required by the farmers, especially the large growers who dominate the farm associations and many local and state governments. Subsidies in various forms—in particular, allowances to finance the relocation of small business—are also required to placate small-scale capital adversely affected by corporate-oriented urban renewal programs.

Financing the budget

In the preceding sections, we have attempted to analyze state expenditures in terms of the development of the forces and relations of production. We have seen that the increasingly social character of production requires the organization and distribution of production by the state. In effect, advanced capitalism fuses the "base" and "superstructure"—the economic and political systems—and thus places an enormous fiscal burden on the state budget.

In the next section, we attempt to submit the major sources of state *financing* to a similar structural analysis. Is it possible for the state to continue to expand traditional sources of financing to meet its growing fiscal needs? Can the state find new sources of financing? Or does modern capitalism produce a permanent "fiscal crisis of the state"?

In general, there are three possible ways that the state can meet the fiscal burdens that modern capitalism heaps on it: the development of profit-making state enterprise, together with the introduction of other measures to increase productivity in the state sector, the creation of a new state debt, and the expansion of taxation. Each of these possibilities requires underlying changes in social relations, either in the production relations between labor and capital or in the relations within the capitalist class.

The first possibility consists of the development of productive, profit-making enterprise within the state sector, and the mobilization of the surplus produced by the workers in these enterprises to finance general budgetary expenditures. From a strictly economic standpoint, there are no barriers to the accumulation of state capital in the directly productive spheres of the economy. Within the state sector there is no shortage of scientific, technical, skilled, or unskilled labor, nor is there an absence of overall organizational and management "know-how." Within the federal government there exists an abundance of knowledge and experience in the areas of labor relations, financing, marketing, and other spheres of modern production. Moreover, lands presently owned or leased by federal and state governments could yield sufficient raw materials, fuels, and other necessary resources.

In fact, these "economic" possibilities are impossible politically. In capitalist society, state investments are confined to non-profit-making spheres. It is in the interests of private capital to seize all possible profit-making opportunities for itself, and resist the encroachment of state capital on its own "natural territory." Private capital also has every reason to compel the state to remain dependent on tax revenues by depriving the state of opportunities to accumulate wealth in order to weaken or "pauperize" it and thus reduce the possibility for popular governments to redirect the allocation of economic resources on the basis of popularly determined, rather than corporate capital, priorities. Finally, from an ideological standpoint, private capital normally monopolizes profit-making activities in order to perpetuate the myth that the state is incompetent to manage directly productive capital.

There have been crisis periods (in particular, World War II) when corporate capital has used the state to develop and manage productive wealth in the interests of general economic efficiency. But with the return to "normalcy" the state is rapidly stripped of its capital assets. From 1946 to 1949, for example, the cumulative percentage decline of state-owned producer durable assets exceeded 40 percent. In the wake of the Hoover Commission investigations and follow-up recommendations by the director of the Bureau of the Budget in the 1950s, the federal government abandoned more commercial activities to private capital. Even in the climate of corporate-dominated federal policy and working-class quiescence of the early Johnson administration, the government was compelled to promise to sell off the few remaining enterprises competing with private business (for example, nuclear fuel production) in order to win a "business consensus" for its (pro-business) policies.[34]

The problem of financing the budget reduces itself to the problem of increasing taxes, specifically the problem of intensifying tax exploitation of the working class, owners of small businesses, and self-employed professionals.

The issue of taxes has always been a class issue; it is still true that "external protection and power, and the enrichment of some classes at the expense of others [are] the purpose of the tax system."[35] Every important change in the balance of class forces has always been registered in the tax structure.

In advanced capitalist states tax exploitation cannot be openly applied or instituted without some kind of ideological justification. Taxes can be either concealed, which is difficult to accomplish in the modern era, or justified on some basis of "tax fairness or equity." Failing this, there is the danger of a tax revolt, in the form of tax evasion or organized political opposition.

Even in the feudal era, the ruling class was compelled either to conceal or to justify tax exploitation. Taxes contained an "equity" criterion when they first appeared in the budgets of the feudal nobility. But they were based on the principle that different persons and classes had different rights and duties. "The nobility of eighteenth century France were serenely certain," Louis Eisenstein has written, "that they contributed special benefits to society that called for a special immunity from taxes. They . . . had incentives that had to be preserved for the welfare of others."[36]

In 19th-century America, the ruling class concealed tax exploitation. The working class was small and a personal income tax was not feasible; the only wealth tax was the property tax. The tariff became the most important source of revenue, one that was hidden from view because it took the form of higher commodity prices. (Because they are easy to conceal, import and export taxes today are held up as models of taxation in underdeveloped countries. Economists have written of the political "advantage" of export taxes because they hide the burden that falls on peasants engaged in export production.) [37]

Today the false reasons given to justify tax exploitation revolve around two ideas —the old concept of "incentives" and the new idea of "ability to pay." Put briefly, the "incentive" rationale asserts that if profits are taxed too heavily, the accumulation of capital, and thus the growth of employment, will diminish. Similarly, the "incentives" of investors, wealthy families, and others who monopolize the supply of capital must not be "impaired." Such statements are in fact true within the framework of capitalism because those who make them threaten to sabotage production if they do not realize acceptable profits. Again in brief, the doctrine of "ability-to-pay" assumes that the benefits of state expenditures accrue to everyone more or less equally, and therefore that everyone should pay taxes according to ability, normally measured by the level of personal income. This doctrine obviously has no basis in reality, and is false, not because of its logic, but because of its premise.

Tax exploitation is still concealed—there are roughly 150 taxes hidden in the price of a loaf of bread, and about 600 taxes concealed in the purchase of a house.[38] Excise and sales taxes still remain important sources of revenue at state and local government levels. But, of more importance, tax exploitation is accepted because the ideology of corporate capital is still accepted. Only recently has this ideology been subject to challenge. Thus, both workers and the individual capitalists identify their

interests closely with those of the state; and workers therefore identify their interests with those of capital.

Concealing and justifying taxes are of crucial importance in the contemporary era because the fiscal burden that the owners of corporate capital place on the state is not accompanied by any willingness to shoulder the burden themselves. Superficially, it appears that the ruling class taxes itself in a number of ways—there are corporation income taxes, property taxes, and inheritance taxes, besides the individual income tax, which place extremely high marginal tax rates on high incomes. In fact, corporate capital, for the most part, escapes taxation altogether except during periods of national crisis (for example, in 1936–39, when Congress legislated an undistributed profits tax, and during World War II, when corporate capital had to pay an excess profits tax) .

First, the corporate managers completely shift the corporate income tax to consumers —mainly wage and salary earners—in the form of higher prices. Although corporate gross rates of return doubled between the 1920s and 1950s, net rates of return remained the same, even though the corporation income tax rate rose from 5 percent to 52 percent during the same period. In effect, the corporation income tax is similar to a general sales tax, levied at rates in proportion to the profit margin of the corporation.

Second, the property tax falls mainly on the working class, not on the business class. One reason is that within the core cities residential properties assume the larger share, and commercial land and buildings the smaller share of the total property tax burden. Property values in the central city show a relative decline owing to the "suburbanization of industry" and to the spread of freeways and the expansion of public parking facilities, office buildings, and other structures that have taken lands off the tax rolls. The flight of well-to-do workers and the middle classes to the suburbs has reduced local revenues from residential property taxes, as well.[39]

Moreover, available studies indicate that owners of tenant-occupied residential buildings usually shift the property tax to their tenants—the vast majority of whom are working people. And about 75 percent of property taxes on local industry and retail establishments is shifted to consumers.[40] Thus, it is not surprising that there is general agreement among economists that the property tax as a whole is regressive.[41]

All in all, however, property taxes are becoming a relatively insignificant source of revenue. In 1902 they raised over 80 percent of all state and local government revenues; today property taxes finance about one-half of the budgets of local governments, and only 5 percent of state government budgets (the largest cities are becoming increasingly dependent on intergovernment transfers, which are financed chiefly by income, sales, and excise taxes). In the past few years, taxpayer groups and politicians in dozens of states have been actively seeking to lower property taxes. And some kinds of property taxation (for example, taxes on personal property) are being eliminated altogether in many localities.

The only other wealth tax in the United States is the inheritance tax. Nominal rates of the federal tax range from 3 percent on $5,000–10,000 to 77 percent on $10 million or more, but the actual average rate is little more than 10 percent. The difference between the high nominal rates and the low actual rates is explained by exemptions for life estates and for gifts made more than three years before death.[42]

This brief survey warrants the conclusion that the owners of monopoly capital pay few taxes on their wealth,[43] and none on their corporate income. There is no general business tax in the United States, and unrealized capital gains go tax-free. To be sure, wealthy individuals who receive dividends and interest income are taxed at high marginal rates under the individual income tax, but top corporate controllers and managers receive most of their income in the form of tax-free interest from municipal bonds and realized capital gains, which are taxed at low rates. Capital thus protects not only its profits from taxation, but also personal wealth and income. This should not come as a surprise; profits are the key to the economic survival, and personal income and wealth are the key to the social and political survival of the ruling class.

In addition to that portion of property and corporation income taxes that falls on the working class, tax exploitation takes the form of social security taxes, sales and excise taxes, and the individual income tax. The most important social security tax is the payroll tax used to finance old-age insurance. This is a regressive tax because a flat rate is applied to taxable earnings without regard to income levels; it is especially regressive for those who do not stay in the labor force long enough to accumulate sufficient credited employment to qualify for primary benefits.[44] Excise taxes are applied by both state and federal governments, and most state and many local governments have general sales taxes. These taxes are altogether regressive, and fall particularly hard on low-income workers.[45] Indicative of their importance is the fact that state governments raised nearly two-thirds of their tax revenues from sales and gross receipt taxes in 1967, while state individual income taxes accounted for only 16 percent of the tax revenues.[46]

The most oppressive instrument of tax exploitation is the federal individual income tax. First passed by Congress in 1894, on the heels of more than a decade of farmer and working-class agitation against big business, the income tax was originally conceived as a class tax. The tax rate was a flat 2 percent and provision was made for a $4,000 personal exemption, and thus the tax would have fallen on only a handful of wealthy individuals. The tax was declared unconstitutional.

The modern individual income tax did

not win acceptance until 1913. The historical reasons for this delay were simple: First, the development of the income tax, and, in particular, the general application of the tax by the expedient of regularly lowering exemptions, was not possible until there existed a massive propertyless working class. Second, by the turn of the century, the United States economy was producing a wide range of substitutes for imported commodities and, as a result, workers were able to avoid tariff excises by reducing their consumption of imports.

Not only was an individual income tax historically possible, it was also ideally suited to the needs of corporate capital. On the one hand, the income tax cannot be shifted to profits; on the other hand, the tax is regressive or proportional in content, although progressive in form. The myth of "tax equity" is preserved, and the reality of tax exploitation is concealed behind an elaborate progressive tax schedule, which in turn contains hundreds of loopholes deemed necessary for "economic growth," "economic stability," and "fiscal justice."

The income tax has increasingly encroached on wage and salary income since it was first introduced. The state has systematically reduced personal exemptions and credits for dependents from $4,000 (for a family of four) in 1913–16 to $2,400 today. In 1913–16 a single person was granted a $3,000 exemption; today, only $700. In terms of actual purchasing power, real exemptions have fallen even more. Further, popular consciousness of the tax burden has been reduced by the introduction of tax withholding—the highest form of tax exploitation. At present, 85 percent of income taxes are collected at the basic 20 percent rate, which applies to two-thirds of all returns.

According to available studies, the average rate of taxation on the highest incomes is roughly 30 percent, chiefly because of the special treatment granted to capital gains income, deductions (mainly applicable to those who receive relatively high incomes),

and income splitting and exemptions (which benefit high income families relatively more than low income groups). In fact, no one apart from independent professionals and small and middle businessmen pays more than a 25 percent rate because of the ease of short-circuiting income into nontaxable forms (for example, expense accounts) and to tax evasion, which is most widespread among farmers and those who receive interest income and annuities. In recent years the state has failed even to pretend that the flat tax surcharge of 10 percent is progressive, and passed a tax cut in 1965 that benefited the rich far more than the poor—for the former the decrease is permanent, but for the latter (whose money income is rising) only temporary.[47]

The tax revolt

In the preceding sections, we have seen that the economic surplus is mobilized for the political-economic programs of corporate capital through the budget. Monopoly capital dominates the state budget and socializes various production costs and expenses, but resists the socialization of profits. Taxation is the only source of state revenue fully consistent with capitalist property relations: the burden of taxation necessarily falls on the working class.

The fiscal crisis consists of the gap between expenditures and revenues, which is one form of the general contradiction between social production and private ownership. The severity of the fiscal crisis depends upon the production and social relations between corporate capital, local and regional capital, state employees and dependents, and the taxpaying working class at large. In the absence of a serious challenge to the ideological hegemony of corporate capital, in particular in the absence of a unified movement organized around opposition to corporate liberal and imperialist budgetary priorities—a movement that seeks to unify the working class as a whole—the fiscal crisis will continue to divide state workers from state dependents (e.g., teachers from parents, social workers from welfare recipients) and state employees and dependents from workers in the private sector (e.g., teachers and students from taxpayers as a whole).

At present, growing taxpayer resistance to heavy, rising taxes both reflects and deepens the fiscal crisis. Although "taxpayers" as a group comprise the small business, professional, and working classes as a whole, tax resistance is not presently organized along class lines. In practice, tax issues are rarely seen as class issues, partly because of the general absence of working-class unity in the United States, and partly because the fiscal system itself obscures the class character of the budget. As we have seen, although monopoly capital dominates the budget, the state mediates between labor and capital, and the working class benefits materially from state expenditures. In addition, monopoly capital has developed an elaborate ideological rationalization of the budget that is integral to capital's general view that material abundance, capital accumulation, and economic growth define social well-being. Finally, as we have seen, the aggregate, effective tax rate on the incomes of both lower- and higher-income families is roughly the same, indicating that tax exploitation is not confined to poor people, who have least to lose and most to gain from radical social change.

For these reasons, tax issues ordinarily are seen as interest group or community issues, and far from helping to unite the working class, the issues act to divide it. In particular, the growth of thousands of autonomous taxpaying units—the "1400 Governments" of the New York metropolitan area and the nearly 500 separate tax-levying bodies in Illinois's Cook County, to cite two examples—and the proliferation elsewhere of autonomous trusteeships, municipalities, and school, water, sewer, and other special districts tend to set community

against community, tax district against tax district, suburb against city. The fundamental class issues of state finance—the distribution of taxation and the division of expenditures between different social classes—emerge in a new form. The core cities are attempting to force the suburbs to pay their "fair share" of city expenditures, while the relatively well-to-do suburban populations not only are defending themselves against the programs of the core cities—tax redistribution, central city income taxes, commuter taxes, consolidation or merger of tax districts and entire metropolitan areas—but also are taking the offensive by offering inducements to private capital in order to establish an autonomous industrial and commercial base.

Apart from the cold war between city and suburb, the most militant form of tax resistance is that against the property tax. Decades ago, the function of the property tax was to finance public improvements for the benefit of property owners. Today there is little or no visible connection between property taxation and expenditures financed by it; rather, there is a tendency to use property tax revenues to finance social programs that many property owners oppose. In many cities, small homeowners are mounting tax referendum campaigns aimed at downtown business interests whose properties are undervalued for tax purposes. In the suburbs, there is widespread sentiment that the property tax should be replaced in whole or in part by other sources of revenue—sentiment that right-wing state and local politicians are successfully exploiting for their own purposes.

Suburban resistance to increased taxation, agitation against the property tax, and the urban-suburban cold war, not to speak of tax avoidance and evasion and the general sentiment against "spendthrift" government, arise not only because of the rising level of taxation, but also because of government expenditure priorities.

The *priorities* of corporate liberalism are under attack, not only by the black movement and the organized left, but also by a significant part of the population at large. A study conducted in the early 1960s concluded that popular sentiment ran against space spending and support for agriculture, and in favor of domestic welfare and education programs. According to this study, no single government program inspired the majority of the population sampled to agree to expand the program through higher taxation.[48] A recent Harris poll stated that "the central motive for paying taxes has begun to disintegrate." Those polled opposed foreign aid, Vietnam War spending, space and defense, and federal welfare outlays (no doubt because of racism and the prevailing ideology that stresses the importance of "individual self-sufficiency"). Favored were aid to education, pollution control, help for the cities, and other domestic programs.

What is the significance of popular attitudes on taxation and spending for the left? The tax issue is complex, and cannot be separated from the questions of the level of state expenditures and spending priorities. In the past, the left has not been able to exploit the tax issue because it has been wedded to the modern liberal tradition that has sought an enlarged government role in the economy with little or no attention paid to the structure and burden of taxation. Chiefly for this reason, the right wing has enjoyed a near monopoly on the issue of taxation.

There are some signs that the left is breaking its self-imposed silence on taxation, and beginning to link up taxes and expenditures. Some unions—in particular, state employee unions such as the Transport Workers Union in New York and sections of the American Federation of Teachers—are incorporating demands that the tax burden be shifted to business into their programs for higher wages and better working conditions. This enlarged perspective on the state finances represents an advance, but it is clear that even a general critique of the relationship between expenditures and taxation is insufficient in and of itself. Of equal importance is a theoretical and practical demonstration of the relation between state expenditure priorities and the pattern and rhythm of *private* accumulation and spending. For example, tax referendum campaigns organized around the issue of the relative burden of property taxation on residential versus commercial property should include a critique of the class character of education and urban renewal expenditures. Clearly, struggles against tax exploitation alone can have only a limited impact on either popular consciousness or the actual tax structure. Past struggles by populist, progressive, liberal, and left movements dramatically show that under conditions of monopolistic industry and administered prices it is impossible to influence greatly the distribution of the tax burden (and thus the distribution of wealth and income) without a simultaneous challenge to *both* state and private capital spending priorities.

Further, the left must begin to demonstrate the relationship between foreign and domestic spending, which, we have seen, public opinion radically separates. Struggles around regressive property and sales taxes, increases in fares for public services, and so on, should be informed by an understanding that domestic and international spending are integrally related; that is, that the maintenance of corporate liberalism at home depends upon the expansion and consolidation of imperialism abroad, and vice versa. Even on the left, it is sometimes not appreciated that foreign economic expansion and imperialism are required to maintain corporate liberalism by *expanding* national income and material wealth, thus muting domestic capital-labor struggles over the *distribution* of income and wealth. And the growth of social and welfare expenditures (and the establishment of class harmony) at home are preconditions for popular acquiescence in militarism and imperialism abroad. The "welfare-warfare state" is *one* phenomenon, and military and civilian expenditures cannot be reduced significantly at the expense of one another. An understanding of the relation between foreign and domestic programs requires comprehension of the *totality* of world capitalism—a difficult but necessary undertaking, precisely because there is presently a large constituency ready to support a massive expansion of corporate liberal domestic programs (except welfare) at the expense of military, space, and foreign aid expenditures.

Movements of state workers and dependents

Partly a reflection of the tax revolt, and partly deepening the fiscal crisis that is producing the tax revolt, is the practical activity—union organizing, day-to-day agitation, strikes, demonstrations—of employees and dependents of the state. On the one hand, the developing awareness of state employees and dependents that they are subject to a gradual erosion of material standards is crucial to a general understanding of their socioeconomic condition and political future. On the other hand, employees, dependents, and clients of the state are also subject to profound *qualitative* changes in their relations with state administrators, politicians, and the corporate ruling class. In actual struggles against the state, quantitative and qualitative issues interpenetrate. The struggle for black studies programs is at once an attempt to win control over state expenditures and to produce fundamental changes in the nature of school curriculum and social relations. Teachers' unionism weaves the issues of control of the schools, curriculum development, programing of classroom time, and racism into the traditional themes of wages and hours.[49] In brief, the

social meaning of the fiscal crisis goes well beyond immediate budgetary issues. For purposes of exposition, however, the two basic themes—the quantitative and qualitative—are analyzed separately, first in relation to state employees, and second in relation to state dependents and clients.

The most important response to the deterioration of wages and salaries of state workers is trade unionism, including strike activity, slowdowns, and other traditional weapons of organized labor. Labor union activity in both the state and private sectors of the economy aims to *protect* the standard of living and conditions of work; that is, unions function essentially as defensive organizations. Thus, for example, the American Federation of Teachers proposes collective bargaining as an answer to such problems as keeping salary schedules in line with those in private industry and ensuring that teachers maintain their "fair share" of control of the schools.

The uncritical acceptance by state employees of traditional modes of organization and struggle is easily understood; the themes of "economism" and corporate liberal reform have monopolized recent labor struggles, and state workers, no matter how militant or radical, have no alternative traditions. Yet traditional unionism is bound to fail the state employee, not only in the profound sense that the labor movement has failed workers in the private economy by binding the working population hand and foot to the corporate-dominated political consensus, but also in the immediate sense that state unionism increasingly will be unable to win wage advances and "deliver the goods."

The reason is that private workers and state workers occupy different places in the society. In the short run, the large corporations pass on wage increases won by private workers to consumers in the form of higher prices. State administrators do not have any equivalent indirect "taxing" mechanism. Instead, wage and salary increases must be absorbed by the taxpayer. In the long run, the corporations have responded to the militant economism of traditional unions by accelerating labor-saving technological change, lowering costs, and augmenting productivity. The corporations have protected profits directly by raising prices and indirectly by raising productivity, and hence over many years have contributed greatly to the absolute volume of goods and services available to the population. In other words, traditional labor struggles have forced the corporations to advance productivity, and, indirectly, real wages, in order to maintain and expand profits. State administrators are unable to increase productivity in the state sector. On the contrary, some are even under pressure to retard the application of modern technology to the state sector, and, in any case, they do not have any operative profitability criteria to guide decision making. In short, there is no way for wage struggles in the state sector to "pay for themselves."

Therefore, the state normally resists state unionism in general, and wage demands in specific, more adamantly than private corporations oppose private unions. Labor struggles in the state sector are increasingly opposed by the taxpaying working class as a whole, and, as a result, the traditional conduct of these struggles tends to *worsen* the condition of state employees precisely because the struggles worsen the fiscal crisis itself. Finally, state unions ordinarily must stay on the defensive, insofar as economic demands are concerned. In the private sector, traditional unions regularly demand that workers get their "fair share" of increases in corporate income arising from productivity increases. Owing to the fact that the income of the state is dependent on the tax rate and tax base, state employee unions are unable to go on the offensive.

To the extent that state workers confine their activity to traditional economism, they are fighting a losing struggle. As yet,

there is no general understanding of the function of the state, and especially of the fact that state employees are employed not by the people but by capital as a whole. That is to say, there is no general understanding that the growing antagonism between state employees and state administration conceals an objective antagonism between wage labor and private capital.

At this point, we can tie together some of the themes already developed. Labor strikes are only effective when they stop the flow of profits and, hence, threaten the social existence of the ruling class. Strikes in the state sector cannot possibly be effective in this sense; state unionism thus cannot uncritically apply the experience of private unionism. Strikes in the state sector merely raise production costs for capital as a whole —leading to increases in prices and inflation—or lower the real wages of the taxpaying working class, or both. Strikes conducted by state unions always hold the potential of dividing the working class, and delaying the development of proletarian consciousness. Objectively, therefore, there is no successful reformist, economistic strategy available to state workers. The only way for state workers to win even substantial material gains is to radicalize themselves. And to radicalize themselves requires that they seek alliances with other workers, especially workers in other branches of the state economy. It is too early to predict the nature of these alliances, the form they take, the issues on which they will revolve, and their general political thrust. One or two conclusions, however, can be drawn from existing practice. It must be emphasized that traditional economic struggles mounted by state employees cannot be expected to win the support of the taxpaying working class; from a narrow economic point of view, the interests of private and state employees are opposed, precisely because the socialization of production costs and the expenses of maintaining the social order, including the evolving corporate liberal consensus, tend to worsen the material condition of state employees. Alliances are more likely to be forged over qualitative issues, even given the great difficulties involved.

There is no easy way for the state administration and ruling class to contain the struggles of state employees. In their frustration and disillusionment, the state workers may line up solidly behind the ruling class (as the police are doing now in many cities) and voluntarily adapt to the right-turning corporate liberal consensus. But this danger is minimal. It is impossible to train a person to perform an essential *social* function, and arm him with the rudiments of critical thought, and subsequently expect him to be oblivious to the essentially *private* character of state power, particularly in a social milieu in which traditional labor organization and activity are largely irrelevant.

If state employees have the possibility of developing socialist consciousness, their potential is nothing beside that of state dependents: the mass of students, blacks, Third World groups, and the poor in general. Also difficult to contain are those in motion around the issue of environmental destruction, another movement that both reflects and deepens the fiscal crisis.

Needless to say, collective bargaining dose not afford a solution to the problems of state dependents if only because of the impossibility of defining appropriate bargaining units. There is no traditional way to formalize, administer, and neutralize these struggles, in particular the struggles of those sections of the black and student movements that have already adopted an anti-imperialist, anticapitalist perspective. The corporate ruling class has begun to take the only available course of action. In the schools, it has mounted an attack on the traditional student-teacher relation, and has sought to substitute a systems approach to education in order to increase its control over the student population. In the black ghettos, it is circumventing both the local and federal bureaucracies and beginning to deal directly with the black militants, especially on the crucial issue of jobs. Politically, it is adopting a divide-and-conquer strategy; on the one side, it is trying with some success to co-opt sections of the black nationalist movement; on the other side, it is trying to smash the revolutionary socialists.

The movements of dependents and clients have many sources. This is not the place for a detailed investigation of them, but only for an analysis of the relation between these movements and the fiscal crisis. In the first place, these movements, insofar as they are responses to declining material conditions, obviously reflect the fiscal crisis. Insofar as they raise budgetary demands, they clearly deepen the crisis. And, insofar as they are redefining the meaning of material and social well-being, their activities may deepen the crisis (for example, demands for free clinics provided by the state) or leave it unaffected (for example, emphasis on self-help, new life styles) .

In the narrow material sense of the activities of state dependents and state employees, to the degree that the latter are struggling for more resources to serve the people, are in no sense antagonistic, but rather perfectly complementary. Alliances between teachers and students, welfare workers and clients, and public health workers and those who use public medical facilities are possible and likely. Unity among those who are directly or indirectly dependent on the state will sharpen the contradiction between taxation and expenditures and, thus, deepen the fiscal crisis.

The problem arises from the intermingling of quantitative and qualitative demands. Students in the fight against authoritarianism must confront their immediate "enemy"—the teacher. City planners, whose technical solutions to problems of renewal, relocation, zoning, housing, and so on, are frustrated by profit-seeking businessmen, confront those in the community who pose a third solution—planning by, for, and of those who reside in the community. Public health personnel trying to protect their "professional" status from the attacks by state administrators confront patients who demand not only technically competent medical services, but also *human* service. Professors struggling to maintain faculty "autonomy," "open campuses," and their traditional scholarly prerogatives confront black students and others who want to develop their own curricula and control their own faculties, and, indeed, redefine the meaning of traditional education.

Of all the service workers, probably the social and welfare workers, whose jobs put them constantly in touch with the lowest income groups, have learned most about dealing with their own authoritarianism. Yet, even welfare workers struggling to redefine their jobs and seek ways to help their clients, and not control them, confront masses of welfare clients with their *own* ideas about welfare and social work. And throughout the state economy, it is more difficult for employees to fight against their own racism because black people and other minorities are typically "clients to be looked after" rather than job peers, as in private production.

In short, state service workers are being proletarianized from above, and socialized from below. Under two general sets of pressures, one seeking to transform them into various kinds of "human capital," the other seeking to humanize them, service workers are subject to contradictory sets of conflicts. The only way for them to negate their proletarian condition is by helping to make a socialist revolution; the only way

to participate in socialist revolution is to fight against their own professionalism, racism, and authoritarianism; and the only way to fight these evils is to relate organizationally to those "below" them—that is, relate as equals, not as professionals—clients, as they must in the context of the structure of the state bureaucracy.

Seen in this framework, it is no wonder that the response of state employees to pressures from above and below has been confused and irrational. It is no wonder that the development of class consciousness is uneven, irregular, and uncertain. It is no wonder that the exclusive repetition of themes of antiracism, anti-imperialism, and antiauthoritarianism alone has not radicalized masses of service workers. And it is no wonder that in the absence of a specifically socialist perspective—which can help people comprehend all issues from the class nature of budgetary control, the determinants of state expenditures, and the nature of tax exploitation, to the process by which the uses of technology itself is decided by struggle—indeed, in the absence of a keen comprehension of the basic contradiction between social production and private ownership itself, unionists, organizers, and demonstrators necessarily function in a vacuum. In the absence of this kind of general historical consciousness, how is it possible for all those in motion to come to grips with even the immediate material, budgetary questions, not to speak of the questions of authority, control, professionalism, and service or, finally, the question of what will be the new material basis of social existence itself?

NOTES

1. U.S. Department of Commerce, *Chart Book on Governmental Finances and Employment, 1966* (Washington, D.C., 1966) , p. 15.
2. Bureau of Labor Statistics study, cited in *Missouri Teamsters*, 5 April 1968.
3. *American Teacher* 52, no. 10 (June 1968) .
4. Grant McConnell, *Private Power and American*

Democracy (New York, 1966) ; Walton Hamilton, *The Politics of Industry* (New York, 1957) ; Gabriel Kolko, *Railroads and Regulation, 1877–1916* (Princeton, N.J., 1965) ; Robert Engler, *The Politics of Oil* (New York, 1961) .
5. Hamilton, *Politics of Industry*, p. 9.

298

6. McConnell, *Private Power and American Democracy*, p. 279.

7. Ibid., p. 244.

8. Hamilton, *Politics of Industry*, p. 9.

9. William Appleman Williams, *The Contours of American History* (New York, 1961) ; James Weinstein, *The Corporate Ideal in the Liberal State, 1900–1918* (Boston, 1968) ; Gabriel Kolko, *The Triumph of Conservatism, 1900–1916* (Glencoe, Ill., 1963) ; G. William Domhoff, *Who Rules America?* (Englewood Cliffs, N.J., 1967) ; David Eakins, "The Development of Corporate Liberal Policy Research, 1885–1965" (Ph.D. dissertation, University of Wisconsin, 1966).

10. Lelio Basso, "*State and Revolution* Reconsidered," *International Socialist Journal* 5, no. 25 (February 1968) : 82.

11. Lucius Wilmerding, Jr., *The Spending Power: A History of the Efforts of Congress to Control Expenditures* (New Haven, Conn., 1943), p. 193.

12. Ibid., p. 195.

13. Basil Chubb, *The Control of Public Expenditures* (London, 1952), p. 1.

14. Wilmerding, *Spending Power*, p. 194.

15. David S. Ott and Attiat F. Ott, *Federal Budget Policy* (Washington, D.C., 1965), p. 6.

16. David Novick, ed., *Program Budgeting: Program Analysis and the Federal Budget* (Cambridge, Mass., 1965), passim.

17. Arthur Smithies, *The Budgetary Process in the United States* (New York, 1955), pp. xiv–xv.

18. James R. Schlesinger, *The Political Economy of National Security* (New York, 1960), p. 109.

19. Jesse Burkhead, *American Economic Review* 56, no. 4 (September 1966), review of Novick, *Program Budgeting*, p. 943.

20. Ott and Ott, *Federal Budget Policy*, p. 36.

21. Schlesinger, *National Security*, p. 111.

22. Ibid., p. 107.

23. Harold D. Smith, "The Budget as an Instrument of Legislative Control and Executive Management," *Public Administration Review* 4, no. 3 (Summer 1944) : 181.

24. Payntz Taylor, *Outlook for the Railroads* (New York, 1960), p. 91.

25. *Wall Street Journal*, 28 June 1965.

26. Roger Sherman, "A Private Ownership Bias in Transit Choice," *American Economic Review* 57, no. 5 (December 1967) : 1211–1217.

27. *Wall Street Journal*, 23 July 1965.

28. Henry W. Broude, "The Role of the State in American Economic Development, 1820–1890," in Harry N. Scheiber, ed., *United States Economic History: Selected Readings* (New York, 1964).

29. Louis Hartz, *Economic Policy and Democratic Thought: Pennsylvania, 1776–1860* (Cambridge, Mass., 1948), pp. 290–291.

30. Good general discussions of these tendencies can be found in Shonfield, *Modern Capitalism*, p. 192, and John Kenneth Galbraith, *The New Industrial State* (Boston, 1967), passim.

31. Maurice Dobb, *Capitalism Yesterday and Today* (New York, 1962), p. 75.

32. William Baldwin, *The Structure of the Defense Market, 1955–1964* (Durham, N.C., 1967), p. 9.

33. Murray Weidenbaum, "The Defense-Space Complex: Impact on Whom?" *Challenge,* April 1965, p. 46.

34. M. J. Rossant, *New York Times,* 7 June 1965.

35. Rudolf Goldscheid, "A Sociological Approach to the Problem of Public Finance," in Richard A. Musgrave and Alan T. Peacock, eds., *Classics in the Theory of Public Finance* (New York, 1958), p. 203.

36. Louis Eisenstein, *The Ideologies of Taxation* (New York, 1961), pp. 222–223.

37. R. Jackson, "Political Aspects of Export Taxation," *Public Finance* 12, no. 4 (1957) : 291.

38. These were the conclusions of a study by the Tax Foundation, cited by Sylvia Porter, *San Francisco Chronicle*, 29 November 1966.

39. Mordecai S. Feinberg, "The Implications of the Core-City Decline for the Fiscal Structure of the Core-City," *National Tax Journal* 17, no. 3 (September 1964) : 217.

40. Richard Musgrave's study of Michigan property taxes, cited in California Assembly, Interim Committee on Revenue and Taxation, *Taxation of Property in California*, December 1964, p. 30.

41. Dick Netzer, *Economics of the Property Tax* (Washington, D.C., 1966), pp. 40–62.

42. Tax Foundation, *State Inheritance Tax Rates and Exemptions* (New York, 1966), p. 165.

43. The best analysis of the political economy of wealth taxation is Manual Gottlieb, "The Capital Levy after World War I," *Public Finance* 7, no. 4 (1952) : 356–385.

44. Ernest C. Harvey, "Social Security Taxes—Regressive or Progressive?" *National Tax Journal* 18, no. 4 (December 1965) : 408.

45. Tax Foundation, *Retail Sales and Individual Income Taxes in State Tax Structures* (New York, 1962), pp. 29–30.

46. Bureau of the Census, *State Government Finances in 1967* (Washington, D.C., 1968), p. 7, table 1.

47. S. D. Hermamsen, "An Analysis of the Recent Tax Cut," *National Tax Journal* 18, no. 4 (December 1965) : 425.

48. George Katona, *The Mass Consumption Society* (New York, 1964), pp. 145–146.

49. See, for example, *American Teacher* 54, no. 1 (September 1969).

The limits of legitimacy*

ALAN WOLFE

The breezy optimism with which partisans of liberal democracy greeted the post–World War II years has changed to a desperate pessimism about whether liberal democracy has a future at all. It is no longer uncommon to hear political observers say things like "it would be no bad thing if the expectations of citizens of democratic states were somewhat reduced,"[1] even though such statements were once considered too far to the right to be taken seriously. A new tone has crept into the usually placid language of political science, as represented by these musings of Anthony King:

Although no one has produced a plausible scenario for the collapse of the present British system of government, the fact that people are talking about the possibility at all is in itself significant and certainly we seem likely in the mid or late 1970s to face the sort of "crisis of the regime" that Britain has not known since 1832, possibly not since the seventeenth century.[2]

The new mood is contagious. Willy Brandt's prediction that democracy in Western Europe will last no more than 20 or 30 years, the feeling among "cold warriors" that communism is about to triumph throughout the Mediterranean, and the defensiveness of Henry Kissinger are all based on the assumption that liberal democracy as we know it has seen its best days.[3] The most relentlessly pessimistic analysis of all has been offered by Robert Nisbet, who sees in the rise of mass democracy an erosion of political civility so extensive that militarism, bureaucracy, and unchecked power become the hopeless condition of modern man. The "tendencies of political centralization and social disintegration" characteristic of the modern state render attempts to restore a sense of political community close to impossible.[4] We seem consigned, in his vision, to a choice among equally nihilistic alternatives.

The manifest popularity of this pessimism should not be surprising. As we have seen, the emergence of late capitalism has seriously altered the nature of the state and the political system within which it operates. The inability of government to achieve its professed ends despite its seeming power, the separation of decision makers from the public, the eclipse of rationality and its replacement by a world of illusions and falsehoods, the bankruptcy of traditional political thought, the replacement of genuine politics by an alienated opposite, the schizophrenic nature of citizenship, the breakdown of mediating mechanisms, and the utopianization of ruling classes—all these processes operating together have contributed to a serious paralysis of the late capitalist state.

The secret, in a sense, is out; liberal democracy no longer works the way it is supposed to. While some, especially politicians, continue to proclaim that happy societies will once again exist, both popular sentiment and intellectual opinion conclude otherwise. The trend toward the exhaustion of alternatives raises the important questions of whether the capitalist

---

* From *The Limits of Legitimacy: Political Contradictions of Contemporary Capitalism,* by Alan Wolfe (The Free Press, 1977), pp. 322–347. Reprinted with permission of Macmillan Publishing Co., Inc. Copyright © 1977, The Free Press, a division of Macmillan Publishing Co., Inc.

state can continue to exist with minimal legitimacy and, if it cannot, what new forms it is likely to take. The legitimacy crisis of late capitalism poses questions too important to the future of Western nations to be ignored.

The attack on liberal democracy

The everyday perception that something is amiss in the world of liberal democracy is now commonplace. One example is a poll taken by *Le Monde* in late 1970, which showed that 47 percent of the French people felt that the state defends the rich, compared to 8 percent who said it defends the poor. In addition, 42 percent felt that the state was unjust or intolerant; 24 percent said that the state leans to the right, as opposed to 3 percent who saw it leaning to the left; 69 percent indicated that the state weighed heavily on their daily lives, while only 27 percent said that it did not; and 73 percent felt that they were impotent in the face of the state, compared to 23 percent who felt that they could influence its actions.[5] A widely reported survey of American political attitudes between 1964 and 1970 showed similar sentiments, proving that the traditional French hostility toward the state is not unique. A few of the U.S. findings are worth reproducing (see Table 1).[6] Moreover, alienation from government in these years cut across class and regional lines, affecting every group in the population.[7] Opinions like these seem to have intensified since 1970. A poll undertaken by Cambridge Survey Research showed that 38 percent of those interviewed in 1972 thought that their leaders regularly lied to them; this rose to 55 percent in 1974, and then to an astounding 68 percent in the spring of 1975.[8] The strongly worded conclusion of Arthur H. Miller of the University of Michigan that "a situation of widespread, basic discontent and political alienation exists in the U.S. today"[9] seems, if anything, too tame. One must wonder how long a society can continue to exist in which over half its members show strong negative feelings toward the government and toward those who occupy positions of power within it.

Survey findings like these have been responsible for a reevaluation of attitudes toward liberal democracy by a number of leading social and political thinkers. Indicative of the new trend is a report of the Trilateral Commission, called *The Governability of Democracies,* which can justly be viewed as a watershed in the attitude of bourgeois social science toward liberal democracy.[10] The Trilateral Commission, an association of "private" citizens from the United States, Western Europe, and Japan, has recently come to public attention through its close connections with the Carter presidency.[11] Under the leadership of men like Zbigniew Brzezinski

TABLE 1
Proportion of the public expressing little confidence in government (percent)

	1964	1966	1968	1970
1. How much do you think you can trust the government in Washington to do what is right?				
Only some of the time	22.0	31.0	37.0	44.2
2. Would you say that the government is run pretty much by a few big interests looking out for themselves . . . ?				
Few big interests	29.0	34.0	39.2	49.6
3. Do you think that almost all of the people running the government . . . don't seem to know what they are doing?				
Don't know what they are doing	27.4	—	36.1	68.7

and other planners of what I call the Transnational State, the Commission has adopted the position that only through the cooperation of all the major capitalist powers—working in harmony with the leaders of Third World countries that control vast resources—can the stability of the present world system be maintained. Because this perspective requires some sacrifice of short-term sovereignty and self-interest in exchange for long-range global planning, the Commission is often viewed as "liberal" in contrast to the aims of the U.S. Republican Party. The Trilateral Commission—which is financed by a number of U.S. and European bankers including David Rockefeller—has come out in favor of national planning, at sharp variance with the laissez-faire rhetoric of men like former U.S. Secretary of the Treasury William Simon. This approach, also, is willing to sacrifice the short-term goals of any given corporation for its long-term benefits. Because of its links with the Carter administration the remarks of the Trilateral Commission on the "manageability" of democracy seem especially important.

The Trilateral Report is divided into four sections: one on Europe, another on Japan, a third on the United States, and some concluding remarks about structural change. The European section, written by Michel Crozier, and the American, authored by Samuel P. Huntington, are the most interesting, though the concluding recommendations, which I will discuss shortly, are the most controversial. In both Europe and the United States, all the usual agencies of "political" socialization are seen as falling apart. People are no longer deferentially accepting as inviolate what established authorities tell them. The value structure has changed, and new expectations have revolutionized political life. Crozier, for example, echoes Jürgen Habermas' *Legitimation Crisis* when he notes that traditional standards of rationality in the West, such as the distinction

between ends and means, have begun to disintegrate. Cut loose from ties of obedience and traditional values, people begin to make political demands on the state. The result is an "overload" of inputs that cannot be met by government. Consequently, in Crozier's words, "the more decisions the modern state has to handle, the more helpless it becomes."[12]

Huntington carries Crozier's pessimism further. What he calls the "democratic surge of the 1960s" was a challenge to all existing authority systems. As people became politicized, their disappointment was inevitable because democratic societies cannot work when the citizenry is not passive. The result is a substantial withering away of confidence in government, such as the University of Michigan survey cited above, of which Huntington makes extensive use. An accompanying decline of faith in the party system, combined with the inability of presidents to finish their terms, gives rise to what Huntington suggestively calls a "democratic distemper" that hinders the political system from carrying out its traditional policies, domestic and foreign. If the system is to correct itself, this "excess of democracy" must be reduced. There must be an emphasis on the fact that the "arenas where democratic procedures are appropriate are limited." Individuals and groups should be depoliticized, since a functioning system requires "some measure of apathy and non-involvement." In general, the demand is one for "balance":

A value system which is normally good in itself is not necessarily optimized when it is maximized. We have come to recognize that there are potentially desirable limits to economic growth. There are also potentially desirable limits to the extension of political democracy. Democracy will have a longer life if it has a more balanced existence.[13]

In order to restore this balance, the authors make a number of controversial proposals. First, they strongly endorse mechanisms for economic planning. Noting that "the governability of democracy is dependent upon the sustained expansion of the economy," the Report implicitly argues that the only way to make people content with political apathy is to increase their income, and this task is too important to be left in the hands of market mechanisms. The authors' hopes for planning are as much political as they are economic, for a workable capitalist economy and acceptance of that structure are, to them, linked. Second, the Report calls for a strengthening of political leadership. Sentiments that one would have thought dead after Vietnam and Watergate are dramatically reborn: "The trend of the last decade toward the steady diminution [?] of the power of the Presidency should be stopped and reversed. The President clearly has the responsibility for insuring national action on critical matters of economic and foreign policy. He cannot discharge that responsibility if he is fettered by a chain of picayune legislative restrictions and prohibitions." Some people never seem to learn; the seeds of a new Watergate have already been planted, even before the old roots have been fully ripped out. Third, the Report calls for attempts to put some life back into dying political parties, endorsing government aid to parties, but calling for balance in the sources of campaign finance. The decision of the state to finance elections to itself, a consequence of the breakdown of mediating mechanisms, is worrisome to these writers. Fourth, unspecified restrictions on the freedom of the press are urged. ("But there is also the need to assure to the government the right and the ability to withhold information at the source.") Fifth, education should be cut back because the democratization of education, minimal as it has been, has raised expectations too high. Assuming that education is related to "the constructive discharge of the responsibilities of citizenship," then "a program is necessary to lower the job expectations of those who receive a college

education." On the other hand, if citizenship training is not the goal of education, then colleges should be turned into vast job training centers. Sixth, the Report calls for "a more active intervention in the area of work," since alienation must be attacked at its roots. German experiences with code-termination are rejected in favor of state aid in experimenting with new forms of work organization. Finally, supranational agencies of cooperation among the major capitalist powers are encouraged, including the mobilization of private groups (just like the Trilateral Commission) to share "mutual learning experiences."[14]

The unusual bluntness of *The Governability of Democracies* violates a taboo of democratic societies, which is that no matter how much one may detest democracy, one should never violate its rhetoric in public. Consequently, this report has generated a full-scale controversy within the Trilateral Commission itself. When it was formally presented, at a conference in Kyoto, Japan, on May 30 and 31, 1975, numerous commission members from the United States and Europe denounced it as too pessimistic, and some even urged that the Trilateral Commission repudiate its own study. In a major speech Ralf Dahrendorf, now head of the London School of Economics, aligned himself with the critics, saying, "I am not, contrary to many others today, pessimistic about the future of democracy."[15] The passion of the Kyoto debates reveals that liberal democracy still has its partisans, the conservative intellectuals by no means unanimously share disdain for it. Yet in spite of the sincerity of those within the Trilateral Commission who have objected to the Crozier-Huntington analysis, one cannot escape the feeling that their commitment to democracy is as much tactical as it is principled, that they are prepared to retain democratic structures only until their breakdown becomes more complete. The seriousness with which *The Governability of Democracies* has been discussed, even by those who object to it, confers legitimacy upon its ideas because it makes reasonable what only ten years ago would have seemed to be an extremist position. Just as during the war in Indochina, the Defense Department continued to adopt "options" that it had shortly before dismissed as extreme, Western intellectuals are now calmly discussing hypotheses that they once would have associated with lunatic fringes. This tendency of social theorists to become chiliastic as the system they defend becomes untenable suggests that the issues in the debate over liberal democracy are about as deep as political issues can get.

Why should liberal democracy, after a sustained period of existence, suddenly become not an assumption that everyone shares, but a hypothesis about which people argue? At one level, the answer lies in the polls cited above, which show the lack of positive affect toward the state characteristic of populations in the 1970s. The authors of the Trilateral Report are very much shaken by these figures. "Leadership is in disrepute in democratic societies,"[16] they note, and without faith in leadership democracy as we know it can no longer exist. Huntington's section on the United States extends this preoccupation. To him, the most basic cause of the "democratic distemper" lies not so much in anything that governments have been doing lately, but in changing patterns of political participation; it is citizens, not leaders, who are responsible for the instabilities of what Maurice Duverger has recently called "plutodemocracy."[17] Huntington is particularly concerned with the increase in political participation among black Americans. Attributing it, rightly, to their increased group consciousness, he concludes that it is not greater education that makes for greater participation, but the degree to which an individual or group

develops a preoccupation with political questions. The rhetoric of democratic values begins to be taken seriously. As Huntington notes:

For much of the time, the commitment to these values is neither passionate nor intense. During periods of rapid social change, however, these democratic and egalitarian values of the American creed are reaffirmed. The intensity of belief during such creedal passion periods leads to the challenging of established authority and to major efforts to change governmental structures to accord more fully with those values.[18]

Democracy, in short, starts to work.

The decline in public faith in government and the demand that democratic values be taken seriously are interrelated. Liberal democracy loses respect because it is not democratic enough, because its liberalism is maintained at the expense of its popular component. At the same time, structural factors inherent in the capitalist mode of production bring about a crisis of disaccumulation, best reflected in the economic troubles of the 1970s. Capitalist societies seem no longer able to deliver the prosperity that has always been the main argument in their favor. With private capital no longer able to generate enough investment to keep the system afloat, the state becomes more and more involved in the economy on behalf of private capital. But this, as James O'Connor argues in *The Fiscal Crisis of the State*, merely shifts the problem from one area to another, because government assistance is, almost by definition, a confession of the failures of capitalism.[19] State aid to private capital in turn reinforces public cynicism toward government, since those who feel that the state only helps the rich are basically correct. In other words, problems of legitimacy and problems of accumulation reinforce each other. At the very moment when capitalism no longer seems to be working, democracy is just beginning to work. As one fails and the other succeeds, the inherent differences between them emerge, so that those whose main stake lies in preserving a capitalism that is no longer viable are forced to become critics of a democracy that is potentially more alive than ever, while those who consider themselves genuinely democratic increasingly become anticapitalist. The legitimacy crisis is produced by the inability of the late capitalist state to maintain its democratic rhetoric if it is to preserve the accumulation function, or the inability to spur further accumulation if it is to be true to its democratic ideology. The Trilateral Commission understands this contradiction:

The heart of the problem lies in the inherent contradictions involved in the very phrase "governability of democracy." For, in some measure, governability and democracy are warring concepts. An excess of democracy means a deficit in governability; easy governability suggests faulty democracy. At times, in the history of democratic government the pendulum has swung too far in one direction; at other times, too far in the other.

Noting that in the late capitalist countries "the balance has tilted too far against governments,"[20] the authors of the Trilateral Report make explicit their preference: accumulation is far more important than legitimation. If democracy has come to interfere with capitalism, there is no doubt which they would choose.

One need not agree with the Trilateral Commission's conclusion to be sympathetic to the analysis. What their argument boils down to is that a legitimacy crisis that can be described as *subjective*—based on the negative attitude of the population toward government—is becoming *objective*—based on structural contradictions within capitalist societies themselves. On this point, I would have to agree with them. The political conditions of late capitalist society, I have been arguing, have locked state action into contradictions from which there is no easy escape. In this situation of stalemate, it is not surprising that the inherent tensions between liberalism and democracy are beginning to surface. The temporary resolutions to this tension have played themselves out, and in the 1970s, the problems that were not resolved in the 19th century have resurfaced with intensity. Capitalism and democracy do face each other as real alternatives, and at some point in the near future—one cannot tell when—one or the other will come to dominate. Thus, the dominant political issue facing late capitalism will not take place *within* the rules of the game but *over* them.

Forces are already lining up on both sides of this issue, and the willingness of the Trilateral Report to make public antidemocratic feelings that have long been in the closet is only one indication of the new political tone. As late capitalist societies are unable to develop new compromises to the tensions between liberalism and democracy, they will find themselves pushed one way or the other. Defenders of the powers that be have begun to make their prescriptions clear. Their programs involve such remedies as cutbacks in democratic expectations, attacks on the principle of participation, and, in some cases, outright proposals for authoritarian solutions. Defenders of democracy have not been as organized and articulate, but there is a growing feeling among dissenting groups that democracy has indeed become the issue. One cannot predict in advance who would win a confrontation between capitalism and democracy, but one can analyze the weapons on both sides.

Authoritarian proclivities

The legitimacy crisis of late capitalism has placed defenders of existing social arrangements in an uneasy position, forcing them to deny once strongly asserted values. As they try to maintain control of a system that they feel is slipping away from them, their liberalism turns into social control, their concern for welfare becomes benign neglect, their faith in democracy is transformed into a penchant for hierarchy, their internationalism is reduced to a carping ethnocentrism, and their dreams of the future suddenly become the nightmares of the present. Retracing their steps, they discover that the world is not quite as they thought, and they are prepared to advocate some extreme solutions in order to bring it back into line with their prejudices and preconceptions. Having carefully admonished their antagonists to play by the rules, they wish to suspend the rules when they no longer work to their benefit. In this section, I want to look at some of the antidemocratic solutions being advocated by defenders of the capitalist mode of production. My argument will *not* be that liberal democracy is about to turn into some sort of fascist state; fascism, among other things, requires a degree of mobilization quite at odds with the depoliticized character of late capitalism.[21] Rather, I will describe three alternatives that seem to be most likely: restricting the activity of government; increasing alienated politics; and moving toward explicitly authoritarian structures. Each of these alternatives has its advocates, though no single one has yet achieved hegemony as the preferred strategy.

By far the most popular tendency, probably because it seems least radical on the surface, is the attempt to restrict the activity of government. This is a reflection of the political theory of resignation, which argues that since solutions to basic problems do not exist, political action to rectify them is useless. This disenchantment with the ability of government to resolve social and economic contradictions flies in the face of the history of the capitalist state, which expanded each time a solution outside of it was not to be found. For this reason, the antistatist urge constitutes a serious reversal of a previously held position. But more is at stake here than in-

consistency. The fact is that most state spending is popular, not in the abstract (people regularly denounce big government in polls), but as it affects specific individuals (social security, hospital, unemployment compensation, etc.). The syllogism is unalterable: welfare spending is democratic; some want to eliminate or substantially reduce it; those who do become undemocratic. The attack on government activity has become, in other words, a not particularly well disguised attack on democracy itself.

Businessmen attack big government the most, and their motive in doing so is a clear distrust of democracy. Contrary to assertions that businessmen supported the welfare state in order to buy off discontent, most corporate executives accepted government spending for social welfare only with extreme reluctance. Now that capitalist economies are in the midst of stagflation, these antidemocratic attitudes, always latent, are shooting to the surface. One study of corporate executives in the United States found that in private, businessmen were unreconciled to the ideal of one man, one vote, and all it implies; their attitudes were not much different from the laissez-faire elitism of the Harmonious State.[22] Which of the following statements were made in the 19th century and which in 1975?[23]

It is one man one vote. And as the poor and the ignorant are the majority, I think it is perfectly certain—and it is only consistent with all one has heard or read of human nature—that those who have the power will use it to bring about what they consider to be a more equitable distribution of the good things of this world.

One-man one-vote will result in the eventual failure of democracy as we know it.

We are dinosaurs at the end of an era. There is a shift of power base from industry and commerce to masses who cannot cope with the complexities of the modern world.

The normal end of the democratic process gives unequal people equal rights to pursue happiness in their own terms. There is a difference between the free enterprise system and a democracy which we also espouse.

In this good, democratic country where every man is allowed to vote, the intelligence and property of the country is at the mercy of the ignorant, idle, and vicious.

The first statement was made by the Englishman J. A. Froude in 1887, and the last by an American businessman in 1868; the three in the middle, though indistinguishable in tone from the other two, were made by American corporate executives in the mid-1970s. There is a direct link between the businessman's distrust of democracy as expressed in statements like these and his distaste for social welfare programs. When the *Wall Street Journal* speaks of "putting a lid on social programs,"[24] what it has in mind is a feeling that people want too much and that a democratic polity is unfortunately organized to make them believe that they can get it. The real cure to excessive spending, in its view, is to curb excessive democracy.

In the past five years this Babbitt-like prejudice of businessmen has been given a certain elegance by various European and American political scientists. Samuel Brittan, who works for both the *Financial Times* of London and Oxford University, has pointed out that "liberal representative democracy suffers from internal contradictions" that have recently made themselves felt. One endemic problem is that "democracy . . . imparts a systemic upward bias to expectations."[25] This results in what Daniel Bell has called "the revolution of rising entitlements,"[26] the feeling that citizens seem to have that their dreams can come true, that economic insecurity, for example, can be abolished. But such demands make it difficult for the capitalist state to govern, since the more money ordinary people receive, the less is available for accumulation, and the more politicized the population, the less the power avail-

able to the state. As Anthony King notes for Britain:

The reason it has become harder to govern is that, at one and the same time, the range of problems that government is expected to deal with has vastly increased, and its capacity to deal with problems, even many of the ones it had before, has decreased. It is not the increase in the number of problems alone that matters, or the reduction in capacity. It is the two coming together.[27]

According to King, the performance of government cannot be substantially altered; hence the only solution is to lower public expectations. Government is compared to an electrical system; it has become, in the favorite word of the new antidemocratic creed, "overloaded."[28] The only sensible thing to do, these writers conclude, is to reduce the current, although building new sockets would solve the problem and keep the lights on as well.

When stripped of its social science rhetoric, the theory of overload or "rising entitlements" is little more than the traditional antidemocratic biases of big businessmen. Moreover, contradictions in both positions make their sincerity suspect. Businessmen want less government, but they also support Aldo Moro's $51 billion plan to "modernize" Italian industry, Giscard's $7 billion pump priming of September 1975, and the extraordinary probusiness budget of Britain's Prime Minister James Callaghan in April 1976.[29] The only proposal to give money to business that business has opposed in recent years was former Vice President Rockefeller's $100 billion energy package, and this was more a glimmer in his eye than a serious policy option. Similarly, the neo-neo-Hamiltonian political scientists (the neo-Hamiltonians were the men around Theodore Roosevelt) speak of the necessity to streamline government, but they also desire a strong presidency, backed by a large military and foreign policy machinery, and increased expenditures for the police.[30] In short, neither the businessmen nor the social scientists are incipient anarchists; it is democracy, not government, that has aroused their ire, and their attacks on the latter are a prelude to restrictions on the former. Liberal society, in their view, can be preserved only if democracy is curtailed.[31]

This unease about democracy cannot be divorced from concern about capitalism itself. As Daniel Bell has noted: "Though capitalism and democracy historically have arisen together, and have been commonly justified by philosophical liberalism, there is nothing which makes it either theoretically or practically necessary for the two to be yoked."[32] There is a strong feeling in certain quarters that capitalism can be preserved only if democracy is held in check. Demands on the government are seen as a kind of "political inflation." Just as inflation is "caused" by groups pushing their self-interest at the expense of the common good, the democratic state's capacity is weakened by the too selfish pursuit of individual and group demands.[33] Controlling runaway inflation requires such noncapitalist measures as wage and price controls and state planning; controlling runaway democracy may also require control on expectations and, if necessary, state repression. As Brittan, following Schumpeter, rightly observes, the contradictions of democracy are inherently economic in nature.[34]

The recessions of the 1970s have intensified the feeling in ruling class circles that if capitalism is in trouble, democratic demands will have to be curtailed. An inadvertent rationale for this point of view has been supplied by Arthur Okun.[35] He argues that a well functioning capitalist economy produces substantial inequality, but that an inflexible pursuit of equality would be economically inefficient. While Okun, in good eclectic fashion, calls for balance, in periods of economic difficulty the argument is easy to advance that economic growth will occur when expectations about equality are lowered. High unemployment, *Business Week* noted in March 1976, "has created an economic situation that is eerily reminiscent of Karl Marx's predictions." When *Business Week* and Karl Marx agree, the situation must be serious indeed. The article also noted: "In the Western world, something has changed radically in political economics. Economists and politicians now agree that by themselves the traditional modes of stimulating economies by government spending or increasing the money supply will not end high unemployment."[36] Neither Democrats nor Republicans have found the answer, according to this assessment. Okun's balance, represented by full employment bills, comprehensive job training, and other government policies, is seen as a stopgap at best. Republican attempts to cut back expenditures are not measuring up to the dimensions of the crisis. Unstated but implied throughout is the feeling that drastic economic conditions require drastic changes in the political system. Democracy, in other words, is under attack because capitalism is not working, when, presumably, it is capitalism that should be under attack, for democracy is working.

Reductions in the activity of government are thus seen as one way of increasing the options of the ruling class. But there is a price. The critique of government spending stands for a disenchantment with equality, one of the key aspects of democratic theory. Citizens whose "expectations" have been reduced are citizens who have become resigned to their lot at the bottom of a hierarchy. Without a myth of opportunity, visible, articulated discontent may be the consequence. Discussing cutbacks in social services for the poor, *Business Week* quoted manpower expert Lloyd Ulman of the University of California: "I'm concerned about the young people, especially the blacks. The

308

less they squawk now, the more of a problem we are storing for the future."[37] The image of an uprising of discontent by a population that has come to expect social welfare programs constitutes the major stumbling block of the whole strategy; cutbacks in welfare are a two-edged sword for ruling classes, enhancing immediate flexibility at the cost of longer run legitimation problems. Not surprisingly, as a result there has been some interest shown in other possible ways out of the dilemma. An increase in "alienated politics" constitutes a second possible strategy for ruling classes in the late capitalist period.

Politics becomes alienated to the degree that the everyday political activity of people is used against them to reinforce passivity, instead of being used by them to advance their own collectively determined goals. Alienated politics is in many ways similar to surplus value. In order to increase surplus value and therefore his capital, an employer, when faced with a working day whose length has been agreed upon, can try to increase the "productivity" of a given worker in that period by instituting a "speedup" which, if the costs of reproducing the worker are held constant, will yield a greater proportion of the surplus product to himself. So it goes with ruling classes. An increase in alienated politics requires some way of enhancing the productivity of political action such that a smaller percentage of the collective social power produced is kept by the citizens. The most obvious method of accomplishing this task is to promote passivity by discouraging active participation in political and social life. If the strategy of cutting back government activity represented an attack on equality, the strategy of increasing alienated politics becomes little more than an attack on participation. And since equality and participation are the twin pillars of democratic theory, reinforcing alienated politics becomes, like lowering expectations, an attack on democracy itself.

The irony of the attack on participation is that there was not very much to begin with. Direct, informed participation in political affairs has rarely been a characteristic of the capitalist state in this country. Instead, solutions like the Franchise State instituted a system of bargaining that Lowi has called "interest group liberalism."[38] Under such a system, direct participation was sacrificed for carefully orchestrated negotiation between the leaders of variously affected interest groups. With the stagnation inherent in late capitalism, writers have begun to argue that even this minimal level of participation has become maximal, that liberal democracy can no longer afford even interest group liberalism if it is to survive unscathed. Samuel Brittan, as we have seen, finds one of the principal causes of the internal contradictions of liberal democracy to be the desire of ordinary people for social welfare, but he includes as an even more important factor the tendency of interest groups to bargain for rewards for their members.[39] The one must be cut back just as surely as the other, he concludes, or else liberal democracy will be torn apart. An even more passionate defense of a similar position took place in 1968, when *The Public Interest* sponsored a symposium on New York City. A summary of the discussion, which included many prominent officials, professors, and writers, asked whether the United States was "witnessing the ultimate, destructive working out of the telos of liberal thought." According to this symposium, New York City at one time represented the essence of a Madisonian politics of incremental interests, in which organized "subsystems" competed for public favors. Because of internal contradictions, however, these subsystems tended to break down. The conclusion, expressed in a memo that was read by President-elect Nixon, was self-evident, given the assumptions:

That the society is breaking down means that the liberal state will no longer do. It must, on pain of anarchy or civil war, be replaced by a regime which explicitly recognizes the necessity of subsystems and which is prepared to create substitutes for those subsystems when they break down. Our problem is that informed opinion is moving in precisely the opposite direction.[40]

In this version, interest group liberalism can be preserved only if the state organizes and constitutes the interest groups. What little democratic participation there is would be reduced even more. "Informed opinion" may be moving the other way because it is not prepared to jettison even the minimal commitment to liberal democracy that exists at the moment.

Nonetheless, *The Public Interest* symposium was prophetic, because its focus was on New York City, and in the mid-1970s New York City was most directly facing the new political realities. New York's troubles have been described as a "fiscal crisis," but that is a half truth at best. What is most significant about the decisions of 1975–1977 is that they have stripped New York of its traditional political system. As *The Public Interest* pointed out, New York's politics was the most advanced form of interest group liberalism in the United States, for in this city bargaining among interest groups held the key to most public policy decisions. In this context, the decision to create agencies like the Emergency Financial Control Board represents an attempt to impose new government structures on the city, which would replace the minimal amount of democracy inherent in a bargaining system with decisions handed down from above. Nearly all the participants in these events have agreed that New York's budget as such is not at issue, but its methods of carrying out public business. Under the veritable coup d'état that has taken place there, citizens had better not only reduce their expectations, but also the idea that their participation in affairs of government would be welcome. For the immediate future, interest group leaders in New York will spend more time imposing the demands of the state on their members than

they will be communicating the desires of their members to the state. *The Public Interest*'s call for the creation of new subsystems turns out to be a nightmare come true.

As New York goes, so may the rest of the world. As far as ruling classes are concerned, participation is clearly an idea whose time has passed, and we are likely to see attempts to roll back the few victories for increased participation of the postwar years. In West Germany, an attempt to obtain parity for labor unions in the system of codetermination was defeated by a coalition that wants economic growth instead. The defeat of *Paritätische Mitbestimmung* is a warning to unions that there are limits to what the capitalist class will accept in the name of participation. Yet attacks on the principle of a nonalienated politics create their own problems. Just as people have come to expect a certain level of social services, they also accept as a right the notion of participation. This does not mean that they want to participate at all times—most people, particularly in the United States, find political participation a bore—but it does mean that they reserve the right to do so when they feel aggrieved. In this sense, to restrict participation not only comes into conflict with democracy; it violates some of the basic principles of liberalism as well. Defenders of capitalist society may find that not only is democracy in contradiction with the liberal need to accumulate, but so may be aspects of liberalism itself. If both liberalism and democracy come under attack, the ability of late capitalism to reproduce itself may be upheld, but at costs so dear that they would transform the political structure into something unrecognizable.

Because restrictions on government activity are antidemocratic and limitations on participation can become illiberal, some have drawn the appropriate conclusion and suggested that capitalist societies will increasingly require explicitly authoritarian political structures. As we have seen, the

Trilateral Commission's Report on *The Governability of Democracies* has suggested as much, and in an interview published after the Report was completed, Samuel Huntington was even more explicit: "There has to be a realistic appreciation that we can't go back to a simpler world—that we're going to live in a world of big organizations, of specialization and of hierarchy. Also, there has to be an acceptance of the need for authority in various institutions in the society."[41] Huntington's point may seem extreme, but already some of the Western capitalist societies are facing the option of authoritarianism. Italy, as so often, may be an indication of the future, for there the theory and practice of Christian Democracy are in serious trouble. The ideology of *interclassismo,* which held that all classes would reap the fruits of big business guardianship of the state, has been unable to stem the appeal of left-wing parties. As Giacomo Sani has shown, public opinion generally desires the inclusion of formerly "antisystem" parties like the Communist Party, while the leaders of the Christian Democrats remain far more cautious.[42] It seems clear that if the latter refuse to accept the former into the government, liberal democracy in Italy will fall victim, not to communism, but to a capitalist party unprepared to accept its own political logic. In this sense, in the short run, to quote P. A. Allum, "the Italian ruling class will be forced to choose between its progressive and authoritarian faces."[43] Any attempt by the Christian Democrats to rule without the left would almost necessarily be authoritarian, given current sentiment in that country.

But, to paraphrase Tolstoy, while all stable political systems resemble one another, each unstable system is different in its own way. There are as many versions of authoritarianism as there are of democracy, and to suggest that explicit authoritarian solutions are a possibility is not to answer any questions, but to raise many.

What forms of authoritarian government are we likely to see if late capitalist societies start to move in that direction? Extrapolating from all the tendencies that I have been discussing, it seems that the most likely form authoritarianism would take is a neocorporatism resembling some of the features of earlier experiments tried out in the 1920s. Early experiments with corporatism ran into difficulty because businessmen were not ideologically prepared to accept the restrictions on their freedom that were necessary to bring it into being. Experiences with the Franchise State may have changed this, and if this is the case, then the late 1970s and 1980s could be a much more fruitful period for corporatism than the 1920s. There is nothing so powerful as an idea whose time is 50 years late.

In this context it is important to make a distinction between corporatism, which characterized the Italian economy in the 1920s, and fascism, which succeeded it and then spread to Germany. Fascism contained overt state direction of the economy and a system of vigilante repression and mass mobilization that businessmen found inherently unstable, even though many supported it. Corporatism is far more compatible with the capitalist mode of production, and it also preserves a closer resemblance to the forms of a liberal democratic polity. Philippe Schmitter has described how a corporatist form could emerge out of capitalist needs:

The more the modern state comes to serve as the indispensable and authoritative guarantor of capitalism by expanding its regulative and integrative tasks, the more it finds that it needs the professional expertise, specialized information, prior aggregation of opinion, contractive capability and deferred, participatory legitimacy which only singular, hierarchically ordered, consensually led representative monopolies can provide.[44]

The following can be considered the major aspects of a corporatist organization of the society. First, the economy would be under the domination of monopolies that would make investment decisions privately. Second, these monopolies would work closely with a state planning apparatus that would be organized to help them further their investment decisions with maximum dispatch. Third, selected representatives of "responsible" unions would be consultants to the planning agencies, charged with the task of ensuring that decisions about wages would be accepted. Fourth, a system of wage and price controls would be instituted to stymie inflation, though the controls would be more on the former than on the latter. Fifth, restrictions on freedom of assembly and speech would be designed to prevent breaks in the continuity of the system. Sixth, social welfare programs would be retained, for much the same purpose. Seventh, depoliticization would be the theme of social and political life in general. Eighth, transnational political units would extend the corporatist framework to all the capitalist countries, since it would be extremely difficult for any one of them to maintain a formal democratic system if the others were abandoning it. It should be clear how a form of neocorporatism could arise out of an extension of already existing late capitalist practices. Corporatism would not come about stealthily in the middle of the night, but would be the product of barely noticed changes in everyday practices. When all effective power has passed from representative bodies to corporate-governmental planning agencies, the institution of corporatism would be complete.

None of the countries could at this time be called corporatist, but each is experimenting with proposals that have a corporatist potential. My description of these experiments is not, therefore, meant to imply that the authors of them are self-conscious authoritarians, merely that their ideas could easily be adapted to conform to authoritarian proclivities. This is the case, for example, with Felix Rohatyn's proposal to reconstitute the Reconstruction Finance Corporation, one of the semi-corporatist schemes of the 1920s.[45] Rohatyn, who played a major role in New York City's Emergency Financial Control Board, is also known as one of the most articulate business spokesmen for state planning in the United States, and his sympathy for spending for social programs has led many to classify him as a "liberal." His RFC plan, as he makes quite clear, is not simply a proposal to give public money to private firms; Rohatyn wants the proposed agency to use its money as a weapon, to force firms to conform to sound planning procedures. In short, his RFC constitutes the political-economic shell for a corporatist organization of the economy. The same conclusion can also be drawn from some of the advocates of state planning in the United States. Planners seem divided into two ideological camps. Those on the left, such as John Kenneth Galbraith, Leonard Woodcock, and Wasily Leontief, support legislation like the Humphrey-Javits bill, which would retain democratic structures while trying to introduce an element of rationality into the accumulation process. But state planning is also sympathetically viewed by some on the right, such as Huntington and the Trilateral Commission, who see it as a way of ensuring social peace while at the same time allowing for rational accumulation.[46] An attempt to steer between these two approaches is a plea by Max Ways of *Fortune* for "a new political stance" for business. Ways, who praises Rohatyn and his plans, is, like all the neocorporatists, critical of traditional business laissez-faire and opposition to social spending, but at the same time he also wants to find a way to keep democratic demands under control:

More and more voters have discovered the possibility of bettering their lives through government action. In itself, this discovery is a legitimate extension of the democratic process. But the U.S. has not yet learned to channel and restrain these exuberant pressures so that they won't be self-defeating.[47]

Presumably, some kind of channeling and restraining agency will determine which actions are "legitimate" and which will have to be curbed.

Given the priorities of late capitalism, planning proposals that originate from the left could easily be adopted by the right and turned in an authoritarian direction. American advocates of planning could learn something from Britain. When a new Labour government came into power after the Conservatives were unable to settle a miners' strike, leaders toward the left of the party like Anthony Wedgwood-Benn supported a National Enterprise Bill (NEB), which would nationalize industries that were in trouble.[48] But the NEB turned out to be something quite different, an incipient corporatist form far more compatible with the traditional Tory fascination for corporatist solutions.[49] Once created, the NEB was headed by Sir Don Ryder, an industrialist with a reputation for toughness. While it is too early at this writing to foresee how the NEB will turn out, the decision of a Labour Party position paper of 1975 to give "priority to industrial development over consumption and even over our social objectives"[50] would seem to indicate that the NEB will be more concerned with private investment decisions than with democratic control over corporations. Unless state planning agencies include active members of consumer organizations and unions, they will in all likelihood pave the way for a neocorporatism that would "reform" the polity by "streamlining" and "modernizing" it along the lines of the economy.

What would be the likely results of an explicit move toward quasi-authoritarian solutions to the political contradictions of late capitalism? There is no denying that a move in this direction could severely damage humane and democratic values. One should never underestimate the de-structive potential of a ruling class that has painted itself into a corner, as every living Vietnamese peasant has come to understand. Late capitalist elites are capable of enormous wreckage before they yield their control over the state. Yet the fascination for corporatism is as much an indication of the defensiveness of late capitalist ruling classes as it is an aggressive plan to control everything in sight. Corporatism remains a solution that was tried and found wanting; an avant-garde notion in 1920, it is quite hackneyed at present. In this sense, authoritarian solutions may intrigue ruling classes because they feel themselves becoming illegitimate, a phenomenon noted some time ago by Antonio Gramsci: "If the ruling class has lost its consensus, i.e., is no longer 'leading' but only 'dominant,' exercising coercive force alone, this means precisely that the great masses have become detached from their traditional ideologies, and no longer believe what they used to believe previously."[51] As ruling classes consider authoritarian solutions like corporatism, one can question whether they would continue to be "ruling classes" at all. If the art of ruling lies in the selection of various options in order to preserve power, then the dominant forces within late capitalism are losing their ability to rule. Thus "rule by force" is a contradiction in terms. Authoritarian solutions are an expression of the inability to rule, of the replacement of choice among options with the requirement of preserving power by any means necessary. What the writers in this section symbolize, as a result, is bankruptcy and impotence, not hardheaded realism; political extremism, not moderation and civility. Those who seek to replace liberal democracy by some sort of authoritarian structure are engaged, not so much in a strategy for the ruling class, as in voicing the decline of the ruling class. This does not make authoritarianism any less of a danger to humane values, but it does indicate the desperation of a system that can no longer preserve itself in the face of the desires of the majority.

Democratic dreams

The antidemocratic intellectuals discussed here base their analyses on the assumption that a historical impasse has taken place in liberal democracies, and that the next few years will consequently see a major transformation of Western society. As I have suggested, there are grounds for believing that their general analysis is correct, but I would disagree with them on some of the particulars. First, one cannot know how long the impasse will last; a historical era may be coming to an end, but historical eras generally take a long time in so doing. A postliberal democratic solution will take a long time to work itself out. In the meantime, existing structures will constitute the political framework within which the transition will take place; for that reason, they will remain important. Second, one cannot know what the future will bring. While it would be satisfying to state with precise foresight what the next stage is likely to resemble, only a fool, an astrologer, or a social scientist would try. The truth is that all possible futures will be decided by people themselves, either by ordinary people producing politics as they see fit or by elites trying to work their way out of intractable contradictions. Those who want to know what the outcome of this struggle will be should look elsewhere; those who wish to know the kinds of issues over which these struggles will be waged might consider remaining here. For as I have suggested, the immediate battles will be over the options that the state can command, and because those options are a product of the way people think and act politically, ordinary people will have much more to say about the political future of late capitalism than ruling elites.

In the long run, democratic dreams are far more important than authoritarian proclivities. Pressure from below has constituted a driving force in the adoption of new solutions to the political contradictions of capitalism and has constituted the major reason for the obsolescence of solutions once adopted. Without that pressure, no tension would be present, for then there would be nothing to prevent the capitalist state from serving as a mechanism of accumulation pure and simple. Democratic dreams have come and gone, sometimes appearing as visions of what a humane world would be like and sometimes turning into perverse nightmares as people become desperate in the search for answers to the pressures in their lives. But even though they may be suppressed momentarily, their existence can never be discounted, for the desire to be part of a meaningful community is a human urge that no historical event has yet completely overcome. What, then, is the status of the democratic dream in late capitalism? Will pressure from below be able to offset the authoritarian inclinations of dominant classes in order to make the immediate future one to which we can look forward with anticipation rather than dread? The question has no abstract answer—only political struggle can determine the result—but one can call attention to the importance of the struggle and suggest some possible forms that it might take.

The dilemmas faced by ordinary people are the opposite of those faced by ruling classes; if the latter wish somehow to expand their options, the former, particularly where class struggle is overt, wish to see them contracted. In this sense, the major objectives of democratic pressure should be to counter the directions emerging within dominant elites: increasing the number of activities in which government is engaged; decreasing the proportion of alienated politics; and thinking constructively and imaginatively about democratic solutions transcending the limitations of the capitalist mode of production.

Those who advocate less government

spending on social programs know what they are doing, for given the accumulation function of the state, the only way by which government activity can be reduced is to attack the most democratic point, which is social welfare policy. But at issue is not some abstraction called "spending" or policy" but the real needs of real people. The most immediate political strategy for ordinary people, therefore, should be directed toward both the preservation and the expansion of government services. A social democratic perspective makes perfect sense in the short run for a number of reasons. First, it is based on a historical tradition, since the welfare state has been in existence for some time. Those who wish to roll back social welfare policies become the true radicals, and their attempt to divorce themselves from the history of their own society should be pointed out. Second, however perverse government activity like welfare becomes, it is still meeting some of the needs of the poorest members of the society, and in that sense it is far preferable, by almost any human criterion, to cutbacks. But third, and most important, extensions of government activity restrict the number of options that dominant classes possess, for each increase in social spending means either a reduction in the accumulation function of the state or an intensification of fiscal and political contradictions. Implicitly understanding this, those in power are prepared to wage a battle against more spending on social programs, which makes the continuation of the welfare state essential to a strategy of realizing democratic dreams.

The most articulate presentation of this option is Piven and Cloward's notion of "exploding" the relief roles of the welfare system, in the absence of fundamental economic changes in the society.[52] Written before the fiscal crisis of the state became acute, what Piven and Cloward envisioned for welfare recipients becomes both the lot of, but also a strategy for, the majority of

the population. Attempts to cut back higher education, medical care, police protection, sanitation, and just about every other aspect of domestic services put everyone, metaphorically, on relief. For this reason, the events in New York City of 1975 and 1976, which constitute a testing ground for ruling classes in their strategy of lowering expectations and brutalizing participation, are also a testing ground for popular demands. In a period of recession, for example, there is every reason why public higher education should expand rather than contract, to absorb the unemployed and make good use of their time, if for no other reason. Similarly, "hard times" in the economy generally are times in which government spending goes up, and with it the dreams of the majority of the population for protection against depression. The fact that this is not happening, that most people seem to have accepted the "necessity" of spending cuts in New York, indicates that the dominant forces are winning this particular struggle. Most people seem to have forgotten that the state owes them a decent life with all the social services that they have every right to demand, and because they have, the first step in a strategy to overcome their demoralization has been lost. In a situation of this sort, the preservation and extension of accepted social welfare programs would become a critique of the notion that business conditions are what determines the nature of public policy.

But an extension of domestic social policy, no matter how necessary in the short run, is not a strategy that by itself will bring about basic democratic changes in the nature of the late capitalist state. The power of the state, I have been arguing, is based on the way people produce and reproduce politics, and in that sense, the most meaningful long-range strategy would be one that maximized the nonalienated character of politics. What this means is that in order to fulfill democratic dreams, people must find ways to use the power generated out of political activity for their own purposes, to minimize the proportion of this power that is reimposed on them for purposes over which they have no say. It would appear that there are two general ways in which this could be accomplished: one by "hoarding" the social power that people produce; the other by expending it on activities that they themselves decide.

Hoarding constitutes a first step in the direction of a nonalienated politics, a negative refusal to have alienated power exercised over oneself.[53] It is often recognized that if workers did not work, if they withheld their labor power, no value could be produced, and therefore the capitalist mode of production would grind to a halt. Similarly, if the citizens of late capitalism were to withhold what could be called their "political production," to hoard their political power for themselves, the capitalist state could not continue to function for very long. There are degrees of political hoarding. Simple apathy toward the organized political process is one, and for this reason the authors of the Trilateral Report are so worried about the subjective decline in positive affect toward government, for such alienation represents a first step in the hoarding of political power from the state. The contradiction of depoliticization is that while it serves the need of reducing demands on the state, it also inadvertently contributes to the sense that the existing political system is unresponsive to people's needs. More organized forms of hoarding also exist. Those who engage in cooperative enterprises—such as neighborhood grocery cooperatives, daycare centers, and other social activities—are in a sense hoarding a certain amount of their power from the state, even if their expressed motive is a nonpolitical one. The same is true of those who withdraw into rural areas to produce their own means of subsistence as much as they can. Even though such activities of the "countercul-

ture" by themselves do not pose any direct threat against the existing order, they are a form of hoarding insofar as they withdraw from the existing political system's definition of what constitutes the productive "obligations" of citizenship. When workers go on strike, they hoard their labor power for themselves; an important strategy for political change would involve a "citizens' strike," in which people would refuse to participate in the organized rituals that go under the name of politics in late capitalist society.

But hoarding is only a negative step, which, like a strike, is necessary to understand the nature of one's oppression, but which must lead in new directions or become self-defeating. Strikes, as participants in them often come to understand, are as important for the solidarity they generate as for the immediate concrete objective, and in a similar manner, citizens' strikes, leading to a hoarding of political power, become important when they release a political energy that mobilizes people to begin to make basic decisions for themselves. The difference can be expressed as a shift from unproductive citizenship to repoliticization. Economists have long made a distinction between productive and unproductive labor, in which the former contributes to surplus value and therefore the accumulation of capital, while the latter does not.[54] The same is true of citizenship. A "productive" citizen in a capitalist society is one who contributes to the political power of the state, and therefore to the imposition of an alienated power over people's lives. Hoarding involves an assertion of unproductive citizenship, which is why whenever people engage in political activity that does not conform to the "rules," their efforts are dismissed as "counterproductive," which in a real sense they are. A significant step involves the transformation of nonproductive citizenship into *re*politicization, the attempt by people to seek genuine politics for themselves outside the formal political arena. Any kind of mobilization, even "reactionary" ones like opposition to school busing, unleashes a political energy that gives people a sense of what their liberation might be about. A repoliticized population is one that is subversive of the dominant tendencies associated with the late capitalist state.

The most compelling form of repoliticization involves the direct expenditure of political power by people on alternatives decided by themselves. Not satisfied with mere hoarding, and searching for a vehicle to express their repoliticization, people associate themselves with organized political movements whose purpose is to share social power with people rather than to hold it over them. It matters little whether this strategy is pursued within, outside, or alongside the existing electoral system, so long as the crucial component is the commitment to a nonalienated politics. Examples outside the electoral arena per se would include cultural and social activities, such as the attempts by the Italian Communist Party to create a viable cultural world within bourgeois society. Such movements, if they work, yield a sense of collective power and competence that is far more significant than winning another seat in the legislature. Examples of liberating activity within the electoral system might include attempts by public officials, generally at the local level, to develop methods of sharing their power and their information with the people who elected them, becoming power builders rather than power brokers. This is the underlying philosophy behind the decision of a number of American radicals to involve themselves in electoral activity at the local level.[55] In other words, behind strategies of this sort is an understanding that the depoliticizing needs of late capitalism must be countered with the liberation of political energy, awakening in people a feeling that they themselves are human and capable of deciding what

to do with their collective power. To be avoided is a strategy that reproduces the depoliticized character of late capitalism within opposition movements, for as Gramsci once warned, "In political struggle one should not ape the methods of the ruling classes, or one will fall into easy ambushes."[56]

What I have been suggesting resolves itself into nothing other than an injunction to be political, which is not so much a strategy as an imperative. It does not tell people what to do but how to do it. Its meaning becomes apparent, not over tactics, but over conceptions. Three examples may make it clear what the injunction to be political means. First, should the question arise as to whether the left should organize a political party, the response should depend on the recognition that no *political* parties currently exist, that the bourgeois parties are not political at all because they express an alienated politics at odds with the original meaning of politics in the West. This recognition does not answer the question (people themselves will have to do that), but it does indicate that if a genuinely political party were to be created, its role would be unique, and consequently its tasks could not be derived from existing institutions called parties. Similarly, if intellectuals are worried about whether they have a major role to play in the transition to a postcapitalist society, the answer is that they do—indeed, their role is a major one. For if struggles over conceptions of politics are as important as I have suggested, there is as great a need for conceptualizers as for organizers; to quote Gramsci one last time, " 'Popular beliefs' and similar ideas are themselves material forces."[57] Finally, the importance of being political does not settle the long dispute between reformism and militancy, but it does suggest that "reforms" depressing popular participation lead in the wrong direction while those arousing and sustaining it create a basis of politicization that can be expanded. The debates over reformism within the left have generally concerned themselves with ends —which is as it should be—but the question of means may be important also.

The ultimate objective of repoliticization, in my view, should be to resurrect the notion of democracy, which is far too important an ideal to be sacrificed to capitalism. The political contradictions of capitalist society, I have been arguing, grow out of attempts to reconcile the need for accumulation, which has been justified by philosophical liberalism, and the need to legitimate, which has given rise to democracy. Accumulation, as Daniel Bell has pointed out, will take place in any complex economy.[58] The problem is not that capitalist societies accumulate, but the way in which they do it. In order for the beneficiaries of accumulation to remain a narrow group, a boundary is established beyond which democracy is not allowed to intrude; you have the political system, or at least part of it, liberal ideology claims, but leave the accumulation of capital to us. With liberalism increasingly becoming irrelevant, even to its most articulate defenders, the time has come to think, not about demolishing accumulation, but about democratizing it. The way to eliminate the contradictions between accumulation and legitimation is to apply the principles of democracy to both—to give people the same voice in making investment and allocation decisions as they theoretically have in more directly political decisions. The democratization of accumulation can be called socialism, but it is not the name that is important but the concept behind it. To suggest that socialism can avoid the political contradictions discussed here is

not to argue that any existing societies that are called socialist have—the degree of democratization introduced into accumulation varies greatly from one to another— but to affirm that the democratization of accumulation will prevent any nonrepresentative group of power holders from perverting the democratic process by warping it to suit their own private aggrandizement. Democracy can become reality only when its logic transcends artificial barriers and is applied to all the fundamental decisions made in a modern society, a task in many ways facilitated by the phenomenal technological capacity developed by these societies.

If a choice has to be made between liberalism and democracy, it is my hope that the overwhelming majority of people in late capitalist societies will pick the latter. Whether they do or not is beyond me or anything I can say. Neither revolutionary optimism nor quiescent cynicism are appropriate moods here. Moods do not determine the outcome of struggles; only the contrasting strengths and weaknesses of the contending parties can do that. One side has the power and control over the means of repression and consciousness, the other the weight of numbers, the flow of history, and the possession of a democratic dream. Neither has a claim to certainty. To understand, though, is to contribute, and it has been my desire to illustrate to ordinary people the nature of the political contradictions of their society so that they may be able to find for themselves ways in which to resurrect the democratic dream. It is, in the long run, their vision that will determine whether authoritarianism or democracy is to be our political condition.

NOTES

1. Anthony Hartley, "The Withering Away of Western Liberal Democracy," in E. A. Goerner (ed.), *Democracy in Crisis* (Notre Dame: University of Notre Dame Press, 1971), 163.

2. Anthony King, "Overload: Problems of Governing in the 1970s," *Political Studies*, 23 (June–September 1975), 294–95.

3. See William Pfaff, "Some Questions about a

318

Crisis," *New Yorker*, April 5, 1976, p. 100. Pfaff's point that pessimism about democracy is most of all an American phenomenon is slightly incorrect; as we shall see, Europeans such as Michel Crozier, Giovanni Sartori, Samuel Brittan, and Anthony King all agree with the American sentiment.

4. Robert Nisbet, *The Twilight of Authority* (New York: Oxford University Press, 1975), 232.

5. Alain Duhamel, "Les Français n'aiment pas l'état, mais ils en attendent tout," *Le Monde*, October 10, 1970.

6. Arthur H. Miller, "Political Issues and Trust in Government: 1964–1970," *American Political Science Review*, 68 (September 1974), 953.

7. James S. House and William M. Mason, "Political Alienation in America, 1952–68," *American Sociological Review*, 40 (April 1975), 123–47.

8. *Cambridge Report 3*, Spring 1975, p. 118.

9. Miller, p. 951.

10. The Trilateral Task Force on the Governability of Democracies, *The Governability of Democracies* (New York: Trilateral Commission, May 1975).

11. On the Commission, see Geoffrey Barraclough, "Wealth and Power: The Politics of Food and Oil," *New York Review of Books*, 22 (August 7, 1975), 23–30.

12. Trilateral Report, chap. 2, p. 3.

13. Ibid., chap. 3, pp. 22–25, 47, 59, 60, 62.

14. Ibid., chap. 5, pp. 19, 22, 31, 34, 36, 40.

15. *Trialogue*, no. 7 (Summer 1975), pp. 7–9.

16. Trilateral Report, chap. 5, p. 7.

17. Maurice Duverger, *Janus: Les deux faces de l'Occident* (Paris: Fayard, 1972), 3.

18. Trilateral Report, chap. 3, p. 59.

19. James O'Connor, *The Fiscal Crisis of the State* (New York: St. Martin's Press, 1973).

20. Trilateral Report, chap. 5, pp. 17–18.

21. I have argued this point at greater length in "Waiting for Righty: A Critique of the 'Fascism' Hypothesis," *Review of Radical Political Economics*, 5 (Fall 1973), 46–66.

22. Leonard Silk and David Vogel, *Ethics and Profits* (New York: Simon and Schuster, 1976).

23. The first quotation was cited in Samuel Brittan, "The Economic Contradictions of Democracy," *British Journal of Political Science*, 5 (April 1975), 146. The remainder are from Silk and Vogel.

24. Jonathan Spivak, "Putting a Lid on Social Programs," *Wall Street Journal*, December 31, 1975, p. 6.

25. Brittan, pp. 129, 141.

26. Daniel Bell, *The Cultural Contradictions of Capitalism* (New York: Basic Books, 1976), 232–36.

27. King, p. 294.

28. See ibid., and also Crozier's section in *The Governability of Democracies;* another use of the term is contained in Giovanni Sartori, "Will Democracy Kill Democracy?" *Government and Opposition*, 10 (Spring 1975), 158.

29. *Wall Street Journal*, December 26, 1975, p. 6; *New York Times*, September 5, 1975, p. 35; *New York Times*, April 7, 1976, p. 1.

30. For an example see James Q. Wilson, *Thinking about Crime* (New York: Basic Books, 1975).

31. This conclusion follows from the analysis of Martin Diamond, "The Declaration and the Constitution: Liberty, Democracy, and the Founders," *Public Interest*, 41 (Fall 1975), 39–55.

32. Bell, p. 14.

33. For an example of this reasoning see Huntington's chapter in *The Governability of Democracies*, pp. 5, 11.

34. Brittan, p. 133.

35. Arthur Okun, *Equality and Efficiency: The Big Tradeoff* (Washington: Brookings Institution, 1975).

36. "Why Recovering Economies Don't Create Enough Jobs," *Business Week*, March 22, 1976, pp. 114–15.

37. Quoted in ibid., p. 115.

38. Theodore Lowi, *The End of Liberalism* (New York: Norton, 1969), passim.

39. Brittan, pp. 142–46.

40. Cited in Daniel Patrick Moynihan, *The Politics of a Guaranteed Income* (New York: Vintage Books, 1973), 76–78.

41. "Is Democracy Dying?: Verdict of Leading World Scholars," *U.S. News and World Report*, March 8, 1976, p. 51.

42. Giacomo Sani, "Mass Constraints on Political Realignments: Perceptions of Anti-System Parties in Italy," *British Journal of Political Science*, 6 (January 1976), 1–32.

43. P. A. Allum, *Italy—Republic without Government?* (New York: Norton, 1973), 250.

44. Philippe Schmitter, "Still the Century of Corporatism?" *Review of Politics*, 36 (January 1974), 111.

45. Felix Rohatyn, "A New RFC Is Proposed for Business," *New York Times*, section 3, December 7, 1974, p. 1.

46. See Huntington's chapter in *The Governability of Democracies*, p. 19.

47. Max Ways, "Business Needs a Different Political Stance," *Fortune*, September 1975, p. 96.

48. See Robbie Guttman, "State Intervention and the Economic Crises: The Labour Government's Economic Policy, 1974–75," *Kapitalistate*, 4–5 (1976), 225–70.

49. See Nigel Harris, *Competition and the Corporate Society* (London: Methuen, 1972).

50. Cited in *Wall Street Journal*, November 6, 1975, p. 19.

51. Antonio Gramsci, *Selections from the Prison Notebooks* (New York: International Publishers, 1971), 275–76.

52. Frances Fox Piven and Richard A. Cloward, *Regulating the Poor* (New York: Vintage Books, 1972), 345–48.

53. I have borrowed the concept of "hoarding"

54. See ibid., and James O'Connor, "Productive and Unproductive Labor," *Politics and Society*, 5 (1975), 297–336.

55. For interpretations of these movements see Manuel Castels, "Wild City," *Kapitalistate*, 4–5 (1976), 2–30.

56. Gramsci, p. 232.

57. Ibid., p. 165.

58. Bell, p. 231.

from James O'Connor's work in progress, provisionally called *The Class Struggle*.

READING 7-3

Crime and the development of capitalism[*]

RICHARD QUINNEY

Marxist analysis has moved us to new questions about the nature of crime in capitalist society. Heretofore our understanding was limited by a narrow set of problems, confined by a bourgeois mentality that promoted the existing order. We have since been forced to reexamine our efforts in the study of crime. In the process we are gaining a new understanding of crime.

The Marxist analysis of crime

A Marxist analysis of crime begins with the recognition that the crucial phenomenon to be considered is not crime per se, but the historical development and operation of the capitalist economy.[1] Any study of crime involves an investigation of such natural products and contradictions of capitalism as poverty, inequality, unemployment, and the economic crisis of the capitalist state. Ultimately, however, to understand crime we must understand the development of the political economy of capitalist society.

The necessary condition for any society is that its members produce their material means of subsistence. Social production is therefore the primary process of all social life. Moreover, in the social production of our existence we enter into relations that are appropriate to the existing forces of production.[2] It is this "economic" structure that provides the foundation for all social and political institutions, for everyday life, and for social consciousness. Our analysis thus begins with the *conditions* of social life.

The *dialectical method* allows us to comprehend the world as a complex of processes, in which all things go through a continuous process of coming into being and passing away. All things are studied in the context of their historical development. Dialectical materialism allows us to learn about things as they are in their actual interconnection, contradiction, and movement. In dialectical analysis we critically understand our past, informing our analysis with the possibilities for our future.

A Marxist analysis shares in the larger *socialist struggle*. There is the commitment to eliminating exploitation and oppression. Being on the side of the oppressed, only those ideas are advanced that will aid in transforming the capitalist system. The objective of the Marxist analysis is change—revolutionary change. The purpose of our intellectual labors is to assist in providing knowledge and consciousness for building a socialist society. Theories and strategies are developed to increase conscious class struggle; ideas for an alternative to capitalist society are formulated; and strategies for achieving the socialist alternative are proposed. In the course of intellectual-political work we engage in the activities and actions that will advance the socialist struggle.

With these notions of a Marxist analysis —encompassing a dialectical-historical analysis of the material conditions of capitalist society in relation to socialist revolution— we begin to formulate the significant substantive questions about crime. In recent years, as socialists have turned their attention to the study of crime, the outline for these questions has become evident. At this stage in our intellectual development the important questions revolve around *the meaning of crime in capitalist society*. Furthermore, there is the realization that the meaning of crime changes in the course of the development of capitalism.

The basic problem in any study of the meaning of crime is that of integrating the two sides of the crime phenomenon: placing into a single framework (1) the defining of behavior as criminal (i.e., *crime control*) and (2) the behavior of those who are defined as criminal (i.e., *criminality*). Thus far, the analysis of crime has focused on one side or the other, failing to integrate the two interrelated processes into one scheme. In pursuing a Marxist analysis, however, the problem of the dual nature of the concept of crime is solved by *giving primacy to the underlying political economy*.

The basic question in the Marxist analysis of crime is thus formulated: What is the meaning of crime in the development of capitalism? In approaching this question, we must give attention to several interrelated processes: (1) the development of capitalist political economy, including the nature of the forces and relations of production, the formulation of the capitalist state, and the class struggle between those who do and those who do not own and control the means of production; (2) the systems of domination and repression that are established in the development of capitalism, operating for the benefit of the capitalist class and secured by the capitalist state; (3) the forms of accommodation and resistance to the conditions of capitalism, by all people oppressed by capitalism, especially the working class; and (4) the relation of the dialectics of domination and accommodation to patterns of crime in capitalist society, producing the crimes of domination and the crimes of accommodation. As indicated in Figure 1, all these processes are dialectically related to the developing political economy. Crime is to be understood in terms of the development of capitalism.

The development of the capitalist economy

Crime, as noted, is a manifestation of the material conditions of society. The failure of conventional criminology is to ignore, by design, the material conditions of capitalism. Since the phenomena of crime are products of the substructure— are themselves part of the superstructure— any explanation of crime in terms of other elements of the superstructure is no explanation at all. Our need is to develop a general materialist framework for understanding crime, beginning with the underlying historical processes of social existence.

Production, as the necessary requirement of existence, produces its own forces and relations of social and economic life.

FIGURE 1
Crime and the development of capitalism

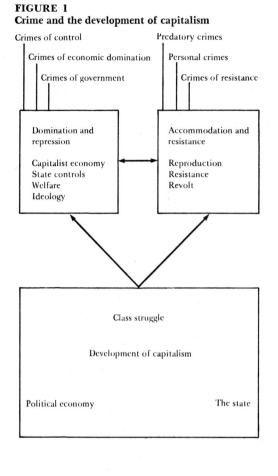

dynamics can be recognized. A class society arises when the system of production is owned by one segment of the society to the exclusion of another. All production requires ownership of some kind; but in some systems of production ownership is private rather than social or collective. In these economies social relations are dependent on relations of domination and subjection. Marxist economists thus observe: "Relations of domination and subjection are based on private ownership of the means of production and express the exploitation of man by man under the slave-owning, feudal and capitalist systems. Relations of friendly co-operation and mutual assistance between working people free of exploitation are typical of socialist society. They are based on the public ownership of the means of production, which cut out exploitation."[3]

All social life in capitalist society, including everything associated with crime, therefore, must be understood in terms of the economic conditions of production and the struggle between classes produced by these conditions. In other words, in capitalist society the life and behavior of any group in the society, or any individual group member, can be understood only in terms of the conflict that characterizes class relations, which in turn is produced by the capitalist system of production. The life and behavior of one class are seen in relation to that of the other. As E. P. Thompson observes, an analysis of class entails the notion of the historical *relationship* of classes:

Like any other relationship, it is a fluency which evades analysis if we attempt to stop it dead at any given moment and anatomise its structure. The finest-meshed sociological net cannot give us a pure specimen of class, any more than it can give us one of deference or of love. The relationship must always be embodied in real people in a real context. Moreover, we cannot have two distinct classes, each with an independent being, and then bring them *into* relationship with each other. We cannot have

The material factors (such as resources and technology) and personal factors (most importantly the workers) present at any given time form the productive *forces* of society. In the process of production, people form definite relations with one another. These *relations* of production, in reference to the forces of production, constitute the particular *mode* of production of any society at any given time. The economic mode of production furnishes society with its substructure, on which the social and political institutions (including crime control) and supporting ideologies are built.

Once the outlines of *political economy* (the productive forces, the relations of production, and the superstructure) have been indicated, the *class structure* and its love without lovers, nor deference without squires and laborers. And class happens when some men, as a result of common experiences (inherited or shared), feel and articulate the identity of their interests as between themselves, and as against other men whose interests are different from (and usually opposed to) theirs. The class experience is largely determined by the productive relations into which men are born—or enter involuntarily.[4]

Hence, class in capitalist society is analyzed in reference to the relationship to the process of production and according to the relationship to other classes in the society.

Moreover, the problematics of *labor* (as the foremost human activity) characterize the nature and specific relationship of the classes. For the capitalist system to operate and survive, the capitalist class must exploit the labor (appropriate the *surplus labor*) of the working class. As Maurice Dobb notes,

the relationship from which in one case a common interest in preserving and extending a particular economic system and in the other case an antagonism of interest on this issue can alone derive must be a relationship with a particular mode of extracting and distributing the fruits of surplus labour, over and above the labour which goes to supply the consumption of the actual producer. Since this surplus labor constitutes its life-blood, any ruling class will of necessity treat its particular relationship to the labour-process as crucial to its own survival; and any rising class that aspires to live without labour is bound to regard its own future career, prosperity and influence as dependent on the acquisition of some claim upon the surplus labour of others.[5]

The capitalist class survives by appropriating the surplus labor of the working class, and the working class as an exploited class exists as long as surplus labor is required in the productive process: each class depends on the other for its character and existence.

The amount of labor appropriated, the techniques of labor exploitation, the conditions of working-class life, and the level of working-class consciousness have all been an integral part of the historical development of capitalism.[6] In like manner, the degree of antagonism and conflict between classes has varied at different stages in the development. Nevertheless, it is the basic contradiction between classes, generalized as class conflict, that typifies the development of capitalism. Class conflict permeates the whole of capitalist development, represented in the contradiction between those who own property and those who do not, and by those who oppress and those who are oppressed.[7] All past history, that involving the development of capitalism, is the history of class struggle.

Capitalism as a system of production based on the exploitation by the ruling capitalist class that owns and controls the means of production is thus a dynamic system that goes through its own stages of development. In fact, capitalism is constantly transforming its own forces and relations of production. As a result, the whole of capitalist society is constantly being altered—within the basic framework of capitalist political economy.

The Marxian view stresses the qualitative changes in social organization and social relations as well as (or in relation to) the quantitative changes in the economic system.[8] Capitalism transforms itself, affecting the social existence of all who live under it. This is the basic dynamic of capitalist development, an interdependence between production, the relations of production, and the social superstructure of institutions and ideas. "For it is a requirement of all social production that the relations which people enter into in carrying on production must be suitable to the type of production they are carrying on. Hence, it is a general law of economic development that the relations of production must necessarily be adapted to the character of the forces of production."[9]

As the preceding discussion indicates, analysis of the meaning of crime in the development of capitalism necessarily involves an investigation of the relation between the concrete stage of capitalist development and of the social relations that correspond to that stage of development. This is not to argue that the superstructure of social relations and culture is an automatic (directly determined) product of the economic substructure. After all, people may enter into relations of production in various ways in order to employ the given forces of production; and it is on the basis of these relations that they create further institutions and ideas. Since human social existence is in part a product of conscious activity and struggle, conscious life must be part of any analysis. Maurice Cornforth, in a discussion of historical materialism, puts it well:

But ideas and institutions are not the automatic products of a given economic and class structure, but products of people's conscious activities and struggles. To explain the superstructure, these activities and struggles must be studied concretely, in their actual complex development. Therefore it is certainly not Marxism, just as it is certainly not science, to attempt to conclude from the specification of certain economic conditions what the form of the superstructure arising on that basis is going to be, or to deduce every detailed characteristic of the superstructure from some corresponding feature of the basis. On the contrary, we need to study how the superstructure actually develops in each society and in each epoch, by investigating the facts about that society and that epoch.[10]

Such is the basic task in our study of the meaning of crime in the development of capitalism.

In addition, the more developed the productive forces under capitalism, the greater the discrepancy between the productive forces and the capitalist relations of production. Capitalist development, with economic expansion being fundamental to capitalist economic development, exacerbates rather than mitigates the contradictions of capitalism.[11]

Workers are further exploited, conditions of existence worsen, while the contradictions of capitalism increase. Capitalist development, in other words, and from another vantage point, creates the conditions for the transformation and abolition of capitalism, brought about in actuality by class struggle.

The history of capitalism can thus be traced according to the nature of capitalist development. The main contradictions of capitalism are concretely formed and manifested in each stage of development. The forms and intensity of exploitation are documented and understood in respect to the particular character of capitalism at each development stage. How crime—control of crime and criminality—plays its part in each stage of capitalist development is our concern in any investigation of the meaning of crime.

The periods of capitalist development, for our purposes, differ according to the ways in which surplus labor is appropriated. Capitalism, as distinct from other modes of production, has gone through periods that utilize various methods of production and create social relations in association with these productive forms. Each new development in capitalism, conditioned by the preceding historical processes, brings about its own particular forms of capitalist economy and social reality—and related problems of human existence.

Any investigation of the meaning (and changing meanings) of crime in America, therefore, requires a delineation of the periods of economic development in the United States. A few attempts at such delineation already exist, but for other than the study of crime. For example, Douglas Dowd in his book *The Twisted Dream* notes briefly three different periods of American development, with particular reference to the role of the state in American economic life: (1) American mercantilism, up to Jackson's Presidency; (2)

laissez-faire capitalism, coming to a climax in the decades after the Civil War; and (3) maturing industrial capitalism, up to the present.[12] Similarly, in another treatment, William A. Williams in his book *The Contours of American History* arranges American history according to the following periods: (1) the age of mercantilism, 1740–1828; (2) the age of laissez nous faire, 1819–96; and (3) the age of corporate capitalism, 1882 to the present.[13] To this scheme, others add that American capitalism is now in the stage of either "monopoly capital" or "finance capital."[14]

It is debatable, nevertheless, in our study of crime in the United States, whether America was capitalist from the beginning, with capitalism merely imported from the Old to the New World, or whether, as James O'Connor has recently argued, capitalist development has occurred in only fairly recent times.[15] For the first hundred years of nationhood the United States resisted large-scale capitalist production. Independent commodity production predominated; farmers, artisans, small manufacturers, and other petty producers were the mainstay of the economy. Only as northern capitalists acquired land from the farmers (thus appropriating their labor power) and as immigrant labor power was imported from Europe did capitalism finally emerge in the United States. American capitalism emerged when capitalists won the battle as to who was to control labor power. Surplus labor was now in the hands of a capitalist ruling class. Workers could be exploited.

For certain, we are today in a stage of late, advanced capitalism in the United States. The current meaning of crime in America can be understood only in relation to the character of capitalism in the present era. Similarly, the meanings of crime at various times in the past have to be understood according to the particular stage of development. Only in the investigation of crime in the development of capitalism do we truly understand the meaning of crime. Concrete research will provide us with knowledge about the role of crime in the development of capitalism.

Domination and repression

The capitalist system must be continuously reproduced. This is accomplished in a variety of ways, ranging from the establishment of ideological hegemony to the further exploitation of labor, from the creation of public policy to the coercive repression of the population. Most explicitly, the *state* secures the capitalist order. Through various schemes and mechanisms, then, the capitalist class is able to dominate. And in the course of this domination, crimes are carried out. These crimes, committed by the capitalist class, the state, and the agents of the capitalist class and state, are the crimes of domination.

Historically the capitalist state is a product of a political economy that depends on a division of classes. With the development of an economy based on the exploitation of one class by another, there was the need for a political form that would perpetuate that kind of order. With the development of capitalism, with class divisions and class struggle, the state became necessary. A new stage of development, Frederick Engels observes, called for the creation of the state:

Only one thing was wanting: an institution which not only secured the newly acquired riches of individuals against the communistic traditions of the gentile order, which not only sanctified the private property formerly so little valued, and declared this sanctification to be the highest purpose of all human society; but an institution which set the seal of general social recognition on each new method of acquiring property and thus amassing wealth at continually increased speed; an institution which perpetuated, not only this growing cleavage of society into classes, but also the right of the possessing class to exploit the non-possessing, and the rule of the former over the latter.

And this institution came. The state was invented.[16]

The state thus arose to protect and promote the interests of the dominant class, the class that owns and controls the means of production. The state exists as a device for controlling the exploited class, the class that labors, for the benefit of the ruling class. Modern civilization, as epitomized in capitalist societies, is founded on the exploitation of one class by another. Moreover, the capitalist state is oppressive not only because it supports the interests of the dominant class but also because it is responsible for the design of the whole system within which the capitalist ruling class dominates and the working class is dominated.[17] The capitalist system of production and exploitation is secured and reproduced by the capitalist state.

The coercive force of the state, embodied in law and legal repression, is the traditional means of maintaining the social and economic order. Contrary to conventional wisdom, law instead of representing community custom is an instrument of the state that serves the interest of the developing capitalist ruling class. Law emerged with the rise of capitalism, as Stanley Diamond writes: "Law arises in the breach of a prior customary order and increases in force with the conflicts that divide political societies internally and among themselves. Law *and* order is the historical illusion; law versus order is the historical reality."[18] Law and legal repression are, and continue to serve as, the means of enforcing the interests of the dominant class in the capitalist state.

Through the legal system, then, the state forcefully protects its interests and those of the capitalist ruling class. Crime control becomes the coercive means of checking threats to the existing social and economic order, threats that result from a system of oppression and exploitation. As a means of controlling the behavior of the exploited population, crime control is accomplished by a variety of methods, strategies, and institutions.[19] The state, especially through its legislative bodies, establishes official policies of crime control. The administrative branch of the state establishes and enforces crime-control policies, usually setting the design for the whole nation. Specific agencies of law enforcement, such as the Federal Bureau of Investigation and the recent Law Enforcement Assistance Administration, determine the nature of crime control. And the state is able through its Department of Justice officially to repress the "dangerous" and "subversive" elements of the population. Altogether, these state institutions attempt to rationalize the legal system by employing the advanced methods of science and technology. And whenever any changes are to be attempted to reduce the incidence of crime, rehabilitation of the individual or reform within the existing institutions is suggested.[20] Drastically to alter the society and the crime-control establishment would be to alter beyond recognition the capitalist system.

Yet the coercive force of the state is but one means of maintaining the social and economic order. A more subtle reproductive mechanism of capitalist society is the perpetuation of the capitalist conception of reality, a nonviolent but equally repressive means of domination. As Alan Wolfe has shown, in the manipulation of consciousness the existing order is legitimated and secured:

The most important reproductive mechanism which does not involve the use of state violence is consciousness-manipulation. The liberal state has an enormous amount of violence at its disposal, but it is often reluctant to use it. Violence may breed counter-violence, leading to instability. It may be far better to manipulate consciousness to such an extent that most people would never think of engaging in the kinds of action which could be repressed. The most perfectly repressive (though not violently so) capitalist system, in other words, would not be a police state, but the complete opposite, one in which there were no police because there was nothing to police, everyone having accepted the legitimacy of that socity and all its daily consequences.[21]

Those who rule in capitalist society—with the assistance of the state—not only accumulate capital at the expense of those who work but impose their ideology as well. Oppression and exploitation are legitimized by the expropriation of consciousness; since labor is expropriated, consciousness must also be expropriated.[22] In fact, *legitimacy* of the capitalist order is maintained by controlling the consciousness of the population. A capitalist hegemony is established.

Thus, through its various reproductive mechanisms capitalism is able to maximize the possibility of control over the citizens of the state. Ranging from control of production and distribution to manipulation of the mind, capitalism operates according to its own form of dictatorship. André Gorz writes:

The dictatorship of capital is exercised not only on the production and distribution of wealth, but with equal force on the manner of producing, on the model of consumption, and on the manner of consuming, the manner of working, thinking, living. As much as over the workers, the factories, and the state, this dictatorship rules over the society's vision of the future, its ideology, its priorities and goals, over the way in which people experience and learn about themselves, their potentials, their relations with other people and with the rest of the world. This dictatorship is economic, political, cultural and psychological at the same time: it is total.[23]

Moreover, a society that depends on surplus labor for its existence must not only control that situation but also must cope with the problems that economic system naturally creates. The capitalist state must therefore provide "social services" in the form of education, health, welfare, and re-

habilitation programs of various kinds, to deal with the problems that could otherwise be dealt with only by changing the capitalist system. These state services function as a repressive means of securing the capitalist order.

Capitalism systematically generates a *surplus population,* an unemployed sector of the working class either dependent on fluctuations in the economy or made obsolete by new technology. With the growth of the surplus population, pressures build up for the growth of the welfare system. The function of expanding welfare, with its host of services, is to control the surplus population politically. Moreover, O'Connor observes, "Unable to gain employment in the monopoly industries by offering their labor power at lower than going wage rates (and victimized by sexism and racism), and unemployed, underemployed, or employed at low wages in competitive industries, the surplus population increasingly becomes dependent on the state."[24] An unsteady alliance is thus formed between the casualties it naturally produces. Only a new economic order could replace the need for a welfare state.

Repression through welfare is in part the history of capitalism. The kinds of services have varied with the development of economic conditions. In the same way, relief policies have varied according to specific tensions produced by unemployment and subsequent threats of disorder. As Frances Fox Piven and Richard A. Cloward write in their study of the modern welfare system:

Relief arrangements are ancillary to economic arrangements. Their chief function is to regulate labor, and they do that in two general ways. First, when mass unemployment leads to outbreaks of turmoil, relief programs are ordinarily initiated or expanded to absorb and control enough of the unemployed to restore order; then, as turbulence subsides, the relief system contracts, expelling those who are needed to populate the labor market. Relief also performs a labor-regulating function in this shrunken state, however. Some of the aged, the disabled, the insane, and others who are of no use as workers are left on the relief rolls, and their treatment is so degrading and punitive as to instill in the laboring masses a fear of the fate that awaits them should they relax into beggary and pauperism. To demean and punish those who do not work is to exalt by contrast even the meanest labor at the meanest wages. These regulative functions of relief, and their periodic expansion and contraction, are made necessary by several strains toward instability inherent in capitalist economies.[25]

Control through welfare can never be a permanent solution for a system based on appropriation of labor. As with all the forms of control and manipulation in capitalist society, welfare cannot completely counter the basic contradictions of a capitalist political economy.

Although the capitalist state creates and manages the institutions of control (employing physical force *and* manipulation of consciousness), the basic contradictions of the capitalist order are such that this control is not absolute and, in the long run, is subject to defeat. Because of the contradictions of capitalism, the capitalist state is more weak than strong.[26] Eventually the capitalist state loses its legitimacy, no longer being able to perpetuate the ideology that capital accumulation for capitalists (at the expense of workers) is good for the nation or for human interests. The ability of the capitalist economic order to exist according to its own interests is eventually weakened.[27] The problem becomes especially acute in periods of economic crisis, periods that are unavoidable under capitalism.

In the course of reproducing the capitalist system crimes are committed. It is a contradiction of capitalism that some of its laws must be violated in order to secure the existing system.[28] The contradictions of capitalism produce their own sources of crime. Not only are these contradictions heightened during times of crisis, making

for increased crimes of domination, but the nature of these crimes changes with the further development of capitalism.

The crimes of domination most characteristic of capitalist domination are those that occur in the course of state control. These are the *crimes of control*. They include the felonies and misdemeanors that law-enforcement agents, especially the police, carry out in the name of the law, usually against persons accused of other violations. Violence and brutality have become a recognized part of police work. In addition to these crimes of control, there are the crimes of more subtle nature in which agents of the law violate the civil liberties of citizens, as in the various forms of surveillance, the use of provocateurs, and the illegal denial of due process.

Then there are the *crimes of government*, committed by the elected and appointed officials of the capitalist state. The Watergate crimes, carried out to perpetuate a particular governmental administration, are the most publicized instances of these crimes. There are also those offenses committed by the government against persons and groups who would seemingly threaten national security. Included here are the crimes of warfare and the political assassination of foreign and domestic leaders.

Crimes of domination also consist of those crimes that occur in the capitalist class for the purpose of securing the existing economic order. These *crimes of economic domination* include the crimes committed by corporations, ranging from price fixing to pollution of the environment in order to protect and further capital accumulation. Also included are the economic crimes of individual businessmen and professionals. In addition, the crimes of the capitalist class and the capitalist state are joined in organized crime. The more conventional criminal operations of organized crime are linked to the state in the present stage of capitalist development.

The operations of organized crime and the criminal operations of the state are united in the attempt to assure the survival of the capitalist system.

Finally, many *social injuries* are committed by the capitalist class and the capitalist state that are not usually defined as criminal in the legal codes of the state.[29] These systematic actions, involving the denial of basic human rights (resulting in sexism, racism, and economic exploitation), are an integral part of capitalism and are important to its survival.

Underlying all the capitalist crimes is the appropriation of the surplus value created by labor. The working class has the right to possess the whole of this value. The worker creates a value several times greater than the labor power purchased by the capitalist. The excess value created by the worker over and above the value of labor power is the surplus value which is appropriated by the capitalist. Surplus value, as exploitation, is essential to capitalism, being the source of accumulation of capital and expansion of production.

Domination and repression are a basic part of class struggle in the development of capitalism. The capitalist class and state protect and promote the capitalist order by controlling those who do not own the means of production. The labor supply and the conditions for labor must be secured. Crime control and the crimes of domination are thus necessary features and the natural products of capitalist political economy.

Accommodation and resistance

The contradictions of developing capitalism increase the level of class struggle and thereby increase (1) the need to dominate by the capitalist class and (2) the need to accommodate and resist by the classes that are exploited by capitalism, particularly the working class. Most of the behavior in response to domination, including the actions of the oppressed that

are defined as criminal by the capitalist class, is a product of the capitalist system of production. In the course of capitalist appropriation of labor, for the accumulation of capital, conditions are established which call for behaviors that may be defined as criminal by the capitalist state. These behaviors become eligible for crime control when they disturb or threaten in some way the capitalist order.[30]

Hence, the class that does not own or control the means of production must adapt to the conditions of capitalism. Accommodation and resistance to the conditions of capitalism are basic to the class struggle. The argument here is that action by people who do not own and control the means of production, those who are exploited and oppressed, is largely an accommodation or resistance to the conditions produced by capitalist production. Thus, criminality among the oppressed classes is action (conscious or otherwise) in relation to the capitalist order of exploitation and oppression. Crime, with its many historical variations, is an integral part of class struggle in the development of capitalism.

Following Marx and Engels' limited and brief discussion, criminals outside the capitalist class are usually viewed as being among the lumpenproletariat.[31] Accordingly, criminals of the oppressed classes are regarded as unproductive workers; they are parasitical in that they do not contribute to the production of goods, and they create a livelihood out of commodities produced by the working class.[32] Much criminal activity in the course of accommodation would thus appear to be an expression of false consciousness, an apolitical expression, an individualistic reaction to the forces of capitalist production.

Many crimes of accommodation are of this lumpen nature. Nevertheless, these actions occur within the context of capitalist oppression, stemming from the existing system of production. Much criminal behavior is of a parasitical nature, including burglary, robbery, drug dealing, and hustling of various sorts.[33] These are the *predatory crimes*. The behavior, although pursued out of the need to survive, is a reproduction of the capitalist system. The crimes are nevertheless antagonistic to the capitalist order. Most police activity is directed against these crimes.

In addition to the predatory crimes there are the *personal crimes* that are usually directed against members of the same class. These are the conventional criminal acts of murder, assault, and rape. They are pursued by those who are already brutalized by the conditions of capitalism. These actions occur in immediate situations that are themselves the result of more basic accommodations to capitalism.

Aside from these lumpen crimes, there are those actions carried out largely by the working class that are in resistance to the capitalist system. These actions, sometimes directed superficially against the work situation, are direct reflections of the alienation of labor—a struggle, however conscious or unconscious, against the exploitation of the life and activity of the worker. For example, workers may engage in concrete political actions against their employers:

On the assembly lines of the American automobile industry, this revolt extends as far as clandestine acts of sabotage against a product (the automobile body) which appears to the worker as the detestable materialization of the social uselessness and individual absurdity of his toil. Along the same lines is the less extreme and more complex example of miners fighting with admirable perseverance against the closing of the mines where they are exploited under inferior human and economic conditions—but who, individually, have no difficulty in recognizing that even if the coal they produced were not so bad and so expensive, their job, under the prevailing conditions, would still be abominable.[34]

These defensive actions by workers are likely to become even more politically motivated and organized in the future. For built into the capitalist economy is the contradiction that increased economic growth necessitates the kind of labor that further alienates workers from their needs. Further economic expansion can only bring with it increased crimes of resistance. For the purpose of class struggle, leading to socialist revolution, a Marxist analysis of crime gives attention to the crimes of resistance, committed primarily by members of the working class.

The effects of the capitalist mode of production for the worker are all-inclusive, going far beyond the workplace itself. The worker can no longer be at home anyplace in the everyday world. The alienation experienced in the workplace now represents the condition of the worker in all other areas of life. Ownership and control of life in general have been surrendered to alien hands.[35] The production of life itself under capitalism is alienated. Furthermore, the natural productive process, of which work is central, has become restricted in the stages of capitalist accumulation. The increasing alienation of work, as Harry Braverman notes,

consists in the narrowing of the base of productive labor upon which the economy rests, to the point where an ever smaller portion of society labors to maintain all of it, while the remainder is drafted, at lower rates of pay and even more demeaning conditions of labor, into the unproductive economy of capitalism. And finally, it consists in the misery of unemployment and of outright pauperization which are aspects of the reserve army of labor created by capital more or less automatically in the accumulation process.[36]

Furthermore, a large portion of workers under advanced capitalism become expendable. For the capitalist the problem becomes that of the kind and size of labor force necessary to maximize production and realize surplus value. The physical well-being and spiritual needs of the worker are not the concern; rather, capitalism requires an "industrial reserve army" that can be called into action when necessary and relieved when no longer needed

—but always available. Marx observed in *Capital*:

But if a surplus laboring population is a necessary product of accumulation or of the development of wealth on a capitalist basis, this surplus population becomes, conversely, the lever of capitalist accumulation, nay, a condition of existence of the capitalist mode of production. It forms an industrial reserve army that belongs to capital quite as absolutely as if the latter had bred it at its own cost. Independently of the limits of the actual increase of population, it creates for the changing needs of the self-expansion of capital a mass of human material always ready for exploitation.[37]

Under these conditions, "the labor force consists of two parts, the employed and the unemployed, with a gray area in between, containing the part-time or sporadically employed. Furthermore, all these categories of workers and potential workers continuously expand or contract with technological change, the ups and downs of the business cycle, and the vagaries of the market, all inherent characteristics of capitalist production."[38] Many workers are further exploited by being relegated to the degradations and uncertainties of a reserve army of labor.

For the unemployed, as well as for those who are always uncertain about their employment, these life conditions have their personal and social consequences. Basic human needs are thwarted when the life-giving activity of work is lost or curtailed. This form of alienation gives rise to a multiplicity of psycho-social maladjustments and psychic disorders.[39] In addition, unemployment means the loss of personal and family income. Choices, opportunities, and even life maintenance are jeopardized. For many people, the appropriate reaction consists not only of mental disturbance but also of outright acts of personal and social destruction.

Although the statistical evidence can never show conclusively the relation between unemployment and crime, largely because such statistics are politically constructed in the beginning to obscure the failings of a capitalist economy, there is sufficient observation to recognize the obvious fact that unemployment produces criminality. Crimes of economic gain increase whenever the jobless seek ways to maintain themselves and their families. Crimes of violence rise when the problems of life are further exacerbated by the loss of life-supporting activity. Anger and frustration at a world that punishes rather than supports produce their own forms of destruction. Permanent unemployment—and the acceptance of that condition—can result in a form of life where criminality is an appropriate and consistent response.

Hence, crime under capitalism has become a response to the material conditions of life.[40] Nearly all crimes among the working class in capitalist society are actually a means of *survival*, an attempt to exist in a society where survival is not assured by other, collective means. Crime is inevitable under capitalist conditions.

Yet, understanding crime as a reaction to capitalist conditions, whether as acts of frustration or means of survival, is only one side of the picture. The other side involves the problematics of the *consciousness* of criminality in capitalist society.[41] The history of the working class is in large part one of rebellion against the conditions of capitalist production, as well as against the conditions of life resulting from work under capitalism. Class struggle involves, after all, a continuous war between two dialectically opposed interests: capital accumulation for the benefit of a nonworking minority class that owns and controls the means of production and, on the other hand, control and ownership of production by those who actually labor. Since the capitalist state regulates this struggle, the institutions and laws of the social order are intended to assure the victory of the capitalist class over the working class. Yet the working class constantly struggles against the capitalist class, as shown in the long history of labor battles against the conditions of capitalist production.[42] The resistance continues as long as there is need for class struggle, that is, as long as capitalism exists.

With the instruments of force and coercion on the side of the capitalist class, much of the activity in the working-class struggle is defined as criminal. Indeed, according to the legal codes, whether in simply acting to relieve the injustices of capitalism or in taking action against the existence of class oppression, actions against the interests of the state are crimes. With an emerging consciousness that the state represses those who attempt to tip the scales in favor of the working class, working-class people engage in actions against the state and the capitalist class. This is crime that is politically conscious.

Crimes of accommodation and resistance thus range from unconscious reactions to exploitation, to conscious acts of survival within the capitalist system, to politically conscious acts of rebellion. These criminal actions, moreover, not only cover the range of meaning but actually evolve or progress from *unconscious reaction to political rebellion.* Finally, the crimes may eventually reach the ultimate stage of conscious political action—*revolt.* In revolt, criminal actions are not only against the system but are also an attempt to overthrow it.

The movement toward a socialist society can occur only with political consciousness on the part of those oppressed by capitalist society. The alternative to capitalism cannot be willed into being but requires the conscious activity of those who seek new conditions of existence. Political consciousness develops in the realization of the alienation suffered under capitalism. The contradiction of capitalism—the disparity between actuality and human possibility—makes large portions of the population ready to act in ways that will bring about a new existence. When people become conscious of the extent to which they are dehumanized under the capitalist mode of production, when people realize the source and nature of their alienation, they become active in a movement to build a new society. Many of the actions taken result in behaviors that are defined as criminal by the capitalist state.

The meaning of crime

A Marxist understanding of crime, as developed here, begins with an analysis of the political economy of capitalism. The class struggle endemic to capitalism is characterized by a dialectic between domination and accommodation. Those who own and control the means of production, the capitalist class, attempt to secure the existing order through various forms of domination, especially crime control by the capitalist state. Those who do not own and control the means of production, especially the working class, accommodate and resist in various ways to capitalist domination.

Crime is related to this process. Crime control and criminality (consisting of the crimes of domination and the crimes of accommodation) are understood in terms of the conditions resulting from the capitalist appropriation of labor. Variations in the nature and amount of crime occur in the course of developing capitalism. Each stage in the development of capitalism is characterized by a particular pattern of crime. The meaning and changing meanings of crime are found in the development of capitalism.

What can be expected in the further development of capitalism? The contradictions and related crises of capitalist political economy are now a permanent feature of advanced capitalism. Further economic development along capitalist lines will solve none of the internal contradictions of the capitalist mode of production.[43] The capitalist state must, therefore, increasingly

332

utilize its resources—its various control and repressive mechanisms—to maintain the capitalist order. The dialectic between oppression by the capitalist class and the daily struggle of survival by the oppressed will continue—and at an increasing pace.

The only lasting solution to the crisis of capitalism is, of course, socialism. Under late, advanced capitalism, socialism will be achieved only in the struggle of all people who are oppressed by the capitalist mode of production, namely, the workers and all elements of the surplus population. An alliance of the oppressed must take place.[44] Given the objective conditions of a crisis in advanced capitalism, and the conditions for an alliance of the oppressed, a mass socialist movement can be formed, cutting across all divisions within the working class.

The objective of Marxist analysis is to lead to further questioning of the capitalist system, leading to an improved understanding of the consequences of capitalist development. The *ultimate meaning* of crime in the development of capitalism is the need for a socialist society. And as the preceding discussion indicates, in moving toward the socialist alternative, our study of crime is necessarily based on an economic analysis of capitalist society. Crime is essentially a product of the contradictions of capitalism. Crime is sometimes a force in social development: when it becomes a part of the class struggle, increasing political consciousness. But our real attention must continue to be on the capitalist system itself. Our understanding is furthered as we investigate the nature, sources, and consequences of the development of capitalism. As we engage in this work, the development of socialism becomes evident.

NOTES

1. Paul Q. Hirst, "Marx and Engels on Law, Crime, and Morality," *Economy and Society* 1 (February 1972) : 28–56.

2. Karl Marx, *A Contribution to the Critique of Political Economy*, ed. M. Dobb (New York: International Publishers, 1970), pp. 20–21.

3. L. Afanasyev et al., *The Political Economy of Capitalism* (Moscow: Progress Publishers, 1974), p. 12.

4. E. P. Thompson, *The Making of the English Working Class* (New York: Random House, 1963), p. 9.

5. Maurice Dobb, *Studies in the Development of Capitalism* (New York: International Publishers, 1963), p. 15.

6. Jurgen Kuczynski, *The Rise of the Working Class* (New York: McGraw-Hill, 1967).

7. Robert Heiss, *Engels, Kierkegaard, and Marx* (New York: Dell, 1975), p. 390.

8. Paul M. Sweezy, *The Theory of Capitalist Development* (New York: Monthly Review Press, 1968), pp. 92–95.

9. Maurice Cornforth, *Historical Materialism* (New York: International Publishers, 1962), p. 59.

10. Ibid., p. 91.

11. Erik Olin Wright, "Alternative Perspectives in the Marxist Theory of Accumulation and Crisis," *Insurgent Sociologist* 6 (Fall 1975): 5–39.

12. Douglas F. Dowd, *The Twisted Dream: Capitalist Development in the United States since 1776* (Cambridge, Mass.: Winthrop, 1974), pp. 42–48.

13. William Appleman Williams, *The Contours of American History* (New York: World, 1961).

14. Paul A. Baran and Paul M. Sweezy, *Monopoly Capital: An Essay on the American Economic and Social Order* (New York: Monthly Review Press, 1966). Robert Fitch and Mary Oppenheimer, "Who Rules the Corporations?" *Socialist Revolution*, no. 4 (July–August 1970): 73–107; no. 5 (September–October 1970): 61–114; no. 6 (November–December 1970): 33–94.

15. James O'Connor, "The Twisted Dream," *Monthly Review* 26 (March 1975): 46–53.

16. Frederick Engels, *The Origin of the Family, Private Property, and the State* (New York: International Publishers, 1942), p. 97.

17. David A. Gold, Clarence Y. H. Lo, and Erik Olin Wright, "Recent Developments in Marxist Theories of the State," *Monthly Review* 27 (November 1975): 36–51.

18. Stanley Diamond, "The Rule of Law versus the Order of Custom," *Social Research* 38 (Spring 1971): 71.

19. See Richard Quinney, *Critique of Legal Order: Crime Control in Capitalist Society* (Boston: Little Brown, 1974), pp. 95–135.

20. Alexander Liazos, "Class Oppression: The Functions of Juvenile Justice," *Insurgent Sociologist* 5 (Fall 1974) : 2–24.

21. Alan Wolfe, "Political Repression and the Liberal State," *Monthly Review* 23 (December 1971) : 20.

22. Alan Wolfe, "New Directions in the Marxist Theory of Politics," *Politics and Society* 4 (Winter 1974) : 155–57.

23. André Gorz, *Strategy for Labor: A Radical Proposal*, tr. Martin A. Nicolaus and Victoria Ortiz (Boston: Beacon Press, 1967) , pp. 131–32.

24. James O'Connor, *The Fiscal Crisis of the State* (New York: St. Martin's Press, 1973) , p. 161.

25. Frances Fox Piven and Richard A. Cloward, *Regulating the Poor: The Functions of Public Welfare* (New York: Random House, 1971) , pp. 3–4.

26. Wolfe, "New Directions in the Marxist Theory of Politics," p. 155.

27. See Stanley Aronowitz, "Law, Breakdown of Order, and Revolution," in *Law against the People: Essays to Demystify Law, Order, and the Courts*, ed. Robert Lefcourt (New York: Random House, 1971) , pp. 150–82; and John H. Schaar, "Legitimacy in the Modern State," in *Power and Community: Dissenting Essays in Political Science*, ed. Philip Green and Sanford Levinson (New York: Random House, 1970) , pp. 276–327.

28. See Richard Quinney, *Criminology: Analysis and Critique of Crime in America* (Boston: Little, Brown, 1975) , pp. 131–61.

29. Tony Platt, "Prospects for a Radical Criminology in the United States," *Crime and Social Justice* 1 (Spring–Summer, 1974) : 2–10; Herman and Julia Schwendinger, "Defenders of Order or Guardians of Human Rights?" *Issues in Criminology* 5 (Summer 1970) : 123–57.

30. Steven Spitzer, "Toward a Marxian Theory of Deviance," *Social Problems* 22 (June 1975) : 638–51.

31. Karl Marx and Frederick Engels, *The Com-munist Manifesto* (New York: International Publishers, 1965; original 1848) , p. 20.

32. Hirst, "Marx and Engels on Law, Crime, and Morality," pp. 49–52; Ian Taylor, Paul Walton, and Jock Young, *The New Criminology: For a Social Theory of Deviance* (London: Routledge & Kegan Paul, 1973) , pp. 217–20.

33. Judah Hill, *Class Analysis: United States in the 1970's* (Emeryville, Calif.: Class Analysis, 1975) , pp. 86–87.

34. Gorz, *Strategy for Labor*, pp. 57–58.

35. Karl Marx, *The Grundrisse*, ed. David McLellan (New York: Harper & Row, 1971) , pp. 132–43.

36. Harry Braverman, "Work and Unemployment," *Monthly Review* 27 (June 1975) : 30.

37. Karl Marx, *Capital*, vol. 1 (Chicago: C. H. Kerr, 1932) , p. 693.

38. Editors, "The Economic Crisis in Historical Perspective," *Monthly Review* 26 (June 1975) : 2.

39. K. William Kapp, "Socio-Economic Effects of Low and High Employment," *Annals of the American Academy of Political and Social Science* 418 (March 1975) : 60–71.

40. David M. Gordon, "Capitalism, Class, and Crime in America," *Crime and Delinquency* 19 (April 1973) : 163–86.

41. Taylor, Walton, and Young, *New Criminology*, pp. 220–21.

42. Sidney Lens, *The Labor Wars: From the Molly Maguires to the Sitdowns* (New York: Doubleday, 1973) ; Jeremy Brecher, *Strike!* (Greenwich, Conn.: Fawcett, 1972) ; Samuel Yellen, *American Labor Struggles* (New York: S. A. Russell, 1936) ; Richard O. Boyer and Herbert M. Morais, *Labor's Untold Story* (New York: Cameron Associates, 1955) .

43. Ernest Mandel, "The Industrial Cycle in Late Capitalism," *New Left Review* 90 (March–April 1975) : 3–25.

44. O'Connor, *Fiscal Crisis of the State*, pp. 221–56.

The problem of religion in modern culture*

JAMES LUTHER ADAMS

"The Reformation must continue." With these words Friedrich Schleiermacher, over a century ago, raised a protest against the Protestantism and the prevailing mentality of his time and pointed forward to a new Protestant realization. Protestantism and its culture, he believed, were in need of a Protestant reform.

These words of Schleiermacher could well serve as the epigraph of the writings of Paul Tillich. This does not mean that Tillich recommends, any more than Schleiermacher did, a return to the Reformation. Like Schleiermacher, who was also a theologian of culture schooled in the dialectic of philosophical idealism, Tillich is concerned not only with the religion of the churches but even more with the religious bases and implications of the whole cultural process. In his view, which is based on a realistic philosophy of meaning, religion has to do with humanity's ultimate concern, the concern with the meaning of life and with all the forces that threaten or support that meaning, in personal and social life, in the arts and sciences, in politics, in industry, education, and the church. It is with respect to the total cultural situation, then, that Tillich would say: "The Reformation must continue"; for we are living at the end of an era.

Beginning as a rediscovery of the prophetic message of the majesty of God and emphasizing the doctrines of predestination and of justification through faith, early Protestantism raised a protest against a hierarchical system that had interjected itself between man and God with "a demonic claim to absoluteness." This prophetic message reaffirmed the unconditional character of God. Sin and guilt, the Reformers asserted, cannot be overcome by any mediating human agency. Union with God is received through grace and faith alone. Through this union the sinner paradoxically becomes justified before God. Man's love is the consequence and not the condition of this justification through faith. Analogously, the concept of predestination was the doctrinal statement of the experience of regaining the meaning of life without human activity, an experience that is God's work and that has an explanation hidden from man.

In accord with these Protestant affirmations, the absolute doctrinal authority of the church, the constitutional authority of the hierarchy, and the independent power of the sacraments were all renounced as blasphemies, as attempts by humans to elevate mankind above God and to subject to outer conditions the approach of God to the soul and of the soul to God. Insofar as humanism set up human reason as the final arbiter and adopted an anthropocentric orientation, humanism was also renounced on the basis of corresponding objections. The Reformers cut through all these mediations; they also cut through church history and returned to the source of the message of justification, the Bible.

The positive element taking the place of ecclesiastical authority found its initial expression in the claim of freedom of conscience to interpret the Scriptures, a freedom that was expected to issue in a new unity supported by a providentially inspired harmony. This Protestant freedom of conscience was an "ecstatic" rather than a purely autonomous, humanistic freedom; it was interpreted as the "pneumatic," or, as Tillich would call it, the "theonomous," response of the individual member of the church to the message of the Bible. Obedience to the hierarchical priesthood was therefore supplanted by belief in the priesthood of all believers. Clerical domination yielded, in principle, to radical laicism. The Bible, it was assumed, would interpret itself sufficiently for salvation. Every individual as a monad in the body of Christ would be able to find truth in the Bible. The saving Gospel is there, and the Reformers believed that it would create a unified church wherever it was proclaimed and listened to in faith. Thus, although Protestantism appealed to the individual consciousness and conscience (guided by Scripture and nourished by the religious community), it relied from the beginning upon a hidden automatic harmony. Tillich holds that much of the history of Protestantism and also of modern culture must be understood in terms of this and of corresponding theories of harmony.

But Protestantism could not carry through unaided its resistance to the previously accepted authorities; nor was it able alone to establish new integrations in church and society. It eventually made an alliance with the humanism which it had at first opposed as strongly as it had opposed Roman Catholicism. Philosophical and linguistic exegesis was required for the interpreting of the Bible. Protestantism joined humanism to overcome Catholic exegesis. Here it was assumed that autonomous criticism and Protestant criticism would fundamentally agree. This same pattern was adopted also for other areas of common interest. Gradually the "holy" legend of the Catholic church was dissolved by the modern historical consciousness and by humanistic-Protestant historical criticism; humanistic education was combined with biblical education; scholasticism was supplanted by autonomous science, in which theology claimed a leading role (later to be lost); monastic and feudal conceptions of work were replaced by an inner-worldly asceticism and activism (especially on Calvinistic soil). Belief in harmony between divine and natural law gave rise to a new amalgamation of Stoic and biblical ethics. To be sure, there have been and there still are countertendencies within Protestantism. In Europe, neofeudal types of authority continued to play a role. Moreover, in many quarters rigid forms of ecclesiastical orthodoxy have ignored the original Protestant protest. As a consequence, they have, in principle, maintained the traditional authoritarian outlook. They have merely substituted for the authority of the Roman Catholic church some new absolute, such as the Bible or the confessions of faith, the "priestcraft of the word."

The alliance of Protestantism with humanism gradually developed into an alliance also with a humanist theory of harmony. This development in its outcome must be viewed as simply another dimension of the changes already described; accordingly, it can be best discerned by observing its characteristic negations and affirmations.

The alliance was possible, if not inevitable, because humanism resisted many of the same things that Protestantism resisted. Tillich, employing a conception familiar in modern myth research, characterizes the pre-Protestant, or Catholic, era in terms of its "myth of origin." In general, this sort of myth expresses man's numinous sense of relatedness to the originating or creative powers of nature and history; it provides a feeling of security and support by relating men to sacred powers of origin rooted in the soil, in the blood, in a social group, or in some other support and sanction of a vital and authoritative tradition. For the Middle Ages the superhuman origin of life was found in a primeval revelation, which was preserved as a holy tradition and guarded as a mystery by the priesthood. This holy tradition found objective manifestation in a sacramental system (which included within it the natural powers of origin). Medieval freedoms, securities, and authorities were supported by this comprehensive myth of origin. Innovation could be introduced only in the name of the "origin." All privileges of "domination," including those attached to the feudal ranks, appealed to the same sanction. Since the system was largely controlled by the priesthood, the latter achieved a certain social independence as the bearer of religion and as the consecrating agent for the sacred powers of origin. Against this medieval myth of origin and the corresponding authorities, both humanism and Protestantism revolted, humanism in the name of an autonomous humanity and Protestantism in the spirit of ancient prophetism and in the name of the doctrines of justification and predestination.

Protestantism, as we have seen, returned to the Bible, where it found not only its own myth of origin but also a sense of mission, a sanction for pushing forward to a new church and society. This does not mean that the medieval myth of origin was wholly eliminated; rather, it was transformed. Just as in ancient Hebrew religion, prophetic and priestly elements were combined, so in Protestantism prophetic elements were grafted onto Catholic sacramental elements. However, in rejecting the claim of the priesthood to be the consecrating agent of the powers of origin, Protestantism initiated a process whereby it would in time weaken its own independence. Partially as a consequence of the principle of radical laicism (implied on the belief in the priesthood of all believers) the modern man has taken a larger share in the shaping of social policy than did his predecessors. Because of these changes, Protestantism has had to depend more and more upon extra-ecclesiastical social forces for support. It

entered more and more, especially after the Enlightenment, into alliance with the developing state bureaucracies or with the bourgeois powers and customs.

Humanism also rejected the old myth of origin and introduced a new conception. According to this new conception, man in his possession of universal humanity was believed to be rooted in the divine *logos*. In its struggle against authoritarianism, humanism can scarcely be said to have developed a myth of origin, but it did create its own "myth of mission" (a term suggested by Michels and not used by Tillich, though it conveys Tillich's idea). This myth of mission drove humanism forward toward the liberation of humanity, which as the bearer of reason and truth was to bring in a new rational order of society. This myth came to its full growth when the enlightened authoritarianism of the early modern period was replaced by liberal and democratic social myths and forms. This full growth took the form of a theory of natural harmony.

In humanism the Judeo-Christian trust in providence was transformed into a reliance upon a pre-established harmony in the cosmos, in the human psyche, and in society. This harmony, it was believed, would progressively engender unity and general well-being if every individual had the freedom to follow his or her own convictions and economic interests; in pursuing self-interests, the interests of the community would be advanced.

This theory of natural harmony may be understood either from the point of view of the human subject—the mind—or from that of the object—nature and the social, productive forces. With respect to the object, the theory of harmony asserted that, in sense perception, nature gives itself to humanity in such a way that a natural knowledge emerges which is adequate for purposes of control; and it asserted that the free sway of all human creative forces—in the cultural area through tolerance, in the economic area through liberal political economy ("laissez faire"), in the political area through the rule of the majority (democracy) —would lead to the rational shaping of society. In other words, it held that the human being may, through a natural harmony, achieve true fulfillment. With respect to the subject, the theory asserted that the categories of the human spirit are the structure-giving elements of nature; hence nature is amenable to rational knowledge and control. Society can be rationally shaped because the human species is undergoing in history an education that will fulfill its rational potentialities. Taken together, then, both the objective and the subjective aspects of the theory of natural harmony presupposed a religious faith in the essential unity and goodness of man and the world and in a spiritual unity between man and nature. It must be noted here that, although certain pessimistic motives of classical Christian thought were ignored, the optimistic worldview that was adopted came primarily from Judeo-Christian, rather than from pagan, sources, as did also the activist, world-shaping impulse (which was given marked impetus through Calvinism).

The developments in philosophy during the period of rationalism and enlightenment may be taken as typical of the trends, both practical and theoretical, which gave expression to the theory of natural harmony. From the 17th century on, one philosopher after another worked out the implications of the theory of harmony: Spinoza, Descartes, and Leibniz in metaphysics; Shaftesbury and Helvetius in psychology and ethics; Montesquieu, Rousseau, and Adam Smith in political and economic theory; Voltaire and a host of others in the progressivist philosophy of history. Reason, both speculative and technological, both revolutionary and formative, working in the individual and in society, was to usher in the kingdom of universal brotherhood. An original motive power in this drive toward emancipation came, of course, from the

recognition of the sacredness of personality, from belief in human rights and human worth. But other ideas also soon appeared, ideas that reflected an increasing tension between the objective and the subjective aspects of the theory.

The enthusiasm for the rational control of nature and society, besides releasing new energies, introduced a new alienation between persons and between humanity and nature, an alienation that would in time disrupt the harmony. Employing a characteristically "existentialist" interpretation of the outlook of modern mentality, Tillich asserts that one of the decisive elements of modern thought is the contrast between "subject" and "object," a contrast that tends to stress the "objectivity" or the "subjectivity" of reality. This dichotomy between subject and object superseded the subject-object unity of the high Middle Ages and became the "prime mover" of Western philosophy and also of modern technological, capitalist society. The sense of the immediacy of the origin, of the creative sources of man's life, was gradually lost. Personality and community became merely objective things, thus losing their intrinsic powerfulness and depth. The attitude toward things followed the same course, partially as a consequence of the developing technology; in the human consciousness "things" lost their intrinsic value and depth. Thus personality, community, and things became the instruments of an autonomous secularism; they became merely objects for control and calculation in the service of man's economic purposes. A spirit of "self-sufficient finitude" invaded the common life. Indeed, religion itself lost its sense of the immediacy of the origin and became one sphere among other spheres; even its God became a "thing" among other things, and the language of religion assumed an "objective," literal character that could only elicit skepticism. In philosophy both realism and idealism exhibited the loss of the sense of immediacy, emphasizing in corresponding ways the dichotomy of subject and object. Romanticism attempted to recapture the lost unity between subject and object (and with it the lost splendor of life) by restoring old myths of origin or by developing new ones, but it achieved only the spurious immediacy of irrationalism, either in the archaism of religious revival or in primitivist organicism and vitalism. Romanticism, however, did not much alter the main trend in capitalist society. Positivism became the characteristic philosophy of a technological society, seeking the domination of the object by the subject. In the spirit of this positivism, the dynamic ethos of capitalist society became increasingly determinative for the Protestant-humanist era.

This characteristic dynamic is epitomized in what Tillich calls "the bourgeois principle." Wherever technology and capital have been at work in the modern world, this principle has been operative. Its success is to be observed in its permeation of almost the entire planet, in a world domination that no one can escape. The definition of this principle can be formulated most succinctly in terms of its goal. The goal of the bourgeois principle is the radical dissolution of the bonds of original, organic community life, the dissolution of the powers of origin into elements to be conquered rationally. Science, religion, politics, art, the relations among the classes—all have been drawn into the crucible of the bourgeois principle. It is true that the bourgeois principle has never been—indeed, it never could be—the sole support of capitalist society. The principle was itself primarily utilitarian and critical; it unconsciously presupposed previously existing creative powers and supports. Just as Protestantism retained and transformed Catholic elements, so modern capitalist society has presupposed and has in varying ways retained contact with the powers of origin. It has not carried through the bourgeois principle in complete consistency. This fact becomes evi-

dent whenever the middle classes feel themselves threatened; they then appeal to myths of soil and blood, to nationalism, as a protection of middle-class interests. Yet the characteristic positive preoccupation following from the bourgeois principle has been the creation of means of objective control; and this preoccupation has displaced the intuitive grasping of intrinsic values; both things and persons have been enervated by subordinating them to economic purposes. The spirit of bourgeois society is the spirit that, after having dissolved the primary ties of origin, subjects a "thingified" world entirely to its purposes. This process of "thingification" has been carried through by the motive power of the theory of harmony and progress.

The amalgam of Protestant and humanist faiths in a principle of harmony has produced the modern age with its tremendous creativity; it has produced the modern ideas of tolerance and education and democracy; it has provided the energy and goal of the age of "free enterprise." The practical implications of the theory of natural harmony become especially clear if one observes the contrast between the social and metaphysical presuppositions of the Protestant-humanist era and those of the Catholic era. Catholicism has relied upon a hierarchy that is supposedly based on an ontological hierarchy of being. It has attempted to make the hierarchical system exercise control in all spheres of society. Where Catholicism has been dominant, it has elicited sharp resistance from these spheres, as, for example, in Italy and France. The Protestant-humanist era, on the other hand, has depended upon a hidden harmony. Accordingly, Protestantism has exhibited a greater cooperation and harmony with the evolving autonomous cultural spheres than has Catholicism. (As we shall observe later, this fact must be taken into account in any attempt to understand Protestant secularism.) Moreover, a certain harmony has prevailed within Protestantism itself, despite the lack of authoritative courts of appeal. "A decisive harmony," says Tillich, "has again and again come about automatically. And so the division of Protestantism into numerous mutually antagonistic churches, sects, denominations and movements did not involve any dangers so long as the common fundamental attitude was both positively and negatively unshaken."

Humanism's faith in harmony was for a time no less confirmed by history than was Protestantism's corresponding faith. The residues of earlier social coherence, expanding markets, and relatively free competition, these and other similar factors made it appear at first that the "law" of harmony expressed the nature of reality. The rise in the standard of living for many, the great increase in wealth, and the "success" of Western imperialism made tragedy in history seem (at least to the middle-class mentality) a thing of the past.

But the prevailing forms of Protestantism and humanism are now reaching their limits. The cunning of history pursues elusive, labyrinthine ways, and it makes unexpected turns. Capitalism, with its religion of harmony, has culminated not in harmony but in contradiction and crisis. This turn is no accident.

What earlier seemed to be the natural laws of harmony turned out to be contingent historical circumstances. The theory of the harmony of interests presupposed the 18th-century society of small producers and merchants, a society not yet controlled by mammoth corporations. Developments unforeseen by classical liberal economics were to bring about tremendous structural changes—and the breakdown of harmony. Already, within a half century after the promulgation of the theory of the harmony of interests, the liberal utopia began to assume the physiognomy of Lancashire and Manchester. Subsequently, the theory of harmony has more and more become an ideology protecting the interests of the new ruling groups and sanctioning an increasingly destructive application of the bourgeois principle. Instead of producing harmony, the structural changes have in the 20th century raised the "storms of our times."

These storms have created a darkness so readily visible that it is now almost a work of supererogation to describe it. Whether we think of the far-flung conflicts among imperialisms and of their exploitations in the domestic spheres or in the colonies, of the growth of monopoly and the concentration of wealth and economic power, of the disparity between increasing powers of production and decreasing purchasing power, of the opposition between the classes, of two world wars within our generation, of the inability of capitalism to use the full resources of the economy except in time of war or of radical depression and unemployment (the normal sequel to "normalcy"); whether we consider the "thingification" of man through the rationalization of industry and through his being made into a mere quantity of working power subject to the laws (or chances) of the market, or the "thingification" of nature through its being viewed as something only to be conquered and used, as something only to be shoveled about; whether we think of the prostitution of education to merely utilitarian ends or of the complacently accepted corruption of politics through special interests; whether we think of the irresponsible and commercial vulgarization of the idea industries (radio, movie, and printing), of the increase of agitation, propaganda, and mass-production methods for the influencing of public opinion (with the consequent weakening of individuality and tolerance and responsible discussion), or of the decline of ethically powerful and uniting symbols in the democracies and in the churches—in each and all these tendencies we discern the causes or the consequences of the disruption of "automatic" harmony. This disruption has created a mass society in which reason has lost its depth and dignity (having created a huge impersonal machine that it does not control) ; in which societal sadism and insensitivity to suffering and injustice are taken for granted; in which the average individual is lost and lonely; in which the fear of insecurity and lack of spiritual roots produce neurosis and cynicism; in which psychiatric hospitals and counseling centers have become major institutions; in which the sense of personal insignificance is compensated by egregious group egotism; in which a flat secularism, the spirit of "self-sufficient finitude," prevails in church and society, exhibiting contemporary man's blunted sense of his relatedness to the creative depths of personality, existence, and meaning; and therefore in which there is a void of meaninglessness, yearning for meaning. This is the world, said Henry Adams in 1892, which is ruled from "a banker's Olympus."

Whether one accepts Henry Adams' dictum in its simplicity or not, one must recognize that Protestantism in its alliance with the evolving middle-class humanism has tended in many respects to become merely the religious aspect of capitalism. Humanist and Protestant harmonisms have together moved from their originally creative phase through a technological stage to become a passionately conservative force. Just as Roman Catholicism first helped to shape the culture of the Middle Ages and then became fettered in the "Babylonish captivity" of the waning Middle Ages and of a petrified Counter Reformation, so Protestantism has helped to form the Protestant era and then, in differing ways in its different forms and countries, has to a large extent become bound in a new Babylonish captivity within capitalist culture. It languishes (all too comfortably) in this prison, or, to change the figure from a Reformation to a biblical one, it is largely a prostituted, a "kept" religion. It has lost its relatedness to an ultimate ground and aim, and thus it has lost much of its original prophetic power. Its God has become domesticated; it is a bourgeois god. In its major effect its ethics are largely indistinguishable from the "ethics" of the bourgeois principle.

As a consequence the Protestantism that offers "religious" embellishment for the bourgeois principle merely aggravates the contradictions of capitalist society. Its appeal to individual consciousness and conscience (detached from the socializing influences of a nourishing spiritual tradition) and its belief that the freedom of the individual by virtue of the centripetal power of harmony moves toward a common center and then issues forth in health and healing for the individual and the society have become a means of evading basic social-ethical issues and of merely protecting the governing powers of the status quo. Philanthropy and social reform emanating from the churches usually assist these governing powers by moving strictly within bourgeois presuppositions. Through its emphasis on economic and spiritual individualism combined with a class-bound moralism, this Protestantism has also helped to dissolve communal symbols and supports. It has been drawn into the general process of dissolution.

It is true that the dissolution described here has not disintegrated spiritual and ethical values in America to the extent visible during recent decades in Europe. As Tillich puts it, "America lives still in a happy state of backwardness." But many of the conditions and attitudes that led to fascism in Europe exist also in America.

The foregoing characterization of the present status of Protestantism is, of course, one-sided and incomplete; indeed, Tillich asserts (as we shall observe presently) that genuinely Protestant motives have persisted in the churches and even in certain aspects of secularism. Yet the tendencies described have been largely responsible for, or have accelerated, the decline of the Protestant-humanist era.

In response to these developments, dynamic movements of revolt have for a century been abandoning the characteristic tenets of burgeois and Protestant-humanist individualism and automatic harmonism and have been moving in the direction of new (and sometimes of collectivist) forms of faith and society. Some of these movements have opposed the churches and liberalistic humanism as the bulwarks of privilege; other movements have appeared within the churches or in the form of neo-humanism. The spectrum of revolt is a wide one. Communism, fascism, and Roman Catholic corporatism assume varying shades of red and black. The Christian socialist movements, neoliberal and neo-orthodox, occupy other positions in the spectrum. In certain areas of the spectrum a desire to "escape from freedom" is evident. The burden upon the individual has become almost too heavy to bear. Consequently, many people relinquish individual religious or political responsibility; they are willing to sacrifice their autonomy in the hope of finding on the path of authority a new meaning in life, new symbols and forms of life. The present attraction of Roman Catholicism and communism must be understood partially in this context. All these movements have been seeking a way out of the Protestant-humanist era.

The whole situation is a paradoxical one for both Protestantism and humanism, the partners of the modern era. Tillich has, in several writings, succinctly described the plight in which Protestantism finds itself. The description applies also to humanism. "That which Protestantism denied at its rise," he says, "is today—*in an altered form* —the demand of the age. That demand is for an authoritative and powerfully symbolic system of mass reintegration: but it was just that—*in a distorted form*—against which Protestantism protested. . . . The Protestant era is finished, after nearly all the historical conditions upon which it rested have been taken away from it." Indeed, the very manner of the rise of Protestantism would seem to have determined its present limitations.

It is clear that if Protestantism is to play a prophetic and creative role in the new situation, it must effect a break and transformation as disruptive and as boldly productive as the changes made at the beginning of the Protestant era; and the transformation must in its effect on the social structure move in a direction opposite to that of the earlier break and transformation.

To inquire, as Tillich does in many writings, as to whether the Protestant era has now come to an end, suggests questions that are importunate for Protestantism and humanism at this epochal moment. It will suffice if we here formulate these questions as they concern Protestantism. Will Protestantism escape its Babylonish captivity and assist reformation again? Will it extricate itself from the disintegration of the mass society of the late-capitalist epoch? Or has it cast its lot irrevocably with the transitory and exhausted forces that now serve as its ideological expression and protection? Will it be able to exhibit again the self-surpassing power of the historic Christian dynamic by disassociating itself from these forces and by giving a sense of meaning, a direction, and a quality of greatness to new forms of thought and life? Or will the coming era take shape in opposition to organized Protestantism? Will it be in any significant sense a Protestant era? Or will it eventually be called a post-Protestant era because of the emergence of some new type of Christianity which will help to determine a new spirit and form of society?

Obviously, no one can today give the answers to these questions (or to corresponding questions that might be posed concerning liberalistic humanism). The questions serve the purpose, however, of giving concrete relevance to a consideration of the problems, the perils, and the opportunities that now confront Protestantism. But they cannot be properly dealt with in the manner of the soothsayer. In considering the problems which they raise, Tillich aims, as he says, "to drive the analysis to a point where the vision of a possible reconstruction" of Protestantism and contemporary society may appear. Hence the title of the volume *The Protestant Era* means to suggest not only that the Protestant era is now approaching its limits but also that the end of the Protestant era would not be the end of Protestantism. Indeed, a new realization might be more in accord with the nature of Protestantism.

A main trend, a characteristic dynamic, of the Protestant era has been expressed, as we have seen, in the bourgeois principle supported by the theory of natural harmony. But the harmony has not come. Instead, men have lost their sense of relatedness to the creative springs of life; community has been frustrated, and neurotic insecurity is the "order" of the day. Insofar as the Protestant spirit has identified itself with the prevailing ethos, it participates in and aggravates the disintegration of our world. The bourgeois principle is insufficient to create community. The questions arise then: By what principle can bourgeois society be criticized and transcended? By what principle can Protestantism regain a prophetic and newly creative power?

Tillich holds that, even if the Protestant era is finished, Protestantism knows a principle that is not finished. Like every other finite reality, Protestantism in any particular historical realization must reckon always with the possibility of its exhaustion. But the principle of Protestantism is not finite and exhaustible. As a witness to this principle, Protestantism is not to be identified with any of its historical realizations. It is not bound to the Protestant era. It can drive forward to qualitatively new creation. It can also, in the name of its principle, protest against the Protestant era and against organized Protestantism itself. The latter are relative and conditioned realities. This does not mean that they are lacking in significance. They are to be understood in the light of the Protestant principle.

Protestantism here confronts the perennial problem of the one and the many, what Emerson called *the* problem of philosophy. This problem, he asserted (quoting Plato), is "to find a ground unconditioned and absolute for all that exists conditionally." The Protestant principle aims to express the true relation between the unconditional and the conditioned. Only by appeal to such a principle can Protestantism transcend its cultural entanglements at any particular time and offer both criticism and creative direction in personal and social life.

This principle is presented in a dual aspect. On the one hand, it is a universally significant principle, pointing to the source and judge of every religious and cultural reality. It points to a moving, restless power, the inner infinity of being, that informs and transforms all conditioned realities and brings new forms to birth. Thus Protestantism can lay no exclusive claim to it. On the other hand, the principle refers to the characteristic possibility, the essential power, of Protestantism as an historical movement. It is the principle by which Protestantism is supported and judged. When Protestantism is not loyal to this principle or when it does not judge itself according to the principle, it is no longer truly Protestant.

Catholicism, in effect, identifies its own historical realizations of the Catholic era with the ground and judge of all religious and cultural realities. Luther called this self-absolutization the "worship of man-made gods." This worship of man-made gods appears in Protestant as well as in Catholic forms, in the sacramentalism of the Word as well as in the sacramentalism of holy institutions and objects. It appears also in the "secular sacramentalism" of capitalism and nationalism. This claim to an absolute authority can conflict with similar claims of other authorities. It can also elicit the resistance of autonomous freedom. At the beginning of the modern era the autonomy that was expressed by humanism and that rebelled against ecclesiastical and political heteronomy, vibrated with a residual religious power. But in both ancient and modern times autonomy has again and again shown itself to be precarious and unstable. It loses its original sense of an unconditional demand for truth and justice; it becomes self-enclosed. As we have observed, this is what has happened in capitalistic society, in which the spirit of self-sufficient finitude now prevails. Increasingly, modern autonomy has degenerated into relativism or into a new heteronomy. Among intellectuals who have been deeply affected by modern historicism, the former tendency is widely evident, but in the culture at large the latter tendency is undoubtedly the stronger. The typical bourgeois man accepts the presuppositions of the capitalist mentality and the societal forms of capitalism with the same rigidity and absoluteness that the Fundamentalist exhibits in his religion. But heteronomy and autonomy do not exhaust the possibilities open to humanity.

The Protestant principle stands in contrast to both these attitudes. The negative implication of the word *Protestant*—a word that arose out of an actual historic protest against ecclesiastical authoritarianism—makes it eminently appropriate to serve as the name and the historical manifestation of the prophetic protest against every conditioned thing that presents an unconditional claim for itself. This negative implication of the Protestant principle has from the very beginning of the Protestant movement included also a protest against any autonomy that forfeits its unconditional source and judge and that rests in its own conditioned self-assertion.

But the Protestant principle is not only negative and critical; it is also creative. Indeed, the critical presupposes the creative

element. This positive element is the formative dynamic that sustains the fundamental attitude of seriousness and responsibility that belongs to all creative endeavor. It points to the ground and source of meaning that is present in a singular way in every relative achievement; but it cannot be exhausted or confined in any realization, not even in a definition. This dialectical principle, which combines critical negation and dynamic fulfillment, is the basis for what Tillich calls the "Protestant Gestalt of grace." The ultimate orientation involved here Tillich calls "theonomy." Before defining "theonomy," however, we must give further consideration to the Protestant principle.

This principle has been apprehended again and again in the history of religion and culture. In the West its lineage derives ultimately from Old Testament prophetism with its message of judgment and fulfillment. For the Christian the decisive expression of the essential power and meaning of reality is (in Tillich's formulation) the New Being manifest in Jesus as the Christ. Here the essential power and goodness reveals itself as *agape,* "love," an ontological and ethical dynamic that overcomes the frustrations, the fragmentariness, and the perversions of human existence, bringing together that which is separated. *Agape* is the source of justice and law, supporting, criticizing, and transforming them. It is, on the one hand, a command, and, on the other, it is the power that breaks through all commands. Thus it relates ethical life to the universal and the unconditional, and yet it adapts itself to every phase of the changing world. The Protestant principle presupposes this original critical and dynamic Christian message and its proclamation of the Kingdom of God near at hand. But there is a peculiarly Protestant statement of the principle.

Tillich finds this characteristically Protestant version of the principle in the Reformation assertion of the unconditional character of God and in the idea that the fulfillment of human existence ultimately depends not upon human devices and mediations (of Catholic, Protestant, or secular type) but rather upon justification through faith. He recognizes, however, that the doctrine of justification has become well-nigh unintelligible to the modern man and even to the modern scholar. The situation is partly due to the fact that in some instances the doctrine has come to mean a rule of faith imposed as a "law"—just the opposite of what was originally intended. Tillich has therefore attempted to give the doctrine a restatement in modern terms by devising a Protestant interpretation of a conception that has been used in existential theology and philosophy, the concept of "the human boundary-situation." This restatement presents Tillich's peculiarly Protestant interpretation of the character of human freedom and fulfillment.

Human existence is the rise of being to the realm of freedom. Being is freed from bondage to natural necessity. It becomes spirit and acquires the freedom to question itself and its environment the freedom to raise the question concerning the true and the good and to make decision with regard to them. But we are in a sense unfree in our freedom, for we are compelled to decide. "This inevitability of freedom, of having to make decisions, creates the deep restlessness of our existence; through it our existence is threatened." It is threatened because we are confronted by an unconditional demand to choose and fulfill the good, a demand that we cannot fulfill. Consequently, each of us as spirit has a cleavage within us, a cleavage that is manifest also in society. There is no place to which we may flee from the demand. And in confronting the demand we can never provide ourselves with absolute security.

The point at which every self-provided security is brought under question, the point at which human possibilities reach and know their limits, Tillich calls "the human boundary-situation." "Right" belief and "right" action, church and sacrament and creed, piety and mystical experience, and also secular substitutes for any of these things, are recognized as false securities. An ultimate and threatening "No" is pronounced upon them all.

But human freedom and existence find support as well as threat at the boundary-situation. This support comes from beyond or beneath the interplay between person and society. What is involved here is the deepest level of human existence. Just where dependence upon the finite creations of spirit is relinquished, a new confidence and a creative impulse arise from the infinite and inexhaustible depths.

This experience of the boundary-situation is not something that takes place in a flight away from the concrete and the temporal. The boundary is, so to speak, at the edge of a particular complex of spiritual and cultural realities. The specific consequences of the experience of ultimate threat and support will therefore be different in the time of Luther or Pascal from what they were in the time of Jeremiah. But always the transcendent significance of, and judgment upon, temporal realities are envisaged anew. One gains at the boundary a paradoxical sense of the immediacy of origin and of threat. Beneath the dichotomy between subject and object a new, a third dimension, the dimension of depth, is discerned. The creative and destructive and recreative powers of being erupt into the consciousness. A new relation to things and people appears. Things are no longer viewed merely as objects for use or as technical means without intrinsic worth. They are seen again in their "powerfulness," which is rooted in the inner infinity of being. In place of "the mutual domination between thing and personality," there appears "a mutual service between personality and things," an "eros-relation." This eros-relation becomes manifest also in a new sense of community and of its depth. In place of the community that breaks the personality and bends it under its yoke, there can now emerge a community of free personalities who know themselves as belonging together through their connection with the ultimate supporting and threatening reality. The personality recognizes something holy and unconditional in the dignity and freedom of other persons; for persons, like things, are seen now to be supported by the inner infinity of being. Here, it would seem, we have Tillich's rendering of Luther's idea of the "love of neighbor"—the consequence of justification.

We do not, however, by our experience of the boundary gain control of the ultimate threat and support. We can *prepare* for receiving the support by exposing ourselves consciously and without reservation to the claims of the unconditional. But awareness of the ultimate meaning and of the possibility of fulfilling that meaning in a particular situation is a matter of "destiny and grace." Neither a church nor any other group can subject the ultimate threat and support to human conditions or techniques. For this reason the radical Protestant attributes only a provisional importance to the church and its forms. Here the radical stands nearer to the secularism that is skeptical of the conventional securities of piety than to any orthodoxy, whether it be "religious" or secular.

In this connection one of the most striking and original aspects of Tillich's rendering of the doctrine of justification should be noted. Luther applied the doctrine of justification only to the religious-moral life. The sinner, though unjust, is "justified" and anticipated. Tillich applies the doctrine also to the religious-intellectual sphere. No act of will accepting "right" belief can be properly demanded by any authority. Devotion to truth is supreme; it is devotion to God. There is a sacred element in the integrity that leads to doubt even about God and religion. Indeed, since God is truth, any loyalty to truth is religious loyalty, even if it leads to a recognition of the lack of truth. Paraphrasing Augustine, the serious doubter may say: "I doubt, therefore I am religious." Even in doubt the divine is present. Absolutely serious atheism can be directed toward the unconditional; it can be a form of faith in truth. There appears here the conquest of meaninglessness by the awareness of the paradoxical presence of "meaning in meaninglessness." Thus the doubter is "justified." The only absolutely irreligious attitude, then, is absolute cynicism, abolute lack of seriousness.

Returning, now, to the consideration with which the concept of the boundary-situation was introduced, we may restate the implications of the Protestant principle as they relate to heteronomy and autonomy. Both these types of "religion" are overcome by what Tillich calls "theonomy" (a concept that had been used previously by Troeltsch and others). In the face of the destruction or weakening of freedom that accompanies heteronomy and autonomy, theonomy goes beyond them both, preserving and transforming an element from each. It emphasizes the commanding element in the unconditional demand for the ultimate good, for truth and justice. This ultimate ground of meaning and existence is not (as in heteronomy) identified with any conditioned reality or social form; yet it calls for obedience. Here an element of heteronomy is retained and transformed. But the unconditional is not arbitrary; it never demands the sacrifice of the intellect; it is not alien to our humanity; it fulfills our inmost nature, our freedom. Theonomy takes over from autonomy this element of intelligibility and self-determination and transforms it. Recognizing that self-sufficient autonomy, as the self-assertion of a conditioned reality, is not able to create a world from within itself and recognizing that every conception of the ultimate good must reflect the cleavage within man and society, theonomy deepens autonomy to a point where the latter is transcended. Theonomy supports autonomy and at the same time breaks through it without shattering it. Thus theonomy brings both heteronomy and autonomy to the boundary-situation, where in differing ways they confront the ultimate threat and support and are transformed. In short, theonomy is the condition in which spiritual and social forms are imbued with the import of the unconditional as their supporting ground and judge.

The critical and creative principle that points to the ultimate threat and support is what makes Protestantism Protestant. It is, therefore, called the "Protestant principle." But it is clear that this principle is no sectarian principle. It cuts through all sectarianisms (both religious and secular) to that which shatters and transforms all self-enclosed forms. Its first word, therefore, "must be the word against religion"; and this means its first word is against every movement that idolizes established forms, whether religious or secular, orthodox or liberal, ecclesiastical or nonecclesiastical. All these idolizations are merely forms of "pharisaism." The Protestant may not attribute a classical status even to the Reformation or to any other period (e.g., the period A.D. 30–33) in a normative sense. "It is of the essence of Protestantism," Tillich says, "that there can be no classical period for it." The principle protests also against any idolization of religious language, whether it be old or new, whether it be in the Bible or in the church confessions.

Thus, Protestantism (or any other religion) always needs the correction that comes from the "secular" protest against any tendency within it to identify itself with the unconditional. In this function, as well as in the challenge of its creative achievement, secularism on Protestant soil may be called "Protestant secularism." The very existence of this sort of secularism shows that grace is not bound up with explicit religion, that is, with those forms whose express purpose it is to serve as a medium of grace. It is "a concealed form of grace," a manifestation of "the latent church." It often serves to remind Protestantism of its own principle and in some cases exhibits a better, even if an unintended, apprehension and application of that principle. Protestantism can appropriate this stimulus only if it stands at the boundary between itself and secularism. When there is a vital relation between church and society, "the church is the perpetual guilty conscience of society and society the perpetual guilty conscience of the church."

These implications of the Protestant principle are given corresponding expression in Tillich's definitions of religion and culture. Religion is "direction toward the unconditional." Culture is direction toward the conditioned forms of meaning and their unity. Despite this contrast, however, genuine religion and vital culture have ultimately the same roots. "Being religious is being unconditionally concerned, whether this concern expresses itself in secular or (in the narrower sense) religious forms." All sharp divisions between the sacred and the secular must be eliminated in recognition of a transcendent critical and formative power which is present in both religion and culture. "Secular culture is essentially as impossible as atheism because both presuppose the unconditional element and both express ultimate concerns." Implied here is a dialectical view of religion and culture. Religion, in order to achieve realization, must assume form and become culture; in doing so it is religious in both substance and intention. But culture, even when it is not religious by intention, is religious in substance, for every cultural act contains an unconditional meaning, it depends upon the ground of meaning. Yet when religion becomes culture, it may lose its depth and its sense of relatedness to the unconditional; it may degenerate into an absolute devotion to conditioned cultural realities. On the other hand, culture, even in the act of opposing "religion," may rediscover the unconditional threat and support, and it may bring forth new religious creation. Accordingly, the major types of explicit religion appear in implicit form in the history of "secular" culture. With Schelling, Tillich would say that the history of culture is in a broad sense the history of religion. The Protestant principle, in pointing to that universally operative reality that judges and supports all meaningful existence, interprets religion as present wherever there is a uniting of negation and affirmation, of threat and support, of judgment and grace, of crisis and form-creation. Perverted religion and perverted culture appear wherever this dialectic is absent.

The demand is always placed before Protestantism, then, to transcend itself at the boundary-situation and to move toward new realization. It must effect this realization directly in relation to secular realities. This means that its prophetic and creative power must become manifest in a concrete historical situation; it means also that it must combine prophetic and rational criticism (as it has done almost from its beginning). The Protestant principle, therefore, relates "the line upward," the reference to the eternal meaning, to "the line forward," the direction toward the temporal realization of the eternal meaning in accord with the demands of a rational understanding of a particular historical situation. In emphasizing "the line forward" as well as "the line upward" and in demanding a dialectical relation between Protestantism and secularism, Tillich turns away from pietistic indifference to "the world" and history, and stresses the world-affirming and world-shaping dynamic of Calvinism and modern humanism.

In the light of the Protestant principle there can be no *official* philosophy for Protestantism, and there can be no official program for the application of the principle. Yet, if the principle is to achieve relevance in any particular historical situation, it requires both a philosophical elabora-

tion and a program for action. His own philosophical elaboration of the principle Tillich calls "belief-ful" or "self-transcending realism," for it combines realism and a faith that transcends realism. Belief-ful realism "is a turning toward reality, a questioning of reality, a penetrating into existence, a driving to the level where reality points beyond itself to its ground and ultimate meaning." It does not look "above" reality to a transcendentalized spiritual world; it looks down into the "depths" of reality to its inner infinity. "Belief-ful realism" may be characterized as an existential and dialectical philosophy of meaning-fulfillment.

The concept of "meaning" has become almost indispensable in discussions of philosophy of culture and philosophy of history during the past three-quarters of a century, especially since Dilthey gave it a central place in his "critique of historical reason." So great a role has the concept played in recent times that Tillich says the problem of the meaning of history has become the problem of the present period in contrast to the previous period's major interest in the control of nature. This shift of interest is a symptom of the crisis in the culture. Tillich started with the twofold idealistic presupposition that all the spiritual life of man forms an inner unity and that this spiritual life, both as a whole and in its parts, is to be understood only in its religious roots. But in his "self-transcending realism" he goes beyond epistemological idealism and the critical-dialectical method corresponding to it. He is always conscious of the tension between any synthesis and the unconditional quality pointing beyond it. Thus he rejects the idealistic conviction that the antithesis should be thought of only as "sublated" in the achieved synthesis. In this way he replaces the idealistic philosophy of Mind by a realistic philosophy of Meaning.

Perhaps the thinker with whom the most instructive comparison can be made is Karl Barth. Tillich has often been classified with Barth as representative of existential and dialectical theology. But, in his article "What is Wrong with the 'Dialectic' Theology?" Tillich questions the classification. Tillich asserts that Barth's neo-Reformation theology at its beginning supplied a powerful and radical religious criticism of church and culture; in the face of Nazism it saved the German Protestant church. But he denies that Barth's theology is dialectical; it is, he says, merely paradoxical. Moreover, by interpreting the divine as wholly other and alien to man, it derogates all human culture. It denies significance even to any human questioning concerning the ultimate. By rejecting humanism and autonomy it has created a new heteronomy. Although it opposed the Nazi "Grand Inquisitor" (to use Dostoevsky's term), it has set up its own Grand Inquisitor "with a strong but tight-fitting armor of Barthian supernaturalism" and scholastic confessionalism. Despite its constant reference to crisis, it has come to view everything as being under judgment—except itself. It has "relapsed into the mere reiteration of tradition." It has forgotten the Protestant protest in the name of which it began and is in danger of becoming a merely weakened form of traditional Catholicism. Moreover, in its criticism of culture it has opposed tyranny only for the sake of the church and not for the sake of human rights. And, as a consequence of its supernaturalism and of its Kantian ethical presuppositions, it has for the most part pronounced only an abstract, formal judgment upon the social order—all things are judged and really nothing is decided. This aloofness to the responsibilities of prophetic religion, an aloofness sanctioned by a supernaturalist pessimism, merely assists (by default) the ruling and dominating powers in society. By this aloofness, Barthianism even helped to destroy the religious-socialist movement in pre-Hitler Germany. And it has not yet been able to explicate a positive conception of fulfillment in history. It turns away from a positive decision with regard to the specific situation "here and now." It escapes backward into an otherworldly traditionalism. Despite its avowed existential attitude, which renounces the spectator attitude, it is unable to find a way forward out of the Protestant era.

Tillich's philosophy is one that looks toward meaning-fulfillment in all areas of life. Although many of his formulations of this philosophy reveal the influence of modern intellectual movements, its deepest roots are to be found in the Judeo-Christian apprehension of human existence and fulfillment. This apprehension, implicit in what we have already presented, may be epitomized in three familiar axioms—and affirmation of the essential, if not actual, unity and goodness of existence (mythologically expressed in the doctrine of the Creation) is combined with the recognition of an underivable contradiction in human existence (mythologically expressed in the doctrine of the Fall—which may not be accepted as an historical event or as an explanation of the human condition but as a description of the cleavage in the human spirit and in human society) and with a confidence that the cleavage, the broken unity and goodness, can be restored by the inexhaustible creative power (mythologically expressed in the doctrine of redemption). This Judeo-Christian apprehension, when truly understood, implies a philosophy of history.

In conformity with the historical thinking of ancient prophetism and of the modern historical consciousness, which is in part derived from it, self-transcending realism affirms that the focal expression of these three elements is to be found in history, though the form-bursting and form-creating power arises from beneath the level of freedom and existence. Self-transcending realism is an historical realism. In and through the historical "here and now," in and through the dynamics and structures of history, we experience in widest and deepest dimensions the realization and the contradiction of meaning. Here we encounter in its critical and creative power the ultimate threat and support of human existence. History in all its spheres is the arena of salvation, the realm in which the demands of the unconditional are confronted. Salvation occurs in time and through community, in the overcoming of the demonic powers that pervert both personal and social life. It appears in those forms and structures that give a local habitation to justice and love and beauty. And it is the work of a gracious, affirming, healing power moving toward the fulfillment of being and meaning.

The depth, the tensions, and the possibilities of existence are not really known until one in faith apprehends them through passionate participation in the struggles of history. In other words, the existential attitude implicit in the demand for participation presupposes that the subject comes to know the human situation only by entering into the process of fulfillment, a process in which thought and being are merged and transmuted in the creative life of spirit. The mark of the fullest intercourse with reality is found, then, in the uniting of contemporaneity with self-transcending relatedness to the unconditional; it is found in a "belief-ful," timely awareness and action in terms of the unconditional demands relevant to the present situation. Such an awareness and action, therefore, demands a venturing decision, the taking of a risk.

When people (or churches) do not direct their deepest existential concern to this focus of decision and participation in the "here and now," they miss an unrepeatable opportunity for the expression of meaning in history; in other words, they miss the *kairos,* the "fulness of time." But action or participation is not sufficient. If the action is not accompanied by a decision for the unconditional, then either demonic self-inflation or lack of seriousness ensues. On the other hand, if decision is not

accompanied by participation, then knowledge will be abstractly formal or "untimely." Only from an awareness of the inextricable bond and tension between the concrete historical situation and the unconditioned depth of being and meaning can humans avail themselves of truly critical and formative power. The unconditionality of prophetic criticism, combined with the timely resoluteness of formative will under grace, can alone bring the fullness or fulfillment of time, the *kairos.* No aspect or area of life is exempt from the demands of this timely criticism and form-creation; that is, timely in the sense of the *kairos.* Only through timely criticism and action can the significantly new come into being; only in this way can the import and demand of the unconditional impinge upon history. This is the practical implication of the Protestant principle.

In viewing the present social situation at the end of the Protestant era, Tillich sees a negative vindication of the Protestant principle in the consequences of the operation of the bourgeois principle, as well as in the degeneration of self-sufficient autonomy into the current heteronomies of racism, nationalism, and capitalism. These heteronomies have often served to protect the bourgeois principle against radical criticism and thus to negate the Protestant principle. A characteristic consequence of the bourgeois principle (which, it will be recalled, always moves toward the dissolution of the bonds of community life through the rationalization of the powers of origin) is to be seen in the dependence of the working class upon the "free" sale of their physical ability to work, a dependence which, in its turn, relies upon the "laws" (or the chances) of the market. Here the perversion of humanity's essential nature assumes tremendous social dimensions. Even in normal times the fateful threat of insecurity confronts the entrepreneur as well as the worker. This threat, as it has expressed itself in the 20th century, has more and more torn away the ideological veil that romantic conservative thought and progressivist liberal economics have thrown over the contradictions of capitalist society.

These contradictions, in their most general economic aspects, are three: first, the contradiction between the rapidity of technical advance and the slowness of the development of societal forms that enable adjustment to the technical advance; second, the contradiction between the increasing production power and the decreasing consumption capacity of the masses (bigger and better factories have brought a higher proportion of unemployment) ; and, third, the contradiction between the assumed liberty of every individual and the actual dependence of the masses on great concentrations of economic power (which determine not only the production and prices of goods but also the manipulation of symbols through the idea industries) .

The way out of the present era can be found only if we can be released from the "possession" of the demonic powers that now carry through or protect the bourgeois principle, only if we can be caught up and transformed by newly creative powers emanating from the depths of being and history. Tillich is convinced that we will not even approach this timely moment unless we come to a passionate awareness of the deep void of meaninglessness that the bourgeois principle and its supporting heteronomies have created. The prevailing "neutrality" of the churches to these issues is only a form of ideological concealment of the perversions of the common life. It is true that no Protestant church can properly espouse an official social philosophy or program; to do so would be to violate the Protestant principle. Yet if the Protestant principle is apprehended in a vital and relevant way, it should lead to a turning-away from the void of meaninglessness and to new creation. It should lead to the forging of a principle pertinent to the present

historical situation, a principle that in the spirit of radical Protestantism can overcome the bourgeois principle.

This principle might be called the "religious-socialist principle." Tillich has written extensively on this theme; apart from certain collections of his essays, his book, *The Socialist Decision*, deals with this subject. Besides this, he was coeditor of a religious-socialist magazine for the Kairos Circle in pre-Hitler Germany. Here it must suffice if we give merely a few hints concerning the meaning of the central principle.

Tillich rejects the legalistic or programmatic type of religious socialism that considers socialism to be the precise demand of the Gospels; it attempts to make the Gospels a socialist textbook. He rejects the romantic type of religious socialism that claims that socialism is itself religion; this type of religious socialism rightly asserts that religion does not confine itself to a special religious sphere, yet it stifles the radical criticism inherent in the Protestant principle. He also rejects the practical-political type of religious socialism that simply tries to bring about cooperation between organized socialism and the churches; it tends to emphasize merely practical strategies and fails to scrutinize the basic presuppositions of either socialism or religion in their actual forms, and thus it neglects the need for fundamental transformation of either of them.

In his religious socialism Tillich attempts in a dialectical fashion to dissolve the static opposition of prevailing conceptions of religion and socialism; he aims to understand them in their deepest roots and to transform both of them in the spirit of prophetic religion. Accordingly, he aims to interpret religion and socialism in such a way as to point toward a new concrete Gestalt, capable in the deepest sense of meeting the particular needs of our time. The goal of this religious socialism is the radical application of the Protestant principle to both Protestantism and socialism, to both religion and secularism, in order to free Protestantism from bondage to the religious sphere as a separate sphere and also to make possible a religious understanding of the socialism and the secularism of the Protestant era. This type of religious socialism works primarily on theoretical problems. It is not concerned with the development of blueprints for a socialist system of society; its practical effectiveness, as compared with the theoretical, is intended to be small.

Whether or not organized Protestantism will continue its class-bound subservience to the spirit of capitalism is largely a matter of conjecture. There are evidences of change in European Protestantism in the direction of socialism. In the United States there would seem to be a persisting disposition in Protestant circles to rely upon automatic harmony, that is, upon capitalism. In any event, the coming years will bring to birth new forms of collectivism, forms that will vary in different countries. Religious socialism aims to accept the responsibility of delineating the principles that will be in conformity with the theological demands of self-transcending realism, with democratic ideals, and with economic necessities.

The widespread opposition between Protestantism and socialism is to be understood as the consequence of perversions within both of them. Protestantism's opposition is due not only to its Babylonish captivity to capitalism and nationalism but also to a widely held supernaturalist conception of the Kingdom of God as purely transcendent; it is due to the complacency of Protestant liberalism and to the "religious" indifference of Protestant Fundamentalism and Barthian neo-orthodoxy. All these tendencies reveal in varying ways and degrees the absence of a really disturbed consciousness of the magnitude of the struggle that must be made against the demonries of our time. In the face of this

situation, religious socialism not only demands that Protestantism should come to a new awareness of the Protestant principle and thus be released from bondage; it also tries to present the special demands of the *kairos* of our time, the demand for a new order of life imbued with new meaning to take the place of an autonomously emptied and heteronomously controlled society.

The opposition of socialism to religion is as false in principle as is the opposition of Protestantism to socialism. The historical roots of socialism are to be found in the prophetic-Protestant-humanist tradition; in the drive forward to the new in history, represented by revolutionary spiritualist movements of the pre-Reformation period and of the left wing of the Reformation; in the autonomous revolt against the powers of origin claimed by an ecclesiastically controlled culture (a revolt moving in the direction of democracy); in the Calvinist and humanist impulse to give a rational, rather than an arbitrary, shaping to society; in the struggle for humanity implicit in all these motifs, as well as in the world-affirming spirit of the Enlightenment. Perhaps the most powerful prophetic element in socialism is what has been called its "epochal consciousness," its awareness of the decisive character of the dynamic structures of a whole period. (The very concept of "the Protestant era" presupposes this prophetic view that the human situation must be understood in terms of the integrating and the disintegrating structures of a period.) Tillich believes that socialism is today more strongly conscious of the *kairos* of our period than is any other movement, conscious of an impending epochal fate and opportunity. But it is perverted by the possession of certain untimely elements that are either residues of the era now in crisis or new forms of idolatry. Some of these elements were originally creative ideas, and they are now, therefore, in their untimely form, all the more dangerous.

Socialism (and especially Marxism) has ignored the transcendent reference of the Protestant principle, and through its false claim to be a science it has degenerated into a new legalism and a new heteronomy. By its merely sociologistic interpretation of the cleavages and corruptions of human existence and by its continued reliance on an unbroken bourgeois principle (with its naïve belief in progress) it has transformed originally prophetic expectations for the future into utopianism. Religious socialism aims to correct the false anthropology of Marxism and to overcome its hereronomous and utopian impulses by the achievement of an autonomy deepened by theonomy and by an insistence upon the remoteness of socialism from the Kingdom of God, however clearly "the decision for socialism during a definite period may be the decision for the Kingdom of God."

The religious-socialist principle points the direction out of the Protestant era by combining elements that have been either neglected or perverted by both capitalism and socialism. It seeks a new theonomous society in which the powers of origin supporting organic community may be broken and yet fulfilled under the demands of the unconditional; it seeks more than a new economic system, it seeks a total outlook on existence in which all cultural areas retain their autonomy. It rejects the metaphysical core of bourgeois harmonism and socialist progressivism, and it adopts a prophetic philosophy of history in which anticipation of the new (as well as the breaking-away from the old) is combined with the responsibility of planning for freedom. On the basis of these principles, religious socialism would overcome the fear, the insecurity, the loneliness, the thingification of the masses of men; in such a way it would overcome the contradictions of our disintegrating world. It is clear, then, that if Protestantism or any other group is to meet the demands of our *kairos*, concern for individual salvation will have to be coupled with a concern for "the ultimate meaning and salvation of groups and institutions." But men cannot merely by decision bring about so great a change as this. A power more than human, a power greater than that of the now ruling principalities and powers, greater than that of the present demonries that have men in their possession, must be released. If Protestantism responds to this *kairos*, the Protestant era will not be at an end. The Reformation will continue. And, surely, in many of these motifs, Tillich may help prepare us for the religious and secular reformation that alone can overcome the crisis of the Protestant era and give new, timely access to what the poet, Gerard Manley Hopkins, has called "the dearest freshness deep down things."

CHAPTER 8

Capitalist society in the world system

It is out of the final development of capitalism that socialist forms emerge. Capitalism is transformed into socialism when capitalism is no longer able to reconcile the conflicts between the existing mode of production and the relations of production, when the contradictions of capitalism reach a point at which capitalism can no longer solve its own inherent problems. Ultimately capitalist relations become an obstacle to the further development of capitalism. New forms of production and social relations develop. In other words, as another form becomes evident, socialism begins to develop. As Marx wrote:

> No social order is every destroyed before all the productive forces for which it is sufficient have been developed, and new superior relations of production never replace older ones before the material conditions for their existence have matured within the framework of the old society. Mankind thus inevitably sets itself only such tasks as it is able to solve, since closer examination will always show that the problem itself arises only when the material conditions for its solution are already present or at least in the course of formation.[1]

The forces within capitalist society, combined with the socialist alternative, create the conditions for moving beyond the contradictions of capitalism. Thus begins the transition to socialism.

The transition to socialism is the ultimate trend of history operating within capitalist society. The transformation of capitalism to socialism thus depends on the prior development of capitalism. Socialism is nothing less than the dialectical abolition of capitalism. The development of socialism is, as Shlomo Avineri writes, "the realization of those hidden potentialities which could not have been historically realized under the limiting conditions of capitalism."[2] Capitalism creates conditions and expectations that it cannot satisfy, thus digging its own grave. At the root of the transition from capitalism to socialism is the fact that "socialism is in practice nothing but what capitalism is potentially."[3] However, since the potential cannot be satisfied under capitalism, socialism becomes necessary.

The transition to socialism does not automatically or completely dispense with the contradictions of capitalism. Some bourgeois characteristics, such as market relationships, "are inevitable under socialism for a long time, but they constitute a standing danger to the system and unless strictly hedged in and controlled will lead to degeneration and retrogression."[4] There is always the danger in transitional societies that there will be retrogressions to former capitalist relations. For example, the problem may arise in socialist state planning:

> Without revolutionary enthusiasm and mass participation, centralized planning becomes increasingly authoritarian and rigid with resulting multiplication of economic difficulties and failures. In an attempt to solve these increasingly serious problems the rulers turn to capitalist techniques, vesting increasing power within the economic enterprises in managements and relying for their guidance and control less and less on centralized planning and more and more on the impersonal pressures of the market. Under these circumstances the juridical form of state property becomes increasingly empty and real power over the means of production, which is the essence of the ownership concept, gravitates into the hands of the managerial elite. It is this group "owning" the means of production which tends to develop into a new type of bourgeoisie, which naturally favors the further and faster extension of market relations.[5]

Within socialist society, as within capitalist society, contradictions develop that require new adaptations. The class struggle continues in the transition to socialism.

Each transition to a new social order is a unique historical process that must be understood as such. Nevertheless, all history is a continuous transformation. Even with the overthrow of class domination, with the eventual transition to communism, the transformation of human nature and social order never ceases. Even after the disappearance of classes, the withering away of the state, the elimination of the crippling forms of the division of labor, the abolition of the distinctions between city and country and between manual and mental labor have been achieved, we are moved to a higher plane where other transformations become possible. As one level of human and social development is reached, another becomes evident. Out of the seeds of the past and present, our future takes shape. We move from one historical epoch to another.

In the final stage of capitalist development the state and the economy may well become antagonistic. Already, for example, monopoly capital is forming into multinational corporations in order to bypass intervention by the national state.[6] A point may be reached (or is already being reached) at which advanced capitalism poses a threat to the continued existence of the state. A real tension is developing between the economy of late capitalism and the interests of the modern state. The antagonism opens the way for a socialist struggle. A world socialist economy is in the making.[7]

That a socialist state will be necessary in the first stages of socialism follows from socialist theory. Socialist society will require direction and planning, since socialism implies the subjection of human creative powers to conscious direction.[8] Yet, as Marx argues, while the state represents the attempt to realize human ideals politically, solutions must be found beyond the state. In concrete terms of historical reality, the dialectic between the state and civil society will be worked out in various ways, differing from one society to another and from one stage of socialism to another. Avineri thus makes the following Marxian observation:

> Since the future is not as yet an existing reality, any discussion of it reverts to philosophical idealism in discussing objects which exist only in the consciousness of the thinking subject. Marx's discussions of future society are therefore more austere and restrained. He never tried to rival those socialists whom he called utopian by construing detailed blueprints for a communist society, since for him communist society will be determined by the specific conditions under which it is established and these conditions cannot be predicted in advance. One can only attempt to delineate some of the dominant features of future society, and even this is very cautiously and tentatively done.[9]

In general, however, in the first stage of socialism private property will be abolished by turning it into universal property, the property of all. Workers will be in control of production as well as owning the means of production. Decisions about collective endeavors will be made democratically, as true democracy can exist only under socialism. With subsequent developments there will be an end to domination by the objective forces of our existence. This can occur only after the birth pangs of the creation of the new society. We will then be free to transcend our objective conditions, no longer limited by the alienation and restrictions of a former age. "Under such a system man's relation to nature ceases to be determined by objective necessity: man, now conscious of his mastery over nature, creates it."[10] Such is possible with the proper organization of our creative powers. Human conditions of life can now be controlled by human consciousness instead of consciousness being determined by the objective forces of circumstance.

Yet, and necessarily, as beings living collectively in this world, we seek a public morality, a social morality. But the question is whether this morality relates to the nation-state, especially when that political unit is based on capitalism, or to some other social formation. That a socially liberating and religiously sacred morality cannot be ultimately established under capitalism is certain from all we know historically, theoretically, and spiritually. It is one thing to conceive of a civil religion in a capitalist society; it is quite another to realize a religious life in a socialist society.[11] The critical issue is between a secular and a sacred religion, on the one hand, and a religion that is or is not related to the political state, on the other. The prophetic expectation is for a sacred religion that will be realized in the struggle for a socialist society— although the particular relation to the political state within that society is uncertain, and will be known only in the struggle that is religious as well as political and social.

A religious socialism goes beyond a civil religion—beyond sacredly rather than secularly. We are beyond the liberal theory of politics and religion which has historically been a defense against radical, socialist democracy. In Europe and the United States, from the 18th century onward, liberalism has been a reactionary response to a revolutionary socialist democracy. Lockean liberalism was as much a defense against radical democracy as it was an attack on traditionalism.[12] Liberalism in the United States has been a substitute political philosophy and practice for any radical impulses fostered by the activities of workers struggling against the capitalist mode of production. The liberal tradition has been part of the process of a secularizing religion—removing a revolutionary and sacredly socialist religion from the politics of the nation. The emphasis has been on a civil religion that gives support and legitimacy to the liberal, capitalist state. The vision of a New Jerusalem on earth—always in relation to a transcendental Kingdom of God—as shared in a religious socialism is quite different (and even revolutionary) from the ideology and reality of a politicized civil religion which supports a secularized capitalist society.

The separation of religion from the state is both a philosophical and a historical phenomenon. Ultimately, as Marx pointed out, the separation between "civil" society and the state is fallacious, and eventually it will be eliminated.[13] The separation isolates people from the human context that is innately and simultaneously political and civil: the two are actually one. Human life is alienated when human society is divided into separate private and public spheres. The division between civil society and the state represents the tension between the actual and the ideal, between particularistic interests and the postulate of universality. The solution will be found beyond the state. Human life can achieve universal content only after the framework of the state has disappeared. And that is in the future, as the existing political and civil structures have exhausted all of their potentialities—as capitalism is transformed into socialism and socialism into communism and communism into the universal community.

Thus, the struggle is for a society that is infused with both the political and the religious. This model diverges sharply from the liberal-capitalist notion of a religion which ideologically and morally legitimizes the state. Civil religion is a secularized religious ideology that is historically specific to the development of capitalism. In the expectant hope of the socialist principle, however, human life is continuously lived in the context of a world that is charged with the presence of God. Our lives will no longer make the artificial distinctions between the moral, the political, the social, and the economic. Of divine origin and reality is the worldly kingdom; and of divine transcendence is the Kingdom of God.

NOTES

1. Karl Marx, *A Contribution to the Critique of Political Economy* (New York: International Publishers, 1970), p. 21.

2. Shlomo Avineri, *The Social and Political Thought of Karl Marx* (London: Cambridge University Press, 1969), p. 150.

3. Ibid., p. 181.

4. Paul M. Sweezy and Charles Bettelheim, *On the Transition to Socialism* (New York: Monthly Review Press, 1971), p. 27.

5. Ibid., p. 29.

6. See Joyce Kolko, *America and the Crisis of World Capitalism* (Boston: Beacon Press, 1974). Also Marty Landsberg, "Multinational Corporations and the Crisis of Capitalism,"

The Insurgent Sociologist, 6 (Spring 1976), pp. 19–33.

7. On the crisis of the world system, in relation to capitalist societies, see Samir Amin, "Toward a Structural Crisis of World Capitalism," *Socialist Review,* 5 (April 1975), pp. 9–44; and Robert Brenner, "The Origins of Capitalist Development: A Critique of New-Smithian Marxism," *New Left Review,* no. 104 (July–August 1977), pp. 25–92.

8. Avineri, *The Social and Political Thought of Karl Marx,* pp. 202–7.

9. Ibid., p. 221.

10. Ibid., p. 227.

11. On civil religion, see Donald G. Jones and

Russell E. Richey, "The Civil Religion Debate," in Russell E. Richey and Donald G. Jones, eds., *American Civil Religion* (New York: Harper & Row, 1974), pp. 14–18. Also Martin E. Marty, *A Nation of Behavers* (Chicago: University of Chicago Press, 1976), pp. 180–203.

12. Sheldon S. Wolin, *Politics and Vision: Continuity and Innovation in Western Political Thought* (Boston: Little, Brown, 1960), p. 294.

13. See Avineri, *Social and Political Thought of Karl Marx*, pp. 17–22, 202–220.

READING 8–1

Toward a structural crisis of world capitalism*

SAMIR AMIN

The previous structural crises and how they were surmounted

The capitalist mode of production is characterized by the contradiction between the increasingly social character of the productive forces and the persistently narrow character of production relations. This contradiction appeared from the beginning, so it does not imply an impending "final breakdown." It has been surmounted for at least a century both by the expansion of the capitalist system and by the renewal of its accumulation model. Marx reminds us that capitalism is compelled to revolutionize production continually. It is therefore also compelled to revolutionize production relations continually to meet the requirements of the continuous development of the productive forces. The history of capitalism is necessarily that of the process of adjustment of production relations to the requirements of the developing productive forces.

This history is not continuous, but contains periods of expansion and periods of "structural crisis." It is possible to distinguish clearly four periods of expansion: 1815–40, 1850–70, 1890–1914, and 1948–67; and four periods of structural crisis: 1840–50, 1870–90, 1914–48, and the period after 1967.[1]

Every phase of expansion is characterized by a particular accumulation model: a type of propelling industry, specific forms of competition, and a definite kind of firm. Each phase corresponds to a certain stage of geographical expansion of the capitalist system, to a particular organization of international specialization, more specifically to a functional division between the center and the periphery, and finally, to a certain balance (or imbalance) among the nation-states at the center. These conditions determine the type of class alliances by which the capitalist class rules, and establish a context for class struggle and political life.

Every structural crisis constitutes a phase of "maladjustments and readjustments" (an apt expression used by André Gunder Frank), in the transition from one accumulation model to another. Crisis means that growth is slowed, and that the class struggle intensifies. From 1914, one may speak of the decline of the system, and we will specify the nature of this decline both in the 1914–48 restructuring phase and in the subsequent phase of expansion from 1948 to 1967.

The first phase of expansion (1815–40) marked the exhaustion of the industrial revolution, which had begun in the last

* From *Socialist Review*, 5 (April 1975), pp. 9–44.

third of the 18th century. It came after the wars of the French Revolution and the Empire (1791–1815). The industrial revolution was based on the steam engine and the weaving loom. Its area of expansion was actually limited to England, Belgium, and the northeastern quarter of France. The accumulation model was still based largely on the successful struggle of manufacturing against handicrafts, while competition among manufacturers was limited. Industry was still primarily a family enterprise, producing for a local or a regional market. Therefore, the confrontations with other businesses of the same branch were restricted. This accumulation model assigned a lesser role to the periphery than it had occupied during the mercantilist period.[2] The periphery was nevertheless still important as a source of raw materials, mainly American and Indian cotton, and as a market for new industrial products (e.g., cotton goods).

At this first stage of the development of mature capitalism, the emergence and expansion of the capitalist mode of production depended on class alliances of the new industrial bourgeoisie with the landowning classes. These alliances took various forms, such as an alliance with the owners of the large agrarian estates in England, and an alliance with the peasant landowners after the Revolution in France.[3]

The deterioration of feudal relations of production occurred well before the Glorious Revolution in England in 1688 and the French Revolution in 1789. As well, the formation and development of mercantile capitalism occurred first in the Mediterranean region from the 13th to the 16th century, and then in the Atlantic region from the 17th century, preparing the ground for industrial capitalism. It seems natural that in these conditions the industrial revolution did not take place simultaneously in England, France, and North America, and on the rest of the European continent. The industrial revolution, which began in the middle of the 18th century, was completed in England before 1815, during the wars of 1790–1815; while it only really developed in France, and sporadically in Germany and northern Italy, between 1810 and 1840.

This process of expansion came to a halt in Western Europe (west of the Elbe, north of the Pyrenees and the Florence region) from the 1840s. The structural crisis culminated in the economic and political crisis of 1848. The 40s witnessed the birth of the workers' movement (English Chartism); in 1848, the *Communist Manifesto* marked the birth of Marxism. The revolutionary attempts in this period failed, however; the French workers' movement was crushed by armies of peasant mercenaries mobilized by the bourgeoisie, and the confused movements dominated by the bourgeoisie and petite bourgeoisie of the less advanced regions—Germany and Italy—were temporarily defeated, though they began the process of national unification.

The second period of capitalist expansion (1850–70) was based on the railway and the steel industry. The development of the productive forces necessarily led to the beginning of a socialization of production relations in the form of arrangements for the association of individual capitalists. The limited liability company and the "société anonyme" were attempts to overcome the inherent contradictions of capitalism within the context of capitalist relations. The railway extended the area of capitalist expansion. The unification of Germany and that of Italy were completed in this phase. Russia, the Austro-Hungarian Empire, and Spain were integrated in the new European capitalist market. The abolition of serfdom in Russia (1861) accelerated the process of transformation of the old precapitalist Russian agriculture into a capitalist export agriculture. The borders of the United States were established, and the Civil War (1861–65) consolidated the predominance of capital in North America.

The international balance was altered. In place of the predominance of two Atlantic monarchies, England and France, in the West, and two decaying empires, Russia and Austria-Hungary, in the East, a sevenfold balance emerged: four advanced central capitalist nations (England, France, Germany, and the United States), one semi-backward country (Italy), and two multinational empires, backward but integrated into the new capitalist system (Russia, Austria-Hungary).

The functions of the periphery declined in relative importance in this phase. The periphery continued to supply cotton, but the new propelling industry, steel, obtained raw materials from the center itself.

This accumulation model was exhausted by about 1870. The crisis began with an intensification of the class struggle, marked by the Paris Commune. It was overcome, and the conditions created for a new period of expansion (1890–1914) by superseding the laissez-faire policy of the 50s, 60s, and 70s (the only real period of capitalist liberalism), by forming monopolies and by imperialist expansion. The first phase of expansion was characterized by the struggle of the new industries against the traditional handicrafts system, the second by a form of "atomistic" competition among a large number of medium-sized firms that were unable, individually, to modify market conditions. From this point on, competition occurs among monopolies capable of affecting the market through unilateral decisions. Price competition is reduced, or even eliminated, and competition through advertising and product differentiation is emphasized. In this phase of capitalist expansion, electricity opened up new fields for industrial modernization, and shipping extended the market throughout the world. The periphery gained a new

importance. It continued to supply raw materials and agricultural products, to import capital for the creation of infrastructures, and to buy manufactured products (which was made necessary by the destruction of its handicrafts and the subjection of its agriculture to capital). But beyond these changes and capital flows, there arose unequal exchange, the unequal remuneration of the labor power crystallized in world goods.

The unequal international specialization and the construction of the periphery in these forms facilitated the swing of the European workers' movement toward revisionism, and the domination of the class as a whole by the labor aristocracy. This was the social democracy of the Second International. At the same time, it helped to reduce Marxism to an economistic positivism and to imbue the working class with the ideology of the dominant class.

International life was still characterized by a relative balance among the four major powers (the United States, Germany, England, and France), with which were associated four backward or young powers (Italy, Japan, Russia, and Austria-Hungary). The first world conflict, which inaugurated the period of the decline of capitalism, erupted from this unstable equilibrium, from the clash of imperialisms in the scramble for the periphery, from imperial neo-protectionism and the resulting coalitions.

The structural transformations in the relations between agriculture and industry, in particular the international specialization between agricultural and industrial countries, should be seen, following this line of analysis, in terms of the adjustment of the relations of production to the development of the productive forces. The embryonic forms of capitalism appeared first in agriculture, in which a transformation preceded that which occurred in manufacturing. The content of the traditional feudal revenues was changed; it became capitalist revenue, though agrarian capitalism remained handicapped by the persistence of feudal social relations. The capitalist mode did not achieve its finished form until industry became central, submitting agriculture to its domination. For a century, the slow development of productive forces in agriculture retarded industrial development. It was only much later, after the First World War, that a second wave of modernization seized agriculture, transforming and deepening its subordination to industrial capital. To the extent that the periphery of the world system was fashioned through agricultural specialization, its dependence and backwardness must be analyzed in terms of the domination of precapitalist rural society by the capitalist mode.[4]

With hindsight, we are now tempted to see this relatively long period (1914–48) as a single period of structural crisis. The propelling industries between the two world wars were the same as they had been before 1914, the accumulation model was more or less the same, and so were the methods of monopolistic competition. However, as it developed, the crisis entailed profound changes in the international system. Europe was weakened by the First World War to the advantage of the United States. The Second World War finally ensured the triumph of the United States. The period between the two world wars was not really a phase of overall expansion; the short boom that followed the reconstruction and the inflation of the first half of the 20s ended in catastrophe in 1929. The production level in 1938 was barely that of 1913.

One of the characteristics of this long crisis was the intensification of the class struggle in the center and its extension throughout the world in nationalist, anti-imperialist movements. Between the initial signs (Russia, 1905) and the October revolution, the first breach in the capitalist system, there were only 12 years. Between 1917 and the beginning of the Chinese civil war, which culminated in 1950 with the first triumph of socialism at the periphery, there were only ten years. Elsewhere, however, the revolution was crushed, under the weight of the reformist social democracy. And the radical criticism of the reduction of Marxism to positivist economism was still incomplete. Leninist bolshevism maintained some aspects of this reduction, which will be discussed later with regard to the failure of the "popular front" attempts and the significance of fascism.

Did this period of crisis, termed too quickly a "general crisis of capitalism" by the Third International, see new forms of competition and a new basic alignment of classes? The theory of "state monopoly capitalism," according to which the interpenetration of the state and the monopolies would have forced the middle strata of the bourgeoisie into opposition, argues that it did. The "anti-monopoly bloc" of the "frontist" politics of the Communist parties was based on this questionable theory. In fact, the state served capital as a whole, beyond the secondary contradictions within the bourgeoisie.[5]

The phase of expansion that opened in 1948 and ended 20 years later with the international monetary crisis, the French May, and the "creeping May" in Italy, presented distinctive features. The propelling industries of this period, in which the growth of the world economy surpassed even that of the exceptional period 1890–1914, were industries producing durable goods. The automobile industry was particularly important, with the accompanying "functional" urbanization. The development of these industries began in the inter-war period, and the accumulation model they reflect took definite form in the United States during the Second World War. The expansion that took place between 1948 and 1967 was entirely based on a process of "catching up," in which Europe's decline relative to the United States between 1914 and 1948 was to be reversed. For Europe and Japan, "catching up" with the United States was the goal, and they were soon joined by the Soviet Union in this effort.

This process expressed the decay of capitalism. The "state monopoly capitalism" that arose during the crisis of the 30s, and the new types of multinational corporations that began operation in the 60s, were not radically new forms of monopoly competition, but rather ways of prolonging the declining stage of the system, particularly by resorting to the state.

The theory of the successive periods of capitalism presented here should not be confused with that of the "business cycle." The course of the cycle, relatively regular for a century of capitalist development, was linked to conditions of non-monopolistic competition. This form disappeared in favor of a more or less controlled conjuncture, beginning in 1930–40, characterized by state intervention, primarily through monetary and incomes policies, and closely related to monopolistic competition and the predominance of social democracy in the workers' movement. Nevertheless, the limits of regulation remain narrow, to the extent that these policies encounter conflicts at the international level.[6]

The expansion phase 1948–67 was accompanied by a change in the structure of international specialization. The industrialization process in the periphery, based on import substitution, began during the Great Depression in some Latin American countries, accelerated during the war and in the 50s in Latin America, the Arab world, and Asia, and began in Africa in the 60s. In this context the old imperial models were replaced by neo-colonial formulas. Inequalities within the periphery grew worse and embryonic "sub-imperialisms" appeared.[7]

All these processes accompanied the absolute predominance of the United States in the industrial, financial, and military spheres. This period was characterized by a highly stratified international order. The dollar was accepted as a universal currency and "Atlanticism" was triumphant. In 1953, the cold war policy of the Soviet Union was replaced by a policy of peaceful coexistence. The term *bipolar*, frequently used to describe the period, is misleading, for the Soviet Union played in this "bipolar" world the role of a "close second" to the United States. We should in fact speak of an almost unipolar world.

But from 1967, this balance began to crumble, well before Europe, Japan, and the Soviet Union "caught up" with the United States. In retrospect, the 1948–67 period appears as a "time of illusions."

We shall now deal with the contemporary crisis and the prospects it opens. But first it is useful to survey the theoretical tools at the disposal of the socialist movement today.

The renewal of Marxism in the present period

The last few years have been important in the history of the development of socialist thought. The revival of Marxism contrasts sharply with the crisis of the dominant ideology. This revival followed a long barren period dominated by Stalinist dogmatism, tempered by technocratic and "apolitical" ideologies, whose influence was first subterranean, then expressed openly after 1953. The eclectic compromises of the 50s soon faded, and since at least 1965 a rigorous Marxist thought has begun to supersede them.

Why has this renewal occurred? Its cause must be sought in the development of the struggle for socialism, along with the deepening of the crisis of capitalism, for the development of Marxism is never the result simply of autonomous academic work. China's direction since 1950, which was quite different from that taken by the USSR, culminated in the Cultural Revolution and made possible for the first time a left critique of the Soviet experience.[8] This is fundamental; until then, no criticism of the Soviet reality, not even Trotsky's, was untainted with anti-Sovietism. The 20th Congress ought to have been the great vindication of Trotskyism, the basis for its advance. Nothing of the sort took place: the persistent sterility of Trotskyism may be attributed to an inability to go beyond the late "prophet." Trotsky retained the economistic positions of his time. His "regret" for the failure of the German revolution, and his assertion of the necessity of "socialist accumulation," in order to "catch up and then overtake" capitalism, thereby reproducing the types of division of labor peculiar to capitalism and shattering the worker-peasant alliance of 1917 by making the peasants finance this industrialization, are evidence of this. On this terrain Stalin was to be victorious.

The Chinese experience made it possible to transcend the narrow debates concerning the "means" of this type of "socialist construction." By refusing to reduce socialism to "capitalism without capitalists," but instead questioning the capitalist models of industrialization, technology, organization, and hierarchy, of the division of labor, urbanization, consumption, education, etc.—by revealing the political character of these models—China had to adopt a radically different approach to the problems of transition.

The Chinese experience also required a re-evaluation of the roles of the center and the periphery in eliminating capitalism. The national liberation movements of the 40s and 50s were offered no alternative other than the development of a national capitalism or the imitation of the Soviet model. But this was followed by a new vision, made concrete by the Vietnamese revolution, which opened the door to a fresh formulation of the theory of the world system and of unequal development.

The radical critique of the positivist and economist interpretation of Marxism that dominated the Second and Third Internationals encouraged, in Rossana Rossanda's words, a "return to Marx." This return was well-received in the developed West, where the Soviet model had very little to contribute. Dissatisfaction with the consumption model of this West, and with the entire civilization of mature capitalism, was finally to be expressed in authentically socialist demands. The onset of a structural crisis throughout the capitalist system, even before Europe and Japan had "caught up" with the United States, the collapse of the economic basis of the prosperity of the previous 20 years, and the sharpening of the social struggles since 1968, especially in France and Italy, made possible a thorough renewal of Marxism. It is in this framework that the theoretical contributions of the last few years can best be appreciated.

The critique of economism has permitted a rediscovery of Marxism, which is neither an economic nor a sociological theory, nor a philosophy, but the social science of revolutionary socialist praxis. The revival of Marxism has had a number of starting points. One has been the internal criticism of marginalist economics. This criticism has undermined the attempts in the West and the Soviet Union, inspired by the technocratic vision of the 50s, to synthesize Marxism and marginalism. These attempts expressed the class nature of the Soviet mode of production and the reduction of Marxism to positivism, and culminated in the "convergence of the systems" which was seen as the triumph of the "natural" lows of economics, irrespective of social system. The rediscovery of the works of the young Marx, particularly the *German Ideology,* was decisive here. Indeed, the Chinese gave these rediscoveries practical relevance. They have conceived the relations between the ideological superstructure and the material base quite differently than the Soviets had. Although Althusser attempted to save Moscow a last time in denying the Marxist nature of alienation, he thereby contributed to the final liquidation of the positivist heritage by pushing it to its extreme.

On this basis, a whole series of problems could be posed correctly, notably the following: (1) the analysis of contemporary capitalism at the center—the particular form of its reproduction at a stage where the contradiction between the social character of the level of development of the productive forces and the narrowness of production relations made it necessary to go beyond the schemas of the second book of *Capital* and to confront active state intervention;[9] (2) the analysis of class alliances in the history of capitalism and their transformations in connection with political and ideological history, particularly that of social democracy; (3) the critical assessment of the strategies of the workers' movements, especially the critique of "frontism" and of the forms of working-class organization defined by the Lenin of *What Is to Be Done?*;[10] (4) the criticism of contemporary capitalism in all its various aspects, the division of labor and its devastating effects, urbanization, etc.; (5) the criticism of the eclectic efforts of Freudo-Marxism (Reich) and of the Frankfurt school (Marcuse, Adorno, etc.), which has only begun; (6) the assessment of the explosive "youth movements," and of the problems involving the function of education in reproduction; (7) the assessment of feminism; (8) and finally, the analysis of the uneven development of capitalism and the discussion of the "periodization" of the world system.[11]

As China had superseded the Soviet experience from the left, it was obvious that the entire world system had to be reviewed. (The obstacle that had stopped Trotskyism might now be surmounted.) Here again the starting points were modest, and were linked to real social movements, such as those for "national liberation" and "development." The failure of development strategies based on integration into the world system (populism and the Latin American "desarrollismo") resulted in the formulation of the "dependency theory," a formulation that is still confused, part nationalist and part Marxist.

The mediocre results obtained from transposing the Soviet model to the Third World—which is the content of the "non-capitalist" path, and of which Egypt is the most advanced example—led everywhere to challenge to the linear view of historical development common to bourgeois scientistic ideology and dogmatic pseudo-Marxism. Decisive advances have been made in all these fields during the last few years. The analysis is still limited to reproduction models at the level of the world system as a whole, but nevertheless it has been possible to specify the concepts of center and periphery, to bring together contributions which had been diffuse and poorly formulated (such as those concerning unequal exchange), and thus to reconsider the history of the birth, development, and superseding of capitalism at a world level. At last the Eurocentrist outlook has been transcended.

The contemporary crisis and the tendencies of the system to overcome it

To say that capitalism is in decay does not mean that it will collapse on its own as a result of an irresistible economic contradiction. This would be a return to the reductionism of the positivist economistic approach.

The reduction of Marxism to positivism is the common philosophical basis of all of the schools of bourgeois social science. It consists in reducing the dialectic by which the relations of production are determined in the last instance by the forces of production to a linear, immediate, one-sided determinism. From this viewpoint, the forces of production must be considered as a "first cause," a deus ex machina, an external force imposing itself implacably on society. This leads to a model centered on a single type of historical evolution, within which transformations are signaled by a succession of modes of production corresponding to the successive stages of the development of the forces of production. This single evolution will be imposed, sooner or later, on all peoples—only occasional detours or delays on this path are recognized. The European ideology of the Enlightenment reappears in this perspective, with its theory of inevitable progress, and its thorough Eurocentrism: clearly the use of the dialectical method disappears, as the concrete analysis of different modes of production is abandoned.

The analysis of the relations between the economic base and superstructure, relations which are different in precapitalist modes of production from those which exist in the capitalist mode, is replaced by a formulation in which ideology can only reflect the base in all conditions. At a stroke, the analysis of Marx, which does not rigidly separate science from ideology, but treats both as ideal productions, was lost. In its place was substituted the pretensions of bourgeois science, for which there exists a "pure science," while ideology is reduced to a fraud.

Marxism is deeply opposed to this linear and mechanical view of history. It is crucial to recognize that the contradictions of a system can be resolved in various ways, and with regard to those that are characteristic of the capitalist mode, the point of departure should be the recognition of the specific features of these contradictions and their possible resolution. In precapitalist formations, the form of the surplus is transparent, and ideology is the dominant moment. Its content, religion (religious alienation), expresses this domina-

tion and the severe restrictions imposed by the dependence on nature, given the limited development of productive forces. In the capitalist mode, commodity alienation is based upon the direct domination of the economy. The essential content of capitalist ideology is thus economism. This displacement testifies both to the development of productive forces and to the alienated form in which this development occurs; it accompanies the absolute triumph of exchange value, and the total subordination of use value, the foundation of previous civilizations.

Thus one can see why and how the capitalist mode is characterized by the constant revolutionizing of the forces of production, why it is compelled always to transform the relations of production. And it is possible to see that there are always two possible outcomes of a contradiction, one capitalist and the other revolutionary. Communism is a possibility, but it is not mechanically inevitable.[12]

Today, then, as throughout the last century and a half, a new stage of the development of productive forces can occur without ending capitalist class relations.

In fact, we can anticipate the new industries that might constitute the basis of a renovated accumulation model: atomic and solar energy, space, genetics, synthetic food production, sea bed exploitation, etc. And we can glimpse what the development of these new branches of industry would mean for the conditions of competition and the role of the state, the international division of labor, etc. It is therefore useful to consider how social forces would operate to ensure the transition from the present situation to new "equilibrium states" based on the development of these new branches —what contradictions would have to be overcome and what are the weak links of the system.

We will call these final equilibria the modalities of "1984" (referring to George Orwell's book). Why? Because the picture of perfection in horror represented by Orwell's world corresponds to the perfect rationality of the capitalist mode of production and to its natural tendencies. It expresses the "barbarian" side of the "socialism or barbarism" alternative envisaged by Marx and Engels in the 1848 *Manifesto. 1984* re-establishes a perfect correspondence between the completely socialized productive forces and the production relations, completely dominated by commodity alienation.

The contradiction between the ever-growing socialization of productive forces and the renewal of capitalist production relations has been surmounted to this point by the continuous centralization of capital (which becomes more and more "abstract") and by the parallel gradual destruction of precapitalist modes. The individual enterprise was replaced by the limited liability company and the latter by the monopoly. From the time of the 1930 crisis, the state has been compelled to intervene actively in the process of reproduction, so as to support the monopolies and to absorb a share of the surplus which could no longer be absorbed by capitalist reproduction itself in the context of monopolistic competition. Nevertheless, what has been called "state monopoly capitalism" is still ambiguous, for it is not a new phase, qualitatively different from that of the monopolies. State intervention in practice has appeared only as a means for sustaining the reproduction process of the monopolies. This intervention occurred during the 1914–48 period of structural crisis and continued in the subsequent phase of expansion.

On the other hand, it is apparent that the new industries of 1984 would require a new kind of firm and a new modification of competition. In such fields as atomic and solar energy, it is difficult to see how the monopolies known to us, including the most powerful multinational corporations, could intervene with the means at their disposal. They would have to be replaced to a great extent by the state. If capitalism is to be perpetuated, it will reach an unprecedented level of centralization and abstraction. The capitalist state would tend to replace fragmented and competing units of capital.

This centralization of capital would certainly change capitalism profoundly. Direct conflict among states would tend to replace the forms of competition with which we are familiar, i.e., monopolistic competition. What is prefigured in the "military-industrial complex" would become essential to economic life in general.

This change would mean a reversal of the relations between the economic base and the ideological superstructure. Economism, that is, commodity alienation, has always been the content of capitalist ideology. But the extraction of the surplus in the capitalist mode is hidden by competition and the market, in which labor power itself is sold as a commodity. For this reason, the dominant factor in capitalism has not been ideological but economic, as opposed to the situation in the precapitalist modes and the Soviet mode. 1984, with the centralization of capital, is similar to the Soviet mode. The extraction of the surplus by the dominant state class again becomes transparent, and the ideological factor thereby acquires a dominant role in reproduction. Marcuse analyzes this contemporary ideology in *One-Dimensional Man;* its totalitarian religious character corresponds to its hegemonic function.[13]

There is nothing cheerful in the barbaric final equilibrium of 1984. Nevertheless, this prospect has some variants. For convenience, we will describe two extreme types (a combination of the two is also possible). "1984A" would be characterized by the following international division of labor: the center would retain all the new industries, and would transfer to the periphery all of the "classical" industries, and "polluting" industries we know today (iron and steel, chemicals, light industry). We are not concerned here as to whether every central region would have precisely the same vocation.

Although the new industries would require a highly skilled and relatively large labor force for their installation, their operation, due to automation, requires very little labor. In the 1984A prospect, the citizens of the center would therefore be engaged in parasitic activities that would undergo a massive development, while the periphery would provide the agricultural and "classical' industrial products necessary for the maintenance of the center. In other words, the masses of the periphery, proletarianized and exploited by the central capital (due to the monopoly of technology exercised by the center) would produce the surplus consumed by the masses of the center. This corresponds to a sort of extension of the South African model to the world level. Apartheid and the racism it supposes are thus not "relics" of the past, but are on the contrary a requirement of this type of "advanced capitalism." The ideological "justification" of the unequal exchange implied (at the periphery, producers of surplus value; at the center, consumers) can only be racist.

The goods produced under these conditions by the periphery for the center are world goods, produced by the most modern means. One could not therefore claim that labor is less remunerated at the periphery on the pretext that the level of development of the productive forces is backward there. However, we cannot compare the productivity in "standard" industries located in the periphery with that in the "new" industries concentrated in the center. (We have dealt with these points in *Le développement inégal* and in *L'échange inégal et la loi de la valeur,* to which we refer the reader.)

In this outcome, the "classical" industries would not be evenly distributed among all the regions of the periphery, but would be concentrated in some of them. This phenomenon, which is still at an embryonic stage and is known as "sub-imperialism," would become general. The sub-imperialist countries would import capital and technology from the center, and would export the products of the "standard" industries mainly to the center and secondarily to the more deprived areas of the periphery. They would recover in this way what they owed to the center for the imported capital and technology. The concentration of "classical" industries in these countries, coupled with the high rate of exploitation of the proletariat, would enable the sub-imperialist bourgeoisies to benefit from a sufficient share of the surplus to ensure the economic and political balance of the system.

The outcome that we will call "1984B" excludes all international division of labor: like the new industries, the "classical" industries would all be concentrated in the center, while the periphery would be completely marginalized. This prospect would necessarily involve the genocide, in one form or another, of the peoples of the present Third World, who would have become completely useless and even dangerous for the reproduction of the capitalist system. Accompanying this, the center would no doubt import a massive amount of unskilled labor, accentuating a trend which is already apparent. The unequal exchange would be internalized, as a result of the development of a systematic racism with respect to immigrant workers.

The different modalities of 1984 share the essential features of a simplified world, reduced to the capitalist mode of production. In 1984 we can no longer speak of social formations in the sense we did for the past and the present, nor of a world system, since the latter implies a diversity of modes of production.

The world of 1984 can be reduced to the

capitalist mode on the world scale. This implies neither equality nor homogeneity, but the inequalities here would be simply class inequalities within the capitalist mode: between bourgeoisie (henceforth state classes) and proletariat, between sections of the proletariat (on a racial basis), between proletariat and parasites. The heterogeneity that reflects the uneven geographical concentration of classes would merely accompany the class differentiation and no longer express, as is still the case at present, the complex character of formations in which dominant and dominated modes are interrelated, the latter modes being characterized by a retarded development of the productive forces.

The 1984A prospect is the most "natural," because the uneven expansion of capitalism throughout the world has been a permanent feature of the system. Mercantilism already supposed a periphery, which fulfilled decisive functions in the accumulation of capital. But, from the industrial revolution to the 1860s, wages in Europe were not better than those in India and were comparable to the real "income" of the slaves in America. The situation changed after 1870; wage differences increased faster than differences in productivity. The "external market" was important for raising the rate of profit, but as we have shown in *Le développement inégal,* it was not essential for absorption. Nevertheless, imperialism was the capitalist solution to the crisis of the years between 1870 and 1890, because it offered the monopolies a new and profitable field of action. The contradictions generated by imperialism led to the nationalist movements of the period from 1914 to 1948. The renewal of the alliance between monopoly capital and the local bourgeoisies, which is the content of neo-imperialism (marked by the independence of the colonies, from Egypt in 1922 to India and southern Asia in the 1940s and 1950s to Africa south of the Sahara in 1960), opened a new field to capital

through import substitution industrialization. The high profits were due, as we have noted, to the greater gap in wages than in productivity.

This evolution permitted the reinforcement of racism and fostered an ideology based on the "inequality" of peoples. In the 1984A outcome, the result would be the strict equality of productivities, the total modernization of the production of the new periphery, but at the same time the maintenance of a gap in real wages.

These two extreme prospects are doubtless caricatures. If the system were to develop according to its own laws, without being challenged by a series of revolutionary transformations, it would probably move toward a combination of both models. Some "classical" industries would be transferred from the center to sub-imperialist countries, while others would be maintained in the center; some areas of the periphery would be progressively marginalized, even destroyed.

What factors would decide in favor of A or B?

To answer this question, we must examine the significance of the transition from the present situation to the final balances described under the generic term of 1984. The accumulation model at present governing the capitalist system has collapsed, because the profitability of the propelling industries (cars and durable goods) on which it was based is handicapped (1) by the huge mass of investments in infrastructure that sustain the expansion of the market for these commodities (urbanization, roads, etc.); (2) by the fact that a considerable portion of the surplus value generated in these industries is wastefully absorbed by the accompanying tertiary services and by the sales services required by the forms of monopolistic competition governing these branches; (3) by the inadequate exploitation of the potentialities of the periphery, limited by the type of international division of labor implied by this model; and (4) by the fact that this accumulation model is politically and ideologically viable only when a dual requirement imposed by the working class of the center is met: full employment and continuous growth in real wages, a requirement that makes the system less flexible, particularly when a decline in the rate of profit necessitates a difficult readjustment of employment and wages.

The transition from the present accumulation model to the 1984 model implies massive investments in new industries. Who will finance these investments? The proletariat of the center and/or that of the periphery?

In such a situation, when the illusions of "easy and sustained" growth have crumbled, it is obvious that the frightened bourgeoisies will first attempt to transfer the burden of the consequences to others. The stronger the bourgeoisie, the greater its economic, political, and military resources, the better its chances to create a zone of influence on which to impose the difficulties of the transition. A weak bourgeoisie, however, can be compelled to make its own proletariat bear more of the burden. Therefore, the strong will incline toward 1984A, the weak toward 1984B; the new period will be marked first by a sharpening of the struggle between the central capitalisms for access to the Third World, and to Eastern Europe. This is the terrain on which the struggles that will decide the new international "balance" are being fought.

In this context, we shall examine: (1) the inter-imperialist struggles on the terrain of the Third World and the resulting contradictions (will the imperialist strategies be checked by the "nationalism" of the periphery?); (2) the integration of Eastern Europe into the new world system and the contradictions arising in the Soviet Union and the other countries of Eastern Europe; and (3) the social struggles in the center that will result from the successes and fail-

ures of these imperialist strategies (where are the weak links?).

The energy and raw materials crisis and the role of the periphery in the new world system

The present oil and raw materials crisis must be viewed in the context of the crisis of the accumulation model as a whole, rather than simply in terms of a readjustment of relative prices in the various regions of the world. The progress made by Europe and Japan in catching up with the United States during the "time of illusions" led to a questioning of American predominance. In the immediate postwar period the United States had an absolute competitive superiority in every industry; in other words, the productivity gap benefited the United States because it was greater than the wage gap. But gradually this relationship was reversed, at least in certain Japanese and German industries. The tendency toward a surplus in the American balance of payments gave way to an opposite trend; thus the United States lost the advantage that had enabled it to acquire strategic positions in Europe through taking over firms and modernizing them. At the same time, the United States found it increasingly difficult to play the role of international policeman, because this costly operation (the war in Vietnam) aggravated its balance of payments problems. For this reason, the crisis burst forth in the international monetary system, and was manifested in the fall of the dollar.

The United States nevertheless was able to formulate a major counteroffensive strategy, which is now being implemented. This strategy was first formulated in the sphere of ideological preparation ("zero growth," "the environment," neo-Malthusianism), then in the political sphere (the United States–Soviet pact, the "peace" in Vietnam, and the recognition of China), before it was actually launched in the economic sphere, with regard to the price increases in oil, raw materials, and agricultural products.

The Club of Rome had sounded the alarm and announced the generalized scarcity and depletion of raw materials, thus preparing the price increases.[14] The "ecology" campaign was conditioned by these preoccupations. The United States improved its balance of payments position by sharply reducing its participation in the war in Southeast Asia. Then, like a thunderbolt, came the announcement by the Shah of Iran of the increase in the price of oil. (This decision was made before the October War of 1973 between Israel and Egypt/Syria.)

It is true that the United States depends on other countries for a substantial part of its fuel and raw materials needs. But it is also a major producer of oil and a wide variety of raw materials and agricultural products. Compared with the United States, Europe and Japan are poorly situated to attempt a reconversion of their economies based on higher relative prices for energy, raw materials, and agricultural products. Indeed, the increase in the price of oil led at once to an improvement in the United States balance of payments and in the position of the dollar.

There are at least three aims of this United States counteroffensive: (1) to weaken Europe and Japan and restore the situation prior to the international monetary crisis; (2) to win over the underdeveloped countries, which on the whole also benefit from this rise in the prices of oil and raw materials (we shall see later how this analysis must be qualified), and thus to detach them from European and Japanese influence, in order to place the United States in the best possible position to develop the 1984A strategy to its own benefit; and (3) to seal the alliance with the USSR, which is more self-sufficient than Europe and Japan, and is not greatly affected by the increase of raw materials prices. (In fact, the Soviet Union is likely to benefit from the increase if its intention is to export more and more of these materials to the West in exchange for advanced technology. The USSR is thus compelled to follow the American lead.)

This operation would not be limited to oil, nor would it be determined simply by the Middle East conflict. A general increase in the price of raw materials, particularly ores, should follow. And, in the American strategy, the same applies to agricultural products. Until now the United States has adopted a policy of low prices for agricultural products, by subsidizing their producers. This policy was feasible so long as the balance of trade showed a surplus, but it was nonetheless costly to American capital. By eliminating these subsidies in order to allow prices to "adjust to the demand," the United States, a major exporter of agricultural products, will improve its external position.

The principal beneficiaries of such measures are the predominantly American multinational corporations. The oil companies, for example, used to face a large growth in demand and the obligation to make major new investments, coupled with low prices. The result was relatively small profits. The situation is now reversed: with the superprofits to be made in oil these corporations can combine to finance the reconversion toward 1984, particularly in the field of atomic and solar energy; that is, they are well-placed with respect to the new leading sectors. The same is true of the multinational corporations dealing with other raw materials. By forcing Europe, Japan, and the Third World to bear the main weight of the crisis, the United States is easing its reconversion toward 1984.

The success realized by the United States in the recent period, as much in the Middle East as in Europe, should not foster illusions. Neither Gaullism nor Nasserism have represented a serious challenge to the hegemony of the United States in the world system during the last 25 years. Such politics, powerful as verbal declarations, are extremely weak in the face of reality. The

American success testifies more to the weakness and inconsistency of its apparent adversaries than to the real force of the United States. In the future, the contradictions among imperialists will sharpen, and on this basis the present international order is doomed.

Will the Third World countries benefit from these developments? The underdeveloped countries as a whole export fuel and raw materials, and import manufactured goods and food products. The rise in the relative prices of the former in relation to the latter improves their external balance, even if this improvement is reduced by the opposite effect of higher prices for imported food. This is clear, and statements about the so-called negative effects of this improvement in the terms of trade of the Third World are curious, to say the least.[15]

Nevertheless, the strategic operation envisaged by the United States is not in the interests of the peoples of the Third World, first because the imperialist perspective is based on the unequal distribution of the benefits among the countries of the Third World. The beneficiaries—the ruling classes —would agree to play sub-imperialist roles. These countries would industrialize at an accelerated rate, in the 1984A perspective, thus offering capital a "cheap" proletariat. The surplus that the center would draw from this exploitation would quickly surpass the advantages obtained at the stage of implementing the new balance. Thus the operation aims to make the peoples of the Third World finance the reconversion toward 1984A, through an alliance with the bourgeoisies of some countries of this part of the world.

Is the integration of Eastern Europe a way out of the crisis?

The USSR already presents the features of a sub-imperialism. In its relations with the developed countries of the West, it exports raw materials and imports advanced technology; in its relations with the Third World, it exports "classical" manufactured goods (including arms) and imports raw materials. Moreover, the deficit resulting from the relations with the West is covered by the surplus obtained from its relations with the Third World.

Strictly speaking, the Soviet Union is at present the only country clearly presenting these features—with South Africa. Those countries already termed "sub-imperialist" —Brazil, India, Iran, for example—are still far from realizing this structure. From the economic point of view, they export almost exclusively to the developed world, and not to the underdeveloped world. But the logic of their growth policies will necessarily lead them toward exporting to the underdeveloped world, and this is their political goal.

Is it possible that the USSR will more and more play a sub-imperialist role, thereby offering an essential outlet (much larger than the Third World) to Western capital? In theory, yes, for it is already a well-formed society, with a large and disciplined proletariat and substantial peasant reserves. The projects for developing Siberia tend in this direction.

The Soviet Union has stated that clearer relations must be established between the external market and the mechanisms of the national economy, that is, the USSR wants to belong to the international capitalist system, and not only to the international capitalist market. According to Agnelli, it is better to manufacture Fiat cars at Togliattigrad, where the proletariat is more disciplined and less costly than at Turin.

But it would be wrong to stop here. For the Soviet Union has a specific mode of production which cannot be reduced to the capitalist mode; it has a world vocation, particularly a military vocation; and it maintains special relations with its sphere of influence in Eastern Europe.

The Soviet mode of production is not the expression of the backwardness of the productive forces. On the contrary, although relations of production are class relations, they are more advanced than in the West, the total centralization of capital prefigures 1984. This gives political power a predominance it lacks in the capitalist mode.

The power of the dominant class on the world level requires the maintenance of Soviet military strength. This compels the USSR to refuse specialization in the "classical" industries, but also to develop the new industries (atomic, space, etc.). To achieve this development, the dominant class must retain the maximum surplus generated by the Soviet proletariat; this seriously limits the prospect of a large-scale installation of "classical" industries intended for the markets of the developed countries.

This is doubtless why the USSR is hesitating, and why it will try to control the process, particularly by playing on the contradictions among the possible partners: the United States, Japan, and Germany. The error of the Soviet opposition of the Solzhenitsyn type is clear: the opening to the West does not "liberalize" the system, first because the "natural" tendency of capitalism is not toward the development of democracy but toward 1984, and second, because this opening is based on the "discipline" of the Soviet working class, on unequal exchange and thus on the continued repression of this class.

Europe—A weak link in the system?

The crisis has burst apart Europe and put at least a temporary halt to European construction at the very time when it seemed to be accomplished, through the integration of Great Britain.

The period from 1948 to 1967 produced the illusion that the gradual formation of an integrated Europe was going to enable it to "catch up" with the United States, due to the advantages of a continental market. But Europe is not the United States, but a collection of unequal nations. As always, the most powerful partner, in this case Germany, wanted to accelerate the movement. Italy, Belgium, and the Netherlands accepted a "comprador" status with respect to Germany.[16] France, on the other hand, sought to improve its position before the European integration was completed, by maneuvering between the maintenance of pre-eminent national institutions and policies and the acceptance of a limited supra-nationality (the policy of the "Europe of Nations"). France was strengthened politically and economically by the dependence of the franc areas.

The high growth rates of the late-comers of the "time of illusions" permitted grand hopes. These hopes were reinforced by the mechanical projections of technocrats. Thus Herman Kahn predicted a glorious future for Europe and particularly for southern Europe (France, Italy, Spain). This sort of exercise means little. A small difference between two growth rates, projected over a long period, is enough to make this difference appear to lead to a qualitative change in the international balance, but in fact, the growing imbalance generates new contradictions which are not considered in the projection scheme. Kahn's analysis appeared just as the phase he was projecting indefinitely was ending.

In northern Europe, advanced industrial capitalism has eliminated the vestiges of the mercantilist period. Agriculture in England was abandoned with the repeal of the Corn Laws in the middle of the 19th century, and the class alliance of capital and landed property lost its basis. In Scandinavia, particularly in Sweden, the heterogeneity of the agrarian structures and the early alliance between the leaders of the workers' movement and finance capital facilitated a pure development of capitalism. In Germany, nazism was the last phase of a policy of complex alliances by which large-scale capital mobilized peasants, petite bourgeois groups, etc., against a revolutionary proletariat. But nazism at the same time liquidated the basis of these alliances; its collapse and the division of Germany after the war meant the disappearance of this 19th-century heritage.

Society in northern Europe, with its simplified structure, required for its reproduction a fundamental social pact between capital and the working class. Thus democracy is pre-eminently the ideology of mature capitalism. This ideology reacts in turn on the material base, by ensuring increased growth through full employment, social security, and a negotiated but continuous increase in real wages.

The system in the United States is similar though still more favorable to the domination of capital. The workers' movement, drowned by the effects of the successive waves of immigrants and the conquest of the West, never managed to transcend the most elementary economism, never reached political autonomy, even social democratic "autonomy." Instead conflicts occurred at another level: between dominant capital (the Republican party) and local interests (more or less in coalition in the Democratic party). With the progress of integration and accumulation, the coalition of local interests gradually lost its force, and the result was the present regime of a de facto single party. The state has nevertheless been forced to adopt the equivalent of a social democratic policy. This was the purpose of Roosevelt's New Deal, and also of the "Great Society" invented by Johnson and then taken up by the Republicans.

There is nothing similar in southern Europe. Industrial capital, weaker than in northern Europe, was compelled to develop lasting class alliances with the remnants of mercantilism: in France and in northern Italy with the small peasantry, in Spain and in southern Italy with the latifundia, everywhere with the urban petite bourgeoisie, the local notables, and the commercial bourgeoisie. This series of alliances drove the proletariat to a more radical opposition, in the anarchism of the 19th century and the relative success of the Communist parties of the Third International.

The political life of southern Europe has been quite different from that of northern Europe. It is characteristic that the expansion between 1948 and 1967 was supervised by conservative and authoritarian governments (Francoism, Gaullism, Italian Christian Democracy). "Frontism" has been the counterpart of this type of regime. When the working class was associated with power in these countries, as in France and Spain in 1936, it has really threatened capitalism. (In the north, the social democratic governments never constituted any danger to the social system.) Each time this association with power lasted only for a brief time, and ended with a sharp move to the right—Francoism or Pétainism. The parties of the working class were attempting the impossible, to win from the bourgeoisie its traditional allies. This led to economic failure and to the return of the bourgeoisie to power, reclaiming its unstable allies from the popular fronts.

But the very process of growth during the expansion between 1948 and 1967 undermined the traditional bases of the power of capital, because this process liquidated the peasantry, the small enterprise, etc. Capital tried to replace its traditional class alliances with divisions in the working class, as a "northern" social democracy was not possible. The policy of increasing wage differences, aimed to win over the middle-level employees and technicians, was formulated for this purpose. This policy failed at the ideological level, as shown by day-to-day events in Italy and France from 1968. Capital was consequently compelled to renew its traditional alliances, as indicated by the tolerant support for the new bourgeois strata growing rich from urban land speculation and the parasitic tertiary sector.

The failure of social democratic integration makes southern Europe a weak link in the present crisis. Its class alliances limit the competitiveness of its capital with respect to the northern countries, and an attempt to make the working class bear the burden of the crisis risks creating an explosive situation in those countries with a revolutionary tradition. The frightened bourgeoisies have hesitated between an attempt to form an anti-American bloc with some areas of the Third World (the pro-Arab and Euro-African choices of the French government) and submission and acceptance of "compradorization" (the choice of the "center democrats" and the independents).

Southern Europe is not the only weak link at the center, although it is the most fragile. Will social democracy in northern Europe withstand the end of full employment and rising real wages? The wildcat strikes in Sweden and the emergence of a Marxist current in German social democracy already indicate the weaknesses of the system. If, in the United States "multinational" capital can exploit the crisis for its own benefit this will damage the sectors of capital tied to the internal market. This contradiction may be minor so long as the working class does not intervene autonomously in the life of the country, but it is not negligible at the level of state policy.

How can these weaknesses be used to move toward a socialist transformation in the center?[17] The working class and its organizations now have a choice between a "defensive strategy" and an "offensive strategy." The former, which consists in defending the "standard of living" of the class, is not very effective in a situation of structural crisis. Further, its possible success would transfer the burden of readjustment to the periphery, accelerating the march toward 1984A. The "offensive strategy" aims at seizing the opportunity of intensifying class struggle to abandon the economist framework and to put forward the "need for communism" (expressed in the crisis of the system of values, of educa-

tion, the active criticism of the division of labor, in Italy and France at least). The "offensive strategy" aims at raising the working class to a hegemonic position. It is too early to say how this strategy might progress.

It is already apparent, however, that frontism and a program of "economic recovery" based on the development of the public sector are not effective means. Frontism supposes that the working class can detach from capital its surest allies, the parasitic sectors it sustains. The strategy of economic recovery presupposes that the crisis is an ordinary recession—this is the diagnosis of the Communist parties—but it is a structural crisis. In these conditions, an expansion of state spending—an additional cost for capital—is not adequate to facilitate the creation of new industries.

To justify the diagnosis of the "ordinary" recession, the modest increase in the rate of unemployment is cited. This is a major mistake. The crisis will not simply repeat the events of the 1930s, because the forms of state intervention and competition are not the same. The present crisis, which will probably not entail a massive, sudden unemployment, is the crisis of a system that is less flexible or capable of rapid adjustments than was previously the case. That is why it is wrong to perceive the choice as one between social democracy and fascism (the alternatives of the 1930s). The present prospect, in the short or medium term, is rather that an authoritarian neo-social democracy accompanied by selective repression will be the means used by capital to delay the fundamental challenging of the system.

Once again: The tempest belt

The characteristic feature of the equilibrium termed 1984A is the existence of sub-imperialism, which might be more aptly designated "lumpen-development." Tendencies in this direction already exist, with at least two variants. The first is marked by the runaway industries of central capital taking advantage of a cheap proletariat, as occurs in eastern Asia and in Mexico. The second is characterized by a more significant association of the local bourgeoisie and the creation of integrated "classical" industrial complexes, as in Brazil, India, etc.

In order to avoid ambiguities and false problems, it is necessary to abandon the term *sub-imperialism*, a term first used by Ruy Mauro Marini to define the Brazilian phenomenon.[18] This expression describes poorly the new stage in the unequal development of the periphery. By referring to imperialism, it suggests the export of capital, when in fact the "sub-imperialist" countries in question, such as Brazil, import capital and technology from the center. What is important is to reach agreement on the content of the term, that is, on the place occupied by a country in the new unequal international division of labor.

The oil crisis has emphasized sharply the importance of these possibilities. Not much imagination is needed to envisage a unified Arab world rich in oil revenues, able to industrialize through the massive import of Western technology, supplying cars to Europe and textiles to African countries. A second wave of Arab nationalism maintained in the east by King Faisal, the emirates of the Gulf, and Egyptian industry, and in the west by Libyan and Algerian oil and the basic industries of the Maghreb, is clearly possible.

This course is far from certain. Here again there are many contradictions, and the new equilibrium presupposes that they can be overcome without upsetting the system. Three series of contradictions are worth mentioning.

The first and most important are those of the class struggle in the Arab world. The "time of illusions"—1948–67—was for the Arab world that of "Nasserist" development, inspired by the Soviet model, first transposed to Egypt and then extended to

Syria and Iraq and renewed in Algeria. It was in Egypt that this model was most systematically applied, through the nationalization of the whole of industry and a radical agrarian reform. It is also in Egypt that its limitations are most visible. The choice is clear for Egypt today: either to give up the accomplishments of Nasserism and to accept a form of Arab unity in which the private capital of Saudi Arabia and the Gulf would predominate, or to go beyond the "Nasserist" model. The violent and repeated struggles waged by the Egyptian proletariat and youth make it impossible to predict that outcome. In Algeria, where the "technocratic" option benefits from the facilities afforded by petroleum, the game is not yet finished either. For in this country, the "technocratic" option leads necessarily to a "lumpen-Europeanization" based on the Turkish model. It puts a definite end to integration into the Arab world.

Second, there are contradictions which will long remain unresolved among the various sections of the Arab bourgeoisies. Who will achieve the Arab unity which is necessary for their project to flourish? The emirs and kings of the desert or the bureaucracies of the densely populated countries? Will the latter accept comprador status after having hoped to achieve Arab unity under their direction?

The third series of contradictions is that between the Arab world and other countries in the Middle East. Israel has been used by the West since 1948 as a first-rate means of checking the development and the liberation of the Arab world. But this state has now lost its *raison d'être:* if the Arab world can be integrated into the capitalist system as a "sub-imperialism," that is the end of the Zionist state's dream of fulfilling this function by submitting to its "peaceful" semi-protectorate the less industrialized and militarily weak Arab countries. But Israel still exists, and nothing proves that the renewal of bourgeois Arab nationalism will be strong enough to deal a final blow to Zionism or to make the Arab peoples definitely accept it. Hardly had Zionism begun to decline when Iranian "sub-imperialism" loomed on the horizon, with its designs on the Gulf. . . .

The Arab world is certainly not the only area in the periphery where there are major obstacles to creating a 1984A model. In Southeast Asia, capitalism has been under attack since 1945, and this may become true in the Indian subcontinent. During the expansion from 1948 to 1967 the Indian bourgeoisie was able to widen the class base of its rule by integrating the country more and more into the capitalist system, through a series of agrarian reforms and an accelerated dependent industrialization. The continuation of this project may be threatened by the present crisis, as shown already by the gloomy prospects for India's foreign balance, and if this occurs, violent struggles are likely, in the context of a weakened state and bourgeoisie.

Should we despair on account of the failures of the 60s in Latin America, culminating in that of Chilean "frontism"? There as well, if the "miracle" of Brazilian "sub-imperialism" were to face stagnation, the situation might become favorable to a new socialist breakthrough. There are many reasons why this "miracle" is apt to reach a ceiling. It has been based on an increasingly uneven distribution of income (real wages have been reduced by 40 percent in ten years), which created a market for durable industrial goods (such as motor cars). These goods have been consumed by the local bourgeoisie and a major part of the growing petite bourgeoisie. Continued expansion will soon require an opening of foreign markets, which will be quite difficult in the face of international competition sharpened by the crisis.

There will be a great temptation for the local bourgeoisies of the periphery to participate in the strategic game of the blocs. Against the United States threat, which is

primary, certain alliances may gain new meaning. The rapprochement begun between France and the Arab world and the expressed will of the French to resist an American stranglehold over Africa must be watched closely. It is the French practice in Africa that often constitutes the best objective ally of American penetration, by facilitating Washington's demagogy toward the weak comprador bourgeoisies. It is important that another strategy be initiated, of a front of the peoples of the Mediterranean region, of Africa, and of the Middle East, a strategy based on these objectives: (1) to get rid of the multinational corporations and substitute long-term state-to-state agreements, giving more autonomy to the underdeveloped nations to define the use of the benefits from a rise in the price of their exports; (2) to reject the project of a new international division of labor (1984A) and develop their economies on the basis of a maximum social and technical autonomy; and (3) to refuse the division of the Third World between lumpen-development and sub-colonies, but, on the contrary, to accelerate the process of unifying large groups of countries and/or regions with the perspective of an equal development of partners.

Revolution or the decay of capitalism?

Evolution toward a model of social organization like that outlined in *1984* or *One-Dimensional Man* constitutes the decay of capitalism. Decay is in fact a possible solution to the further development of contradictions in the capitalist world system. In the absence of a revolutionary transformation of the relations of production, this solution permits the transcendence of these contradictions through a period of evolution characterized by political unconsciousness. The complete centralization of capital that characterizes 1984, like the Soviet mode, means that for the first time capitalist relations of production would not be able to adjust to the development of the forces of production without surpassing certain arrangements heretofore essential to capitalism. In a sense, one hesitates to characterize the society of 1984 as capitalist. It is rather a question of a new kind of class society, identifiable, as is capitalist society, by alienated labor and commodity fetishism, but different in that ideology—totalitarian ideology—would again become dominant (as in precapitalist societies, where religious ideology dominated economic life).

The prospects for this nonrevolutionary outcome are conditioned by the perpetuation of the ideology of capitalism, an ideology damaged by serious attacks but nevertheless able to retain hegemony among the masses. An evolution of this type is always possible, as is attested to by the example of Roman decline. The history of capitalism bears a peculiar resemblance to that of the Roman Empire: a long period of preparation (five centuries in each case), a very short zenith (one century in each case, 1814–1914 for capitalism), and finally a long decay.

The Roman Empire was already dead before it came to the realization that it was dying. When Constantine declared himself a Christian, it was two centuries too late; Marcus Aurelius had earlier been unable to adapt the pagan ideology to the demands of renovating the empire. Feudalism, which developed slowly out of the ruins of the empire, bears witness to the failure of this attempt. This type of evolution contrasts with that of the finished centers of tributary ("asiatic") civilization —Egypt and China—where ideological renewal often permitted a reconstruction of the imperial state and of civilization itself, thereby avoiding the disintegration of the empire into feudal estates.

Decline manifests itself in the impossibility of a renovation of ideology, the dominant instance. The debasement of the system of social values reveals this failure.

Such a situation produces a perpetual delay of political strategy; intervention occurs, but each time too late. By the time Roman citizenship is conceded to the barbarians, they are already there in force; by the time the Empire recognizes the *colonat*, it is already the dominant form of social relations in the countryside.

Capitalist society offers certain analogies to the declining Roman Empire. In its most advanced center—the United States— the capitalist system of values is crumbling without producing a political consciousness capable of going beyond the system. "Hippieism," like Christianity in the Roman Empire, is the route to political unconsciousness; it arose in the United States because it is in that country that use value was truly suppressed by the total triumph of exchange value, of capitalism as the "moment of negation."

Fortunately, use value is far from forgotten outside the United States. And this is probably the reason that capitalist ideology is in a state of crisis in Europe, and that in the societies of the periphery this ideology remains without real impact. The inability of the system to recover by imposing the ideology of "one-dimensional man" will be as fatal to the capitalist mode of production as the failure to renew the ideology of paganism was to the Roman Empire, because the centralized neo-capitalism of 1984 requires the domination of capitalist ideology, of exchange value and alienation.

Simultaneously, the decline is revealed by the system's incapacity to renew the model of the reproduction of its dominant class. During the 19th century the reproduction of the bourgeoisie was assured by the inheritance of fortunes (via the family) and by a humanist and elitist education. The ideological content of such an education was clear; it rested on a false social science that perfectly fulfilled its function. Industrial development, however, required an education in the natural sciences, and called for an ever-growing specialization. The organizational model of the natural sciences was transferred to the study of society, to meet the need for an elaboration of an alienated social science; social reality could be observed from the exterior—social laws, notably economic laws, impose themselves much like the laws of nature. Empiricism and positivism are the philosophies of this reduction. In these circumstances bourgeois education does not have as its object the elaboration and development of conscious mastery over society. On the contrary, this mastery is abandoned to the alienation of the bourgeois himself, who learns to submit to the working of natural "economic laws." Such an education prepares the system's politicians to become ideologues.

Both aspects of the reproduction of the bourgeoisie are in crisis. The centralization of capital suppresses the role of the individual capitalist, in pulverizing his functions. Inheritance loses its major importance; the transmission of power and wealth occurs within an institutional framework. Indeed, the family enters into crisis. The schools are expected to fulfill increasingly important functions, approaching the creation of a "mandarin" elite stratum. These tendencies correspond well to the evolution toward 1984, that is, toward a class mode of production where the extraction of surplus is transparent, and in which ideology again becomes the dominant instance.[19]

But the present system is proving incapable of passing from the type of education of the 19th century to a new type of "elitist" education, that is, the system is not able to renew its ideology.

Why not? In the domain of natural science and technology, specialization is no longer scientifically efficient. Science must now play the role of justifying an increasingly elaborate division of labor and hierarchy of rank and salary, as the substitute for the class alliances that previously formed the basis for the domination of capital. But this division of labor creates new contradictions, and the revolt against it threatens the system at its roots.[20]

The decadence of social science has been particularly advanced. The attempts to reply to Marx by a return to economism failed badly, and in 1914, on the European continent, Marx remained the dominant figure. In England, where capitalist alienation is more profound, philosophy has been reduced to empiricism and Darwinist scientism, and there emerged an eclectic melange that was successfully transferred to the United States. In the United States the social sciences are driven toward absurdity, a "super-specialization" in which economics is content with studying the formal properties of general equilibria ("universal harmonies"), and sociology puts forward innumerable strains of functionalism and behaviorism. This banality, coupled with the quantitative growth of the universities, results in total decadence; "knowledge" is no longer of any use, neither practically nor ideologically.

Thus there are two possible resolutions to the present crisis. The revolutionary resolution would permit the dialectical transcendence of precapitalist class societies and of capitalism (the moment of negation) by communism. The nonrevolutionary resolution would solidify a new type of class society.

A communist resolution would not signify the end of history, only the end of prehistory. The new society would have its contradictions. These contradictions, in a society in which individuals would be realized for the first time, would be located largely in the domain of interpersonal relations—more than that one cannot say today. But to believe that Marxism can be superseded today—while class society remains a reality—by proposing the primacy of these interpersonal contradictions is to be condemned to powerlessness. The in-

378

fantile stammerings of American "psychologism" about the irrelevance of the class struggle for social change reflect the immaturity of American society, and not, as people there often think (with the conceit of a "New World" mentality), a penetrating avant-garde vision.

If history should lead to the disaster of 1984, would this be the end of history? It is difficult to imagine the nature and the forms of expression of contradictions in this new type of class society. (So difficult that Marcuse did not envision them at all.) What we can say is that the universal harmony that characterizes 1984—a harmony of horror—is impossible by definition, since harmony—the absence of contradiction—does not exist for the living; perfect harmony only defines death. In fact, we can abandon the exercise of imagining the class struggle in the society of "one-dimensional man," for it can only be a futile exercise.

The real problem today is to analyze the contradictions that block an evolution toward 1984, and on the basis of that analysis, to elaborate strategies of socialist transition. Until now one has often thought that only the periphery of the capitalist system would know "problems of transition," problems which might be summarized as: how to develop the productive forces without simultaneously recreating class relations of production? In fact, immense problems of transition await the center as well, where the problem is posed in opposite yet complementary terms: how to enlarge progressively the domain of use value without surrendering the level of development of the productive forces attained on the basis of exchange value?

NOTES

1. This periodization is quite close to that proposed by André Gunder Frank, in a work not yet commercially published, *Multilateral Merchandise Trade Imbalances and Uneven Economic Development* (Dakar: IDEP, 1974).

2. Frank, *Multilateral Trade Imbalances*, and Samir Amin, *Le développement inégal* (Paris: Les Editions de Minuit, 1973).

3. On the issue of the relations between capitalism and agriculture, see Samir Amin, "La rente foncière et le capitalisme," in *La question paysanne et le capitalisme*, by Amin and Koslas Vergopoulos (Paris: Anthropos-IDEP, 1974).

4. On the problem of revenue from land in the theory of capitalism, the relations between agriculture and industry in different periods of capitalism, and the corresponding class alliances, see Amin and Vergopoulos, *La question paysanne;* Pierre Philippe Rey, *Les alliances des classes* (Paris: Maspéro, 1973); Gilles Postel-Vinay, *La rente foncière dans le capitalisme agricole* (Paris, Maspéro, 1974); Alain Lipietz, *Le tribut foncier urbain* (Paris: Maspéro, 1974).

5. This criticism of the content of "frontism" has been developed by Nicos Poulantzas, in *Political Power and Social Class* (London: New Left Review Editions, 1974).

6. For a theory of the cycle, see Amin, *Développement inégal,* chapter 2, section 4.

7. See A. Faire and J. P. Sebord, *Le nouveau déséquilibre international* (Paris: Grasset, 1973).

8. See K. S. Karol, *The Second Chinese Revolution* (New York: Hill and Wang, 1974), and Charles Bettelheim, *Revolution culturelle et organisation industrielle en Chine* (Paris: Maspéro, 1973).

9. P. Baran, *The Political Economy of Growth* (New York: Monthly Review Press, 1957); P. Baran and P. Sweezy, *Monopoly Capital* (New York: Monthly Review Press, 1966).

10. Concerning points (1) and (2), the work of P. P. Rey, N. Poulantzas, and the "Manifesto" group in Italy should be noted (cf. *Il Manifesto*, Le Seuil, 1971).

11. For a history of the theory of the world system, and a bibliography, see Amin, *Développement inégal,* especially chapters 3, 4, and 5. See also the brilliant synthesis of Fernando Henrique Cardoso, "Dependent Capitalist Development in Latin America," *New Left Review* 74 (July–August 1972).

12. I have tried to develop systematically this nonlinear approach in *Développement inégal* as well as in "In Praise of Socialism," *Monthly Review,* vol. 26, no. 4 (September 1974), pp. 1–16, in contrast to the linear approach shared by bourgeois science (perfectly summarized in W. W. Rostow, *The Stages of Economic Growth*) (New York: Cambridge University Press, 1971

[second edition]), and pseudo-Marxist dogmatism, with its "five stages" (primitive communism, slavery, feudalism, capitalism, socialism).

13. Herbert Marcuse, *One-Dimensional Man* (Boston: Beacon Press, 1964).

14. D. Meadows, J. Rangers, W. Behrens, *Halte à la croissance* (Paris, 1972). [The Club of Rome sponsored a study on the "Limits of Growth" conducted by a research group at MIT, published by Universe Books, New York, 1972.—Eds.]

15. [See the exchange between Angus Hone, "The Primary Commodities Boom," *New Left Review* 81, and Arghiri Emmanuel, "A Note on the Primary Commodities Boom," *New Left Review* 85.—Eds.]

16. A. Faire and J. P. Sebord, *Le nouveau déséquilibre.*

17. The elements of a response to this question constitute the essential work of *Il Manifesto,* the Italian daily newspaper. See especially: *Il Manifesto* (Le Seuil, 1971); Lucio Magri, *Il Manifesto,* 13 January 1974; Valentine Parlat, "Spazio e ruolo del reformismo," *Il Mulino,* 1974; and the articles of Magri, Sebord, and Granon that follow.

18. Ruy Mauro Marini, *Subdesarrollo y revolución* (Mexico, 1969). [See also Ruy Mauro Marini, "Brazilian Subimperialism," *Monthly Review,* vol. 3, no. 9 (February 1972).—Eds.]

19. This is not the place to develop a critique either of feminism or the school. See S. Amin, I. Eynard, and B. Stuckey, "Féminisme et luttes des classes," *Minuit* 7 (Paris, 1973).

20. Here it is not possible to develop this critique of the development of science and technology in relation to the division of labor. See Yvon Broudet, *La délivrance de Prométhée* (Paris: Anthropos, 1970).

READING 8–2

Capital accumulation on a world scale and the necessity of imperialism*

AL SZYMANSKI

Persistent debates have occurred in radical circles both about the question of whether imperialism is a necessary aspect of monopoly capitalism *and* around the question of the relationship between imperialism and capital accumulation on a world scale. Although recently these debates have often tended to occur separately, these two questions in fact address much the same issue. The controversy between Luxemburg (1913), Lenin (1917) and such social democrats as Hobson (1902) and Kautsky, which peaked around World War I, centered on the question of whether or not imperialism was a necessary *condition* of the capital accumulation process (and thus on whether or not capitalism could function without imperialism), or fundamentally a *policy* (which could be changed without abolishing capitalism altogether). At the heart of this early debate was the question of capital accumulation on a world scale and the role of imperialism in this process. In the last few years there has been a renewed debate around both the questions of the "necessity of imperialism" and around the question of "capital accumulation on a world scale."[1] Today, however, these two debates are occurring pretty much separately. This paper will attempt to clarify the issues in these debates, show the essential unity of the two questions, and offer a tentative answer to these vital questions based on a look at recent trends in the economic relations of the U.S. to Third World countries.

Some clarifications

By the term *imperialism* I mean the political and economic domination of one or

* From *The Insurgent Sociologist,* vol. 7, no. 2 (Spring 1977), pp. 35–53.

more nations by another nation, normally in the interests of the dominant group in the dominant nation. For the purpose of this paper I will examine only part of the general phenomenon of imperialism: the economic and political domination of the poorer and more technologically backward countries of Asia, Africa and Latin America and their outlying islands (what can loosely be referred to as "the periphery"), by and in the interests of those that dominate the advanced capitalist countries of North America, Western Europe and East Asia.

This paper will deal empirically only with the U.S., far and away the leading imperialist power in the generation after World War II. If it can be shown that capital accumulation in the U.S. and the process of capital accumulation on a world scale are not irredeemably dependent on metropolitan imperialism vis-à-vis the Third World, then it is also shown that the proposition that imperialism is an indispensable aspect of advanced capitalism, and specifically that it is a requisite of the world capital accumulation process, cannot be valid. This should be true whether we take a world system approach which considers all the advanced capitalist countries as essentially *one* unit (the metropolis) within which the U.S. plays the leading military and political role performing essential functions for the capitalist system as a whole and from which other metropolitan nations benefit; *or,* whether we consider each major advanced capitalist country to be the essential unit, in which case the U.S. is merely the largest (and also typical) example. In either mode of conceptualization of the problem of the indispensability of imperialism for capital accumulation on a world scale, the examination of the relationship between the U.S. and the Third World is absolutely key.

Much confusion has occurred in the debate around the question of the "necessity of imperialism" because of the frequent posing of the issue as either "imperialism is a necessary condition for the existence of capitalism (i.e., advanced capitalism could not exist without it) " *or* that "imperialism is merely a policy which can be changed by a progressive state administration *without* changes in the fundamental economic and social organization of society." When the question is posed in this dichotomous way it is relatively easy for the proponents of the first position to "prove" their case by showing that imperialism is not merely a policy, *and* for proponents of the second position to "prove" their case, by showing that advanced capitalism is indeed not irredeemably dependent on imperialism (i.e., that only a relatively small proportion of the GNP, total profit, investments, trade, etc., can be attributed to imperialism). Consequently, much of the recent debate is rather futile, with neither side really coming to grips with the strong arguments of its opponents.

Quite obviously there is another position on the relationship between advanced capitalism and imperialism, a position which sees imperialism as growing organically from the very logic of advanced capitalism (and in that sense a *necessary outgrowth* of capitalism) *but not* as a *necessary condition* for the continuing existence of capitalism, i.e., that advanced capitalism could survive and the capital accumulation process continue even if there were no imperialism. It is the position of this paper that this latter position is both correct and, that in the event that forces such as the universal victory of national liberation movements were to defeat imperialism, advanced capitalism would nevertheless remain viable and the capital accumulation process continue in the metropolitan countries; although in all probability, only with some rather important political and economic reorganization (which however need not be outside of the limits of capitalism). Further it will be argued that this is also the position actually proven by Magdoff and others in the *Monthly Review* tradition (although they themselves confuse their actual argument for the organicness of imperialism with their suggestion that imperialism is a necessary condition for the existence of capitalism) ; but *not* the position maintained by Lenin, Luxemburg and the orthodox Marxist-Leninist tradition (including the Chinese today) , which maintains that accumulation *could not occur* without imperialism.

The capital accumulation process must result in the expansion of the *total value* encompassed in the capitalist system since by its very nature it implies the reinvestment of profits above and beyond the mere replacement value of capital equipment. The failure to find sufficient new investment outlets for profits necessarily results in economic stagnation and contraction of the system. The process of capital accumulation must thus either expand or wither.[2] Logically, there would seem to be two directions in which capitalist expansion could occur: intensively, i.e., within the geographical limits of a metropolitan capitalist area; and extensively, i.e., by expanding into the areas which do not have fully capitalist relations of production, expanding the number of people engaged in capitalist social relationships and increasingly incorporating the periphery. Intensive capital accumulation assumes a sufficiently rapidly growing source of purchasing power in the metropolitan country which allows for the realization of profits from new domestic investments. The extensive capital accumulation process does not assume that purchasing power in the metropolitan countries needs to grow. The debate about the relation of capital accumulation on a world scale to the necessity of imperialism in good part focuses on the relative possibilities of extensive and intensive capital accumulation.

The position that capital accumulation cannot proceed without imperialism (i.e., that imperialism is a necessary condition

for the existence of monopoly capitalism) tends to focus on *three* major arguments: (1) the *absolute need* of advanced capitalist countries to export capital in order to avoid underconsumption and economic stagnation; (2) their *absolute need* to secure export markets (dictated by the same considerations) ; (3) their *absolute need* to control their sources of raw materials. The first two of these are variants of the same general theory which is based on the underconsumptionist argument. These two maintain that capitalism during its monopoly phase is absolutely unable, because of the low living standards of the masses and the inability of the state to spend enough on the public welfare, to find sufficient domestic markets for all it produces, and that consequently outlets for otherwise unrealizable profits must be found in ways that result in the domination of Third World countries if the capital accumulation process is to continue. The structure of the third argument, while it does not assume underconsumption, also can be interpreted as arguing that capital accumulation in the metropole will not occur without the control of essential raw materials at their source.

A fourth argument exists within the Marxist tradition although it is not emphasized much by 20th century Marxist theorists of imperialism. It has been argued that the tendency for the rate of profit to decline, caused by the tendency of the organic composition of capital to rise more rapidly than the rate of exploitation—processes which are the most advanced in the most developed countries—channels capital investment overseas where costs are lower (namely, wages and construction costs) and hence the rate of profit higher; and further generates greater imports which cheapens the costs of both variable capital and especially organic capital (thus increasing the rate of exploitation and lowering the organic composition of capital in order to increase the rate of profit). Imperialism could well be considered to be a necessary condition of capitalism (or the capital accumulation process on a world scale) because of this factor.[3]

It should be noted that parallel arguments are also given in support of the position that maintains that imperialism is an organic product of the capitalist mode of production but is not a necessary condition for its existence. In my opinion all these later types of arguments *are* valid. We must be careful not to confuse the indispensability with the organicness position. In this paper I will closely examine the evidence for the three major arguments listed above.

Underconsumption type arguments for necessity and capital accumulation

The two variants of the underconsumption type argument for the indispensability of imperialism (i.e., that imperialism is a necessary condition for the very existence of advanced capitalism) are integrally related to the arguments about the process of capital accumulation on a world scale. The first of these variants, the argument that overseas outlets for capital accumulation are central, was the traditional position of most revolutionary Marxists and continues to be the position of both the Soviets and Chinese. The two most important classical arguments that imperialism is a necessary condition for the existence of advanced capitalism are probably those of Lenin (1917) and Luxemburg (1913). Both argued that the process of capital accumulation *could not proceed* without imperialism and thus that the logic of the capital accumulation process absolutely required imperialism so that it could break out its national boundaries and operate on a world scale.

The export of capital

For Lenin and Luxemburg, it is not merely a question of whether or not over-

seas investments are *more* profitable than domestic investments but rather one of whether or not *any* profitable investment outlets can be found, i.e., whether or not capital accumulation can proceed:

It goes without saying that if capitalism could develop agriculture, which today frightfully lags behind industry everywhere, if it could raise the standard of living of the masses, who are everywhere still half-starved and poverty-stricken, in spite of the amazing technical progress, there could be no talk of a surplus of capital. This "argument" is very often advanced by the petty-bourgeois critics of capitalism. But if capitalism did these things it would not be capitalism; for both uneven development and semistarvation level of existence of the masses are fundamental and inevitable conditions and premises of this mode of production. As long as capitalism remains what it is, surplus capital will be utilized not for the purpose of raising the standard of living of the masses in a given country, for this would mean a decline in profits for the capitalists, but for the purpose of increasing profits by exporting capital abroad to the backwards countries. In these backwards countries profits are usually high, for capital is scarce, the price of land is relatively low, wages are low, raw materials are cheap. . . . The necessity for exporting capital arises from the fact that in a few countries capitalism has become "overripe" and (owing to the backward state of agriculture and the poverty of the masses) capital cannot find a field for "profitable" investment. (Lenin, 1917: 759–60)

Lenin maintained that a significant amount of intensive capital accumulation within the advanced capitalist countries was impossible and that therefore capital accumulation required the export of capital to previously noncapitalist areas, and further that the political and economic domination of Third World countries was essential in order to secure profitable overseas investment opportunities. The lack of profitable investment opportunities in the advanced capitalist countries, in good part caused by the fact that capitalism by its nature could never raise the living standards (and hence purchasing power) of the working class, meant that only external markets and capital export could allow the accumulation process to go on.

Rosa Luxemburg insisted, even more firmly than Lenin, that the only way that the capital accumulation process could continue was through overseas expansion, and hence that imperialism was an absolute necessity for advanced capitalism. She argued that in order for capital accumulation to occur *at all* new consumers had to be continually brought into the system of capitalist market relations. The additional surplus value generated in each phase of the expanding reproduction process of capital accumulation according to Luxemburg cannot be realized except through new consumers previously outside of the capital accumulation process. People already in that process could not buy any more than they were already buying. Only previously noncommercial rural classes and populations in industrially backward countries, not yet committed to capitalist markets, could possibly buy the additional production thereby allowing the realization of the additional surplus value. Capitalism, then, was forced to continually expand or die. Indeed Luxemburg predicted that the final economic crisis and collapse of capitalism would occur once there were no more noncapitalist areas into which capitalism could expand. Consequently, capital must be exported to the less developed areas of the world to avoid a cataclysmic economic depression which would be produced by the absence of investment possibilities within the system.

Realized surplus value, which cannot be capitalized and lies idle in England or Germany, is invested is railway construction, water works, etc., in the Argentine, Australia, the Cape Colony, or Mesopotamia. . . . There had been no demand for the surplus product within the country so capital had lain idle without the possibility of accumulating. But abroad, where capitalist production has not yet developed,

there has come about, voluntarily or by force, a new demand of the noncapitalist strata. . . .

The important point is that the capital accumulated in the old country should find elsewhere new opportunities to beget and realize surplus value, so that accumulation can proceed. . . .

Enlarged reproduction, i.e., accumulation is possible only if new districts with a noncapitalist civilization, extending over large areas, appear on the scene and augment the number of consumers. (Luxemburg, 1913: 426–29)

The arguments of Lenin and Luxemburg were in good part a response to the arguments of such social democrats as Karl Kautsky and John Hobson who argued that it was indeed true that capital export was the main motive force of imperialism and that capital export was made necessary by the lack of profitable investment opportunities in the advanced countries caused by endemic underconsumption, a product of the lack of purchasing power in the hands of the masses of people (i.e., imperialism was an organic part of monopoly capitalism) . But they maintained that imperialism was not a necessary condition for the continuing existence of capitalism. Hobson and Kautsky, both arguing within the social-democratic tradition, maintained that a process of reforms which would redistribute income to the working class and break up the monopolies would eliminate the problem of underconsumption, create sufficient investment outlets in the advanced countries and destroy the logic of imperialism, and hence allow for its elimination without abolishing the capitalist mode of production:

Aggressive imperialism, which costs the taxpayer so dear, which is of so little value to the manufacturer and trader, which is fraught with such grave incalculable peril to the citizen, is a source of great gain to the investor who cannot find at home the profitable use he seeks for his capital, and insists that his Government should help him to profitable and secure investments abroad. (Hobson, 1902: 55)

Everywhere appear excessive powers of production, excessive capital in search of investment. It is admitted by all busines men that the growth of the powers of production in their country exceeds the growth in consumption, that more goods can be produced than can be sold at a profit, and that more capital exists than can find remunerative investment.

It is this economic condition of affairs that forms the taproot of Imperialism. If the consuming public in this country raised its standard of consumption to keep pace with every rise of productive powers, there could be no excess of goods or capital clamourous to use Imperialism in order to find markets. . . . (Hobson, 1902: 81)

It is not industrial progress that demands the opening up of new markets and areas of investment, but mal-distribution of consuming power which prevents the absorption of commodities and capital within the country. The oversaving which is the economic root of Imperialism is found by analysis to consist of rents, monopoly profits, and other unearned or excessive elements of income. . . . (Hobson, 1902: 85)

The assumption in the type of argument presented by both Lenin and Luxemburg is that the process of capital accumulation on a world scale should result in the less developed peripheral or semi-feudal areas, industrializing in relation to the most advanced areas where profitable investment outlets cannot be found.[4] For example Lenin argues:

The export of capital influences, greatly accelerates the development of capitalism in those countries to which it is exported. While, therefore, the export of capital may tend to a certain extent to arrest development in the capital-exporting countries, it can only do so by expanding and deepening the further development of capitalism throughout the world. (Lenin, 1917: 761)

Capitalism is growing with the greatest rapidity in the colonies and in overseas countries. Among the latter, new imperialist powers are emerging (e.g., Japan). (Lenin, 1917: 789)

"Uneven development" for Lenin was used to mean the rapid growth of poor countries like Japan in relation to Europe. In contrast "uneven development" for Baran, Frank, Amin et al., means the more rapid growth of the metropolitan countries.

This question became a major point of contention in the Communist International in the 1920s, with some arguing that capital tended in balance to flow away from the wealthy areas of the world to industrialize the poorer regions and in consequence create a large industrial working class in the Third World areas, and others, arguing that since the effect of imperialism was to "underdevelop" the Third World, or at least to keep them backward, there could not be a significant flow of capital to the periphery (see DeGras, 1960: 526–28). The issue was resolved at the Sixth International Conference of the Comintern in 1928 when the official resolutions supported the second position. Consequently, this later position became the dominant one in Marxist circles and has remained so down to the present. The 1928 position of the Comintern was further developed by and popularized in the English-speaking world by Paul Baran, Paul Sweezy, Harry Magdoff, André Gunder Frank and others in and around the journal *Monthly Review* in the 1950s and 1960s. All these later authors have argued that (1) the direction of capital flow is from the less developed to the most developed capitalist countries and (2) that the process of surplus extraction from the poor to the rich countries results in the latter's underdevelopment. Stated in another way, the capital accumulation process on this world level operates to speed up the accumulation of capital in the advanced countries while slowing it down in the less advanced countries, the opposite of what was argued by Lenin and Luxemburg.

Paul Baran, who made the classical and most influential statement of the *Monthly Review* position (1957), argued that capital flow from the periphery to the metropolis, mainly in the form of interest and dividends, accelerated the capital accumulation process in the latter.

Profits derived from operations in underdeveloped countries have gone to a large extent to finance investment in highly developed parts of the world. Thus while there have been vast differences among underdeveloped countries with regard to the amounts of profits plowed back in their economies or withdrawn by foreign investors, the underdeveloped world as a whole has continually shipped a large part of its economic surplus to more advanced countries on account of interest and dividends. (Baran, 1957: 184)

André Gunder Frank made an even clearer statement of the same position:

Economic development and underdevelopment are not just relative and quantitative, in that one represents more economic development than the other: economic development and underdevelopment are relational and qualitative, in that each is structurally different from, yet caused by its relation with the other. Yet, development and underdevelopment are the same in that they are a product of a single, but dialectically contradictory economic structure and process of capitalism. . . . One and the same historical process of the expansion and development of capitalism throughout the world had simultaneously generated—and continues to generate—both economic development and structural underdevelopment. (Frank, 1967: 9–10)

Samir Amin in his recent and influential book made the same argument in terms of the logic of capital accumulation on the world scale.

Relations between the formations of the "developed" or advanced world (the center), and those of the "underdeveloped" world (the periphery) are affected by transfers of value, and these constitute the essence of the problem of accumulation on a world scale. Whenever the capitalist mode of production enters into relations with precapitalist modes of production, and subjects these to itself, transfers of value take place from the precapitalist to the capitalist formations, as a result of the mechanisms of primitive accumulation. These mechanisms do not belong only to the prehistory of capitalism; they are contemporary as well. It is these forms of primitive accumulation, modified but persistent, to the advantage of the center, that form the domain of the theory of accumulation on a world scale. (Amin, 1974: vol. 1, p. 3)

If the arguments of Amin, Baran, Frank et al. are correct then it logically follows that the argument of Lenin and Luxemburg, that intensive capital accumulation in the metropolitan countries *cannot* occur because of lack of expanding markets there, must be wrong. In other words imperialism is not necessary in order to insure that the capital accumulation process in the home countries proceed. Further not only are investment outlets not blocked in the advanced countries but also, according to Amin, Baran, Frank et al., the process of capital accumulation in the metropolitan countries is actually *facilitated* and *sped up* by the flow of capital from the rich to the poor areas (the exact opposite of what Lenin and Luxemburg argued). That what was the principal aspect of imperialism for Lenin and Luxemburg, the export of capital, is not central to those of the *"Monthly Review* school" who defend the necessity position can be seen by examining the works of Harry Magdoff:

Attractive as lower costs are, their appeal is not necessarily the main attraction of foreign investment. It is merely one of the influences. Much more important is the spur of developing raw material resources, creating demand for exports, and taking advantage of "monopoly" situations.

The commonly held notion that the theory of imperialism should be concerned largely with investment in underdeveloped countries just isn't correct. The fact is that profitable investment opportunities in such countries are limited by the very conditions imposed by the operations of imperialism. Restricted market demand and industrial backwardness are products of the lopsided economic and social structures associated with the transformation of these countries into suppliers of raw materials and food for the metropolitan centers.

The stage of imperialism, as we have tried to show, is much more complex than can be explained by any simple formula. The drive for colonies is not only economic but involves as well political and military considerations in a world of competing imperialist powers. Likewise, the pressures behind foreign investments are more numerous and more involved than merely capital to backwards countries. (Magdoff, 1969: 37–39)

The traditional link between the theory of capital accumulation on a world scale and the argument for the necessity of imperialism has been severed in the arguments of those around the journal *Monthly Review*. In its place is put the argument that the process of capital accumulation in the rich countries is facilitated by the exploitation of the poor regions whose capital accumulation process is consequently inhibited. In this later construction of the relationship of imperialism to the capital accumulation process it is argued essentially that the advanced capitalist countries are imperialist in order to increase profit opportunities for their giant corporations and the size of funds available for investment in the metropolis to increase (not decrease). It is not, and cannot be, claimed by the *Monthly Review* school, that imperialism is an absolute necessity because of the need to guarantee investment outlets.

The export of goods

Although the principal aspect in both the arguments of Lenin and Luxemburg (who argued that imperialism was an indispensable aspect of advanced capitalism) and of those underconsumptionsists like Hobson (who argued that reforms would be able to generate enough buying power to create profitable domestic investment outlets) was overseas investments or capital outflow, all understood that the export of goods, as well as the export of capital, could logically accomplish the same function of allowing the capital accumulation process to proceed. Export of goods, by providing markets for the domestic industries, could create profitable domestic investment out-

lets, even in the absence of expanding domestic demand. The advantages of the export of capital over the export of goods for the capitalists, however, are: (1) the lower wage and construction costs in the peripheral countries building the same plant; (2) the lesser transportation costs of shipping the goods from their point of manufacture to those with purchasing power outside of the home country; (3) the ability to slip under the tariff barriers of the country buying the goods; and most importantly, (4) avoiding the problem of having to purchase imports from the country to which exports are sent—a problem caused by the necessity of selling goods for local currency which can only be used to purchase local goods unless one's own currency is available to the locals from the sale of their goods to the metropolitan country. Exports necessarily generate *either* imports *or* overseas investments (which can be paid for in the local currency acquired through exporting). This last point is probably the most crucial reason why arguments that imperialism is a necessary condition of the capital accumulation process must base their case primarily on the export of capital rather than on the export of goods.

Those who today assert that imperialism is necessary in order to guarantee export markets tend to base much of their case on the argument that advanced capitalism requires the export of goods. For example, Harry Magdoff argues:

For the sake of protecting profits and capital investment, the avid exploration of sales opportunities in the world markets must accompany the inexorable expansion of capacity. (Magdoff, 1969: 24)

Foreign markets are pursued (with the aid and support of the state) to provide the growth rate needed to sustain a large investment of capital and to exploit new market opportunities. In this process, the dependence on export markets becomes a permanent feature, for these markets coalesce with the structure of industrial capacity. (Magdoff, 1969: 36)

Magdoff explicitly downplays the role of foreign investment in the capital accumulation process by interpreting such investments primarily as a way to expand demand for exports:

For investment is an especially effective method for the development and protection of foreign markets. The clearest historic demonstration of this was the export of capital for railways, which stimulated at the same time the demand for rails, locomotives, railway cars and other products of the iron, steel, and machine industries. (Magdoff, 1969: 36)

Just as the argument about the relationship between capital export and the need for imperialism has been reversed since the time of Hobson, Lenin, and Luxemburg, so too has the argument about the relationship of the export of goods and the need for imperialism. The works of both Samir Amin, especially *Accumulation on a World Scale,* and Arghiri Emmanuel, namely *Unequal Exchange,* focus on trade between the metropolitan and peripheral countries as the principal means by which value is transferred from the latter to the former, and hence, the reason why capital accumulation proceeds more rapidly in the metropolitan areas of the world than in the periphery.

Emmanuel argues that the different levels of wages in the metropolis and periphery, given the equalization of profit on a world level, necessarily produce a transfer of value to the high wage countries in the process of trade:

Once a country has got ahead, through some historical accident, even if this be merely that a harsher climate has given men additional needs, this country starts to make other countries pay for its high wage level through unequal exchange. From that point onward, the impoverishment of one country becomes an increasing function of the enrichment of another, and vice versa. The superprofit from unequal exchange ensures a faster rate of growth. (Emmanuel, 1972: 130).

Samir Amin, although the overall argument is more complex than that of Emmanuel, makes essentially the same point. He too argues that unequal exchange between the metropolitan and peripheral countries accelerates the process of capital accumulation in the former at the expense of the latter:

The relations between "advanced countries" and "underdeveloped countries" cannot be understood within the context of analysis of the capitalist mode of production. This question is actually a matter of relations between different social formations: more precisely, between those of the capitalist center and those of the periphery of the system. Analysis of these relations forms the essence of a study of accumulation on a world scale. It reveals the contemporary forms assumed by the mechanisms of throws little light on the positive side of that is, the exchange of products of unequal value (or more precisely, with unequal prices of production, in the Marxist sense) the social formations of the center (since the appearance of monopolies) and of the periphery (where the precapitalist economy provides reserves of labor power) allowing of different rewards for labor with the same productivity. (Amin, 1974: vol. 1, p. 134)

In the models of Hobson, Lenin and Luxemburg the motive force for the export of goods was the inability to realize surplus value in the metropolitan countries and hence the necessity to attempt to realize it overseas where there was available purchasing power; i.e., trade results in the net transfer of value to the periphery. It was this process that both Lenin and Luxemburg argued contributed to making imperialism a necessary condition of the capital accumulation process. But in the arguments of Amin and Emmanuel, trade serves the opposite function. Rather than acting to allow the capital accumulation process on a world level to continue by transferring value to the periphery, it accelerates *intensive* capital accumulation in the metropole by incorporating value produced in the Third World. Amin and Emmanuel thus *in fact* reject the argument that imperialism is a necessary condition of capital accumulation in favor of the organicness position.

Military spending and capital accumulation

Paul Baran, Paul Sweezy, Samir Amin and others in and around the journal *Monthly Review* have recognized that imperialism is not a necessary condition of capital accumulation because of any absolute necessity to export either capital or goods. As Baran and Sweezy argued in their influential *Monopoly Capital:*

For an understanding of the state of the world today—in particular its division into economically advanced and underdeveloped areas and the dialectics of their interaction—there are few subjects more important than foreign investment. For the moment, however, this range of problems does not concern us: we are only interested in foreign investment as an outlet for investment-seeking surplus generated in the corporate sector of the monopoly capitalist system. And in this respect it neither does nor can be expected to play an important role. Indeed, except possibly for brief periods of abnormally high capital exports from the advanced countries, foreign investments must be looked upon as a method of pumping surplus out of the underdeveloped areas, not as a channel through which surplus is directed into them. (Baran, 1967: 104–105).

. . . it is of course obvious that foreign investment aggravates rather than helps to solve the surplus absorption problem. (Baran, 1967: 108)

Samir Amin concurs:

Like Baran and Sweezy, I maintain that neither foreign trade nor export of capital really offers a means of overcoming the difficulties of realizing surplus value, for trade is equally balanced for the central regions of capitalism taken as a whole, and export of capital gives rise to a return flow that tends to exceed it in volume. (Amin, 1974: vol. 1, p. 117)

Paul Baran and Paul Sweezy argue (and Samir Amin concurs, p. 118) that the problem of "realizing the economic surplus" (of

preventing underconsumption), and thereby allowing the capital accumulation process to proceed, is solved not by extensive processes (exports and foreign investments), but by intensive processes, most importantly the expansion of military expenditures by the metropolitan states.

. . . given the power structure of United States monopoly capitalism, the increase of civilian spending had about reached its outer limits by 1939. (Baran and Sweezy, 1966: 161)

. . . the difference between the deep stagnation of the 1930's and the relative prosperity of the 1950's is fully accounted for by the vast military outlays of the 50's. (Baran and Sweezy, 1966: 176)

Gigantic and expanding military expenditures serve the dual functions of acting to: (1) as Baran and Sweezy say, "contain, compress, and eventually destroy the rival world socialist system," or in other words make the world safe for the profit making of U.S.-based transnational corporations (and hence facilitate the transfer of value from the periphery to the metropole accelerating capital accumulation in the latter); and (2) allow the capital accumulation process in the metropolitan countries to proceed even though the masses of consumers have inadequate purchasing power.

What Amin, Baran, Frank, Magdoff et al., really show

Amin, Baran and even Frank and Magdoff are forced in fact to reject the traditional argument that imperialism is a necessary condition of capital accumulation and in its stead, argue that imperialism is an organic outgrowth of capitalism which allows the transnational corporations to make greater profits than they otherwise would and which results in greater economic stability and growth in the metropolitan countries. For example Baran and Sweezy argue:

[The giant multinational corporations want] monopolistic control over foreign sources of supply and foreign markets, enabling them to buy and sell on specially privileged terms to shift orders from one subsidiary to another, to favor this country or that depending on which has the most advantageous tax, labor, and other policies—in a word, they want to do business on their own terms and wherever they choose. (Baran and Sweezy, 1966: 201)

Harry Magdoff argues that because the interconnections between imperialism and monopoly capitalism are so multitudinous and complex it is impossible to separate the two phenomena:

Our point of view is that the separate parts must be understood in the context of their interrelations with the social organism of world monopoly capitalism. Further, it is important to recognize the essential unity of the economics, politics, militarism, and culture of this social organism. We reach the conclusion that imperialism is the way of life of capitalism. Therefore, the elimination of imperialism requires the overthrow of capitalism. (Magdoff, 1970: 29)

Magdoff compares the question of the necessity of imperialism to the question of the necessity for the U.S. of keeping Texas, New Mexico or Manhattan:

"Does the U.S. Economy Require Imperialism?" Imperialism, however, is so intertwined with the history and resulting structure of modern capitalist society—with its economics, politics, and ruling ideas—that this kind of question is in the same category as, for example, "Is it necessary for the United States to keep Texas and New Mexico?" We could, after all, return these territories to the Mexican people and still maintain a high-production and high-standard-of-living economy. We could import the oil, mineral ores, and cattle from these territories and sell U.S. goods in exchange. Any temporary decline in our Gross National Product would surely be a small price to pay for social justice. And given our growth rate and supposed ability to regulate our economy, continued economic growth should soon make up any losses resulting from the return of stolen lands. (Magdoff, 1970: 20)

The answer to Magdoff's question is that of course Texas, New Mexico and Manhattan are integrally related in every way to the U.S. and that therefore the U.S. would not give them up without a fight, but that nevertheless if the U.S. were forced to surrender these territories, just as France was forced to surrender Alsace-Lorraine to Germany in 1871, Germany was forced to cede it back to France in 1918, and capitalist Germany lost her eastern half in 1945, the capital accumulation process in the rest of the U.S. need not suffer (any more than the capital accumulation process suffered in France or Germany). In other words, imperialism, like national economic integration, is a result of the logic of capital accumulation, but not a condition of its continuing existence.

By thus posing the question Magdoff admits that the capital accumulation process in the metropolitan countries would go on in the absence of imperialism (i.e., that Lenin and Luxemburg were wrong), and thus that imperialism is not a necessary condition for capital accumulation but rather merely an organic outgrowth of capitalism. In his response to S. M. Miller et al., Magdoff explicitly rejects the absolute necessity position in favor of the organicness argument:

It takes no deep perception to recognize the limits of the "necessity" formula. Thus, a substantial part of the world, notably the Soviet Union and China, has chosen the path of economic independence and therefore broken the trade and investment ties with the imperialist network. The advanced capitalist countries adjusted to these changes and have in recent decades achieved considerable prosperity and industrial advance. . . .

The relevant question is not whether imperialism is necessary for the United States, but to discover the "rationality" of the historic process itself: why the United States and other leading capitalist nations have persistently and recurrently acted in the imperialist fashion for at least three-quarters of a century. (Magdoff, 1970: 21)

The argument of Magdoff about the complex interconnections between imperialism and capitalism and the point emphasized by Amin, Baran, Emmanuel, Frank et al., that imperialism results in speeding up the capital accumulation process *in the metropole* at the expense of the periphery, as well as the point emphasized by many that the transnational corporations, which dominate the metropolitan states, make enormous profits from imperialism, merely show that capitalism causes, produces or generates imperialism; i.e., that imperialism is an organic outgrowth of capitalism, not that capitalism could not survive if the contradictions within the world capitalist system, or an external factor (such as the expansion of socialism), cut off the peripheral areas from imperialism. The traditional argument of Lenin and Luxemburg which continues to be the position of the mainstream of orthodox Marxism-Leninism (e.g., that of the Chinese) is thus rejected by the above-cited authors who have justifiably retreated to the organicness position (although they do not always clearly enunciate the fact).

An examination of the evidence

If arguments like those of Lenin and Luxemburg are correct, i.e., if imperialism is a necessary condition of capital accumulation, then we would expect to find that either (1) there is considerably more capital export out of the metropolitan countries than is repatriated to them *and/or* (2) that there is considerably more export of goods to peripheral countries than is imported from them. By "considerably more" is meant something like at least a majority share of the pool of funds available for investment. If empirically it cannot be shown that net capital flows, or the balance of trade, serve as major mechanisms which allow the capital accumulation process to proceed, it cannot then be maintained that capitalism in the advanced metropolitan

countries could not continue without imperialism (unless it were shown that essential raw material imports could not be obtained and as a result capital accumulation could not go on in the metropolis). In the absence of showing that either investment or trade with the periphery is essential for the continuation of the capital accumulation process in the metropolitan countries, all the evidence in the world about the complex and multifaceted interlinkages between peripheral and metropolitan countries, and reams and reams of evidence about the immense profitability of the domination of the periphery by the metropolis, merely show that imperialism is an organic outgrowth of advanced capitalism; not, as Lenin and Luxemburg claimed, that capitalism would be impossible in the absence of imperialism. Let us carefully examine Tables 1 and 2, which compare two key indicators of the economic surplus seeking investment, after tax corporate profits and domestic capital investment (nonresidential, private fixed investment), with the appropriate measures of capital flows and trade, as well as with the size of state military and nonmilitary spending over the years 1950 to 1974.

From these tables it can clearly be seen that not only does capital consistently flow from the peripheral countries to the U.S. (in the period 1970–74 the ratio of repatriated profits to new investment outflow from the U.S. was about 3.6×), but over time the tendency is for net capital flow to the U.S. to grow, rather than decline, in relation to either the pool of corporate profits or the size of domestic capital investments.

It can also be seen from Tables 1 and 2 that even the total new capital outflow from the U.S. (ignoring the effect of repatriated profits) is very small in relation to either corporate profits or private nonresidential fixed investment (in 1970–74 it represented only 2.1 percent of corporate profits and

TABLE 1

U.S. foreign investment, exports and military and nonmilitary expenditures in relation to corporate profits and domestic capital investment (billions of current U.S. dollars)

	Corporate profits after taxes	Domestic capital investment (private nonresidential fixed investment)	U.S. new overseas investment in Third World	Net capital flow (outflow— repatriated earnings) between U.S. and Third World	U.S. exports to Third World	U.S. balance of trade (exports-imports) with Third World	U.S. military expenditures	U.S. nonmilitary government expenditures
1950	$25.4	$ 27.9	$0.185	$— 0.689	$ 4.205	$—1.107	$18.4	$ 51.9
1951	21.6	31.8	0.198	— 0.913	6.002	+0.390	—	—
1952	19.5	31.6	0.390	— 0.653	5.595	—0.235	48.2	51.6
1953	19.9	34.2	0.241	— 0.847	5.082	—0.962	53.6	56.5
1954	19.8	33.6	0.234	— 1.032	5.313	+0.199	49.3	62.0
1955	26.1	38.1	0.235	— 1.133	5.777	+0.207	43.5	67.2
1956	26.0	43.7	0.818	— 0.618	6.548	+0.551	43.4	72.4
1957	24.5	46.4	1.375	— 0.152	7.750	+1.638	47.5	78.0
1958	20.4	41.6	0.468	— 0.935	6.764	+0.860	47.6	87.3
1959	25.1	45.1	0.304	— 1.067	6.256	+0.064	49.7	96.1
1960	22.6	48.4	0.210	— 1.289	7.131	+1.166	48.9	102.4
1961	24.8	47.0	0.446	— 1.236	6.923	+0.999	51.2	113.7
1962	26.9	51.7	0.195	— 1.689	7.213	+0.926	55.2	121.0
1963	29.4	54.3	0.478	— 1.552	7.380	+1.150	56.4	128.6
1964	35.2	61.1	0.537	— 1.681	8.234	+1.568	57.3	139.1
1965	43.1	71.3	0.807	— 1.445	9.023	+1.878	55.8	149.8
1966	46.8	81.6	0.547	— 1.803	10.112	+2.350	60.8	164.0
1967	45.9	83.3	0.645	— 1.994	9.960	+2.279	74.6	183.2
1968	47.8	88.8	1.146	— 1.802	10.813	+1.950	83.9	198.7
1969	42.8	98.5	0.760	— 2.513	11.278	+1.905	84.5	223.8
1970	34.7	100.6	0.935	— 2.158	12.993	+2.551	84.3	248.7
1971	46.1	104.6	1.397	— 2.343	13.405	+1.853	79.9	289.5
1972	57.7	116.8	1.117	— 3.201	14.577	+0.223	81.1	316.3
1973	72.9	136.8	0.921	— 3.808	20.963	+0.651	78.1	354.5
1974	85.7	149.2	1.718	—10.747	32.698	—6.773		

| Sources: | HS (924) SA: 1975 (504) | HS (229) SA: 1975 (381) | SCB (Various) | SCB (Various) | HS (550) SA: 1975 (814) | HS (550, 552) SA: 1975 (814) | HS (1120) SA: 1975 (226) | SA 1975 (253– 254) |

HS = U.S. Department of Commerce, *Historical Statistics of the United States from Colonial Times to 1970,* 1976.
SA = U.S. Department of Commerce, *Statistical Abstract of the United States,* 1975.
SCB = U.S. Department of Commerce, *Survey of Current Business.*

only 1.0 percent of domestic capital investment). Thus even if we did not subtract the effect of repatriated profits the total effect of new capital outflow could barely be considered to have any effect at all on the surplus seeking investment, never mind, as Lenin, Luxemburg and the orthodox Leninist tradition argue, be the primary mechanism of capital accumulation on a world scale.

From Tables 1 and 2 it can be seen that the U.S. balance of trade was positive with Third World countries from 1954 to 1973, i.e., some surplus was realized by exporting more than was imported from the peripheral countries (it represented 3–4 percent of

TABLE 2

The ratio of U.S. foreign investments, exports and military and nonmilitary expenditures to corporate profits and domestic capital investment (period averages)

Period	New overseas investments	Net capital flow	Exports	Balance of trade	Military expend- itures	Nonmilitary expend- itures
Ratio to corporate profits						
1950–54	1.2%	−3.9%	24.7%	−1.6%	200%	262%
1955–59	2.6	−3.2	27.1	2.7	190	329
1960–64	1.3	−5.4	26.5	4.2	194	435
1965–69	1.7	−4.2	22.6	4.6	159	406
1970–74	2.1	−7.5	31.9	−0.5	137	509
Ratio to domestic capital investment						
1950–54	0.8	−2.6	16.5	−1.1	133	175
1955–59	1.5	−1.8	15.4	1.5	108	187
1960–64	0.7	−2.8	14.0	2.2	103	231
1965–69	0.9	−2.3	12.1	2.4	85	217
1970–74	1.0	−3.7	15.6	−0.2	67	249

Source: Computed from data in Table 1.

corporate profits and 1–2 percent of non-residential fixed investment during this period). However, this is hardly enough to create more than the slightest of effects on the capital accumulation process on a world scale. Even if exports are not discounted by imports they have averaged only about 25 percent of corporate profits and 15 percent of domestic investment over the last 25 years, clearly not the greater part of either profits or investments as the argument that imperialism is a necessary condition of the capital accumulation process maintains. It is of interest to note that as of 1974 the U.S. began importing more than it exported from the Third World countries, and thus that the net effect of trade with them, became the same as the net effect of invest-ment in them, to *aggravate*, rather than alleviate, any problem of finding outlets for investment funds in the metropolis. Neither investment nor trade, then, in fact, acts to facilitate the continuation of the capital accumulation process by acting as a mech-anism for extensive capital accumulation. The Third World is not used as an outlet for surplus capital as Lenin and Luxem-burg argue.

Tables 1 and 2 suggest that both the state's military and nonmilitary spending play central roles in the capital accumula-tion process. The importance of military spending, however, has declined consider-ably from averaging 200 percent of total corporate profits and 133 percent of total nonresidential fixed private investment in 1950–54 to 137 percent of total corporate profits and 67 percent of domestic capital investment in 1970–74. In spite of this de-cline, military spending continues to be far more significant than either exports or new overseas investment, and unlike either one of these factors has a net effect of pro-viding investment outlets for the corpora-tions which invest heavily in military hard-ware. The factor which, contrary to what Paul Baran and Paul Sweezy suggest in their book *Monopoly Capital*, seems to play both the greatest and the most rapidly ex-panding role in facilitating the capital ac-cumulation process is nonmilitary spending, especially social expenditures on educa-tion, welfare, medicine, housing, etc. In the period 1950–54 total government ex-penditures on all levels (local, state and federal) in the U.S. was almost evenly bal-anced between military and nonmilitary spending. Further, military spending had only very recently come to play such a predominant role. It clearly, as Baran and Sweezy point out, was the difference between the stagnation of the 1930s and the prosperity of the 1950s. However, nonmilitary spending has become more and more important in the economy, until in the early 1970s, it grew to about four times as large as military spending. Nonmilitary spending in the period 1970–74 was 509 percent of corporate profits and 249 percent of domestic capital investment. The evidence thus strongly suggests that the most dynamic element in facilitating the capital accumulation process in the advanced capitalist countries is now state spending on *nonmilitary* factors, especially social expenditures. Table 3 gives a more focused picture of the trend of military versus social expenditures in the U.S.

Instead of showing that imperialism is a necessary condition for capital accumulation in the metropolitan countries (the argument of Lenin and Luxemburg), the data shows instead merely that there are multifaceted links between the metropolitan countries and the Third World. These undoubtedly increase the profitability of the transnational corporations based in the U.S. and tend to accelerate the rate of capital accumulation *in the U.S.* by *expanding*

TABLE 3

The ratio* of total U.S. federal social expenditures to total U.S. military expenditures, 1960–1975

1975	1.79
1974	1.56
1973	1.46
1972	1.26
1971	1.08
1970	0.85
1969	0.73
1968	0.66
1965	0.61
1960	0.45

* The ratio is the sum of federal expenditures for community and regional development, education, manpower and social services, health and income security divided by expenditures for national defense.
Source: Computed from data in U.S. Department of Commerce, *Statistical Abstract of the United States*, 1975, pp. 226, 253.

the pool of funds available for investment, through repatriating profits from Third World investments and providing markets for big corporations that are thereby more able to operate at a higher level of efficiency, lower all-around costs and realize all-around greater profits than in the absence of export markets. The works of Magdoff and others are full of statistics which back up these latter points. He shows, for example that the earnings on foreign investments of U.S. corporations are over a third of corporate profits and are rising rapidly, that military demand plus exports represents 20–50 percent of total demand in almost all major industrial sectors, that the rate of profit is higher in peripheral countries, that the biggest corporations tend to acquire a higher share of their profits from overseas operations than smaller firms, etc. All this evidence presents a convincing case that imperialism is organically a product of capitalism, but it fails to show what Lenin and Luxemburg claimed when they made their argument for necessity, i.e. that the capital accumulation process could not continue without imperialism. If Latin America, Africa and Asia become severed from the world capitalist system we should fully expect the capital accumulation process to continue in the U.S. even though the multifaceted links and high profitability of the transnational corporations would no longer exist. Lenin and Luxemburg are wrong. Capitalism can survive and prosper without imperialism.

Raw material import, capital accumulation and imperialism

Those that have tended to reject the argument that imperialism is a necessary condition for the capital accumulation process because of the necessity of finding investment outlets or markets in the peripheral countries tend to argue that imperialism is indispensable in order to obtain the raw materials from the peripheral countries which are required by the technologically advanced economies of the metropolitan countries, i.e., that the capital accumulation process would be stalled in the metropolis without the key raw materials unobtainable without imperialism.

Heather Dean has made one of the most straightforward and important statements of the position. Rejecting the underconsumptionist type arguments of Hobson, Lenin and Luxemburg, she argues that intensive processes within the metropolitan countries are fully adequate to allow the capital accumulation process to proceed and thus that the root cause of imperialism is the drive to obtain raw materials:

. . . the development of capitalist economies has shown an almost limitless capacity for internal expansion. Legalized unions, welfare, public works, defense spending, planned obsolescence, space programs, consumer credit, ad-created markets and fad spending—techniques beyond the wildest dreams of the Social Democrats [of Lenin's time]—lead one to suspect that the last cataclysmic convulsion of capitalism just isn't coming.

Not only have capitalist economies succeeded in expanding internally, but they have observably not exploited market and investment opportunities in the underdeveloped countries. The feudal economic and political structures of the Third World provide neither purchasing power nor opportunities for investment in industry. . . .

American investors do make a tidy sum each year on their overseas investments, and it would be naive to suppose that the corporations involved would be too altruistic to fight to maintain them. But the degree of expansion has been so limited, the profits so peripheral to the American economy, that it takes a peculiar sort of demonology to believe that they are in themselves adequate justification of the three wars and countless lesser military actions by which the United States has gained and maintained control of the Third World. (Dean, 1971: 140)

Gabriel Kolko (1969) and Harry Magdoff (1969) have made similar arguments:

The economic control, and hence the political control when dealing with foreign sources of raw material supplies, is of paramount importance to the monopoly-organized mass production industries in the home country. In industries such as steel, aluminum, and oil the ability to control the source of raw material is essential to the control over the markets and prices of the final products, and serves as an effective safety factor in protecting the large investment in the manufacture and distribution of the final product. (Magdoff, 1969: 195)

Like the arguments about the relationship between capital flows and exports, the arguments about the relations of imports of raw materials from the peripheral countries can be made either in the defense of the position that imperialism is a necessary condition of capitalism *or* that imperialism is an organic product of capitalism. To maintain the first, it would have to be shown that there could be no other way to obtain a secure source of raw materials at a price which would allow profits to be made and the capital accumulation process to continue other than through the imperial domination of the peripheral countries. To maintain the second, it need only be argued that it is *more* profitable and more *secure* to obtain raw materials through imperialism. This latter position is in fact what Harry Magdoff shows in his *The Age of Imperialism*, although once again he takes a jump in suggesting that he has proven necessity. Magdoff rightfully argues that imperialism allows the metropolitan countries, and more importantly the transnational corporations based in them, to guarantee themselves a cheap and secure source of raw materials. In fact, this drive to guarantee raw material supplies at their source is at least as much motivated by the pursuit of profits vis-à-vis transnational corporations based in other countries as it is to insure that necessary raw materials will be available in their home country. Magdoff himself weakened his original position in his response to S. M. Miller et al.:

The concentration of economic power in a limited number of giant firms became possible in many industries precisely because of the control by these firms over raw materials sources. The ability to maintain this concentrated power, to ward off native and foreign competitors, to weaken newcomers, and to conduct its affairs in accordance with monopolistic price and production policies depended on alertness and aggressiveness of the giant firms to obtain and maintain control over major segments of the supplies of raw materials—*on a world scale*. This has been the underlying rationale of foreign investment in the extractive industries during the era of modern imperialism: not only in oil but in a spectrum of products, especially minerals.

The issue, therefore, is not dependency of the United States on foreign mineral supplies, but the dependency of monopoly industry qua "monopolies" on the control of these supplies. (Magdoff, 1970: 28)

The position that the control of raw materials at their source is a necessary condition for the maintenance of profitability and capital accumulation in the metropolitan countries would have to demonstrate: (1) that the only source of at least some crucially necessary raw materials is Third World countries; (2) that there are no more expensive substitutes available in the metropolitan countries, and thus that it is essential that supplies come from Third World countries; (3) that there is a real motive for the Third World countries to not supply the metropolitan countries with their essential and unsubstitutable raw materials at a price which would allow profitable capital accumulation to continue in the metropolis without imperialism; and (4) that the solidarity necessary among the politically highly diverse Third World countries to run an effective and long-term boycott could be maintained. The position that the control of raw materials at their source is merely more profitable for the transnational corporations, on the other hand, need only demonstrate that imperialism results in considerably greater profits

for the raw material extracting corporations.

Magdoff and others tried to prove the first argument, but in fact demonstrate only the second: i.e., that the quest for raw materials is organically linked to capitalism, but is not a necessary condition of its continuing existence. Magdoff, like others that focus on the raw material argument: (1) greatly overemphasizes the importance of the peripheral countries as sources of supply for raw materials; (2) confuses the reality of raw material imports from these countries with the question of whether such imports are the *only* way to obtain such materials, or are merely the cheapest; (3) neglects the possibilities of the development of ersatz materials which would be more expensive but which would nevertheless perform the functions of materials available only from peripheral countries; (4) falsely suggests that the peripheral countries have an interest in stopping the flow of crucial raw materials to the metropolitan countries, while in fact they merely have an interest in increasing their price; and (5) neglects the fact that effective long-term boycotts require more or less complete adherence under great pressure on the part of a large number of nations, some of which are socialist, others progressive noncapitalist, some capitalist and others semi-feudal nations—which are at different economic levels, have different needs and interests, are differentially under the influence of different metropolitan powers and have great antagonisms among themselves.

It can be seen in Table 4 that, although

TABLE 4

U.S. imports from Third World countries

	1955	1960	1965	1970	1972	1974
As a percentage of all U.S. imports	49	41	33	26	26	39
As a percentage of the U.S. GNP	1.40	1.18	1.04	1.07	1.25	2.33

Source: *Statistical Abstract of the United States*, 1970, 1973, 1975.

there has been a sudden upturn in the most recent period, most U.S. imports continue to come from other advanced capitalist countries and that total imports from Third World countries still do not amount to an especially significant share of the U.S. GNP. The mineral imports from Third World countries in 1974 totaled 33 percent of total U.S. mineral imports (35 percent of all unprocessed and 33 percent of all processed minerals). Two-thirds of U.S. mineral imports are from other advanced capitalist countries. On the other hand, it should be noted that 76 percent of U.S. imports of fuels and lubricants in 1974 were from Third World countries.[5] While the aggregate value of imports from peripheral countries *is small*, it may very well be the case that imperialism could be indispensable in order to obtain small quantities of rare but absolutely indispensable materials *qualitatively* necessary for advanced industry.

Let us examine more closely the important minerals from Third World countries and their impact on the U.S. economy. Table 5 lists U.S. mineral imports from Asia, Africa and South America as a percentage of total U.S. production and imports. This table underestimates somewhat the dependence of the U.S. on mineral imports from Third World countries since it excludes Central America, the West Indies and the Pacific Islands from its definition of Third World.

This list of 40 minerals includes the basic minerals which were on the U.S. government list of strategic minerals to be stockpiled in 1973 plus the other minerals reported in the summary tables on production and imports in the annual editions of the U.S. Department of the Interior's definitive *Minerals Yearbook*.

Of all the basic 40 minerals listed the U.S. in 1971 had to import more than 25 percent of its consumption from Third World countries only for antimony, chromium, cobalt, columbium, manganese, tin and bauxite (which should be on this list

TABLE 5

The percentage of U.S. mineral production and imports imported from Asia, Africa and South America†

	1965	1971
Antimony	24%	80%
Asbestos*	11	5
Bauxite	18	24
Beryl*	100	0
Bismuth*	35	15
Cadmium*	5	11
Chromium*	81	65
Coal, Coke	0	0
Cobalt*	44	32
Columbium*	55	59
Copper	0	3
Fluorspar*	2	1
Gases (natural and manufactured)	0	0
Graphite*	21	0
Gypsum	0	0
Iron	13	12
Lead*	13	3
Magnesium	1	0
Manganese*	95	91
Mercury	2	5
Mica*	10	5
Molybdenum	0	1
Nickel	1	0
Petroleum (crude)	16	8
Phosphates	0	0
Platinum*	7	18
Potash	19	2
Salt	0	0
Silver*	23	12
Sulfur	0	0
Talc	0	25
Tantalum*	43	11
Tellurium	2	10
Tin*	95	—
Titanium	7	0
Tungsten*	11	1
Vanadium	0	0
Uranium and Thorium	9	12
Zinc*	10	6
Zirconium	0	0

* Indicates that this mineral was stockpiled by the U.S. government as a strategic material in 1973.

† This list includes the basic materials included in the U.S. government stockpile of strategic materials in 1973, plus the minerals listed in the summary tables for mineral production and imports in the *Minerals Yearbook* in either 1965 or 1971. Some figures must be considered to be approximations since for some minerals production figures are not released and hence production data had to be roughly estimated from consumption figures. For the most part scrap and waste are excluded from these figures, although there are a few exceptions. For a few minerals the categories employed by the *Minerals Yearbook* may have changed from 1965 to 1971.

Source: U.S. Department of the Interior: *Minerals Yearbook*, 1965 and 1971.

since a large share of the U.S. consumption is imported from Jamaica which is excluded from the definition of Third World employed in Table 5). With the exception of these 7 metals at least three-fourths of the U.S. supply of 40 basic minerals in 1971 was either produced domestically or imported from other advanced capitalist countries. It should be noted however that during the mid-1970s the U.S. has become increasingly reliant on crude petroleum imports. In 1974 crude petroleum imports from the Third World accounted for about 30 percent of total U.S. consumption.[6]

In the period 1965 to 1971 the U.S. increased its reliance on mineral imports from Third World countries in the case of only 11 of these 40 minerals, and *decreased* its reliance on imports for 20. Of the seven minerals for which the U.S. is definitely dependent on Third World supplies, that dependency has increased in the case of three: antimony, bauxite and columbium, and decreased in the case of three: manganese, chromium and cobalt. On balance raw material dependence on the Third World would appear if anything to be decreasing, *not* increasing as the defenders of the indispensability argument usually suggest. In sum, it does not appear that the U.S. is as dependent on critical raw material imports as proponents of the raw material dependence argument for the indispensability of imperialism maintain; i.e., neither quantitatively *nor* qualitatively does the U.S. appear to depend so heavily on raw material imports from the Third World as to justify claims of the indispensability of imperialism.

It is argued by Magdoff (1969) and others, that the need to secure raw material supplies required to maintain a technologically advanced military establishment is among the primary motive forces of imperialism. Leaving aside the fact that most of the "esoteric" minerals required by space age military technologies can be obtained outside of the Third World this is a rather circular argument; i.e., a powerful military establishment must be maintained in order to secure the supplies of raw materials, so that a powerful military establishment can be maintained to secure the supplies of raw materials . . . A drastic reduction in the U.S. in *per capita* military spending, to put it on a par with that of the other advanced capitalist countries, would significantly reduce the U.S.'s dependence on the crucial metals the secure supply of which is one of the motives of U.S. imperialism.

Since this paper concentrates on the relationship between theories of capital accumulation on a world scale and theories of the necessity of imperialism I cannot treat at length the arguments for and against the availability of more expensive sources of raw materials outside of the periphery, the availability of ersatz materials, the motives of peripheral governments in cutting off or threatening to cut off raw material supplies and their ability to maintain solidarity. All I can do here is to raise some serious questions about the arguments of those, such as Magdoff and Dean, who suggest that imperialism is an indispensable condition for guaranteeing raw material supplies.

Much of the U.S. importation of raw materials from the Third World occurs not because potential supplies don't exist elsewhere, but because much richer deposits of the imported minerals exist in Third World countries than in the U.S. or in other advanced capitalist countries. That is, much of the raw material imports occur because it is simply more *profitable* to import them than to mine or recycle them in the U.S; in fact most of the raw materials obtained by U.S. transnational corporations have traditionally been sold in Europe and Japan.

The Allied blockade of Germany in both world wars was premised on the assumption that cutting Germany off from raw material supplies would lead to the destruction of its military capacity. This assumption proved wrong in both cases. The Germans were able to develop adequate, although sometimes expensive and inefficient, substitutes for all the purposes necessary to maintain their fighting machine and keep German industry rolling at full capacity. The resource base available to the U.S., even if it were cut off from all the rest of the world except Canada, is significantly greater than that available to the Germans in either war. This together with the more efficient and resourceful technologies presently available to the U.S. would seem to more than counterbalance the increased demand for a few esoteric metals required by the more sophisticated technologies of the 1970s.

It would seem to be demagogic to argue, with the apologists for imperialism, that there is a real likelihood of all the Third World sources banding together in order to indefinitely cut off the supply of raw materials to the advanced capitalist countries. The Third World countries are for the most part more dependent on the industrial exports of the advanced countries than the advanced countries are on their raw material exports. The preservation of the privileges of the local elites and/or the prosperity and economic order of the Third World countries is thoroughly dependent on the continuation of raw material exports. What Third World countries (whether socialist, capitalist or state capitalist/bureaucratic) are interested in, is not in cutting off the supply of raw materials (which would destroy their own economies), but rather in securing significantly better terms of trade for themselves. Even if the average cost of raw material imports from Third World countries to the U.S. increased by a factor of five times—hardly likely because of inelasticities in demand (alternatives are developed when the cost becomes too high) — this would represent only about 8 percent of the GNP of the U.S.

Even if a majority of Third World countries tried to band together to cut off raw material exports it is most unlikely that they could long maintain a solid front given the tremendous political diversity in their regimes and the tremendous domestic pressures that would develop to break ranks and make extraordinary profits (as the OPEC oil boycott of the 1970s showed). It should also be noted that historically it has been the advanced capitalist countries that have been able to effect disciplined boycotts against the poorer countries, far more than the reverse; e.g., the boycotts of the Soviet Union in the 1920s, China by the U.S. in the 1950s and 1960s, Iran in 1953–54 and Cuba by the U.S. after 1960. In all these cases, it was the industrially backward countries that, because they were hurt the most by suspensions of trade, sought the hardest to normalize trade relations. In summary, the argument that raw material imports absolutely require imperialism cannot be demonstrated.

The evidence presented by Dean, Kolko and Magdoff on the relationship between imperialism and the needs of the capital accumulation process in the metropolitan countries does not in fact show that capital accumulation in the metropolis is necessarily dependent on controlling the sources of raw materials in the periphery. Rather it merely shows that transnational corporations prefer the security of having cheap and stable sources of raw materials, both to gain an edge over their competitors (domestic and foreign) and in order to make especially high profits by monopolizing the world raw material markets, and that the U.S. military establishment prefers to control raw materials at their source. Indeed the evidence they and others provide is most convincing: imperialism results in considerable profits for the transnational corporations which control raw material markets, and perhaps for the U.S. domestic corporations that might benefit from more secure and cheaper supplies (although it is in fact doubtful that a U.S.-based transnational would supply raw materials to another U.S. corporation at a cheaper price than that offered by a Japanese or German firm); and also that imperialism tends to structure the terms of trade between the peripheral and metropolitan countries in such a way as to accelerate capital accumulation in the metropolitan countries and slow it in the peripheral countries. While capital accumulation in the metropolitan countries is in all probability accelerated because of raw material imports, imperialism is not a necessary condition for capital accumulation because of the need for raw materials.

The contradictions of imperialism and their resolution within the logic of the capitalist world system

Imperialism is an organic product of the capitalist mode of production. Magdoff, Sweezy and others have demonstrated this quite conclusively. Capitalism, especially monopoly capitalism, *does* have a strong tendency to expand geographically. The relentless process of capital accumulation is a powerful force leading to the expansion of the world capitalist system both intensively *and* extensively. But, if obstacles to extensive accumulation develop, so long as the avenues for intensive accumulation are open, the capital accumulation process can continue and capitalism can thrive. Imperialism is a necessary result of capitalism in exactly the same sense that all objects in the earth's gravitational field necessarily tend to fall toward the center of the earth. Although this latter tendency is absolute it can be negated by greater counterforces propelling objects away from the earth, i.e., a rocket's thrust.

Large segments of the capitalist class benefit from extensive capital accumulation, the repatriation of profits and the control of cheap and secure raw materials, while others benefit more from intensive capital accumulation. So long as serious losses do not accrue to one or the other set of capitalists, each will support those economic processes which benefit the other. However, if the cost of imperialism becomes too great for those that do not benefit from this mode of capitalist growth, it is possible that they would eventually support a restructuring of the economy to facilitate intensive accumulation without imperialism.[7] Although the cost of transition to a non-imperialist capitalism would be great when the contradictions of imperialism, namely the rise and victory of national liberation movements, liberate greater and greater areas of the world, capitalism can reorganize itself on a profitable basis and the capital accumulation process continues.

The period of direct colonialism from the middle of the 19th century to the immediate post–World War II period was most advantageous for the major business interests in the advanced capitalist countries. Profitable investment outlets were fully guaranteed against expropriation and unfriendly restrictions; highly profitable monopolies of cheap raw materials were obtained; and export markets were protected from prohibitive tariffs or quota restrictions. As long as (1) the natives could be taxed to pay for the state which guaranteed their exploitation and drafted into the colonial army to preserve the colonizers' rule, and (2) the working class of the metropolitan country could be taxed to make up any deficit in the financing of the empire and drafted to handle any crises in colonial relations, then the economic benefits accruing to the powerful business interests in the colonizing country were greater than the costs.[8]

But once a popular resistance movement grows up in response to imperialism the costs of maintaining formal rule escalate. The advanced countries have to pour in vast sums of money as well as troops in order to maintain their domination. In the process of national liberation struggles, even when the natives consistently lose the major military battles, the profitable investment outlets dry up, export markets evaporate and raw materials cease to be cheap and secure. The costs of suppression are manifested in domestic inflation, balance of payments deficits, lower standards of living and growing domestic opposition and instability. The colonial powers eventually are forced to recognize that the benefits of direct rule are now far outweighed by the costs.[9] In order to cut their losses and maintain a good deal of the profit possibilities from their investments, exports and raw material imports, the colonizers must retreat to indirect rule or informal colonialism. Although not as profitable for most capitalist countries as direct rule, at least in its initial stages indirect rule is much less costly. Formal decolonization brought with it increasing economic control of the secondary economic sections by natives. But the economy as a whole tended to remain dominated by metropolitan-based transnational corporations.

In almost all of the new states created in the postwar period of decolonization a class of native rulers developed which came to serve as the intermediaries between the old colonizers (or in many cases the U.S. which replaced them) and the vast majority of the native peoples. The feelings of freedom and self-determination which formal independence brought "cooled-out" the anti-colonial movements for some time. Gradually, however, the reality of continuing *de facto* domination and exploitation by the advanced capitalist countries, together with the increasingly self-interested rule of the new native leaders, has reawakened the old movements which have come increasingly to join the struggle for *de facto* independence and authentically popular rule.[10] This process is the principal characteristic of the present period of relations between the advanced capitalist and the less developed countries.

The U.S. in recent years has been faced with growing worldwide opposition to its hegemony in the Third World. It is becoming more and more costly for the U.S. to maintain its informal empire. Since it became apparent that the U.S. could not win in Vietnam (more or less in 1968) the U.S. has been retreating from indirect rule to mechanisms which have been referred to as the "Nixon Doctrine."[11] In order to further cut its losses, while at the same time trying to preserve much of the profit-making opportunities from its Third World activities, the U.S. has tended to back a few relatively powerful and stable conservative regimes around the world (e.g., Brazil, Iran, Israel, Indonesia, South Korea), which are expected to exert local hegemony to protect U.S. interests, while at the same time, as in the OPEC countries, allowing the local governments to nationalize the key sections of their economies while the transnational corporations try to keep overall control through continuing to dominate both the world market (distribution of raw materials) and the means of advanced technology (the development of resources). This new mode of imperialism saves U.S. troops and money, and tends to avoid the prohibitive social, economic and political costs that direct intervention and outright ownership necessitate. Like its predecessor, indirect rule, the Nixon Doctrine of indirect rule once removed, accepts some loss in profits as the cost of hanging on to a good share of profit possibilities and reducing the prohibitive expenses of empire.

This further retreat from direct colonialism and direct ownership of the key sectors of the peripheral economies itself has serious contradictions. On the one hand the local ruling classes cannot be expected to indefinitely do the dirty work of the U.S. Eventually and perhaps gradually they can be expected to use their position to further their own interests even at the expense of the U.S. business interests, either by acting on their own, or, perhaps more likely, by looking for a better deal with another advanced capitalist country. The Nixon Doctrine thus tends in the long run to intensify inter-imperialist rivalries. On the other hand the working classes of these countries cannot be expected to indefinitely pay taxes and die for the preservation of U.S. business interests. Their opposition to being used by the U.S. can be expected to mount. Thailand in 1973 apparently experienced a rebellion of this kind. But such imperial mechanisms, while they are not as reliable, at least hold out the short-run hope of maintaining a good share of the profits of empire while cutting its costs.

Imperialism has two basic effects on the rapidity of the capital accumulation process in the leading metropolitan countries. On the one hand, to the extent that real value is transferred to the metropolitan countries through trade and the repatriation of profits, the process is *speeded* up in relation to that in the periphery. This process affects *all* the metropolitan countries whether or not they are directly imperialist. On the other hand, imperialism carries with it heavy costs in the form of military expenditures and all that being a leading military power entails in terms of allocation of the most productive plant, scientific resources and technology away from productive pursuits. This drag effect affects only the *leading* capitalist country. A comparative analysis of the advanced capitalist countries suggests that the freeing of resources from the military-industrial complex is probably the necessary condition for increasing productivity and hence the rate of growth.[12] The rate of overall economic growth, as well as the rate of growth in the industrial sector, in the U.S. has been among the slowest in the entire world (in comparison to either the developed or less developed countries). In the case of the leading military power in the world capitalist system (the U.S. since World War II and Great Britain before World War I) the very heavy costs of empire prove to be ultimately destructive. The leading metropolitan country must pay the costs not only of preserving the interests of its own transnational corporations, but also of functioning as the "world's police-

man," i.e., creating an imperial umbrella under which the lesser capitalist countries such as Switzerland, Sweden, Japan, Belgium, etc., can operate to great economic advantage for themselves *without* having to pay the costs of military hegemony. This is a true contradiction. Maintaining economic hegemony in the world requires maintaining military hegemony as well. But the cost of military hegemony is the undermining of economic hegemony and allowing one's competitors to gain. What happened to Britain before World War I is today happening to the U.S. as well.

The competitive pressure of its competitors, which increasingly push it out of world markets (as the U.S., Germany and Japan did to Britain before World War I and as Japan, Germany and other European countries have been doing to the U.S. since the 1950s, implies that the leading country in the world system must cut back its military expenses and reallocate resources to increasing its productivity (as well as slowing down the rate of increase in real wages of its working class) so that its commodities can remain competitive in the world market. The state must increasingly subsidize both research and development and wages for the major corporations so as to reduce their costs. This means both increasing the state's economic role in the economy, in order to guarantee the overall capital accumulation process and the level of profits, *and* the relative growth of a social-industrial complex at the expense of the older military-industrial complex.[13]

Given the slow rate of growth of the British and American economies during the later years of their world hegemony it would appear that the process of capital accumulation and the level of overall profitability could very well *gain* if these economies' imperial links could be severed and the draining effect of military outlays discontinued. The effect of the transfer of value from the periphery to the metropolis caused by imperialism does not appear to even balance the drain due to the military expenditures required to maintain an empire. In the secondary metropolitan states of the world capitalist system, whose economies are able to participate in the extraction of surplus value from the periphery without having to pay the costs of this process, however, the ending of imperialist domination of the periphery could only slow down the rate of capital accumulation (e.g., as in the effect of OPEC on the economic growth rates of Japan and Western Europe). Thus the overall effect of the cessation of imperialism on the metropolitan countries would seem to be an acceleration of capital accumulation in the leading country (the U.S.) and a deceleration of capital accumulation in the secondary countries (e.g., Japan, Germany, Sweden, etc.).

Even if the liquidation of imperialism proved to be profitable for the capitalist class as a whole, large segments of it—especially the transnational raw material based corporations—would stand to suffer immensely and therefore, of course, should be expected to violently oppose any fundamental shift in U.S. policy. Further, because of the heavy costs of transition, virtually all of the monopoly capitalist class should, at least at first, resist transition to a nonimperialist capitalism. To appease these groups with alternatives for profit making and to compensate for the slack in military spending's function of absorbing the surplus, thus allowing the capital accumulation process to continue, a great expansion of the state's role in the economy would be necessary.

A nonimperialist capitalism would require a dominant social-industrial complex which would stress developing productive technology and increasing productivity, especially in exportable commodities, and subsidizing wages (e.g., national health insurance, increased welfare programs, public housing) so as to preserve and increase the U.S. competitive advantage in both domestic and international markets, in the process absorbing the economic surplus and thus allowing profits to be realized and capital accumulation to continue. The data presented in Table 3 shows that the development of the social-industrial complex is already well advanced. A nonimperialist capitalism would also involve considerably more economic planning than presently exists (of the order currently practiced in Japan) but need not involve any significant infringements on profit-making possibilities. Economic planning could reduce the level of unemployment and increase the rate of growth of the U.S. to the level of the other advanced capitalist countries as well as negate most of the potentially disruptive effects of the possible loss of export markets, problems with raw material supplies and the loss of foreign investment opportunities and profits.

In the last few years the Chinese Communists have been predicting that world war will break out between the Soviet Union and the United States—the two "superpowers"—which are allegedly being driven into worldwide competition with each other because of the inexorable logic of imperialism which Lenin outlined in his *Imperialism: The Highest Stage of Capitalism*. Because the Chinese consider the Soviet Union to be a capitalist country, and because they accept the argument of Lenin that all capitalist countries must export capital in order to continue their capital accumulation process, they maintain (following Lenin's argument) that the USSR must inevitably come into military conflict with the U.S. because of necessary conflicts with the U.S. over protected areas for their respective overseas investments. They see a more or less exact parallel between the contention of the "two superpowers" today and the period before World War I which Lenin analyzed.

Another important consequence of the analysis presented in this paper is that if both Lenin and the Chinese are *wrong*, that is, if capital does not require capital export to survive, then it does not necessarily follow that the USSR (even if it were capitalist) and the USA are inexorably headed for another world war in order to redivide the world. World war might come, but it would come because of miscalculations, accidents or the aggressive policies of one or the other country, not because of any necessity within the world system. Neither the American nor the Soviet system requires imperialism as a condition of its survival.

This paper does not try to prove that the U.S will necessarily cease being imperialist, but only that, since there is no inherent absolute economic requirement for a monopoly capitalist economy to be imperialistic in order to survive, imperialism *could* be eliminated without a radical transformation of the U.S. class structure.[14]

The politics of necessity

Beneath the debate on the question of whether or not imperialism is a necessary condition of capitalism lie the political implications of the various positions. Traditionally, the radical left has often felt it necessary to argue that imperialism is indispensable in order to try to channel antiwar and anti-imperialist movements into the struggle against capitalism and for social revolution. On the other hand, reformists who thought that capitalism could be saved by being doctored up, and that social revolution was not necessary, felt compelled to argue that an abuse of the system which all leftists condemned—war and imperial domination of the poor countries—would be eliminated by a *policy* of social reform. To have argued otherwise would have forced them to become revolutionaries. In the post–World War II period, however, the implications of the theory of indispensability have changed. The *Monthly Review* school, which has steadfastly defended the necessity position also

has, over the years, consistently maintained that the primary contradictions of advanced capitalism were imperialism (in both its international and domestic manifestations) and economic stagnation (which necessitates tremendous military spending). If imperialism is indispensable then the antiwar, anti-imperialist and anti-racist movements can *only* win through the collapse of capitalism. These struggles then are inherently and necessarily anti-capitalist. Further, anti-capitalists should focus on these struggles, not the struggles of the U.S. working class, which under modern conditions have become reformist.

The implications of the modern day defenders of necessity are the opposite of the theories of Lenin and Luxemburg. While the early radical defenders of indispensability were trying to convince the workers that their oppression by militarism and imperialism could only be ended by social revolution, the modern indispensability theorists use their argument *against* the struggles of working people. It is blacks as blacks, it is the anti-war movement, and most importantly of all it is the peasants and economically marginal populations of the Third World who will make the revolution. All we can do in the mother country is lend a helping hand. Further, also implicit in this argument is that the struggles of Third World peasants and marginal urban populations *cannot* succeed without bringing about the collapse of capitalism. Hence it is expected that the U.S. will fight to the last against National Liberation Movements. Revolutionary groups thus have no realistic hope of winning short of a collapse of capitalism in the U.S. Both of these political implications of the modern day defenders of indispensability are highly questionable, as the events of the last few years are making clear.

The argument against indispensability can be *either* revolutionary *or* liberal. Liberals like to believe that imperialism is neither indispensable *nor* organic to capitalism They are comfortable with the notion that imperialism is a result of mistakes, bad leaders or faulty policies. Conservatives such as George Wallace, on the other hand, feel quite comfortable with the notion of indispensability. It can be an effective demagogic argument when presented to workers in the defense industries, or, for that matter, to great numbers of working people worrying about full employment and the rising standard of living. The argument *against* indispensability and *for* the organicness of imperialism on the other hand has revolutionary implications. If the National Liberation struggles (which fight against the imperialism organically produced by capitalism) in the Third World *can* win with-

out bringing about the destruction of capitalism in the U.S. and Europe, then these struggles, although certainly progressive and deserving of wholehearted support, are *not necessarily* anti-capitalist. Authentic anti-capitalist struggles in the metropolis can only be centered in the metropolitan working class. To the extent that the struggles for peace and against imperialism may be winnable within the framework of capitalism they are *objectively* reformist. But the struggles of working people for self-determination and against being treated as objects of capital accumulation are inherently unrealizable without the complete liquidation of the capitalist system and its replacement by socialism.

NOTES

1. For some of the major contemporary statements of the necessity position see Dean (1971) and Magdoff (1969, 1970). For some of the major critiques of this position see Erlich (1973), Miller et al. (1970), Perlo (1963), and Steward (n.d.).

   For the debates around the question of capital accumulation on a world scale see Amin (1974), Baran (1957), Chase-Dunn (1975), Emmanuel (1972), Frank (1967), McMichael et al. (1974), Murray (1976), Sutcliffe (1972), Szymanski (1974b), and Warren (1973).

2. See Karl Marx, *Capital*, vol. 1, part 7, Paul Sweezy, *The Theory of Capitalist Development*, parts 2 and 3, and Paul Baran and Paul Sweezy, *Monopoly Capital*, chaps. 3–8 for discussions of the capital accumulation process.

3. See Karl Marx, *Capital*, vol. 3, chaps. 13 and 14 (especially section 5 of chap. 14). Also see Samir Amin, *Accumulation on a World Scale*, pp. 122–23.

4. See Szymanski (1974b) and the debate in vol. 8:2 of the *Review of Radical Political Economics* for a discussion of this argument.

5. See U.S. Department of Commerce, *Highlights of the U.S. Import and Export Trade*, December 1974.

6. See U.S. Department of Commerce, *The Statistical Abstract of the U.S., 1975*, p. 686, and U.S. Department of Commerce, *Highlights of the U.S. Import and Export Trade*, December 1974.

7. Perlo (1963) uses data on the costs and profits of imperialism to show that large segments of the capitalist class lose more than they gain by imperialism.

8. For discussions of the economic losses suffered by the working classes in the imperialist countries because of imperial policies see Hobson (1902) and Szymanski (1973a).

9. This has been vividly illustrated in the early 1970s by the case of Portugal which was bled white by its futile attempt to preserve its direct colonial rule in Africa.

10. See Frantz Fanon (1966) for an excellent description of the process of formal decolonization and the reawakening of the freedom movement. Magdoff (1969) and Frank (1967) give excellent accounts of the mechanisms of indirect rule.

11. See Michael Klare (1972).

12. See Melman (1965) for the development of this argument. Also, Szymanski (1973b) for the correlation of military spending and rates of growth.

13. See James O'Connor (1973) for an analysis of the growing role of state social expenditures in the U.S. economy.

14. The structure of domination in the world economy is becoming more pluralistic with the relative decline of the U.S. (Szymanski, 1974a). This situation brings with it better prices for many of the raw material exports of the Third World countries which are able to use the competitive struggle among the advanced capitalist countries to their own advantage. Growing conflict among the advanced capitalist countries may well be the result of the decline in the hegemony of the U.S. (see Rowthorn, 1971).

REFERENCES

Amin, Samir
1974 *Accumulation on a World Scale*. New York: Monthly Review Press.

Baran, Paul
1957 *The Political Economy of Growth*. New York: Monthly Review Press.

Baran, Paul and Sweezy, Paul
1966 *Monopoly Capital*. New York: Monthly Review Press.

Chase-Dunn, Christopher
1975 "The Effects of International Economic Dependence on Development and Inequality." *American Sociological Review,* December.

Dean, Heather
1971 "Scarce Resources: The Dynamic of U.S. Imperialism" in K. T. Fann and Donald Hodges. *Readings in U.S. Imperialism*. Boston: P. Sargent.

DeGras, Jane, ed.
1960 *The Communist International, 1919–1943 Documents*. vol. 2. New York: Oxford University Press.

Emmanuel, Arghiri
1972 *Unequal Exchange*. New York: Monthly Review Press.

Erlich, Alexander
1973 "A Hamlet without the Prince of Denmark" in *Politics and Society*, Fall, pp. 35–53.

Fanon, Frantz
1966 *The Wretched of the Earth*. New York: Grove Press

Frank, André Gunder
1967 *Capitalism and Underdevelopment in Latin America*. New York: Monthly Review Press.

Hobson, J. A.
1902, 1965 *Imperialism*. Ann Arbor: University of Michigan Press.

Kalre, Michael
1972 "U.S. Military Strategy after Vietnam." *Monthly Review,* February.

Kolko, Gabriel
1969 *The Roots of American Foreign Policy*. Boston: Beacon Press.

Lenin, V. I.
1917, 1960 *Imperialism: The Highest Stage of Capitalism* in *Selected Works in Three Volumes*. Vol. 1, Moscow: Foreign Languages Publishing House.

Luxemburg, Rosa
1913, 1964 *The Accumulation of Capital*. New York: Monthly Review Press.

Magdoff, Harry
1969 *The Age of Imperialism*. New York: Monthly Review Press.

1970 "The Logic of Imperialism," *Social Policy,* September–October, pp. 20–29.

Marx, Karl
1887 *Capital*. Vols. 1 and 3. Moscow: Foreign Languages Publishing House.

McMichael, Philip, Petras, James and Rhoades, Robert
1974 "Imperialism and Capitalist Industrialization," *New Left Review,* May–June, no. 85.

Miller, S. M., Bennett, Roy and Alapatt, Cyril
1970 "Does the U.S. Economy Require Imperialism?" *Social Policy,* 1:2, September–October, pp. 13–19.

Murray, Martin
1976 "International Capital Flows and the Meaning of Capitalist Expansion," *Review of Radical Political Economics,* 8:2, Summer.

O'Connor, James
1973 *The Fiscal Crisis of the State*. New York: St. Martins Press.

Perlo, Victor
1963 *Militarism and Industry*. New York: International Publishers.

Rowthorn, Bob
1971 "Imperialism in the '70's: Unity or Rivalry." *New Left Review,* September–October, no. 69.

Steward, Michael
n.d. "The Decline of American Imperialism and the Growing World Conflict." A pamphlet published by the International Socialists (U.S.).

Sutcliffe, Bob
1972 "Imperialism and Industrialization in the Third World" in Roger Owen and Bob Sutcliffe, eds. *Studies in the Theory of Imperialism*.

Sweezy, Paul
1942 *The Theory of Capitalist Development*. New York: Monthly Review Press.

Szymanski, Albert
1973a "American Imperialism and the U.S. People." *Social Praxis,* 1:1, Summer, pp. 81–92.

1973b "Military Spending and Economic Stagnation." *American Journal of Sociology,* 79:1, July, pp. 1–14.

1974a "The Decline and Fall of the U.S. Eagle." *Social Policy,* 4:5, March–April, pp. 5–13.

1974b "Marxist Theory and International Capital Flows." *Review of Radical Political Economy,* 6:3, Fall, pp. 20–40.

Warren, Bill
1973 "Imperialism and Capitalist Industrialization." *New Left Review,* September–October, no. 81.

The transition to socialism*

PAUL M. SWEEZY

The subject of this essay is so large that I must confine myself to a few aspects of what could easily constitute the content of an entire course of lectures. This necessarily means that I will assume much that is neither obvious nor uncontroversial. It may therefore be useful at the outset to make explicit some of these assumptions.

1. There is no such thing as a general theory of the transition between social systems. This is not because relatively little attention has been paid to the subject—though this is undoubtedly true—but because each transition is a unique historical process which must be analyzed and explained as such.

2. Nevertheless, a comparative study of transitions can be extremely valuable. In particular the study of past transitions can help us to ask fruitful questions about present and possible future transitions, to recognize similarities and differences, to appreciate the historicity and totality of the process under examination.

3. Transitions are never simple or brief processes. On the contrary, they typically occupy and even define whole historical epochs. One aspect of their complexity is what may be called multi-directionality: movement in one direction may turn back on itself and resume in a forward direction from a new basis. In some places the reversal may be prolonged or conceivably even permanent.

4. Transitions from one social order to another involve the most difficult and profound problems of historical materialism.

"Herr Proudhon does not know," Marx wrote in *The Poverty of Philosophy*, "that all history is but the continuous transformation of human nature" (Marx/Engels, *Werke*, vol. 4, p. 160). This view can be squared with the principle, as stated in the sixth thesis on Feuerbach, that "the human essence is no abstraction inherent in each single individual" but "the ensemble of social relations," only if it is possible to relate the transformation of human nature to the transformation of social relations. How this is to be done is also indicated in the *Theses on Feuerbach* (the third):

The materialist doctrine that men are products of circumstances and upbringing, and that therefore changed men are the products of other circumstances and changed upbringing, forgets that it is men who change circumstances and that the educator must himself be educated. . . . The coincidence of the changing of circumstances and human activity can be conceived and rationally understood only as *revolutionizing practice.*

Here, in the concatenation of human nature, social relations, and revolutionizing practice, we reach the heart of the problem of the transition from one social system to another.

Let us begin with a few reflections on the transition from feudalism to capitalism in its decisive European theater. There are, I believe, many unsettled questions in this area relating to such matters as the causes of the decline of feudalism and the origins of

* From *On the Transition to Socialism*, 2d ed., by Paul M. Sweezy and Charles Bettelheim, pp. 107–122. Copyright © 1971 by Monthly Review Press. Reprinted by permission of Monthly Review Press.

capitalism, but they are not my present concern. Whatever positions may be held by different scholars on these questions, it seems to me unlikely that any would disagree that both the decline of feudalism and the beginnings of capitalism can be traced far back into the Middle Ages, that is to say, into a period when there is no doubt that the dominant European mode of production was feudal. In other words, there is no doubt that capitalism made its appearance, not as a theory or an aspiration but as an actual social formation within the confines of feudal society. Oliver Cox has argued very persuasively that Venice in the Middle Ages was already a thoroughly bourgeois city-state, completely oriented toward profit-seeking commerce, with significant capitalist production (e.g., in shipbuilding) and a typically bourgeois political and ideological superstructure. The same can be said with even greater certainty of a considerable number of Italian and Northern European cities in the later feudal period, and of course the discovery of America and the opening up of sea routes to the Far East in the 15th and 16th centuries generated a burst of activity (including plunder and piracy as well as trade) which by no stretch of the imagination could be called "feudal." There is room for dispute about precisely how and when capitalism finally triumphed, but there can be no contesting the fact that the process involved an ongoing struggle between two actually existing social formations for supremacy, i.e., for state power (monopoly over the means of coercion) and the right to organize society in accordance with their respective interests and ideas. Moreover the process was a prolonged one in which the "new" social formation had ample time to prepare itself, both economically and ideologically, for the role of undisputed dominance.

What does this mean in terms of the transformation of human nature? It means that "bourgeois man" was born and ma-

tured in a feudal world. The establishment and expansion of capitalist economic and social relations were practical human activities which gradually molded human beings with appropriate attitudes, motivations, "instincts"—cupidity, means-and-ends rationality, individualism, and so on. For centuries bourgeois man lived alongside feudal man, sometimes in uneasy accommodation, sometimes in mortal combat, but always advancing and reaching out for more power, eventually conquering and even assimilating his ancient rival. When the time finally came for bourgeois man to step forward as the master of his universe, his nature was fully formed and faithfully reflected the newly emergent "ensemble of social relations." In retrospect we can see that in this case the "revolutionizing practice," which in Marx's view is the key to understanding changes in society and hence also changes in human nature, was precisely the centuries-long process of building capitalism within the framework of feudal society.

If we turn now to the subject before us, the first thing we notice is that the transition to socialism does not, and in the nature of the case cannot, take the same course as the transition from feudalism to capitalism. Not that this road has never occurred to anyone, or even that it has never been tried. Quite the contrary. The distinguishing characteristic of pre-Marxian or Utopian socialism was the deliberate selection (though not the conscious copying) of a road to socialism similar to that which had led from feudalism to capitalism. Small socialistic communities were to be, and in many cases actually were, established. These were to be both schools of socialism and bases from which the new society would spread, undermining and eventually overwhelming their capitalist matrix. There were many reasons why this strategy could not work, perhaps chief among them that the small socialist communities—unlike capitalism in the interstices of feudal society—had nothing positive to offer the dominant system and hence from its viewpoint their success would be an unmitigated disaster. Add to this that they had neither the ability nor the desire to compete against capitalism on its own terms and one can see that the obstacles to their survival, let alone development, were so enormous that they were in effect doomed from the outset. Instead of creating a new socialist human nature, they served only to buttress the characteristic bourgeois view that human nature is, after all, unchangeable.

Marx of course shared none of the illusions of the Utopians and, as we have already seen, was fully aware of the complex interrelation of social systems, human action, and social change. (It is worth remembering that both the *Theses on Feuerbach* and *The Poverty of Philosophy*, from which I quoted earlier, were written in the period 1845–47, i.e., early in Marx's intellectual development; and there is not the slightest reason to believe that he ever changed his mind on these absolutely fundamental questions.) What, then, was his conception of the *modus operandi* of the transition to socialism?

The answer, at least in broad outline, is well known. Socialism itself cannot take root and grow within the confines of capitalist society, as capitalism had done under feudalism. But in Marx's view capitalism has a special, perhaps historically unique, characteristic which not only makes possible but guarantees the existence of a different road to its transformation.

The essence of capitalism is the self-expansion of capital, which takes place through the production and capitalization of surplus value. Production of surplus value in turn is the function of the proletariat, i.e., the class of wage workers who own no means of production and can live only by the sale of their labor power. Since the proletariat produces for capital and not for the satisfaction of its own needs, it

follows that capitalism, in Marx's words, "establishes an accumulation of misery corresponding with accumulation of capital." The proletariat is thus both essential to capitalism and its essential victim. As capitalism grows, so does the proletariat; and the very processes of capitalist development prepare the proletariat for its historic role. Hence the concluding sentences of the first section of the *Communist Manifesto:* "What the bourgeoisie therefore produces, above all, are its own grave-diggers. Its fall and the victory of the proletariat are equally inevitable."

This theory of the revolutionary mission of the proletariat is of course central to Marxism and has been endlessly expounded, criticized, and debated. It is not my present purpose, however, to enter this discussion but rather to point out that, considered as a theory of the transition to socialism, it is only half a theory. What it deals with is the overthrow of capitalism; what it omits is the construction of socialism. Does Marxism contain, or imply, a complementary theory of the construction of socialism? If so, what is it? These are the questions to which I should like to address myself next.

For our purposes we do not need a definition of socialism, nor do we need to compile a catalogue of its characteristics. But we definitely do need to be perfectly clear that Marxism has always conceived of socialism as the negation of capitalism, operating according to radically different laws and principles. Capitalism treats people as means to the expansion of capital, which is the root of its manifold contradictions and evils. The main point of socialism is to reverse this, to enable people to take over and to arrange not only their productive activity but their whole lives with a view to satisfying their truly human needs. This reversal implies, among other things, the abolition of private property in the means of production and of incomes derived therefrom, a high degree of equality in all things, allocation of resources by plan rather than by the blind forces of the market, the elimination as rapidly as possible of invidious distinctions between manual and mental labor and between city and country, and the ultimate replacement of all money and commodity relations by direct human relations.

Now it is clear that capitalists and those imbued with capitalist attitudes and values would neither want nor be able to build and operate such a society. Their bourgeois human nature would be totally incompatible with the ensemble of social relations of socialist society. An attempt to combine the two would be doomed from the outset: either bourgeois human nature would have to be transformed into socialist human nature, or socialist relations would have to be transformed into bourgeois relations.

Let us recall at this point that this dilemma never arose in the case of the transition to capitalism. Bourgeois relations grew up within the framework of feudal society and molded bourgeois human nature over a period of several centuries. When capitalism finally conquered feudalism, it did so not merely as a revolutionary class but as an entire social order in which the correspondence between human nature and social relations was already fully developed. The element of dissonance represented by the continued existence of feudal remnants was of course there and in some (superstructural) respects was even important, but it posed no serious threat to the functioning of capitalism.

As we have seen, socialist human nature could not emerge through the revolutionizing practice of socialism within the framework of capitalism. Are there other possibilities, and if so what are they?

Not so long ago, I argued, in a discussion with Charles Bettelheim, that Marxism, at least up to the time of the Russian Revolution, had a clear answer to this question:

In classical Marxian theory . . . the proletariat . . . referred to the wage workers employed in large-scale capitalist industry who, in the advanced capitalist countries, constituted a majority of the working class and a very substantial proportion of the total population. These workers were assumed to have acquired, as a consequence of the capitalist accumulation process itself, certain specifically proletarian (and anti-bourgeois) attitudes and values: solidarity, cooperativeness, egalitarianism, etc. Historically speaking, the proletarian was seen as a "new man" formed by capitalism and possessing the interest, the will, and the ability to overthrow the system *and* to lead the way in the construction of a new socialist society.

I wrote this not after research in the relevant texts but from my general understanding of Marxian theory formed over a period of many years. Subsequently I was challenged to support this interpretation, and I must confess that I was unable to do so. It is easy to cite dozens of passages from the works of Marx and Engels affirming the revolutionary role of the proletariat in the overthrow of capitalism. I have not, however, found any which are specifically addressed to the question of the proletariat's ability or readiness to build a socialist society; and at least some of their formulations, especially those which analyze the effects of the division of labor on the worker, clearly imply a negative evaluation of the proletariat's qualifications. Consider, for example, the following from the famous chapter on "Machinery and Modern Industry," in the first volume of *Capital* (repeated verbatim by Engels in *Anti-Dühring*):

Modern industry, indeed, compels society, under penalty of death, to replace the detail-worker of today, crippled by life-long repetition of one and the same trivial operation, and thus reduced to the mere fragment of a man, by the fully developed individual, fit for a variety of labors, ready to face any change of production, and to whom the different social functions he performs are but so many modes of giving free scope to his own natural and acquired powers.

As a statement of one of the central aims, I would even say necessities of socialism, this is magnificent. But when Marx says that modern industry "compels society" to follow the course indicated, he deliberately sidesteps the question of the nature of the revolutionizing practice which will turn a mere fragment of a man into a fully developed individual.

When in doubt about the correct interpretation of Marx, it is a good idea to consult Lenin. What were his ideas on this subject?

Perhaps Lenin's most systematic analysis of the characteristics of the proletariat was in *What Is to Be Done?*, written in 1902. There, as is well known, he argued that "economism" comes naturally to the proletariat: "The history of all countries shows that the working class, exclusively by its own effort, is able to develop only trade union consciousness, i.e., the conviction that it is necessary to combine in unions, fight the employers and strive to compel the government to pass necessary labor legislation, etc." (*Selected Works,* vol. 1, part 1, pp. 233–234). Socialism, i.e., the conviction that it is necessary to overthrow capitalism and replace it by an entirely different system, was, according to Lenin, introduced into the proletariat by revolutionary intellectuals. It was they who took the initiative in educating the advanced workers to their real interests and organizing them into a revolutionary vanguard party whose functions were both to lead the proletariat in revolutionary struggles and to imbue it with an ever sharper socialist consciousness. The clear implication of this view for the problem which concerns us is that it is not capitalism as such but the revolutionary struggle to overthrow capitalism which creates men with the will and ability to go further and begin the construction of socialism. Revolutionizing practice, in Lenin's view, was nothing more nor less than the practice of revolution.

We are often told, especially by learned opponents of Marxism, that it was precisely in his denial of the spontaneous revolutionary potential of the proletariat that Lenin differed most markedly from Marx and Engels. This is supposed to be the basis of his conception of the nature and role of the vanguard party, which is widely believed to constitute a Leninist deviation without roots in the teachings of the masters.

Certainly there is no doubt that it was Lenin who was responsible for developing the vanguard party, both in theory and practice, as we know it today. But is there really any inconsistency between the Leninist conception of the party and the ideas of Marx and Engels?

It seems to me that it would be correct to give an affirmative answer to this question only if it could be shown that Marx and Engels believed that the proletariat was capable of developing, exclusively by its own effort (in Lenin's phrase), a revolutionary *and* socialist consciousness. As I indicated earlier, I used to think that this was indeed their view but an effort to prove it convinced me that I was wrong. Not only does one look in vain for specific statements attributing revolutionary socialist spontaneity to the proletariat, but the lifelong practice of the two men would be incomprehensible if they had held such a view of the character of the proletariat. From the Communist League in the 1840s through the First International to Engels's last years when he acted as consultant to socialist parties all over the world, they were tireless in their efforts to do just what Lenin said it was the function of revolutionary intellectuals to do, i.e., introduce a revolutionary socialist consciousness into the proletariat. And it is of course obvious that one of the examples Lenin had in mind when he wrote *What Is to Be Done?* was the founders of scientific socialism. The weight of the evidence, it seems to me, is that in this as in other matters Lenin's ideas and activities were fully consistent with those of

Marx and Engels. For them, no less than for him, revolutionizing practice was the practice of revolution.

I would like now to attempt to draw some of the implications of this view for the transition to socialism. Bourgeois human nature, as we have seen, was formed in a centuries-long process of actual capitalist development within the framework of feudal society. When capitalism had grown strong enough to challenge and defeat feudalism, there was no real possibility of a return to feudalism. Bourgeois man was at home only in bourgeois society: there was no conceivable reason for him to reactivate or recreate feudal social relations. (This is not to deny of course that capitalist power could here and there be defeated by feudal power, resulting in local and perhaps even prolonged setbacks to the progress of capitalism. Such occurrences, however, could not arrest the general advance of the new system.) It is altogether different in the case of the transition to socialism. Socialist human nature is not formed within the framework of capitalism but only in the struggle against capitalism. What guarantee is there that this will occur on a sufficient scale and in sufficient depth to make possible the construction of a new socialist society? For we should be under no illusion that the social relations specific to a socialist society could exist in anything but name in the absence of the kind of human material which alone could give them sense and meaning. That Marx himself understood this, even if he did not explore all its implications, is shown by a passage from the *Enthüllungen über den Kommunisten-Prozess zu Köln* in which he distinguishes between the propaganda of his group in the Communist League and that of an opposed minority group:

While we say to the workers: you have to undergo fifteen, twenty, fifty years of civil wars and popular struggles not only to change the relations but to change yourselves and prepare yourselves for political mastery, they tell them on the contrary, "We must come to power immediately, or we can forget about it." While we make a special point of emphasizing to the German worker the underdeveloped state of the German proletariat, they flatter his national feeling and the craft prejudice of the German artisan, which to be sure is more popular. (*Werke*, vol. 8, p. 412)

Here Marx puts his finger on the central issue: the proletariat must not only change the relations of society but in the process change itself. And unfortunately more than a century of subsequent history proves all too conclusively that there is as yet no guarantee that this can be successfully accomplished.

As far as the industrially advanced countries are concerned, capitalism proved to have a great deal more expansive and adaptive power than Marx suspected. Under the circumstances, their proletariats succumbed to the economism which Lenin saw as natural to them but believed could be overcome by a conscious revolutionary vanguard. What actually happened was the opposite: the vanguards, whether calling themselves Socialist or Social Democratic or Communist, instead of converting the proletarian masses to revolutionary socialism were themselves transformed into economistic reformers. There are of course those who see in this a temporary aberration and believe that a new revolutionary period has opened in which the proletariat will once again play the role attributed to it in classical Marxist-Leninist theory. (For an able presentation of this argument, see Daniel Singer's recently published work, *Prelude to Revolution*.) I for one fervently hope that they are right, but as for now the most one can say is that the case is unproved.

When we turn to the countries where the old regimes (either capitalist or a feudal-capitalist mixture) have actually been overthrown, we are confronted with two very different experiences which, for obvious reasons, can best be exemplified by the Soviet Union and China, respectively.

The October Revolution proved the validity, under conditions existing in Russia in 1917, of the first half of the Marxist-Leninist theory of transition to socialism. The industrial proletariat, though relatively small, was able, under resolute revolutionary leadership, to overthrow the bourgeois regime which had come to power in the February Revolution. But with regard to the second half of the theory—the capacity of the proletariat to lead the way in the construction of socialism—the Russian experience is at best inconclusive. Small to begin with, the Russian proletariat was decimated and dispersed by the four years of bloody civil war, hunger, and chaos which followed the October Revolution. The Bolshevik government, preoccupied with problems of survival and economic recovery, was obliged to rely on the old, obviously profoundly anti-socialist state bureaucracy and to add to its size and power in the ensuing years. Nevertheless, the period from roughly 1922 to 1928 was one of revolutionary ferment—in the arts, education, sexual relations, social science, etc. —which, had it not been cut short, might have generated powerful socialist forces and trends. What brought this period to an end was the fateful decision to subordinate everything else to the most rapid possible economic development. It would take us too far afield to discuss the reasons for or justification of this decision: suffice it to point out that it entailed what may almost be called a cultural counter-revolution together with the imposition of an extremely repressive political regime. Under the circumstances, revolutionizing practice tending to produce socialist human nature almost totally disappeared. Instead, the reconstituted and expanded proletariat which came with forced-march industrialization was repressed and atomized, deprived of all means of self-expression, and terrorized by an omnipresent secret police.

While the Russian experience thus throws little light on the positive side of the problem of constructing socialism, it does provide devastating proof of the impossibility of infusing seemingly socialist forms—such as nationalized means of production and comprehensive economic planning—with genuine socialist content unless the process goes hand-in-hand with the formation of socialist human beings. The idea, assiduously promtoed by Soviet ideologists, that raising material living standards of the masses will by itself foster socialist consciousness never had anything to recommend it and has been shown by Soviet (as well as American!) experience to be nonsense. Some of the negative potentialities of the Soviet Russian system were, paradoxically, held in check for a time by the Stalinist terror: a bureaucrat abusing his position too blatantly was likely to find himself in a labor camp, if not worse. But after Stalin's death these restraints were largely removed, and the true nature of the situation was soon revealed.

A recent Chinese critique points to the heart of the matter:

From production to distribution, from economic branches to government organizations, the forces of capitalism run wild in town and countryside. Speculation, cornering the market, price rigging, and cheating are the order of the day: capitalist roaders in enterprises and government team up in grafting, embezzling, working for their own benefit at the expense of the public interest, dividing up the spoils and taking bribes. Socialist ownership by the whole people has degenerated into ownership by a privileged stratum, and is directly manipulated by a handful of capitalist roaders and new bourgeois elements. . . . This has been a painful historical lesson! ("Socialist Construction and Class Struggle in the Field of Economics—Critique of Sun Yeh-fang's Revisionist Economic Theory," by the Writing Group of the Kirin Provincial Revolutionary Committee, *Peking Review*, April 17, 1970, p. 9)

I would stress particularly the statement that "socialist ownership by the whole people has degenerated into ownership by a privileged stratum" with the *caveat* that this is to be interpreted *de facto* rather than *de jure*. It is a privileged stratum—what Charles Bettelheim has called a new "state bourgeoisie"—which controls the means of production and thereby decides how the fruits of production are to be utilized. Regardless of legal forms, this is the real content of class ownership.

It is noteworthy that the foregoing characterization of the situation in the Soviet Union could be applied with little or no change to almost any capitalist country, the main difference being that under capitalism a large part of the activities alluded to are perfectly legal. This underscores the fact that no legal system, using the term in the broadest sense to include the system of property relations, can effectively control men's behavior unless it is in harmony with the historically formed human nature of its subjects. This condition is patently not fulfilled in the Soviet Union.

This of course does not mean that there will never be socialism in the Soviet Union, still less that the failure of the first effort to introduce it has been without positive effects. The earliest appearances of capitalism were also abortive, but they left a precious heritage of experience (including, for example, the invention of double-entry bookkeeping) without which later capitalisms might also have failed or at any rate found development much more difficult. It was through the Russian Revolution that the crucially important science of Marxism-Leninism reached the peoples of Asia, Africa, and Latin America; and it is probably no exaggeration to say that it was only the negative example of later Soviet experience which enabled other countries to see the necessity of protracted revolutionizing practice to the building of socialism. "The restoration of capitalism in the Soviet Union and certain other socialist countries," said Lin Piao on the 50th anniversary of the October Revolution, "is the most important lesson to be drawn from the last fifty years of the history of the inter-

national Communist movement" (quoted in *Le Monde Weekly,* January 13, 1971, p. 8).

It was not, however, only the negative lesson of Soviet experience which impelled the Chinese to pioneer a different road to the construction of socialism. The situation in China differed in important respects from that in Russia. For one thing, the Chinese proletariat, though smaller than the Russian, was never seriously plagued by economism. As Mao wrote in 1939, "Since there is no economic basis for economic reformism in colonial and semi-colonial China as there is in Europe, the whole proletariat, with the exception of a few scabs, is most revolutionary" (*Selected Works,* vol. 2, p. 324). To this consistently revolutionary force there was added another even larger one formed in the quarter-century-long military struggle against capitalism, feudalism, and imperialism, which culminated in the triumph of the Revolution in 1949. In the words of the editors of *Hongqi* (no. 5, 1964): "Owing to the education and training received in the people's army, millions of ordinary workers and peasants and many students and other intellectuals of petty-bourgeois origin have gradually revolutionized themselves [in thinking and action] and become steadfast, politically conscious fighters and mainstays in revolution and construction." (The square brackets are in the original text.) The prolonged civil war in China combined with the war against the Japanese invaders thus fostered a vast growth in both the size and the maturity of the revolutionary forces, while a much shorter period of civil war and resistance to foreign invaders in the Soviet Union seriously weakened the revolutionary forces there. The result was that China, on the morrow of the Revolution, was much more richly endowed with revolutionary human material than Russia had been. Finally, in Lenin and Mao Tse-tung Russia and China were fortunate to have two of the greatest revolutionary geniuses of all time; but Lenin died before the process of constructing socialism had really begun, while Mao's leadership has already lasted more than two decades since the victory of the Revolution.

Both men were well aware of the enormous difficulty of the task that lay ahead after the overthrow of the old regime. In his "Report at the Second All-Russia Trade Union Congress" (January 20, 1919), Lenin said:

The workers were never separated by a Great Wall of China from the old society. And they have preserved a good deal of the traditional mentality of capitalist society. The workers are building a new society without themselves having become new people, or cleansed of the filth of the old world; they are still standing up to their knees in that filth. We can only dream of cleaning the filth away. It would be utterly utopian to think this could be done all at once. It would be so utopian that in practice it would only postpone socialism to kingdom come.

No, that is not the way we intend to build socialism. We are building while still standing on the soil of capitalist society, combating all those weaknesses and shortcomings which also affect the working people and which tend to drag the proletariat down. There are many old separatist habits and customs of the small holder in this struggle, and we still feel the effects of the old maxim: "Every man for himself, and the devil take the hindmost." (*Collected Works*, vol. 28, 424–425)

Mao was even more explicit when he wrote, as the People's Liberation Army was about to win its final victories in March of 1949:

To win country-wide victory is only the first step in a long march of ten thousand *li*. Even if this step is worthy of pride, it is comparatively tiny; what will be more worthy of pride is yet to come. After several decades, the victory of the Chinese people's democratic revolution, viewed in retrospect, will seem like only a brief prologue in a long drama. A drama begins with a prologue, but the prologue is not the climax. The Chinese revolution is great, but the road after the revolution will be longer, the work greater and more arduous. (*Selected Works*, vol. 4, p. 374)

After only two decades we can see how right Mao was. The drama has continued to unfold, moving from one climax to another. Despite all its initial advantages, China has never been free of the danger of slipping back into the old forms and relations which for centuries had molded Chinese human nature. The old "ensemble of social relations" continued and still continues to exist in the minds and consciousness of hundreds of millions of Chinese. As Marx expressed it in *The Eighteenth Brumaire*, "The tradition of all the dead generations weighs like a nightmare on the brain of the living" (*Werke*, vol. 8, p. 115). To overcome this ineluctable fact—not to nationalize property or build heavy industry or raise material living standards, important though all these things are—is the central problem of the transition to socialism. And it was the Chinese revolutionaries under the inspired leadership of Mao Tsetung who grasped and internalized this truth to the extent of making it the conscious basis of their revolutionizing practice.

This is not the occasion for an attempt to analyze this revolutionizing practice, nor do I have the knowledge and competence which would be required. What I wish to emphasize is that *for the first time* the problem has been fully recognized and correctly posed. Until that was done, there was not even a chance of finding a satisfactory solution.

It is as well to close on a note of caution. In politics, as in science, the first step in solving a problem is to recognize and pose it correctly. But the first step is usually a long way from the final solution, and when the problem is nothing less than changing human nature this *caveat* is doubly and triply relevant. Fortunately, Mao knows this better than anyone else, and we can hope that the knowledge will become a permanent part of his legacy to the Chinese people. Ultimate success or failure will probably not be known until all of us are long since gone and forgotten. Said Mao in 1967 at the height of the Cultural Revolution:

The present Great Proletarian Cultural Revolution is only the first of its kind. In the future such revolutions must take place. . . . All Party members and the population at large must guard against believing . . . that everything will be fine after one, two, three, or four cultural revolutions. We must pay close attention, and we must not relax our vigilance. (Quoted in the concluding chapter of Jean Daubier, *Histoire de la révolution culturelle prolétarienne en Chine* [Paris: Maspero, 1970])

All history, Marx said, is the continuous transformation of human nature. What is Mao telling us but that even after the overthrow of class domination the positive task of transforming human nature never ceases?

CHAPTER 9

Conclusion

The revolution that is socialist and the reformation that is religious continue. We are in the struggle for a culture that joins the realms of finite existence and eternal essence. The historical roots of the struggle are in the prophetic tradition. And in the prophetic element of socialism we are conscious of the decisive character of our development.

In the emerging socialist culture we are aware of and motivated by the transcendent nature of the prophetic principle. We have an image of our essential nature and the possibilities for our human existence. This essence, however, has become separated from the conditions of this world, contradicted by social and moral life. The cleavage between reality and essence can be overcome only by human action through the creative power of redemption. In the dynamics of history we experience meaning that both guides and transcends our history. History and the transhistorical—time and the eternal—support our human existence.

In our own time the world has been broken apart by the development of capitalism. Not only has existence become separated from an essential nature, but our minds and spirits have all but lost the ability to comprehend and move beyond the separation. Bourgeois thought, appropriate to a capitalist society, analytically broke the world apart for the purpose of examination and control. Being and living in the world whole again is the mission of a prophetic social criticism that is materially and theologically joined in Marxism and the Judeo-Christian tradition.[1]

Prophetic criticism is in sharp contrast to the ethos of the contemporary scientific method. Prophecy has very little to do with predicting the specific events of the future. In comparison to scientific prediction, with its explicit emphasis on human manipulation and control, prophecy is a form of address that calls human beings to an awareness of their historical responsibility and challenges them to act in ways that will change the existing human condition. The prophets of the Old Testament sometimes used the rhetorical device of visions of the future, "but they used them to try to rouse the people of Israel out of slumber and into the wakefulness and responsibility required by God."[2] The prophets foretold doom, but only if the people refused to keep the promises they had exchanged with their image of God. Human fulfillment was found in the exercise of moral will in the struggle for a historical future. The pessimistic character of a deterministic and predictive social science is overcome in the prophetic hope for a humane and spiritually filled existence.

As social critics we are working in the realm of a critical sociology that is informed by a prophetic theology. We are positioned in the long tradition of critical and religious reflection, inspired by the prophetic spirit. Social criticism—prophetic criticism—interprets historical and contemporary events with the intention of revealing and proclaiming their deepest meaning. And that meaning is grounded ultimately in the unconditional being that is in the process of knowing itself. We discover what the Kingdom of God means in the process of struggling for our personal and collective history.

The prophetic voice brings to social criticism the unity of the temporal and the eternal, the secular and the sacred. A critical sociology that does not consider the sacred meaning of our existence systematically excludes the full potential and essence of our being. Prophetic criticism brings together the historical and the transhistorical, allowing us to truly understand the present meaning of our social and moral condition. Prophetic criticism—in a sensitivity to what the moment demands, rather than foreknowledge of the future—takes place with an awareness of divine involvement in history.

A cultural form that has the objective of reconstructing the social and moral order necessarily draws from the fundamental character of our religious and intellectual experience: the prophetic. The prophetic that forms the basis of our social criticism has the embracing qualities of having a long tradition, of being radical, and of being comprehensive. Prophecy is firmly rooted in the tradition of the Old Testament, furnishing the basic intellectual and spiritual tradition continuing in the present. Moreover, the prophet is the radical critic of the time and place, witnessing to the divine judgment. And the prophet speaks on behalf of all the people, discerning the signs of the coming Kingdom of God. A cultural criticism founded on the prophetic is thus profound in its source and its purpose.

Our prophetic heritage perceives the driving force of history as being the struggle between justice and injustice. We the people—in a covenant with God—are responsible for the character of our lives and our society, for the pursuit of righteousness, justice, and mercy. The social and moral order is consequently rooted in the divine commandments; morality rests upon divine command and concern rather than on the relativity of reasonableness. We seek to realize God's concern and command, the essence of perfect justice and love. The prophetic presence is real: "God is a living entity, closer than one's hands and feet, not a philosophic or theological abstraction."[3]

The prophetic furnishes us with the perspective for understanding the world and for working to change it. Out of our understanding of the present social and moral order, with all of its problems and contradictions, we are prepared to work for the creation of a new society. The essential task of prophetic criticism is to disclose the present so that our future may be constructed, all in terms of an image of the union of the historical and the transcendent. We learn from the prophet, whose eye is directed to the contemporary scene yet whose ear is inclined to God.[4] Through prophetic criticism we are reminded of the moral condition of the times and of our moral responsibility for changing that condition. Prophetic thinking and acting bring the world into divine focus.

The concrete form in which divine revelation takes place, as the theologian Karl Rahner indicates, varies historically and is conditioned by the historical context in which it occurs.[5] The prophetic element has taken many forms in the historical development of our world, but its presence has been continuous. In our secular age, prophetic criticism brings to us the prophetic element. In times that are less dark, divine prophecy will be manifest in a more religious form. We accept the prophetic in the form in which it comes to us. In faith, with the grace of prophecy, we struggle to build a better world.

Prophecy—and the extent to which it exists in prophetic criticism—proclaims the divine concern for justice. The idea and belief that "God is justice" means the divine support and guidance for such human matters as the demystification of conventional thought, the humanization of work, the democratization and socialization of the economy, and the elimination of oppression of all kinds.[6] Apparent material issues are thus conceived of in terms of the transcendent, adding the necessary element that is missing in a strictly materialist (and this-worldly) analysis. Prophetic criticism is as much theological as it is sociological. In fact, the dialectic of both types of analysis gives prophetic criticism its power as a critique and an understanding of justice and injustice in this world.

To the prophets of the Old Testament injustice (whether in the form of crime and corruption or the condition of the poor) is not merely an injury to the welfare of the people (which it certainly is), but is a threat to existence itself. Moral comprehension, in other words, is rooted in the depth of the divine. This is a sense of justice that goes far beyond our modern liberal and legal notions of justice. For the prophets, the worldly virtue of justice is founded on the understanding that oppression on earth is a humiliation of God. Righteousness is not just a value for the prophet, as Abraham J. Heschel observes, but "it is God's part of human life, God's stake in human history."[7] The relation between human life and the divine is at stake when injustice occurs. Prophetic criticism for us seeks such grounding in its concern for justice. Justice is more than a normative idea; it is charged with the transcendent power of the infinite and the eternal, with the essence of divine revelation.

For the prophets, justice is like a mightly stream, not merely a category or a mechanical process. "The moralists discuss, suggest, counsel; the prophets proclaim, demand, insist."[8] Prophetic justice is charged with the urgency of the divine presence in the world.

> Let justice roll down like water,
> And righteousness like a mighty stream.
>
> (Amos 5: 24)

In Heschel's phrase, "What ought to be, shall be"[9] Prophetic criticism has a similar sense of urgency and depth.

Justice—and its lack of fulfillment—is a condition of the whole people. An individual's act expresses the moral state of the many.

> Above all, the prophets remind us of the moral state of a people: Few are guilty, but all are responsible. If we admit that the individual is in some measure

conditioned or affected by the spirit of society, an individual's crime discloses society's corruption. In a community not indifferent to suffering, uncompromisingly impatient with cruelty and falsehood, continually concerned for God and every man, crime would be infrequent rather than common.[10]

Prophecy is directed to the whole world as well as to the inner spirit of the individual. The purpose of prophecy—and I am arguing for prophetic criticism as well—is to revolutionize history. Divine compassion is expressed in our own time. And we are all judged collectively in the presence of corruption and oppression:

> From the heavens Thou didst utter judgment;
> The earth feared and was still,
> When God arose to establish judgment
> To save all the oppressed of the earth.
> (Psalm 76: 9–10)

It is the source of the prophet's experience that gives prophecy its certainty and its ugency. "The certainty of being inspired by God, of speaking in His name, of having been sent by Him to the people, is the basic and central fact of the prophet's consciousness."[11] The experience without a confidence in its source would diminish if not negate the prophetic consciousness. But the prophet is in an encounter—a communication—with the transcendent. The self is surrendered—however momentarily—to the divine; consciousness is with another. From knowing God, rather than from an absolutely mysterious experience, divine inspiration comes to the prophet.

The prophet, in turn, conveys the demand and judgment to others. Prophecy becomes social as well as divine. While prophetic criticism necessarily lacks the *sui generis* quality of the Old Testament prophets, it is nevertheless aware of being subject to a transcendent intensity. Prophetic criticism, even in the most secular of times, is compelled to listen to the divine source of inspiration. Communication is with both worlds.

The prophetic, even today, is open to those who are concerned about ultimate matters. In listening and addressing ourselves to the dialectic of the temporal and the eternal, history and the divine, we are in contact with the most profound questions of our personal and collective being. We are not looking for a mystical vision, but we are ready to consider profoundly the meaning of our present condition and our future possibility. Our prophetic stance in this secular age attempts to recover some of the essential quality of the prophecy of a time when the sacred was realized more fully.

Prophetic criticism is a form of understanding that leads us to the human actions that move us to a world which is closer to our essential nature, a world that is constantly aware of the coming of God's Kingdom. Prophetic criticism provides us with direction, giving us a hope that is both temporal and transcendent. The meaning of our history is revealed—made known to us—in our own time.

A prophetic social criticism is based on the recognition that being human is being in contact with divine guidance. The purpose of prophetic criticism is to establish the right relationship between human life and the transcendent.

Thus, the ultimate—that which is divine—is to be found in the everyday life of human existence and in our human history. In an analysis of history and our time we search for the signs of providence. In the living of our lives we seek that which has unconditional meaning. Yet our understanding and our being are both within a concrete and historical engagement. Spiritual life and historical praxis are one.[12] Our human history—our present condition—is thus to be understood in relation to the divine.

Not only do we know history through an apprehension of the infinite, but we incorporate that history and a sense of the unconditional into our daily lives. What I am arguing is that all historical events have their ultimate significance in a reality that transcends them. In 2 Corinthians 4:18, Paul writes, "Meanwhile our eyes are fixed not on the things that are seen, but on the things that are unseen: for what is seen passes away; what is unseen is eternal." Likewise, the culture (including the social and moral order) of any society or collectivity has a significance that transcends it. The ultimate meaning of the substance and form of any culture transcends all the empirical realities of finite existence—although the signs of infinite reality are to be sought in the substance of human forms and these forms are where the infinite i concretely realized. The forms we create and the substance we give these forms have a profound unity with the spiritual depths of our personal and collective being.

I am following here Paul Tillich's notion of the interpenetration of culture and religion, that "as the substance of culture is religion, so the form of religion is culture."[13] Everything in our culture is in some way an expression of the religious situation. And "every religious act, not only in organized religion, but also in the most intimate movement of the soul is culturally formed."[14] Culture is that which encompasses all human productions, including politics, economics, and science, as well as art, literature, philosophy, and the patterns of social life. As human creative production, culture is an expression of the ultimate— an enterprise of infinite importance. Culture and religion are joined historically in the social and moral order of any society.

It is through the sacred element of culture that finite and infinite reality are united; and it is in the arena of everyday social and moral life that the sacredness of culture is manifested. Thus, in our symbolic affairs there is no real distinction between the sacred and the profane. The culture we create is in this sense "supernatural," and has the goal of raising us above nature, assuring us "that in some ways our lives count in the universe more than merely physical things count."[15] We know that we are truly represented in something which exceeds ourselves.

Culture is essentially sacred in seeking the perpetuation and redemption of human individual and collective life. In the search for meaning in the universe, culture is the constructed means of transcending the material world. This transcendence moves us not only into a symbolic world (apart from the physical world), but transports us into the realm of infinite concern. Through the culture of this world we reach out to that which remains beyond definition, that which is beyond ourselves and our concrete existence. Through culture we participate in the ultimate, in the ground of our essential being. We attend to the infinite, and are inspired by the unconditional.

Culture, in other words, is theological. The "theology of culture," as Tillich called it, recognizes "that in every culture creation–a picture, a system, a law, a political movement (however secular it may appear) –an ultimate concern is expressed, and that it is possible to recognize the unconscious theological character of it."[16] Within every cultural creation–including the substructure of the economic order as well as the superstructure of ideas and social institutions–there is a spiritual expression. Given this concept of the unity of the sacred and the profane, Tillich can observe that "there are no persons, scriptures, communities, institutions, or actions that are holy in themselves, nor are there any that are profane in themselves. The profane can profess the quality of holiness, and the holy does not cease to be profane."[17] The religious substance of culture is manifest in all aspects of human culture; every person is in some way related to the unconditional ground of being. And the creation of human culture, let us realize, has within it the touch of divine inspiration.

Yet there is the continuous attempt in contemporary culture to divide the religious and the secular into separate realms. Although our essential nature requires the presence of ultimate concern in all areas of our life, the tendency is to establish a separate realm for the religious–apart from the rest of the world. The human predicament is determined by this situation, by an estrangement from our true being. "One could rightly say that the existence of religion as a special realm is the most conspicuous proof of man's fallen state."[18] Nevertheless, beyond the actual predicament, the secular and the sacred are rooted in the experience of ultimate concern. "To the degree in which this is realized the conflicts between the religious and the secular are overcome, and religion has discovered its true place in man's spiritual life, namely, in its depth, out of which it gives substance, ultimate meaning, judgment, and creative courage to all functions of the human spirit."[19]

To the extent that life in capitalist society is divided into separate compartments for religion, on the one hand, and secular pursuit on the other, to that extent human beings have lost the dimension of depth in their encounter with reality. Capitalism has made impossible the construction of a meaningful cultural existence. Capitalism itself has become the symbol of a "self-sufficient finitude."[20] The end result is the estrangement of our relation to our selves, to others, and to our ultimate being. Autonomous individuals cut off from their roots and from their nature find little support in a human community. The sacred is unfilling and unfilled in such a world.

The project is to create a theonomous culture, a sacramental community–"a more righteous social order, established in the prophetic spirit."[21] The answer to the human predicament is a salvation achieved through the overcoming and healing of the disparity between existence and essence. The sacred and the secular are integrated into the expectant symbol and reality of socialism. The human predicament produced by capitalism is transcended in the creation of a prophetic, socialist faith. The ancient split between secular wisdom and religious faith is thereby overcome in a religious socialist culture. And in socialism's final expectation a new being is created: "a radical transformation of human nature, and in the last instance–since human nature constantly grows out of nature as such–a transformation of nature and its laws."[12] Human existence is redeemed through the grace of providence.

NOTES

1. The ideas in this chapter are developed further in my forthcoming book *Providence: The Development of Social and Moral Order,* especially chap. 1 and the epilogue.

2. Harvey G. Cox, "Foreword," in Arend Theodoor van Leeuwen, *Prophecy in a Technocratic Era* (New York: Scribner, 1968), p. 10.

3. Edgar R. Magnin, "The Voice of Prophecy in This Satellite Age," in Harry M. Orlinsky, ed., *Interpreting the Prophetic Tradition* (Cincinnati: Hebrew Union College Press, 1969), p. 108.

4. Abraham J. Heschel, *The Prophets* (New York: Harper & Row, 1962), vol. 1, p. 21.

5. Karl Rahner, *Visions and Prophecies* (London: Burns & Oates, 1963), p. 15.

6. See Dorothee Soelle's review essay of *Marx and the Bible* by José Miranda, in the *Union Seminary Quarterly Review,* 32 (Fall 1976), pp. 49–53.

7. Heschel, *Prophets,* vol. 1, p. 198.

8. Ibid., p. 215.

9. Ibid., p. 213.

10. Ibid., p. 16.

11. Heschel, *Prophets,* vol. 2, p. 206. Also see pp. 207–226.

12. José Míguez Bonino, *Doing Theology in a Revolutionary Situation* (Philadelphia: Fortress Press, 1975), pp. 72–73. Also see Walter Leibrecht, "The Life and Mind of Paul Tillich," in Walter Leibrecht, ed., *Religion and Culture: Essays in Honor of Paul Tillich* (New York: Harper & Row, 1959), pp. 16–17.

13. Paul Tillich, *The Interpretation of History* (New York: Scribner, 1936), p. 50.

14. Paul Tillich, *Theology of Culture,* ed. Robert C. Kimball (New York: Oxford University Press, 1959), p. 42. Regarding the term *religion,* Carl J. Armbruster in *The Vision of Paul Tillich* (New York: Sheed and Ward, 1967) notes that Tillich means two things: "In the narrow or ordinary sense it refers to organized religions and their external trappings such as sacred books, creeds, rituals, priests, sacraments, and so forth. In the broader and more basic sense, religion is faith, the interior state of being grasped by an unconditioned, ultimate concern. Sometimes he intends both meanings under the term 'religion'; at other times, only one, and this is made clear by the context or by an express designation" (p. xviii). The concept of *culture,* on the other hand, includes (as in the German *Kultur*) the wide range of phenomena that social scientists designate by both the terms *social* and *cultural.* In reference to Tillich's concept of culture, Hammond writes: "Included in the scope of this concept (which may be rendered loosely as "civilization") are all material products and modes of production, all social institutions, all patterns of thinking and acting, all artistic creations. Tillich understands all of the products of human culture to be aspects of man's self-creation, which is one of the basic functions of life." Guyton B. Hammond, *The Power of Self-transcendence: An Introduction to the Philosophical Theology of Paul Tillich* (St. Louis: Bethany Press, 1966), p. 39.

15. Ernest Becker, *Escape from Evil* (New York: Free Press, 1975), p. 4.

16. Tillich, *Theology of Culture,* p. 27.

17. Paul Tillich, *On the Boundary: An Autobiographical Sketch* (New York: Scribner, 1966), p. 71.

18. Tillich, *Theology of Culture,* p. 42.

19. Ibid., p. 9.

20. Paul Tillich, *The Religious Situation* (New York: Meridian Books, 1956), p. 82.

21. Tillich, *On the Boundary,* p. 90.

22. Paul Tillich, *The Socialist Decision,* tr. Franklin Sherman (New York: Harper & Row, 1977), p. 111.

NAME INDEX

SUBJECT INDEX

This book has been set VideoComp, 10 and 9 point Baskerville, leaded 2 points. Chapter numbers are 14 and 30 point Baskerville and chapter titles are 18 point Baskerville. Reading numbers are 10 point Baskerville and reading titles are 16 point Baskerville Bold. The size of the type area is 33½ by 49½ picas.